The Von Balthasar Reader

Hans Urs von Balthasar

THE
VON BALTHASAR
READER

Edited by
Medard Kehl, S.J.,
and Werner Löser, S.J.

Translated by Robert J. Daly, S.J.,
and Fred Lawrence

T. & T. CLARK
38 George Street
Edinburgh

1985

The Crossroad Publishing Company
370 Lexington Avenue, New York, NY 10017

Originally published as *In der Fülle des Glaubens: Hans Urs von
Balthasar–Lesebuch* © 1980 Verlag Herder Freiburg im Breisgau

Printed in the United States of America

Library of Congress Cataloging in Publication Data

Balthasar, Has Urs von, 1905–
  The von Balthasar reader.

  Translation of: In der Fülle des Glaubens.
  Bibliography: p. 432
  Includes index.
  1. Catholic Church—Doctrinal and controversial works—
Catholic authors—Addresses, essays, lectures.
  2. Theology, Doctrinal—Addresses, essays, lectures.
  I. Kehl, Medard. II. Löser, Werner. III. Title.
  BX1751.2.B234   230'.2   82-5193
  ISBN 0-8245-0468-2   AACR2
  ISBN 0-8245-0720-7 (pbk.)

Contents

The Church Today 304

LIFE IN FAITH 319

Faith as Agreement with God 321

Turning to God in Prayer 325

Spiritual Stances and Ways of Carrying Out One's Life 348

Theology—a Ministry in the Church 356

Translators' Preface

This translation has been a work of love: love for the church and for the fullness of faith that characterizes von Balthasar's life and work, and love for the catholicity of vision which drives him to see all things in relation to each other and to their triune source and center. Von Balthasar's is a holistic theological view of divine-human reality, the kind of theology which the theological technicians of the present age may tell us is nothing but a relic of another, simpler time; but it is also the kind of theology which the believing heart of that same theological technician all the more yearns for in this age of fragmentation. Impressive as the depth and breadth of von Balthasar's knowledge is, even the most humble graduate student will be able to point out some statement or attitude in these pages which does not reflect the most accurate information, the most reliable consensus of up-to-date scholarly opinion. Nor does von Balthasar think that such information is unimportant. But he is aware that information is not everything. The Bible is, after all, filled with inaccuracies and inconsistencies. Thus, while repeatedly anguishing over the imperfection of what he produces, and although deprived of the naiveté that may have enabled writers from a former age to produce comfortable visions of a simplified reality, von Balthasar goes on building a worshipful theology that dares to be "catholic" in the fullest sense of the word, a theology born from, nourished by, and drawn to a fullness of faith.

The nearly impossible task of rendering von Balthasar into comparably good English might have been better achieved if it were possible to devote more years to it. We must apologize for not fully succeeding in rendering into modern, nonexclusive English passages written on another continent and across the space of several decades. The even more demanding challenge of recreating the Balthasarian rhetoric in English has scarcely been met, but we hope the English reader may still get a sense for the way von Balthasar molds both word and image, the logical and the aesthetical, together to form a powerful medium of worshipful theological expression.

Everything in this selection has been translated from the German edition. In a few cases this was done with broad reliance on earlier translations, but only after extensive comparison with the original, and not without significant revisions.

The 112 passages* were arranged by the editors in five great headings—The Human Being, God, The Church, Life in Faith, Consummation—in order to provide a systematic access to the breadth and fullness of von Balthasar's faith vision.

Robert J. Daly, S.J.
Fred Lawrence

---

* Of the original 120 selections in this reader, 8 have been omitted. They are all from *Herrlichkeit* which is being translated by another team of British and American scholars. These passages (with their respective numbers) had the titles: (8) Great World Theater: King David; (10) Eros—According to the Song of Songs; (13) Death According to the Old Testament; (16) Sin According to the Old Testament; (17) The Human Being as "Image of God"; (40) Old Covenant as Type of the New Covenant; (41) Argumentum ex prophetia; (111) People of the Church: Georges Rouault.

Editors' Preface

Hans Urs von Balthasar reached his seventy-fifth birthday in August of 1980. For a long time he has been known to the public, above all in the church, as a publisher, translator, and author of theological works. His first published works were written in 1925, that is, over fifty-five years ago. In the meantime his work has grown like a great tree which has thrust its roots deep into the fertile ground of holy scripture, church tradition, and human culture, and whose powerful trunk supports an extensive system of branches and leaves. Nor is there any sign that this tree is beginning to wilt. On the contrary, it is still developing. The reports are that Hans Urs von Balthasar is presently working on another volume of his *Theodramatik*, and further writings continue to appear in periodicals and books.

Hans Urs von Balthasar's work is eminently worthy of serious attention. It contains a great wealth of insights which are today rather badly needed by the church and individual Christians. And yet very few have a real chance so to study and meditate on the greater part of von Balthasar's total work as to form a living and accurate impression of it. It is just too extensive. This anthology should provide a helpful point of entry for those who would like to come into contact with von Balthasar's theology, for it points beyond itself and will have ideally fulfilled its purpose if it leads the reader to the complete editions of von Balthasar's works.

The texts gathered here were chosen to reflect the thematic and systematic nature of the Balthasarian theology as accurately as possible. At the same time the choice reflects the intention of including from von Balthasar's work a characteristic text on all the important affirmations of the Christian creed. A substantial "portrait" which precedes the texts casts some light on the person and work of Hans

Urs von Balthasar. It can contribute to a deeper understanding of the texts.

This anthology can help students of theology begin an acquaintance with a significant project in contemporary reflection on the faith. For preachers of the word it can be a stimulus to those prayerful reflections on which they must constantly rely both for their personal spiritual life and for their catechetical and liturgical activity. Finally, for all Christians it can be a storehouse of texts which have the happy quality of presenting theology in a spiritual way and spirituality in a theological way.

The editors conceived the book together. The Portrait comes from the pen of Medard Kehl, S.J., the texts were chosen by Werner Löser, S.J. The editors considered it superfluous to provide the anthology with a subject index. The chapter and text titles provided in the table of contents give sufficient information about what questions are handled in which place.

With the publication of this reader the editors would like to give heartfelt thanks to the Reverend Doctor von Balthasar for all that they themselves and many others have received from him over the years.

Medard Kehl, S.J.
Werner Löser, S.J.

INTRODUCTION

Hans Urs von Balthasar:
A Portrait

by Medard Kehl

BIOGRAPHICAL DATA

Hans Urs von Balthasar was born in Lucerne on August 24, 1905. After attending the grammar school and the Gymnasium of the Benedictines in Engelberg and of the Jesuits in Feldkirch, he went on to the universities of Vienna, Berlin, and finally Zurich where, on October 27, 1928, he completed his doctoral examinations in Germanistics and philosophy. The title of his dissertation was: "The History of the Eschatological Problem in Modern German Literature." On October 31, 1929, he entered the Society of Jesus. After his two-year novitiate in Feldkirch, he studied philosophy from 1931 to 1933 at the Jesuit philosophical faculty, the Berchmanskolleg in Pullach near Munich, and then theology in Lyons (Fourvière) from 1933 to 1937. He was ordained to the priesthood on July 26, 1936. From the Autumn of 1937 to the Summer of 1939 he served as an associate editor of the journal *Stimmen der Zeit* in Munich. The latter half of 1939 was occupied with tertianship (concluding phase in the training of a Jesuit) at the Berchmanskolleg in Pullach. From the beginning of 1940 he worked in the university student chaplaincy in Basel. Since 1950, after leaving the Society of Jesus, he has been living in Basel as the spiritual leader of the *Johannesgemeinschaft* (Johannine Community), publisher (the *Johannesverlag*), and theological writer. After the Second Vatican Council he became a member of the Papal Theological Commission, all the while continuing his varied activity as a lecturer and retreat director.

A "CONSERVATIVE" THEOLOGIAN?

The name of Hans Urs von Balthasar carries with it a particular tone in today's church. Some, who judge him predominantly from his great theological and historical-theological works, see him—transcending all preliminary labels—as one of the most significant figures in theology today. Many others, however, who know him only from some smaller controversial works, paperbacks, and newspaper articles, content themselves with placing him—approvingly or disapprovingly—on the "conservative" side of the church. There are certainly grounds enough for this. For many years he has done battle with a sharp tongue against certain post-conciliar "trends" in the church in order to uncover in them numerous hidden ambiguities and inclinations which would "lighten the ballast of what is Christian." Examples of this would be: the "trend" to the Bible (with a neglect of the whole subsequent tradition), to the liturgy (which frequently dissolves into spiritual managing and community self-satisfaction), to the ecumenical movement (at the price of leveling one's own tradition), to the "secular world" (with a simultaneous devaluation of the "sacred," the "mystical," and the "monastic").[1] He has directed the sword of his pen against the theological justification of a nameless, "anonymous" dissolution of the Christian into the worldly in which—when necessary—even the explicit ecclesial and preserving confession of faith becomes secondary,[2] or against the fashionable plea for a theological pluralism from which a sense for the "symphonic" unity of the whole seems to have disappeared,[3] or against the fixation on a historical-critical demythologization of the faith at the expense of its "eschatological center of gravity."[4] And finally, he has vigorously opposed the increasing spread of an "anti-Roman feeling" which would like to separate the concrete papacy from the mystery of the church, etc.[5]

Besides "going against the stream" of many trends in the church, Balthasar has, in relation to some particularly controverted ecclesiastical questions of the day, repeatedly taken a position which stands in opposition to what "progressive" and "critical" streams in the church consider desirable. An instance of this would be his attitude toward obligatory priestly celibacy or women's ordination. He has said a clear no to the desire for regulations of another kind and has supported this with biblical-traditional arguments which, to many ears today, sound incomprehensible, if not "scandalous."[6] It is the same when talking about "identification with the church" which, in Balthasar's conviction, in no way can be lived just "partially."[7] Nor does he have any patience for the currently much discussed possibilities of a "temporally" limited state in the church ("temporary priest," "temporary pope," "temporary marriage," "temporary religious life," etc.).[8] Further, the superiority of a purely "contemplative" form of life entered into out of truly Christian motives over all charitable, social, or political action is for him absolutely certain.[9] He also takes a reserved position with regard to "political theology" or to "liberation theology," as long as the specifically Christian aspect of the universal "liberation" given by God in the crucified and risen Christ is not sufficiently emphasized ahead of all human action.[10] Or, in comparison with a clearly theological-spiritual interpretation of institutional forms in the church, he holds sociological reflections on structure to be relatively unnecessary or not very helpful, etc.[11] This list could easily be extended. But instead I would like to mention one final reason why most public opinion in the church usually places Balthasar among the "conservatives."

The *sources* of his theological thinking and speaking lie not only— as is quite common today—in sacred scripture, modern philosophy, modern theological movements, and the investigations of the human sciences, but above all in the great tradition of the church. The writings of the church fathers and the great saints and spiritual masters of the church are for him more than a presupposed background of his theology. As the decisive milestones in the "effective history" of the Old and New Testaments, they provide him with a living and always richly available basis of argument from which to approach the theological questions of the present. This tradition-conscious starting point makes him today subject (subconsciously or openly expressed) to the occasional complaint that, with all his knowledge of modern intellectual history, he still has basically no proper understanding of the modern age and its changed problematic. The symbolic-holistic understanding of the fathers of the church and not the critical-analytic reflection of the moderns is what forms the real horizon of his thought.

We will see later what is justified in this characterization. But one should not easily lose sight of one particular point: precisely this "congenial" and also, in relation to our present situation, hermeneutically precise opening of the great tradition of the church signified, in the three decades before the Second Vatican Council, a very decisive liberation of Catholic theology from the constricting chains of neoscholasticism. Ultimately, Balthasar belongs with Przywara, de Lubac, Fessard, Daniélou, Bouillard, Congar, Hugo Rahner, and Karl Rahner, among others, to that generation of theologians who, precisely with the help of the church fathers, gave the final deathblow to the "two-storey-thinking" of the neoscholastic doctrine of grace and thereby overcame the unhealthy—for the encounter of the church with modern consciousness—dualism in Catholic thought between nature and grace, history and revelation, experience and faith. Without this tremendous and laboriously achieved theological advance, which had to bear up under massive criticism from the teaching office of the church well into the fifties, neither the decisions of the Council nor the majority of the basic theological assumptions in force today would have even been possible. What H. W. Gensichen (in a quite different context) holds against many modern critics fully applies here as well: "they forget that they can look farther because they are standing on the shoulders of giants."[12]

THE CENTER: CATHOLIC "FULLNESS OF FAITH"
IN THE CONCRETE CHURCH

But when one tries not only to avoid this forgetfulness but also to avoid letting one's picture of Balthasar the theologian be stamped just by his positions on certain inner-church questions and tendencies, the cliché "conservative" will get left behind very quickly, and one will hit upon a capacity of integrative breadth and penetrating meditative depth that is truly astonishing.[13] In a small contribution to the celebration of Balthasar's sixtieth birthday, Karl Rahner calls the versatility of the editor and inspirer of eighteen "series," translator and commentator of past and present theological and poetic works, original historian of theology and systematician, passionate hagiographer and spiritual writer, "really breathtaking":

> He writes minute patristic monographs on ancient church fathers (basically, he is *the* discoverer of Evagrius of Pontus), and with the same scrupulousness does a commentary on an almost forgotten section of Thomas's *Summa* and makes a part of the theology of Aquinas come alive again; but he can also sketch out magnificent collective portraits of the fathers (on Origen, Gregory of Nyssa, Maximus the Confessor . . .) as hardly anyone else can do. . . . He writes an intellectual history of the nineteenth century. . . . He is also a systematic theologian: he writes a *theological* aesthetic, the only one that has ever been written, a work that makes the bold claim of pointing out to theology its unique and definitive center; what he says about Christian eschatology, about the relationship between nature and grace, about the Catholic position on Barth, the modern Protestant church father, about the theology of history, and much more . . . all that has become an integral part of contemporary systematic Catholic theology. He is a spiritual writer who writes about contemplative prayer, unlocks the scripture for meditation, gives a Christian interpretation to existential angst, praises the heart of the world in a Christ-book of hymnic flight, and who says something important to the German-speaking world about the nature of modern secular institutes. He is an apologist in the best sense of the word

who answers the God-question in a way that makes sense to a person of today. He is a philosopher not only in his interpretation of German idealism in his *Prometheus,* but also in his work *Wahrheit.* He is a translator of rank not only for Origen, Augustine, Gregory of Nyssa, Ignatius of Loyola, but also for Claudel, for whom he has become *the* decisive mediator to Germany, and for Blondel.[14]

"CATHOLIC"

This versatility, impressive enough in terms of mere external quantity, is also immediately matched by an ability to integrate qualitative contents which does not simply receive or put together what fits into the "system," but which enters into discussion with a truly universal openness. The tolerance and decisiveness of this openness enables him both to go and meet the other side in all its positive substance and also, precisely in this meeting, to preserve and bring into play his own position in its full identity. Reflected here is doubtless more than just an "almost French curiosity of thought" of an intellectual interested in everything;[15] and more too than just the "impatience" of a perplexed writer always dissatisfied with himself and his products.[16]

No, what is revealed here is the main feature of a life that can be characterized with nothing other than with the original full sense of the word "catholic." Balthasar is a truly "catholic" person—far from all confessional narrow-mindedness, living and thinking out of the boundless "fullness" of the self-revealing love of God not only in order to proclaim this experienced fullness well beyond the ecclesiastical area of faith and into the whole breadth of human reality, but also to experience it there ever anew in its most hidden and mysterious forms. Not for nothing did Balthasar twice translate H. de Lubac's great work *Catholicism* (1938) into German;[17] for this book became for him and many others the "basic book" of theology.[18] He was able to discover there that "catholicism of fullness"[19] which was still present in the fathers of the church and which now needs revitalization, that self-understanding of a "Christianity which reaches out in thought to the limitless sphere of the earth's peoples and hopes for the salvation of the world."[20] "Catholic," in the understanding of the ancient church, means this fundamental Christian attitude which, in complete openness, allows itself to receive from the fullness of the incarnate love of God and to be taken up by it, and which—simultaneously communicating and ready to receive—is open to the whole of human reality and is thus able to integrate in itself everything that human beings experience as positive in the (preliminary, fragmentary) knowledge of truth and actualization of freedom. This "catholic" does not consist primarily in being limited by itself but in comprehensively integrating to the extent that the other proves itself open to integration in love.[21] The theology of the letters to the Ephesians and the Colossians form the biblical foundation of this concept: because the fullness of God (*plērōma*) has communicated itself in a bodily manner to the world in Christ, the world can and must be drawn into this fullness, mediated through the service of the church, "the fullness of him who fulfills all in all" (Eph 1:23).

But here the question we raised at the beginning again arises even more sharply: does not this basic "catholic" position which lives and thinks out of the "fullness of faith" stand in striking contradiction to the picture that Balthasar offers to a rather large public in the church because of his often very blunt antitheses and objections? How can this "Christian universalism" of an unlimited openness to discussion be consistent with those numerous opinions in which Balthasar not only takes a very decisive position which also draws clear lines within the church and is thus one-sidedly presumptuous, but also disputes predicating "catholic" of other positions? One actually hears the question quite often: how can such a fundamentally world-oriented theology still be at the same time so "conservative"? Surely it desires—in the good sense of the word—"to be true to the fullness";[22] but can this really be done with such clear setting of limits and "elucidations"? Where does it get the distinguishing criterion to come out so decisively against certain abbreviations and diminutions of this "fullness"?

"Concrete Universality"

With this question we come to the point where the key to an adequate approach to the complex "phenomenon" of Balthasar lies: it is the special understanding of what "Catholic universality" means for him. For Balthasar it has absolutely nothing to do with a naive, uncritical syncretism which mixes everything together into a peacefully amicable potpourri of a Christian world view. It is just as sharply to be set apart from a religious liberalism which levels all contours between true and false interpretation of the revelation-event and reduces faith to some general "reasonable" principles that can be tolerated by everyone. No, the only defensible "liberalism of Christian love"[23] is revealed in its origin as a wholly "concrete universality": in other words, the universality of the love of God which chose incarnation and crucifixion as its means of remaining present in the world. The eternal Son of the Father, who lives completely from the fullness of love *received* from the Father and whose "very own being" consists precisely in this unlimited and thankfully received love which he is for this reason able to bestow on human beings even "unto the uttermost" (Jn 13:1), up to the final emptying of death and "descent among the dead," this Jesus Christ is the concrete *form* within which the universal *fullness* of the love of God is once-and-for-all bound up, and in which alone it will remain effective in history. God's all-including love is not simply a "general" (cosmo-politan) love; rather it takes on the "special" form of the "poor (i.e., all-receiving and all-dispensing) love" of the incarnate and crucified One. Only in this "form" does it become universally "fruitful" like the grain of wheat that falls into the earth and dies. That is, only there can it demonstrate its all-liberating—because integrating in the fullness of the three-fold love of God—power, where people in faithful discipleship allow themselves to be taken into this "poverty" of love where they thus "clear out" and empty their hearts com-pletely from all that is self-aggrandizing in order to allow the love of God to be given to them "in fullness" and go with him along the concrete way of this love "unto the cross." The community of such people is the church; it is thus nothing other than the abiding "form" of the universal love of God in Christ translated into the social dimension. This community finds its personal exemplar in Mary, that "poor" handmaid of the Lord who allows the love of the incarnate God to take place in her.

For Balthasar, this is where the decisive criterion of the "Catholic" lies: it is the love which, in the (marian-stamped) following of the Son, is owed to the Father as "received fullness" and allows itself to be "used up" by him in the *forma servi*, in the form of the One crucified unto the uttermost for our salvation. Where human self-understanding and action in any (perhaps even quite hidden and unexpected) way is in harmony with this concrete form of love, it is integrated or able to be integrated into what is Christian; where it is not in such harmony, it must allow itself to be firmly corrected and "oriented" anew by this criterion. The exemplar of this definitive standard is and remains Jesus Christ; he is therefore the *universale concretum*[24] which bears and stamps everything: infinite *fullness* of love in the concrete *form* of absolutely "poor" receiving and selfless, all-including giving. In the church, this "paradox of Christ" of con-cretely determined form and universal breadth is continued through history; the church receives the Spirit of Christ and with it the char-acter of a truly "catholic," that is, universal, integrating love.[25] Bal-thasar sees here, precisely in the very concrete, resistant *structures* of the church, which inevitably foster human self-glorification, a genu-ine expression of the cruciformity of the universal love of Christ. For insofar as the sinful person who makes himself the measure is es-tranged from the Spirit of the love of God, this love often takes the form of a "law" making demands on him from without and convict-ing him of sin. And this is precisely what meets him—in concrete, socially tangible fashion—in the objective, not at the disposal of the individual, predetermined, official sacramental structures of the church. They are the "institutional framework into which the Spirit takes the sinner in order to lead him to what faith, hope, and love *really* mean."[26]

Should individuals wish to receive an undiminished share in the "concrete universality" of the love of Christ, they must allow themselves in their whole existence to be taken up and transformed into this concrete ecclesiastical "form"; they must really become "Christ-formed" and—as a mediation to that—"church-formed," as offensive as this may sound. The tradition of the church fathers speaks here of the *anima ecclesiastica*: this refers to those persons who allow themselves in faith to be "dispossessed" of every purely subjective, self-complacent form of existence, and at the same time to be led into the form of existence of Christ the servant. In the history which issues from the death and resurrection of Jesus, this form is in fact always a church form. For it is only in the concrete church that the individual's imitation of Christ finds that objective form which helps "expand" his private I and make it disponible for the simultaneously quite personal and yet universally valid mission for others for which God has him in mind. Precisely in this "deprivation of what is one's own," in this "renunciation for the sake of responsibility" does the believing person receive "what is truly his": namely the *forma Christi* in the "form of the church," the "transformation of the individual devout soul into an *anima ecclesiastica*."[27] Wherever this fundamental attitude is accepted and visibly lived, Balthasar sees preserved the fullness of "what is Catholic" (and also of what is Christian in general; for he sees the two concepts as identical on this level). This lived unity of God's all-encompassing love *and* concrete Christian-church form alone guarantees by itself that the unforeshortened universality of faith within history will be brought to full recognition. Where even only a shadow falls on this unity, which is always new and of the most sensitive equilibrium, Balthasar raises his warning, doubting, critically discriminating voice. Whether progressive or conservative, liberal or orthodox—that is not his concern;[28] the only important thing is that the *universale concretum* of God's love *both* in its whole reality-encompassing fullness *and* in the binding concreteness of its ecclesial form are preserved by us and handed on without any falsification or diminution.

PROBLEM OF "CONCRETIZING"

This understanding of "concrete universality" can also provide a possible explanation for the contradictory impression which Balthasar makes on many Christians and to which I have already briefly referred. First, with respect to the "ecclesiastical concreteness" which he emphasizes so much: in its deeply spiritual meaning, it is not intelligible to every Christian today. For could it not also be that the ecclesial structures in this theological argument are raised too quickly into a spiritual-theological sphere which makes them quasi-incomprehensible and unattackable? Is the human and the all-too-human aspect of the institution precisely according to its own socio-logical laws really given its due? Is not sin itself often made manifest in it so that it is simply not experienced as the "form" of love? Balthasar in no way disputes this. But he sees the power of God's love which overcomes human sin so prominently in the foreground that the dark, humanly sinful side of the church always seems to be outshone by this "transfiguring" light of God's love. There is something else too: precisely when it comes down to not simply listing one after the other both sides of the polarity (universal fullness of love–concrete ecclesial form), but mediating them with one another in such a way that neither gets the short end, and in such a way that each one is fully unfolded and given its due only by being connected with the other, then it can hardly be denied that this very difficult mediation does not, always and in every respect, turn out to be the perfectly balanced and convincing answer to every question that arises. In my opinion, it is quite possible—as also with every other philosopher and theologian—thoroughly to share in Balthasar's basic insight and intention without, on that account, having to take over his position in all particular concrete questions. For in the application of a basic option to specific, concrete problems, numerous other points of view and motives play a role which lead to judgments which do not always necessarily follow in strict coherence from the principle. No really good "system" which is open to the vast multiplicity of phenomena will be so rigorously consistent that its basic suppositions, even in the most concrete outcomes, allow for just *one* consequence and not quite a few equally coherent alternatives. Thus one does not do justice to Balthasar if one judges his theology wholly or predominantly by simple inferences from certain statements on particular controverted questions or tendencies in the church. One must take the opposite way, take the trouble to work through to the "im-plicative" center of his thought in order to be able to judge from that point, with approval or disapproval, its many explicitations.

LIFE FROM A "SENDING"

We believe we can make this center somewhat graspable conceptually with the term "concrete universality" (further understood as the "fullness of the love of God, constituted in ecclesial form, and being bestowed on the world"). In terms of its contents, this concept is proven clearly not to be a rounded-off, definitively conclusive formula which tries to bring the variety of this thought under one simple denominator. No, precisely in its mediating tension, never fully satisfied but always needing to be balanced anew, it breaks through all simplifying formulas and lets the breadth and dynamic character not only of his theology but, even more, of his whole life shine forth. The portrait of a human being should (without tendentiousness of course) represent the inner unity of person and work, in this case of biography and theology, from which it becomes clear that the whole many-sidedness of a life and activity are unified, as it were, under a central "guiding conception" and formed into a harmonious picture. Now this "guiding conception" in our case is not just a construct personally worked out just by Balthasar or a motif picked up at whim from the history of theology. No, he understands it as the most beautiful and most demanding gift passed down by the Christian tradition; affected persons must place themselves both thankfully and obediently at the disposition of this gift. Hence a "guiding conception" becomes a "sending" which forms the life of a human being into a unified "Christian gestalt" in which all centrifugal individual traits are bound together and permeated by this one sending.

The knowledge of being commissioned by God with the mission to give witness as a theological writer to the world-encompassing love of the crucified God in the midst of the concrete church was given to Balthasar fundamentally in the Spiritual Exercises. Here we must mention his encounter through the Exercises with Ignatius of Loyola, who was the one who united in himself in a singular way a passion for the ever greater glory of God (*ad majorem Dei gloriam*) and fidelity to a clear, unequivocal form of service in the church. In his first thirty-day, so-called "long retreat" (in 1929 under Father Kronseder, S.J.), the decisive turn in Balthaser's life took place. He later said that this is where, finally, "the good hand of God siezed him as he once seized Habakuk together with his basket and destined him for a true life."[29] For during those days the inadequacy of the existential and intellectual alternatives for which the study of modern intellectual history had increasingly prepared him now became clear. Whereas there, the goal and high point of modern thought seemed to lie in a subjectivity absolutely positing itself, identifying itself with God, continually circling about itself and grounded only in itself; here, in his encounter with Ignatius a whole other world opened up. Here all at once there emerged into the foreground something with which the modern age thought it had long ago dispensed: there was no longer the decision of the reflecting "I," but the call of God; no longer the planning and calculating choice of someone sure of himself, but the allowing himself to be chosen of someone obedient; no longer the constructing of a self-conceived form of life, but the following of the crucified Christ. The immediate encounter with the calling, addressing, and choosing Word of God in the Exercises remains the experiential foundation of Balthasar's whole theology.

Along with this experience of the sovereignty and freedom of God who needs us for the work of his love on earth and by whom we can allow ourselves to be used without being "annihilated," there is yet another decisive motif: that of "indifferent" (in the Ignatian sense) obedience within a concrete form of life in the church. The call of the *Deus semper major*, of the ever greater God, is indissolubly joined in the Exercises with the Ignatian *sentire in ecclesia*, the "sense of the church." That is, the Word of God to the individual here establishes unequivocal contours inasmuch as it brings the exercitant ineluctably face to face with the question of whether and how he is ready to follow the crucified Lord and his serving love within the church. In this way this "zealous," "choosing," "exclusivity-demanding" love[30] creates in the so-called "evangelical counsels," which apply equally to everyone (whether in the religious or secular state), its very particular ecclesial form of expression. All who seriously wish to follow the way of the Lord, no matter what particular state they may choose in so doing, must enter into this. For when the Lord calls someone to follow him, it is always a matter of the unconditioned "leaving everything behind" without reserve; but this not just "somehow" but in the ecclesially concrete way of "poverty, chastity, and obedience." For Balthasar these are basic attitudes of Christian existence which are not reserved just for those in "religious life"; religious only live them in a special way.

It is right here that the "guiding conception" of "concrete universality" has its deepest existential basis in the life of Balthasar: the obedient response to the call of Christ experienced in the Exercises binds the human person into a form of life in which—analogous to the cross and resurrection of Jesus—the universal love of God can work unimpeded for the salvation of the world.[31] "For this form of life is the salt of the earth which may not lose its savor; it alone as 'yeast,' can inject life into the 'secular world' by occupying the 'last place' by 'foolishness,' 'weakness,' 'despicableness,' 'being cursed and maligned.' "[32] From this living experience of the Exercises Balthasar not only continually draws his theological intuitions and thoughts ever anew; no, from this he "lives" entirely: "I translated the exercises and must have given them a hundred times: if anywhere, this is where Christian joy holds sway. If anywhere, this is where it is disclosed what being a Christian in one's 'origins' means: the attentive listening for the Word that calls and becoming free for the expected answer. This is where, more than any place else, there is also intimate contact with the sense and genius of the reformation from Luther to Karl Barth."[33]

In a third step of our introduction we now ought to try to reveal, in the variety of his biographical paths and theological thoughts, this form-giving center of his sending which he experienced in the Exercises. In an integrally lived life, neither of these can be separated from the other: Balthasar's theology is indistinguishably intertwined with the history of his life; it is formed through his life in and with his church *communio*. Through the mediation of this *communio* he receives his sending as theologian; for it he puts his theology to work.

UNFOLDING OF THE CENTER: THEOLOGY IN ENCOUNTER AND DISCUSSION

We are not attempting a complete biography of Balthasar in the context of this portrait. Instead we are only viewing those decisive "pieces of the mosaic" out of which the unity of structure mentioned in our "interpretative formula" has been formed both in the course of his life history and in his theological work. But, because of the great variety involved, the most important "formative elements" of his life and thought cannot be easily determined. Nevertheless, *one* pervasive characteristic of his life stands out: Balthasar is a person guided to his own form of life by (direct or literary) *encounters* with some extraordinary contemporary figures in the church. This happened in such a way that the whole wealth and the inexhaustible fullness of the Christian faith was opened to him in these meetings. Balthasar can "learn" from the great believers of his time, go to school with them, let himself be guided by them to the key figures and ideas in the history of the church, and receive in them that faith in which is contained the whole "height and depth" of the love of Christ which has been revealed in the long history of the *communio sanctorum* without ever being exhausted by them. In concrete encounters with believing people Balthasar experiences at once the essence of ecclesial *communio* and his own vocation in it: to take full and undiminished cognizance of the received fullness of Christ in the church, to appropriate and give it to others. The general life-principle of the *communio* is thus taken as his own: it is verified in him as much in the praxis of theological work as in the theory of theological thought. With regard to praxis, Balthasar does not give any emphatic assurances that he is basically indifferent as to whether he writes his own works or translates, edits, and comments on those of others. The long list of names and works made accesible to the public by him speaks for itself. He realizes that he has been called to be a theological mediator of the whole fullness of faith which has been entrusted to the *communio*. Balthasar does not perform this task in the manner of a colorless interpreter but instead, through a very independent appropriation, forgotten or hidden things are made to speak in an original and often surprisingly up-to-date way. "If there were nothing original in my work there would remain only the passion with which it hands on what it has received, because it is unknown to so many, and the assignment to do this for the missions one is given, more than one's talents, are what individuate the Christian."[34] The same holds for the *theory*, for the central contents of his theology into which we are going to enter more exhaustively. At least this much is clear: the guiding idea of "concrete universality" or of "received fullness which is given to others" has in Balthasar a clear "situation in life"; it takes on historical, bodily shape in a form of life and thought which is represented essentially in encountering, receiving, and mediating. How does that take place in detail? What are the decisive encounters in which Balthasar's own vocation took form?

IMPULSES

As with every human life, so here too, not all encounters are of the same importance. Many provide so to speak only the first important impulses which, with the course of time, continue to work quite independently of the ones who released them and take their place as a matter of course in the whole of a life's work. Others, however, establish irrevocable milestones and road signs which almost visibly determine the whole further direction of a life's work. These are the few encounters from which a person ultimately "lives," from which he never can nor wants to separate himself because they continually stimulate and support.

In Balthasar's life many famous but also many forgotten names belong to the former category. From his student years in Vienna, the first to be mentioned is Rudolf Allers. As doctor, psychiatrist, philosopher, and theologian he communicated to his young friend "the view of love of the fellow human being as the objective medium of human existence . . . ; in this turning away from the I to a reality full of you lay philosophical truth and the psychotherapeutic method for him."[35] At the same time Balthasar heard the Plotinus lectures of Hans Eibl: there being was basically interpreted as *bonum diffusivum sui*, as the self-communicating good.[36] From Romano Guardini came the impulse to contrast Kierkegaard and Nietzsche.[37] It was in relation to these two figures that the fundamental alternatives in the modern view of man and God ("either Christ or Dionysius") dawned on Balthasar: here the affirmation of the finite through its being taken up in the infinite movement of life, thus the identification of humanity with eternal longing and transcendence towards the over-man—there the affirmation of the finite through its being definitively affirmed by the transcendent God who gives himself to the finite and yet in doing so remains transcendent. "God is dead; I have killed, sacrificed him. That is Nietzsche's conclusion. God is dead; he has sacrificed himself, but he has never stopped living. That is Kierkegaard's paradox."[38] In this connection stands also Balthasar's intensive occupation with the philosophy of German idealism by which he was "profoundly affected . . . from the late Fichte, from Novalis and Hölderlin, and again and again by Goethe."[39] It was not in Kant or Schiller or Hegel, these exponents of critical, modern subjectivity reflecting on itself, that Balthasar found among the idealists a philosophical world view that suited him, but in Goethe. He appreciated in him "the late Aristotelian and his inerrant objectivity,"[40] his sense for "the indissoluble, unique, organic, developing gestalt. . . ,"[41] but above all his unconditionally world-affirming, fundamental attitude which raised into word the "hymn of praise to being."[42] "God radiates from worldliness"—for Balthasar this (in itself pantheistically intended) phrase of Gottfried Keller hits off Goethe's work in an acceptable and convincing sense; for it can be nicely joined here with its theological obverse: "the world radiates from God."[43]

For the same reasons Balthasar felt himself drawn early to Paul Claudel.[44] Claudel's "celebration of the finite world" which, in its universal breadth and colorfulness, forms the horizon of the dramatic play of the human being before God, fascinated Balthasar. In Claudel it comes from a "Catholic heart"[45] which knows that "the question of the horizon can be solved only in God. He knows further that into the solution, through all deaths, the unlimited fullness of the earth must enter. This double knowledge is decisive for his Catholicism. . . . No worldly value may be despised out of pride or ressentiment. Every good is necessary for the Catholic person; he cannot allow himself the smallest no when he stands before a worldly good."[46] This same tension between gospel and world, between being tied into the objective-ecclesial form of faith and affirmative openness to the totality of experienced reality, is discovered by Balthasar in Charles Péguy, Georges Bernanos, and Reinhold Schneider.[47] Again and again, in different renditions, all of them echo this same theme that so impresses Balthasar. In Péguy it is love for the non-Christian (communist) brother which has grown out of an unbroken hope and is ready to carry through its worldly involvement to martyrdom on the cross (as symbolized by Joan of Arc). In Bernanos, the "seemingly wild subjectivist," it is precisely the sacraments of the church which give his eccentric fictional characters at once their form and their freedom, and through which even the angst of modern man can be assuaged in the redeeming Mount of Olives angst of Jesus. In Reinhold Schneider it is finally the conscious "antipsychological ethos of service and of the representation of a divine royal order"[48] which formed the great historical conflicts between the holy imitators of the poor and crucified Christ on the one hand and the powerful agents of a Christian responsibility for the world on the other (as in the symbol of Francis of Assisi before Innocent III). Even his encounter with the "little" Saint Teresa of Lisieux becomes for Balthasar an occasion to emphasize the priority of the "objective sending" before all psychology, the childlike, simple doing one's duty of the "little way" as a necessary counterbalance to the subjectivity of high spiritual mysticism (as in the "great" Saint Teresa or John of the Cross).[49] The list of such encounters could go on and on;[50] they all played their (small and large) parts in the fact that Balthasar became continually more conscious of his own task, namely, to present in all his work as a theologian the apparently paradoxical unity of a universal affirmation of the world and a concrete adherence to the church.

COURSE-DETERMINING ENCOUNTERS

Nevertheless, much more decisive than all of those are four encounters with friends in which the fundamental structure of his life and thought was given its abiding form: his meetings with Erich Przywara, S.J., Karl Barth, Henri de Lubac, S.J., and Adrienne von Speyr.

Encounter with Erich Przywara

Balthasar was together with E. Przywara (1889–1972), the philosopher of religion and theologian from Munich, during the time of his dry, neoscholastic philosophical studies at the Jesuit seminary in Pullach (1931–1933), and in a brief period as an author with *Stimmen der Zeit* in Munich (1937–1940). In Przywara, the thinker of "analogy," Balthasar found an "unforgettable guide," the "greatest mind I was ever privileged to meet," and the one to whom he owes his own philosophical foundations.[51] The close connection with Przywara is also the ultimate reason for the decisive difference between Balthasar's and Rahner's theology which, in its turn, is largely derived from Maréchal. Because Balthasar's basic philosophical categories and his theological starting point developed in this encounter with Przywara, we must dig here somewhat more extensively and insert a brief review of the history of theology.

SURMOUNTING NEOSCHOLASTICISM: THE "UNITY OF REALITY"

Przywara and Maréchal stand (among others) as the great surmounters of the neoscholasticism which was generally dominant in the Catholic sphere to the middle of our century. Their criticism was directed above all against so-called "extrinsicism" in the doctrine of grace and in the whole of Catholic theology. Briefly, this is the theory that there was something like a self-contained human "nature" (*natura pura*) equipped with its own natural goal to which grace is then added as an undeserved "supplement" and endows the human person with an additional "supernatural" goal. Nature stands, in relation to this supernatural gift, as neutral and indifferent; it is at best not in opposition. The critics of this "two-story thinking" objected that grace remained completely outside nature, thereby favoring a self-satisfaction in the natural person. For why should such a one need grace at all? The constitutive character of a grace-bestowed salvation for the human person *as* human being was forgotten in favor of an overly strong emphasis on the undeservedness of salvation whereby grace was devalued to an "ac-cident" of nature.

In their new beginning, most of the critics of this theory returned to the "method of immanence" of the French philosopher of religion, M. Blondel. At the end of the last century (in *Action*, 1893, and *Lettre*, 1896) Blondel had attempted to posit, against this externalizing of grace, an inner demand for the supernatural as a necessary part of the human spirit. Between the "nature" of the human person and "supernatural" grace, then, there existed an inner relationship of correspondence. The "supernatural" therefore cannot be something that accrues to "nature" externally, but rather something that necessarily corresponds to the human being, fulfilling and completing his or her nature in the most integral way. And yet neither the historical event nor the contents of "supernatural" salvation are thereby derived from this religious demand and made dependent on "religious needs" (as was done, e.g., in "modernism"). No, salvation must instead be received on the level of historical freedom and accepted in free decision as that which encounters the human being in an underivative fashion. The goal of this "method of immanence" consists in showing forth the inner unity of history and revelation, experience and faith, nature and grace, without doing away with their differences. This idea of the "unity of reality," together with a strict maintenance of the differences, stands at the beginning of a new epoch in the Catholic theology of this century.

Two important lines of development issue from this starting point to the present: One—proposed by Maréchal and systematically erected by Karl Rahner—attempts, by mediating classical Thomistic metaphysics with German idealism's philosophy of spirit (Kant, Fichte, Hegel), to unfold theologically the idea of the "unity of reality." The outcome is "transcendental theology." Following the model of the mystical uniting of God with the human person, it sees the real place of the union of divine and human reality in the spirit of the individual subject: the human being as spiritual subject is, as such, always oriented to God as the infinite transcendental horizon of being. In the mode of an infinitely encompassing horizon which makes all human knowing and willing possible, God (the holy mystery) is, as such, always present—but not as an object—in the self-realization of the human spirit. On account of this, in every concrete intellectual knowing and doing, the human person has something like a "transcendental experience" of God. In it there then also occurs primarily the supernatural "ordinary revelation" of God in which God's general salvific will is offered and communicated to the human spirit for its ultimate salvation. This transcendental experience of God finds its highest, unsurpassed, unique and—for every other subjectivity—foundational self-interpretation in Jesus Christ. Here, in the person of the "absolute bringer of salvation," general human self-transcendence arrives at the holy mystery, at its goal, in which God accepts this person as his own self-communication to humanity. In Jesus Christ there is achieved in a unique and fundamental way that "unity of reality" to which the human spirit is, as such, always oriented, and which it can therefore find only in—explicit or anonymous—relation to Jesus Christ.

The other great line of the Catholic theological development of this century—suggested by Przywara and theologically unfolded by Balthasar—remains sceptical toward the project above. For does not the absolute transcendence of God and his irreducible, unfathomable historical self-revelation in Jesus Christ get mediated a bit too "harmoniously" with the human dynamic of spirit, and thereby in some way or other (unintentionally, of course) adapted to human standards? Do not human self-transcendence and divine self-communication simply merge into each other too smoothly? Is the radical otherness of God and his historical activity really preserved? For this reason—and driven by the same basic intention—Przywara travels another path, on which Balthasar has followed for quite a distance. He rejects a mediation of classical metaphysics and German idealism, but undertakes—in dispute with idealism and distancing himself from it—the attempt to restructure traditional Thomistic metaphysics on a new basis.[52]

"ANALOGY" AS FUNDAMENTAL PRINCIPLE

The starting point of this approach correlatively lies not in the subjectivity of the human being, in its intellectual self-realization, in order to find there the authentic experiential locus of the "unity of reality" (of God and world). With traditional scholastic metaphysics it begins instead "more objectively," with the whole of reality that we encounter, and tries to discover *in it* the locus of unity between God and world. This objective worldly reality (thus the human being in his or her world) is characterized according to Przywara by a twofold polarity: inner-worldly, by the tension between *Dasein* and *Sosein* ("existence" and "whatness or essence"); "supra-worldly" through the relationship creature—creator. Przywara sums up this double tension in the formula of the *analogia entis* (analogy of being): finite reality is profoundly analogous in its being, that is, simultaneously similar and dissimilar to the being of God. It is similar in so far as it really "is," and thus it forms a union between *Sein and Wesen* (being and nature), and between *Dasein and Sosein* (existence and essence); yet it is dissimilar in so far as it does not mean any full identity or any unity consequent upon an inner essential necessity, but only an external, factually posited "unity of tension." Thus, finite reality, in itself, could just as easily not be; it "is" only because it receives from God its *Dasein and Sosein* (being-there as existence and being-such as essence) from God in whom these two moments form an inner unity necessarily given in the essence of God. Now analogy grounds (on account of the "similarity") the positivity of the finite: it is to be affirmed and loved unconditionally because it is in itself a reflection of the full identity of God the creator to whom it owes its (imperfect) identity. But on the other hand, the analogy of created being grounds (on account of the dissimilarity) the necessity of transcending it again and again and of breaking out to the greater, absolutely transcendent reality of God. These two sides of analogy stand by no means on the same level of importance. The dissimilarity of the creature over against its creator is unequally greater than any merely possible similarity could be. At this point Przywara brings into play the famous formula of the Fourth Lateran Council (1215): "As great as may be the similarity, so much greater must the dissimilarity between creator and creature be preserved." The suspended center of the analogy between equality and full inequality between God and the world does not mean, according to this formula, a peaceful, balanced, pendulum-like swinging between creator and creature. On the contrary, the contradiction always cuts right through the center of every approximation and similarity. And it does so in such a way that the inexorable difference between God and world grows beyond every degree of correspondence preserved by God. This "dynamic" principle of analogy demolishes any merely possible identification of God and world and points to their continually-increasing differentiation. In this is expressed the creature's own uncompletable movement toward the *Deus semper major* (Augustine), towards the always still greater and "more dissimilar" God. The creature can never comprehend God, reduce him to a concept, and thus get "a hold" on him. Analogy in Przywara's sense precisely does not transfer the human person to an elevated place from which he or she could now look over, compare, and contrast God and world. No, analogy brings the human person with his or her whole existence and knowledge into this movement of the incomprehensibility of God which surpasses and leaves behind every similarity and commonality.

In a unique and singular way this "movement of analogy" is made manifest on the cross of Jesus: despite the inexorable bonds of love (identity) between them, the Father gives the Son over to the abandonment and hopelessness of sin and death (difference), permits him there to take on the form of that which is radically other than God, the form of the "sinner" and the "accursed" (cf. 2 Cor 5:21; Gal 3:13). In this figure of the crucified, God identifies himself in growing unfamiliarity and contradictoriness with what is other than himself, the sinner, the God-estranged and the God-forsaken. But precisely in this paradoxal way he reveals himself, in ways that humanly speaking are absolutely incomprehensible and unthinkable, as saving and healing love, as the really "totally other" who, with his life and with his love, fulfills and overcomes the sinful and death-infected world from within.

Accents

While Przywara increasingly emphasizes the contradiction, the nonidentity which he allows to "swallow up," so to speak, the identity (in a kind of "insatiability towards nothingness"),[53] for Balthasar the "positivity of the finite" and its unconditioned affirmation retains its abiding importance. This is precisely where their ways separate. To be sure, analogy is also for Balthasar *the* comprehensive form of thought for thinking about the relationship creator–creature as well as the relationship nature–grace, reason–faith. But the accents which he places in a different way than the late Przywara and which characterize his theology and anthropology lie in the following:

1. Every possible relationship between world and God is founded in the gift of God's relationship as creator to humankind; all movement of the human to God rests on this relationship: "Every comparison and relatedness of the creature has therefore its measure in a converse relatedness of God to the creature."[54] This is the reason for Balthasar's unfailing adhesion to the primacy of God who always acts first, setting himself in (creational) relationship over against all human movements of ascent and transcendence.[55] These are by no means devalued, but they receive their deepest meaning only from the prior relationship of the creator to humankind. This is what first makes ascent and transcendence possible and sets them in motion.

2. The reality of the world has, through its creational relationship,

received a value of its own, a positivity of its own. The fundamental communication of the truth, goodness, and beauty of God to creation turns creation itself into a real revelation of God, into a genuine "self-representation and self-interpretation in the worldly material of nature, human being, and history."[56] The Thomistic principle, "Grace presupposes nature; it does not destroy it but completes it," is in Balthasar received and applied in a new way in the sense of analogy.

3. In every analogous correspondence between nature and grace, between the orders of creation and redemption, Balthasar highlights both the uniqueness and the incomparability of the definitive self-revelation of God in Jesus Christ. Even if the creature represents a presupposed reflection of the creator and his love, the historical event of God redeeming us in Christ does not result from this presupposition. The positive content of the analogous correspondence between the created order of nature and the historical order of salvation lies precisely in the (gratuitously given) *openness* for the, once again, "totally other," underivable completion of the self-revelation of God in Christ which could never be calculated from creation itself and which thus is to be received only as pure gift. This takes place by no means as a self-perfection of creation, but as a totally free act of the loving God for his creature. The revelational form of his love, Jesus Christ, is absolutely unique. All that creation can produce in love, in meaning, in truth and beauty, does not converge on this figure of Christ in such a way that it would logically, so to speak, grow out of it. No, everything created remains fragmentary in itself; it comes up against a not to be transcended limit that is native to all imperfectible and ephemeral things. Only the historical "new beginning" of the loving God himself brings, with Christ, the possibilities of creatures to their definitive fulfillment. It is exclusively in God's reaching to us that our stretching to God reaches its goal. And as near as God may come to us in this movement downwards, as close, too, as the union between God and us through the mediator Jesus Christ has become, it is precisely here, nevertheless, that God reveals himself as the totally other, as the "unfathomably highest reality of love" which the human person can neither expect nor understand, but only humbly receive. "Precisely in the movement in which the creature sees and feels itself drawn to the heart of God, does it experience unto the depths its own not-being-God, does that all-dominant relationship of absolute and relative, of divine and worldly being get brought home to it relentlessly and without any possibility of appeal."[57] The revelation of God in Christ remains—despite every possible demand for it and in every real fulfillment—still the absolutely unimaginable new and other which is already given in no "transcendental experience."

Encounter with Karl Barth

This emphasis in his understanding of analogy is largely due to another dialogue which played a decisive role in Balthasar's life and thought: that with Karl Barth (1886–1968). This Reformed theologian, one of the very great renewers of evangelical theology in our century, had already been one of Przywara's most important dialogue partners from the evangelical side. Balthasar willingly took up and intensively carried on this dialogue. In a very close, friendly, and neighborly encounter of the two Basel theologians over a long period of time, a mutual give-and-take shaped a theology which, in each of them, took on a quite unmistakably unique form, but which nevertheless clearly manifests their far-reaching common ground and influence on each other. The most important molding elements of this for Balthasar are the following:

ANALOGY OF BEING—ANALOGY OF FAITH

At the outset stands the clarifying controversy about the fundamental philosophical concept of Przywara and Balthasar, the "analogy of being."[58] For Barth, this formula is the ultimate expression of Catholic thought and—as he once said—ultimately the single absolutely convincing reason for not becoming Catholic; for this formula is for him "*the* invention of the Anti-Christ." For Balthasar on the other hand, it remains the only solution for being able to make Christian theology work responsibly between the gutters of a philosophy of identity (God and the world are basically one) and an absolute dialectic (God and the world stand in complete opposition to one another). Over against the "dialectical" Barth of the *Epistle to the Romans* Balthasar emphasizes the necessary presupposition of a creation-grounded and indestructible common ground between God and the world. Only within this is the contradiction of the sin of the creature understandable, if creation and sin are not simply to be identified with each other: "Every real 'contra' presupposes a constantly to be understood relationship and thus at least a minimal community in order to be really a 'contra' and not a totally unrelated 'other.' Only on the basis of an analogy is sin possible."[59] But even for the salvation-historical order of redemption in Jesus Christ the creational analogy between creator and creature remains significant. The dialogue with the Barth of *Church Dogmatics* operates in the meantime on the commonly accepted basis of the *analogia fidei*, the "analogy of faith"; but the role of the *analogia entis*, the "natural analogy" of creation, remains controverted.

Analogy of faith, in Barth's sense, means that, through the incarnation of God in Jesus Christ, God first and only God creates a community between himself and the world. Only in believing in this saving message does the human being attain to a relationship of having something in common with God. Balthasar admits that, in the concrete order of salvation, *this* form of analogy does indeed represent the "final form" of the relationship between God and humanity intended from the beginning; but he firmly maintains that in this relationship the presupposed relationship of creation is permanently elevated and brought to its perfection. To be sure, the orders of creation and salvation find this ultimate meaning only in Jesus Christ, but precisely in him they also remain distinct from one another. For in order that definitive salvation in history can really appear *as* such, that is, as the absolutely unmerited and unsurpassable gift of community with God—by internal logic—the other part of itself, the creature, is presupposed; but not as something totally other and different (in that case how could any kind of a relationship with it be taken up?), but as something standing over against it which has been empowered by the God of creation to accept and respond to the offer of salvation. The contradiction of sin against the relationship between God and creature established in creation indeed profoundly corrupts but does not completely annihilate this relationship. For this reason the so-called "natural theology," the philosophical doctrine of God, maintains its right of place in Catholic theology. It is by no means the expression of a sinful "grasp on God," starting "from below," to get control of him—no more so than in all the other pre- and non-Christian religions—but a sign of that presupposition which the revealing God already provided in creation itself in order not only to correct it in Christ ("from above") but even more to save and integrate it into perfect community with himself.

CHRIST—THE CENTER OF THEOLOGY

The redeeming God is no other than the God who reveals himself in Jesus Christ: the saving message of Jesus Christ stands for both Barth and Balthasar in the center of their whole theology which, in its innermost center, is shown to be *christology*. I would like to make special mention of three aspects of this so-called "christocentric" theology of Balthasar which also took its shape precisely in dialogue with Barth:

Incarnation of the Word

The beginning of this christology lies with a comprehensive biblical theology of the Word of God: *Verbum Caro*—the incarnation of the divine Word, the historical self-emptying of the eternal self-interpretation of the Father in the Son—that remains for Balthasar the fundamental affirmation of faith in the light of which the earthly life of Jesus, his message, and his fate must be read.[60] As "figure of figures" (*Gestalt der Gestalten*), Jesus Christ is "God's own appearance," "in whom the whole fullness of the divinity is bodily present" (Col 1:19); he is the "appearing freedom" of God which in him is bound to a limited form and precisely in this way is revealed in its own reality as love. "The God whom we know now and in eternity is the *Emmanuel*, the God with us and for us, the self-revealing and self-giving God. Because he shows and gives *himself*, we know him not only from outside, not only 'economically,' but also we may possess him 'theologically,' from within, as he is."[61]

This presence of the eternal Word of God becomes manifest among us in the innerhistorical sphere primarily in the unique *claim* which Jesus makes from the beginning and which Balthasar summarily reflects upon theologically in the johannine words, "I am the way, the truth, and the life." This claim of Jesus intends the fact that the fate of all human beings is exclusively and definitively decided in his person. Jesus appears with an "eschatological authority" which can only be that of God himself, in which the I of Yahweh himself rings out in a new way that surpasses all prophetic revelation. In this authority Jesus is already carrying out the final and definitive judgment of God on humankind and its orders; in it he is already mediating eternal salvation or damnation, each according to the believing or unbelieving answer of the one called. Such a "claim to absoluteness" must inevitably be looked on by sinners as a hybrid presumptuousness. It would have to lead to the condemnation for blasphemy, to the cross as its consequent movement downwards, as being shattered upon his own "transcendent" claim. But against this is balanced the proclamation of the resurrection: the claim of Jesus and the dying on the cross as final consequence of this claim are confirmed and justified by this new action of God.

Theology of the Cross

Just as christology stands unequivocally in the center of Balthasar's theology, it in turn has its own center: *the cross*. This too shows his proximity to Karl Barth: for him as for Balthasar the atoning event on the cross is the real why and wherefore of Jesus' incarnation and human existence. All God's action in relation to human beings points to this event in which this action receives its enfolding center and from which alone it can make any sense at all. Neither theological statements about the essence of the person of Jesus as "true God and true man," nor speculative reflection on the essence of the "one God in three Persons" and thus on the possibility and reality of the incarnation of the second divine person form the systematic first principle of this christology. No, only the *event* of the death on the cross alone has this importance for Balthasar. The absoluteness of God and his love is revealed once-and-for-all in the *history* of Jesus which has its *concretissimum*, its high point and its converging peak of meaning, in the event of the cross. Only from this starting point does it become definitively clear who God is, who Jesus Christ is, or what the redeeming love of this God is all about. The essence of God and his self-revelation in the person of Jesus is on this account hardly dissolved in the event of the cross; God does not first get "constituted" on the cross of Jesus; nor is his essence simply identical with this event.[62] But all faithful speaking about God and every theological desire to understand his essence has an unsurpassable standard set by this event of the cross in which God has so incomparably revealed himself to humanity. Because God has chosen the history of Jesus, and within that his death on the cross, as the focus of his self-revelation, we can adequately recognize the absolute only in this concrete history.[63] All other ways to the absolute run towards this center, or proceed from it, whether they explicitly know it or not.

But what is it in terms of its content that turns the history of Jesus and above all the event of the cross into the place of God's self-revelation? To what extent precisely *in* this history with its high point on the cross does God himself definitively and unsurpassably make his appearance? For Balthasar, who perceives the figure of Jesus predominantly from the definitive perspective of the Gospel of John and reads the synoptic texts from this perspective, the decisive revelational content of the whole Jesus-event lies in the *obedience of the Son.* Already the "measureless" claim of Jesus can just on that account not be understood as self-arrogation because he acts in obedience to the Father whose absolute authority he wishes to bring to realization. The obedience of Jesus (described by Balthasar also as *fides Christi,* faith of Christ) is manifested throughout as "the absolute precedence of the Father, of his essence, his love, his will and command over all his own wishes and inclinations," as "resolute perseverance in this will, come what may."[64] Jesus lives his mission as God's saving Word to humankind in an utterly "transparent" relationship to the Father who sends him. This attitude of obedience is expressed especially in the unconditional way in which Jesus leaves himself under the Father's guidance with regard to the decisive "hour" which "only the Father knows" and in which the mission of the Son reaches its high point. It is the hour of the passion toward which the incarnation, as beginning of the self-emptying, and the whole earthly existence of Jesus, as existence in obedience, are directed.

Thus the cross becomes the place where in the utmost powerlessness of the Son, God's splendor is most clearly revealed. Precisely in this johannine dialectic of "glorification" in the "poor" dying of the grain of wheat and in the being raised up on the cross does Balthasar's theology find its center. For here, the figure of the obedient Son appears as the purest self-representation of the triune love of God; here the human *obedience* of Jesus corresponds completely to the divine *love* between Father and Son in their common Spirit. What God is in himself, namely, eternal, groundlessly free, loving, self-emptying, is revealed in the obedient self-giving of the Son on the cross (who allows himself to be "delivered over" by the Father to sinners and at the same time gives himself in full agreement) within this world as the totally free, loving self-emptying of God for sinful human beings. The obedience of Jesus, the "delivered-over" servant of God, who vicariously takes on himself the God-forsakenness of the sinner and in so doing suffers through all the power of sin in the world, its deepest and most final no against God, thus hell itself, is revealed; this obedience of the utmost solidarity with sinners is not just the highest instance of an attitude of human faith and obedience towards God. No, within the realm of sin and death this obedience represents the absolutely unique "transference of his eternal love as Son towards the ever greater Father."[65] Who God is in himself is definitively made known only on the cross: the crossing-over-toward-humankind unity (Spirit) of infinitely pouring-forth love (Father) and infinitely receiving obedience (Son):

> Only in his holding-onto-nothing-for-himself is God Father at all; he pours forth his substance and generates the Son; and only in the holding-onto-nothing-for-himself of what has been received does the Son show himself to be of the same essence of the Father, and in this shared holding-onto-nothing-for-themselves are they one in the Spirit, who is, after all, the expression and personification of this holding-onto-nothing-for-himself of God and the eternal new beginning and eternal product of this ceaselessly flowing movement. If one of these Persons steps out of this circling life in order to offer to the world what is the totality of God, his style of life will not be the grasping demeanor of a pantocrator but the opposite: the Son lays bare the heart of the Father as he becomes the servant of all and breathes out into the world his Spirit of service and of the last place.[66]

This happens on the cross of Jesus; and therefore right here, where in the formlessness of death every form (even of love) produced by human beings shatters, arises that form of the inconceivably highest in love which can only be God's very self and which bears in itself the evidence of being the unique and unsurpassable one in contrast to all human forms.

All Balthasar's thinking strives toward this theology of the cross in all theological questions. Here alone are these questions solved for him—not in the sense of a rounded-off, all-explaining systematic formula, but as being able to entrust our searching and questioning to the ever greater God of love as well as accepting from him an answer which does not theoretically "enlighten" us but calls us into the practical imitation of his Son. Only in this praxis does faith find its truth and all theological contemplation its goal, which for this reason is more redemption (*Er-lösung*) than solution (*Lösung*). Thus Balthasar emphasizes rather often that all his theological labor moves between the two poles of John and Ignatius: what constitutes for the former the center of his believing meditation, namely the revelation of the splendor of God in the dying grain of wheat, is put into practice by the latter (through the Exercises) in the concrete ecclesial form of the imitation of the crucified.

Theology of History

A third important moment in this christology which also owes a great deal to the encounter with Karl Barth lies in its historical-theological ramification. Because of his "doctrine of universalistic predestination," Barth has become for Balthasar the great catalyst of his own sketch of a "theology of history."[67] This means that Barth fundamentally overcomes the dualistic doctrine of predestination coming from Augustine that determines the Calvinist tradition, according to which, by God's eternal decree, some are predestined to salvation and others to damnation. According to this (Calvinist) theory, mercy and justice are balanced, with God himself as the scales, as it were. For Barth this is unacceptable: Jesus Christ, God's saving Word for all men and women, is already present and active in God's eternal plan of creation as the that-from-which of creation; and this creation is at the same time directed from the beginning toward him as its perfected that-to-which. For this reason the whole reality of creation is effectively determined by God for salvation: his grace in Christ has already eliminated every possible counterweight of sin (Rom 5!) and made a favorable decision in its regard. The tension between this eschatological promise of salvation to all, and God's selecting choice of some few in the history of salvation, is sustained by the "representation" of Jesus Christ, the *one* chosen bringer of salvation *for all*; in him God has had mercy on all, has called all into his eternal salvation.

Balthasar takes up this universalistic starting point and joins it in an original way with the Logos christology of the ancient church, especially as it was represented by Origen. From the confluence of these thoroughly different, but still common, "Word-theologies" proclaiming the universal atonement of history in Jesus Christ, Balthasar shapes his own theology of history which can be summarized in a pointed formula: Jesus Christ is the *universale concretum* of history as a whole. In the unique "concrete" person, Jesus Christ, and in his history, the meaning of "universal" history (and of the nature underlying it) has been fulfilled. This means not only that in him the endlessly many individual histories of people and nations find their meaning-giving center and ultimate purpose, but that this fulfillment lies still deeper and more fundamentally. The general "logos" of history (i.e., anything in the world that manifests something of reason, of natural regularity and moral norm, of meaning and value, of development and freedom) is integrated and brought to completion in the one particular Logos, the incarnate Word of God. In this person, the "monstrously wide abyss" (Lessing) between the universally valid (of reason and its ideas) on the one hand, and on the other hand the historically particular (of history and its facts) has been closed. Not a universal idea or a universal doctrine of salvation (e.g., the "morally good" or "freedom" or "love" or "world peace"), nor any kind of universal structures which, in the process of their historical self-unfolding, gradually are prosecuted in concrete particulars as well (e.g., the *humanum* or a "classless society"), create in a definitive way this synthesis of universal significance and concrete historical fact. In the historical person of Jesus Christ only and alone do these poles come together in such a way that in him not only every concrete history and its uniquely singular destiny but also all universal structures, values, and ideas are really "sublated," that is, preserved and brought to their full meaning as they are. The "concrete" Jesus Christ is absolutely significant for the meaning of reality as a whole; he alone gives everything its final meaning.

Consequently a twofold claim is made for Jesus Christ: on the one hand, he is the *absolutely unique one* who can in no way be subsumed under universal concepts and norms (e.g., founder of a religion, redeemer, humanist, prophet, etc.); these, instead, must measure up to him in their content, or they are put in relation to Christ and, judged from his history, they are rejected in their false sense or adopted and fulfilled in their partially true sense. Over against everything "relatively unique" in history (to which every human being as an individual and every concrete interhuman relationship belongs) Jesus as "*the* way, *the* truth, and *the* life," claims really to be "absolutely unique." At the same time, however, everything else is in no way divided and excluded from him; he does not stand out as a completely unrelated monolith in the historical landscape. As "type," as *the* original model of humankind, he is at the same time the *infinitely integrating one* who makes room in himself for *everything* truly human and creaturely and in whom alone all this finds its fulfillment, its completed form. Thus, for example, all non-Christian religions, world views, philosophies, moral and value systems are not judged through Christ simply as false, superfluous, or superseded, but are taken in their (fragmentary) truth-content, brought into the comprehensive truth of Christ, and in that way brought fully to themselves. Perfect "exclusivity" (i.e., to be incomparably unique) and perfect "inclusivity" (i.e., to be infinitely integrative and perfecting) are not excluded in Christ but require and promote one another.

This is possible only because in Jesus, the Logos of God himself, the eternal Word of the Father, has become human. In this Word the whole fullness of the love of God is communicated to men and women, in the form of the obedient Son and servant which is represented to humankind as pure "existence in receptivity" (*Existenz im Empfang*). And precisely as such, it can become the center and integrating source of meaning for all of history. Because the Son-become-human wills in his existence to be nothing other than the open, limitless allowing-himself-be-granted by the Father's love, he can, in the receiving of this infinite love, simultaneously hand it on without limits; he can—without himself becoming lost or "dissolved"—open himself infinitely to every reality he encounters and integrate it in affirming or correcting love into the all-redeeming, Spirit-filled event of this love between Father and Son. In this event alone does universal history come to its goal—already anticipated now in the "fullness of time"—and find there its deepest meaning.

HISTORY OF SALVATION: OLD AND NEW COVENANT

This theology of history forms the larger context of the important dialogue which Balthasar has been having for many years with Judaism and one of its best representatives, Martin Buber.[68] The relation between Old and New Covenant, between old and new people of God, between Israel and the church, is a problem with which Balthasar is constantly struggling anew. For the Christian faith, Christ is unequivocally the "fulfillment" of all Old Testament promises; as such, his form takes up as necessary "material" so to speak all the preparatory "images" and "figures" of the Old Testament which are still not unified under one figure (e.g., the Messiah, the servant of God, the mediator, the kingdom of God, the resurrection of the dead, etc.) and brings them together into an integrating synthesis. All Old Testament pre-images converge on this synthesis; but it still cannot be simply derived and construed from them, but has been created only by God's own new beginning in Jesus Christ.

Even more problematic for Balthasar than this promise-fulfillment scheme (which also characterizes the creation-redemption relationship) is the relationship, which comes for the very history of Jesus, of Israel rejecting the new people of God. The question which continually moves Balthasar in this connection is, how can one talk of the universality of Jesus and (derivatively) of his church when the old people of God in its entirety (apart from the "holy remnant") closed itself to the proclamation of Jesus and the Word of God definitively revealed in it? Has there not right from the beginning, that is to say, in Israel's rejection both of the claim of Jesus and then also of the church's preaching, a "chasm" been established straight through the middle of the one people of God? And in such a way that neither the figure of Jesus nor the gathered people of God are really all-encompassing or universal, and that neither of them can therefore be an efficacious-representative sign of the universal reconciliation of God with men and women and of men and women among themselves? The concern for a proper understanding of Romans 9–11 characterizes Balthasar's theology of history; according to this text even the refusing Israel, which remains precisely that in the history of the world, has its enduring meaning for the new people of God. This applies even now, in the middle of history, and not just in the eschatological completion of the one people of God "out of Jews and pagans"; the mercy of God still applies to Israel even "now," in the midst of its disobedience (cf. Rom 11:31). Thus the old people of God makes its way through history not just beside the church; it is instead—because of the mercy of God in the crucified Christ—already "part" of the church, of the new people of God, in such a way at any rate that in her midst it "keeps schism and chasm open."[69] The universality of the love of God appears within history under the sign of a people already separated and divided from the beginning; in this people the church shares in the fate of the crucified who, in his death, lets the refusal of Israel become visible as such, and at the same time still draws it into his universally atoning suffering "for all."

Encounter with Henri de Lubac

With this last point we have already moved into an area in which the ecclesiology of Balthasar must be discussed more explicitly. This is unfolded above all in his encounter with another great theologian of our time with whom, to this day, Balthasar remains in friendly exchange: Henri de Lubac, S.J. (born 1896). Balthasar studied theogy with him in Lyons (1933–1937); with him he found what I would call his "theological home." De Lubac, whose strength also lies less in rigorous systematics than in the meditative-theological elaboration of the treasures of church tradition, was able to pass to his younger friend an "ambience," a so-to-speak Catholic atmosphere in which he could live and think creatively. Balthasar seized upon many inspiring impulses in this encounter, and as much as he united them with other influences and reworked them into his own form of theology, the whole bears undeniably the characterizing mark of this man.

But externally too, even prescinding for the most part from content, many striking points in common dominate between these two theologians. There is, for one thing, the almost unsurveyable number of publications on all possible questions of intellectual and theological history, on systematic themes from philosophy and theology which, at first glance, may seem very much like a "wilderness,"[70] but on more careful examination come together into an "organic whole" with a clear center and some unequivocal fundamental options which recur again and again in the most diverse variations. Further, both feel that they are mediators of the tradition, especially of the fathers of the church. Their own work often merges indistinguishably with what they take from the past or from a hidden present in order to offer it as a valid answer to contemporary questions of faith. Their interest is not in the originality of their own work but in mediating what is valid. And finally, both have made their own a churchliness (*Kirchlichkeit*) borne by an almost mystical optimism. We of today can barely imagine what these and other theologians in the postwar years (to the eve of the Council) suffered under the integralistic-restorative spirit of the church and its then dominant (even in the magisterium) theology. Even if in retrospect many a sharp word on this is spoken,[71] a deep bitterness, spirit of opposition, or resignation never managed to take root in them. A specific postconciliar "suffering from the church" disturbs them more painfully: namely, about the way that—in their judgment—many treasures of the tradition of faith restored in the Council are being too thoughtlessly thrown away at the price of a cheap, progressivist secularization of the faith. But even here their criticism and polemic remains for the most part free of bitterness and resignation; their love for the church and their trust in the "power of the Spirit" bestowed on it by the Lord allow them to bear such disappointments with a certain nobility.

But deeper still than all these more formal, common qualities lies the relatedness in terms of the contents of their theological projects. Out of their mutual inspiration are always formed two distinct faces of one theology. We will briefly mention in turn the most important themes which Balthasar's theology owes to his meeting with H. de Lubac.

THE PARADOX OF THE HUMAN

As with the other theologians we have mentioned, so also with de Lubac, the *nature-grace* problem plays a decisive role. For it was precisely in relation to this question, how the *constitutive*, inner orientation of the human person to the grace of the self-communicating God and the absolute *undeservedness* of this grace may be joined

together, that the representatives of a more neoscholastic prove-
nience or of a—however they may have differed in particular—*nou-
velle théologie* went their separate ways. We have already referred to
this problematic many times. The foundational insight which for de
Lubac and also for Balthasar brought about the liberating solution
and from then on determined their whole thinking on the relationships of God-man, grace-nature, faith-reason, salvation-creation is
their insight into the "paradox of the human being." What does that
mean? Well, the human person is not simply to be arranged univocally with all other creatures under the concept "nature." As personal
body-spirit nature, humankind occupies in the whole of creation a
unique position which also stamps the relationship with God in a
unique way so that it is not to be brought with other "things" under
the general title "nature." An original axiom of high scholasticism,
freed of all post, late, and neoscholastic constrictions, comes into
play again here—but also drawn out by the ever stronger influence of
personalistic-intersubjective thought within theology (e.g., M. Buber,
F. Rosenzweig, F. Ebner, R. Guardini, and others). This axiom states
that "that being which strives after the perfect good, even though it
needs outside help to do so, is more noble than the being that desires
to attain only imperfect good out of its own strength."[72] In other
words, it is constitutive of the "nobility" of the "nature" of the human being that with all that he or she is and can be capable of, a man
or woman strives for supernatural goodness, for a personal, salva-
tion-creating encounter with the triune God, without being able to
attain or even demand this out of his or her own natural power. Yet,
this "striving" (*desiderium naturale visionis*) is truly human only to
the extent that it is ready to allow itself to be granted its fulfillment,
its salvation as pure grace from God. As *person* the human being finds
his or her salvation only to the extent that he or she can accept it as
gift and not produce it from his or her own achievement. Only this
readiness *to allow* oneself, unrequired and unowed, to be loved by
God in personal, freely-given love constitutes what is unique in this
human "striving" which reaches beyond "nature" and ultimately
aims at adoration, at glorifying God, and *therein* at his or her own
blessedness and fulfillment. From its personal nature the human being is thus thoroughly inwardly, constitutively ordered to the communication of God's love and of course in such a way that this love
can be received *only* as an unowed free gift.

A phenomenology of human love confirms this paradox in an analogous way: being completely oriented to the love of the other in order
to find there alone one's fulfillment, *and* at the same time an unconditionally free, undemanded ability to accept this love, do not exclude,
but mutually condition, one another. Required or indeed coerced

love, on the other hand, destroys itself and the partner of the relationship. The most profound reason for this personal-paradoxical character of love lies in God's authentic creative intention: because God wants to communicate himself to one other than himself in the fullness of his love, he posits this other as a free other which is wholly established for this gift of God's self-communication. This creature carries in itself as it were the "wish" of the creator for love in itself, but in just such a way that it can accept this love really *as* free gift, and only on that account can also answer and give back in freedom.

THE WORLD OF THE CHURCH FATHERS

Balthasar's encounter with de Lubac was especially revelatory of the world of the church fathers. He discovered in them a fullness of Christian faith development which fascinated him and in whose breadth, from now on, his whole mission as a theologian in the church took place. Origen above all, in whom he "recognized with awe the most superior mind of the first centuries,"[73] captivated him; he remained for Balthasar the "most ingenious, the most comprehensive interpreter and lover of the Word of God. Nowhere do I feel so comfortable as with him."[74] In the anthology *Geist und Feuer* (*Spirit and Fire*, 1938), and in numerous other publications, he awakened to new life this theologian, who was often forgotten and misjudged by the tradition, by purifying him of his "gnostic garnishings" and laying bare the "true countenance" of an abidingly relevant theology of the Word of God. Origen opened for him the paths to Gregory of Nyssa, to Maximus the Confessor, to Irenaeus, to Evagrius of Pontus, to Dionysius the Areopagite and to many other church fathers whose works he translated, commented on, edited, and in whose service he placed his own theologizing. Their voice should not be lost in the popular theological business of the present.[75] But can we give more precise information how in particular this working with the church fathers has had its effect on Balthasar's theology? That this is where he developed his fundamental intuition of the *universale concretum*, the unity of the universal (Catholic) love of God in Christ related to the whole world and its concrete church-institutional form, we have already seen. Beyond this I would like to treat here only two further points.

Theological Method: the Whole before Its Parts

It seems that it was precisely in his encounter with the church fathers that Balthasar's theological *method* was developed. It has appropriately been described as "theological phenomenology."[76]

What does this mean? Balthasar is always concerned, before and in all particular theological questions, to get a view of the *whole* of

Christian faith as such. That "whole" is more than the (subsequent) sum of its parts because it represents primordial unity which precedes every "critically" dissecting analysis and every simple listing of elements one after the other. The *one* fundamental Christian mystery—God's love for the world in the gift of his Son and in the sacrament of his church—should be recognized in its original "infold" (*Ein-falt*), so that it can then also be continually recognized again in its detailed "un-foldings" (*Aus-faltungen*, i.e., in the most varied expressions of faith, dogmatic formulas, sacramental and liturgical forms, social and legal structures of the community of faith, etc.). For Balthasar the original synthesis has its place in theology ahead of all analyses (of a historical-critical, hermeneutical, historical-doctrinal, psychological, and sociological kind). This synthesis integrates in itself all individual moments of faith and brings them forth from itself, but without ever releasing them from this unity. Therefore each individual theological question can be answered only through the demonstration of its connection with the center of faith; the "resolution back into the mystery" (*reductio in mysterium*) must be carried through in every individual instance if the answer is to be correct. This emphasis of the "whole" before the "parts" of the Christian mystery of faith in no way hinders Balthasar from taking up the results of historical-critical exegesis, history of doctrines, or other modern studies. But these results do not stand by themselves, they rather keep their helping function in order to make the total shape of Christian revelation, perceived in faith and firmly held against all critical relativizing, stand even more clearly in its historical profile and in the wealth of its aspects.

But in order to get this whole truly in view, there is a need, before all legitimate and necessary theological analysis, of that fundamental contemplative attitude which opens itself in all "infolding" (*Einfalt*) to Christ, his Word, his Spirit, his love, and which first accepts this self-revelation of God as what it offers itself to be: the most beautiful and most unexpected gift of his love. For Balthasar good theology is contemplation brought to conceptualization; it attempts to think through and speak the mystery of God's love experienced in the hearing of the Word of God and in the action of the imitation of Jesus, in order that it can always be freshly and convincingly communicated in the respective horizon of understanding of a given age. Balthasar took his self-understanding of theology from the church fathers, from their contemplative exegesis of the Word of God and their symbolic-wholistic understanding of the salvation-event.

Understanding of Sacred Scripture
An essential moment of this method is its special understanding of the Word of God as it has been written down in the sacred scripture.

Balthasar is clearly indebted on this point to Origen, that great Word-theologian of antiquity. What he learned from him is, briefly stated, a sacramental-symbolic concept of the scriptural Word: the incarnation of the eternal Logos is continued beyond the historical incarnation and beyond the church, the primordial sacrament, in its furthermost concretion, namely in the Word of scripture. As with the incarnation of the Word in Jesus and with the taking on of a social body in the church, so the Logos of the letter of scripture serves as the bodily-real symbol of his spiritual presence in the holy scripture. These three modes of presence of the Word are indeed distinguished from each other, but not separated: they are indissolubly interrelated moments of the one self-emptying of the Word of God into history; only in their unity do they form the one sacramental *mysterium* of the self-revelation of God which is then unfolded in many individual sacraments of the church. Coming, therefore, from this symbolic consideration of scripture, it can never be for Balthasar only or primarily a document of the history of faith which could be adequately studied by a neutral historical-critical interpretation. No, the "real symbol" of the eternal Word requires, to be sure, a completely faithful verbal-literal interpretation which, however—for the sake of its faithfulness—must necessarily pass into the "spiritual-pneumatic" where the real encounter with the Word of God begins to take place—in faith.[77] This faith sees the whole of the mystery of the incarnation present in every letter of the holy scripture; a separating ("heresy") of the individual statement or word or book of scripture from the whole Spirit-filled faith-understanding of the church is for him absolutely impossible.

But with this view care is also taken that the "Spirit" does not precipitate into individual "letters" and get hardened in them. There is proper to this kind of symbolic understanding of scripture a dynamic which moves beyond every rigid fixation on the letter, law, rite, or institution toward the Spirit of the eternal Word, which indeed joins them together but never dissolves them; it is instead always going beyond them. A most reverent acknowledging of the letter (as the real symbol of the Logos) and a most free relativizing of the form toward the ever greater "fullness" of the self-revelation of God is truly the art in which for Origen (and his faithful students, de Lubac and Balthasar) is demonstrated true interchange with the scripture.

THE FORM (GESTALT) OF THE CHURCH

Finally, out of this spirit of the church fathers also grows Balthasar's *ecclesiology* which—inspired by de Lubac's *Catholicism* (1938)—presents in new form the symbolically pregnant patristic image of the church with its central concepts of Body of Christ, Bride of Christ, *communio sanctorum* (Communion of Saints). We will only point out here the basic characteristics of this theology of the church.[78]

Participation in Distance

For Balthasar the Christ-event stands, from the beginning, in closest correlation with the church-event. Christology can, therefore, be done only in union with ecclesiology. But in this very point also resides another paradox of Christian faith: that there can even be such a thing as "imitation" in relation to the absolutely unique and singular figure of the incarnate Word. The distance of this unique "human being *for* human beings" in relation to us, the "human being *with* human beings," is established insuperably in the loneliness of his death on the cross, his vicarious suffering of the sin of the world. And yet there is a "participation in distance"; there is an analogy which, from Christ, is given to those who put themselves unconditionally at his disposition and allow him to stamp them with his own form of existence, the *forma servi*. This obedient readiness to let this happen to oneself, in which the "investiture of the form of Christ" can be achieved,[79] forms the "central concept" which brings together the two incomparably different poles (Christ and us). Now the sphere in which this universally intended modeling of the human person after Christ initially takes place is the church; it is what Christ himself brought about as the "form of response" to the form taken by the Word of God in human history. Church is understood as the "place where the formation of humanity in the likeness of the person and event of Christ is introduced, where human beings give themselves in attentive-obedient faith to this event, become sacramentally shaped by it, and through their existence seek to make it effective in the world."[80]

Mary—Exemplar of the Church

This general ecclesial attitude of allowing oneself to be formed after Christ in an exemplarily personal way is concretized in Mary; in her, the complete "identity" of the forming love of God and of the obedience of the human being allowing itself to be formed, as this happened in Christ, is ecclesially "imaged." In this "pure correspondence" the human answer untaintedly (*immaculate*) reflects the Word of God's love and allows it to become manifest for the first time in its glory: "for the Lord does not want to see his church standing there as a unique, evident failure, but as a glorious bride worthy of him."[81] Proceeding from Mary, this "unscathed nucleus" of the church, the further "shaping" of the human person after Christ, takes place. But it remains always contained in and supported by Mary and the "fundamental marian attitude." For in her "Let it be done to me according to your word," Mary is the fundamental "type" or "exemplar" of the church, that is, the "form" of the church which founds, supports, and includes everything else.

Within this comprehensive sphere come next the other corresponding "types," those models of Christian existence which belong to the original "christological constellation": thus above all the Twelve (as original models of the all-abandoning imitation), and among them especially Peter (as the embodiment of office), and John (as representation of the "church of love"), and finally Paul (as exemplary unity of apostolic office and existence). After these early church figures come, most appropriately, the saints of the church; they alone form church in the full sense of *communio sanctorum*. This is why for Balthasar the church in its core is a "network" of concrete persons who are however already "objectivized" into a determining form for every other possible existence in the imitation of Jesus. All believing persons must commit themselves to this exemplary form of imitation, and the more they are successful here in obedient expropriation for the Lord, the more do they themselves become a supporting form for others, so much the more do they bring the church to realization.

Understood this way, it is fundamentally impossible for the church to be an interfering intermediate link between the individual and Jesus Christ. Its only function is to mediate the immediacy of Christ, the communal shaping into the form of Christ in individuals. It has no form of its own apart from Christ; everything in it must stay transparently related to its origin, to Christ, just as Christ is related completely transparently to the Father. Thus, the church must, of its nature, share in performing the double "diminishment" of Christ— towards the Father and towards the world. It will, to the extent that it remains true to itself, not establish itself any more than he did as a third figure between God and world (in Arian fashion!) but solely as the "pure possibility of their encounter." This ecclesial mediation therefore does not estrange individuals from themselves but liberates them from their own attempts to respond which are subjectively narrow and necessarily backward in relation to the exemplary obedience of Mary and the saints.

Body of Christ—Bride of Christ

Distinction from Christ, the absolutely unique figure, and at the same time (analogous) participation in him through being obedientially formed in his likeness: these are the weight-bearing pillars of Balthasar's ecclesiology. In it he makes frequent use of the biblical-patristic images of the "body" and the "bride," in both of which, in different ways, the unity and difference between Christ and the church is illustrated. As "body of Christ" the church is not an independent reality which exists of itself and is understandable of itself: "it is, and it cannot be other than, an extension, a communication, a sharing of the personality of Christ."[82] But the church is this precisely as not identical with its Lord, but as the "bride" which Christ loved and for which he gave himself on the cross. She exists, then, just as essentially outside of his person, and only on that account can Jesus Christ have for her besides the "somatic-identifying" also a really "personal-differentiating" relationship. This dialectical union, church as body of Christ and in this at once as his bride who is distinct from him, who serves him as virginal maid[83] and whom he loves, is seen by Balthasar especially, in connection with Ephesians 5:21ff., as realized by Christ and the church in the mystery of the marital being-one-flesh as sacrament of the being-one-Spirit. The marital similitude ("wedding aspect") for this reason stands at the midpoint of this ecclesiology: it comprises (1) both the personal difference (bride-bridegroom), (2) the being-one-body-and-one-Spirit (head-body), and finally also (3) the fundamental, abiding difference of the persons in this being-one (male-female). Marriage thus becomes a "sign of redemption."[84]

Eucharist

This bridal-bodily relationship between Christ and the church finds its completed *communitary* form in the Eucharist. On the part of Jesus, his passion, this obedient "being disposed of" in the "hour" of death, appears here unequivocally as a personal, active deed of his freedom. For here he makes anticipatory disposition of his being-disposed-of in the passion; he gives himself, whose body and blood will be "delivered over" and "poured out" in the passion, in free and loving self-giving to human beings. His sacrifice appears in the sign of the meal: only thus does he become "food for the world," because his self-emptying into the final abandonment of God and humans is here symbolically embodied in his "kenotic condition" as "bread to be chewed . . . and wine poured out." It is primarily in the abiding form of the eucharistic self-pouring out that the self-giving of Jesus can be quite really accepted by human beings so that they really become "one body" with him. The appropriate attitude of human beings toward this self-giving can only be a complete being-in-agreement with the sacrifice of the Lord. It is precisely in this agreement of the participants in the meal that the community of the church is constituted: for here human beings let the sacrifice of Christ take place in them; they accept the offering of his life for the many and allow themselves to be taken along with it into this sacrifice, into this being-given-up for the salvation of all. In the upper room the bodily-marital formation of the church to Christ is completed, insofar as here the indivisible unity in the abiding, radical difference of self-offering Lord and accepting maid is brought to completion. The church, in agreement with the offering of Christ (which is sealed in the reception of the food), is taken in a quite real way into the sacrifice of Christ, really united with it, without this act of the church (its "sacrifice") being able to be equated with the act of Christ offering himself for his own. But, "it is still complementary to Christ's act, and not externally but internally united to it through the same obedience which has the suffering of the cross as its presupposition."[85]

Institutional Office in the Communio

Within this eucharistically stamped "form or response" of the church, office and everything institutional in the church has its genuine place. Since Balthasar considers all essential structural elements of the church first in their exemplary personal realization, in "typical" church figures, it is in the indissoluble ordering to each other of Mary (and John) on the one hand and Peter on the other that he expressed this relationship between a loving-obedient church and the office formed in it. This means that in every official mandate which Peter (and in him every ecclesiastical officeholder) receives as an "objective," fully empowered mission coming only from Christ, namely "to feed the flock of Christ," the proper acceptance of this responsibility, the "subjective" faith-stance of the holy church, is always presupposed. We find it fully realized only in Mary: it is demanded of Peter but he continually fails and, as a penitent sinner, must have this readiness of faith given him again and again. Because the "subjective spirit" of the officeholder never corresponds to the "objective spirit" of the office conferred, or to the mission and authority conferred by Christ, but always lags behind in sinful deficiency, the "marian principle" must intervene in the church. Through this principle the identity of objective office and subjective holiness is ecclesiastically guaranteed. But on the other hand, in Mary, the subjectively holy church, the fullness of the "objective spirit" of word, office, sacrament, and law in the church is not intelligibly and administratively exhausted. No, it furnishes instead for the office conferred on Peter only the *foundation* of the adequate response into which the officeholder with his personally deficient response must insert himself and out of which he can then legitimately fulfill his mission to the church and to the individual believer.

Balthasar here largely adopts Augustine's teaching on the truly loving church, the *columba* ("dove"), and the communion of saints. She is, through her fundamental unity of objectively conferred grace and subjectively realized holiness lived by the saints, also the really effective church, if the love of God is supposed to be mediated in a human way in office and sacraments. This "church of love" is already in union with Christ. He works through *her* love, and the efficacy of the "official church"—even of the sinful officeholder—has only mediating power when it is anchored in this comprehensive ecclesial love, when it represents *her* and hence also brings Christ into play. It is clear then "that between the official representatives of the holy church . . . and this [church of love] no difference holds sway when they carry out their office with the right attitude of love; but that, in case they do not do this, a difference sets in between them as persons of office and the church of love represented by them, a difference which, according to their natures . . . cannot exist between the latter and Christ."[86]

But this difference is now in the church as a matter of fact, and the sign of the cross (as sign of the contradiction of sin against love) is always stamped on the church precisely by church office and its sinful bearers. It is given to the "holy" church, in its following of the Lord, and assigned it again and again, to carry out this contradiction, without shattering on it, without therefore letting church office break away from this love. Exactly at this point it is shown that church office is always reliant on the love of the saints, on "John"—the type of this church of the saints. For there accrues to the "beloved disciple" (and following him the saints in the church) the special ecclesial mission of playing the "mediating role"; consequently of preventing the "Petrine" office from falling away from the fundamental ecclesial form of "marian" holiness, by virtue of the charism granted it. It is the "service to the center" which John, in his stepping back from office (Jn 21:2–25!), gives to the church; he communicates as it were to church office (Peter) his "greater love" so that Peter can give the response appropriate to his mandate and so be able to be installed in his office as pastor of the community:

> Peter needs the johannine love in order to give the Lord the required response appropriate to his office, and he gets this love as well. By the same token the johannine love has its place henceforth in Peter. But Jesus' missions do not disappear; John maintains . . . his own, distinct from that of Peter. Neither can it be said that love is absorbed in church office (or that church office coopts the love for itself), nor can it be said that office and love stand opposed to each other like two adequately separable structural elements. . . .[87]

Balthasar's theology of church office is an attempt to integrate fundamentally the ecclesiastical-institutional with the totality of churchly love and community. It should therefore—no matter how

much abuse there is—never be understood as a historically conditioned degeneration from an originally institution-free church as
"fraternal community." For everything official in the church is based
on the common love of the *communio sanctorum* and has therein its
special mission which belongs essentially to the church: namely, in
the following of the "Good Shepherd" to perform the service of a
"shepherd" and thus, like Jesus, be prepared "to give his life for his
own" to the last ounce of his being. The reality of sin gives this service
a specific face; for, taken advantage of by sinners and effective for
sinners (which we all are), this service represents in the form of the
cross the love of God in the midst of the church. Just as in Jesus's
passion (e.g., in the agony in the Garden), the "alienness" or even
"objectivity" of the will of the Father and the obedience of the Son,
forced by the sin of the world, comes to the fore more starkly than the
abiding intimacy of this love, the same thing, analogously, takes
place in the institutional church. For in it the Spirit of love between
Father and Son which is always present in the *communio* of the
church, takes, precisely with regard to sinners (and hence above all
the officeholders themselves), the form of a "law," making objective
demands of and correcting and restricting the resisting freedom of
the sinner. It is thus felt to be foreign and constricting. And yet, even
in this salvation-historical "hidden form," it remains an expression
of the love of God.

Encounter with Adrienne von Speyr

Already present in these ideas is the theme of passion and sin
which, through another encounter, moves more and more into the
center of Balthasar's theology. In 1940 the physician Adrienne von
Speyr (1902–1967) became a convert under his direction. His encounter with this woman, with her special mission for the church, and
with her mystical experiences became for Balthasar a decisive
moulding influence in his life:

> It was Adrienne von Speyr who pointed out the fulfilling way
> from Ignatius to John, and thus laid the foundation for most of
> what has been published by me since 1940. Her work and mine is
> neither psychologically nor philosophically separable, two halves
> of a whole which, as center, has but one foundation.[88]

Even if the whole of Balthasar's theology and course of life has
without doubt been "impregnated" so to speak by this encounter and
it cannot easily be determined what, in particular, is due to one or the
other (thus, e.g., with regard to the emphasis on the obedient letting-
it-happen-to-oneself as the fundamental attitude of the human per-

son before God, or the veneration of the saints, especially the Mother of God, Saint Ignatius, Saint Thérèse of Lisieux, among others, or the preference for the johannine writings in the New Testament, or the trinitarian dimension of all theology and mysticism), I would still like to lift out two moments from which it will be clear how Balthasar's own mission has here received its very special contours and its most profound spiritual substance.

THE FORM OF LIFE OF THE SECULAR INSTITUTE

One of these moments concerns the external *form of life* in the church which Balthasar, through this encounter, has recognized as the appropriate one and, generally, most sensible one for the present church. Soon after the conversion of Speyr came the idea to found together something like a "secular institute"; an idea which was for them ever more clearly a God-given and thus absolute commission. The attempt to bring about this new foundation within the framework of the Society of Jesus failed because what was so clear to him was not so clear to his superiors. So, with a heavy heart, Balthasar left the Jesuit order in 1950, but in his whole way of life and spirituality he remained a true son of Saint Ignatius. This new foundation, the *Johannesgemeinschaft* (Community of John), served also by the publishing house, *Johannesverlag*, which he directs, is inspired by the idea of living, in an appropriately modern way, the radical "all-abandoning" imitation of Jesus according to the three evangelical counsels in the middle of the world, in a secular vocation. The idea was to present the "true unabbreviated church program for today" in a community form of life: to present

> the greatest amount of power radiating into the world through the immediate following of Christ. There, where the tension between being a Christian and being a fellow human being is most intense, so intense really that it must appear to the natural human being as disruptive and "psychologically" unbearable, and appear to every harmoniously whole human person as simply asking too much, there not only is the external ("eschatological," i.e., world-overcoming) sign set as a productive provocation, but the reality itself, visibly or invisibly . . . is made present.[89]

For Balthasar the so-called "secular communities" (*Instituta saecularia*) are the existential clamps which are best suited to hold together in a living way (and not just theoretically) the "concrete universality" of the Christian faith in all its tension and to bring it to a socially attainable form. The visible effectiveness of his own Community of John clearly does not correspond fully to the original expectations: yet this form of life remains for Balthasar fundamentally *the* opportunity for the contemporary church to represent, in a way that is also symbolically effective, the unity of the fullness of Christ's love, both as received and being shared with the world.

MYSTERY OF HOLY SATURDAY

In the center of von Speyr's mystical experiences stands the grace, given to the sinner for whom it is most profoundly humiliating, of participation in "the vicarious suffering of Christ for the many." In this a very special importance is given to a moment in the passion of Jesus which it otherwise rather neglected in theology and spirituality, namely the article of faith, "descended into hell," into the "realm of death," in which von Speyr sees the real *mystery of Holy Saturday*. This concentrating of soteriology (i.e., of the theology of Christ's suffering *"for us"*) on Jesus' being dead with the dead assumes an increasingly quite decisive role in Balthasars's christology and eschatology. What does it mean?

What stands in the foreground of the saving event in the mystery of Good Friday is the active readiness of the living and dying Jesus to endure the power of the "sin of the world" venting its rage on him and, by his obedience, his loving letting-it-happen-to-him, to take away and destroy this power once and for all. In this vicarious suffering of the sins of all, the mystery of Holy Saturday goes still a step further: it reflects on the passive solidarity, which the Father uses, of Jesus with the dead, and precisely with those who are "dead" in the theological sense, with those, then, who have definitively separated themselves from the love of God and for whom the biblical tradition of faith has coined the word "hell."

> Into this finality (of death) the dead Son descends, no longer active in any way, but stripped by the cross of every power and initiative of his own, as something purely to be disposed of, as someone lowered to pure matter, absolutely indifferent in obedience, incapable of any active entering into solidarity—that is how he first comes to that "sermon" to the dead. He is (out of a final love, however) dead together with them. And in this he disturbs the absolute loneliness sought after by sinners. Sinners, separated from God, wanting to be damned, in their loneliness find God again, but God in the absolute powerlessness of love who, unfathomably, makes himself one in the place-without-time with the self-damning. The words of the psalm, "If I make my bed in Sheol, thou art there" (139:8), thereby take on an entirely new meaning. And even "God is dead" as the autocratic decree of the sinners for whom God is something done away with, receives an entirely new, objective meaning provided by God himself.[90]

These statements cannot be written off as mythology; they are the attempt of a contemplative theology to gain a deeper understanding of the article of faith, "descended into the realm of death." And indeed in such a way that in that attempt both the confidence in universal salvation of the Eastern church fathers (above all of Origen) and the pathos for freedom and responsibility of Western theology (Augustine) come fully into their own. This means that on the one side, the concern is to proclaim the all-encompassing redemptive power of the crucified love of God; it gives us reason to hope that all human beings will be saved and none lost in the end despite the definitively intended No against God on the part of the human being. This is the Orthodox meaning of the so-called "doctrine of *apokatastasis*" of the Eastern church fathers, that is, the doctrine of the eschatological reconciliation of everything. But on the other side, the freedom of the human being and his or her responsibility before God may not be devalued. Human decisions cannot be degraded to an ultimately insignificant child's game which God in his paternal goodness and wisdom can simply annul any time he wants. But, conversely, do human decisions have so much power that they—in the form of their no—can make God's love for the sinner ultimately ineffective for them? How does the universal, liberating love of the Son of God dying on the cross go together with the abiding freedom of the human person to say no to this love? This ultimate mystery of faith is simply not capable of being "dissolved" by theological reasoning. But Balthasar's theology of Holy Saturday attempts—inspired by the existential experiences of Adrienne von Speyr who consequently is to be ranked in the number of those mystics of the church who have been given an experiential share in the "night of the cross"—to reflect on this mystery and find an access to it through meditation on the Christ who "descended into hell" and entered into solidarity with the dead. The answer which this meditation gives allows the universal power of the love of God, with full respect for human freedom, to hold its full validity—exactly as power of love, which does not overpower sinners and "force them to salvation" against their will, but rather which accompanies them, in the wordless gesture of just being there, into their final loneliness. It must remain open just how human beings experience in themselves such "companionship" (somewhat like beatifying "salvation"). For the universal hope of faith, this alone is all-important:

> Only in absolute weakness does God mediate to the freedom he has created the gift of love which shatters every prison and loosens every confinement: in entering into solidarity from within with those who refuse all solidarity. *Mors et vita duello . . .*[91]

SYNTHESIS

In this portrait we have given at least some indication of the almost unsurveyable variety of Balthasar's theological writings, and have put them in the historical context of those encounters which have given his life and thought its characteristically unique form. The result is a theology which springs from encounter, which puts into words the event of these encounters (in receiving, shaping, and handing them on) and which directly through these encounters lets it be mediated (existentially and theologically) to the meaning-giving center of every interhuman event and history as a whole: to the encounter between God and human in the unique but abidingly valid event of the self-revelation of God in Jesus Christ. This unique quality of Balthasar's theology, namely, its unfolding as a unity of (experienced) event and (reflecting) thought, is also reflected very clearly in that theological collective project which has been in the making since 1961, and in which Balthasar would like to harvest the fullness of his Germanistic, literary, philosophical and theological, exegetical and systematic knowledge into a theological synthesis.[92] It is arranged as a trilogy, which, under ever different aspects, intends to unfold the center of Christian faith, namely, the revelation of the "poor" love of God in the crucified Christ. The three guiding points of view are taken from the medieval teaching of the "transcendentals" according to which the fundamental and comprehensive ("transcendental") qualities of the "true," the "good," and the "beautiful" belong to being as such. But these qualities also apply, analogously, to the revelation-event which, therefore, can now be considered, while maintaining the ever greater difference, in union with the whole of reality as capable of being experienced. In the incarnate and crucified *Word* of God, the *Truth* which grasps and answers every human question and knowing is revealed; in the *event* of the self-emptying of God in incarnation and cross, the human person is given a *good* and love which gathers together and completes in itself all his or her striving and love, everything that is worthwhile in creation; in the human *form* of the Son obedient and broken unto death, a *glory* (*Herrlichkeit*) becomes visible which surpasses and integrates all natural beauty, all human demands for beauty, and all our fragmentary attempts to give shape to things. Theology, then, has to be set in motion within these three dimensions: as theological "aesthetic," as theological "dramatic," as theological "logic."

Herrlichkeit

Within this enterprise, theological aesthetics (*Herrlichkeit*—glory, splendor) forms the fundamental and only suitable access to the mystery of revelation; this is where the trilogy begins. But it is important, before anything else, to have a view of this revelation as a historical phenomenon, to perceive it as the nonteleologically free and therefore "beautiful," attractive, and loveworthy gift of the love of God. Balthasar understands theological aesthetic as the doctrine of the perception of the beauty of this completely "to-no-purpose" self-outpouring love of God, precisely of its "appearing glory" (in the Old Testament: *kabod Yahweh*; in the New Testament: *doxa* and *charis*, *gloria* and *gratia Dei*). It is decisive for this perception of the form of revelaton that it does not depend primarily on the spontaneity of the one perceiving it, who, by peering into the depths, as it were, catches sight of what is hidden in himself, brings it out into the light and pours it into an objective form. No, when we are talking about taking in and accepting from God the truth and goodness of his love, just the opposite is true. As opposed to all human spontaneity, receptive openness has the primacy, because this allows what is appearing to begin to show itself and be as it is in itself and as it wishes to appear. This attitude is "servant to the object" and not a dominating take-over of the subject with its categories. Only in this way can the love of God in Christ begin to be perceived at all as "form," as the infinite fullness of the goodness and truth of God's goodness and truth present in a hidden way in finite human form and yet still being revealed therein.

What is uniquely "attractive" and convincing in this form of Christ lies precisely in the fact that a perfect "harmony" reigns between finite form and infinite fullness being represented in it. All individual traits of this figure necessarily "go together" in some way; they all converge on this one and unifying meaning of its life: to be nothing but self-revelation of the love of the Father. Therefore this life also appears (comparable to a unique work of art) in the eyes of a person looking at it from outside, as a gift that could not be invented, put together, or in any way controlled, as the wonderful play of freedom of God who wills to present himself in this form. This successful unity of necessary harmony and free self-presentation constitutes the evidence of the form of Jesus: whoever perceives it in this way can only accept it as grace (*charis*), as the "Glorious reality that was beyond surmise and graciously offers itself for our participation."[93]

Such an experience of the form of revelation does not, of course, happen to uninvolved observers who consider the gift being offered them in a neutral, distanced, objective way, or who persist in a pleasurable aestheticism. Theological aesthetic has nothing to do with such aestheticizing *l'art pour l'art* (art for art's sake). For the act of "perception" is only the first step; it necessarily moves to the state of "being enraptured." That is, only those who allow themselves to be seized, "swept away," and "enraptured" by this appearing love of

God really perceive the form of Christ. Believing persons, by their contemplation of this form, will allow themselves to be set into a movement that takes them away from themselves and into the revealed event of the love between Father and Son in the Holy Spirit. For Balthasar this is "Christian eros," the "enrapturing" into the event of divine love of the person who allows himself or herself to be loved by God. Thus, every quiet repose in the "vision of God" has become impossible. For the person so affected is at the same time the person who is being "formed" by the revealed form of love, made like it, and "shaped into" it.

THEODRAMATIK

At this point the aesthetic opens of itself into another dimension of theological reflection on the mystery of revelation. For the "form" which has been perceived is not something flat and static (like a statue or a painting), but appears instead as a dramatic "event," as an action of God on and with the human being. And so the *Theodramatic* must stand *at the central point of theology*: it is the doctrine of the human person's letting-it-happen-with-him in the drama of God's love which God himself stages among us. The "being-good" of God that really encounters us in God's historical action, in the very praxis of the life and death of Jesus, is the real content of the gift of revelation; God's "glory" and his "truth" are based on his "freedom" with which he loves us and draws us into his love. Thus the aesthetic categories of "form," "expression," "meaning," "symbol" are not simply left behind; they are moved beyond into categories of action, such as, "deed," "decision," "choice," "play," "role." Theatrical drama provides precisely the appropriate point of contact for the transition from "aesthetic" to "dramatic"; for here the necessary "toolbox" of concepts and representational ingredients lies ready to express the unity of an existentially experienced and aesthetically represented "drama of life":

> Nowhere is the character of existence represented more clearly than in acted drama: we want to see it for ourselves, no matter for the moment whether we are in search of ourselves or in flight from ourselves, whether they are putting on before us the serious or the playful, the annihilating or the transfiguring, the meaningless or the hidden depths of the meaning of our being. Through this play of relationships inherent to theater, the questionability and ambiguity not only of the theater but also of existence too which holds it up to the light, becomes clear as perhaps nowhere else.[94]

But the analogy of the theater brings so to speak only the formal and contentual material together (which is done extensively in the first volume of the *Theodramatics*), "in order to get from it categories and forms of expression for the principal undertaking."[95] This principal undertaking is the representation of the unique "drama" which God plays on our historical world stage and into which we are "cast" by him as his fellow actors: "Our play plays in his play."[96] But then the concepts of the theater are no longer adequate for this; they have to let themselves be changed into those of history and anthropology. "Freedom" now becomes the decisive word for understanding the mystery of the playing together of God and human, creator and creature. Because an *analogia libertatis*, an "analogy of freedom," exists between God and humanity,[97] a common action, a common history can be genuinely possible: God's infinitely creative freedom sets up the human being as a free "other" who, in his or her finite, *owed* freedom, is called to play with and act with God. God's action in relation to human beings is the decisive action in the whole history of the world; it is ultimately, *Theo-dramatic*. But human beings do not stand there as spectators or puppets, they are drawn as partners of a dialogical event of love. They belong to the "characters of the play" (thus the title of Volume II of *Theodramatics*), and only play the role given them as "human beings in God" (first subvolume) correctly when they allow themselves to be "chosen" and "sent" to "perform" consistently the "play" of God and his love in his own existence. It is in these familiar concepts of "sending" and "choosing" that Balthasar's theological anthropology peaks also within the framework of his *Theodramatics* as well. There is no question that this doctrine of the human being and his or her owed freedom can be sketched only from the decisive "Person of the play," as it were, starting from Jesus Christ and heading toward him. From Balthasar's theological point of departure, human beings can really be true co-players with God only as "Persons *in* Christ" (thus the title of II/2). This being taken into the drama of love between Father and Son in no way restricts the freedom of the people playing with them and the openness of their history: because it is the event of *infinite* love, it takes away the boundaries surrounding the finite freedom of man and woman and their future, and leads it into the unlimited sphere of the life of God.[98]

"THEOLOGICAL LOGIC"

The planned conclusion of the trilogy will consist of the "theological logic." It concerns the truth of this action of God in history. The question is, in what words and concepts does the divine Logos understandably interpret himself in his historical-dramatic self-revelation? In what actually does the intelligible "reason in the history" of God with humanity, its inner "logic," and thus the generally valid and understandable meaning of this absolutely unique historical form of revelation, Jesus Christ, consist? How does the general human-philosophical knowledge of truth relate to the particular historical truth of revelation?

It is to be wished that Balthasar will yet receive from God the time and the strength to finish this comprehensive project; it would be the only Catholic theology of our century which would show this universal breadth as well as synthetic overview. Yet Balthasar himself is skeptical of this undertaking; as early as fifteen years ago he wrote, looking ahead to the "theological logic":

> In the small space left to a sixty-year-old, neither images nor concepts remain decisive, only the deed; for its sake even the deed of writing books should be buried; God grant that not *only* the paper decay, but that at least *one* grain of wheat come to the grace of resurrection! Everything paper belongs also to the way that is wide. Not that the patient gets pressured, but that the impatient flesh be pressured and pressed to see whether a few fruitful drops will spring from it. It must be pressed in order not to miss the narrow road, the small gate and perhaps even the microscopic eye of the needle which, invisible to human eyes, leads into the Kingdom.[99]

NOTES

1. Cf. *Wer ist ein Christ?* (Einsiedeln 1965).
2. Cf. *Cordula order der Ernstfall* (Einsiedeln 1966); *Rechenschaft 1965* (Einsiedeln 1965).
3. Cf. *Die Wahrheit ist symphonisch* (Einsiedeln 1972).
4. "Warum ich noch ein Christ bin," in H. U. v. Balthasar and J. Ratzinger, *Zwei Plädoyers* (Munich 1971).
5. Cf. *Der antirömische Affekt* (Freiburg 1974).
6. Cf. *Pneuma und Institution* (Einsiedeln 1974), pp. 369ff; *Neue Klarstellungen* (Einsiedeln 1979), pp. 109ff.
7. Cf. *Pneuma und Institution*, pp. 162ff; *Wer ist ein Christ?*, pp. 86ff.
8. Cf. *Klarstellungen* (Freiburg 1971), pp. 176ff.
9. Cf. *Klarstellungen*, pp. 116ff; *Verbum Caro* (Einsiedeln 1960), pp. 245ff; *Sponsa Verbi* (Einsiedeln 1961), pp. 349ff and passim.
10. Cf. International Theological Commission (ed. Karl Lehmann et al.), *Theologie der Befreiung* (Einsiedeln 1977), pp. 155ff; *Einfaltungen* (Munich 1969), pp. 38ff.
11. Cf. *Der antirömische Affekt*, pp. 254ff.
12. H. W. Genischen, *Glaube für die Welt* (Gütersloh 1971), p. 14.
13. Even a fleeting glance over the writings of Balthasar can show this expansive manysidedness of his literary work; cf. in this volume: Bibliographic Guide IV. I refrain from offering a new list here.
14. K. Rahner, "Hans Urs von Balthasar," in *Civitas* 20 (1964/65):602.
15. *Ibid.*, p. 603. There is no question that his perfect command of German and French, which he has enjoyed since childhood and which has enabled him to be at home in both cultures, has had a strong influence on his thought as well as his style with its elegance of poetic imagery (but has also often made it hard to understand).

16. H. U. v. Balthasar, "Kleiner Lageplan zu meinen Büchern," in *Schweizer Rundschau* 55 (1955):212: ". . . but isn't it better for me to come out immediately with the confession that I am an impatient person, for whom there is no question about one thing: the book that has just been finished again contains nothing of what really should have been said, demonstrated, and made clear. The next one will be the product of final desperation. This will at least be some relief; it is the willingly undertaken penance for the drop of too much pleasure that lies in every author."

17. 1943: *Katholizismus als Gemeinschaft* (Einsiedeln); 1970: *Glauben aus der Liebe* (Einsiedeln).

18. *Rechenschaft*, p. 6.

19. "Kleine Lageplan," p. 221.

20. *Rechenschaft*, p. 6.

21. H. de Lubac: Being catholic "is the only reality which, in order to be, doesn't find it necessary to be in opposition; thus, anything but a closed society" (*Glauben aus der Liebe*, p. 263); H. U. v. Balthasar: "Final fullness through integration of all that is temporary and partial, and in this sense totality" ("Die Absolutheit des Christentums und die Katholizität der Kirche," in W. Kasper [ed.], *Absolutheit des Christentums* [Quaest. disp. 79: Freiburg 1977], p. 134.

22. H. de Lubac, "Ein Zeuge Christi in der Kirche: Hans Urs von Balthasar," in *Internationale katholische Zeitschrift* 4 (1975): 397.

23. Cf. H. de Lubac, *Glauben aus der Liebe*, p. 266.

24. Cf. *Theologie der Geschichte* (3rd ed; Einsiedeln 1959), p. 69.

25. Cf. *Pneuma und Institution*, p. 6.

26. *Pneuma und Institution*, p. 229. We will come back to this again.

27. *Herrlichkeit* I, p. 246; on this set of issues, cf. M. Kehl, *Kirche als Institution* (2nd ed; Frankfurt 1978), pp. 248ff.

28. Cf. his, at that time, very "progressive" plea for an "unentrenched, world-oriented church," in *Schleifung der Bastionen* (Einsiedeln 1952).

29. "Es stellt sich vor . . . ," in *Das neue Buch* (Lucerne) 7 (1945): 43.

30. "Kleine Lageplan," p. 214.

31. When Balthasar emphasized obedience so strongly in almost all his writings, he is by no means arguing for an immature, weakminded readiness to be pushed or directed, but for just the opposite: for this free agreement with the love of God which engages the whole person with all its powers.

32. *Rechenschaft*, p. 13.

33. *Ibid.*, p. 8. In the article "Zwei Glaubensweisen" Balthasar expressly contrasts Luther and Ignatius as "types" of different modes of an existential faith, in *Spiritus Creator* (Einsiedeln 1976), pp. 76ff.

34. "Kleine Lageplan," p. 213.

35. *Rechenschaft*, p. 34.

36. Cf. W. Löser, "Das Sein—ausgelegt als Liebe," in *Internationale katholische Zeitschrift* 4 (1975):416. In this article and in the introduction to W. Löser, *Im Geiste des Origenes* (Frankfurt 1976) is to be found much helpful biographical information.

37. This investigation then also formed the foundation piece for his philosophical dissertation in Zürich (1928) on the "Geschichte des eschatologischen Problems in der modernen deutschen Literatur," which was expanded some years later onto the voluminous work, *Apokalypse der deutschen Seele. Studien zu einer Lehre von letzten Haltungen* (Salzburg 1937–1939). It brought together Germanistic, philosophical, and theological studies on Lessing "in a comprehensive Christian presentation."

38. *Geschichte des eschatologischen Problems*, p. 130.

39. "Kleiner Lageplan," p. 224.

40. *Ibid.*

41. *Herder-Korrespondenz* (2, 1976), p. 76.
42. "Kleiner Lageplan," loc. cit.: A phrase from a very early article of Balthasar remains characteristic for his whole life: "He who affirms more is right in the end."
43. I found this delicate play on words in Alois M. Haas, "Hans Urs von Balthasar— Träger des Gottfried Keller-Preises," in *Neue Züricher Zeitung*, 9 January 1976, foreign edition, no. 5: 21.
44. Besides *The Satin Slipper* and *The Tidings Brought to Mary*, Balthasar has translated all of Claudel's books of poetry.
45. Cf. Claudel, *Fünf grosse Oden* (3rd ed; Einsiedeln 1964), p. 40: "O rounded credo of things, visible and invisible, I affirm you with a catholic heart!"
46. Epilogue to Claudel, *The Satin Slipper* (Freiburg 1965), p. 357.
47. Balthasar found access to the French poets through a friendship with the writer Albert Béguin, who became a convert under him in Basel.
48. *Rechenschaft*, p. 23. On R. Schneider: "Nowhere have I found in so pure a form what I was looking for everywhere: the antipsychological instinct, the natural knowledge of role, service, mission, a Catholic form that lives not in the castles of an order and 'political catholicisms,' perhaps not even in already organized orders, but in the soul of the persons commissioned, whether they be kings or founders" ("Kleiner Lageplan," p. 233). Balthasar excludes from this characterization the later Schneider (*Winter in Vienna*), who according to Balthasar failed in his own mission and himself destroyed this objective form.
49. He consciously superscribes the biography of Saint Thérèse with "History of a Mission" precisely as a counterproposal to I. Fr. Görres, "History of a Soul."
50. One should mention here Gustave Siewerth to whom Balthasar owes many fundamental ideas of his metaphysics (cf. *Herrlichkeit* III/1); he charmingly calls him "the man with the mind of a lion and the heart of a child, fearsome in his philosophical anger against those who forget being, in order to speak smilingly and gently of the mystery of the heart of reality: of the God of love" (*Rechenschaft*, p. 36).
51. Cf. *Rechenschaft*, p. 34; "Es stellt sich vor . . . ," p. 44; Kleiner Lageplan," p. 213.
52. There are, of course, many different influences on this new beginning: Ignatius of Loyola, Newman, Augustine, Karl Barth, etc. We cannot go into that here. But cf. H. U. v. Balthasar, "E. Przywara," in H. J. Schultz (ed.), *Tendenzen der Theologie im zwanzigsten Jahrhundert* (Stuttgart 1966), pp. 354–59; W. Löser, *Im Geiste des Origenes*, pp. 15, 29ff.
53. Thus Balthasar on him in H. J. Schultz, *Tendenzen*, p. 358.
54. "Analogie und Dialektik," in *Divus Thomas* 22 (1944):176; cf. on the whole section also W. Loser, *Im Geiste des Origenes*.
55. It is precisely this primacy that he sees as not wholly preserved in the transcendental theology of Maréchal and Rahner.
56. *Herrlichkeit* I, p. 112.
57. *Glaubhaft ist nur Liebe* (Einsiedeln 1966), p. 30.
58. Cf. on this point the passages mentioned in the book of W. Löser, *Im Geiste des Origenes*.
59. "Analogie und Dialektik," p. 196.
60. The articles collected in *Verbum Caro* revolve predominantly about this theme; its partner in dialogue is expressly Karl Barth (cf. *Rechenschaft*, p. 16).
61. *Herrlichkeit* I, p. 147; with this concept Balthasar means the ordinary theological distinction between the "inner-divine" and the "salvation-history-revealed" threefold reality of God.
62. Balthasar, when he sets this under the phrase, "God's being *is* in his becoming," is in no way following a radical event-christology such as, above all, E. Jüngel believes he has discovered in Karl Barth.

63. Thus it is that *theodramatic*, reflection on the *event* of the cross, forms the center of the theological synthesis which Balthasar proposes in his great "trilogy" (aesthetics-dramatics-logic). More on this below.
64. *Sponsa Verbi*, p. 53.
65. *Theologie der drei Tage* (Einsiedeln 1969), p. 62.
66. *Pneuma und Institution* (Einsiedeln 1974), pp. 114f.
67. On this cf. *Theologie der Geschichte* (3rd ed; Einsiedeln 1959); *Das Ganze im Fragment* (Einsiedeln 1963); *Karl Barth. Darstellung und Deutung seiner Theologie* (Cologne 1951).
68. Cf. *Einsame Zwiesprache. Martin Buber und das Christentum* (Cologne 1958).
69. "Die Absolutheit des Christentums und die Katholizität der Kirche," p. 146; Balthasar borrows this expression from Karl Barth.
70. Thus Balthasar in *Henri de Lubac. Sein organisches Lebenswerk* (Einsiedeln 1976), p. 19.
71. *Ibid.*, pp. 10ff, 20ff.
72. *Ibid.*, p. 57.
73. "Es stellt sich vor," p. 44.
74. *Herder-Korrespondenz*, p. 81.
75. On this, cf. above all W. Löser, *Im Geiste des Origenes.*
76. *Ibid.*, pp. 9ff.
77. Precisely here it is necessary to mention the closeness of Balthasar to de Lubac whose studies on the "fourfold meaning of scripture" in the fathers and in the middle ages strongly influenced the exegesis of Balthasar.
78. Cf. the extensive treatment of this in M. Kehl, "Christliche Gestalt und kirchliche Institution (H. U. v. Balthasar)," in *Kirche als Institution*, pp. 239–311.
79. Cf. *Sponsa Verbi*, pp. 108f.
80. *Herrlichkeit* III/2/2, pp. 416f.
81. *Sponsa Verbi*, p. 168.
82. *Ibid.*, p. 151. This is where the patristic doctrine of the "church from the wounded side of the crucified One" has its theological place.
83. To be sure, the church often falls short of this service; she is, in herself, just a "sinful maid" (*Casta meretrix*, "Chaste prostitute") which only through the love of Christ does not fall completely out of her marian constitution. On this cf. the extensive treatment, "Casta meretrix," in *Sponsa Verbi*, pp. 203–305.
84. *Pneuma und Institution*, p. 218.
85. *Spiritus Creator*, p. 194.
86. *Der antirömische Affekt*, p. 146.
87. *Ibid.*, pp. 120f.
88. *Rechenschaft*, p. 35. Cf. also the book which Balthasar published shortly after her death (1967), *Erster Blick auf Adrienne von Speyr* (Einsiedeln 1968). Nearly 50 books by Adrienne von Speyr have appeared (mostly from the *Johannesverlag*), mostly Bible commentaries, witnesses of a "deep, continuous contemplative prayer life" (*Erster Blick*, p. 85). Since her death Balthasar has published twelve large posthumous volumes (notes from conversations, things dictated, diaries, etc.) as private publications from the *Johannesverlag*. In them the visionary mystical insights of A. v. Speyr are shared with those who are "sufficiently endowed with ecclesial discretion" (*discretio spirituum*) and who, in all the often so strange and even shocking expressions, are able to judge the truth-content of this mission for the church today.
89. *Rechenschaft*, p. 13.
90. *Pneuma und Institution*, p. 408.
91. *Ibid.*, p. 409.

92. Cf. in the bibliography the five volumes of *Herrlichkeit* and three volumes of *Theo-dramatik* which have appeared to date.
93. "Warum ich noch ein Christ bin," p. 30.
94. *Theodramatik* I, p. 17.
95. *Theodramatik* II/1, p. 17.
96. *Theodramatik* I, p. 20.
97. On this cf. the review by W. Löser of *Theodramatik* II/1 in *Theologie und Philosophie* 53 (1978):309f.
98. Volume III (*Die Handlung*) and Volume IV (*Das Endspiel*) still remain to come. Before Balthasar presents the actual dramatic event of the love of God in the history of Jesus Christ, he first presented the "characters in the play" (human beings as free creatures in their special salvation historical qualification "in Christ," above all in the typical form of Mary and the church "of Jews and pagans"; then also "angels and demons" and finally as the crown of it all, *Deus Trinitas*). These persons are of course not to be understood independently of their "play." Nevertheless, Balthasar presents them before the actual "presentation of the drama" in order to avoid the danger of allowing God and the other persons in the play to be absorbed into their historical action so to speak, and thus to be simply identified with their history. Nor can the historical action be simply identified with their history. The historical action can neither be simply understood only as the unfolding of the possibilities already ready-made and placed in the "essence" of the person, nor can the "essence" of God or Jesus Christ or the human being be simply made equal with the historical "event" of love. The grounding of this event in the analogous "freedom" of the persons avoids both extremes; and that is why it comes in the *Theodramatic* before the presentation of the event itself (Vol. III) and its eschatological fulfillment (Vol. IV). On the whole work as trilogy, cf. M. Lochbrunner, *Anologia Caritatis. Darstellung und Deutung der Theologie Hans Urs von Balthasar* (Freiburg i. Br. 1980), which also includes a comprehensive index to the secondary literature.
99. *Rechenschaft*, p. 33.

The von Balthasar Reader

1 · The Program: Profession of Allegiance to the Fullness of Faith

Allegiance professed to that abiding reality "which was from the beginning" and not led astray by all the confusion of our times is the only thing that really gives any hope for the future, because it is greater than any divisiveness and stronger than any compromise, watering-down, or political calculation (left or right). Allegiance professed also to those "differentiating doctrines" which, in dialogue with other Christians, one would like to consider as peripherally insignificant in order to come to a supposed agreement on "essentials," but which belong mostly to the most intimate and most delicate parts of God's loving self-revelation and therefore must be protected from within from misuse and from without from misunderstanding. Allegiance professed to an openness to the world which feels at home in all of creation and God's history with the world, because the center of world and salvation, Christ, has already come to the borders of creation and of history toward which the Catholica is striving: "Everything is yours, you are Christ's." Allegiance professed unerringly, even though the visible form of this Catholica goes about disguised, as it follows in the footsteps of its Lord hidden in suffering: "I know whom I have believed."

THE
HUMAN BEING

· 2 ·

Human beings were created not to be satisfied
with themselves but that, dead to self, they
might, in Christ's possession, possess all
things in him.

The Miracle of Human Existence

3 · A Riddle unto Itself

We recall that the maxim *Gnōthi sauton* ("know yourself") originally stood chiseled on the entrance of the temple at Delphi. On entering a temple, one automatically lowers one's voice, especially when one encounters such an inscription which in its original meaning is actually saying, "Enter into yourself; allow yourself to be told by God that you are only a human being." Beside that stood the other maxim, *Mēden agan* ("Nothing in excess. Don't go too far"). To the Prometheus depicted by Aeschylus, to this *surhomme révolté* (superman in revolt), Oceanus gives the advice, "Know yourself! Change yourself! Adopt new customs! You know that a new lord is in power even over the gods. . . . Let go, unhappy one, of that resentment in your heart, and don't stir up your body against the good." Oceanus, of course, underestimates the seriousness of the disruption between the Titan and Zeus; it is only in the remote conclusion of the trilogy, which has not come to us, that the chasm will be bridged. Nevertheless, all the outcry of the great heroes of tragedy, Ajax, Philoctetus—and to them one can add Job—is of no help in bringing their question, "What is man, what am I, that I must suffer so?" shouted to the silent heavens, any nearer to an answer. The human being carries its question mark and exclamation point painted on placards in an on-strike march of protest through creation, and yet knows full well that its invisible opponent thereby only recedes into a deeper silence. There is no negotiation. When the one on strike turns self completely into a question, he deprives that self of the very hearing that might be able to perceive an answer. In its crude claim, "If I am already a riddle, someone owes me its solution," in its pretentious "anticipatory grasp" (*Vorgriff*) for the answer in order to get noticed before the time when the answer is ready, humanity attains nothing. The impudent questioning at the beginning of *Faust* accomplishes nothing except to bring out the devil and with him the principle of dialëctic, the creative negation. The embittered lament of the prophet Jeremiah that he was misled and betrayed by God can speak from the good fortune of becoming considered at all worthy of an answer, which occurs so harshly and cuttingly that it extinguishes the flaming pathos and restores, so to speak, the zero-point, the pure distance between God and humanity. Thus we come again to the inscription at Delphi which Juvenal said came from heaven: *E coelo descendit gnōthi sauton* (XI, 27). Presumably here the Faustian West should for once have quite simply gone to the school of the East. For there "the beginning of Wisdom" consists in creating within oneself a space for silence in which something like an answer even if wordless, could be made at all. The abandonment of all demands is the presupposition for the mysterious principle of hope's (*Prinzip Hoffnung*) even coming into play.

Gabriel Marcel impressed on us again and again (and at the same undefinable boundary as usual between philosophy and theology as Haecker and Guardini) that "at the root of hope lies something that is literally *offered* to us, and it is given to us to respond to this hope just as we respond to love" (*Homo Viator*, p. 84). "Properly understood, it is given as the creature's answer to the infinite Being to whom it owes everything and over against whom it cannot set the slightest condition" (p. 63). Unfortunately, there are here, says Marcel, some imperceptibly shifting transitions: "I am hoping for" becomes "I am expecting"; "I am counting on," and finally "I am sure of," "I demand." Once again the human being is marching up and down with placards before the court of last appeal.

Let us suppose that the human being remains essentially a puzzle unto itself, and that it would thus be a contradiction if it solved its own puzzle because it would then no longer be this enigma (how dully a finished crossword puzzle stares up at us; it belongs in the wastebasket). Supposing further that no other being in the world can give it the solution (that is obvious), it is no less meaningless to add as a trump the notion that its puzzling character is the very solution to the puzzle, and that, in other words, the open freedom to be able to make of itself everything, *le diable et le bon Dieu*, is itself answer enough. Then indeed that Eastern "beginning of wisdom" will provisionally be the best entrance: the pouring of the oil of a final resignation, pouring a letting-be into the wound of one's own questionability, no matter how painfully it may burn. In the end it could still turn out to be true, what Paul said to the Greeks in the Areopagus where once the questioner Socrates was condemned: "The God who made the world and everything in it, has made from one every nation of men to live on the face of the earth, having determined allotted periods and the boundaries of their habitation, that they should seek God, in the hope that they might feel after him and find him. Yet he is not far from each one of us" (Acts 17:24–27). *Seeking* is the heart of this statement, joined with a "in the hope that they might" and an optative which neither promises a finding nor presents it as a likely eventuality, but leaves the chances for it undetermined. But what is meant here by seeking? Certainly not the search for a familiar, accidentally mislaid object. And certainly not a blind groping about without awareness that there is something findable there.

Let us put ourselves for a moment in the situation of Adam in the paradise story. Does he really know what he is looking for when he gazes among the animals, recognizes and names them, but finds among them no suitably helpful complement? One could answer, on the level of the sexual which he recognizes in the pairing of the animals, he could register a demand from his own maleness. But then, of course, the point of the story would be missed. This man just doesn't know what human encounter is, and so he cannot ask for it. According to the story the answer slumbers within him next to his heart but first the rib must be taken from him, and, by God's creative act, be brought to face him as a living you. One could almost say that the answer to his quest lay so close to Adam that he himself couldn't find it.

But is our whole question, as Feuerbach thinks, answered in the encounter with Eve? Do two puzzles which reflect each other provide the solution for each other? For who mediates between two human freedoms whose creative capacity for decision is in no way exhausted by the decision to belong to each other? All due reverence for the dialogic principle which is really only today being recognized in its anthropological significance and given its due, but it is also something that we absolutely must transcend. Not only do most dialogues remain superficial and full of misunderstandings, they can also falter or end; and there where a person opens himself or herself to a lifelong exchange of love, he or she draws the power to persevere from the store of a silent solitary-resolute fidelity at the innermost I which is somehow eager, by means of that fidelity, to find an answer to a confusing, still unsolved question which comes up precisely because one is being loved. The question is, Why do you love me? Why *me*? It is perhaps only blind chance, for you might just as well have met someone else and been able to bind yourself in fidelity to him or her; is our union, which gives meaning to our being, based on no necessity at all? But this question stirs up from further below, perhaps for the first time in my life, yet another scurrilous, almost crazy question: Who really is this present within me which says I? More briefly, Why am I precisely I? Pure chance? There are, of course, millions all around me who happily prattle their I, each from his or her own never-questioned, not once reflected-on center. This I-saying is a phenomenon of the human species. Only because human being is a bit preferable to mice and crows does one speak of it in terms of persons instead of individuals. And now it really has come about, by means of a comical but really incomprehensible accident, that, as product of a completely extraneous sexual process that didn't concern me at all, there came into being this I which says not merely I— as every I continually does—but that I *am*, that that *I* is condemned to be I, in a lifelong prison which does indeed have many windows to many people and things and tasks and world-changing plans, but through none of these windows can it crawl out of itself—*in una noche oscura*.

If I look into the pit of this question, I can see there several ladders which lead into various depths. First, the many-branched ladder of the anthropological sciences, each of which investigates an aspect of human existence and thus contributes some indispensable stones to the building on the pinnacle of whose highest tower the self-expressing I is balanced. The whole of physics and chemistry, anatomy, physiology, and psychology, and sociology (each working from the lower animals up to the human animal), the whole theory of evolution which each human person variously recapitulates, the theories of heredity and character—they all belong to this massive substructure from which, infinitely conditioned, determined, and colored, there emerges the face of the person which, despite all this, in an ultimate point of identity, is incarnated unconditioned and free in this whole structure. In the first aspect is the human being, who, in the words of Haecker, is like a reversed mirror-image of God who presupposes absolutely nothing and creates everything, while the human being presupposes absolutely everything in the cosmos and creates nothing. In this first aspect self-identification can always be further questioned, and such analysis of self-consciousness is pursued today in an especially tenacious way. In this, many empirical comrades since Marx, Darwin, Freud, and Jung have joined themselves to speculative German idealism. This aspect makes clear to us why, for the I, no flight from the world is possible, nor concentration on the mere point, for this remains completely empty without the Odyssean journey into the fullness of the shaped and to-be-shaped world.

But it is surely just as clear that if the human being wanted to linger at this first aspect, it would never arrive at a self-identification, but would always have to be seen instead only as the product of a prepersonal process which, to our annoyance, we cannot claim that we have guided it to ourselves. At best we could try to identify our empirical I in an incomprehensible point with the absolute I which would then be responsible for the whole guidance of the process, and indeed would necessarily coincide with it (as with Hegel). But that would once again signify the dissoluton of this specific I, the I which I am and not you, in a universal subject.

This is the reason why not only Plato and his followers, not only the dualistic gnosis, spiritualism, not only Scheler and Klages, but also the empiricist and philosopher of nature Aristotle, have held that the spirit is inserted in human beings *thyrathen*, from outside and above, that in this earthly existence it is ultimately not even bound to the body, does not originate in conception like the other souls, and therefore will also not be affected by the dissolution of the body. This massive tension at the center of human existence is taken into account by the philosopher in all its ambiguities, that in itself the spirit is simultaneously actual and potential, realized in itself and yet quite thoroughly being utterly realized through its progressive experience of the other and of itself. But according to Aristotle this very paradox cannot be projected into the sphere of the divine; for God has no need of going into the world in order to be pure self-consciousness. This paradox marks humanity a chimera throughout the whole history of philosophy. Its saving I is always at once interrogated by the anthropological sciences, and yet in the self-evidence of its self-being as I it cannot be found by inquiry for it is a beacon, exposed to every storm, wavering and yet inextinguishable. The I can in happy amazement experience how deep down into the organic and the physical its mysterious center is immersed—as heart, imagination, feeling, emotion, mood, eros—so much so that it would like never to be separated from this being-at-home in body and cosmos. And it can at the same time be convinced that it is not just a subtle balancing act of world force, but a center which possessed all its substructures in virtue of an ultimate point of freedom and from an ultimate point of truth can infuse light and power in them right down into the darkness of the unconscious.

> What sort of freak then is man! How novel, how monstrous, how chaotic, how paradoxical, how prodigious! Judge of all things, feeble earthworm, repository of truth, sink of doubt and error, glory and refuse of the universe! Who will unravel such a tangle? . . . What then will become of you, man, seeking to discover your true condition through natural reason? . . . Be silent. . . . Learn that man infinitely transcends man.*

Pascal is looking here for a platform beyond scepticism (for there really exists the truth of the sciences) and beyond dogmatism (for all its truths must continually be verified on the basis of a never fully

---

* From *Pascal, Pensées*, trans. A. J. Krailsheimer (Penguin Books: Harmondsworth, Middlesex, England, 1966), pp. 64–65.

countable experience). He leads us straight to the goal of our brief reflection. Our most poignant question is, Who am I? Why am I precisely I? Before this the idea remained in the forecourt, in the generality of the problem: Who is man (*Mensch*)? And even here, only a paradoxical answer was attainable. For each who is willing to be content with such an answer, or with a part of it (for example, with a merely psychological or sociological answer), we can here only regret whether such satisfaction can be sufficient for his or her way. But we would like to stick with the question. Who am I? A human being burdened with an ineradicably paradoxical nature, but not identical with it, not simply an instance of it. I appeal once again to the anticipatory knowledge invoked at the start which tells me none of the possible answers that can arise within the horizon of the questioner will ever give me satisfaction. I will not take part in the cheerful masquerade today, once again so much in vogue, where one ties on this or that store-bought or self-designed definition of human being, today this one, tomorrow that.

Might not the old Lessing, with that maxim of his that was relentlessly attacked by all right-thinking Christians, still in some way have been right, that were God to give him the choice, he would prefer the seeking to the finding? And that was precisely because the inner imperfectibility of the human being, as person and as society, was so evident to him. How would a utopian hope in a total change of the future world be of any help to us in fact, since *hic et nunc* we still have to do with nothing else than the human being of today, the human being of yesterday, and, to be sure, with the human being of tomorrow as well? And just how is a rounding off of the human being of the day after tomorrow (something wholly beyond imagining and thus not even targetable) supposed to answer all these questions with one blow, with a kind of *sanatio in radice?* Certainly we should cooperate with all our might in the cleaning of the physical and spiritual swamplands of humanity; but, soberly considered, will we ever be able to do anything other than sew new patches on an old cloak?

4 · Indebted Existence

The act of coming upon oneself in being for one endowed with consciousness and freedom, if the light of being has not been fully obscured, is experienced as a good bestowed upon one without one's doing or merit. It is possible that once in a while other values seem higher, values of the community to which one belongs for instance, or values of the absolute before which one retreats, or values of nonbeing when one's own existence seems no longer worthwhile. But in the awakening of consciousness to one's own being and being-free there lies an instinctive and unrestricted Yes to the reality that has been bestowed. Whoever speaks this Yes knows himself to be somehow affirmed, gifted with the Yes of being. Really to be is precious.

What we have to do here is to grope around behind a certain blindness toward the basic value of being, a sickness called positivism which arises from seeing in what is real only that which one comes upon unquestionably—the expression "the given" would already be saying too much since no one "gives"—from seeing as real only that something before which one puts just one question: what can I do with this material? Blindness to the prior question is the death of philosophy and thus especially of theology as well. When philosophy begins with astonishment at the fact that I, as this individual, am in being, and consequently, that all the rest of being is in being together with me; when it begins, therefore, with amazement over an incomprehensible having-been-gifted-ness; then theology begins—from the realization that eternal freedom is the eternally self-giving and therein Son-generating One—with listening to a You spoken to me.

"Today I have begotten you," says the Father to the Son. Today I have created you, says the eternal One to the finite freedom. That no human I can awaken to itself unless it is addressed as You by another I, is only the inner-worldly rehearsal of what we mean here. For through the human I, in the act of addressing, is manifested an absolute—the human I is, of course, only the You of another I—an absolute which was always being generated as an equally absolute You and which is, with him, in the Holy Spirit, One God. Precisely this bringing forth and being received and being-one of both in the Holy Spirit allows the absolute preciousness—we call it the *Holiness*—of absolute being in its boundless self-affirmation and freedom to shine forth. Never is God for himself what one comes across in the positivistic sense, but rather the "most improbable" miracle: that the self-giving-without-remainder of the paternal origin truly generates the coeternal Son and the meeting and union of the two truly lets the one Spirit, the perfect hypostasis of the gift, proceed.

Only in setting forth from this miracle can the finite freedom that has been given to itself know itself as a You that has been addressed and characterize itself, in relation to the one bestowing, as an I. Yes, from this being-addressed it must draw the consequence and address the infinite freedom in turn with You. This You is an extravagant word because God, in himself, is Other to no one but is the all-encompassing (*Non-Aliud*). On its own the finite could at most *worship* this all-encompassing reality as all-discharging and all-bearing, and *praise* it in its unconditionedness and self-affirmation as what is most precious. But to address it with You is something it can dare only if it thereby responds to a You addressed to it from the inner essence of the absolute—from God's Tri-unity. Both mutually condition one another: that God appears to me as the "highest good" first comes to light when I experience that for him (in the Son) I am an absolutely affirmed good, which guarantees my being gifted with being and freedom. Once I experience that, for God, I represent a good and a You, I can then put full confidence in the gift of being and freedom presented to me, and coaffirm myself as really affirmed from all eternity.

Dimensions of Human Nature

5 · Between Spirit and Species

When one keeps in mind the original unity of being and good, reality and love, it is not enough to say that all worldly knowledge is determined by the constitutive, undeducible difference between being and essence (*esse* and *essentia* in the Thomist sense); rather, this difference attains a much broader fundamental meaning: what obtains between the reasonable and ethical "mastery" of profane situations and the consciousness of a never-to-be-mastered, never-to-be-met capacity of existence, of a graced being allowed to approach and enter into the realm of being as a whole. This consciousness arises out of the primordial experience that one reaches a share in the world-community of being through a call from outside of one's own I. Not in virtue of one's own plenitude of power has one entered here. Nor does it make any difference that the mother, from whom the call sounded herself, as it later is clear, was someone called, and not just her but all beings invited to the table of existence. All it says is that each one of these beings once entered the hall with the same hesitant breath, although it soon felt itself at home with the rest. How is it that I got in here? An irremovable accidental character clings to the individual and lifts him up right away from the universal. The individual cannot reckon this accidentalness together with the accidentalness of all the rest of the beings in the world into a general, equalizing necessity. He discovers the same determinacy in the heart of hearts of the others as well. It is—even though irreducibly my question and my wondering—still at once the common question and wondering of everyone: Why there is a world at all, rather than none at all?

For the individuals, the idea of the terrible accidentalness of their sexual causation remains a salutary reminder. This idea is hardly bearable, and if it points to the total causation of their existence in the world, it could also lead the being which has been generated to cynicism and despair. But even the person who has a living idea of God and can understand the heart of his or her personal being only from God, as something immediately created by God, will nevertheless reflect only with reserved awe on the incomprehensible linking of God's creative act with the accidental generation of nature. God did not, so to speak, will him unconditionally; instead, God connected his own creative act in the light with quite dark and blind cocauses. In view of this last point, the expression "thrown into being" does not seem inappropriate for what is conceived and born of an animal is also called the litter it casts forth. Between sex and spirit there yawns in being something like a geological fault of terrifying depth. Vladimir Solovieff (following other Platonists, like Gregory of Nyssa) built his system of ethics on this. It should be interpreted neither demonically nor tragically, but it also should not be minimized; it appears definitively in the face of death. The sexually generated being is, from the beginning, ordained unto death. Among purely natural beings, death has to be expected as the necessary counterpart to birth; but what does dying mean for the spiritual person who exists immediately from and toward God—and still does not know himself or herself differently than as fellow-citizen of the natural world?

But even from this same enigmatic point, light is shed on a fundamental law of human existence. The space which the material, the vital, and the biological occupies in the human being can be ever so great, and it can, besides, be overwhelmingly dominated by statistical and evolutionary laws which integrate humanity within the whole of nature; and yet, with its spirit it is immediate to God no matter at what stage of personal and world development the human might be. And if, in the age of technology, the natural element in human being is subjected ever more strongly to arbitrary manipulation right to the extremes that have nowadays come so threateningly close to us, there still remains for man and woman this consolation: the supportive substructure of the spirit, in its statistical laws as well as in the mysterious but undeterrable dynamic goal-orientedness of its evolution, is, for all its impoverishment of spirit, so thoroughly permeated with spirit that the human being, as the reasonable and free being that it is, does not need to feel that it is demonically at the mercy of this apparent supremacy of natural power. Weak individual that he is, he certainly did not bestow on himself this substructure, of which he himself is the final result; the whole of humanity, too, which stands at the pinnacle of evolution cannot have been the efficient cause of this substructure. That is why, behind the seemingly alien factor of nature on which he rests and which pervades him to his highest capacities is ultimately an eternal Spirit, related to his own spirit, with whom, as spirit, he can interact only in an immediate way, and from whom he is not seriously removed by the process and mediation of the natural world. He would not be able to seek God as a natural entity in the infinite cosmos unless he had already discovered God as a spiritual entity; that is, as his or her origin in love, whose anamnesis can never be completely obliterated, and which remains the secret or open horizon according to which he measures the things of the world. Two things will come about in doing so: he will be able to arrange worldly realities in a certain sequential order of approximation to the absolute measure (in an evolutionary world view there could be a chance that this sequential order could also be temporally related to the vanishing point of absolute salvation—the *omega* day), but he will also know at the same time that no worldly reality as such can bring him to the point of absolute salvation, but rather that absolute love can turn toward him only from itself and in freedom. But this cannot be derived with necessity from the world of nature, since "grace" cannot be postulated by "nature." Nevertheless, the mere fact that subspiritual nature can be grounded in the Absolute Spirit (and thus in love) implies a promise written in nature itself—a promise that this free fulfilling of ever worldly and existential quest (*eros*), after its definitive encounter with love—in brief salvation—will one day become reality.

6 · Course through Time

The life of the human being is development in time; he is seed and suckling, child and boy, man and old man. He cannot be two of these at the same time. His nature which passes through the changes of the years is subject to a mysterious law: in every stage he is a full and complete human being in the creative thought of God. The child and the youth, in spite of their "immaturity," are not, as was inevitably assumed outside Christianity, incomplete, merely half-realized adults. In his development a human being does not become a human being; he is already. And if ages have characteristics which exclude one another, then the "mature" person, even the old person, will always long to get back to what was possessed as a child and a youth and has now been irrevocably lost. Nevertheless, the ages are not timelessly and absolutely linear, like completed pictures in a gallery; they are joined together in the stream of time, and the flowing itself has its meaning right in this "pro"-gress with its irreversibility. The loss this entails is outweighed by the gain which the passing of time brings, even if this gain finally leads to the deprivations of age, to the helpless wisdom of its poverty, and even to the clouding of reason.

People who have mastered the art of living manage only incipiently to integrate the seasons of life: to take their childhood with them into their youth, and their youth into their maturity. Generally, it is the second and third generations that afford the aging person refreshment because the sadness of leave-taking is transfigured by the stirring of renunciation for the sake of the young. Full integration of temporal life could only be hoped for in a time-beyond in which, with the eternal significance of every moment, there would also be salvaged the sense of direction of the river of time.

It is true that such hope corresponds to the dreaming longing of humanity—all the myths play variations on making the temporal immortal, free from the limitations of growing old and dying. But today, now that the mythical friezes on the temple walls of human memory have faded almost to unrecognizability, who would concede even a glimmer of probability and proof to their fulfillment?

7 · Speech

Human speech is the free revelation of one's inner personality to others in perceivable phonic signs. It comprises three elements:

1. The self-possession of the spirit-person, which is present to itself and so knows and understands its own truth. Therefore its word is not just mere lallying, an incoherent effort to express an obscure inwardness, but an exact, precise process. This is precisely what characterizes the utterances of Yahweh in contrast with the mystical stammerings and impotent speechlessness at the higher reaches of other religions: "I, Yahweh, speak with justice and proclaim what is right" (Isa 45:19).

2. Presence-to-oneself as truth means perfect freedom. Consequently the word which the free person chooses for purposes of self-expression cannot be a necessary word. Human speech, bound as it is with imagery, must at its center rest basically on a free positing of expression. The risen Christ has become, even in his bodily aspect, spiritual, that is to say, free. Thus he is no longer recognized in a natural, passive fashion but rather lets himself be known of his own accord whenever he wishes. Herein is the fulfillment of the *Verbum Caro*, for now all flesh has become available to the Word for its expression.

3. In the truth and freedom of self-presence, the personal spirit is the *universal* and *necessary* element. This means that it has already

gone beyond its subjectivity to the you (in principle to every you) and exists as intersubjectivity. It is communion and mutual intercourse from its very origin. Speech therefore is no mere epiphenomenon of human beings but an integrating part of their very being; and those more recent thinkers who begin with the phenomenon of speech are choosing the quickest way. According to them the *verbum mentis* that arises in inmost being, and the love that lets it arise and accompanies it, does not turn the person solipsistically in on itself (as a superficial interpretation of Augustine's *imago trinitatis* might lead one to think), but rather reveals the mystery of being itself in the mutuality of one's consciousness in love. The human word reveals, if it is true, what being means. It is original participation in being which is already illumined in the Spirit, and thereby also in the Word already uttered in the heart of being by eternal love. In this Word everything was made and has its condition of being; and everything was made with it in view. For human nature (which bears within itself an unfathomable promise) was destined from the first to find its fulfillment in the free and gracious revelation of the eternal Word.

But truth, freedom, and love do not yet characterize speech as specifically human. It is only human when it transcends itself in two directions—in the direction of its provenance and in the direction of its goal.

1. The free spiritual speech of the human person emerges from a deep-lying context of nature, revealed for the first time by modern biology and paleontology, which makes humans the summit of the whole material and organic creation and its mouthpiece before God. Just as human beings as spirit indwell being in its totality, so through their bodies do they indwell the whole of nature, and can never be detached from it. They speak a corporeal organic language, one of natural sounds and gestures. This is what brings about the marvelous give-and-take and endless interplay between nature and spirit in our speech, the gradual transition from natural images to half-emancipated symbols and then to freely chosen signs. These transitions from the speech of the whole body (as in the dance) to that of the tongue and of letters, from physiognomy to abstract logic and grammar, all this wealth of resources, give us some hint at what an inexhaustible openness is the nature of human being. Nor must we forget what modern biology tells us of the speech of animals, the unsuspected exactness of the means of their communications and their signals, the incipient abstraction and the schematization of their expression in the play of gesture, their often long and complicated rituals and liturgies which come astonishingly close to the sign language of primitive humans. It is only in our technological age that a great part of this familiarity between humanity and the nature which gave it

birth has been shattered. The romantics sought to recover this dimension of speech when it was almost extinct; but it was too late. Nonetheless the human being remains, whether voluntarily or not, a natural entity that will never be able to be freed fully from the sphere of natural signs. Mathematical logic will never be a human logic or even its substitute.

In this connection we might refer to the sacraments and the liturgy. Both correspond to the way human beings belong to nature. Both are much less the effect of a free, positive ordinance of divine arbitrariness than of an accommodation of divine revelation to the actual laws of creation. Guardini illuminated well the extent to which the liturgy is related to the sacred drama as a function shared both by individuals and all peoples. We now know that Jesus did not invent any sacramental signs. He takes baptism from John, the meal of bread and wine from the contemporary assemblies of the devout; confession, also required by the Baptist, is a general human practice to be found in all religions and even in Buddhist monasteries. Anointing with oil and the laying on of hands were part of the Jewish ritual in which the liturgy of the mass was foreshadowed in important parts.

2. Now for the second transcendence of speech, toward its end. Speech is not completed in itself; it intends life. It intends action and making. It is already incipient deed and goes beyond itself in works and in involvement with life. The moment arrives when speaking is not enough because the testimony of the whole person is needed, as in the love between man and woman, in political activity, in the apostolate, in martyrdom. On the human plane, truth does not exist without the virtue of truthfulness, wherein alone is shown whether the true, just word has measured up to being itself and has not in some way fallen short. Thus in the Bible the whole range of truth (*veritas, veracitas, fidelitas*) is covered by the one word *emet*. God himself, no less than the human being, has bound himself by his word. Both God's word and the human word is open to existence. In contrast with dumb idols incapable of a true word because they possess no fidelity and no reality, it bears within itself the witness and power of the vitality of the living God. And after having long enough exercised its prophetic office the word passes into a new stage, that of the Eucharist and the Passion.

John calls this "going unto the end" (*eis telos*).

What the spoken word could not do—it only provoked increasing resistance—can be done by the sacrificed Word which trickles out in the words of the cross and finally fades away in the tremendous inarticulate death cry which sums up everything spoken, unspoken, and inexpressible, that God had to communicate to us. Of speaking there would be no end ("the world would not be able to contain the books"); the deed writes the period. But even of deeds there would be no end; suffering and death is humanity's last word, in which it pulls itself together before the Father. It is testament: the witnessing and final sealing of life. In its death, the time and word of the human being has turned into the unity God willed in his grace, the unity which he chose as the highest expression of his own divine unity, the unity of his revelation as well as his triune nature.

Now just as, in connection with the first transcendence toward nature and toward organic gesture, we mentioned the sacraments and the liturgy so here also must we speak of them in connection with the second transcendence. For in the liturgy and the sacraments the word of Christ becomes deed; his truth, witnessed and assured to us, becomes effective and triumphant in us. This second transcendence is attained only in complete self-donation. There is no Christian liturgy without the sacrifice of the cross; one could even say that the two are ultimately identical.

This, therefore, is how the human being speaks: as free spirit-person who knows the truth, he expresses at once both nature and himself in his existence.

8 · Man and Woman

The polarity of man and woman can stand as the paradigmatic instance of the thoroughgoing communal character of humanity. After the "very good" of the first creation account, one hears the "not good" of the second: "It is not good that man should be alone." Therefore God gave him the "woman" as "helper," as "counterpart." The special character of this complementary mutuality becomes clear from the context: God forms the existing animals in pairs and brings them before Adam; he can give them names and thus rule over them, but he finds among them no counterpart fit for himself. This counterpart must thus be both cosmic (sexual) and, to be fit for Adam, metacosmic, touching the *theion*.

The animals are named and ruled even if Adam cannot fully enter into their sensate life. But the "counterpart" which is brought to him, although formed from his rib, although "at last his flesh and bone," is for him eternally unrulable. Up to its last cell, the male body is determined in a male way, the female body in a female way, and so, correspondingly, is the whole of empirical experience and ego-consciousness. And this within a human nature that is identical in both, but which in no place reaches neutrally beyond sexual difference as, so to speak, a place of possible understanding. There is here no *universale ante rem,* as all theories of an asexual or bisexual (androgynous) primordial human would have it. The human being is, when creation is completed, a "dual unity," "two different but mutually inseparable realities of which one is the fullness of the other and both oriented to an unfathomable definitive unity"; "twofold, without multiplying the unity by two, simply two poles of one single reality, two different realizations of one single being, two *entia* in one single *case,* one existence in two lives, but in no sense two different fragments of one whole which, after the fact, must be put together again like a puzzle. . . ." It is with such grouping formulations that one attempts, yet never successfully, to describe the mystery that man as human beside his counterpart, woman, has always been. And the same is true of woman in her relation to man: it is, if this relationship is taken as paradigm, the human I, in continual search for the You, reaching and also finding it ("That's it, finally"), without ever being able to take possession of this otherness. This is the way it is not only because the freedom of the You from the I cannot be mastered by any transcendental overarching concept, since all human freedom in its place is open only to the absolute, to the divine, but also because of the "embodying" of this shortcoming in the diverse and complementary constitution of the sexes.

When this difference is brought together with the body-spirit tension, which is where the cosmic-metacosmic character of the human being first appeared, the attempt could be made to place the difference of the sexes under the cosmic side of humanity and elevate it as spirit above that. But then we would be looking only at the upward movement (from body to spirit) and not the always complementary downward movement (spirit into embodiment). Adam in Genesis fails to find his companion among the animals not because of the lack of exchange from spirit to spirit, but he fails to find the counterpart in which he encounters the bodily in a spiritual way and the spiritual in a bodily way. This becomes even more clear when one adds the story of the formation of woman from the rib of the man.

In the natural order, the sexually differentiated human appears as a cosmic quintessence, a microcosm. And the metaphysics of all cultures have been concerned to describe the male-female difference as the fundamental rhythm of being in the world. The difference is most graphically visible in the mutuality of heaven and earth, the former fructifying and vivifying with rain and sun, the latter answering from its own potential power (*materia-mater*), with, of course, the pervasive danger of equating the male-heavenly with the "spirit" and the female-earthly with the "matter," or at least (in modern parlance) with "nature," and correspondingly, devaluating the latter. This is what we have from Plato (*Timaeus* 90e, 91a; *Laws* 5, 739c) to

Aristotle (woman as "material" and thus "object to be used" [*Poetics* 15, 145a 20], as the *aischron*, "shameful," in contrast to the *kalon*, "beautiful" [*Physics* 19, 192 A 13–14]), and from there to the well known misogynist utterances of the fathers and scholastics. The danger even grew in proportion to the way the "image of God" of the human being in early Christian theology was increasingly transferred to the purely spiritual side of human nature (and correspondingly, by way of the cosmic principle, into the male principle). This devaluation of the female accounts somewhat for the countlessly recurring variations of the myth of the "holy marriage" (*hieros gamos*) between heaven and earth in which the reciprocal tension between anthropology and (a divinely completed) cosmology, as described at the beginning of the chapter, is the properly characteristic point: the projection of the humanly sexual into the world of the gods and the great world of nature—and a reflected repetition, through human beings, of the divine-cosmic marriage (acting, as it were, through the king for the fruitfulness of the earth, the prosperity of the people, etc.). The already pre-Taoistic world principles Yang and Yin affirm every comprehensive form of polarity, that of the sexes among many others; they stand for the equality of the sexes but not for their primary meaning; so, too, in the *I Ching* where both first signs are the male-creative one of heaven and the female-receptive one of the earth and form the foundation for all succeeding variations. The fundamental theme is that of transitoriness ("Book of Changes"); the opposing principles are, so to speak, only the presupposition for their mixture.

One would have to say that no metaphysical polarity can provide a clarifying explanation for the human sex differential; it is either interpreted by those polarities one-sidedly or misleadingly, or the whole attempt does not get past the tension of a mutual illumination in which neither of the two phenomena to be clarified themselves come into the light. But this tension, as we have shown, rests on the fact that the relation between the cosmic and the *theion* itself remains in tension; this is, precisely at this point, inevitable. For if the divine is one-sidedly made the exemplar of the sexual, then the sexual becomes the copy of a univocal sexuality of the divine world—whether it be as marriage of the gods among themselves or with earthly beings, or as gnostic *syzygies*, or as the insertion of the sexual into the Christian God (sophiology), all of which, theologically, lead to the fantastic; but if on the contrary the cosmic is made the exemplar of the sexual, then human being is locked into the cosmos as an "instance" (perhaps the "highest instance"), and its transcendence is seen no more.

One can see in this how terribly difficult it is for pre-Christian anthropology to situate the phenomenon of sexuality within a total interpretation of being. Its problematic remains more acute than that of the two other tensions; even in Christian interpretation it will remain a neuralgic point. Once again it is revealed, but in a more dramatic way, that in the cosmic-hypercosmic situation of human sexuality, there is not just a tension but a rupture.

In order to gain an unbiased access to the phenomenon, one can bring in the two creation accounts of Genesis in which is contained much human legendary material, purified of mythic one-sidedness, while on the other hand the transition to the Christian interpretation is still distant. The beginning of the Bible makes room for a phenomenology of the sexual that can be viewed first of all in the sober context of *creatureliness*. Nowhere is humanity more conscious of its contingency than where each sex must convince itself of its relatedness to the other: neither can be in itself the whole human being; "opposite to" it there is always the other way of being human inaccessible for it. And it cannot be claimed that sexual union takes away this contingency and (as Feuerbach thinks and as even Aristophanes already seemed to be hoping for in the *Symposium*) lets the union turn into the absolute, sufficient to itself: because normally, in this union, a child is begotten, which allows the objective finality of the union to transcend the subjective experience and to perpetuate the process of contingency. Thus the other side of creatureliness sets disclosed: that henceforth, every progressively becoming human being owes its existence to a sexual process, generation and birth.

9 · Marriage—Event and Institution

A marriage that is unfruitful in a bodily way is neither a failure, nor a necessarily unhappy marriage; precisely for this reason one cannot characterize the generation of progeny as the primary purpose of matrimony. Instead, it has to do primarily with a radicalization (deep into the bodily sphere) of what chiefly would be said here about personal encounter. The radicalization lies in the embodiment of personal self-giving whose exclusivity—*this* man and *this* woman—is the temporal-spatial form in which the absolute uniqueness of the personal encounter is incarnately represented. This uniqueness of the other's freedom nevertheless includes its bodily sphere.

But the decisive point will only be seen when one recognizes the fact that the mutual readiness to receive one another leads through the inclusion of the bodily sphere to that mutual dispossession and self-surrender of which Paul speaks: "The wife does not rule over her own body, but the husband does; likewise the husband does not rule over his own body, but the wife does" (1 Cor 7:4). If this is true, however, then both are dispossessed because of their free availability and self-surrender to one another so that, basically, no person can dispose of a bodily encounter for which two consents are needed. And this is true no matter which of the two seizes the initiative for the encounter. The personal coming together of the two dispossessed people is possible only in the third, which—long before the coming of the child—is that objective reality which is made up of their two freedoms: their marriage vow in which each one definitively affirms the freedom of the other and its mystery and surrenders himself or herself to this mystery. It is to be called objective only because it is more than the proximity of their two subjectivities, although on the other hand, it is the creative product of these subjectivities: their will now become one (to belong to each other), which is placed over and between them because neither of the two can claim the resulting freedom for himself or herself. It is objective because both, in order to act together correctly in their mutual dispossession, must look at this product of theirs, more at this than at their partner who, in the ideal case, is ready and disposable in his or her full dispossession.

This objective, which is also what inspires their common love, can without qualification be called the spirit of their covenant of love and this covenant itself as the institution towering over both. This is true even within the purely personal point of view. For there is also, naturally, the other, societal point of view according to which a marriage is a social, public event that has its place and plays its role in the structure of society, and must be taken account of by the community, put in its proper place, and also regulated within certain limits for the sake of the common good. Here a marriage law gets formulated, to which the married are subject, which should indeed have consideration for the personal nature of the marriage, but which has as its direct concern the common good, or, more precisely, the best possible balance between the good of the single family and that of society. That objective, inspiring reality between two who are fully given to each other evades almost totally the applicability of this law. For the law reckons first of all with the average human nature and thus also with its egoism and inconstancy, and tries to limit the damage they cause; while the mutual, perfect, personal dispossessing represents almost the limit-case, and the special objective spirit of such a covenant of love is only the product of a complete mutual transference of possession. Of course the principle of Paul that in marriage each partner belongs bodily to the other is formulated as a general principle, but the ecclesiastical norm—also that of church law—which he here establishes has in mind the ideal character of Christ in whose sphere such dispossessing is possible, as the following sentence shows: "Do not refuse one another except perhaps by agreement for a season, that you may devote yourselves to prayer, and then come together again" (1 Cor 7:5). The inspiring common spirit appears here as a spirit of prayer, concretely as Holy Spirit, who, in his impulse to this common time of continence, betrays his origin. This holds for Christian marriage in general; the thoroughgoing, sober realism of the whole chapter shows it.

Greatness and Limitation of the Human Being

10 · Being unto Death

The human being sees himself as the sum and perfect image of the cosmos. All the realms and genera of living things converge in him; no animal species is totally alien to him. He carries them all within himself as superseded and sublimated forms; he can mirror himself in them and, as in fables, recognize the features of his own character. Even scholastic embryology knew that in his ontogeny humanity recapitulates the states of the natural development from which it emerged. This is confirmed by modern paleontology and biology. In this respect humanity today is no more and no less closely bound with the natural cosmos and the universe than the human of mythical ages and of antiquity, insofar as he also thought of himself as "microcosm."

If this is so, however, it is obviously not the result of an external summation of separate cosmic realities; he is, as their epitome, neither plant nor animal nor anything else apart from himself. "Micro-" also suggests a kind of concentration of meaning which takes the human being, as synthesis of the world, and raises him above it. In this exaltation above the immediate he is that which mediates itself to itself; he is spirit and person. He looks openly into the openness of being in general, which, of its nature, can be bounded only by nothingness. Although always a single individual, he cannot but be orientated toward being in general. He receives his freedom from it and in relation to it: freedom from any constraining bond to any particular being adequate to his individuality. Such proportionate beings do exist, of course, but only so that they may be illuminated and liberated in the whole.

This openness of his situation and the directing of his gaze inward does not detach the human mind from the ground of nature, but enables him to realize his roots in it more reflectively, more insistently, more intimately. Animals are swept away by the cycles of sexual drive as by a flood tide that ebbs again, whereas humans can experience and understand eros more spiritually, inwardly and, through spiritual love, make for it a lasting abode in their illuminated hearts. They can also do the opposite (as the German romantics well knew), and embody the infinities of their spiritual dimensions in those of the dark maternal forces of nature, thus giving back to them through their spirit, the sacredness that nature had accorded them. For nature was never without spirit in humanity, just as the human child never climbs onesidely from lower nature to become a spiritual being, but always awakes out of spiritual depths to consciousness and freedom.

How can a being so constituted be perfectible? As epitome of the world, his perfection would be possible only if the world were fulfilled with him and in him. But inasmuch as he transcends the world as spirit and is open to being in general, the fulfillment of the world is not enough to bring about his perfection. The human being is personal, transcending the world and its being. Person is more than nature which is always predictable of a multiplicity of things; person is unique. It is that which ontologically justifies the insurpassable finality of an essential love. Although every human being is a person, and thus possesses this quality of incomparability, this characteristic may not be predicated of him as a quality of his being. As "spiritual nature," human beings, right up to their most individual traits, have in common generic qualities but in the same spiritual nature, inasmuch as they are persons, these qualities are so distinct that subsumption under one generic term is impossible.

If the question of perfectibility is asked—at this stage, purely formally—then from the outset one thing is excluded: that the person disappears into the race, however, its total final purpose is interpreted—statically or dynamically, or in terms of a materialistic, biologistic, or even theologico-mystical evolution. Complementing this veto of such a subordination of the person to the world's being is that of the equally inadmissible "acosmistic" (Scheler's word) conception of the person, which sees its perfectibility as something which is possible only beyond the world's being (and hence, logically, beyond its own corporality).

The pattern of human love points forcibly to the indissoluble interconnection of spiritual nature and personhood. For in virtue of its being as nature and as person, the human being can find its enlargement and happiness only in the you of another human being, based in the sexual difference (revealing the most profound wisdom) which was devised by *natura naturans* for the most intimate encounter and unity. It lies at the heart of the nature of the species and roots it in eros; it is precisely in this way, through the natural difference itself, that it lets human beings experience the eternally unsurpassible and unfathomable difference between one spiritual person and another. And yet this appropriately elusive love does not exhaust a person's relations with the world. The human being (as a cognitive, conative nature), in spite of any individual tie to a you, remains open to the whole world, hence to a world of labor, a world of research, a world to be built and realized in the human community. In addition, in order to remain open to the world at all, an individual remains open to the whole realm of being beyond it, which he mistakes if he would apprehend it in a quantitative sum of "world material" (say, in interplanetary expansions of his area of habitation and power). He makes this "technical" plunge into the quantitative only because a philosophical plunge into the qualitative has to miscarry from the start; namely, somehow or other to catch sight and get possession of the endless "realm of spirits" as the epitome of the qualitative personal. This was a dream that Leibniz, Herder, the young Schiller, Hölderlin, Novalis, and Hegel dreamed but, obviously, did not carry into their waking thoughts.

Neither the other you as the beloved, chosen one, nor the universe as a place of work and achievement, nor the producible totality of all yous gives an answer to the human being's deepest needs. Ultimately, only absolute being itself can answer him, but as spirit-person, beyond the difference between spirit and nature, beyond the even profounder difference between the personal (as absolute uniqueness) and being (as absolute universality and totality). No transition is possible between the two poles in an inner-worldly manner.

Don Juan tried the mediation of the difference by starting from the individual you and thus destroyed his very starting point: the fidelity and exclusivity of the love from you to you. The pantheist tries it by starting from the totality of the world to which he transfers personal love; this can lead only to an illusory intoxication. The average human being quickly makes do with a compromise between the two halves of human existence which can never be completely integrated: friendship and study, family and the office, private and political life. In renouncing the possible capacity to be whole, one can draw a certain satisfaction from the fact that these two spheres, although never fully penetrating each other, can complement and enrich each other; and from this unresolved tension one may attain feeling for life which preserves one from an ultimately rigid bourgeoisification and expect the possibility of a new beginning.

This essentially gaping, unbridgeable chasm in human beings puts a negative margin around the locus of the relationship with God.

Wholeness would be possible if the inwardness of the natural and spiritual I-you and the sovereign, abstracting freedom for knowing and shaping the world could be encountered within an inclusive third relation which would not only ground both outreaches as not origin, but also definitively rescue both as the final goal. Quasi infinite love between two finite beings is possible only if infinite love in the ground of being reigns; that is, if that which the lovers swear to each other does not necessarily need to be an intoxicated exaggeration, or a "trick of nature" (which subsequently explains it in a cynical way), or a tragically disruptive *hubris*. Equally, if a spiritual being loses himself in the abstract demands of a political or technical world of work, it is no betrayal of spiritual depth to a mere anonymous, antlike existence, made palatable by promises of a utopian future, not for humanity as personal, but as a species. The individual will maintain mental honesty, if, behind and above the objective spirit to which he must sacrifice himself, there is an infinite subject toward which, in all the activities of his freedom, of his control and service of the world, he is moving, with the same or even greater intimacy of love than that which he has come to know in the womb of parental, familial, marital love and friendship.

The happiness caused by such a lightning-like insight into the possible wholeness of human existence within a religious relationship, the unfathomable promise it contains, fades into inadequacy as soon as we would reach for it directly. It is not enough to indicate the place where the higher third entity must let itself be found, if existence is supposed to be completed; for the question remains whether, as it is constituted, it can be completed at all. If, however, it cannot be completed in its totality, according to its whole basic structure, then all partial, fragmentary fulfillments are ultimately of no use to it. Any partial significance is constantly under attack and, rightly, negated by the lack of meaning of the whole. The one who doubts and despairs, who constantly exposes any partial significance of love or knowledge or virtue or achievement as meaningless from the standpoint of the one encompassing, is irrefutable. If, however, the human being is merely a fragment and as such incapable of completion, then it would be better if he did not exist at all and nothing remains for him to do but to curtail and reduce his own contradictory nature until the contradictions fall away and he can achieve, on a lower, more modest level, some kind of completability.

But this disquieting puzzle is not yet lucid even when the idea of an infinite God is proposed as the horizon in terms of which a human in his finitude could be brought to completion. It thus only seems to become all the more deeply disquieting. How could God as the infinite, hence in need of nothing and blissful in himself, help this creature which, from the whole structure of its being, is obviously incapable of being completed to wholeness? For its existence is not only finite and in the world; it is mortal. Death, it would appear, is the great rock thrown across the path of all thinking about possible completeness. Even if one explained its sunderability as something subsequently inserted in its original nature, the ending of earthly life would still pose one unavoidable question: How can a natural being, which must necessarily die (which is what we are as part of a species and a race), be conceived as united, to the point of identity, with an infinite spiritual and personal being with infinite claims of knowledge and love?

One does not fend off the question by letting the human being be made of a "mortal" body and an "immortal" soul; the connecting boundary is—as has already been shown—a different one; that between the cosmic spirit-soul of nature and the supercosmic person in direct relation to God. It is also a falsification to see the cosmic soul, with Origen, as a state (*katastasis*) of self-alienation of the spirit. The acts in which the spirit-soul experiences, knows, and loves in the world have at least their uncorrupted, purely creaturely side, by virtue of which they contain eternity and are unsurpassable. However indissolubly (according to Augustine) vanity and futility may have infiltrated the form of creation, thus definitively turning earthly life into a sphinx, the pure original shape of creation, now reconstructable, was itself a hieroglyph.

The centaur-like nature of the human being manifests something uncompletable which points beyond it to a manner of integration which is for it undiscoverable by it alone—which is formally sketched and negatively framed in the relation to God. The manner of fulfillment, however, is left open and, indeed, must be left open, if the relationship between God and humanity is to be determined and shaped in its dialogical drama by God alone.

In death the uncompletability of human beings becomes obvious to the point of pure contradiction, because their break-up in the denaturing process drags down with it any vague remaining hope of integration. When the beloved face loses it color and starts to decay, a curtain is lowered which separates definitively; this unique being has gone forever. No transmigration of souls, no reunion on other planets can be a satisfactory substitute or continuation. But death, which attacks the sense of life at its core in this way, is not simply an external catastrophe, the "Fates" cutting the thread. It seems to reveal a total decline of life that already turns in the opposite direction from the view toward wholeness.

Death is neither an external accident, nor is it to be rendered comprehensible—in its opposition to the meaning of human existence—as a constitutive element of existence, however much with desperate rigor one seeks to show this. After all, one cannot swear eternal fidelity for a period of time. The only reason that hearts do not constantly rebel against the dark omnipotence of death is because its fateful wind has always inclined the forests of the soul toward it, because the powers of infidelity, of injustice, of betrayal, of psychic debility and physical illness and infirmity, are familar to us from childhood in all their destructive consuming strength. They are forces that are not only above us, but within us, with which we seem to have already made a compact incomprehensible to ourselves, into which voluntarily, yet against our will, we must have entered in a locale to which we no longer have access.

This is Kafka's problem: How these alien "powers that be," the worst of which is guilt, first come to us from without, then penetrate us layer by layer, until we are "compelled" to acknowledge them as our own corruption and declare, "I am guilty." The horror of their alienness nevertheless does not abate. Therefore, the heart that is supposed to confess itself as guilty—not adventitiously, but on the very level of its existence—is always close to rebellion against the human existence that has been forced on it. It casts about for a tribunal to definitively release it from this sentence which has bowed it down under such a fate and which can only have been spoken by a "God."

But in the meanwhile these powers claim the whole human being; turn wherever it will, it cannot escape them. It has been unable to awake to the consciousness of its dignity and its mission in the world without already finding the worm that gnaws at the kernel of its freedom and love. It recognizes a moral imperative, not just as an indifferent law to which it is subject, but as that which will lead to its true freedom. But it also feels a displeasure in following this leader, a laziness that weighs it down, a sluggishness of the heart that would rather abide by itself than embark on the strenuousness of love. Self-conquest is the cost of love, and so even the child already seeks a way of having the pleasure of love without self-conquest, to gain the you and the world without exerting the I. This is the essence of nonlove disguised as love; this is lust.

This uncanny fate circling between not being able to do something and not wanting to do it, from which the child who starts to experience sin for the first time tries violently to escape, is always inevitably and degradingly accompanied by the elemental forces of the *mana* whose deceitfulness the heart first sees through but whose crushing superiority eventually wins because it must admit the hopelessness of radical protest. The world of the adult is right, and in the adult world *adikia*, unrighteousness, is obviously an integral part. And I myself am moving toward this world of adulthood, and therefore must come to terms with injustice. There may be attempts in this world, both in the private and in the public sphere, to dam in the destructive powers; to associate oneself with these attempts will be noble and praiseworthy, but nowhere, either privately or publicly, will humanity be able to deal finally with the Hydra. It carries it around with itself as its enemy; it grows with it and often it seems as if, with the increasing effort to conquer it and transform the world into a paradise, the snake head doubles itself after every blow.

In the region where it intends to be able to register something like real "progress," in the organization of a moral world order, this putative progress appeared paired with more deeply gaping apocalyptic abysses. Measurable progress, not only in the technological, but also in the cultural and social fields, can, of its nature, take place only within the natural order of humanity. But the personal depth of an individual whose home is in the eternal, resists being reduced to a means within a genus. The optimism of progress of a technological culture must make so much noise because it must cover more and more death cries of the ravaged person. Even such an antisocialist as Nietzsche, who appears to have been concerned only with single outstanding individuals, must in the critical moment, reassess all personal values through nature and try to derive them from the biological. The superman has to be "bred" and for this purpose are all moral valuations (which bring forth in us a profound incapacity for good, what Kant called radical evil) to be dissolved into a real biological strength. That Nietzsche's theory thus leads inevitably to that of his bitterest opponents, history has in the meantime shown and, thereby, indicated also that Nietzsche's legitimate concerns can be solved only on a basis other than his.

11 · Changes in the Understanding of Death

What follows is not intended to describe the opinions of well-known modern philosophers with a perusal of what they have said about death; it will be, instead, a much more modest consideration of what might be characteristic of modern philosophical thought on this subject, as against other periods of intellectual history. No one of sound mind will regard death as a phenomenon to be understood on the first try: it remains till the end just as mysterious as existence itself (birth), indeed still more mysterious, because, on the one hand, it radically sublates what is already posited and yet, on the other hand, cannot sublate. Perhaps progress in thinking about death consists in the fact that every period of thought takes this riddle more seriously, and therefore reflects on it even more incisively than its predecessors.

We can distinguish three such periods: the mythic-magical, the theoretical (or philosophic-contemplative), and the existential. We stand in the third and cannot go back into the first two.

The first attempt to master the mystery of death by thought presupposes a stage of spiritual development in which the mind is still imprisoned in image (myth); the general, unrestricted horizon of being (and that means spirit) is still geographically and culturally limited; and thus also the consciousness of the individual has still not come to a full detachment from the tribe (or at best the nation) and thereby from the whole life of nature. Here the individual person can be sensed to be a somehow incomplete and therefore transitory realization of a whole life including birth and death. The "realm of the dead" is then (in a dialectic which the human being does not further attend to or resolve) both "realm of the shades" (because it does not have the color of this life) and also "realm of real life" (because the whole life into which the "forebears" are again integrated is, in duration and power, far superior to the transitory individual life which is subject to fate). Hence the decisive human action (that contains both "philosophy" and "religion") consists in "magical rapport" with the dead: to be assured of their power, to get control of them, to pray to them in oaths, to get on their good side, to live in anticipation already as a living one among the dead. Even ethics becomes magic (cf. the "negative confession" from the Egyptian *Book of the Dead*, Chap. 135). This stage, which we find most clearly defined in China, Mesopotamia, and Egypt, is, as a primitive stage of the development of the human mind, irrevocably gone. Its positive aspects, its convictions of a more than temporal human life, is inseparably bound with what is dubious in it: deficient individuation and thus, magic.

The second attempt is that of the Greeks. Greek natural philosophy fundamentally overcomes the myth and replaces it with *theōria*, the intellectual view of things and of being as a whole. Hence magic also disappears in principle, as does relationship with the beyond as "rapport" (naturally, remnants survive for a while, but that is not our concern). Individuality comes to the fore and fixes its attention on the whole of being, but thereby it also stands more isolated in fate and more severely affected by death. The task is to find an intellectual remedy for this and, faced with the cup of hemlock, Socrates found it. It is perhaps the most prodigious moment in the development of human thought. The nature of a human being is spirit, and it is so precious that it—the Greek *sees* this!—cannot be assailed by death. It is not true that the human being dies. The human being is spirit: the spirit however is immortal; what dies is the body which is "wrongfully" connected with the spirit because of a "fall," a self-estrangement of the spirit from which it through death, if rightly done, can become free again.

Only that which does not really belong to the human dies, only that which drew the person, who is really immortal spirit, down into the sphere of the transitory. Socrates-Plato does indeed rely on the Eastern tradition: the transitory external and bodily world is in its essence already in the process of dissolution, it is without consistency, it is illusion (*doxa, maya*); only the internal, the spiritual core, is perduring and eternal. Those from India already knew that. But Indians (imprisoned in the world of magic) had from time immemorial equated the "self" of the human being with the all (*atmabrahma*); it lacked the Greek, Socratic sense for *spiritual* individuality which now, as such, is posited eternally for the first time. The flash of this platonic intuition is so electrifying that the millenia remain blinded by its brilliance and do not notice its deficiency, or even the devastation it has caused. For Plato rescued the soul, but at the price of the body. He destroyed the metaphysical unity of humanity; and this for the sake of "conquering" death. One must, of course, add that Platonic spiritualism is tempered in Greek thought by the Aristotelian-Stoic contemplation of nature which takes certain traits of the old magical way of thinking and purifies them into natural philosophy. Here the human being appears as a transitory articulation of the living totality which is now also understood as the total reason (*physis* as *logos*), and it appears to the Greek as a noble sacrifice, worthy of the philosophical spirit, to concede the transitory individuality generated in the individual in favor of the universal reason being generated in it, which is already commanding it (Seneca, Marcus Aurelius). Because the Greeks see the world like a huge house with stories (from the highest god beyond the gods and the demi-gods, to the humans, and to the animals), in which one can easily climb up and down, because they (the Greeks) have indeed discovered individuality but not yet the person, for them the dialectic between the Platonic and the Aristotelian-Stoic conception of death does not yet need to appear to them to be deadly for thought.

It is not the purpose of this sketch to describe the encounter of Christendom with the ancient doctrine of humanity. Everyone knows that the message of the total salvation of humankind through the death and resurrection of Jesus Christ brought with it its own enclosed image of human being, but that this picture of the human— human as body-soul, called in Christ to an eternal body-soul blessedness—had to wage a hard battle with the old view. It could be said that, as far as the philosophical view of man is concerned, for the first millennium and a half, Platonism dominated the background. This was most clearly reflected in the fact that everything essential for the human being seemed to be salvaged when a "soul" was with God (even without the body it can attain to eternal happiness and to the vision of God [Const. *Benedictus Deus* from 1336; Denz. 530; DS 1000], and that thus the resurrection of the body seems almost to be only an accessory that could just as well be ignored).

To start balancing this inconsistency was left for the third period which we (for lack of a better word) call "existential." It emerges where the human being begins to step from the "shell" of the cosmos that surrounds and dominates it: the natural sciences shatter that picture of the world in which "heaven" is at once astronomically and theologically the place of God, place of the blessed, of the angels, of the immutable heavenly bodies, as well as the whole anthropology and eschatology that goes along with it. It is hard to say to what extent the becoming-aware of the human being as "person" is the cause, and to what extent it is the effect, of this process. It is, in any case, its complementary inner side. True, as a bodily being, the human being remains embedded in the cosmos and more than ever obliged to it (because now it becomes ever more clear that the human has not fallen down from heaven into a body, but that the whole cosmic ascendancy is itself the human being's becoming body). But the cosmos now no longer seems to be the dominant factor, "divine" in its uppermost parts; it seems rather to be the "footstool" of the human being who is its quintessence and the goal of its becoming and who thus, more than before (and perhaps really for the first time), stands as ruler over creation.

The consequence of this is that the human being can, in the end, no longer be "dissected" and "explained" cosmologically. (The "spirit" belongs in heaven; the "soul," in any case [Platonically], to the *anima mundi;* the "body" to the earth; the human being is the con-crete reality grown together from all its parts which is dissolved again in death.) Instead, the consequence is that the cosmological first stages (plants and animals) must be interpreted as pointing to humanity. The unity that is the human being, as it exists, is the center of the world, in relation to what is below as it is to what is above (the human is no longer, as with the platonizing theologians, the lowest level of "angel"). At the peaks it is always lonely, and the human being has become lonely at the summit of creation. It has nothing with which to shield itself from God. The human being stands now eye-to-eye with the absolute. The world does point it towards God, but the world is for it no longer really the ladder to God: the human being itself stands on the highest rung. It has, in order to understand itself and God, nothing better than just itself. Not the naked individual, without world, without history, but humanity itself so far as it integrates all nature and all history as into its center. Humanity itself as meaning of the world—in its dialogical being before God.

12 · Guilt as Denial of Love

In this love of God which humans meet in Christ, they experience not only what true love is but also at the same time, and uncontradictably, that they, sinners and egoists that they are, have no true love. They experience both aspects in one: the creature's limited love, and its guilty frigidity. They certainly have something like a preunderstanding (*Vorverständnis*) of what love is; if they did not they could not make out the sign Jesus Christ. It would be objectively insoluble and contradictory, because here has appeared the love of God in the form of flesh, that is, in the form of human love. But they cannot proceed beyond this preunderstanding to a recognition of the sign without a radical conversion; conversion not only of heart—and with it the admission that in the light of this love one has never loved—but also of the mind with the realization that one must start from the beginning to relearn what love really is.

Let us take the limited nature of love first. Without a doubt nature brings the reality of love to us from our subhuman roots; for love is built into the foundations of living beings. No unmasking theory of a "will to power" or "a will to happiness" can stand up to the truth of this evidence. We can see the play of eros raised beyond purposiveness; the animal's dedication to its young; the individual's self-renunciation for the sake of the whole. In the human being this transitory relationship enters into the sphere of spiritual and transtemporal meaning. Temporal eros can be a door to a life of fidelity that outlasts it. Thus the animal relationship to offspring can be deepened into a natural-spiritual family love. A dying giving-way of the individual to the superior might of the surviving race can provide an opportunity for the rise of the idea of self-sacrifice of one individual for the good of the community, the clan, the people, or the state; and death can, as it were, bring together the whole of existence in which self-abandonment and an intimation of the sense of love hidden in being itself occurs. But all this is more a direction indicated than a journey completed, for other equally strong or stronger forces limit the movement of love; the race for a place in the sun, the terrible fencing in of the individual in environment and clan and even in the family; the struggle for survival, for which nature supplies the strength and the weapons; the law of passing time. Friendships that seemed everlasting grow cool; people lose touch or drift apart; attitudes and opinions alter and so hearts are estranged; physical separation makes it worse and love must be unusually obstinate and strong in order to fight against it. Vows of love that were to be eternal are broken because the tide of eros receded, another new love intervened, the faults and limitations of the loved one became oppressive, and for a still deeper reason perhaps, because the finitude of human love seems itself to speak against it. "Why love only one woman when a thousand could be loved?" asks Don Juan, who is protesting against the limits of finitude out of an intuition which was originally perhaps just as valid as Faust's. But where the former missed, in his succession of women, the meaning of love itself, the latter lost, in the very multiplicity of moments, the eternity promised him.

Even in the family, love is limited by nature. If it depends at first without question upon the tie of blood, the very closeness of the blood bond can become an impediment when the spirit begins to stir; too much mutual insight can dull the expectation of the gifts to come. The freedom needed by the new generation may perhaps not be allowed by parents whose horizon begins to close in around their own center which lies in another time. All our activities—farming and hunting, politics and war, household and business, scholarship and scientific research can be motivated in part by love, but love can never mold them completely or domesticate them; the other forces of human existence retain their independence and their power; and, as Nietzsche averred, when a human being tries to make human love into an absolute, at the expense of its vital forces, it contradicts itself biologically and culturally. The ordinary zone of human existence, the interchange with the environment, is at best a sort of middle zone where love and self-interest, love and the absence of love, temper one another.

The death of the individual is a solemn moment, for the community experiences within itself the forces of a fate that encompasses humans. It can be undergone by him, to be sure, with "nonresistance" as to a dispensation in fate, which in its severity perhaps also allows him an inkling of the traits of a wisdom and gentleness not to be debunked. Whatever thinkers influenced by Christianity may have said, it is beyond the horizon of human nature to unite that resignation with a personal human love. Although death may lead into a realm of immortality, into a purifying but also a surely to be feared judgment, and into a somehow eternally divine sphere—but even if the soul expects a happy destiny there the whole process embracing the particular events cannot be addressed in the name of love. And still less so, the more the image of a personal God fades, and then later with the mystical divinity and glory of the cosmos growing dim, a personal providence becomes questionable. Even under the Old Covenant—where the love of the covenant Lord for his covenant people (and with them for all of creation) is placed at the center of the interpretation of human existence—death and the afterlife remain a liminal twilight zone.

Finally, human love is snared in an insoluble contradiction implicit in an existence which is both spiritual and mortal: the personal love which lovers vow one another in moments of exaltation intend finality, a love that lasts beyond death; but "eternal love"—"for a period of time" is a contradiction which no one can live. And yet nothing in the household of visible nature warrants the survival of a (fully) human, not just "psychic," continued existence where this existence, as what was meant by love, is not just that of a freefloating intangible soul, meant and not meant: what is now is supposed to be eternal—and at the same time should not be allowed to be eternal (so as not to become an unbearable hell): the heart does not understand itself in this way at all. The exalted moment of love is full of promise: an openness, not closed in upon itself, the fruitfulness of which is revealed naturally in the child, though spiritually it remains veiled. Human love, sheerly as created, is a strange hieroglyph: grammatically speaking, it is ever only an inchoative which cannot translate itself adequately into an indicative mood.

And then there is the question of guilt. It has already been remarked that it is only Christian revelation that really brings guilt into the light of day. It is face to face with Christ crucified that the abysmal egoism of what we are accustomed to call love becomes clear: when the question is put to us in ultimate seriousness, we say no where Christ in his love said yes, and in our lack of love we say yes without a qualm to his bearing our sins: all is right for us, if he is willing to do it! That is why sinners are not asked by God about their agreement with the cross; only the consent of the lover to the most terrible thing, the death of the beloved is retrieved (Jn 12:7; cf. Lk 1:38; Jn 20:17). In the event of the passion, humanity—whether Christian, Jew, or pagan—is stripped naked in the light of its own truth: in the incorruptibility of this unmasking "every mouth is made dumb" and "every human being" who speaks of love is convicted "as a liar." "No one is just, not even one; . . . they are all going astray, there is no one seeking after God . . . they do not know the way of peace; reverence for God is alien to them" (Rom 3:4–19 passim).

But there is also an internal human consciousness of denial that cannot be shifted into the foreground where failures are balanced against expiation. If that were sufficient, then what is good and just could always be fully restored again. But deeper within lies a consciousness of being crippled, of corruption and hardness of heart, that no norm of love, no matter how vaguely conceived, is sufficient. It dares not believe in the possibility of such a fulfillment of human existence. So lacking in strength is humanity that it feels it necessary to accuse some authority higher than its own heart, a heart which could indeed always go a further piece than it really does, but is well aware that it can never go the whole way. All the less since no one can imagine where such a way might lead. The stages cannot be deciphered, but get lost immediately in impenetrable night and thus guilt collapses into a natural resignation. There it is protected and hidden from itself—unless it knows how to find repose in the ethical domesticity of "guilt and expiation."

The finitude of human existence seems to be a permanent justification for the finite limits of love which—in a framework where total life in the cosmos cannot be interpreted in terms of love— withdraws into little islands of mutual sympathy: islands of eros, of friendship, of patriotism, even a certain universal love based on the nature identical in all human beings, or even on a *physis* identical in all profane beings animated by a common *logos*. The identical "nature" that draws two lovers together to such an island of love is expanded into a universal principle by going beyond and overlooking the differences. For example, in Buddhism and stoicism, a sort of love for one's enemies does become possible: the other person's hatred and opposition is simply overlooked and only the community of nature and of being is considered.

13 · The Human Being as "Person"

Let us begin with a very simple consideration which prescinds from all history of theology. It will teach us that we can do without the concept "person" much longer than we are accustomed to think. All living beings (beginning at least from the higher animals and including humans) manifest the puzzling peculiarity that they share in a species of nature which is identical in all individuals, but that each one always possesses it in a unique and immediate way. The being-for-itself of the individual pertains to the particularity of its species (and beyond that to the genus animal); it is eliminated neither by communication between the individuals, nor by the herd instinct, nor by the ability to reproduce. The species concept thus can not abstract from this incommunicable each-for-itself of the individuals which realize the species, even if their number and individual characteristics are not deducible from the species. What now on the level of the animal indicates the inclusion of all individuals of a species in every instance of it (whereby the species never exists other than in the form of fully exclusive individuals), on the level of the human, signifies in the same way the inclusion of all spiritual subjects (with *reflexio completa* of self-consciousness) in human nature which, again, exists only in mutually exclusive individuals. The universal presence of this same paradox of inclusion and exclusion becomes manifest in the "ever-mineness" manner of speaking on the part of the possessor of this species of being. This "ever" belongs to all beings of the species, and thus characterizes every last one of them, while it at the same time points to the uniqueness and immediacy of their individuality.

The spiritual subject knows *that* it is such a being, and hence that it is a human being in a unique and immediate way. But does it thereby also know already *who* it is? In other words, in virtue of what is it not only quantitatively but also qualitatively distinguished from all other spiritual subjects? It can ascribe to itself such a qualitative whatness (*haecceitas*), but not positively describe it. It has two ways of getting closer to the incomprehensible that is central to it. One way is the accumulation of empirical characteristics which are peculiar to it as this single being and which surround its individuality: "Form, figure, relationship, personal name, home, time and place" (Albert the Great). In this way it is not, of course, defined in the strict sense, but rather, as already the ancients used to say, only "sketched." If it totals these characteristics as well as those which come to it from within, like heredity, and those which grow with it organically, like upbringing, encounter with personalities, etc., it does not get beyond an accumulation of accidents. Under other living conditions it could have become a quite differently determined subject.

A second way is the interpersonal, to the extent that it is clear that a spiritual subject can awaken to itself and to its own actuality only if it is addressed by one or more others who find it valuable, perhaps indispensable. When a child learns from its mother that it is "her treasure," there is awakened in it not only the consciousness of its "worth" (*dignitas individui*) but also precisely that of its own uniqueness. But the question remains whether this assertion is really enough—it could actually be taken back!—in order to build on it an abiding consciousness of qualitative uniqueness. Ultimately, no fellow human being can say to another who this other really is. The strongest assertion can only declare who the other is for the one who treasures and loves. And with the indeterminability of its qualitative identity the spiritual subject can also gain no categorical giving of meaning for its existence (how accidental it is, considered from the standpoint of the act of conception and birth!), for its task in the world, for the existence of others and for their tasks. Everything remains stuck in a mesh of relative and mutually temporary evaluations and reevaluations, recognitions and denials.

In all this it is significant for us that up to now there is no reason whatever to introduce into this complementarity of general and individual spirit-nature of man a concept "person" which must or even could be lifted from that of the spiritual subject. One must concur with Paul Galtier when he says that self-consciousness as such belongs to the "nature" (and not to a person contradistinguished from the nature).

The lack of assuredness, not of the That, but rather of the Who of the spirit-subject, will, if no further security is added, again and again seduce one to a surrender of the individual, that is supposedly limited in itself, in favor of a something that is somehow encompassing. Not even the self-sufficient feeling individual of the Stoa dared to attribute immutability to itself, still less the Buddhist I-consciousness; and how seductive for the middle ages was the Arab thesis of an "agent intellect" common to all spirits, how seductive for the moderns is an absorption into the collective, vitalistic, or materially conceived universal life (*Alleben*). Idealism was correct to demand a sublimation of the purely natural individual into the realms of the objective spirit, but it often enough allowed the individual to disappear completely in this absorption. And the great opponent of this idealism, A. Günther, thought he had done enough when he opposed the sphere of nature to that of self-consciousness or spirit and identified the latter with person; but precisely this identification (which he also could propose only by taking over Christian concepts) appears questionable as long as the guarantee of the who of the individual spirit has not been assured.

But this guarantee cannot come from the sphere of the impersonal world (which confers empirical characteristics) or from the sphere of fellow humanity (where no one can give another more than doubtful, precarious assurances), but rather only from the absolute subject, from God. There, where God tells a spirit-subject to its face who it is for him, the eternally abiding and faithful or truthful God, where he tells it in the same breath why it exists—thus conferring on it its divinely attested mission—there it can be said of a spirit-subject that it is person.

In Search of God

14 · Longing for God: Mythological— Illustrated from Greek Tragedy

The meeting of these two words, "tragedy" and "faith," is deeply significant, for what is broken in the tragic presupposes a faith in the unbroken totality. But when being broken is a fact of experience, a knowledge, then that totality which is breaking or has broken into splinters can now be only an object of *faith*, perhaps against all reason. Still, this abstract statement is not intended to show or prove anything, but at most to calm in advance a smouldering prejudice against the title of our reflections.

What is the tragic? One can try to give endless verbal definitions, which are all neither true nor false, because the question remains as to what object they are even trying to address. Therefore, let's leave the word alone for a while and look to the matter itself, to the place where we encounter it centrally. It is from the center, and not from what could belong to it only peripherally, that the understanding and then finally also the definition will have to come. The *tragōdia* were made by the Greeks in the classical age; discovered, so to speak. The primary imprint from that time remained the matrix for everything that came later, as with Seneca and the French (Corneille and Racine) who imitate and vary it, but surely for the Germans too, although here a properly new source discovers it in the old Nordic cycles, in the Nibelungen, with Shakespeare, Schiller, Hebbel. The mother lode of Greek tragedy is the myth, that is, that bright zone of human existence that opens luminously in the distinction between heaven and earth, gods and mortals. Decisive in this is that the human being in this zone is not understood as a god who has come down—as in the East where finite existence stands under the sign of illusion and folly, and as it is to some extent again later in Orphic-Platonic philosophy where the soul has fallen from heaven and is consumed in longing for its origin—but that instead the human being in its finitude and beauty and questionableness is affirmed, whereby indeed this finite existence attains its whole noble grandeur from the fact that it stands in the zone of the light of the gods and is interpreted only in that light.

Homer who, according to Aristotle, is the father of tragedy, opened this zone of light for the West once and for all: There above, composed and in need of nothing, the blessed gods, who nevertheless share decisively in the fate of humanity, who, as patron gods guide the heroes and their destinies, as counterforces impede and threaten them, until the threads of this heavenly play and counterplay in a hidden plan of the "father of the gods and mortals" inscrutably converge in the tapestry. There below the humans, demonstrated and represented in their natures by their heroes and kings: how they stand out in the zone of the gods' fate and still are not manipulated in it like puppets, but act freely and magnificently, in the full weight of their mortal uniqueness, but pray, sacrifice, trust in the divine guidance, fear the black fate, rejoice in the light of success and fame; a play in which the eye of Zeus takes pleasure and which can be replaced by no feast of the gods.

This full weight of finite human existence which exists out there in the divine light is the foundation of Greek tragedy. It is even the foundation of the philosophy that followed, which in the age of Greece is introduced by the tragic death of Socrates, who succeeded in turning the full weight of his existence into a martyrdom and thus into a witness for the truth; later through the tragic death of Hermias who died for the beloved beauty of philosophy, *tas d'heneken philiou morphas*, as Aristotle wrote in a passionate hymn to his dead friend; again through the tragic death of Seneca; again, as prelude to medieval philosophy, through the tragic death of Boethius in the arms of the consoler, philosophy; and once again through the tragic death of Kierkegaard, the witness of truth in our times, who put the question, "May one allow oneself to be struck dead for the truth?" and who demanded that as preacher of the truth one must "gesticulate with his existence."

But back to the Greeks. When the great tragedians, descending from the light of Homer, place the human being in an eclipse of God where God is really still present but has become invisible and alien and yet continues to determine the meaning of human existence, where then does the core of the tragic lie for them? We would like to make three comments on this, but first remind ourselves that the Greek tragedy was a liturgical play in honor of Dionysius, that it thus presented to the praise of God in a revelatory way the fate of humanity in the dark light of the gods.

1. Existence is tragic because its essential lines cannot be completed. In man's standing in the divine sphere, goods become visible to him which need to be affirmed and loved and which nevertheless evade him. There is the love between husband and wife, but Admetus is called away from the wedding banquet to his death: his loving spouse, Alcestis, freely offers herself unto death in his place to save her beloved, but Admetus now becomes the one who has been robbed; and since his beloved has died, life for him too has lost its allure. There is dignity, but it is humiliated, ground into the dust, trampled on unto the last indignity: thus Queen Hecuba, before Troy in flames, is divided with her daughters like merchandise among the victors. There is fidelity, but this, in Sophocles' Deianira, who sends her husband Heracles the robe of Nessus, is fiendishly outmaneuvered; and in the Heracles of Euripedes, just when the hero comes to free his threatened family, fidelity is duped by a demon of insanity so that, in this insanity, he himself kills his children.

2. Here my second comment comes into view: the essential lines of existence are not only unfulfillable, but they cross one another and turn human existence into a contradiction. Orestes exactly obeys the god Apollo in killing his mother Clytemnestra, because she murdered her husband; but for this he is delivered to the furies. Antigone obeys the unwritten law of the gods of love for family in burying her dead brother, but for that, without a god intervening, she is buried alive by the guardian of the law of the city who had forbidden this. Hippoly-

tus obeys the goddess Artemis, whom he loves, by remaining unmarried, but in doing so he insults the other goddess, Aphrodite, whose nature and law he spurns. It is the same in the Danaides. Prometheus confirmed himself as the friend of humanity against Zeus who wanted to eliminate them, and thus became the enemy of the highest god. In this contradictoriness human existence can become absolute pain; many tragedies show substantially nothing other than this apparently insurpassable state of pain, like that piece which represents the seven mothers of the seven heroes slain before Thebes, or the women of Troy we have already mentioned. To this belongs the continually recurring situation of the "Hiketes," hardened almost to a requirement in Euripedes, someone fleeing for protection, as the precise starting point of a drama: the person is placed right away in a state of homelessness and lawlessness, in a state of being outcast which holds his whole existence, as it were, suspended in the air over the abyss. It is the utmost illustration of existence outside of itself: it becomes a subsisting question for the gods and for one's fellow humans, to have mercy on him or not, to practice hospitality, perhaps despite very weighty misgivings, or not.

3. But now my third comment. At the basis of the contradiction, to the point of pure pain and to the ultimate emptying, there lies an impenetrable guilt. It is basic and, as foundational, can be somehow exposed but not really taken away. It is, although evidently there, still not clearly locatable. Is the individual guilty? Oedipus for example? Yes, at bottom, his guilt comes on the day he killed his father and married his mother; but pointing to that all along was a decree of fate, a doom from afar: as hereditary curse. So much so that Oedipus, in the second play depicting his death, considers himself pardoned: he had done nothing wrong intentionally, and bitterly repented of the deed. The inherited guilt can occasionally, as with the Atridae, be traced to a beginning; in other instances it points to a divine wrath unleashed by insults which remain unknown to the humans (as in the insult to Artemis in the *Iphigenia in Aulis*) and yet require the most severe atonement, atonement which leads to new guilt. The human becomes guilty insofar as he acts responsibly, but he acts in an association with the gods whose thoughts and plans are unfathomable. Thus guilt develops the human in an even greater network of guilt from which he can be freed in no other way than by the rooting out of his whole existence. And on the other hand to the extent that the gods, as conceived by Homer, are only partial aspects of the whole of providence, they themselves have an overview of only part of fate; they too can become entangled in something overarching— like Apollo who commands the matricide and who, when it is a matter of the final solution, does not dare to get involved but has

Athene represent him. Such a collective doom ("Twilight of the Gods") binding together gods and mortals becomes visible above all in the coarse and abrupt Germanic myths. Thus, guilt is present; it is not denied out of hand; it goes beyond just the individual, without on that account fully exonerating him.

When we consider that such a disclosure of the human situation in its exposure to the gods is intended as a worshipful liturgical act, that here the human being is held into the light and into the darkness of the gods just as the flesh and blood of Christ is raised at the consecration so that all those standing around can see it and the divine Father himself can cast his eye on it, then suddenly one can see as well how exposed is this act of disclosure itself. In many tragedies indeed it borders close to rebellion against the gods, to a quarreling against its fate and mandate: it is a glorious exhibition of human lamentation in its frightfulness which almost or even entirely outweighs in existential significance the significance of an existence of the gods.

The drama which holds the human situation, for a moment made visible, as a sacred symbol in the light of truth—the absolute truth which holds between God and humanity—is like a sacrament that contains something like grace and redemption in sensible form. This grace is mysterious enough. It does not consist in getting control of and removing the fundamental contradictions of existence; it consists in the fact that such a frightful, pain-formed being might stand at all in the light and the darkness of the gods. This is the incomprehensible power of the Greek heart: that, in the darkness as well as in the light, it says Yes to this existence. A hushed Yes which has carefully gathered all the reasons for saying No in order to overcome them, in spite of everything. The unity of all tragedies lies in this Yes, which almost makes a pleasure of gathering together so much that is questionable, indeed as unexplainable as possible, and presenting it to those who are together experiencing and celebrating the tragedy, in order to make known the greater power of the affirmation. To the No belongs also rebellion in every form: the rebellion of the titans against the gods, rebellion against death, against outrageous injustice, blindness (Ajax), against the powerlessness of sickness (Philoctetus), insanity (Heracles), and against the apparently senseless, contradictory, arbitrary ordinances of the gods. In the Yes to everything rests the unity of the tragedies. For there are many individual solutions which cannot be reduced to one denominator: the solution of the metaphysical-mythological process (as in the Aeschylean trilogy we have mentioned); the solution of a purification through suffering to the brink of holiness and divinization (as in the Oedipus at Colonus and also in the Deianira); the utopian or fairy tale solution (as in the Alcestis where Heracles tries to trick Death of the dead wife and lead her back to her husband); the solution of simply leaving open every horizon of suffering, as it often is in Euripedes; the solution of an intervention of God, which is minimized as a *Deus ex machina*, unjustly because, after all, a knot that is tied by a god can only be untied by the god.

The key to Greek tragedy does not lie in these individual paths. It lies in the paradox that human existence transcends the sphere of dumb subhuman nature and stands in a zone determined by the fate of gods; so that it thus comes into an extreme darkness beyond all earthly reckoning, but in honor of the gods is not oppressed in the face of its own tragedy, but affirms it as its own incomprehensible greatness surpassing perhaps even that of the gods. What Aristotle calls *catharsis*, the purification of the spectator through the shared experience of this process, through the reception of this kind of sacrament and the grace hidden therein, is no more to be understood than the process itself—psychologically not at all, because we are dealing here with an existential process, with an elevation from particular, unpurified (because blind) standpoints to the vision of the real situation of humanity before which one can only reverently, as in the presence of something in which God has had a say, keep quiet.

15 · Longing for God: Philosophical

For the nonbiblical person, the fundamental experience can at best be, I am not the absolute, not the whole, not the one, or that which is without any differentiation and what I know about myself I know about all other beings in the world. The nonbiblical person can, insofar as he or she has this elementary experience, at the same time have the complementary experience of an equally elementary longing to move from this limitedness and nonabsoluteness toward that one, which is without any differentiation. Indeed, both experiences are only like the front on back sides of one single reality. And precisely because both are so indissolubly connected with each other they can bring the nonbiblical person to the idea that his or her own nonabsoluteness might possibly relate to the absolute like the part to the whole or the spark to the fire, so that the religious problem would consist essentially in bringing about a knowledge of the process of integration and in translating it into reality.

Let's stay for a moment with the presuppositions and consequences of such a conception. The presupposition is that at the same time there exists the one without opposition and the other (even if secondary and transitory) nevertheless opposed to it, of which I also am one. This fact seems contradictory and it is surely, in its facticity, inexplicable. For when the one is without opposition, how can anything be set over against it? There are three ways, complementary to one another, of solving this puzzle. The first explains the relation of the one to the not-one (which are the beings of the world) by means of the relation between being and appearance: then the religious way consists in the seeing through of the appearance and in the knowledge that I am ultimately not an "other" but the one itself. The second way would explain the being-other with the category of guilt, of falling away from being included in the one; then the question remains, who committed this guilt and why, and according to each answer the path of purification from this guilt is planned. The third way will think of the one in such a way that it contains every being-other already subsumed *as such* into itself, so that the individual that I am is simply understood as contained and integrated into the whole and must comport itself existentially in accordance with this. Each of these three ways has its limit, its contradiction, which lets it become a dead end and point further to one of the two other ways. The first idea, that the not-one is only an appearance not only destroys the I as individual (it would be for the mystic to make the best of this way), but also every individual thing in the world and thus interprets every historical event as empty of meaning, at best (but even this idea cannot be thought through to the end) as a self-terminating process. The second idea which speaks of guilt can, as already indicated, assign no subject of it, unless it gets lost in gnostic speculation about aeons which, however, explain nothing because right from the beginning it is not clear how there can even be a limited number of aeons within the unopposed one; and that is even before dealing with the question why one of these aeons can fall out of the "plenitude" and cause the material world. Here then, right from the outset there is placed in the one the other which is capable of setting itself against the one of its own free will: what is supposed to be explained is actually presupposed. It is the same with the third idea which operates as if there is no contradiction at all, as if the individual were both an individual in itself and at the same time something integrated or assimilated in the whole. Here the notion of a way eliminates itself in principle: what, considered by itself, is "underway" is already at its goal when considered in the one. While the third way thus allows the problem posed so urgently from basic experience to disappear as nonexistent, the second way tries to establish the distance between the one and the many as what-should-not-be and toward whose dissolution one must work; but it fails to give an answer to the equally pressing question of how we came to this what-should-not-be, or why I must conceive of my being an individual me (*Einzel-Ich-Sein*) as guilt and concern myself with getting rid of it. Since these problems are insoluble, we are thrown back upon the first way which explains the individual, in the precariousness of its temporal coming to be and passing away, as not at all existent, and thus turns the religious way to a seeing through of the non-being of all appearance, to the negation of any meaning of plurality, of dialogue, of interhuman love, of history as a whole.

16 · The Inconclusiveness of the Human Search for God

Let us bring to mind the dialectic of the idea of God as it has developed in the religions and philosophies of the world.

1. The first image of God, that of the *myth*, could be described as the religious projection of the primordial experience of loving human fellowship, woven through of course (and not a little obscured) with the existential feelings which humanity feels in view of the strangeness and superior force of nature and being as a whole. If we strip this image of its expressly natural traits—power, as it is encountered in the beast, in the thunderstorm, in the elements, in light, fire, darkness, and in natural catastrophies, overwhelmingly panicked anxiety, reverential awe for what encompasses one in every respect, i.e., for conception, birth, and death, for the ancestors who embody one's origins—if we then do this, there emerges at the heart of things a mysterious, undefinable "for me," behind which must stand a You that can provide me favor, protection, and help, a grace promised in the first experience of childhood and which just is unable to be fully granted by parents or one's fellow humans at all. This god is (as the mother was) a "Someone," unreflectively understood as *One* (among possible others), just as the mother, the father, the friend or relative is one among others who are not for me. My enemy will have his own god who will, logically, be the enemy of my god. This "For me" or, when we are dealing with a tribe or country or kingdom, this "For us" of God is his unconditionally most important quality: he is person, endowed with the power and freedom of a person; he turns, he is moved, by the appeals of the humans who need him, to new manifestations of love, protection, and favorable hearing. The veneration, the personal prayer, and its empowerment through personal sacrifice (as a sensible expression of one's readiness to give all for God) are a continuation of the act of answering, self-giving love of the child to its mother. The name of the god who helps gain the favor of love can be without number across the nations and ages; always God is this One, special One who is interested in me, in whose circle of protection I am sheltered, listened to, and safe. A wonderfully

enlightened late form of the living myth are the divine patrons of the heroes in Homer: Athena is the goddess of Odysseus in whom he trusts absolutely, in an entirely asexual mutual love, to whom he complains that in his long, dangerous journey he has never seen her (*Od* 13:314f), and who assures him that she has never abandoned him even in misfortune (331). And since there is a personal god for every hero and his tribe, and the gods must therefore be numerous and split among themselves in their protective interests, there arises a Zeus who orders and plans the whole of destiny, who listens to the concerns represented by the gods and ties all together in a hidden plan of providence. Somewhere in the realm of god is something like free omnipotence which, however, cannot call in question the "For me/ For us" in the myth. The Egyptian Re is all-powerful and yet is there for Egypt. Among the gods of Babylon the one at any given time addressed looms as the important one, who stands above the others, in the sense of Hölderlin's "shed your favor on us, the sons of the loving earth, so that we, grown so used to the feasts, celebrate them all, and do not count the gods; one is always for all" (*Festival of Peace*, Sketch 1). For the understanding of the Bible it is important to see that Yahweh does not introduce himself above all as a god who corresponds to an abstract-universal concept of god, but as the "God for . . . ," just as Israel is his chosen people, a "people for . . . ," that he thus establishes the rivalry with the other gods and only in a long history steps forward as victor over all others, as the truly all-powerful, who therefore shows the others to be "nothings." Thus it is not that he refuted and demythologized the concrete "sacred legend of origin" (which is called myth), but rather that he fulfills it from within and shows its universal validity in its concreteness.

2. Nevertheless the mythic idea of God shows its inner finitude and gets surpassed in a few decisive intellectual steps by *philosophy*. That primary-dualistic emergence of being into an immortal divine world and a mortal human world, as Pindar acknowledges (*Nem* 6:1–7) and even the tragedians presuppose, puts inappropriate limits on the divine in its power and freedom and makes it dependent on what is despair-engendering, dark and unutterable (*Moira*: fate). It is of the essence of the divine (a) that it is ungrounded and unconditioned (absolute), and only as such related to the world. In Plato this absolute can still, as "the idea of the good" (*Pol* VI: 505A) and the all-radiant sun (508B), be the cause of all being in that it "surpasses reality in sublimity and power" (509C), but it just cannot (except perhaps once again somewhat in the Timaeus myth) be presented as personal love. Now love always falls more on the side of the person longing for God (*Symposium*), of the world enthralled by the absolute and kept in motion by eros (Aristotle). (b) A further, very confusing idea coher-

ently follows: the absolute can, basically, have no antithesis. The world is full of antithesis and if it is thought of as finite, it has its antithesis to God. But God himself has no antithesis. He is, as Nicholas of Cusa said with perfect logic, *Non-Aliud*, the not-other. Already for Heraclitus God was "that which rests in change," which at once embraces and goes beyond the antitheses. Plotinus completes this in that he transports the "One" without antithesis beyond the "Spirit" which lives in the tension between thinking and thought, between loving and loved, between I and You. The "One," fount of all love and insight, can itself not be a loving You. From this follows necessarily a final step. (c) The divine-absolute, that cannot stop being the object and goal of all human religious striving, disappears into the inexpressible. "You-less": it is that which is loved to which all good must be attributed, but which remains personlessly the beloved unrestricted by every I-You, so that also only he obtains it who leaves his personal being behind him like a confining box and presses forward to that which is without antithesis. The mystics of the most varied stripe in East and West are found together here, but Karl Barth is not wrong when he sees at the subtle heights of philosophical mysticism the necessary reversal to atheism. The contentless absolute becomes a logical form (Hegel), a law of process (Marx), and the whole center of gravity slips back to a quasi-divine interhuman love (Feuerbach).

3. The idea of God remains uncompletable for humanity as a whole because it cannot do without either of the two points of departure but, when it builds from the two pilings, the idea cannot complete the bridge span. Purely philosophical religion, above all as civil, cannot exist; it must depend, at least secondarily, on the mythical, where alone there can be prayer and sacrifice. It was in this sense that Rome made concessions to the old cult of the gods (cf. Varro's triple division of religion into mythical, natural, and social, and Augustine's criticism in *The City of God* IV, 4:3); but, out of political considerations, it gathered together the mythical cults of the annexed nations and put them together in an artificial Pantheon, about which Hegel made a sharp and clear judgment: the unity of power to which these shadow-deities are related "is Rome, is domination" (*Philosophy of Religion*, 1832, p. 135). Artificial too is the renewed mythicizing of Plotinian philosophy by Porphyry and Iamblicus: the powers of the one All are personalized in order to make the cultic accessible, but that (especially in Egypt) acquired a very strong magical character. Conversely also, the attempts to push through from an individual mythical world system to the breadth of philosophical universality— as is attempted in the fantastic world-dramas of gnosticism and in the Hermetic writings—remains paper-like and lifeless, pure abortions of a conjecturing imagination which of course has a certain

knowledge of true religious concern, but tarnishes it into the sensational, sectarian, often lascivious, and always intellectual elements. But civil cult does not rest on personal love and self-giving; it is for the most part a technique for coming to agreement with divine fate; in its sacrifices it is an official discounted payment for various offenses and a propitiation of the *numina*. Standing isolated between them is the figure of the pious Aeneas, this highest approximation to the true source-point of religion: existence as calling to a future work and complete docility (on condition of painful renunciations) in the hands of the gods: not for nothing did the Christian West place its religious poetry under the sign of Vergil.

From the foundation of human personal existence in the call and in the response of love, one can accordingly formulate something like an *a priori* postulate for the form of religion, but cannot of oneself sketch in this form concretely because a dialectic (between "heart" and "reason") seems constantly to require the repeated sublation of every set form: the heart (Pascal) demands a God as You and an absolute love between the two; but reason prohibits God from being grasped as such a You, because he must be absolute (and therefore in need of nothing), because he overcomes from the outset every antithetical tension and hence is best understood as an anonymous, generously self-bestowing all-goodness, but not as the personally addressing and person-awakening One.

The *God of Israel*, with his first historical saving action, sets the foundation for that unity of the idea of God which humankind seeks to grasp in vain—in vain even as just a possible idea. God shows himself here as powerful and good, in that he "goes looking for" (Deut 4:34) and "chooses" (Deut 7:6) for himself a people, and he brings all this about, in the act of calling and saving (from Egypt) by election above all as subject and partner. Any merit, any reason for preference toward Israel, is lacking (Deut 7:7; 8:17); it becomes what it is by means of the call, the "nation for Yahweh." The ground of the choice is groundless love (Deut 7:7, 9), which may be answered only by total, unlimited love (Deut 6:5): the core of the I to the core of the You. This event is unique, as David's prayer wonderingly expresses it: "Is there, then, any other nation on earth like thy people Israel whom God went to redeem to make of them his people . . . and drive out before him the other nations and gods?" (2 Sam 7:23) From the uniqueness of the event, a total and presuppositionless love, which as such betrays omnipotence (for God could just as well have chosen another nation; all "belong to him" and are "as nothing before him": Is 40:17), demonstrates the one choosing to be the unique One (Is 43:10–12): The absoluteness of his love demonstrates the absoluteness of his being.

17 · The Coming God
as Perfection of Humanity

Where does the human become complete? Where does humanity with its freedom cease being an open question mark? At the start, we can exclude any solution which reckons the free individual human being as a means toward the planning of the future of humanity. That an individual may place his life also in the service of a "better future" (and indeed must, after what we have just said) is clear. But were his liberty compelled to surrender itself entirely to such plans, then his very nature would be both denied and destroyed.

One free agent is constantly searching for another. And the happiest thing that can happen to a human being in its finite condition is to be recognized for his true worth and affirmed in freedom by a free you. Without doubt, part of the meaning of human existence is satisfied when people meet and live together in such a relationship. But what about the whole meaning? For the more irrevocably two natures love one another in freedom, the more tragic appears their mortality. It may well be of some consolation that after the death of the beloved, be this spouse, or child, or friend, the wound is healed, albeit gradually, by the biological laws of life, and that there follows a guilt-free kind of unfaithfulness; this may well help to maintain the human species. But such gentle cynicism calls into question all that is most precious and unique in human freedom of choice, and thrusts the human being down into the domain of nature. The contradiction between irrevocably intended self-giving and death (or quite simply, the law of transformation) remains insoluble; the human being in his finite existence is this contradiction.

Ancient religious cultures including Christianity have seen all this quite plainly and have therefore related human being to a supernatural and divine sphere of existence. Let us confine ourselves to the Christian view. Thomas Aquinas, who summarizes the voices of the past (Augustine in particular) and the future to the present, can teach us about the paradox of this transcendence. After having shown that there are not many ways in which human freedom is able to find complete fulfillment, and having discoursed on particular goods which in every case fail to bring fulfillment—on riches, honors, and fame (or posthumous reputation); on power (!), health of body, sensual pleasure (coarse or sophisticated), and inner tranquility of soul—he then shows that only the eternal God can fulfill the longing gaze of human freedom (*ST* I. 2 q.2.). But if in the encounter between two people, neither power nor magic may give one control over the freedom of the you but this intimacy must open itself of its own accord, then all the more will the absolute infinite you be able to open himself to human beings only in perfect freedom and in pure, unmerited grace. There is essentially no "claim" the human being can make on God, even though in the last resort the human being is unable to fulfill itself without God's free opening of himself. In the light of our present-day personalist and dialogical philosophy, our conclusions concerning the paradoxical nature of humanity's inmost being are shown to be both necessary and fully justified. For if the free turning of one person to another cannot be brought about by compulsion, how much the less can we compel God's gracious self-disclosure of the absolute inner godly space. The highest dignity of the human being that raises it above all the orders of nature, is to be oriented in its freedom toward him who is freest of all. Thomas is fully aware that nature has furnished humanity (as she has all other natural beings) with the necessary resources and equipment to enable it to fulfill its immediate aims and purposes on this earth. The human being is also aware, however, that when the question of the ultimate meaning of its freedom arises, the laws of its natural being go into abeyance, and another principle takes precedence (which Thomas borrows, out of courtesy, from Aristotle): "Nobler [he writes] in his constitution is the being who is able to attain the supreme good even though he stands in need of assistance from outside to attain this end, than he who attains a lesser good by the aid of his own resources" (Ibid., q. 5 a 5). Thomas takes seriously the image of the human being from Paul's speech in the Areopagus, which portrays humanity in its limitation of time and space (God has determined for us "allotted periods" and "boundaries of their habitation") and sets it therein to the purely groping search for the absolute (" . . . that they should seek God, in the hope that they might feel after him and find him": Acts 17:27); throughout all of which God reserves himself the right to meet humans in their searching and to satisfy their questing whenever and in whatever way he chooses.

In his book *Surnaturel* (1947; no E.T.), which was at first subject to some criticism but which in its expanded version (*Augustinisme et théologie moderne* [1965; E.T., *Augustianism and Modern Theology*, 1969] and *Le mystère du surnaturel* [1965; E.T., *The Mystery of the Supernatural*, 1967]) is quite beyond reproach, Henri de Lubac drew attention to the whole paradox of humanity as represented by the entire classical tradition. He does so by dismissing as both superfluous and unrealistic modern naturalistic models of humanity which give the impression that humans might conceivably have been created by God in a state of "pure nature" and in this state have been able to attain by nature a final and satisfying end within this world; and further that God by only a secondary, positive determination orientated humanity toward a supernatural end within the godhead for which he then provided them with the means of grace necessary to the achievement of this end. In this view, humanity is reduced to the level of a "natural being" who belongs essentially to this world, and its capacity for transcendence and entry into the sphere of the freedom and love of God is seen as a mere chance epiphenomenon; God's whole involvement for the world in Christ's incarnation, cross, and resurrection (in which, indeed, according to Eph 1:3–10 the creator's original design for the world is revealed) is virtually demoted as something superadded, to be dispensed with if necessary, and humanity is simply made more attentive to the satisfying of its needs and aims in this world.

De Lubac's radicalism, however, which in itself is but a modern exposition of the radicalism of all great Christian thinkers, is of considerable consequence for our whole concept of Christian involvement in the world. For only the Christian, who has found his own fulfillment in the person of Jesus Christ, senses clearly how basically unsatisfying it is for a human being, both as an individual and as a social being, to have as his ultimate goal the civilizing and humanizing of the world. Some brilliant Christian thinkers of recent times, such as Maurice Blondel in his book *Action* (1893) and Emmanuel Mounier in some of his personal manifestoes (1934), have recognized this to be of fundamental importance. Teilhard de Chardin has taken this into account too when he refuses to allow that the story of the natural inner-historical evolution of humanity (as seen in history) leads automatically to the final transcendant Omega point, but represents instead all humanity's cultural activity and its greatest efforts to civilize, socialize, and personalize the world as being but a *preparation d'un holocauste*, the building of a great funeral pyre, into which from on high alone and out of free grace can descend the lightning which transforms the whole, world and God, into a blaze of marital union ("2me Memoire du P. Teilhard," in *Blondel et Teilhard de Chardin; correspondance commentèe par H. de Lubac*, 1965, p. 43; cf. p. 91): "The whole of our work [he writes] must ultimately be directed to forming the material for the sacrifice made ready to be kindled by the living flame from heaven." In this, Blondel and Teilhard are at one.

If it is true, however, that humanity is endowed by its very nature with the capacity to begin the work of making the earth its subject and of humanizing the world, and to step out beyond the limits of the entire natural order towards a goal which in its own strength it cannot attain, then only the Christian, and he alone, since he knows God's involvement for the world in Christ, will be able to direct aright human strivings in this world and his efforts to attain transcendence. This does not mean that, by dint of sheer human superiority, he is in a position to offer his fellow humans a "synthesis" of nature and supernature, like some ready-made manipulatable design for freedom. For this synthesis lies solely in the view and possession of God; it is essentially eschatological; it far exceeds the limits of all inner-worldly conception. The risen Christ, who appears to his disciples in a "strange form," then each time allows himself to be recognized in a flash and afterwards immediately withdraws, is certainly not a principle of which to make use and handle like some working hypothesis. It is at best the goal of both our Christian and human hope which, amid the "futility," keeps our efforts alive and oriented in a definite direction. On the way toward this goal where the divine involvement and human strivings are finally to coincide, there is no clear pattern of development. And this because the human being in his creatureliness has been purposefully sketched in only a fragmentary way.

Set within the teleological framework of this world, supplied with tasks whose purpose lies within the limits of this world, which altogether like humanity itself remain preliminary to a goal, which cannot be reached by his own efforts—this, as Thomas says, is what constitutes human nobility.

18 · The Human Being before the God Who Chooses

All ancient peoples have their gods. The God of Israel, however, is distinguished from all other gods by the fact that he brings into being, by his own free sovereign act of choosing, the people who worship him. Whether we look at the first presupposition of this choice of a people—at the choice of Abraham—or at the choosing and leading of the people from Egypt by Moses (who himself had first to be called by God), thus making something akin to a nation from a miserable collection of uncultured and demoralized slaves; at the primordial beginning, in each case, there is a free act of the divine initiative which from no standpoint whatsoever can be foreseen, demanded, deduced. The choosing of the whole people can, at most, be traced to that of the patriarchs who received an initial promise. This choice, however, is not governed by an obvious principle.

> It was not because you were more in number than any other people that the Lord set his love upon you and chose you; for you were the fewest of all peoples; but it is because the Lord loves you, and is keeping the oath which he swore to your fathers, that the Lord has brought you out with a mighty hand, and redeemed you from the house of bondage. (Deut 7:7–8)

It is true that later Israel set her calling within a wider frame of reference, when she began to suspect that she had not been called for her own sake, but in order that she might be a leaven for the world. Then it was that she inserted the convenant with Noah before the covenant with Abraham and Moses, as representing the peace concluded between God and the whole of creation and human history, and in so doing Israel correctly recognized her role. It never occurred to her, however, to relativize her role and to see the covenant with Abraham and that on Sinai as a mere epiphenomenon of the general covenant between God and humanity. In the Christian era, the fathers, St. Augustine in particular, were to express the view that the *civitas Dei*, the polity or city of God among humans, was in existence from the very beginning of the human race, but they do not thereby deny that the meaningful center of this presence of God in the world is Israel, and after Christ, the church of the New Covenant. For as Israel could only view the covenant with Noah in the light of the covenant with Abraham and the covenant on Sinai, so too Augustine could only view the presence and nature of the *civitas Dei* in the light of Christ himself.

The free choice and initiative of a God who is ever free always constitutes the concrete form under which grace is manifested among human beings. We could suppose that this unfathomable sovereign act of God robes him in the character of a despotic potentate and degrades humans to the status of slaves, condemned to a life of mere obedience. This free choosing, however, is not primarily a revelation of power but of love. The text which we have just quoted supports this. And if this act of God in choosing is first and foremost an act of boundless love, then the response expected and indeed required by such love is certainly a gentle obedient yes of submission and willingness to comply, from the beginning a simple return of love in gratitude for love given. The response is obedience. God will bring his people from Egypt, make them pass through the Red Sea, destroy their persecutors, give them food and drink in a miraculous manner in the wilderness, and God himself will go before them and as a pillar of cloud and a pillar of fire mark the places where they are to rest. Wherever the cloud descends, there must the people pitch their tents; when it rises again, the people must break camp and march on, always following God as he leads. It is inconceivable that Israel should ever take over the leadership and that God should follow behind his people. For what is first required of Israel is that she should obey and live in harmony with the ways of the God who has chosen her. At the same time, however, she knows that what God does is her liberation. That he has liberated her from the slavery of Egypt cannot result in bringing her into a new state of servility to Yahweh but only, by her following of the free God, to lead her into her own freedom. The foundation of the choosing, God's freedom, must coincide with the purpose of choosing, namely participation in the freedom of God himself. All obedience is education into this freedom. The text "Be holy, as I am holy" means, properly understood (but at what sacrifices must such an understanding be purchased!), "Be free, even as I am free."

The desacralization which begins in the Old Testament and is fully carried out in the New is a liberation from the sacred character of the cosmos and from its powers to the point where the human being itself appears as "holy" in its act of entrusting itself freely to the perfect freedom of God. Slavery lies behind us; it is the point of departure. Perfect freedom lies ahead of us; it is our eschatological goal. Certainly, the people of the Old Covenant above all know that God is power; but precisely the power which frees from slavery. But it knows more than this: his power is his love which demands my love in return. And love can only be given freely: "Hear O Israel: The Lord our God is one Lord; and you shall love the Lord your God with all your heart, and with all your soul, and with all your might" (Deut 6:4–5). That is the archetypal situation which will never become a mere fact of past history; it is the living source from which we must never withdraw. These premises must never be forgotten even when—and precisely when—their consequences are being worked out. Our freedom is inseparable from the fact that we have been made free.

> And when the Lord your God brings you into the land which he swore to your fathers, to Abraham, to Isaac, and to Jacob, to give you, with great and goodly cities, which you did not build, and houses full of good things, which you did not fill, and cisterns hewn out, which you did not hew, and vineyards and olive trees which you did not plant, and when you eat and are full, then take heed lest you forget the Lord, who brought you out of the land of Egypt, out of the house of bondage. (Deut 6:10–12)

We shall find again and again that docility to God is and always shall be the inmost ground and drive of human initiative, and that it is always demanded and put into practice suddenly, out of the blue. The testing of King Saul is a scene, which, at first sight, almost defies our comprehension. Before going into battle against the Philistines, he is supposed to wait for Samuel, who is to offer a burnt sacrifice. Samuel fails to arrive on the appointed day, the enemy attacks, and the army is already in disarray. It is high time; Saul himself offers the sacrifice. For this action, he is deposed by God, for God requires obedience, and not sacrifice (I Sam 13:8ff; 15:22). This condemnation applies not only to the use of sacrifice, but also to the use of elementary political cunning, as we can see in the similar case of Hezekiah who, being forbidden by the prophet Isaiah to offer resistance to the

Assyrians encamped before Jerusalem, saved the city by his obedience and not by military tactics (Is 36). In a similar situation Jeremiah warns King Zedekiah against rebelling against the supremacy
of Babylon (Jer 27—29); but the king prefers to rely on his political
expertise and seeks an alliance with the Egyptians which Jeremiah
knew would be fruitless (Jer 37:7–8). His attempt to escape when the
city is taken is in vain and, after witnessing the murder of his children, he is blinded and carried away to Babylon. These are but a few
examples which illustrate the theology of history of the Deuterono-
mists who monotonously trace one single theme through Israel's history: obedience to the Lord of the convenant and his visible leadership, turning her heart from him, punishment, conversion, and
salvation at the hand of God. To think we know better how to fight
our way to freedom by ourselves, leads us inevitably back into the
bondage of Egypt (Hos 9:1–3).

GOD

· 19 ·

The love of God is great beyond comparison. It has no ground except itself and always comes from farther away and leads still farther on than I could have thought and imagined. In my limitation, therefore, I must unceasingly add an "and"; but what I thus bring about has already long ago been brought about by the love of God.

20 · God as Triune Love— Manifest in Jesus

Who is Jesus Christ for me? The only man in the history of the world who dared make a claim how God had established him in the Old Testament; who for that reason was looked upon as crazy and possessed (Mk 3:21f) and was crucified. For modesty is becoming to a wise man, and it is becoming for a prophet to say "Word of the Lord," not "but I say to you." God the Father confirmed this claim with the resurrection of Jesus, and thus was established the primitive Christian core of dogma: God is love; the immanent Trinity is revealed in the economic, and precisely as God's "orthopraxis" in the giving of his Son to divine abandonment and hell, which is the greatest possible conception of God; he is (with Hegel) identity of identity (God is all; he is eternal life) and of nonidentity (God is dead, insofar as he had identified himself with godlessness). He is so full of life (so very much love) that he can afford to be dead.

No religion or world view has dared to think and proclaim something of this kind about God, human beings, and the world; therefore Christianity remains without analogy, and it rests not on an "idea" but on a fact—Jesus Christ—which, in the unity of claim, cross and resurrection, remains an unsplittable atom. It depends on him whether we can dare to address being as love, and thus all beings as worthy of love, an idea to which the face of the world would otherwise have hardly brought us.

21 · Jesus—Proof of the Prevenient Love of God

If Christ were no more than the supreme example of natural human being, and Christianity only the sublimest form of natural religion, it would now no longer be worthwhile being a Christian. Value judgments about historical things fluctuate and some past or future person might dispute Christ's preeminence. Since in Christ God became human, Christianity is bound, in the eyes of unbelievers, to take on the guise of the merely human. But for the believer this view is not simply a partial misunderstanding; it is a complete misapprehension, a scandal, however great the religious pathos in which it is enacted, as in the high priest's rending his garments, when he heard the answer of Christ. For faith, all human religions and philosophical systems seem to approach one another ever more closely on one side, and Christianity seems to become more and more isolated on the other. No matter how variegated the market display of human world views may be, seen from a bit of distance its stalls and attractions soon come to take on a common air, all equally of human provenance and human proportions.

But this standard is limited, and so too are its possibilities of application. What one can achieve unaided, what one can discover and sketch in the way of world views can, even if not in all its details, still in its general lines be surveyed, even classified. However bold one's mental flights, whether in a dirigible or a rocket, one invariably takes oneself along on the journey. In other words, human thought, philosophical or religious, starts out from the human being, ascends with him, operates on his scale. This does not thereby make it "immanent in the world," confined to the human being and its world. It is, rather, essentially "world-transcending" in its intention; in the sense of Pascal, *L'homme passe infiniment l'homme.* Yet however much a person transcends himself, the act of transcending is as the very word betrays, an act posited, ventured, in reference to the human being. Even when one negates onself in order to affirm the other, one can only understand the affirmation in relation to what one negates.

It would be ungrateful to the creator if one would want to represent this power of transcending as nugatory, this mode of contact with what is beyond the world as a mere *fabrica idolorum*, and necessarily already blasphemous. But it would be just as ungrateful to the redeemer and giver of grace if one would not see in grace something wholly new and other, crowning and perfecting human attempts, precisely because it first shatters and overturns them. The natural human being and its reason operate in a "transcending" fashion; God's grace, which we grasp in faith, operates in an "immanent" fashion. It is not our movement toward God, but God's movement to us. It is heaven irrupting into our world. It is a participation in the divine nature, ontologically as sanctifying grace, consciously as faith, hope, and charity. The one is the human being who is seeking God; the other is God who has found the human being. The one is the human being who brings to bear all his powers of investigation, in a kind of spectral analysis of his own being, so as to figure out from that the composition of the star from which it came forth as a ray and with which it must have some sort of kinship; the other is the descent of the divine light among human beings not only to shine on, to illuminate, to purify and to warm them, but, through grace, to make them also shine with a light not of this world. It should never be forgotten that these two movements move in opposite directions. That the first was created for the sake of the second; that the first thus, in some way, remains the presupposition for the second; that ultimately the first cannot be understood, in the creator's design, apart from the second, which is its justification and the key that interprets its riddle; all this is to be treated elsewhere.

Jesus, the Absolutely Singular

22 · Relative Singularity

If a philosophy that reflects upon reality as a whole will always resist identifying a part of the whole with the whole, it could perhaps come a bit closer to its presumptuous claim in trying to show that, in the contingent part of reality, which as such is subject to the critique of reason as encompassing it, significant aspects of the whole truth can still be concentrated—perhaps for the first time—so that one will always have to attribute such a significant concentration to this historical event.

On the one hand, it is not difficult to establish the temporal contingency of the Jesus-event. Modern scholarship is uncovering more and more evidence of contemporary forms of thought and historical events and presenting them even more irenically and without controversy.

Moreover, the *aggiornamento* program, in all the difficulties experienced in trying to put it into practice, shows very clearly how firmly the gospel truths are attached to that point in time, and how hard it is for us to translate the gospel into more accessible images and categories, even if we clearly sense the time-conditioned aspect of the expressions and perhaps their supratemporal meaning.

On the other hand, the universal significance of the Jesus-event—from the point where his break into history took place—can be all the more reliably underlined for succeeding eras because Jesus himself called for discipleship, and beyond that, promised to bestow his own divine Spirit on his faithful disciples, and (according to Luke) this promise was fulfilled on the day of Pentecost.

Church, as the community of those reconciled with God in the Holy Spirit and given God's life and light, has since then mediated to the world something what in Jesus is at first alien and unique, but which nevertheless seems to stand in an analogy with other relatively singular events in history. It is worth looking for a moment at at least three forms of singularity within the encompassing whole.

1. A great work of art appears like an original creation, an inexplicable miracle on the stage of history. Just as no sociological law can predict the day of its arrival, neither can any law explain it in retrospect. Of course, the work of art has its presuppositions without which it cannot come into being: such conditions may be effective stimuli but do not provide a full explanation of the work itself.

Shakespeare had his predecessors, contempories, and models; the whole atmosphere of the theater by which he was surrounded. He could only have emerged within that context; yet who would dare offer to prove that his emergence was inevitable? Mozart's *Magic Flute* was preceded by a number of Viennese and Italian suggestions and models; there was a considerable amount of material available, but who can explain how the unique form got stamped on this material?

At most, we can point to or guess at the propitious moment—the *kairos*—but never whatever it is that, flowing in it, lets loose that lasting form. This takes over; no sooner is it there, than it leads. It *speaks the word*. Its unique utterance becomes a universal language.

A great work of art is never obvious and immediately intelligible in the prior, immediately understandable language that lies ready to hand, for the new, unique language that is born with it is its interpreter. It is "self-explanatory." For a moment the contemporary world is taken aback, then they understand, and begin to speak in the newly minted language (e.g., "the age of Goethe") as though they had invented it themselves. The unique word makes itself understandable by itself. The greater a work of art, the more extensive, generally, will be the cultural sphere it dominates.

The *Magic Flute* is accessible to every child who hums the Papageno arias, but even a really fastidious ear never tires of hearing them: the Pamino recitative, the Tamina arias, the farewell trio remain mystery, inexhaustible.

Hence, a final point—a great work of art has a certain universal comprehensibility but discloses itself more profoundly and more truly to an individual the more attuned and practiced are his powers of perception. Not everyone picks up the unique inflection of the Greek in a chorus of Sophocles, or of the German in *Faust*, Part II, or of the French in a poem by Valéry. Subjective attunement can add something of its own, but far more important is the objective attunement, the adequate organ for distinguishing the noble from the commonplace.

Philosophies of art—Schelling's and Hegel's, for example—try to project the great, irrationally and arbitrarily erupting imagery and the world-content manifested in them against a horizon of universal understanding. And is there any reason why they should not partially succeed? Yet the "miracle" that is the achievement of a great work of art remains inexplicable.

2. *Genuine love between persons* is probably more rare than one thinks—although most people believe that they have some share in it, and perhaps they do attain it for brief moments. It may well be as rare as great works of art, which tower here and there above the mass of what is also called art.

I am not thinking about the misfortune of passion which, as in the *Tristan and Isolde* of Gottfried and again of Wagner, relates the whole world to this one absolutely fixed point, and with it gives itself to disaster, but about something that can be much simpler and that to succeed requires a Christian predisposition: a dedication of one's whole life to a you in whom the lover sees the quality of the absolute shine forth, and with it the inclusion of the whole world.

Such dedication is a risk that can make sense in the end only if related to an absolute venture: to the calling out of Israel by the electing of God, apparently arbitrarily, from among all other nations (Deut 7:7), and to the call of Jesus to this and to this person alone to follow him.

The brilliance of the loving choice from the regions of the divine raises the individual, lost in the anonymity of the species, to the uniqueness of a person. In this ultimate mutual acknowledgement between two lovers, *eros* is able not merely to offer the initial spark, it can go along the whole way, if only it allows itself to be purified into transfigurations beyond itself: Dante and Beatrice, Hölderlin and Diotima, Claudel's *Satin Slipper*, Teilhard's *Hymn to Beatrice*.

Indeed what a pure foretaste is there in the *Alcestis* of Euripides. Line 242 and following tell of the vicarious death of the wife for her husband who, at the moment of farewell, realizes that he will "live on, lonely upon the earth. For if you die, I live no longer: you are my life and my death, for your love is holy to me" (lines 277–79).

In *The Meaning of Sexual Love* (1892–94) Soloviev praised the sublimity of such love, unexplainable by any cunning of intellect. In the eyes of the world it always looks like folly, for the stream of life flows on (Hofmannsthal has depicted the immanent "wisdom" of this "un-faithfulness" in many ways); it sets itself deliberately and hardhead-edly against the current laws of life; and somehow it interprets itself eschatologically: in the midst of time not only has a "moment" of eternity shone forth for this love, but a lasting, lived faithfulness has sprung perpetually beyond all immanence.

3. What is seldom achieved by love is offered as a possibility to everyone at the moment of one's own death when one comes to understand oneself not merely as a transitory individual in the ever-flowing stream of life—"to yield oneself up to which is delight"—but as a unique person who must carry out his own unique commission against a finite, and not even controlled, future horizon, and who in the end cannot do so.

What is distinctive here is this radical loneliness of dying on ac-count of which the individual who, unlike the animals, sees what is ahead, can become conscious of his own personal uniqueness. On this point Scheler (*Death and Afterlife*, 1911–12) and Heidegger are cor-rect. And if the biblical revelation stresses more starkly the spiritual solidarity of all, thus introducing something like a corporate human history, a supraindividual though not cosmic and cyclical time, then it lets us (under both the Old and the New Covenants) become thor-oughly aware, in contrast to the idea of solidarity, of the finitude of personal life in the face of the loneliness of personal death.

Departure from the community of life for the judgment of the electing God, for that refining fire, through which the individual must pass, and in which is demonstrated the worth of one's deeds upon earth—empty straw or solid metal (1 Cor 13:12f)—is a completely lonely step.

Here in earnest, it is *monos pro monon*; there can be no quick reference to the merits of others. Here no one can intervene for me: "Each will be rewarded according to his deeds" (Ps 62:13; Prov 24:12; Sir 35:24; Mt 16:27; Rom 2:6; I Cor 4:5; 2 Cor 5:10).

The communion of saints, even at the judgment, can be spoken of only dialectically, in conjunction with this posited loneliness. Death and judgment are primarily an interruption of every horizontal, dialogic situation; indeed, such a situation will be responsibly en-tered into only from a nondialogic situation that answers to God alone.

From this we must conclude logically that true time is primarily that of the individual toward this death and judgment, whereas common "world-historical" time, which is made into a chronological continuum by bracketing-off personal deaths, is a secondary phe-nomenon, because precisely in it the whole moment that constitutes the seriousness of temporality is suspended.

A philosophy of the future, which accounts for the whole ethos of humanity in the time to come when the philosopher himself or herself will no longer exist, can address us only as members of a species and not as persons. The problem of how an individual person can incorporate into one's finite time any notion of humankind's future ultimately demands a christological answer.

I have chosen three points at which a—at least a relative—singularity stands out from the encompassing horizon of human reason. These points were not systematically arranged, just taken up symptomatically. But they do have something in common that is worth mentioning. In each case the human being is differentiated from a sheer datum, acceptance of which determines his rational conduct toward it.

In order objectively to apprehend and then judge the unique work of art, one must create for oneself the appropriate mode of receptivity. In order to love personally, one must let there be opened in the beloved a value already present to one, which may perhaps be reserved for that person alone to see and to come forward to encounter. In order to approach one's death responsibly, one must accept this frontier and project one's actions toward it. At each of these three points we find the provocation of uniqueness, in that each eludes the tribunal of the comprehensive.

As Paul says, "Not that it makes the slightest difference to me whether you, or indeed any human tribunal, find me worthy or not. . . . The Lord alone is my judge" (1 Cor 4:3f). Yet all three situations may be reckoned among the general, human, mundane sphere. They stand in a dialectical relationship to the universal that finds expression in a certain secrecy, defenselessness, and often shame. The true artist, aware of his own worth, presents his work arrogantly but leaves it to the course of its fate. It may be carried on high in triumph, or it may remain in the shadows (Schubert) only to be exhumed later, as if by chance. Great personal love can remain utterly esoteric; and the responsibility that comes from facing death will always be silent. Whatever is aware of its own uniqueness surrenders itself unhesitatingly to relativity.

23 · Jesus, the Absolutely Singular

The modest action of the overtowering gets apparently abandoned at the point where a human being, Jesus of Nazareth, claims that he is the way, the truth, and the life. The fact that the claim is actually made with modesty, or rather with humility—"I am meek and lowly of heart"—in no way weakens it, but makes it seem all the more strange.

He is represented as the one who is absolutely unique: "No one has gone up to Heaven except the one who came down from Heaven, the Son of Man who is in Heaven" (Jn 3:13). And in the echo of his disciple: "The spiritual man judges everything while he himself is judged by no one" (1 Cor 2:15).

This is said loudly and clearly. Would a wise person raise his voice in this way? Do the wise not speak more softly? And what of the constant stress on his own boldly pronounced "I"? "It was said of old to your fathers, but I say to you." The whole gospel is full of this resounding "I." We cannot shut our ears to it.

There are those who would like to turn Jesus into an apostle of love of one's neighbor who stands for the poor and the oppressed, and declares his solidarity with sinners. But then they would have to bracket-off all these provocative references to his own person, and the measuring of others by their relationship to him: "If anyone . . . is ashamed of me and of my words, the Son of Man will also be ashamed of him when he comes in the glory of his Father . . ." (Mk 8:38).

It is immaterial whether or not they distinguish the "I" from the Son of man. They would have to excise the provocation in the question, "Who do people say I am . . . who do you say I am?" (Mk 8:27ff), and the command to leave all "for my sake" (Mk 9:29) immediately and without first fulfilling the basic duties of piety (Mk 8:21f). All these words and actions are characterized by a cutting hardness comparable in tone and manner with nothing else that can lay claim to greatness in the history of the world.

Whoever presents himself in this way, must realize how much of a challenge he presents. The disputes with the Jews, reported by John, are one long unrelenting provocation. A man who uses such peremptory tones must be resigned to and prepared for anything. He must have some weapon that gives him the assurance to challenge the whole world. He must have the consciousness of being able to step forward with complete authority: in the midst of history, as this one individual, reaching in anticipation to include all things proleptically from beginning to end: "Before Abraham was, I am." "You will see the Son of Man coming." "I am the alpha and the omega." He must see clearly that in him the end, the *eschaton*, is on the scene.

But how can he be the end if he stands as a mortal man in the midst of history, which will flow on after his death? He will have to make the apparently mad claim that on the course toward his own death, he embraces the course of all history toward its very end. He will need to possess such a powerful, primary mortal time that it holds within itself all derivative time—emptied of death.

If he is correct, something equally crazy must happen: that all that he is, his life and death taken together, must prove to be ultimate. His death will belong essentially to this proof, for altogether speaking and acting and even suffering never reveal the whole truth of his existence. But if the claim stands, however, the whole truth must also possess an absolute weight that can be counterbalanced by nothing, and—because it is a matter of truth—be able to show that this is so.

The stone in one pan of the scales must be so heavy that one can place in the other any or all the truth there is in the world, any religion, philosophy, world view, every complaint against God, without counterbalancing it. Only if that is true is it worthwhile being a Christian today.

If anyone knew any weight capable of raising, ever so slightly, the Christian side of the scales, and lifting it into the sphere of relativity, then being a Christian would become a matter of preference, and one would have to decide against it unconditionally. From some quarter or other it would be contained. To take more than a historical interest in it would be a waste of time. The gospel is full of miracle stories. They are disturbing to us. One does not prove one's truth by working miracles. Truth must prove itself. But how could Jesus' claim prove itself if his life has still not reached the end of the world and of time, if the proof will be conclusive only when all life and death has run its course?

Miracles are in themselves no proof of what really matters; but they can be signs in a twofold sense: signs that what was intended from the beginning—the eschatological "miracle" of God which breaks the very bounds of profane reason—has come upon the scene in Jesus Christ, has started to occur; and second that the consummation of the event, if it occurs, must have such a manner of conclusiveness that in the one decisive point it puts all mundane knowing right out of joint and appears to it as "miracle."

We could try, beginning with the Christ-event, to explain it as the all-controlling systematic formula and with it to penetrate all reality to the outermost reaches of the thinkable. All would be bound to converge on this center: God and world. The world would find its ultimate genuineness in its self-transcendence toward the Son of God, and God would manifest himself as all in all, by presenting himself above the Son of God, the head of the "body of the church" and ultimately of the whole world, as the quintessence of all becoming, and as the one who brings about all his creative possibilities.

Nothing could be left out of this all-embracing principle; one would in the end define absolute truth as the identity of identity (God) and of nonidentity (the world distinct from God); and could be aware that from this formula only nonbeing—that is, nothing—could apparently be excluded. In terms of the Christ-event no matter how "free" God's self-disclosure in Christ may be conceived to be, God, the absolute truth, has nevertheless now become visible, knowable, and accessible to thought. But whoever has thought the absolute, has essentially grasped everything.

We know that after Hegel's claim came two jokers: Kierkegaard who in his "absolute paradox" summed up in Protestant style the patristic axiom, *si comprehendis, non est Deus*; and Marx, who from an alleged intellectual grasp of God, drew the correct conclusion that if everything has been played out in the brain of the thinker, then it is sheer speculation that sublates itself because truth lies not in thinking but in the world-changing deed that the human being retrieves from the estrangement of its thought-games. Both are right: absolute philosophy is not the last word, for it has grasped God but not changed the world.

If Christian life is to have an eschatological emphasis it must be shown as such in a way that at no point "explains" the mystery of God—even though God reveals himself therein—but at the decisive point actively changes the world. The provocation in the assertion "I am the way, the truth, and the life" cannot be dulled by mediation. There is no point from which it becomes accessible. It remains isolated in the midst of history. Everything rests on this utterly unconstruable point. It does not result from the combination or synthesis of Jewish and Hellenistic expectations. It is incapable of being expected; and when it suddenly is there it immediately demands belief without allowing a moment's pause for reflection.

Always the essential thought is this: that that which is conferred by grace can be comprehended as such, but can never be reconstructed by intelligence in retrospect. I cannot say, that is what I have always "really" expected, or what my mind and heart have always been oriented toward and determined so that only a slight impulse from outside was required to allow my preunderstanding to crystallize into perfect insight. What is offered with the basic character of free grace can never be overtaken rationally without destroying its distinctiveness. And in-so-far as it can never be captured it constitutes a continuous source of bliss for the recipient. What grace gives is also never a definitive given, but remains within the originating act of self-giving. It thus keeps on bearing meaning from itself, and this once again prevents understanding from closing in upon the meaning already revealed. On the contrary, the more meaning revealed, the more confident faith the recipient is able to shoot ahead of that which gives itself.

24 · Jesus as "Gestalt"

In the articulation in which the faith of the early church presents him, Jesus Christ is a clear figure (gestalt), but one which uses not only transcendental points of reference in order to be propagated and thereby (somewhat like Socrates) become tragic, but also which, from its own special points of reference, overcomes this—actually undergone—tragedy for the first and only time. Jesus' life stands under the sign of his claim to be preaching the ultimate prophetic inspiration above and beyond Moses and the previous prophets; his "I am" and "But I say to you" is a direct resonance of the "I" laid claim to by God himself in the Old Testament. This claim is immediately perceived in the oldest gospel as hubris, insanity (Jesus' relatives, Mk 3:21), or demonic possession (the scribes, Mk 3:22). In a religiously conceived polis, hubris is unbearable: priests and politicians immediately take counsel on how to eliminate him (Mk 3:6): "Who do you claim to be?" (Jn 8:53). They want to stone him for blasphemy, "because you, being a man, make yourself God" (Jn 10:33). Again and again they try to seize him; he escapes. But the gibbet that threatens him from afar finally wins its prize. This combination of presumption and failure produces "not a gestalt . . . but a frightful breakdown" (Guardini). One could perhaps stylize this fate after that of some great figures, Socrates for example, inasmuch as one looked at Jesus' apparent self-importance together with his humility and interpreted it as obedience to the mission he was given (just as Socrates obeys the Delphic Oracle), and inasmuch as one construed Jesus' fate of death according to his own eschatological interpretation: superseding all mundane political schemes, it comes down to the final point, the resurrection of the dead. The content of his message would then be, centrally, political nonviolence: the poor and the meek will be, as the effective eschatological reserve in contrast with every violent implementation of earthly power or even justice, the true victors in world history. This manner of bracketing the worldly from the eschatological would then stand at about the level of Buddha or Epictetus. The gospels, however, which reflect the faith of the primitive church, say something different, they proclaim the "resurrection of Jesus on the third day": the eschatological horizon (characterized in Jewish apocalyptic by the general resurrection) is reached by the unique Jesus (while the witnesses are found incomprehensibly still in the middle of the course of history); from the experience and witness of this attainment the primitive church interprets the cross as a grouping of the eschatological dying of the sinful world on the judgment day of God—Jesus' death was vicarious for all (the pre-pauline *pro nobis*: Rom 4:25; 1 Cor 15:3, etc.). This makes explainable the whole weight of Jesus' claim which, in its personal exclusiveness, goes far beyond that of a Socrates or a Buddha. It is from the resurrection that the Christian faith comes to an understanding of its content (as the evangelists ingenuously concede again and again) and that the figure of Jesus for the first time is closed within a real gestalt: the claim, the cross, the resurrection are its articulations which mutually depend on and prove each other in a dynamic circuit. This gestalt is the superabundant fulfillment of everything sketched earlier which claimed and used expressly transcendental points of orientation in the coming to be of their gestalt, but it supersedes their tragedy in that the absolute shattering on the cross of all mundane fulfillments is overtaken by the resurrection from the dead which justifies everything and precisely this total tragedy as well. For this means nothing less than the breaking through of the deadline of all human existence, the justification of every frustration in this world by the bringing home of the bodily-spiritual existence of humanity as a whole to the eternal life of God. This justification and home-bringing is, from the world's standpoint, inconceivable; its unsatisfactory substitute was the Hegelian world history as the Golgatha, "skull-place of the spirit," evolution or utopianism. For what is called "resurrection of the dead" cuts straight across the dimension of world-historical succession and can only be understood as an act of God the creator of the world and human beings. This act would have to be then God's first, all-encompassing intention with world and world history (Eph 1:4–10), the original meaning of his promise (Rom 4:17–25), his definitive, conclusive word to his creation, identical with the existence of Jesus Christ. His resurrection as witnessed fact (of God) allows the utopian hope of a justification of the whole of history (not just of its final generation for which the rest sinks to Golgatha) to become a really grounded utopia. Consequently, the gestalt of Jesus thereby comprehends the horizon of the world-spirit with its gestaltless, unending diastasis between prophetic-tragic individual gestalt and political event. The life of the world is given a "change of life" (Guardini) by the gestalt of Jesus.

25 · Faith and "Objective Evidence" of the Gestalt of Jesus

If Christian faith is not primarily a holding-true of propositions presented in the kerygma as true but a taking hold of the event by which the one coming to faith has already been caught (Phil 3:12), then it is also—as elementary as always—an allowing of oneself to be inserted into the form of this event: into the faith-obedience of Christ himself. This faith-obedience is the not conditioned, from every conditioned absolute, self-donation to the total will of the Father; Christian faith is like this when at its core it raises no barriers to the believed ("I believe, as long as I can see into," "as far as I can justify," "as long as I am not spiritually and existentially pushed beyond my limits," etc.). But then, such an unconditional self-giving can be demanded only by the absolute object of faith, that is, by God;

otherwise such a self-giving would amount to being "led astray" by "dumb idols" (1 Cor 12:2). Therefore, in the event presented in the kerygma, God himself in his divine absoluteness must shine out so that the unconditional assent of faith can be given to the event. How is this possible? How does the divine quality become visible in the quality of this event?

In no other way than in such a manner that something shines forth in the event of the cross and resurrection of Christ which paradoxically has the property of being and remaining both essentially and eternally incomprehensible—and at the same time of being manifested in this incomprehensibility as the superseding (*a priori*) of *all* possible notions of God. One can situate the unique evidence that shines from this event between the two formulae of St. Anselm of Canterbury: God is *id quo maius cogitari nequit* (*Prosl.* 3), and the human being *rationabiliter comprehendit incomprehensibile esse* (*Monol.* 64). If both are valid for the knowledge of God (as Anselm thinks), they must be no less, and indeed first and foremost valid at the point where God reveals himself to humanity itself in the most definitive way; but then it is no longer valid just *a priori* (deduced and formulated from the idea of God as such), but verified *a posteriori*, empirically, in the revelation of God. The human being then who in faith grasps the revelatory act of God in Christ as what it is, must be able to "see" therein that something shines forth here *quo maius cogitari nequit*, the manifestation of absolute divine love, which in contrast with everything that the human being could deduce as being above and beyond the self-revealer, would be evidently outstripped. (How paltry, for example, would all apocalyptic and gnostic initiations into heavenly mysteries be when compared with the love of the Son of God who for all sinners and for me goes to death into the night of God and of hell, etc.) This evidence, that here the highest possible form of love becomes visible, cannot be led astray by the abstract objection that God, in his infinite freedom and power, could always invent and bring to reality something greater. The "figure" which God poses—between his own freedom and the freedom of his creature whom he permits to sin (because it is free and must be free), and which he then can still bring back in love without doing violence and stepping all over it in his omnipotence—is obviously a *summum* (greatest possible). Nothing greater can be conceived. That is understood. *Comprehendit.* Not only in feeling, enthusiastically, but in the clear light of spiritual understanding. *Rationabiliter comprehendit.* But precisely what is seen in this way as an insurpassable reality, is incomprehensible and remains therefore (in correction of the first formula), *quiddam maius quam cogitari possit* (*Prosl.* 15).

We come now to the specifically Christian turn which, because of the self-revelation of God in Christ, is distinguished from every abstract speculation about God and the representation of God. This turn takes place in such a way that the "philosophical" incomprehensibility of God's essence which is expressed in the rules of thought of *theologia negativa* is changed into a "theological" incomprehensibility of the love of God (for the Christian knows what the philosopher does not know: "God is love"). It is utterly incomprehensible that the absolute love (which in the triune life is completely satisfied in itself) should, for the sake of the sinner (which I am), empty itself of its divine form and go into the outermost darkness to die. Up against this ludicrous absurdity all "negative theology" is nugatory. But precisely this laughable absurdity is what, in the "figure" which God places before me in his revelation, rushes upon me with an overwhelming, even deadly, threatening force. Now it might be possible to evade this in such a way as would emphasize only what is paradoxical, unlikely, and thus unbelievable in this figure, fixing upon only the product of priest-ridden invention, a grotesque unwarranted affront to normal thinking people which one must indignantly reject and ought to detoxify and make harmless by demythologization. But right away the opposite moment announces itself again: *rationabiliter comprehendit*. In this "figure" there resides an inner harmony which resists every division into parts as well as every combination of parts. Should one want to designate the individual figures of the Old Testament as such "parts" which, by combination, would result in the figure of Christ, prophet, king, priest, sacrificial lamb, servant of Yahweh, Son of man, etc., then we would have to say that the simple whole is greater than the sum of its parts, that Christ lived his simple, indivisible life without anxious worry about integrating all possible partial aspects, and that only the event of cross and resurrection, which was "arranged" neither by him nor by his disciples, made the convergence of the partial aspects appear in its superior unity.

This integration of the individual images into the whole image (the relationship of promise and fulfillment, therefore) could and can indeed be a real support for the Christian faith, but only as a supporting confirmation, not as the core of the evidence itself. In any case, Christ's disciples did not come to their own proof of faith through such combinations but from their simple impression made by the existence of Christ himself.

This evidence, however, does not replace but actually categorically demands faith; for what is recognized is the evident presence of the unknowable, comprehensible through no concept, but about which one knows at the same time. It is manifested here in its own uniqueness, and this proclamation cannot be replaced by, or even be in competition with, any other figure or any other event. But that Christ in his attitude as one who obeys does not present himself as the ultimate source of love, does not make his human existence into a revelation of his own eternal love, but into a transparency of the love of the Father, lifts the paradox definitively out of the realm of the comprehensible, insofar as at the same time it still brings this closer to existential understanding: on the one hand it lifts the person of the one who obeys here to the side of God and makes him the trinitarian "Son" and "Word" of the Father, but on the other hand through his life-style of obedience it gives the believing disciple a starting point for discipleship, opens a door of entry: in this last removal of the mystery of Christ into the sphere of the pure object of faith, there is then once again perfected the evidence that here the Old Testament covenant (in the *diastasis* between God and human being as well as in their meeting and *unification* in the life of the covenant) has attained to its superabundant fulfillment.

26 · The Biblical Picture of Jesus and Modern Exegesis

Many Christian lay people are deeply upset by the incessant incursions of modern exegesis and by the retreat, indeed even paralysis, of dogmatics which has apparently been caused by this. On whatever text of the gospels (this, most of all, is what the problem is about) one would like to stand and be secure, some critic or other pulls it out from under our feet. There seem to be practically no words or miracles of Jesus left that are certain. The general biographical and geographic framework of his life is redactional even in Mark (and John arranges it completely differently). Practically all Jesus' statements about himself go: Jesus preaches not himself but the kingdom of God coming into reality. The titles of majesty go (Messiah/Christ, Son of God, *Kyrios*); only "Son of man" is still sharply disputed, although many have long considered it to be secondary. A great many of the miracles go, especially the nature miracles, even if many healings are indisputable. The trappings of individually transmitted expressions in (pseudo-)historical scenes go, and of the sayings it is pretty well established that they have been subsequently transferred into a different context of meaning, as is palpably obvious in the different treatments in Luke and Matthew of the words that come from the logion source (*Q*). To avoid attributing unacceptable contradictions to Jesus, one must push aside many of his words (for example, the final sending of the disciples into the whole world, or the presupposition that the gospel must be preached to all nations before the end of the world) as insertions of the community. How much of the history of the passion would have been shaped very early (pre-Markan) according to Old Testament themes, only then to be glossed later by Matthew with an "according to the scriptures" is hard to say. The classical motif of the just man who suffered and was rescued by God had been intensified in late Judaism to that of an unjustly condemned martyr or powerless ("poor") one with an atoning effect for the nation: to what extent did this theme have an effect on the interpretation of the cross in the primitive community, in Paul, and finally in the gospels ("ransom for many")?

Whoever reads the text of the gospels with eyes schooled in form criticism and redaction criticism in every pericope and often in every verse, runs up against gaps, seams, patchwork, artificial bracketings, and "upheavals" of geological strata; behind almost every word lies a dramatic story which usually can be explained on the most recent levels, but which then, the closer one comes to the original form, to the word, deed, and being of the historical Jesus, recedes into the uncertain, at times into complete darkness. The simple believer can, in reading and prayer, despite these difficulties, trust in the Holy Spirit who has inspired the whole of scripture: thus scripture provides an adequately secure ground for the Christian faith just as it has been presented from the start as a documenmt of the faith and belief of the primitive church. But doesn't that plunge us into a vicious circle? Faith of that time and faith of today circle around each other, while exegetical research tries to uncover on what this faith originally rested: perhaps even on feet of clay. Did not the faith form the word of revelation in such a way as to justify itself? In any case, dogmatics will have to reflect on this suspicion quite explicitly if it does not want to build its house on sand.

And yet, behind all the post-Easter paintings, a firm core of historical truth stands: That Jesus was crucified *sub Pontio Pilato* he owed without any doubt to 'his, for Jewish ears, intolerable claim to be the interpreter—superior even to the Torah—of the will and intention of God, to represent God so personally that he takes it upon himself to forgive sins and actually takes the sides of sinners in the name of God against those who by their zeal for the law sought to justify themselves before God. In this claim the hardness of his No against all self-justification was only the converse of the gentleness of his Yes for anyone who in humble trust surrenders himself or herself to the mercy of God. Jesus' conduct was a reflection of God, which in genuineness was possible only on the basis of an absolutely unique mission from God; otherwise he would (as one of his doubtlessly genuine words says) "have driven out the demons by Beelzebub." With his existence—according to his central and genuinely authentic proclamation—God's rule in the world was "in the process of coming." Neither simply here already nor still to come in the future, but "about to happen," "on the threshold"; between him and the coming kingdom there was room for no further prophet.

The claim was intolerable, much more intolerable than that of the earlier prophets to whose fate Jesus links his own. To what extent he may have hoped to win acceptance with his mission in Israel may be impossible to say. But it is possible, even looked at in a purely human way, to hope for something even when one knows ultimately that it is not realizable. In the life of Jesus there is on the one hand a limited task for the time of his active mission, "the lost sheep of Israel," and on the other hand an unlimited task for the total period of his human existence: in johannine words, to draw all things to himself, "to gather and make into one not only the nation but the scattered children of God." The hardly otherwise explicable words of the Eucharist, "poured out for you and the many," show this level of meaning. So little was his public mission a private undertaking, but a showing forth of God in a mission, so little is his death a private one, but rather the culmination of this presentation of God: the event "on the third day" demonstrates to faith that God stood by his "interpreter," that therefore his presentation was not only correct but also effective and decisive for the whole world.

One speaks here of "implicit christology" and supposes, correctly, that it is more rich in content than any translation into explicit word. If that is true—and it is true!—then both exegesis and dogmatics and their mutual relationship are subject to form and law. Thereby, the highest principle to be held is this: the Word which God in Jesus speaks to the world ("the Word was made flesh"), is spoken in full only with cross and resurrection. The words and deeds of the mortal human being Jesus are only a fragment of this Word. To whomever fell the task of integrating this fragment into the total Word—to the risen One himself or to the Holy Spirit or to the faith of the primitive church or to the formulators of that word which was in the end to become the finished gospel—that person had in any case to carry out a transposition. From this we understand also—and will explain it even more closely—to what extent for Jesus himself the kingdom of God in its earthly existence was "only just" in the process of coming, "only just" dawning. Only his own fate which he could no longer actively shape, to which he could now only surrender himself, would change the kingdom into a "having come," and him, however, into the "kingdom itself" (the *autobasileia*) and hence from the proclaimer into the simultaneously proclaimed. How much modern exegesis needs contemporary and future dogmatic theology as a caution against a speculation which proceeds lineally and in a priori fashion, but how little it can do without dogmatics in its own business, may be illustrated in conclusion by an especially critical example, that of Jesus' horizon of consciousness. The horizon of a genuine human person—and Jesus was one—is necessarily finite. Now a rather large number of texts, however, show undeniably that Jesus expected the arrival of the kingdom of God and with it the end of the world in the very near future; "some of those standing here" will experience this event before their death. The device of shifting this "apocalyptic imminent expectation" away from Jesus and attributing it primarily to the primitive church just doesn't work. Every means has been tried in order to read into some texts the supposition within Jesus himself of an "interval" between his death and his second coming, without striking success, we think, since one is dealing there with late levels of tradition or interpretations or churchly adjustments (to explain the delay of the *parousia*). Was Jesus then mistaken and—what is almost worse—did he mislead the primitive church to its unequivocal imminent expectation? Many, and not just liberal exegetes, flatly concede this in view of the textual evidence. Can the dogmatic theologians be satisfied with such information, or must they not, from their understanding of Jesus as the authentic interpreter of God, provide interpretative assistance? And can the dogmatic theologian do this without putting a muzzle on the text?

How would it be if Jesus had been completely right for himself? The ultimate horizon (says the dogmatic theologian) out of which he speaks is not the general apocalyptic of his time but the tremendous mandate of his Father to accomplish the atonement of the whole world with God, to "be finished with" the world, to reach the end of the world. As John puts it, to take away the sins of the world. He does not have to know in advance how this will be possible; enough that "the hour" of the Father will come, which no one ("not even the Son") knows; enough that the "hour of darkness" will be, which however introduces the end, brings the solution: "God made him to be sin," "in order to have mercy on all," says Paul. It is judgment and salvation at once, and this through Jesus' fate ("I must be baptized with a baptism . . ."). Once again, he doesn't have to know anything about the cross, nay, he *should not* in order to achieve full obedience, know anything precise about it; the exactly spoken prophecies of the passion could be *vaticinia ex eventu*. But something horrible for him is coming, through which he will attain the end of the world, that he knows. And now it is extraordinary that this horror that stands before him does not force him to any kind of apocalyptic haste; he can project an ethic for believing existence which is not an "interim ethic" for a short time that is left but sounds as if all time was available to live it. That too is an expression of his perfect obedience, that he lives in the presently given day and leaves worry for the morrow to his Father. The only thing that is important is that each day be filled to the brim with doing the will of his Father. To that end he presses on, and not ("apocalyptically") to the approaching "hour" of the Father—and of darkness. For his active work he had his program, Israel, but in many ways pagans are already coming into his sphere of activity. Israel had long since been open to the nations in one way or another. Within this earthly mandate takes place the call of the Twelve, helpers in the mission, representatives to and judges of the tribes of Israel. He does what is possible within his active mandate whose horizon remains confined by his absolute obedience to the Father. Jesus *is not allowed to,* and will not, anticipate; in John 17 he entrusts his own, for the time of the passion, to the protection of the Father. Cross is end of the world (Matthew depicts it quite explicitly in these terms); Easter is a new world beyond the timeless abyss.

And the church belongs to the "new creation." Did Jesus "found" it? It depends on what one understands by founding, or how one conceives the act. He took the representatives of the finite Israel with him to the end and to the new beginning (also by distributing his Eucharist to them in anticipation); and his spirit breathed out on the cross he breathed into them at Easter. It was not part of his mission to worry about a chronological afterwards: he leaves this task to the divine Spirit which "takes from what is mine," in order to "guide you into all the truth." After he has eschatologically borne the sins of all, he is able to be distributed to all, and discovered in all ("what you do to the least . . ."), the unity of all. Those who live after him will in a short time misunderstand his form of life, valid for him, as their own chronological imminent expectation, but without damage, as is shown by the magnificent example of Paul who is expecting the Lord, and in doing so has time to think through and carry out his mission plans unto the ends of the earth, and who thereby spares us from entering here into the intricate problems of individual gospel verses.

But notice that what the dogmatic theologian is saying here is absolutely antimonophysite. Jesus was no superhuman who looks out over all the time. His horizon was "economically" confined to his mission to be fulfilled in obedience. But again on the other hand, this confinement is also not the general-anthropological one (for that time the apocalyptic one); it is completely unique (conditioned by the hypostatic union of God and man), because only in a human mission can he get to the end of the (old, sinful) world. This explains his awful urgency ("work as long as it is day," "today, tomorrow, and on the next day I must go . . ."), which nevertheless is without any overhastiness but rather accepts everything in a childlike way from the hand of the Father.

If that is right, then this example makes it clear that exegesis and dogmatic theology need each other. And if today the predominant impression has arisen that dogmatic theology has been dethroned by exegesis and in many aspects become deeply confused, so could it be more deeply true that it has been freed by genuine exegesis from many illusory problems and led back to its true object.

27 · Jesus—God and Human Being— New Interpretation of the Dogma of Chalcedon

Where God says to a spiritual subject who that subject is for him, the eternally abiding and true God; where God says to it in the same breath why it exists—thus bestowing on it its divinely attested mission—at that point it can be said of a spiritual subject that it is a person. But that has taken place once, archetypally, in Jesus Christ, who was given his eternal "definition"—"You are my beloved Son"—when his unique and universal mission was bestowed on him from time immemorial, and with it the most precise knowledge of who he is not only for God but also from the beginning with God (Jn 1:1). Yes, it must be said that the combination of an exact definition of the personal uniqueness and the universal meaning of this uniqueness which lies in the mission of Jesus is the incontrovertible expression of his divinity. It is this way because it is a matter of mission, a received divinity, but which then is no contradiction in itself only if it is not merely God's sharing with a creature but the giving over of divinity to one who is God (*Deum de Deo*).

Everything which, beside Jesus, still merits a claim on the title "person" can raise it only on the basis of a relation to him and derivation from him. There can be no talk about the identity between I and mission, as it exists in Jesus, in regard to any other person; but only of the endowing of their spiritual subjectivity with a part or aspect of his universal mission.

Jesus lives his human consciousness completely as mission: he has in the Holy Spirit the mandate from the Father to reveal the essence of God and God's attitude toward human beings. And not just one-sidedly (as represented so gladly these days) merely as God's taking the part of sinners and the needy, but especially in as much as he reveals all the other qualities of God in his sensible human existence: God's wrath (e.g., over the sinful desecration of the place of his cult), God's disgust at having to endure so long among these people without understanding, God's grief and tears at Jerusalem's refusal to accept his invitation, indeed one can even say, God's abandonment of sinners in the cry of abandonment on the cross, and so forth. Jesus' whole existence, even in what was the cause of such embarrassment in the Greeks, in his *pathē* (suffering), stands in the service of his proclamation of God. This does not prevent him from doing this in a completely human spiritual subject which, as such, simultaneously brings to light the perfect truth of the human being, and to be sure—since he is primarily revealing the truth of God—of the human being as God sees us: of the human being as we should be, as we are, and as we will be again (through the advocacy of Christ). But this latter takes place *concomitanter* (simultaneously): Jesus lives not in order to produce himself as the highest examplar of the human race, but rather solely to do the will of the Father.

The next point to be noted is that Jesus reveals God not by order of the Trinity but of the Father; and more still, he wishes, as the only Son who alone knows the Father completely as he is (Mt 11:27), to make him known, to interpret him (Jn 1:18). He reveals God essentially, but in the mode of the personal, and he does this compelled by the Holy Spirit, that is, not *ad libitum* but under the pressure of a mission that absolutely must take place (that reaches from the *dei** of the twelve-year-old [Lk 2:49] through the *dei* of action [Lk 13:14; Jn 9:4, etc.] to the *dei* of the passion [Mt 16:21], etc.), wherein is revealed at once his highest free resolve and resolute freedom to want to live for nothing else than for his mission. Just as, once again, the artist or scholar who is possessed by his or her mission knows himself or herself freely and totally only if he or she can pursue this most personal mission. But it needs to be repeated: the identity of this personal freedom with his mission (from time immemorial, not discovered after the fact), excludes every impression that Jesus is following an alien decision made prior to the world's existence (as in the belief in rebirth one lives out a *karma* which has been formed in another existence). Between his acceptance of the Father's mission and its conclusion no intermediary authority is inserted. He is the one who has always said Yes to this mission—"for this have I come" (Jn 10:10)—even when it now, while it is being carried out, points to the final incision of the "hour" for which he can only wait because then he will no longer have control over the mission but the mission will dispose of him (beyond all human capacity). It is like a human dread in the face of this hiatus, and then a resolute leap through abandonment to the Father: "Now my soul is troubled. And what shall I say? Father, save me from this hour? No, for this purpose I have come to this hour" (Jn 12:27).

Here, where the subject suffering the hour is the Son speaking immediately with the Father, the disputed "theopassionist formula" is correct: "One of the Trinity has suffered." The strict Antiochenes

---

* The word "it is necessary" with which the New Testament authors express the necessity of Christ's redeeming life, death, and resurrection. Trans.

did not like this since only the humanity of Christ, but not God, can suffer. To be sure, Gregory Nazianzen had already coined it: "We needed a God who took on flesh and was put to death," a "crucified God." The twelfth of the condemnatory propositions of Cyril set forth the affirmation almost provocatively: "Whoever does not confess that the Logos of God suffered in the flesh, was crucified in the flesh, and tasted death in the flesh, in order then to be the first-born of the dead . . . let him be anathema." Through its insertion into the "Thrice Holy" (*Trisagion*) it could be related to the whole Trinity, but even here it should mean only the divine Son, and in this sense it was recognized as orthodox by the Emperor Justinian and Pope John II. And if it is true that one in God took suffering upon himself to the point of abandonment by God and acknowledged it as his own, then obviously it was not as something alien to God that does not touch him inwardly, but as something most profoundly appropriate to his divine person, to the extent that—to say it once again—his *missio* by the Father is a modality of his *processio* from the Father.

Although in the *analogia entis* there is no common measure for the absolute and the contingent, it is therefore not possible to attribute a double consciousness to the incarnate Logos. The mission of which Jesus is conscious is the mission of the only Son. He knows that he as a human being does freely what he as the Logos wants to do, or, what comes to the same, the human being Jesus knows that what he does in freedom is the action of the Son of God. He carries out not what someone else has decided to do; he is also in temporality always the one who offers himself to the Father for doing the work of redeeming the world; in the moments when its massive difficulties humanly overpower him, this offer becomes newly evident (cf. the just-quoted passage from John 12 and the scene in the Garden of Olives). In no way does Jesus as man obey himself as God, nor does he obey the Trinity, but as Son in the Holy Spirit he obeys the Father. The "trinitarian inversion" which stands at the origin of his human existence and accompanies it to his breathing out of the spirit on the cross does not contradict this. For as the one who, henceforth, is the absolutely "inspired one," he does not begin his mission like a constraint, a fate imposed on him, but on the contrary as that with which he identifies himself in freedom with all his heart, all his soul, and all his strength.

There of course remains the mysterious reverse side of this identification of Jesus with his divine mandate, which is the mandate of the Logos, namely the identification of the Logos with the consciousness of a human spiritual subject. Since this spiritual subject begins to exist in a moment of time, there must be for the Logos the moment in which the Logos as this human person comes "into the world" (Jn 1:9; Hebr 10:5), since he, as Irenaeus says, "accustoms" himself as a human being to live among human beings, and since he thus encompasses the immeasurable space of the *analogia entis* and, he who is God, identifies himself with this nature at the edge of nothingness. Or better, since this nature does not preexist him but *ipsa assumptione creatur* (Augustine): he allows himself to be sent to be this nature. Since for Jesus the identity of his I with his mission is from time immemorial, the event or, if you wish, the process of this identification must actually have taken place from the first moment of his conception, which does not necessarily mean that the child Jesus in his mother's womb must have already led a conscious life of the worship of God and acts of atonement. But the form of the actuality of a humanly still-slumbering consciousness remains, as we have already said, deeply mysterious, and in any case not determinable by mere negations.

We must, according to biblical revelation, avoid splitting the Son of God, as he exists in his mission, into one who fulfills his mandate on earth and one who meanwhile abides unchanged in heaven and observes the one who is sent. The one sent is one single unity who abides in time as eternal one. His allowing himself to be disposed of from the form of God into the "form of a slave" and "human likeness" (Phil 2:6f) is an event which involves him as the eternal Son. Whether one says that here eternity enters into time "for a period of time" or that here eternity assumes a time-period and its quite temporal contents into itself: neither explains how such a process is possible. One can call it *kenosis*, as in Philippians 2, but this affirms no mythological change in God, but can only express one of the infinite possibilities in the free eternal life: namely that the Son who has everything from the Father "leaves behind" his "divine form" with the Father from whom he has it in order to concentrate in all seriousness and realism on his mission (which is one possibility of his going from the Father). This is so little a mere as-if that the result will be the abandonment by God on the cross. This "infinite distancing" which brings into itself the mode of the estrangement from God of the sinner will still however always be the highest worldly revelation of the *diastasis* (difference) between Father and Son in the Holy Spirit within the eternal nature of God.

28 · The Expectation and Proclamation of the Approaching Rule of God

Let us for once presuppose that the theology of the Gospel of John is a correct interpretation of synoptic theology. After all John was there and his reverence for the Lord as well as for the church would never have permitted him to sketch free-handed additions onto the teaching of the Lord. His words then can be taken as valid discourse about or as key to the events they report.

The kingdom is near, it is imminent, *engys*, breaking in, *en thurais*, proclaims the synoptic Jesus. If he thereby points to the future as God's arrival, he is still distinguished from the old prophets by the fact that he connects this future to his person and existence. None of the prophets had connected the time of God's word about the coming kingdom to the time of the prophet's own mortal existence. After them other prophets can come; after Jesus comes only God.

Now what this quite precisely means is that an equation takes place between the dimension of an earthly, human, temporal, mortal existence and God's promise of the coming kingdom. The statements "I, this human person" and "God is coming" are identical, and indeed not just for the first time in the explicit johannine equation "The Word was made flesh"—that is, the Word of God of the promise of salvation became identical with the temporal presence of a human person. They are already thoroughly synoptic. There occurs in Jesus a decisive step over and beyond the presence of a prophetic human person endowed with God's word and power proclaiming God's salvation: the there-being of this human being is the *coming*, the *becoming* of the kingdom.

But a human person is itself an entity that becomes ever striding into the future, but also ever walking toward death. Presupposing that identification then, one has to say, inasmuch as Jesus is striding into his human future, to his death, the kingdom is coming. Not simply in such a way that he, running ahead so to speak, would generate, spin it out of himself—to this extent the formula of Origen that Christ is the *autobasileia* (himself the kingdom) is short-circuited—one must instead stay with the expression that leaves things open: inasmuch as he is going the kingdom is coming.

We want to understand what that means, first, for Jesus' consciousness and, second, for his activity. Jesus is a genuine human being, and the inalienable nobility of the human being consists in the fact that he or she can and even has to direct his or her existence in freedom towards an *unknown future* and that, if he or she is a believing human being, this future into which he or she throws and projects herself or himself is God in his freedom and immensity. To take away this opportunity from Jesus and allow him to walk toward a goal known in advance but not yet realized in chronological time would simply mean depriving him of his human worth. The word of Mark *must* be genuine: "No one knows that hour . . . not even the Son" (Mk 13:32).

If Jesus is a genuine human being, he must furthermore fulfill his work in the finiteness of a human life, even if its worth-content and its later effects greatly transcend this finitude. A human being cannot say, this part of my mission I will complete before my death, and since I know that I will rise again, I can always carry out the rest of it afterward. Someone speaking like this would perhaps be a heavenly spirit playing around a bit on earth, but would certainly be no human being bearing the burden and dignity of temporal finiteness.

And so it is: if the eternal Word of God which can say of itself, "Heaven and earth will pass away but my words will not pass away" (Mk 13:31), has become seriously human, then, for the consciousness of this human being—as paradoxical as this may sound—his walking towards death must coincide with heaven and earth's approach to their end, or, put in a better way, the free self-project of this human being through his death toward God must coincide with the survival of this Word of God beyond the passing away of heaven and earth.

Jesus is not only a human being, he is a Jewish human being who lives in the horizon of prophecy and who himself is obviously permeated with the prophetic spirit. He lives not only into the future opened by God's word, but also looks prophetically into it.

Now this prophetic vision or knowledge that Jesus makes his own must at once be distinguished from something like a "second sight," a quite natural possibility of a purely material so to speak photographic registering of future events or dangers. This is excluded here because biblical prophecy is in content and extent ever bound to the free decisions of contemporary people as headed for salvation and ruin. From the standpoint of the one prophesying, it is therefore closely bound to its saving mission by God. In this sense Jesus certainly possessed a prophetic knowledge of the destruction of the holy city and its whole economy as immediately bound with his saving mission and its rejection by Israel.

Prophetic knowledge must be delimited in the same way from properly apocalyptic knowledge which, where it is genuine (and not merely literary imitation), in Daniel and John then, unconditionally presupposes ecstasy. *Egenomēn en pneumati* (I was in the Spirit), says John (Rev. 1:10). In a special obedience of the prophet to God, the seer is snatched from the subjective, free context of life on earth in order to transpose the seer for a moment, as if in brackets, to an unlocalizable place of pure objective vision, neither in heaven nor on earth. Only in the state of transport is a glimpse into the salvation-history drama between heaven and earth possible, in image-codes which, as in a cross section, uncover ever new aspects of this drama without being interested in its chronology in the earthly, world-historical sense.

Such apocalyptic vision is, seen theologically, a helping function for the prophetic perspective and prophetic existence, but it is nowhere visible in the life and words of Jesus and does not need to be presupposed. The erroneously so-called minor apocalypses of the synoptics (Mark 13, par.) are in truth prophetic vision and speech which does not look vertically from above into the event, but ahead horizontally into the dimension of the future of the human being unto God and the future of God unto human beings. But while the Old Testament prophet can see and proclaim the saving events completely beyond his own time of life as well, that prophet who is the Word of God's promise in person can do the impossible, because as much as chronological time may continue after his human death, *he* steps proleptically toward the kingdom in which he includes and surpasses every possible world future. Therefore it is not a confusion in the text but theologically precise speech when Jesus sees his end coinciding with the end of the world, when he thus lets the expectation of his infallibly proximate death be congruent with the so-called *imminent expectation* of the end of the world. (And this vision does not even need to be disturbed by a continuation of chronological time, whose ontic dignity and quality is thoroughly inferior to the time of Christ.) For within his advance towards the unknown coming "hour" of the Father he must also, in accord with his mandate, have done with all the forward march of created and sinful humanity toward the coming of God. The texts which cause difficulty because they postulate proximate end-times (Mk 9:1: "There are some standing here who will not taste death before they see the kingdom of God come with power"; Mk 13:30: "This generation will not pass away before all these things will take place") are speaking within that equation we have mentioned which is the foundation of the theology of the incarnation. *Ho logos pachynetai, ho logos brachynetai:* The Word of God is (by incarnation) "made palpable," "cut down" into finitude—statements of Gregory of Nazianzus and Evagrius, commented on by Maximus the Confessor. For with the death of Jesus we have reached the judgment of the world and with his resurrection the horizon of the resurrection of the world.

Consequently, the imminent expectation of the disciples and the primitive church was to a large extent a chronological *misunderstanding* of the ontotheological imminent expectation of Jesus, a partial falling from the tremendous density and infallible truthfulness of his statements into a worldly-neutral dimension of time which was also affected not only by faith, love, and hope but partly by fear of judgment and partly by a certain eschatological curiosity.

This leads immediately to our second point: the action of Jesus with a view to his future, that is, to the Kingdom imminently breaking in.

* * *

This acting self-conduct is characterized by the words obedience and fulfillment. *Fulfillment* (predominantly synoptic) as the coming-

true of every promise, *obedience* (predominantly pauline and johannine) as the ontological reason *why* Jesus' action is fulfilling. As fulfillment of the attitude demanded in Israel from time immemorial,
his action can and must be understood as archetypal faith, as the
perfect attitude of the earthly covenant partner in relation to God, as
the self-entrusting of the servant of God in the covenant, as step by
step existence in instruction, as pilgrimage under the exclusive leadership of God, and thereby as the perfect self-sacrifice to God as all
this is described in the Epistle to the Hebrews which calls Jesus the
"pioneer and perfecter of our faith" (Heb 12:2).

Into this temporally advancing perfect faith which is, in itself, absolute hope in God, comes, on and on, step by step, the kingdom. It
enters from *ahead* as well as from *above*. Now in that Jesus, the
human being and servant of God, heading toward his death as limit,
at the same time as Word of God, *takes along with him* the whole truth
of the world and its sin into this course and death, in dying he must
come to his end in absolute darkness, and *precisely this headlong fall
into judgment and estrangement from God, into Sheol and hell, in which
all headlong falls of the Old Testament, indeed of the whole human race,
accumulate* is the inbreak of God, the resurrection of humanity: here
the name is made holy, here the kingdom comes, for here the will is
done on earth exactly as it is in heaven, here the Father gives over
judgment to his redeeming Son.

But this fulfilling obedience is now definitively interpreted by John
as *love* beyond faith and hope, and indeed not only as the revelation of
the fatherly goodness of God through the man Jesus' love of God and
of human beings (as the Enlightenment or Harnack think), but *as the
revelation of the trinitarian love between Father and Son. That is what
the preliminary movement of the synoptic Jesus toward the ever approaching kingdom of God has for its depth and presupposition.* When
this Jesus expects the coming kingdom as *imminent* because *after* him
no one else is coming but God, because for this reason no one stands
before him but God, because he thus seeks *first* the kingdom of God,
then everything else, human beings, the cosmos, the world mission of
Jesus has no place except in the advance of the obedient Son towards
the ever approaching Father. Not *behind* this advance (so that one
first obeys God in order to turn to the world *afterward*); not beside it
(so that one would have to make a synthesis of turning to God and
turning to the world), but quite exclusively *in it.* The Son, advancing
toward the Father, in virtue of his obedience takes the world with
him to God, brings it to its end and beyond its end. Insofar as Jesus
first fulfills the will of the Father (John), he therein fulfills consequently also the Torah and the Prophets (Matthew, all the evangelists), and therein every law of God in the world.

Hence, the legacy of Jesus to the world after him cannot really be a work which begun is to be continued, developed, completed by others, by the church. There cannot be any future of Jesus in this sense (as Moltmann, by forcing the text, tries to make plausible); the legacy can only be the totality unique to Christ which *in itself* provides room for advancing with him, believing with him, obeying with him. Human-mundane striving draws its power from Jesus' long-since having-arrived and the striving human being's long-since "having-been-arrived-at" by Jesus (Phil 3:12); and such striving is Christian only in anticipatory grasp of hope and obedience above and beyond all intramundane concern and cultural-technical planning and construction. Whatever our planning in the future of this may be—mandate of creation, or God-opposed titanism, or often both together—it can, as Christian, lay claim to no other space than in the advance of Jesus to the Father, in an obedience so strict, in an imminent expectation so urgent that, between Jesus and the Father whose will he does, no needle can fall to the ground. The whole salvation event from the beginning to the end of the world takes place on this most narrow path, through this needle's eye: it occurs within the divine intersubjectivity, as it has been opened in Jesus Christ in order to let us enter. It is not primarily in our human intersubjectivity that God occurs (as Feuerbach thinks); *we* come to pass nowhere else than in the inner-trinitarian conversation, at the place of exchange, of the Holy Spirit. Thus, without trinitarian thinking, one does not understand the first statement about Jesus or about the historical and temporal horizon of his human existence.

29 · Mysteries of the Life of Jesus (I): Conceived by the Holy Spirit, Born of the Virgin Mary

When the light of Easter dawned over the life of Jesus, there was no more holding back—the question simply had to be asked: Who was this man in reality; from what realm does he originally come? So the question of his origin is posed to which originally the proposition of the creed we are now about to consider communicates the answer: "Conceived of the Holy Spirit, born of the Virgin Mary."

The history of faith had begun with Abraham who first had an ordinary son, Ishmael, by the fertile Hagar, but to whom however, when he was a hundred years old, God promised another son, the son of promise, Isaac, from his barren wife Sarah. The same sign is repeated with the birth of Sampson, again with the birth of Samuel from the hitherto barren Hannah, and a final time with Elizabeth who, likewise barren, conceived the precursor, John, by means of an explicit miracle of God: "And behold, your kinswoman Elizabeth in her old age has also conceived a son; and this is the sixth month with her who was called barren. For with God nothing will be impossible" (Lk 1:36–37). This motif, perduring from the beginning to the end of the Old Testament era, haunted Jewish thinking; reflection revealed ever more clearly that it was God himself who had the major part in those generations and conceptions; God's power vivified the dead seed and the barren womb. Of Abraham Paul said that he had generated "in his faith in God who gives life to the dead and calls into existence the things that do not exist. . . . He did not weaken in faith when he considered his own body which was as good as dead, . . . and likewise the womb of Sarah" (Rom 4:17–19). And of Isaac Paul said similarly that he was "generated through promise" (Gal 4:23), "born according to the Spirit—*kata pneuma*" (Gal 4:29).

But as long as we remain within the Old Testament, the relationship of the human father to his son, despite all God's activity, is decisive. Not the Holy Spirit but Abraham is eminently the father of Isaac. While they were on pilgrimage to Mount Moriah, "Isaac turned to Abraham and said to him, 'My father!' And he said, 'Here am I, my son.' He said, 'Behold the fire and the wood; but where is the lamb for a burnt offering?' " (Gen 22:7). Before the birth of Sampson, the angel of the Lord does appear first to the woman, whose name of course remains unmentioned; but the decisive action takes place with the husband, with Manoah of Zorah of the tribe of Dan (Jud 13:2–24). The story of the barren Hannah also begins with an extensive description of her husband Elkanah, son of Jeroham, etc., from Ramathaim, who is going to Shiloh on pilgrimage with his wife to offer sacrifice. And after Hannah's prayer begging for a son, it says of them both, "They rose early in the morning and worshiped before the Lord; then they went back to their house at Ramah. And Elkanah knew Hannah his wife, and the Lord remembered her" (1 Sam 1:1–19). And how clearly, in the first chapter of Luke, did the priest Zechariah of the division of Abijah have the ascendancy over his wife: he it is who meets the angel as he offers the sacrifice of incense; he receives the details of the prophecy about his son who, filled with the Holy Spirit, will prepare the way of the Lord in the power of Elias.

It is Zechariah who is struck with dumbness because of his lack of faith, who is later asked at the naming ceremony of his son, and finally, is the singer of the Benedictus: "His father, Zechariah," it is written, "was filled with the Holy Spirit, and prophesied, saying, 'Blessed be the Lord God of Israel' " (Lk 1).

After this introduction, one would obviously expect to hear something about Joseph, the man from the tribe of David, as the one on whom the whole promise depends. But the whole scene of the annunciation, both in Matthew and in Luke, passes over him and is played with Mary alone. Here for the first time the angel of the Lord is turned toward a woman, and she is the one who passes the Spirit she has received to another woman, her cousin Elizabeth, who is only then filled with the Spirit and receives the sign of the child leaping in her womb. Mary alone sings her Magnificat. It is quite clear that much more than the question of "biological generation" is at issue here; for we are dealing with the decisive emergence of God as the unique Father, which excludes in Jesus another father-relationship just as much as Jesus' marriage relationship to his bride, the church, excludes a different marriage relationship to him.

Abraham's loins had been blessed by the Holy Spirit as a newly awakened source of life. The old servant Eliezer had to touch those loins in order to take his oath to make the arrangements for the bride of Isaac. Just think how Joseph's sources of life would have had to be praised, from which, now at last, the longed-for offspring of David was to come forth! But no. The whole process of bodily generation, yes the whole question whether a man or a woman is fertile or barren, becomes unimportant in the New Covenant. Joseph crosses the threshold to the New Covenant only as one making a renunciation. As such he becomes the foster father of him who will himself be chaste and open a whole other source of life through his most radical renunciation: His crucified body will become, as a whole, capable of generation and will bring forth, according to Paul, his immaculate bride without wrinkle or blemish, the church.

With this central emphasis on renunciation rather than upon human generation, we stand at the threshold to our confession of faith; the threshold is, of course, not yet crossed; the step from the barren Elizabeth to the virginal Mary remains to be taken. But how characteristic for the origin of the motif of the virgin birth in the Bible that the angel of the annunciation puts the hand of Mary into the hand of her cousin Elizabeth, that the angel thus derives the origin of the motif and its foundation quite clearly from the Old Testament promise. Everything in the depiction of the conception and birth of Jesus in Matthew and in Luke is completely understandable from the Old Testament; nothing, on the other hand, refers to pagan mythology, whether to Egyptian or to hellenistic parallels where the descendants of the Pharaohs or various kinds of heroes are begotten from a virgin by gods. The most that one could grant here would be that such remote parallels (but the differences are greater!) point to a vague expectation of humanity that a great human being could come directly from the world of the divine. But we must make a correction here right away: according to the Jewish idea of God, one can't even talk about a physical sonship of God.

On the one hand, the account in Luke points directly to the prophecy of Isaiah, that the young woman (*almah*) would conceive and bear a son whom she would call Immanu-el (Is 7:14). The Hebrew word "young woman" is translated in the Greek bible as *parthenos*, which means "virgin" and thus forms the transition to the event at Nazareth. In Judaism, however, virginity was not surrounded with any bright light; on the contrary, all the light fell on the fertile woman. For this reason it once again is an Old Testament note when Mary, in her song of praise, notes that God has "regarded the low estate of his handmaiden." Further, the words, "the Holy Spirit will come upon you and the power of the Most High will overshadow you," also point wholly to the Old Testament: nowhere in there does God unite himself with a human being in a "sacred marriage," but rather, from his unapproachable height, the power of his Spirit turns his will into deed. And yet we also here cross—and we are talking about the virgin birth!—the threshold from the Old to the New Covenant and should not hesitate to see in this "Holy Spirit" that power of God which in the Christian reflection on the events is characterized as the third divine *hypostasis* or person. That *pneuma* stands here (as often in the New Testament) without article, while it is used elsewhere with article, *to pneuma*, is not a decisive objection against this point (the texts change at times from one verse to the other, as for example, at the baptism of Jesus: "He will baptize you with [the] Holy Spirit. . . . And behold the heavens were opened and he [Jesus] saw [the] Spirit of God descending like a dove. . . . Then Jesus was led up by the Spirit into the wilderness" (Mt 3:11, 16; 4:1). Much more important is the fact that, right in the scene of the annunciation, the threefold address of the angel brings the three hypostases of the divinity onto the scene for the first time: "The Lord is with you" (Yahweh, the God of Israel, whom Jesus will call his father), "You will bear the Son of the Most High," "[the] Holy Spirit will come upon you." If the Father as the all-governing One remains in high heaven, and if, on the other hand, the Son allows himself to be borne in the womb of the virgin, thus allowing his incarnation to take place and not actively carrying it out, then the Holy Spirit as the third divine *hypostasis* remains the truly active one, as the Spirit will always be in the prayers and sacraments and charisms of the church.

30 · Mysteries of the Life of Jesus (II): The Last Supper and the Eucharist

The next starting point in our reflection is formed by the words of institution (we need not get involved here with the differences among them): "This is my body which is given for you" (Lk 22:19), "This is my blood, . . . which is poured out for you" (Mk 14:24). The "being given" clearly signifies, as the parallel "being poured out" shows, the crucifixion; the Lord's Supper is its anticipation. And if the primitive church and Paul can from the fact of the resurrection conclude the universal salvific meaning of the cross (which remained unrecognizable in the process itself)—"Put to death for our trespasses and raised for our justification" (Rom 4:25)—this truth resided already evidently as a "sacred-public mystery" in the gesture with which Jesus proffered his flesh and blood at table as given up, poured out. The gesture of self-giving precedes in time the violent event of the passion and thus shows that the free self-sacrifice is also the ontological reason and presupposition for the fact that the following gruesome event can attain universal salvific meaning. The free self-giving wills to go "unto the end" (Jn 13:1), and the end consists in this disposing of oneself which passes over into a pure letting oneself be disposed of and becoming disposed of. The passivity of the passion, with chaining, scourging, nailing, piercing, is the expression of a most highly active will to self-sacrifice which, precisely for this reason, transcends the limits of self-determination into the limitlessness of the pure letting-oneself-be-determined. On the other hand, such a will to sacrifice which, in the eucharistic gesture of delivering oneself among the disciples donates itself beyond all confines of human finitude, would really appear to be Promethean hubris if it were itself not already the expression of a prior act of being determined and disposed of. This Paul and John see exactly when they depict the whole self-giving of Jesus to his own and to the world as the concreteness of the self-giving of the Father who, out of love for the world he created and in fidelity to the covenant he has entered with it, gives what is most precious to him, his Son (Rom 8:32; Jn 3:16). Because Jesus is the one and the only who comes down from above, from heaven, as Paul and John say, there resides already in his becoming man God's infinite will to self-giving which (as un-finite) becomes manifest in the fundamental will of the Son nowhere to dispose of himself but in all things to be at the disposal of the Father and his driving Spirit. This is clear: the human reality of Jesus (his "flesh and blood" or his "life": Jn 10:15) is, because of becoming man, already predisposed for Eucharist, insofar as it is the personified gift of God to the world; and the realization of this self-giving in the Lord's Supper, passion, and resurrection is nothing other than the actuation of this always intended, really planned and begun self-giving.

Before we go further, we must note here that this self-giving in our fallen world was intended soteriologically from the outset: the Son is "sent" by the Father onto the God-forsakenness of the cross because he really "takes on himself" (Jn 1:29) the sins of the world, represents them in their entirety (2 Cor 5:14, 21; Gal 3:13; Eph

2:14–16). As mysterious as the *how* of this representation may remain, *that* it is so should not be made problematical. The "for us" of Jesus is in no way meant just juridically-morally-satisfactorily but, over and above that, in a real way, or "physically," if you will. It is my God-forsakenness which is there in my sin, in my dying into remoteness from God and into the darkness to eternal death, that he experiences in his "being delivered," and indeed experiences more deeply and more definitively than any mere creature can experience such a thing. Only the unique Son of the Father whose food it is to do the will of Father can definitively and insurpassably realize and experience what it means to have to do without this food and to undergo the absolutely hellish "thirst" (Jn 19:28). His unique, hypostatic suffering underpins every possible temporal and eternal suffering of a created human being. That is why he who was so definitively dead and lives in eternity holds "the keys of Death and Hades" (Rev 1:18). Precisely through the removal of any food by God—and perhaps there really is in Mark 14:25 (par.) also a freely chosen eucharistic fast of Jesus, as J. Jeremias thinks—God makes his Son into the food for the whole world. In suffering his whole human substance is made to flow in order to be able to enter into human beings; but this happens in such a way that he makes flow with himself the stone blocks of sin which dam the stream of God's flowing being, and dissolves them in that experienced God-forsakenness of which they secretly consist.

Now the decisive point may be formulated. The eucharistic gesture of Jesus' distribution of himself to his own and through them to the world is a definitive, eschatological, and thus irreversible gesture. The Word of the Father become flesh is definitively given by him, passed around, and will never again be taken back. Neither the resurrection from the dead nor the ascension as "return to the Father" (Jn 16:18) are a counter-movement to becoming man, passion, Eucharist; the farewell discourses speak clearly enough here: "I am going away and am coming to you" (Jn 14:28); "you see me because I live, and you will live also" (Jn 14:19). Or when Jesus says he gives up his life in order to take it back again, that he gives it voluntarily, he has the power to give it, and the power to take it back again (Jn 10:18), then the addition "and I give them eternal life" (Jn 10:28) shows that here there can be no talk of a taking back of what has been given or of the gesture and its state of self-donation. The setting into flow of earthly substance into the eucharistic substance is irreversible; it also lasts not only (as a "means") until the "end of the world"; it is rather the radiant core about which (according to the vision of Teilhard de Chardin in his youth) the cosmos crystallizes, or better, from which it becomes radiant. One must realize what theological depth of meaning gets expressed with the showing of the wounds on the risen One: that the state of being sacrificed during the passion has positively entered into and is taken up into the henceforth eternal state of Jesus Christ; and that between his "heavenly" state and his "eucharistic" state no difference can be added which would affect its inner constitution. The total self-surrender of Jesus—after his sharing at the Last Supper where he leaves his fate and the meaning and shape of his saving work to the discretion of the Father, the interpretation of the Holy Spirit, and for the promotion and fructification of the church—is so conclusive that it can in no way ever go back to a disposal over himself. And this is true even though through his obedience he has been "exalted" (Phil 2:11) and "made to be Lord" (Acts 2:36). He is "Lion" (Rev 5:5) only insofar as he is for ever "Lamb as though slain" (Rev 5:6) in the middle of the throne of God. This says much more than that he, on the basis of the earned merits, stands before the Father as intercessor, even more than that he merely makes his "self-giving" brought to completion in a bloody manner on earth to continue in an unbloody manner in heaven. It means ultimately that the Father's act of self-giving, with which he pours out his Son through all space and time of creation, is the definitive opening of the very trinitarian act in which the "persons" of God, "relations," forms of absolute self-donation and loving flow. In the Eucharist, the creator has succeeded in making the finite, creaturely structure—without breaking it or doing it violence ("no one takes my life from me": Jn 10:18)—so fluid that it is capable of becoming the bearer of triune life. The "language" of human existence—in its spontaneity as in its condition of being disposed of by the superior strength of suffering and death as a whole—has become the language of God and his self-expression. Of course we stand here in the midst of the most impenetrable mystery, for we cannot conceive of a human being in any other way than as a being who brings itself together within itself in order then to bestow this self (this being-present-to-oneself) on another as well. And in fact the resurrection accounts show us just such a self-possessing one who lets himself be known in the utmost freedom and sovereignty, when it pleases him, and withdraws himself in the same way, and disposes of himself in highest fullness of power. And yet this human being is at the same time the Word and the Son of the Father who, in giving up his "divine form" with his kenotic self-giving, has gone to the ultimate, and he does not do away with but rather lets his self-donation, sacrifice and *kenosis* be demonstrated as the authentic power and glory of God. The crucified One, and he alone, is the risen One. For being allowed to give himself in such a way, he gives eternal thanks to the Father as the substantial Eucharist of the Father which, as such, never becomes past or mere remembrance.

31 · Mysteries of the Life of Jesus (III): Prelude to the Passion—the Agony in the Garden

Important as the deeds, teachings, and miracles of Jesus' public life were and remain, they still are only the entrance and prelude to his decisive deed: his gathering together into himself the sin of the world which offends the goodness of the Father, in order to consume it in the fire of his passion. The Father is supposed to perceive it only as fuel for the love of the Son: "Behold the Lamb of God [the scapegoat], which takes away [into the desert, into the invisible and inaccessible] the sin of the world." Since the Son has allowed the monstrous darkness of sin into himself, he is as if robbed of his power, he has "emptied" himself, in order, in his weakness and hence in being completely overwhelmed, to bear the unbearable burden. At the temptation in the desert, all the enticements of the world—of an easy, humanly attractive way—stood against the will of the Father; but the latter could be victorious in him because he stood before Jesus' soul as the ever-greater One, worthy of adoration. Now the temptation is a different one. The choice is not between the Father and the world, but between two images of the Father: the image of the God familiar from time immemorial and before the inner darkening as all-powerful and all-good, who could adopt completely different ways to the same goal—and the image of this severe God of justice as that of the Father as seen and experienced through the heart and eyes of sinners, who now appears to the Son. The sun of love has disappeared behind the clouds; only the threat of the divine thunder can be sensed. This situation belonged to the trinitarian plan, but the Son is now wholly the sin-bearing man, and the Holy Spirit represents the fatherly will to him only like the obvious contradiction between what is simply assigned to him and what simply overwhelms him.

In the terrible fear of not being able to perform what is demanded, he must be convinced of a Yes. It is a struggle with himself; he has to wring his "your will be done" in the exertion of utmost weakness. The words about the sweating of blood show this, words which were removed by many transcribers but which are genuine gospel text. Neither the sleeplessness which Jesus demands ("watch and pray"), nor the purely human fear and agitation before the suffering ahead can explain this outbreak of his innermost substance; only a conflict between God in heaven and God the representative of sinners on earth can explain it.

The gospel says that Jesus interrupted this struggle several times in order to seek sympathy, support, and help from his disciples, the representatives of the visible church, arranged by the Lord himself at certain distances: eight disciples left further back, three brought nearer to him, apparently to take part. We see their refusal; they sleep out of sadness, hopeless confusion, but indeed also out of a refusal of their obedience which cannot speak the yes of faith unto the end. This faith is not awake and prayerful enough. This is the church in its average condition, precisely then, too, when we regard the three as representatives of those especially chosen to the state of the counsels and priesthood, of whom a stricter obedience of faith is demanded than of the others. These give a general, as it were somewhat abstract, yes to the faith of the church and its most important precepts; but they do not live in the daily tested form of a concrete obedience to a superior or to a bishop. The disciples do not live up to their vocation; they leave the Lord alone.

He must go back to his lonely struggle which does not move on so to speak, but remains stuck at the same point of his inability to cope. He prays "with the same word," even if "still more earnestly."

32 · Mysteries of the Life of Jesus (IV): Jesus' Death on the Cross— Fulfillment of the Eternal Plan of God

The deeper the suffering, the more our concepts fail us. Before the last station at which God's living word is nailed by human beings into deadly motionlessness, every word goes dumb. It is the hour of the Father when the triune eternal divine plan is executed to clean away the whole terrible mess of the world's sin and consume it in the fire of suffering love. This fire has burned eternally in God as the glowing passion of commitment to the eternal good in which, according to God's plan, the world too should have a share. This good is the commitment of the divine persons to each other, the triune radicalism which here reaches over the world. The mystery of the cross is the highest revelation of the trinity.

The generation of the Son proceeds to an ultimate level of releasing; the connection of the source with what has flowed out seems broken down: the concentration of everything contrary to God in the Son is experienced as being abandoned by the Father. The fountain from which the Son eternally lives seems to be empty, and hence everything the Son did under the pure mandate of the Father loses its meaning; it was in vain. Nor is it by any means just the earthly fiasco in this ending of life that gives the Son this feeling, but, much deeper, his inner bearing of the irreconcilable contradiction between the sin he has within him and the salvific will of the loving Father. As the embodiment of sin he can no longer find any support in God; he has identified himself with that which God must eternally turn away from himself. And still he is the Son who can proceed and live only from the source of the Father, hence his infinite thirst for the inaccessible God. It is a thirst which burns in him like eternal fire, bodily, psychically, spiritually. The Holy Spirit which accompanied him through his whole life as the Spirit of the Father, is now just the enkindler of this thirst: the Spirit unites Father and Son while stretching their mutual love to the point of unbearability. In this infinite difference both are exposed: the infinite difference within God which is the presupposition of eternal love and gets bridged by the Holy Spirit; and the salvation-historical difference in which the alienated world is reconciled with God.

This is what makes the cross the dramatic *peripeteia* from the old to the new. Not only from the Old Covenant in which so much was said of the anger and wrath of God, of his bloody wine press, but also from the whole of the old fallen world; and not only to the church which becomes the visible sacrament of God's reconciliation, but also to the whole new world which is here born invisibly and is brought to completion in the final transfiguration of creation. It is the turning, the transition, the Pasch. And in the turning point, in the crucified, these coincide: God's wrath which will not come to terms with sin but can only reject it and burn it out, and God's love which begins to disclose itself precisely at the point of this inexorability.

The crucified One, as this turning, is the Word which the Father addresses to the world. At this moment, the Word cannot hear itself. It collapses into its scream for the lost God. And it will really be an interpretation of his heavenly meaning, as it were, of the voice of the Father and the Spirit in the Son when the evangelists write the words, "Forgive them . . . ," "Today you will be with me in paradise," "It is finished." We should receive such words as spoken to us by the Father through the Spirit in the suffering of the Son.

But we share in still more. If the church's hour of birth lies in this great turning, since from that point the body of God's Word, flooded to the very end with the divine fullness (Col 2:9) but also with the assumed substance of the world, can be eucharistically distributed, and the water and blood of the sacraments flow forth from the pierced heart, this body does not forget its provenance and its connection with the body of its mother. And the body of the mother of Jesus could bear this fruit only on the basis of her anticipatory agreement with his whole mission; that is why Mary is present under the cross where the incarnation of God comes to its completion and the church begins. She suffers with him, in her spirit she undergoes with him the death of the Son, and the stab of the lance which pierces the dead body strikes her, the one who must keep on living, as the sword which was promised her. The disciples have received communion, sacramentally they are already Christ's body, objectively the church which they form is already with Jesus on the cross; but subjectively they are not there except for the Beloved Disciple who represents them.

33 · Mysteries of the Life of Jesus (V): Jesus' Death on the Cross— Substitution and Descent to Hell

If one wished to apply the discernment of spirits to the question of who in the church really believes in the undiluted mystery of Jesus Christ and who remains stuck in an outer court—"Whom do people think that I am? Whom do you think I am?"—one would have to go back to the source of primitive Christian christology, which doubtless lies in the phrase *pro nobis*, that is related to the cross and proven valid through the resurrection. The Nicene Creed formulated it explicitly: *qui* propter nos *homines et* propter nostram *salutem . . . , crucifixus etiam* pro nobis" But Paul was not the first; even before him the earliest Jerusalem reflection on the scandal of the cross had been instilled with the idea of substitution: from this soteriological change of place light is cast on the genuine essence of Jesus, and from him on the true picture of the (trinitarian) God. The suffering of Jesus is not only a symbol in which one can read the always present but not yet clearly highlighted atoning will of God, but is the very act of this atonement: "God reconciled the world to himself *in* Christ" (2 Cor 5:19). But the suffering of Christ is also not—the other extreme—a magical event through which an angry, justice-demanding God would be changed into a gracious one (as an externalized satisfaction theory, coming from a misunderstanding of Anselm, sometimes claims): "for *God* so loved the world that he gave his only Son" (Jn 3:16). Between these two extremes emerges, in the *event* of what happened on the cross, the true image of Christ as well as the true image of God, Jesus Christ. For this *pro nobis* to be effective, Jesus Christ has to be, unconditionedly, truly human, for only in that way could he take on himself and suffer from within the vicarious experience of the world's sin. But he must also be more than a human being, more than a creature, for within the world no being can completely assume the place of another free fellow nature: this would offend against the dignity of the self-responsible person.

More needs to be said about this right away. The image of God, however, considered from the standpoint of this christological-soteriological event, becomes alive in an unheard-of new way. It is not as if God became dependent on temporal events in a mythological or gnostic fashion, for he is the one indeed who sends the son of God, the one who lets him suffer and die in God-forsakenness, and he does not then enter into any dependence on the dark powers of the world. Instead, he proves to be so living, so mobile, that he can reveal his life precisely even in death, his trinitarian communality even in abandonment, and that here his fundamental properties of justice and love neither fall together in an undifferentiated way nor get separated unrelatedly, but, in a most sublime drama, are shown to be correlated, and finally identical.

But now it is significant that this oldest core of christology from which the whole dogmatic theology will develop doubtless arose in view of Isaiah's songs of the servant of God whose suffering was understood as a vicarious work of atonement for "the many"; and that furthermore these songs did not arise in the Old Testament in an unmediated fashion, but had their manifold roots in the offers of substituion of the great founding figures: from Abraham, who put his friendship with God in the balance (Gen 18:20–33) in order, in solidarity with the sinners, to rescue them from threatened catastrophe; from Moses who, in solidarity with the idolatrous people, begs to be wiped "from the book of life" in place of them (Exod 32:32); from the many prophets who, inwardly and outwardly, have the burden of the sinful people laid on their shoulders. Is the unique event on the cross interpreted by an already-known category which is somehow understandable in general human terms and thus stripped of its incomparable character? To answer this one must ask the opposite question: how could what is unique and valid for all times and places even be understood by human beings at all unless some kind of preunderstanding for the meaning of substitution had been present? And what there is of this that emerges into understanding in the Old Testament remains strangely fragmentary, inchoate: Abraham's offer remains ineffective; that of Moses is only partially accepted (completely only in a late idealizing interpretation: Deut 1:37; 3:23–28; 4:21–22); the fate of Jeremiah and Ezekiel does not avert the punishing judgment. Everywhere are found allusions to a mysterious substitution (first of all in the choice of the one in place of the other, and *for* him); but even in the songs of the servant of God the whole event remains indefinite (as far as the subject is concerned), and is sung in an almost dreamy, premonitional, prophetic atmosphere. Everything is looking to the real deed transcending the limits of national particularity.

The central problem has already been indicated; it comes clearly to the fore in Kant's treatment of the problem of the idea of substitution. For him the puzzle can "not be worked out by insight into the causal determination of the freedom of the human being . . . , thus not theoretically, for this question exceeds the whole speculative capacity of our reason" (*Religion Within*, A 163). Kant is right in the sense that the theologian, who tries to think from the affirmations of the New Testament, also runs against a necessary puzzle to solve which in an oversimplified way in this or that direction has been the twofold temptation of the history of theology, with Origen on one side and Augustine on the other. The basic affirmation is that God, by substituting for all sinners on the cross, has brought humanity into a new mode of being—"If one has died for all, then all have died"—into the mode of being of a relatedness to that point from which the uprooting from the first way of being took place: "And he died for all, that those who live might live no longer for themselves but for him who for their sake died and was raised" (2 Cor 5:14–15); cf. Rom 14:7–8: "None of us lives to himself, and none of us dies to himself. If we live, we live to the Lord, and if we die, we die to the Lord." This unheard-of modification of the human mode of being without doubt touches the personal freedom of the individual, but without over-whelming it. Paul emphasized both: that through the substitution the sinner is liberated to his own freedom (Gal 5:1), but therefore attains a new responsibility placed upon him, so that he remains responsible before God for what he does or does not do, for his Yes and No (Rom 14:10–12). The first moment, the touching of human freedom, could verge on the magical; how is anyone supposed to manipulate my freedom from outside without my becoming aware of it and giving or refusing my consent or assent to it? Of course, Paul does not shy from such an *a priori* when he establishes that "Christ at the right time died for us sinners [i.e., at the time], while we were yet helpless [and unable to help ourselves]" (Rom 5:6). The second moment: the per-during self-responsibility of human beings, however, could, in case they refused liberation through the cross, still not give themselves power over God himself with the possibility of frustrating his plans.

It is very difficult to decide whether creatures, who through the grace of the creator have received a share in his absolute freedom, thereby possess an absolute or only a relative freedom. The latter seems to be a contradiction in itself, but the former seems to step too close to God's sovereignty. One would still be able to say that God gives human beings the capacity to perform what seems for human beings to be a definitive (negative) choice against God, but which does not need to be judged/evaluated/assessed by God as definitive. And not of course in such a way that the human person's choice is called into question from outside—which would amount to a disregard of the freedom bestowed on it—but rather in such a way that God, with his own divine choice, accompanies the human person into the most extreme situation of his (negative) choice. This is what happens in the passion of Jesus.

To be sure two aspects of this mystery can be distinguished here; the one is more related to the event on Good Friday, the other more to the event on Holy Saturday. There is in the suffering of the living Jesus the readiness to drink the "chalice" of wrath, that is, to let the whole power of sin spend its fury on him: he takes on himself the blows and the hate contained in it and pays it so to speak through suffering. The weakness of suffering (and the active readiness in it) outlasts all the force of the pounding sin. Its impatience is—also as sum of all the world-historical sinful impatience against God—finite and exhaustible in comparison to the patience of the Son of God. This grasps from underneath and upsets it. Of course, it is not quantities that are here opposed in rivalry, but qualities. The quality of the loving obedience of the Son of God toward the Father (who in this manner, through his Son become man, wishes to conquer sin from within) is beyond all comparison with the quality of hate spending its fury on him.

But on Holy Saturday there is the descent of the dead Jesus to hell, that is (put very simply) his solidarity in the period of nontime with those who have lost their way from God. Their choice—with which they have chosen to put their I in place of God's selfless love— is definitive. Into this finality (of death) the dead Son descends, no longer acting in any way, but stripped by the cross of every power and initiative of his own, as one purely to be used, debased to mere matter, with a fully indifferent (corpse) obedience, incapable of any active act of solidarity—only thus is he right for any "sermon" to the dead. He is (out of an ultimate love however) dead together with them. And exactly in that way he disturbs the absolute loneliness striven for by the sinner: the sinner, who wants to be "damned" apart from God, finds God again in his loneliness, but God in the absolute weakness of love who unfathomably in the period of nontime enters into solidarity with those damning themselves. The words of the Psalm, "If I make my bed in the netherworld, thou art there" (Ps 139:8), thereby take on a totally new meaning. And even the cry "God is dead" as a self-made decree of the sinner for whom God is something done away with takes on a totally new meaning objectively established by God himself. The freedom of the creature is respected, but it is retrieved by God at the end of the passion and seized again in its very foundations (*inferno profundior*: Gregory the Great). Only in absolute weakness does God will to mediate to the freedom created by him the gift of love that breaks from every prison and every constraint: in his solidarity from within with those who reject all solidarity. *Mors et vita duello.*

34 · Mysteries of the Life of Jesus (VI): Resurrection

"If Christ has not been raised, our faith is in vain" (1 Cor 15:14). Without resurrection there would be no evangelical witness. The whole life of Jesus, even his passion, was arranged for this purpose. The admission of the disciples that, before the resurrection, they had really not understood what it was all about, the description of their unbelief, even in the face of the fact of the resurrection, the complete turn-about of a Magdalene, of the Emmaus disciples, of a Paul, all belong to the Easter proclamation.

The resurrection is a trinitarian event. With his death on the cross the Son of God fulfilled his mandate to return to the Father with his human spirit, the Holy Spirit of his mission. As a human being he himself cannot rise from the dead; it is the Father who, as "the God of the living" (Rom 4:17), raises the Son from the dead so that he, as newly united with the Father, might send the Spirit of God into the church.

Without the resurrection the whole trinitarian salvific plan would be incomprehensible, and the work begun in the life of Jesus would remain meaningless. For the world, and also for the Old Testament, this life was one singular provocation, since Jesus raised himself above the authority of the Law as its goal and meaning. Israel must permit itself to be stretched beyond itself—in a blind faith of Abraham—in order to come to its fulfilment. That it does not want to do this becomes clear at the beginning of Jesus' preaching; he knew what his provocative mission would inevitably bring to him, but went "with his face firmly set" toward his death. The disciples followed full of amazed fear (Mk 10:32). And this fearful trembling remains in their bones even at the resurrection (Mk 16:8; Lk 24:22, 27). They do not have the slightest preunderstanding for what a resurrection—not "on the last day" but in the midst of their own time—could be. That Jesus himself in his suffering has "finished his business" with the world, and also with the future of the world which for him is the Last Day, while the disciples still abide in time, took quite some time to dawn on them. And still more difficult will it be to understand that the whole life of the church was from then on supposed to be stamped by the two-in-one event of cross and Easter. To understand this, even more to live it, the disciples had to become partakers of the Spirit of Christ which is at the same time the Spirit of the all-planning and all-accomplishing Father.

But to receive the spirit of Christ and of the Father means at the same time to accept the essential gift of God: the body and blood of the Son which the Father extends to the world through the efficacious power of the Spirit. Receiving the Spirit and Eucharist are two sides of the same thing. There, where Jesus emphasizes with the deepest urgency the inexorableness of the eating of his flesh and drinking of his blood (Jn 6:53), he adds, "It is the Spirit that gives life, the flesh is of no avail" (Jn 6:63). After the Spirit accompanies the incarnation of the Son and in him has as it were an experience of the world, it remains forever inseparable from flesh and blood.

Therefore the church assembled at Easter will encounter a Spirit-filled but bodily Christ—he breathes his Spirit into them (Jn 20:22), but also wants to be touched so that it will not be thought that he is "a spirit" (Lk 24:39). And after the ascension the church will await both the promised Holy Spirit and the Lord who will come again, whose arrival they anticipate, as instructed, in the celebration of the breaking of the bread. The witness that the disciples receive and must hand on is, according to John, only complete when "water (baptism), blood (Eucharist), and Spirit" are together (1 Jn 5:7). Encounter with the Lord at Easter must culminate into receiving the Spirit so that the Lord may be known and so that he can send the one who does the knowing and empowers possession of the Spirit to nothing other than the proclaiming and witnessing that God the Father has given us his Son, the Son who died and rose for us.

But the church is now the church founded on the cross: the gathering together of the faithful around those endowed with office, with Mary in their midst. To her, as the core of the church, the Son without doubt, appeared first (Ignatius, *Exercises*, no. 299). She is the one who, sought out by the Spirit before all others, received the body of the Word. Gathered close around her, the church prays that what primordially happened to Mary may also happen to it. And Mary herself prays anew for this event; she prays now *as* church, as the centerpoint of the community of saints, that the incarnation completed in cross and resurrection may be communicated to the whole community.

When we look ahead to the exaltation of this prayer as narrated in the Acts of the Apostles and continued in church history as a whole, it then becomes clear that the Holy Spirit comes ever anew, and ever anew the Spirit places the witnessing church under the sign of Jesus Christ: humiliation, persecution, cross. The Acts is simultaneously filled with persecution of the church—the apostles are scourged, Peter imprisoned, James killed, Paul particularly chosen for the suffering that is dramatically described towards the end of the book—and with the victorious procession of the church "from Jerusalem to Samaria and to the ends of the earth." Both belong together; the first is the sign of the genuineness and credibility of the second. If Paul finally goes as an exemplar the way of Christ, given by his Christian brothers to the Jews and by these to the pagans, and if his journey to

Rome leads to a violent shipwreck, then the gospel of Paul is that of the crucified but definitively risen Lord: "The Lord is the Spirit" (2 Cor 3:17), "Death no longer has dominion over him" (Rom 6:9).

This brings the inconceivable paradox of Christian life into the full light of day. The Christian must take up his cross daily in order to daily rise anew with the dead Lord: "For while we live, we are always being given to death for Jesus' sake, so that the life of Jesus may be manifested in our mortal flesh" (2 Cor 4:11). Neither is it the case that the church dies only in an earthly-historical way in order to rise into the pure beyond, nor is it the case that the church in an earthly-historical way moves into a pure life of resurrection for which the cross would be only a means of development. The first would be a denial of the incarnation, the second would be a relapse into a (secularized) Old Testament hope. Easter is reality on earth, but it leads not away from the cross but back into it anew. The whole Pasch, the whole passing over from death to life, is forevermore real.

Jesus, the Fulfillment of the Hopes of Israel

35 · The Essential Incompleteness of the Old Covenant

The Old Covenant gives us the classical model for the more general theological question about the unity of the Bible. Two millennia of Christian theology have thought of the relationship of Old and New Covenant in the scheme of manifold promise and single fulfillment, of many types and one antitype. If that is true, then Pascal is right once again: *La figure a été faite sur la vérité, et la vérité a été reconnue sur la figure* ("The type was made according to the truth, and the truth was recognized in the type").

An essentially temporal religion, as was the Old Covenant, can, *a priori*, possess no purely supertemporal truth recognizable in overview: faith means following behind the God who walks ahead and shows the way through time without one's being able to know in advance where the path leads. The situation of Abraham (Gen 12:1) and of the people in the desert cannot be mastered. At any time God can give new instructions. Therefore the Old Testament is to be interpreted and fixed neither on the basis of its original situation (as Deuteronomy did with a certain partiality, but which still considers this origin as a "today"; or as Martin Buber did when he measured everything later against the original pure theocracy), nor is it to be interpreted univocally as on-the-way as such (e.g., the now-arriving word of the prophets; because the prophets themselves always point back anew to the beginnings in order to keep Israel's faith alive), nor is it to be fixed unequivocally toward the promise of the future (as the apocalyptic prophets would have loved to do), because that which is coming remains as such undisclosed and the images which point in that direction may not be taken in the sense which human beings would like to take them (this narrowing, which is practically unbelief, will be the cause of Jesus' death; he does not correspond to the Jewish image), but in a sense, which leaves everything open, which corresponds to the first obedience of Abraham. The inner temporality of the religion of Israel makes wholly impossible the absolutizing of one temporal aspect.

Everything temporally alive "develops" in some way: it moves from implicit to explicit. Let us take a few examples that come to mind: the "Ten Words" of commandment formulate on the one hand a single idea of the living God which clearly transcends the "religion of the fathers"; on the other hand they sum up the ethical statute of the twelve tribes by which these tribes, giving up their individual statutes, subject themselves in a binding way. But the decalogue, which represents a transparent end-point, is in its turn transcended in the synthesis of Deuteronomy: there it is written that the people at Horeb perceived nothing besides the "Ten Words"; filled with fear, they sent Moses ahead to receive the further instructions of Yahweh, which they would then obey. The decisive thing that Moses heard and gave to the people at the end of his life as a testament, is the *Shema*: the command to love back with every human power the God who choose then from his groundless love; this would then quite correctly be conceived as the quintessence and synthesis of the "Ten Words" and all the other directives of God. But once again the great prophets transcend this deuteronomic conception when they throw the images of Israel's origin into the future and make the fulfillability of the Old Covenant as a whole dependent on a definitive saving action of God which will judge, purify, and sanctify Israel and embody God's word in its heart.

A being living in time is not only in "development," but is also moving continually closer to end-points where something is completely fulfilled and then must lose something of its gestalt in order to make room for further development. The blossoms must fall if the fruit is going to ripen. Israel's history is full of such "dead-end streets" at the end of which a gestalt was usually formed which, in its perfection as image (figure, type), cannot go any further in time.

Another couple of examples: the original theocracy, as classically expressed in the decree of Gideon (Jud 8:23), is no longer tenable at a certain point in time (the Philistine wars) and, under the influence of unclear ideological struggles (many early and late voices are all mixed together in 1 Sam 8), turns into a monarchy which, after a rather catastrophic history simply cannot be justified and vindicated just by the fact that, according to the Books of Chronicles, an earthly king "sits on the throne of Yahweh" (1 Chron 28:5; 29:23; 2 Chron 9:8; 13:8).

One can also ask when this people consisting of twelve tribes, this amphictyony or confederation, really came into existence as the true partner of the covenant agreement with God. Certainly not at Sinai. And by the time it is raised to a theological concept, at the time when Deuteronomy and Joshua are written, it had long since ceased to be historical reality. It lives on like a ghost in the War Scroll of Qumran, and Jesus' choice of the twelve as judges of the tribes of Israel is a historical reflex back to it.

The precise point where the spheres of God and of the people come together in the covenant is a highly sensitive, explosive place. Moses stands there as mediator: with God's words he comes down to the people; with the people's concerns he climbs up to God. Prophets will carry on above all the first part of this role; but the more visible it becomes how little the covenant is observed and realized the more the mediator also turns into one who makes expiation, into God's whipping boy who must vicariously carry the people's guilt. So it was already with Hosea, with the Moses of Deuteronomy, Isaiah with his "children," Jeremiah and Ezekiel, and at the end of the series, the "servant of God" of the anonymous author from the exilic period who put the final stamp on the full idea which had slowly unfolded through the centuries. And never was an end and a breaking-off any more abrupt than here: from the Exile to Jesus the line is not continued, even if, here and there, a weak echo of the tremendous event might be detected.

We know what questionable things are associated with ritualism, with the ark, tent, and temple. The idea behind all this is near at hand and so far from being dispensable that even after the exile, when the presence of the glory of God in the new temple seemed unsure and became more and more questionable, the sacrificial cult—even the bloody cult—does not stop in order to be handed over so to speak as unblemished "figure" at the threshold of the New Testament: "Without the shedding of blood there is no forgiveness of sins" (Heb 9:22). There was no expectation in Israel of a gradual spiritualizing of worship which was moving toward the incarnation of God where a questionable temple of stone was to be replaced by an unmistakeable temple, Spirit-filled but resting on the bodiliness of Jesus—the church.

In the time after the exile, everything, even the best and most necessary, becomes problematic; it has to demonstrate its inner fragility, the fact that it is just-a-figure. The touching attempt of Judaism from then to continue living the previously so scandalously broken covenant by means of doubled zeal in the painfully exact observance of the Law shatters upon the silence of the divine partner. concerning whom one literally does not know whether he is still cooperating or not. And still the figure of "perfect obedience to God's directive" was needed.

What is to be said of "wisdom" which, after dubious political beginnings in the time of Solomon, acquires some depth and within the Bible turns into an area of "connecting points": first to the Egyptian and ancient oriental cultures, and then to hellenism? Its figure was not dispensable, as is shown by the broad stratum of wisdom thinking which permeates the whole New Testament; it even becomes somehow the basis for the proclaimability of the gospel to the whole world. But it remains questionable in itself and (in a temporal-historical religion like the Old Testament) practically a foreign body, as Alexandrian Judaism shows with Philo who was unable to achieve an inner transposition of the religion of Yahweh into Greek philosophy.

In Daniel apocalyptic lightning bolts had pierced through the dark sky and pointed out the gestalt of the preexistent Son of man to whom God entrusts judgment. It is very problematic when a whole apocalyptic literature takes these lightning bolts under its sway, climbs onto the very "places" reserved for God, and establishes a previously unheard-of traffic between heaven and earth: and surely one has to ask whether, without this dimension, the New Testament event would have had enough conceptual materials to express itself.

Everywhere are either temporally discontinuous or inwardly limited figures which—and this is really the decisive point—even by projecting into the future cannot be brought together as a unified picture.

Certainly the human need for integration cannot but make the attempt to line up the great symbols beside each other, to superimpose them on each other to some extent. Indeed, New Testament exegetes search with sparrow-hawk eyes after the traces of such combinations in the late Jewish period before Christ. The results are minimal. If, for example, a certain atoning function is attributed to the martyr, no one thought of equating a martyr with Isaiah's servant of God. The Davidic Messiah, Daniel's Son of man, the promised prophet equal to Moses (Dt 18:18), the perfect high priest, the servant of God, the temple itself, the Passover lamb, the scapegoat and all that sacrifice was—of all these things no one thing quite covers any other. Precisely the time-conditionedness of each gestalt worked against its inner opening to and communication with the others: *Tout est figure.*

And behind all the individual figures there remained the riddle of their origins: the open question between Abraham and Moses; the one-sided promise of God to Abraham who must respond to this with total faith, and the, in some measure, necessarily two-sided covenant with the people; for a powerful king who makes a covenant with a vassal, no matter how much he acts out of royal favor, there still remains a mutual obligation. Yes, the more favorably the powerful king acts, the more he rightly expects a return from the vassal. Faith and Law stand—as Paul will proclaim almost too sharply—in a barely dissolvable tension.

The more deeply one thinks about the unsolvable problems toward which the Old Testament leads, the more one gets taken up with both their theological urgency and their insolubility, all the more wonderful does their solution appear in the New Covenant. For here alone the Old Covenant has its unity; it cannot find this in itself. But in what way and under what conditions can Jesus Christ create the unity of the Old Covenant?

36 · Jesus—the Unifying Goal of the Old Covenant

The evangelists provide the key—each in his own way—by attesting that the synthesis achieved by Jesus dawned on them only after Easter, and because of Easter. This clearly means that Jesus did not spend his earthly life reconciling the contents of the honorific titles of the Old Testament with each other, and that he presumably did not even attribute them to himself. He lived and fulfilled the will of the Father unto the end: the titles and their substance fell to him one and all like pieces of booty. He fulfilled his mission in a place which afterward proved to be precisely that place towards which—in a way that did not lend itself to construed—all the figures of the Old Testament converged. But this place could not possibly be found on the level of the figures, for the figures contradicted each other (on their own level) sometimes diametrically. Only because Jesus transcends the figures and persists in a royal freedom in their regard, they fall to him as if by-the-way—and yet centrally, since they could belong to no one but him.

The transcendence of his event is shown in the fact that in his historical existence he effects a *breakthrough* which immediately di-

vides into a breakthrough upward—toward God—and downward—
toward death and hell. To the extent that he is *Verbum-Caro*, God and
human, he is at the same time the covenant realized and the resolution of the riddle of tension between Abraham and Moses: with his
whole human "achievement" he is the Word of the Father returning
to God, and this human achievement is precisely the "full faith," the
pure obedience. From this standpoint the double breakthrough becomes understandable:

Upwards the picture of God is enhanced in such a way that God is
seen not only as freely choosing love in relation to Israel and eschologically in relation to the whole of humanity and the world, but much
more, that God is love in himself, namely absolute, that is, triune
love, which has no need of human beings in order to possess an object
of love. For if one did take this idea seriously (that God had this need),
the human being would undeniably acquire power over this God who
needed him; and this road would lead relentlessly either to Hegel
(because then the human being sees to the depths of God: God really
becomes God only through the necessary unfolding of his creative
possibilities, through the creation of his counterpart, through whose
release and return home again he himself first experiences who he is
as God and what he is capable of as God), or it would lead to the
homme révolté at which one almost arrives with Job and which has
become for many moderns a shibboleth of authentic humanity itself,
because the freedom of human beings is released to them for the
purpose of making known the weakness of God and of exploring in
this perverse way "the depths of God" (1 Cor 2:10) or also "the deep
things of Satan" (Rev 2:24). Only the identity of freedom (of choice)
and love in God himself, only the mystery of the Trinity which God
opens to humanity in the disclosure of the New and eternal Covenant
in Christ supersedes definitively and insurpassably the self-revelation
of God in the Old Testament; this *mysterium* is *id quo majus cogitari
non potest*, but it is revealed not as "doctrine" but as active self-
manifestation, since God loved the world so much "that he gave his
only Son, that whoever believes in him should not perish but have
eternal life" (Jn 3:16).

In this thesis the opposite abyss is also open: the possible ruin of
the creature endowed with freedom and the self-giving (giving-up-
for-lost) of the Son by the Father in order, downwards, to retrieve the
person lost in death and hell. This bursting of the gates of hell did not
by rights exist in the Old Testament; the covenant partner of God is
the mortal human being, and the realm of the covenant is mortal life.
All apocalyptic or moralizing anticipation must in fact "wait" (Heb
11:39–40) for the *Descensus Christi*, in order to be realized in rising
with him in the Easter event (Mt 27:53).

The new foundation of Christ, his church, is a communication to human beings of the divine *pneuma* which is the place, actuation, and attestation of the love between Father and Son. Henceforth, the church consciously and the unbelieving world unconsciously exist within the trinitarian love which here has proven to be the ultimate, the *eschaton*. The result is that this love, in opposition to itself—in the "hell" of lost human freedom—was able to be itself, as the perfect obedience of the love of the Son, even in the realm of death.

There is therefore in the New Testament one, single, overall truth, one single dogma which in its center is christological, but in its immediate implications is trinitarian as well as soteriological, and indeed is soteriological (*descensus* and resurrection) *as* trinitarian. The Christ-event thereby fulfills not only all figures of the Old Covenant, but also is—as the apocalypse of the ultimate mystery of God— *always far ahead* of every possible world revolution and all "figurations" that could still come to the surface in them, which is why Christianity has nothing to fear from any evolutionism.

This single dogma has once and for all unrolled the absolute horizon for all the partial views which the Old Testament had opened; for faith (Abraham), for good works (Moses, who gave away his goods to the poor), for knowledge (the Book of Wisdom), and for prophecy (the prophets): all of that, on this Old as well as the New Testament level, is eschatologically "stopped," set off course (1 Cor 13:1–3, 8–10), in view of the love of God which never ends. Inasmuch as this love was revealed in its self-proclamation in Jesus Christ, every surpassing of this love by gnosis is excluded. This particular reality will never be changed into a "universally valid principle." But even though the *id quo majus cogitari non potest* was really revealed in the fact Jesus Christ, all revelational positivism on the other hand is also excluded; so that Paul was right in using a dialectical formula, "To know the love of Christ which surpasses knowledge" (Eph 3:19); as was Anselm in seconding him no less dialectically: *rationabiliter comprehendit incomprehensible esse.*

37 · Jesus' Obedience as the Consummation of Old Testament Faith

In its center the Christ-event, as superabundant fulfillment of the Old Testament covenant-event, is even less a doctrine than the covenant. It is the absolute saving act of God, the miracle of the infallible and yet free covenant agreement between God and humanity which, before all verbalization by the church, in the sovereign disposition of God's deeds and laws, is something set forth once and for all; God's word no longer on lips, no longer as proclaimed mandate which promises or judges or blesses, but Word in flesh, in the realization of the spiritual and psychological, of what is thought and intended—right down to the fingernails, down to the heart opened and poured out. However important may be what is said before and after the cross, or about its looking toward the event or reflecting on it, compared with the reality, with the event itself, it is of secondary importance. An endless number of things can be said about this, but all spoken words taken together never equal the accomplished Word, let alone replace, supersede, or get beyond it.

The event is described more clearly than in words by those deeds which have been done as a result of or in anticipation of the cross: the fundamental deeds of the Old Covenant which head toward the cross, and the deeds of the saints in the church permitted and loosed by the cross. The deeds of the Old Covenant which are illuminating here contain something in anticipation of the incarnation of the Word of God: they take place where a human being under God's mandate places his existence at God's disposition (thus becomes obedient to the point of flesh and blood) so that the Word can take place in the space provided. Let us take the clearest case, because it is the highest as well, the attitude of the servant of God: "That I may know how to sustain with a word him that is weary, the Lord has awakened a word. . . . Morning by morning he wakens my ear to hear as those who are taught . . . but I was not rebellious, I turned not backward, I gave my back to the smiters, and my cheeks to those who pulled out the beard; I hid not my face from shame and spitting" (Is 50:4–6). The total attitude toward God of letting-things-happen of themselves becomes the total attitude toward human beings letting-things-happen; the nonresistance is the same in both cases (because it is complete), and in the identity of this attitude the saving will of God can be incarnated. It is not only the hearing of a limited word of God, to a certain degree of acceptance, of understanding, of transmission; it is rather the entire existence as ear, the entry of the whole loving will of the Lord of the covenant into the whole existence of the covenant people made really present in the prophet through beating, pulling out the beard, shame and spitting. In this nonresistance, in this obedience and only in it, what cannot be united thus comes definitively together: eternal love and temporal hate, eternal fidelity and temporal nonfidelity, God and the human being. In this nonresistance, in this obedience and only in it, the two paths cross: the path of God to the sinful human being and the path of the sinful human being to God. These crossing paths are hostile to each other unto death; but that they should even meet requires a wholly real "battlefield" where the conflict can be decided. For as real as the institution of the covenant by God and his offer of salvation to men and women are, just as real is their refusal to dwell in this sphere of grace; and human beings know this for they have had to get exact knowledge of the reality of the two paths and affirm this knowledge: life and death, blessing and curse (Lev 26; Dt 28). Sin does not get simply forgotten and become nonexistent. It is a fact of enormously real import in that space opened by God's covenant grace where humanity can and should live. The attitude of the servant of God is then the battlefield: existence as the making present of God's word and simultaneously of all words against God, and such an existence is of course essentially death. Note that only in this place and from it is the covenant definitively concluded, and that therefore only in this place as well has the unity of love of God and love of neighbor (human beings) actually taken place.

All the acts of obedience of the Old Covenant come together in the servant of God: from the sacrifice of Isaac on Mount Moriah, to the fully vicarious obedience of Moses in Deuteronomy, to the total degradation of the aged David in the face of the death of his rebellious son ("Would I had died instead of you!" 2 Sam 18:33), to all the expropriations of prophetic existence for the becoming human of the Word, the marriage of Hosea with the prostitute, the prohibition of marriage imposed on Jeremiah, the forbidding of Ezekiel to mourn his beloved deceased wife, etc. Consequently, it is an existence which is not lived according to human laws and determinations, but which has become the showplace of inner divine life. "It is nothing less than if the prophet . . . were separated in a special way from himself, from his personal feelings of inclination and disinclination, and incorporated into the pathos of God himself, nothing less than if not only the knowledge of historical plans but also the passions of the divine heart were transferred to him: anger, love, concern, disgust, and even perplexity." "It can be asked whether this entrance of the Word into the bodily existence of the prophet will not already come close to what John the Evangelist means by the incarnation of the Logos" (G. von Rad).

The situation of perfect obedience (as perfect nonresistance) is concretely that of the doubly borne wrath because of the doubly perfect solidarity. So Moses is in perfect solidarity with the sinful people which he represents before God when he attempts to interrupt God's wrath (Exod 32:11–22). He is just as much in solidarity with God in whose anger he breaks the tablets of the covenant before the people (Exod 32:19–20). And should a prophet, who once has given himself to be the conductor wire, want to escape its high tension, he is in extreme danger of being inwardly consumed by it (Jer 20:7–9). Only in giving himself up for dead can he live. That is the Old Testament path towards the Christ-event. A path with clear footprints which all head in the same direction. A path made up of individually readable figures which point to that "no form" (Is 53:2) which sums them all, since, in comparison with this "super-figure," the prophetic figures are all only signs and pointers and not themselves "the picture" itself.

It is the same way with the "pictures" of the saints of the church which derive from the super-figure of the cross and are readable only in its light. They too stand constantly, in one way or another, in the burning point of the covenant, in the place where the paths between God and humans meet and cut across one another, and they can do this in any case only in that unconditioned obedience which in the course of church history has received different names and yet always remained the same: *apatheia, Gelassenheit, indiferencia.* It is always the point of being in fundamental agreement with the embodiment of all God's will and therefore a place of death (of the death of Jesus naturally: 2 Cor 4:10), whether this death is now expressed as "dark night" (John of the Cross), as "dying to be able not to die" (Teresa of Avila), as readiness to let oneself be shared in any way (the Little Flower), as love without reason (Eckhart), or in various other ways. Certainly an elementary love of neighbor will always grow from this attitude, but the important thing is that it does not set the standards for itself, that the fruitfulness of the life given to God for the world and for humanity is, in the end, controlled by God alone.

The paths toward the cross in the Old Covenant and from the cross in the New Covenant point from both sides toward the place where the whole covenant, the new and eternal covenant, is made and sealed. This is the place where God effects the wondrous, so that from both sides, that of the God of grace and fidelity and that of the human being of sin and infidelity, nothing remains to be accomplished. It is the place where every no to God's offered love is gathered, is received and borne as "blow" and "beard-plucking" and "curse" and "spitting," as far as the perfect yes, because the yes to God (and to the will of God which will save the world) bears all that and makes it into an expression of this yes in the night without vision and formlessness of God-forsakenness, and because this perfect yes to God actually incarnates the perfect yes of God to the world: in this night and nowhere else. In this night everything is wordless and becomes, the deeper it sinks into absolute death, ever more wordless; the Word made flesh becomes a soundless Word, growing ever more deeply silent into the abyss of death. It is unword, because the dialogue with the Father stops, after which no dialogue with sinners is any longer possible. It is also unword because no spoken and understandable word can shine down into the shafts of this abandonment. Word is communication, and the conclusion of the covenant in the night is the breakdown of all communication—in the identity of obedience which indifferently contains the whole salvific will of God and the whole sin of the world and brings it to expression.

But if there can be absolutely no adequate word about this event (the Word itself is in the process of sinking and dying and ends in a great inarticulate scream), if then everything which, backward (to the Old Covenant) and forward (to the church), is anyhow given as an expression of the wordless event, is absolutely secondary to and far behind the event itself, then from the event springs right away two truths which make it real and possible and without which it would have to collapse and be extinguished. One of these is the difference between the ordering God, the Father, and the One descending into the infinite, obeying, indifferent, Not-Disposing but Disposed Of. And the other difference is that between the violent human being, from whose ranks no one can be separated, not even a prophet or a saint, and the all-pure who, in order to bear all things for everyone, must be God himself, but God the Son.

Both these differences springing out of the identity of the cross attain their confirmation in the resurrection of Christ. That Christ, coming from the deepest night, sets vitally experienced in the life of God—seen, heard, touched—is God's verification of what happened in the silence of death (ultimately in the absolute wordlessness of Holy Saturday, of the descent into hell).

38 · Jesus—The Fulfillment of the Hopes of Israel

The Christ-event is understood as the fulfillment of "all the promises of God" (2 Cor 7:19; Heb 7:1–2). This is understood in a concrete way because all the promises and all faith in them, from the very beginning, had been aimed at resurrection from the dead.

Abraham was the first to believe the promise. He believed in a God "who brings the dead back to life and calls into being what does not exist" (Rom 4:17). By so doing he set up and unleashed a dynamic process that was to go far beyond the symbolic confirmation of his act of faith: he received the son of promise although "his body was past fatherhood—he was about a hundred years old—and Sarah too old to become a mother" (Rom 4:19).

This faith in a God who can raise the dead resounds like a general bass tone beneath all the single promises to Israel. Hence the oldest Christian credal statement (which materially is not to be justified but is formally exact): "Christ died for our sins, in accordance with the

Scriptures; . . . he was buried; and . . . was raised to life on the third day, in accordance with the Scriptures" (1 Cor 15:3f). The whole faith of Israel is a single assault upon the frontier of death, with a dynamic that, in contrast to all other peoples, approached death not as some posited power to be neutralized by some religious means or another (despite the apparent and tentative resignation of the Old Testament) but as a power that had to be broken under all circumstances.

A test of this may be designed from present-day Jewish thought; and one will acknowledge how relevant this mediating second circle—the transcendance-dynamic of the Old and New Covenant—is for world-history as a whole. The presupposition is the mysterious affinity of the two entities "law" and "death" (cf. Romans 7). Both barriers fall or relativize one another together.

Paul puts Abraham's faith before the law that "came after," and was thus able to attribute to him a longing for a goal that lay on the other side of the law and of death. But even this faith too had to be superseded and deposed, for its object is boundless, as the Letter to the Hebrews expounds, using the analogy of the superiority of Melchizedek, the immortal "king of peace" who is "like the Son of God" (Heb 7:3). Israel will constantly find itself refusing to pay tithes to this mysterious king. It will try to follow three roads of escape from the dreaded gates of death and of the underworld:

1. The platonic road leading straight from the sphere of law and death into the spiritual sphere, whether in its contemplative or ethical form. This was the road followed by Josephus and Philo of Alexandria, as it is followed by idealist-liberal Jews today (Cohen and Brunschweig). But this represents a digression into the general, as we find, say, in Hegel the anti-Semite. Death is regarded as a necessary moment in the dialectic of becoming; and it is folly for the finite individual to run against it. It becomes serious in the other two schemes.

2. Israel owed its origin to the "mighty acts of God," in which, however, it was an active and fighting participant. The prophets projected the imagery of the origin (Exodus) materially into the future, at the same time making the people feel urgently their coresponsibility for the advent of the eschatological kingdom—lying temporally in the future.

The apocalyptic writers see God (in the form of his messiahs and angel hosts) fighting with Israel in their breakthrough battle against the nations. The plan of battle, which redeems Israel from all fallenness, subservience, and self-alienation is meticulously developed in the Qumran writings as "the battle of the sons of light against the sons of darkness."

Modern Marxism lives from this prophetic-apocalyptic pathos of the breakthrough from oppression into freedom. (At the end of its development would have to be placed Nikolai Federov's "philosophy of common work" [1906]: the resurrection of already dead generations by means of all the earth's elemental and technical forces so that they can enter into the condition of the redeemed world.) This refers to the zealot and Zionist bringing about of the kingdom, which is to come for Israel, but also through Israel.

3. Yet perhaps it is unnecessary for material imagery, which in the end must always be finite and regular, to be projected into the future by the dynamism of prophetic, hopeful faith. Perhaps all imagery, like the law, is only something that has "slipped in between": a transient and surpassible projection of the empty formal drive forward which itself creates the framework in order to prove itself the stronger when it is discarded.

It occurs, to begin with, (a) in the *Lebensphilosophie* developed by the early Bergson and in detail by Simmel; (b) in the instinct philosophy of Freud and all his successors down to Marcuse, in open contradiction of Paul's correlation of *epithymia* (libido) with "sin" and "death," constantly aggravated and found guilty by the law; (c) in Ernst Bloch's philosophy of hope in which the absolute drive forward rejects the principle of legal rule from above (God). This last idea is rooted in Job's rejection of the injustice of a God who lays upon life more of a burden of suffering than it deserves, and who appeals from this God to a transdivine court. Kafka's indictment of the law bears an affinity to this, as does the destruction of all that has been and is, in favor of a reality that is yet to be inaugurated (G. Landauer: "There is nothing at all; we still have to make everything"): perennializing apocalyptic.

The presence and actuality of this unique, irrepressible drive forward, which stems from the biblical sphere and deflects any appeasement in the Christ-event, becomes a lasting proof of the actuality of Jesus' claim to be the meaningful culmination of this dynamic.

It is thus logical, and forms part of the proof of the validity of this claim, that Christians who contest the eschatological aspect of Jesus' claim, fall victim to the biblical dynamic that precedes it. For them, Jesus becomes a political theologian who at least tolerates zealots among his disciples, and by his sympathy with the people is forced to do all that is humanly possible in his attempt to fulfill his mission— the coming of the kingdom of God upon earth.

In reality, however, to be the meaningful culmination of this dynamic and to know himself as such implies that on Jesus' road toward his death (which is also the end of the world) lay an absolute suffering, for in his petition to God, "Thy kingdom come" must have been the ultimate in self-offering: let it come through my whole existence and substance, through my being used right to the last drop of sweat and blood. And if it is true that the kingdom has fundamentally been reached and has come through Jesus' victory over death and his resurrection, then it has not by any means come by Jesus' sheer waiting patiently for some act to be accomplished by God alone, but by an equally impatient pressing forward of total effort, which then coincides with being totally used and consumed as well. "I have come to bring fire upon earth. . . . There is a baptism I must still receive, and how great is my distress till it is over!" (Lk 12:49f). "Learn that today and tomorrow I cast out devils and on the third day attain my end. But for today and tomorrow and the next day I must go on" (Lk 12:32f).

And if the resurrection is not the self-actuation of the one who died (for the living God, Father and Spirit, raise him), it is still his innermost act and self-offering that go into the resurrection as the substance which alone is worthy of being raised to share the eternal life of God: "He has entered the sanctuary once and for all, taking with him . . . his own blood" (Heb 9:12).

The difficulty of being a Christian, both in the sense of believing in Jesus and in following him, is this: the passionateness of the Jewish drive forward has to be taken over by the Christian, and then fulfilled as Christ fulfilled it. The whole utopian urge toward the advent of the kingdom of God—"on earth as it is in heaven"—must, therefore, be carried until it includes the laying down of one's life (for until we have committed ourselves unto death, we have not yet wholly given ourselves); but giving one's life to be taken over by God constitutes the ultimate renunciation of self-determination in favor of being at God's disposition, and such sacrifice raises the fulfillment of the claim to a dimension that lies beyond life and death.

Does this mean that all that is visible eludes the Christian, and that his or her creative endeavors for the future of this world are to no avail? To a purely immanent way of thinking it appears so, for then Christianity would not be a meaningful culmination but the abrupt cessation of movement, a betrayal of the earth.

But Jewish thought nevertheless, as prophetic and apocalyptic, goes far beyond mere immanence; it is essentially utopian. As a material projection and as formal dynamism this utopia comes up empty. It is only the preindication of the goal attained, the resurrection of Jesus, that provides forward-looking hope with a real basis. It is a "pledge" or "downpayment," as Paul puts it. Christianity is no less utopian than Judaism, but it is factually utopian.

Jesus, the Proof of the Triune Love of God for the World

39 · The New Image of God and the New Image of the Human

On the biblical stage, the world-historical battle about the meaning of life and of history is fought to the right and the left of the cross. At the same time, however, the object of strife has become the whole, corresponding to Jesus' original claim to be the way, the truth, and the life in relation to everything.

Israel remains caught in the paradox of being but one nation which, as a chosen people, was supposed to have received an eschatological redemptive significance for all nations. This paradox, not resolvable by proselytism, is at times endured by transferring its apocalyptic restlessness to the world.

The gospel, on the other hand, by its very nature, moves beyond the biblical sphere and into the pagan *oikoumenē* (inhabited world). Its implicit claim that it had received and was able to proclaim all truth is soon organically transformed into the demonstrations of the apologists as to how the scattered seeds/*Logoi* of the religions and philosophies are to be assimilated by the superior eschatological synthesis of Christ.

The final task, therefore, is the demonstration of how the claim made by Christ presents a challenge to every world view—religious or secular—a challenge to be measured against this claim; and of which criteria are applicable in assessing the conflicting claims on both sides. The careful treatment of this theme would require a book. Only a few pointers can be given here. The human being, individually and socially, is centrally affected by the resurrection of Christ from the dead. For it completely revalues the whole of individual human life and, in virtue of the end of history having being reached in the death of Jesus, the history of humanity as well. This takes place, however, only because in the Christ-event God, as Father, appears in his Son and in the communication of the Holy Spirit, so that an equally new image of God emerges from which we must take our departure if the image of human being conditioned by it is going to show forth its full import.

The Christian image of God is determined by the pauline and johannine eschatological statements which interpret the Christ-event theologically, and refer back to the great Old Testament election texts (e.g., Hos 11:8ff; Jer 31:20f; Deut 6 and 7): "God loved the world so much. . . . God is love." In view of the state of this world no religion other than Christianity could responsibly make such a statement. God could, at best, be the peace that lies beyond our deadly dissensions, the "nothingness" beyond our intolerable, meaningless existence, the world of archetypes above the alienated copies. He can at best bend with compassion and grace over suffering creatures; but how, as creator, can he be responsible for all their agony?

Two answers are insufficient here. First, instruction, even if it did teach the skill of overcoming suffering for oneself; for there remains the majority of those who do not know, or are unable to walk along, these secret paths. The second insufficient answer is the idea of a power of God to which is imputed the possibility of preserving the creature whom he has liberated, by means of a surplus of grace, from falling away from God, from guilt and its consequent disaster. Such a God of power—even if his power were that of grace—would never have dared, or been able, to be fully serious about giving the gift of freedom to his creature. The father did not withhold what was asked from the younger son who wants to get his inheritance in advance so that he could go to a foreign land. Is it still possible for God himself to lose his game of creation when the liberated creature gets lost? Only a very mysterious possibility, for which we do possess a certain human preunderstanding, but whose final mystery we can have given us only in the gratitude of faith; namely the way of a genuine sharing in the suffering, and for that reason a vicarious suffering, silent accompaniment into complete desolation. In the parable of the Prodigal Son one figure is absent: the narrator himself—Jesus. The father not only waits for the return, spontaneous or constrained by need, of the Prodigal, but sends his love in the form of his son into his desolation. He allows his son to identify himself with his lost brother. And actually by this very power of identifying himself—without keeping a respectable distance—with his complete opposite, God the Father recognizes the "equality of being," the divinity of the one he has sent as his redeeming Word into the world.

He recognizes that this Word, become man, has been able to do what the Father intended when he generated and uttered this Word: to make himself audible and intelligible to anyone who does not want to hear any more about God. In other words, that Jesus could become the brother of all the very least and of the lost, revealed first by deed more than by word; that God, as all-powerful, is love, and, as love, is all-powerful; that he is this intrinsically, in the mystery of his trinity, which alone can explain the total opposition—between being with God and being abandoned by God—within God himself.

This mystery can be revealed in its full reality as accompanying the sinner only *sub contrario*, in hiddenness, because otherwise it would not have been revealed as reality. But because God (and God is only God as eternal and living) reveals himself therein as love, he cannot have become love first only on the basis of the release of the creature; he has no need of the world and its process in order to become himself, but manifests himself precisely in the cross of Christ, in his abandonment by God and descent into hell, as the one he always was: eternal love.

God is so much, as three-in-one, eternal love, that within his life even temporal death and the hellish desolation of the creature, taken over out of love, can become transmuted into an expression of love. (We might add that the necessary hiddenness of a vicarious accompanying into lostness also results in a certain hiddenness of the resurrection in the eyes of the world: an event involving divine cosuffering which can be accepted only by an act of receptive faith could not become a neutral datum of world-historical public opinion.)

The eschatological emphasis of the Christian image of God consists in the fact that God is not immanent in everything mundane and historical in a general philosophical sense, merely because he (incommensurable with the world) is the one who is transcendent—the one with no opposite (*Non-Aliud*), wholly other than all other beings who all have their opposites—but because he realizes this relationship in a way that the world cannot discover or guess, and which is completely free; and this manifests him as the God who in himself is absolute love (and hence trinity). This love cannot be reconstructed by any kind of gnosis: everything that we can "understand" about it places us ever again before "the love of Christ, which is beyond all knowledge" (Eph 3:19).

Christianity's image of the human is thus sketched: the human being has been endowed by God with genuine freedom and self-responsibility for a work that is both himself and the world to be formed in a humanly worthy way; both his own human work and (creative) cooperation in the work of God the creator.

On the one hand, the human being is set off from any embrace of a naturalistically conceived immanent, or even transcendent, "providence," which would relate his actions and decisions far beyond him to a goal unknown to him. Here we find limits set to all optimism concerning a court of appeal that overrides either developmentally or dialectically upon human freedoms.

There can be laws of the species which permit certain harmful tendencies to be balanced, yet which create more or less beneficial preconditions, although never determining an ultimate personal decision. We cannot rely on technical progress, for the increased power this puts in our hands can be used both for good and for ill. Concentrations of power, moreover, unleash demonic temptations to misuse them.

Just as little can the dialogical principle and the hoped-for mediations between personal freedoms be an escape from the ongoing loneliness of personal decision. Dialogue between individuals always must be begun from the beginning again, returning to the same basic questions and fundamental options. Freedom as such is not perfectible; indeed all the educational aids to right choice may indeed be useful, but they cannot compel; all sociological structures remain ambivalent: the proved injustice of one set of structures is no proof that another, which might redress this specific injustice, will not bring with it new and perhaps greater injustices. If a system of government needs several hundred prisons with millions of inmates in order to keep itself going, it will hardly commend itself as a road to freedom.

Nothing can be relied upon except humans themselves and their freedom. But with this they would truly be lost if it were that solitary absolute out of which they could make themselves from their own nothingness into "God" as well as "the devil." Even this concept of freedom is a sign of lostness and dislocation.

Human freedom gets a location from God's freedom in Jesus Christ to accompany humanity bearing as well all the consequences of its lostness. Externally this looks like mere "sharing our common humanity"—and it is that too—but it is essentially more, because this sharing our common humanity proves itself to be effective in the end in virtue of its being God-with-us. It assists us precisely at that point where mere sharing our common humanity no longer helps: in the loneliness of death, of abandonment by God, of the fall into ultimate desolation.

Jesus' companionship is not primarily earthly and humanity-sharing in order to become eucharistic in its final phase, but is eucharistic from the very start: on the cross, in the God-forsakenness of his broken body and shed blood put at the disposal of his fellow humans.

Because of this ultimate point, Christian companionship of one's sisters and brothers must carefully assess every provisional and earthly social configuration by the principles of social justice (explicitly adopting the ethical demands of the Old Testament), but it is constantly inclined to go beyond the criteria of utility and success, and to accompany the sister or brother into the darkness of earthly meaninglessness.

Genuine Christian charity always preferred to take these paths: to tend the dying, the helpless, the lepers, the mentally defective. Again, Christian human compassion does not wish to begin there, nor should it, thus allowing itself to be more and more suppressed by increasing non-Christian welfare institutions. It begins, rather, in the midst of common, human social concerns, but must be distinguished by the fact that it—from its foreknowledge of God's ultimate way with humans—goes along tranquilly and continues in places where others quit.

The motive that makes the Christian go further is the knowledge that what is humanly meaningless and utterly negative has succeeded, through the companionship of God in Christ, in transforming the loneliness of death and of broken dialogue between God and humans into a situation of companionship in suffering, and in turning merely passive resignation into an expression of the sublimest action of self-surrender to God.

This is something unique in the whole realm of human thought and behavior, for it presupposes precisely faith in the action of the triune God in the cross and resurrection of Christ. The fulfilling expansion of the image of the human in Christianity is correlative with the completed fulfilling expansion of the image of God in the Trinity and in christology.

One should be aware here of taking seriously Nietzsche's reproach that Christianity is a religion of the weak which turns negative into positive values. It is instead the religion of those who understand positively even those things which all others see as negative. One should therefore also beware of giving too much weight to Bonhoeffer's idea that Christianity ought not to address human beings principally in terms of their weak limit situations, but in the concentrated strength of their existence. For it will reach the heart of the strong ones in its midst only if simultaneously it permits them a glance at the periphery of existence, so that freely and positively they are able to face every situation—terror, sickness, weakness, loneliness, and spiritual darkness.

Today these limit-situations come into collective consciousness, hence the panic-flight into anarchy and into the dreamland of drugs, into artificial spirituality with its compulsive devaluation of personal freedom, its silencing of death, its destruction of childhood where the immature person is dependent upon loving friendship.

Teilhard de Chardin will be right in his opinion that Christianity alone could offer to a world that doubts its capability of building up peace and contentment from its own resources, and is on the brink of foregoing all hope (hence the hysterical talk about hope), a motive for continuing.

40 · The Trinitarian Dimension of the Existence of Jesus

The synoptics show us the existence of the human Jesus predominantly *in actu*, in verbs. Paul and John interpret it predominantly in a retrospective which lifts out the kernel of the event, in nouns. There we see the lived obedience to the Father in the Spirit; here the obedience is expressed in words: Rom 5:19; Phil 2:6–11; Jn 6:38, etc. John, who provides the definitive formulations and emphasizes so strongly the unity between Father and Son, is also the one who speaks most clearly of a mandate of the Father (Jn 10:18; 12:49; 14:31). This mandate encompasses everything. Jesus is not a human being who is found in earthly existence in order, reflecting on himself from that level and asking about the purpose of his existence, to catch sight of God's will and do it. His existence is not *Geworfenheit* (a matter of chance); instead, in his human existence he is the result of a mission (Jn 4:34, etc.) and thus of obedience. The same thing is expressed on the other hand by the statement that God's Word has become flesh (Jn 1:14), or that God has appointed his Son heir of all things for the sake of his suffering death (Heb 1:2; 2:9), or that in the Son of God "all the promises have found their Yes" (2 Cor 1:19). Jesus is thus, as the incarnate mandate of the Father, also the (super-) fulfillment of all Old Testament prophetic existences.

The pauline and johannine statements on this obedience clearly exclude Jesus' fulfilling any will but that of the Father. He obeys neither "his conscience," his "conviction," nor does he as human being follow the will of his own divinity; such statements, even if they were the outcome of theological conclusions, would obscure the principal statements which can be maintained and illuminated only by a trinitarian presupposition: that the One, who now stands before us in Christ as a human being, is doing the will of the Other, and that both wills stand in opposition to each other in a terrifying nakedness at the Garden of Olives: "Not my will, your will." Two remarks here should be made immediately.

The first concerns the role of the Holy Spirit. It is made visible in the descent of the Spirit of mission at the baptism of Jesus, but it is already anticipated by Luke to some extent in his infancy narrative, as in the action and certitude of the twelve-year-old of having to be (*dei*) where the Father is and wants to have him. (The presence and activity of the Spirit at the conception, the visitation, and the presentation in the temple can be understood as making visible the theological *a priori* both of the election of Jesus and of his will to obey.) The

Spirit of mission "drives" Jesus, just as he too will "drive" the Christians as children of God (Rom 8:14). Nowhere is there any mention to the effect that Jesus the human being in his mortal life would somehow breathe the Spirit together with the Father, so that he together with the Father (in a kind of "divine majority") codetermined his mission which would be incorporated in the Spirit. This divine communality in the breathing out of the Spirit is first received by the human Jesus when as man he has "breathed out" his spirit of mission, and when as the exalted One, united again with the Father and receiving from him power over the Spirit (Acts 2:33), he can send and breathe it into the church. As long as he dwells on earth the Spirit hovering over him concretizes for him the Father's will, to do which is his food. And when the Spirit "drives" him toward the hour which will bring him the ultimate point where too much is asked, the Son speaks his innermost Yes to this being driven ("How I am constrained," and at the same time "It makes me anxious": Lk 12:50), which also leads him necessarily forward, "where you do not wish" (Jn 21:18), not only into death but into the realm of opposition to God, into the inner essence of "sin," which he, without setting himself apart from it, is supposed to bear (2 Cor 5:21).

The second point to keep in mind is the Son's being accompanied by the Father which is also expressed precisely in the presence of the Holy Spirit. This accompaniment has, for us, a hardly imaginable intimacy which is expressed in the Son's prayer-life and, moving from this, in his whole existence. Words like the following, "The Son can do nothing of his own accord, but only what he sees the Father doing; for whatever he does, that the Son does likewise. For the Father loves the Son, and shows him all that he himself is doing" (Jn 5:19–20), shed light into the depth of the contemplative prayer of the Son. The word "love" shines here as the innermost ground of complete mutual disclosure. It is without doubt not only opened or believed but also experienced love: love of the Father which, in its self-disclosure in the Son, becomes its answering coactuation or realization, so that, as the next verses show, the Son's actuation of this love in his loving obedience becomes the presence of the Father's authority in the world: the Father "has given all judgment to the Son, that all may honor the Son, even as they honor the Father" (Jn 5:22–23). This fullness of power is raised to the highest power reserved solely to God the creator: the power to raise the dead to life (Rom 4:17; 2 Cor 1:9).

But both aspects, perfect objective obedience and perfect subjective love, have, in the manner in which the divine *pneuma* is bestowed on the Son—as mandate (institution) and as its loving fulfillment—always been one. Being invested with the highest authority, independence, and responsibility joins in Jesus Christ with the absolute self-giving of himself to the loving will of the Father as the Other. And even more, this most profound contemplative and dialogic intimacy in which the Father accompanies the Son is the essential presupposition for the dialogue in the Garden of Olives where the Father as love hides himself and formalizes himself into a purely demanding will. It is the presupposition for the way in which all love in the Son is concentrated into the pure, demanded, asking-too-much obedience, into the all-deciding "test of strength" of the divine love in which the Son becomes the "Servant of God" and thus, in his exaltation, the Lord. In this, also according to Paul, the justification of all the believers and the salvation of the cosmos takes place; in this, according to John, the exalted One on the cross draws all things to himself. The freedom for which "Christ has set us free" (Gal 5:1) was "bought with a great price" (1 Cor 6:20; 7:23) and cannot prescind one moment from this price: "By one man's obedience . . ." (Rom 5:19). The cross is the test-case of love, and the becoming man has, on the whole, no other goal than this test-case; it is the path toward it and as work of obedience (*kenosis*) already has a part in it. The test-case for Jesus is obedience to the complete asking-too-much; for how could a human being "take away the sins of the world"? How could he be "made into sin"? What he cannot do, that for which no human power is sufficient, that burden is laid on him who, in his impotency, has the consciousness of being unable to do it. What he bears is, only as seen by the Father, "according to his strength"; as seen and experienced by him it is "absolutely beyond his strength" (2 Cor 1:8).

41 · The Holy Spirit as "Rule" of the Life of Jesus

It is possible also to contemplate the individual economic pattern of the divine *pneuma*, the way it fits into the total gestalt of Christian revelation. It is, in the overshadowing of Mary, the *pneuma* coming from above which, breathing into her, embodies the Word of God in her. But at another time in the baptism of Christ it is the *pneuma* coming from the Father—whose voice rings out—which "abidingly" inspires the Son to proclaim and do nothing but the living will of the Father. Both times the descending movement of the *pneuma* appears as a determining movement, concretizing definitively from above what is historically already predetermined. Mary as well as the Jesus of the baptism-event are, compared with the *pneuma*, accepting, indifferent; the decisive difference comes to them from the *pneuma*. This has, in the economy of salvation, the tendency to a pattern. One can think back to its preunderstanding in the realm of art: inspiration for the artist is not a vague condition predisposing to all possibilities, but on the contrary that which—within what is materially already prepared but not yet given form—indicates the direction towards the pattern, allowing its shape to dawn, gathering up and setting in motion toward it. And the artist opens, not really passively but with all senses, listening to and obeying the guiding Spirit over him or her and in him or her in order to keep all human powers and prepared materials at its disposition. The example is arbitrary; one could also choose such an example from the realm of the moral or the political, from every realm where something genuinely constructive is to be accomplished. Of course the inspired works of this world, insofar as they make a historical appearance, all remain under the "judgment" of the encompassing world-Spirit which gave them their relative superiority over their own narrow personal horizon; this is recognized in the fact that their understandability is mostly a relative, time-conditioned one and they, as much as they are a valid concretization of the eternally valid for their epoch, can disappear in a later time.

This demonstrates the difference from the *pneuma* which inspires Jesus at his baptism. The incarnational tendency of this *pneuma* is not that of the world-Spirit but that of the will of his divine Father who in the expression of the Holy Spirit is so concretized for the Son that a process of universalizing abstraction is not possible on any level. This will is in the Spirit both absolutely universal and absolutely and definitively concrete, neither subjectively nor objectively surpassable.

The world-Spirit will, even after the appearance of Jesus Christ, continue its work. It does this, because history continues, and thus it can do nothing but try to represent even the *pneuma* of Christ as one of his offspring, perhaps or, say, in categories of the general philosophy of religion. But on a deeper level it remains encompassed by the normativity of the incarnational tendency of the Holy Spirit. This tendency, in the instituting of the pattern of the living, dying, rising Son and of the institution of the church in which Christ lives, demonstrates its unsurpassable determinateness and power to determine. In fact, the inspired character of Christ's pattern is not universalized into the church on the basis of his resurrection in such a way that the concreteness of its nature as pattern dissolves into something merely *pneumatic*; but rather the inspired character of the church of Christ is thereby proved as genuinely Christian, so that it leads the paradox of Christ through all the ages of history: to be simultaneously universal and definitively determined in a patterned (organic) way.

This form of the activity of the divine Spirit points to God's own divine essence by which the Spirit is both God's final freedom and his final determinateness. The Spirit in God is the last to proceed and is thus determined by the relations between Father and Son, by the generation of the Son, by his being generated and related to the Father, and by their mutual unity which breathes forth the Spirit. But it is precisely in this way that the Spirit is the last positive freedom of God which—as opposed to the freedom of the world-Spirit which prescinds from the individual patterns in order to "sublate" them within itself—in its procession from the Father and the Son, never surpasses their special nature whose expression it truly is. The world-Spirit also seems, in the moment of inspiration, to be actually incarnated in the shape of the particular institution with which it is then involved. But in this situation it has a secret proviso which allows it to break free again at the proper time in order to take shape in another institution. The Holy Spirit knows no such proviso because it does not need to abstract in an inner-divine way from the particularity of the Father and the Son in order to be communal with them. Thus, according to the divine economy, it can represent, in a most perfect way, the incarnational tendency of the fatherly or triune will in relation to the Son become man.

The will of the Father which is communicated to the Son in the *pneuma* is, in fact, the eternal trinitarian plan for the reconciliation of the world. In eternity the Son and the Spirit share in this decision just as much as the Father, even if now, during the economic becoming human of the Son, this trinitarian will comes to the Son through the Spirit as the Father's will, as all four gospels clearly testify. It becomes clear, when one reflects on this, that the inspiration of Christ through the Holy Spirit not only brings him unequivocally the will of the Father in economic terms, but also, deep within this, his own trinitarian will. The Father's will which the Spirit ever-now brings to the Son is thus the opposite of something that comes over him from outside and above—whether as duty imposed on him or as an extraneous Dionysian transport. Rather, even in the distance of the economy of salvation, it is something eternally at home. Insofar as Jesus as human being stands before the Father, the will of the divine Father is *bestowed* on him through the Spirit, and he also accepts it in obedience as a gift of the love of the Father. He knows nevertheless in the same inspiration of the Spirit, that he has already said his Yes to this gift in an eternal, by no means merely passive, agreement with that will of the Father. And even if, in the earthly economy, this will of the Father will appear to him more and more as an "imposed," even incomprehensibly imposed institution—up to the struggle in the Garden of Olives—there still remains, right into the depth of this necessary darkening, in virtue of the inspiration of the Spirit which continually breathes between Father and Son, the wordy affirmation painfully wrung from him—"Your will, not mine"—in the depth of the reverberating harmony of the eternal trinitarian consent.

42 · The Holy Spirit
as the Inner-Trinitarian Life of God

The mysteries of the inner-divine processions remain undisclosable to us; no analogy from creation and the economy of salvation can suffice to afford an unbroken statement about the life of the Trinity. Most confusing is the *economy-of-salvation reversal of the relationship between Son and Spirit*. While the Spirit proceeds within the divinity from the Father and the (or through the) Son, the Son becomes man through the Spirit and is guided in his mission by the same Spirit. As the one who, in the self-emptying of his divine form, places himself under the will of the Father, he also allows the Spirit proceeding from the Father and governed by the Father to attain over himself the power of a rule of his Father's will in order to have this Spirit, resting on him in fullness, flow forth from himself at the end of his mission in death and resurrection (and Eucharist): both to the Father ("into thy hands . . . ") and to the church and world ("then he breathed on them . . . "). But in this reversal it becomes clear that the Spirit shares internally in this economic event.

For the Spirit, who assumes the leading role in the incarnation—the Son *allows* himself to be directed—and presents the will of the Father (and with that the trinitarian plan of salvation) to be obeyed—the Son obeys the Father in the Holy Spirit—also gives up an aspect of its divine form: to be the superabundant product of the love between Father and Son. One can rise saying that insofar as the Spirit is this inner-divine product, it represents the archetype of what at the beginning was depicted as the transcending of a perfect human being-for-one-another. For in fact the divine Father is actually the inexhaustible, externally flowing source of the divinity, but yet in such a way that in his paternal act of generation he keeps nothing of the divinity back for himself, nothing that he has not always entrusted to the Son, which is why the Son, as the perfectly responding image of the Father, likewise can keep nothing back for himself that he does not gratefully and willingly offer back to the Father.

Precisely in this mutual lack of holding anything back in their "for-one-another" does the starting point for the procession of the Spirit rest. As seen from the standpoint of the human experience of an unconditioned "for-one-another"—thus in the "image and likeness" of human analogy—mutual love always appears as a more-than-understandable, more-than-calculable reality: something happens to both lovers that transcends the anticipated horizon of their self-giving, which nevertheless is no impersonal fate but is experienced only as a miracle stemming from their personal love. In view of the biblical revelation of the *pneuma*, one could also say that a miracle, like the "personification" of their mutual self-giving, appears as the "gift in person." Looking at it again anthropomorphically, the never-ending surprise that mutual love conceals more in itself than in the lover would have been able to surmise the experience that love is beyond comprehension, even though it is the nature of comprehension to be perfected in the "letting be" of the other, so that what is breathed out by the lovers does not appear again as something strange (a "bottled spirit"), but what is commonly "really meant" by both together, what is "bestowed" on them in their union: both the representation of the form of this mutuality and its testimony. As fruit of this, the Spirit is then as much the manifestation of the innermost "subjectivity" of the encounter of Father and Son as its "objectivity," in relation to which those totally given to one another attain a measure of their love which, because it is something eternally immeasurable, becomes an ever-new incentive for their self-giving.

At the point where, in the economy of salvation, the loving readiness of the Son toward the Father empties itself out in obedience (which, however, is not an estrangement of this loving readiness but only its metamorphosis into a soteriological form), that is the place where the aspect of the subjectivity of the Spirit must also coactuate a corresponding hiddenness within its objective aspect, so that the economic obedience will be possible in the first place. This explains the initiative of the Spirit which goes before the Son: it is through this that the authority must be fashioned in relation to which obedience can be performed: already in the act of becoming man in which the Son allows himself to be directed, as in the incarnate One who now stands over against the Father in his representation or objectification through the Spirit. This representation of the Father through his Spirit, proceeding from him but primarily presenting him objectively, is the consequence of and correspondence to the (kenotically) self-emptying love of the Son for the Father in the mode of human obedience.

43 · The Unknown God

Is not the desire to curb an inflated use of the divine name an indication of a healthy instinct in modern man? Nor is one likely to be mistaken if one places responsibility for this inflation on the shoulders of Christians. Among them God became all at once a continually speaking and acting subject in the midst of the world and among us.

The Jews scarcely dared to utter the word "God" at all. The more deeply they learned to know him, the more unutterable became his name, the more inconceivable he became himself. A more intimate communion with God lay far back in the early period of Judaism when Moses was allowed to see God face to face and when God tented with his people in the desert. Perhaps it was that the concept of God at that time was still too limited, too much a part of folk religion. Or was it perhaps that the Jews of a later period projected their longing for such a naive communion with the unutterable onto their portrayal of that primal period? There were, too, times in Christian history, above all at the end of the patristic period, which were epochs marked by an elemental trembling in the face of the total otherness of God, who in his very being transcends every concept and, even more, every statement. Let us leave aside the question how far such epochs were influenced by Greek philosophy (which we can summarily describe as "natural theology"). We are concerned not with questions of historical influences but with questions of substance and truth.

The question may be put as follows. Does God cease, when he reveals himself in his Son, to be the wholly other, the incomprehensible? If he allows himself to be touched, captured, bound, condemned, and crucified in Jesus of Nazareth, does he then come within the reach of human beings? Does he then become an element among their rational concepts and calculations? *Si comprehendis non est Deus*, says Augustine, echoing those Greek fathers: "If you think you have conceived something, then it was certainly not God." In the Eastern church this sense of awe in face of the incomprehensibility of the mystery soon led to the liturgy's being performed in concealment behind the "iconostasis." About the year 500 an unknown figure, probably a Syrian monk, who called himself Dionysius the Areopagite, set the course of Christian theology for a thousand years by placing at its center the total otherness of God and a sense of deep liturgical awe. His influence on the middle ages in the West was scarcely less persistent than that of Augustine. The great scholastics wrote commentaries on his writings; he it was who again and again prevented theological speculation from presumptuously forcing its way into the darkness of the divine mystery.

In our times two German thinkers have again taken up this cause. First, Erich Przywara gave positive expression to it, taking as his starting point the formula of the Fourth Lateran Council (1215) and from there formulating his principle of *analogia entis* as follows: "That, however great the similarity between creator and creature may be, the dissimilarity always nevertheless remains greater." The "however great" refers not only to the character of the created spirit as "image and likeness of God," but just as much to the supernatural self-revelation of God in Jesus Christ and to the gracious participation in the divine being which is offered to humans in the outpouring of the Holy Spirit. What Przywara saw clearly was that, even in so intimate a communion between God and humanity as is portrayed in the Christian doctrines of grace, of the church, of the "infused virtues," faith, hope, and love (which have their origins in the divine life), of the love of God and one's neighbor, in all this God is still nevertheless always other, the dissimilarity remains always greater. It seems clear that this insight into the best theological tradition had become increasingly strange to modern Christians—with a few exceptions, as, for example, Newman. It was then in our times only by a violent struggle, both in a spirit of reaction and revolution, that the traditional sense of the divinity of God could again be recovered.

The second thinker is Gustav Siewerth who in his book *The Fate of Metaphysics from Thomas to Heidegger* (1959) portrayed negatively the tragic history of the loss of the sense of the divine mystery with a relentless, at times biting, logic. For him the tragedy begins within Christianity and within theology itself. God, so it appeared to Christians and theologians, has eliminated his hiddenness in his self-revelation in Jesus Christ; from now on we know him even in the very depths of his heart. The Holy Spirit who "searches even the depths of God" has also "been bestowed on us" so that we may "understand the gifts bestowed on us by God" (1 Cor 2:10–12). So that, once God in the folly of his love had revealed to us his own deepest secrets, people now armed with the weapons of the spirit bestowed on us began to advance into the divine arcana, and to take possession of his mysteries, with the consequence that for Hegel the divine spirit is no longer distinguishable from the human (for there can only be one single absolute spirit) and that then logically for Feuerbach, Marx, and Freud the spirit once divine is now replaced by the human spirit which searches its own psychological and sociological depths.

It is more than instructive to read Siewerth's account of the individual stages of this spiritual development which led from a theological rationalism which laid claim to precise knowledge about all the mysteries of God to the final declaration that "God is dead"—a progression which had its own terrible logic. But we may also ask whether it is truly the case that this tragic history goes back only as far as the onset of nominalism after Thomas. For it may be that the dogmatic formulations of the great councils of the first centuries, in which the Trinity and christology were conceptualized, were at least very dangerous pointers in this direction. The answer is as follows. Even such formulations as these, like any other theological "knowledge" of God, must become dangerous from the very moment when humans cease to know and to be conscious of whom they are dealing with. The Catholic principle "Grace presupposes nature, elevates, and perfects it" is perhaps nowhere more important than here; for the natural person, if he had not already been artificially corrupted, does have a sense of awe in the face of the hidden mystery of human existence, in the face of the ultimate origin and destiny of the world, of matter, of life, of evolution, of the fate of the individual and of humanity.

Every religion, from the most primitive to the most sophisticated, lives essentially on this awe. Goethe and Albert Schweitzer have given us great examples of such religion, and even the humanitarian world views which today describe themselves as religionless draw their strength, at least in the cases where they do not publicly proclaim their cynicism and demonism, from a primal pathos. They have been gripped by a sense of the urgency of the reconciliation to be produced of the human being with the being of the world as a whole; hungering and thirsting after ultimate righteousness are not possible without a sense of awe in the face of the mystery of being. Religious Judaism which, as we saw, is deeply rooted in this sense of awe, has again and again produced utopian speculations reaching into the unconditional. That this is so has its grounds in the incomprehensible fact that the eternal incomprehensible God has at a particular time and place in history revealed himself to this people.

But at the moment when the mystery of God bears in upon us so overwhelmingly as it does in the incarnation, death, and resurrection of Jesus Christ, a highly dangerous situation arises. On the one hand, those who are confronted with this mystery are enjoined to preach it and consequently to put it into intelligible words and concepts and even, in certain circumstances, to translate it into broadly descriptive formulae in order to *protect* his overwhelming greatness, to frustrate human attempts to master it with their reason and to fit it into human forms of thought or to frustrate one's attempts to bring it down to the level of human wisdom about life (as, for example, "being a Christian is nothing other than the brotherhood of man taken seriously"). On the other hand, the wire which is set round the mystery to protect it can only too easily and almost fatally become a snare to trap humans. This, either in the sense that it makes the approaches to the mystery difficult or almost impassable for the one who draws near in a sense of awe (by either a literal or a figurative iconostasis), or in the sense that for educated and uneducated alike the impression may be created that it is in the wire itself that the mystery has been captured and tamed, that the unknown God has been made known. The "even greater degree of dissimilarity" is then forgotten; for where can one find a work of dogmatics, ancient or modern, which gives it significant expression? Certainly the theological textbooks seem to have lost every trace of such a sense; but do we find it unequivocally in the monumental work of Karl Barth? Or are the texts of the last council formulated primarily on the basis of such a sense? Or must one go looking among the "liberals" like Paul Tillich to find such a sense?

*   *   *

It is no easy task to find one's way back from the "all too familiar" God to the truly unknown God. One makes no headway simply by throwing overboard all formulations, by rejecting all the work of theology, of the magisterial office, of the councils as dangerous aberrations. One simply saws through the branch of tradition on which everything historical sits, and falls into the void. This can be seen most clearly where attempts have been made to make a clean sweep of things: for instance, where one discards even the earliest expressions of the mystery of Jesus of Nazareth in the formulae of faith of the early church (which for the most part make use of Old Testament concepts) and fumbles one's way back into a great darkness. For here one finds nothing on which one can lay firm hold, because all the witnesses to the historical Jesus are formed in part by the Easter faith and confession. If one discards the truth of the way in which in faith the early church was overwhelmed by God as of no importance for such an investigation and as not binding on us, then the whole overpowering deed of God was in vain. Nothing remains of it except the fact that Jesus was an "outstanding example,"* alongside Buddha, Marx, and others. The modern theology of secularization and the death of God does in its way open the way for the old negative theology. Indeed it scarcely needs to open it but simply points to the fact of its existence as it brushes to the side, like so many dead leaves, the withered formulae of a Christianity which would know too much. Even the dogmas of the first ecumenical councils fall victim to this purge; the "unknown God" cannot at the same time also be a known God. But, on the other hand, we must also be quite clear that precisely those fathers who helped decisively to formulate the trinitarian and christological dogmas, Athanasius, the Cappadocians, Hilary, wrote clearly to expound the transcendence and unintelligibility of the divine nature in the course of their relentless struggle against the Arian and Eunomian rationalism. It is this which makes it clear that the conciliar definitions of the patristic age are to be taken as attempts to protect the mystery against one-sided "ratonalization," attempts repeatedly made always in the consciousness of their inadequacy.

It is true that in Jesus Christ the mystery of the ground of the world

---

* Piet Schoonenberg, in *Die Antworten der Theologen* (Patmos 1968), p. 54.

burns more brightly than anywhere. But, on the other hand, it is precisely in this light that for the first time and definitively we grasp the true incomprehensibility of God. It is here that God breaks *forever* all the "wisdom" of the world by the "folly" of his love which chooses human beings without reason, by his entering into the chaos of the history of humanity, by his bearing the guilt of his lost and fallen creatures. This incomprehensible love of the God who acts in the event of Christ raises him far above all the incomprehensibilities of philosophical notions of God which consist simply in negating all statements about God, which may be ventured on the grounds of our knowledge of the world, out of regard for his total otherness. But this more powerful incomprehensibility of the biblical God only remains in effect so long as the dogmatic formulae protect it against renewed attempts at rationalization. Like the cherubim with their fiery swords, they surround the folly of the love of God, scandalous both for Jews and Greeks, and protect any cabbalistic or Hegelian attempts to overthrow *agape* with *gnosis*.

John makes the claim that God is "love" on the basis of the experience which in Jesus Christ we may have of him. However, according to the teaching of the disciple, God is not love because he has found in us an object worthy of his love which before he lacked, in the sense, that is, that we were necessary to him in order that he might be love. Rather, he is love in himself. But one cannot define love even when one meets it in this world. Where it is genuine it transcends in its sovereign freedom every why and wherefore. It has its necessity only in itself. It can be encompassed by no concept. Even more, the ground of the absolute divine love outstrips immeasurably all human thought. And so, too, the statement that God needs no creature in order to be love, the statement that God is love in himself, begetting and begotten, communing with himself in such a way that from this communion there proceeds again and again the eternal fruit and witness of love: the statement therefore that God is "triune," all this is and remains discourse about an incomprehensible mystery. It is only analogously (where the similarity is overruled by a greater dissimilarity!) that we can speak of persons in God; only analogously (where the similarity is overruled by a greater dissimilarity!) that we can speak of "begetting" and either "spiration" or "breathing forth"; only analogously (where the similarity is overruled by a greater dissimilarity!) that we can speak of "three," for what "three" means in relation to the absolute is in any case something quite other than the inner worldly "three" of a sequence of numbers.

It might then seem that it would be better to abandon any attempt to speak and think of God if he always remains, even when he reveals himself, wholly and then most truly unknown. But we no longer have authority to do this, for he came to us in an event—which had its climax in Jesus Christ—of such self-giving, defenseless, inviting power (or powerlessness) that we understand at least so much: he wants to be *for us*, he wants to gather us into the abyss of his own inner trinitarian love. We do know that this love is in no sense the I itself, that it is also not the We of fellow humanity; we experience, further, that it addresses me and us as you; it is indisputable that Jesus teaches us to reply to this address of love also with you; that we may and must entrust ourselves to it unconditionally is the mounting demand of the whole Bible and this demand is justified with the "proof" which God has given of his love to the world (Jn 3:16; 1 Jn 4:9).

The Christian centuries and millennia have repeatedly erected towering theological buildings around these mysteries. From time to time it becomes necessary to stress the insufficiency of much which has been thus piled up in order to make room for new attempts. Everything remains a beginning, an attempt, an approximation, just as the life shared between two lovers remains to the end a beginning, an attempt, an approaching toward one another, but only as each allows the other his or her own freedom. Woe to the lover who, by whatever means, were to seek to tear from the loved one his or her final mystery! Not only is such an attempt impossible, but also by it the life of love is killed. Only that which is given by the unsearchable freedom of love has revelatory value. And so analogously (the similarity is overruled by the greater dissimilarity!) the free self-disclosure of the divine heart sheds over all our existence, thought, loving, and action an incomparable light; and yet it comes from the God "who dwells in unapproachable light, whom no one has ever seen or can see" (1 Tim 6:16). And yet we are to draw near to the inaccessible one "in boldness and confidence through our faith in Jesus Christ" (Eph 3:12) who has "expounded" to us the inaccessible God "whom no one has seen" (Jn 1:18).

Christians today must be capable of withstanding the tension which is contained within these statements. On the one hand they must refuse every attempt to penetrate into the hidden and free being of God with unbaptized reason; on the other they may reject no path which God himself offers us into the mystery of his eternal love. They may neither on the one hand push God away into a realm of inaccessible transcendence which then ultimately becomes a matter of indifference for them, nor on the other hand so draw the human being into the historicity of the world that freedom over the world is forfeited and they fall victim to human *gnosis*.

44 · The Personal God

Can we dare to apply the concept person, personality, to the unutterable hidden ground of being from which has proceeded and ceaselessly proceeds the mysterious multiplicity of the world in all its evolving and declining forms? These forms, of which we are one, stand unprotected in the cold wind of existence. Perhaps from time to time we lean against each other to find a measure of support, perhaps from time to time another person's house seems to offer us something like home and security. But how precarious such dwellings are, hurriedly erected huts in the icy wind of fate which whistles around us on all sides and which unpredictably tears away our or another's roof under which we had thought we might for a while find shelter. And if indeed we are so exposed to fate and if all our insurances against accidents, against old age, against illness are simply powerless attempts to protect ourselves against an overwhelming power, against the ultimatel destructive blizzard of death, if our abandonment is indeed as extreme as this, no human fellowship can protect us against our loneliness, no hope for the future can alleviate the frightening situation of the world *now*. If, finally, no historical past provides us with the consolation which we fail to find in the present—because human beings have always lived in the same exposure—then where shall we muster the confidence to feel ourselves truly secure in that deeply concealed womb and primordial ground from which we have been cast without our asking and into which we will at the end fall at the will of fate? If it is true that (according to Nietzsche) everything which is mature wants to die, then that is not to say that it wants to return to the primal ground into which, dying, it falls.

Paul in his speech at the Areopagus offered the Greeks an unusual definition of our existence. God, he said, has scattered people over the surface of the earth and has given them determinate and limited dwelling places; that is to say he has set them in the midst of the finitude of space and time with all its questionableness, with all its painful edges and corners. "They were," he says, "to seek God, in the hope that they might feel their way toward him and find him." Searching is the basic characteristic of the human being. It is a continual leaving behind one of the past results which have proved unsatisfactory. Now, of course, one would not keep on feeling one's way forward—after all the disappointments—if one did not know that there was a gap which must be filled at all costs. But what follows—"that they might feel their way toward him"—betrays a strange sense of helplessness. To feel their way toward him: that is the manner in which blind men behave. "In the hope that perhaps" makes it appear questionable whether such feeling will meet with success. It will apparently be a matter of pure luck, a mere chance hit, if those who are feeling after the truth should happen on anything of decisive importance. And what do they then find?

What is it that the Greeks to whom Paul turns have found? What is the concept of God to which they have fought their way? At the beginning of the Greek culture stands Homer. For him there are many gods who wear a personal face. Above them stands the father of all, Zeus, who governs the fortunes both of Hellas and of Troy. But behind Zeus and the personal gods stands as a final authority the impersonal, unsearchable, inscrutable abyss of being: fate. It is the question mark of fate which concludes the beautiful, sunny poetry of the Greeks. It is in this fate that the great heroes of Greek tragedy stand, and to this fate and not really to the friendly or inimical personal gods that they address their questions.

And then follows philosophy: Plato, Aristotle, the Stoics; and what does it do? It takes over from the personal gods of mythology their anthropomorphic, good, and comforting characteristics: goodness, their readiness to care and provide for others, faithfulness, the love which is without envy. It lifts these characteristics like a cape from the shoulders of the personal gods and drapes them around the impersonal absolute. This was an enormously bold step. It required an unheard-of courage to be, the courage to affirm existence. Now the ultimate principle which bears all things is the *idea* of the good or *providence*. The question is, however, whether such a view of things can in the long run be upheld. As soon as philosophy arises, two ideas come into prominence. The first is the idea of Heraclitus: "The world is no more than a heap of sweepings scattered at random," and it is precisely these sweepings, precisely this terrible chaos and lack of order, this juxtaposition of extremes, precisely this which, according to him, is providence. The other idea comes from Parmenides: the sweepings, the contradictions and opposites in reality do not exist. In truth there is only one thing and that is being, that is God. The first says, the world as it in fact exists is God, or at least God takes responsibility for it, he is the sense which mediates between all this lack of sense. The second says, the world, conceived of as distinct from God, does not in reality exist and is consequently meaningless. Meaning can only be found beyond all distinctions in the very ground of things. Either God is absorbed in the world, or the world is absorbed or resolved in God. The sphere of being is round and what could fall outside its compass? Only nothingness. And so consequently for philosophy which, as such, always wishes to reduce its subject matter to an explanation in terms of some one ultimate concept, God and the world are finally united and one in the sphere of being. And this philosophical tradition stretches via Plotinus and the

Arab philosophers of the middle ages to Hegel, who was the last philosopher to make the attempt once again to embrace everything within absolute knowledge.

The man Hegel who thinks this all-embracing knowledge is a person, a professor in Berlin. The all-embracing knowledge which he thinks is not a person. All finite beings are sacrificed to the one whom he names the "world spirit." Personal immortality, even the resurrection of the flesh, are for Hegel a laughable presumption on the part of the tiny individual in all his questionable mortality. What remains? Karl Marx replies: that which was there at the beginning before philosophy began—the questioning one standing out in the icy wind of fate who must attempt on the basis of his own strength alone to build a house which is protection against the storms of fate, to tame and domesticate the terrifying strangeness of the world, to humanize inhumanity. Where theory could provide no answer practice takes over. Practice at least does what it can: it attempts to provide for the person of tomorrow a house in which to live. To the questions which the person of yesterday and today put to it, shouting them out in distress, practice can and wants to give no answer. Is there nowhere a unity of these fragments of theory and practice? Is there not anywhere beside all the false trails a road which will take us through the forest of being? If so, then there is only one. Something would have to happen which the blind person's fumbling cannot take into account in the search: namely, that suddenly another hand would seize his and take over the lead. This other hand would not be the hand of a fellow human, promising us for a moment such shelter and refresh· ment as his or her hut could provide; for tomorrow we will both be again confronted by the same fate and death. The hand of one's fellow human could offer us great promise and hope, but only if it was empowered to seize the hand of the searching person with the power of unconditional love.

What conditions must be satisfied if a hand—the hand of God, of the living, free, personal God—is suddenly to reach out and seize the fumbling hand of the human being. Under all circumstances, that the terrible suffering of this human being, his exposure to the night and wind should lose nothing of its weight. Fine words do not bring comfort, even if they are divine. Existence is not only *maya*, a bad dream, from which one can awake, a veil or a net which one can tear asunder: it is reality. A real living God will have to recognize this terrible reality; indeed, if he is to help and to provide strength, he will have to take it more seriously than a human being can. The one who embraces humanity will have to face up to the force of reality, not by virtue of an omnipotence which from the outset disempowers that might but from a position in which that one could experience the terribleness of the power of the world. For only then would he be credible. The cross of Christ on which God takes upon himself the burden of the whole suffering of the world is the authentication of the living God. It does not matter whether or not it resembles the myths of dying gods; for why should not the myths be a premonition, as it were, an empty form of that which must occur in true history and yet which cannot be fathomed in terms of it? Sayings, teachings, wisdom of all kinds would not in any case have sufficed. Much penetrating thought can be pieced together. It was necessary that there should be a word which is no word but a silent deed, a nonword, which Paul calls the folly of God. Such a word was necessary if the first condition was to be fulfilled.

Supposing that this condition were fulfilled—and for the Christian it is indeed fulfilled in the event of the incarnate Word and Son of God—why in that event should not the one who wishes to be *sought* stretch out his hand in order to let himself be *found*? The Bible bears witness to such a God; he gives proof of his vitality and personality most clearly in the fact that he again and again leads the people of Israel along paths which they do not want to follow, which they resist with all their instincts, stubbornly, in a stiff-necked way, their hackles raised. For "my thoughts are not your thoughts and my ways are not your ways. As the heavens are high above the earth, so are my ways above your ways and my thoughts above your thoughts" (Is 55:8f). Will clashes with will, plan with plan. Whoever the God of Israel may be who redeems them from the house of bondage, who drags the unwilling people through the desert, imposes on them a law, gives them his promises; whoever this mysterious one may be who never yields up his name—"I am who I am, who I will be for you," whom you will always know from my dealings with you, even if you do not know my proper name, my hidden nature—whoever this free and living one, hidden and forcing himself on them, may be, one thing is certain for Israel: he *is*. He is the *other*, even if he is "all things" (Sir 43:27). He acts and speaks, he guides, promises, and fulfills: "He leads humans into the underworld and leads them up again."

Philosophers attempt to find and express something of the nature of God. Israel does not philosophize. It does not seek to grasp God, for God has already grasped it, already has seized it by the scruff of its neck. With its mother's milk it learns the reality of the divine you. An I, a people, can only exist in relation to this you. Pascal's alternative is vindicated: not the God of philosophers and of the learned, but the God of Abraham, Isaac, and Jacob, the God of Jesus Christ. The God of the philosophers is a mild, timeless, diffuse light, Plato's sun of justice, the light of the enlightenment. But the God of Israel is, to use

Pascal's words, "Fire!" Or in Jeremiah's words, "Does my word not burn like fire? Is it not like a hammer which smashes the rocks?" (23:29).

Other people too have had their gods and have addressed them as you in prayer. But none of them has had anything remotely like the bitter experiences of its God that Israel underwent. No god has so relentlessly pressed its people on toward its goal, through thick and thin, through defeats, exiles, abandonments, till it reached the goal to which it wished to bring its people through this history, till it had brought them to the place where in the deepest hiddenness it could unveil to them its face on which no person had ever set eyes—or rather not unveil it but make it discernible as absolute love. "No one has ever seen God," but "we have seen and bear witness that the Father has sent his son as savior of the world: beloved, if God has shown us such great love" (1 John 4:12, 14, 11): and "God who has said: Out of darkness shall light shine! he it is who has made it to shine in our hearts, so that we were enlightened by the knowledge of the glory on the face of Jesus Christ" (2 Cor 4:6). These are paradoxical sayings which speak of not seeing and yet seeing, without canceling each other; sayings which transcend the laws of human language, because they are the self-interpretation of a deed which has been achieved; incarnate words in which the flesh more and more receives the primacy over the word; practice before theory. They break the sound barrier of that which for human beings is unutterable, they outstrip every hermeneutical problem for they confront us with something done, so self-evident that it "stops the mouths" of many who would question it. And that which is done—"the fact"—is not simply cast before humankind, before the people of Israel at the end of God's ways, as a unilateral action on the part of God, but in the Word becoming man the personal God creates for himself as it were in advance a personal answer. Out of the catastrophes of the disobedience of the Old Testament he has elicited for himself so much obedience that, as the fruit of the history of the people since Abraham, he can produce one woman who can say, "I am the handmaid of the Lord, let it be unto me according to thy word." And even her word is more deed than word: she permits the active word of God to occur. And the fruit of this fruit is Jesus, who is obedient to death on the cross, but who at the same time knows that in this obedience to the other, to the Father, he has finally brought to light that God's hidden, always concealed name is love. Out of his love God the Father gives that which is most precious to him, his Son, for us. Out of his love the Son goes into the utmost darkness of the world, of death and hell, in order to bear the guilt of all his human brothers and sisters. And this love is given to us as the fruit poured into our hearts: God's holy spirit of love.

* * *

The human being in its search for truth can never arrive by philoso-
phizing—of however simple or academic a kind—at the statement
"God is love." For against this statement the world, as it appears,
raises a categorical objection. At best we can push our way forward to
the statement that God is the reconciliation of the contradictions
internal to the world, a place of peace, where one no longer suffers,
where one can forget life, where the painful boundaries between
individuals finally fall away, where we may be taken into the realm of
that which is without distinction. Unless, that is, the human being
should prefer to dispense with such a peace *beyond* this earthly realm
and to attempt to rise by his own heroic efforts to an affirmation of
the world as it is in the *midst* of existence with all its divisiveness, as
did Nietzsche; to say yes and amen in all eternity to this ruminating
monster, this will to power. But such an affirmation may not exclude
a single one of the concentration camps. Let one attempt it and see
whether sanity can be retained.

There was only one way to approach the statement "God is love."
God first had to reveal himself as the one for himself, who in his
freedom disposes over all existing things, who predestines and promises, in brief, to show himself as the absolute person, the someone
who takes our fumbling hand firmly, only too firmly, in his. The
result is Jesus Christ. For him there is only the personal God, whom
he addresses as *Abba*, tenderly loved Father. One can perhaps argue
that Jesus was not objectively the unique son of God. But one cannot
dispute historically that he was conscious of his unique status as the
one who in his origins stood in an incomparable relationship to a
thoroughly personal God, and that all his efforts were directed towards bringing us into relationship with his Father as his children.
When you pray then say, "You, our Father. . . ." If one reflects for a
while on this, keeping in mind the whole fate of Jesus up to his cross,
then perhaps the realization might begin to dawn that here occurred
God's final, never-to-be-exceeded self-revelation. That in this existence and in this dying abandonment by God, God has proclaimed his
final "word" which from that point rings undiminished down the
centuries. What more then could be said than this? And yet has
anyone ever penetrated so far into this final revelation that it does not
always stand before him as his future?

But what is Christian does not oscillate uncertainly between past
and future; by virtue of its unique form and figure it lends support to
the present at every stage. For what distinguishes and sets Christian
faith above all other religious beliefs is this: the hand of the loving
Father, who grasps the fumbling child, is the hand of a *human* you.
The hand of our neighbor: " 'Who is neighbor to him who fell among

robbers?' He answered, 'He who showed mercy on him.' And Jesus said to him, 'Go and do likewise' " (Luke 10:36f). The fact that God's hand is the hand of *one particular* fellow human being makes of the hand of every fellow human being something quite new. We may sense through its uncertainty the firmness, the trustworthiness of the divine hand. We can within a Christian marriage join hand in hand in the faith that weak human love will be strengthened by the love of God with an eternal power. Reliability and faithfulness from person to person bear fruit in the fact that we are together carried by a personal God who shows us his faithfulness in human form. Only where God is person is the human being taken seriously as a person. Every human being is addressed personally as you by God and experiences here his irreplaceable value. It is with this insight that biblical religion, and in particular Christianity, has entered history. But this insight is in danger of being submerged and lost wherever God is no longer understood personally as freely loving. Moreover, he is only credible as a person where he does not stand against the suffering of the world, teaching and pouring comfort on it with words, but where he acts by going to the cross. The personhood of God, the cross of Christ, the dignity of the human being, and human love are indissolubly interrelated. One may imagine that one could advocate human dignity without believing in God's person, indeed precisely by denying it. But the logic of history will again level, either existentially or collectivistically, the persons who have thus been absolutized. It will turn them into cannon fodder and the objects of experiments, into manure for evolution. Only the personal God himself whose love is truth and whose truth is love can give to the I and you between human beings a truly personal value, so that in the exchange in trust between the two something unique, something irreducible occurs, not an erotic illusion, not a trick of nature, not something which psychoanalysis can reveal as egoism, but pure truth.

45 · The Incarnation of God

The statement "God became human" is without question central to the Christian witness. For any other religion—quite apart from other world views—it is an intolerable, basically self-contradictory statement. It isolates Christianity from all other philosophies and confessions. For the point is not simply that God who has all names and yet is without name, who is wholly other and (beyond this indeed) not other, because without opposites, that such a God at particular points and in particular people in the world and its history becomes "transparent." That is indeed an all too fashionable word today and, with its help, it may appear possible to reduce to a common denominator with the basic Christian message Indian *avatars* and prophetic or mystical personalities—for example, in Judaism or Islam, or even in other religions. Rather, what sets Christianity apart from other religions is the scandalous claim that the one who bears all names and yet is without name, who as the scripture says "is everything" (Sir 43:27), has once and for all declared himself identical with a tiny something or someone in the vast cosmos and among the countless millions of swarming humanity—identical with someone who then can make such monstrously exclusive statements about himself as "I am the door . . . all who have come before me are thieves and robbers" (Jn 10:7f) and "No one knows the Father but the Son and him to whom the Son will reveal it" (Mt 11:27). Of course, once one has admitted that the "all" can become identical with the tiny "someone," then one will be compelled to accept such unbearably intolerant claims on the part of this "someone." But does not the very absurdity of claiming that all the broad rivers which link people of all cultures and religions with the unutterable ground of all things flow through this—his!—narrow gorge show that the very presuppositions of such a claim must be absurd and consequently undermine those claims? Moreover, quite apart from the logical nonsense of attempting to identify the whole with a part of itself (being with individual existents), is it not apparent that such an act would run directly contrary to those broadening, liberating effects which a religion ought indeed to have, namely of gathering up into an all-embracing peace that which within the world is rent asunder in opposing camps, in a perpetual struggle, and so might it not seem that it is in effect designed "not to bring peace but the sword" and "to divide" people even in their households and families (Mt 10:34f)? May not Christianity, with its intolerant history of persons burned at the stake and religious wars, be a terrible step backward from a religious and political universalism which was beginning to show itself in the Hellenistic-Roman world, and which Christianity at its outset cripples? And may not Christianity, in its post-Christian, secularized form, have to be made responsible for the spirit of impatience and division which today, against the general direction of technical progress, delays and indeed demonically questions the unification of the world?

This indeed is how it appears if we approach the basic Christian claims from outside, in the abstract, unmediated, independently of the forms by which they are mediated to Christians, without making the effort to view them in their whole context, which context is indispensable for their understanding. The tender shoots at the top of a pine tree presuppose the whole powerful tree down to its deepest roots. But precisely the effort to think through the whole anew and more deeply in the light of the highest claims is what is demanded by Christianity; or rather, it is the fact that from its highest point it sheds over the whole a light which makes possible such a new and deeper appreciation. This light does not simply show the weakness and frailty of all religious and nonreligious philosophies of humanity, of all attempts to find one's way to an understanding of the mystery of the existence of the world; on the contrary, it brings such attempts and efforts to a fulfillment which far outreaches anything which might be expected, by setting the truths contained in such philosophies in their proper place and integrating them with the whole. What we shall attempt in the three following sections is to move from an abstract pair of opposites ("all"—"something," "God"—"human") into the realm of the concrete.

The primordial ground of being from which finite things arose—things which require an explanation not only for the way they are but for their very existence—was addressed by Plato with the name of "the good." For even assuming that our experience of worldly existence would lead us to hesitate before declaring as "good" the existence of a world which is not identical with the primordial ground, in particular the existence of a world full of inexplicable suffering, and would further lead us to experience our distance from the ground of being, our falling away from it into a "region of dissimilarity" (*regio dissimilitudinis*), as a disaster; even assuming, that is, that what we regard as our worldly being, in its strangeness, inexplicableness, estrangement, was to be experienced rather as something to be overcome than as something for which we should be grateful (as for example in Buddhism); even so, the primordial ground of which one would then have to speak (by contrast with worldly existents) as the "not-existing" would, in spite of all, be the good and that which was to be striven for by stripping oneself of the estranging illusion of finitude. It is impossible to conceive of the primordial ground itself as evil, demonic, as that which is to be cursed. The "guilt" for the estrangement which attaches to finite existence (not, that is, simply for its mere otherness from the primordial ground) is attributed therefore by the religious always to a secondary factor; for example, to the freedom of the preexistent souls (Plato, Buddhism), or to a "demigod" (gnosticism), or in radical modern utopianism to a principle of the past which stands in opposition to the absolute which is to come. Setting aside this utopianism, which cannot be thought through without contradiction, primal goodness still remains a justification of everything which in this mixed world can be called truly existent and positive; in this sense it is a diffusion of itself beyond the bounds of its being as ground, communicating itself to its effects (*bonum diffusivum sui*). This principle which unites the religions is taken from the biblical revelation of the Old and New Covenants and integrated into the complementary notion that the causing of a finite world by the good did not occur because the (infinite) good *needed* this (finite) world in order to be the good. In other words, God does not produce the world naturally because he is God, which would then mean that the world would be in the same measure divine and necessary as God himself; rather it is an absolute *freedom* which is the ground of the self-effusion of the ultimate good. This in turn has two consequences: that God in himself and independently of his relationship to the world is the good, or in Christian terms, is love, and that the ultimate cause of the creation of a world can only be the free, loving communication of divine goodness to created beings. If one thinks this through, then one will have to say, over and above this, that precisely in the freedom of the love of the divine ground of being lies the possibility of there being such a thing as a world (which is not God, not the infinite and the all) at all. Indeed the final point may emerge dimly as a kind of limiting notion which will find its confirmation in the central assertions of the Christian faith: the primordial ground can only be called the good as free love, if it possesses *in itself* a spiritual *life* of love; that is to say, if there is within it a self-giving, a communing, a communality which does not impugn the identity of the absolute but indeed is the necessary condition of its truly being the absolute good.

* * *

If from this point of view we consider creatures, which find their highest form in human beings, then it appears that they also, precisely as individuals, are not only a tiny something (as opposed to the all-embracing all) but are something whose being and nature are fashioned and determined by the good which communicates *itself* to them. The human being is "in the image" of God. As spirit—that is to say, in so far as he knows and thinks spiritually and wills freely—he is open to everything and to every entity, which is possible only if he is open to the horizon of being itself (he is *quodammodo omnia*). As he knows that he is not God, so too he knows that his being is from God, a knowledge grounded in a basic experience which may perhaps use other concepts, ideas, and words but which envisages the same matter as we have attempted to express here. His concern is with the question of the meaning of the world and existence as a whole. It is a secondary matter whether he seeks this meaning in a mysterious peace within the riddle of the world (a peace which, however, must lie beyond the pain which he experiences and can be found in an ascetic, mystical, perhaps technical overcoming of the painful states), or whether he denies the being of the world in the form in which he finds it, in order to find peace beyond it (for example, in the "idea" of the world as it is in God), or whether finally he despairs of his ability to find a solution and, while trying to make the best of his mortal life, sets the riddle aside. But if he encounters the idea that he, as this particular human being (as indeed every human being is a "particular individual"), is the image of the freely loving God who consequently also wills him of his freedom, then a strange and special light will be shed on his existence. On the one hand, it will occur to him that the free divine good has intended him to be this particular person, this unexchangeable person, and has consequently freely released him into his freedom and insight and responsibility; but that this, on the other hand, cannot be simply a matter of dismissing him, of sending him off without further interest into an estrangement from God. Rather he must realize his being as a human with free, intelligent responsibility precisely by relating the image to the original, not by turning away from but by turning to God. Here a realm of intimate inwardness is opened which may take many forms and names: contact with the primal image, cherishing and contemplating memories and recollections, prayer, the attempt to make human insight and freedom in every life situation transparent to absolute insight and freedom. It is an openness, ready to be formed and fulfilled; it is a making room for the one who may come to dwell, a readiness to be the womb which shall bear fruit each in one's own particular human worldly activity and efforts.

* * *

In these first two steps in thought we have clarified and simplified what is ambiguous, dark, and impure in the many religious attempts of humanity to understand this world and its reality in the light of the Christian answer, clarified moreover in such a way that the path from the universal, human understanding of the world to the Christian understanding could be shown here as a possible, intrinsically intelligible and knowable one. Does this mean to say that such an exercise as such has already led us to the Christian faith, perhaps indeed has postulated it *a priori*, constructed it, shown it to be necessary? No. Two elements must be added if we are to get it clearly in view. First, the extent and scale of the negative decisions of human freedom when measured by the standard of the absolute goodness of God—a standard which remains decisive where the human being's behavior toward God and toward the world in which he lives is to be measured. These negative decisions are both individual ("sin") and social ("common guilt," previously known as "original sin") in character. The historical world is consequently in a state of such deep confusion that it is totally beyond the power of any individual to outweigh the consequences of personal as well as of social guilt by his own decisions and enterprises. The concrete, unnatural figure of death sets on human existence the seal of futility and makes the history of the world internally imperfectible—because the bloody way which may lead to a relatively final happy state can never be justified by this state itself—and remains for ever a warning and a reminder of this insuperable guilt. It thus constantly exposes the perilous and indeed imperilling character of every program which would seek to lead humans toward a greater freedom. For this always remains a freedom of choice, for better or for worse, so that all mundane optimism vis-à-vis the future is not only naive but pernicious.

If, however, these are the consequences of the risk which God has taken in entrusting his creatures with genuine freedom (freedom ultimately to deny and to destroy themselves), then ultimately God could only take such a risk if he threw himself into the balance, assumed the risk himself, and of himself opened a way where there was no way. It is here that the biblical message interposes and proclaims, "God with us," God on our side! It proclaims not only "covenant" which assures us of God's faithfulness, even in spite of our breaches of that covenant and in spite of his just judgements ("if we are faithless, he remains faithful—for he cannot deny himself"; 2 Tim 2:13), but a coming over to our side in order to open a way for us from within our helplessness and hopelessness—yet without in any way overtrumping that situation with his omnipotence; without, that is, impugning our freedom in any manner. A way which leads through death into life. Dying freely and obediently, God turns death, the sign of our guilt, into a monument of love.

Here, of course, our thoughts begin to stumble. The mystery begins. And how could it be otherwise if it is God who comes to our side? In order that this one life and death might become significant for all, the divine gracious freedom had to coincide with human obedient freedom; only the self-interpretation of Jesus' human existence allows us to sense how this occurs: God's word of promise, his wisdom, his law, his faithfulness, are "sent" bodily to our side (so that consequently the mission of all other earlier mediators, wise ones, and prophets is absorbed and superseded by this mission). At first one sees the man, Jesus of Nazareth, who, like the prophets and yet more radically than they, obeys the spirit which has been given him from above and surrenders himself to the task given him by God to the point where he identifies his life (and death) with that task, until it becomes clear that he in his whole being has become the statement of God. But he could only become this if, regardless of the process of becoming, he had always been so from the start. God's Word does God's purposes for the world in the form of a man: the salvation of humanity by God's own absolute initiative for it. We cannot here unfold the meaning of this statement, but only point to it. For the "incarnation of God" to be possible in a Christian sense, God must be *able* to come to our side without leaving his own "side"; but this opposition presupposes essentially that eternal opposition of which we spoke when considering the life of love within the godhead. The world with its freedom finds a resting place in the final plan of God between God the Father and God the Son and is allowed to participate in that highest freedom which, Christianly speaking, is the divine spirit, the shared spirit proceeding from the Father and the Son which gives expression to their unity of love. Because the opposition within the godhead is overcome in him and (in faith) becomes visible as a presupposition of eternal love, the opposition between God and humanity, which is a scandal to reason, can (in faith) be understood as a presupposition of the one, free, self-giving of God to his world in his Holy Spirit.

And so the isolated position of Christianity, which at the beginning appeared only as a sign of its intolerance, finds its explanation. It signifies nothing else than the from now on intelligible claim of being the utmost gesture of God and hence his ultimate self-donation and self-proclamation. This cannot be transcended because God, who is "all things," here out of his free love goes not only into that which is "other" than himself, into the creature, which is a "something" and "nearly nothing," but also into that which is contrary to himself as he gathers into himself the sin and the lostness and so the abandonment by God of his creature, and takes it upon himself. He does not thereby cease to be himself; indeed he shows precisely through this what he is in himself, what he is and what he can do. God can be dead without ceasing to be eternal life and he can, acting in this manner, prove finally that he is life and love and the goodness and grace which pours itself out in selfless self-giving. That is definitive, "eschatological," and it would be a self-contradiction if it, relativizing itself, should set other relationships alongside itself (which perhaps contain pointers toward this ultimate truth) as of equal importance. The heart is pierced, its spring uncovered, water and blood pour forth, there is nothing more than this.

What is the consequence of this death for the world? If it is what Christians believe, then the answer is that it gives meaning to the futility both of our individual existences and of the history of the world, that it gives hope to those who live under the rule of death, hope in a life with God which overcomes death. The way forward is for the individual, and for humanity as a whole, a way toward final meaning; it is a way to a "peace" such as the world cannot give (Jn 14:27), even if it should make progress in pacifism, because it is first and foremost peace between heaven and earth, between God and human being (Lk 2:14; Eph 2:14; Col 1:20). It is from this peace that we are sent to work with all our power for the pacification of the world. There are Christian existences which radiate such peace, which are blessed for it and called "children of God" (Mt 5:9).

46 · The Human Being— The "Brother for Whom Christ Died"

Christian thought occupies a lonely station, because it is indeed in the world but not of the world. Even as a "fact" it protrudes only partly into history, as witness for something that is as worldly as it is heavenly and eschatological. What is witnessed to is not directly verifiable in this-worldly terms; it is introduced as an offer in whose interior the solution for the agonizing riddle of existence is supposed to be found: "Do that and you will live" (Lk 10:28). Testimony is given that the crucified man, Jesus, is alive, has completed the break-through through the barrier of death, doom, and the powers of fate. And that he has done this from the beginning not for himself but "for us," as the testimony stubbornly insists, and from both sides too: from the experience that the crucified lives, as well as from the outrageous claim and the blasphemous self-interpretation of the man who because of his hubris was nailed to the cross. Like a quintessence of the three moments which constituted his existence, stand the sayings: "Take, eat, this is my body which will be poured out for you," "for you and for many," that is, for all.

One can dispute that the witnesses speak the truth. One cannot dispute that this is what is meant: The particular person Jesus Christ—a special person in his outrageous and yet simply proposed claim—has died for all and that is confirmed by his "resurrection from the dead." One can dismiss it as a myth, but one can not dispute that—whether the witness is true or not—its *idea* was and is a motivating force of quite unique power, of course only for such as grant a real "factual" character to this idea. For as idea without reality what was attested would have had at most the power of a "memorial"—like the one Jan Palach erected—but not the power of a reality which encompasses all in advance, not just those to whom it comes.

In Christianity the believer who proclaims and gives witness to its truth can come only as far as the reality of the attested is already true. Christ has died and is risen for all the brethren, all of whose existence is affected by this event. And this self-giving of Christ is attested to us as an expression of the reconciling will of God who has in him reconciled the world to himself (2 Cor 5:19), who with the gift of his most precious possession, "his own son," has given us *everything* (Rom 8:32), and hence has given witness to his unsurpassable love (Jn 3:16). To all other results and consequences the assurance is given in advance: This love of God which in Jesus Christ has taken in and borne every human being, and suffered through the fate and doom of every human being, has actually gone that far. One draws no conclusion from this that church, proclamation, and sacrament thereby become superfluous or are reduced to an external sign. But one also does not conversely conclude that the action of God in Christ for the world, which does not come into contact with the message or reject it, remains meaningless. The choice of messengers, their being sent into the world, belongs to the core of the Christian phenomenon, no matter how paradoxical a Christian existence—each is in some way or other commissioned—may always be in the world. They are sent not only to preach, but to proclaim with their whole being, to make present here and now what in Jesus Christ is really posited as already present. What does that say to us today? In answer, one can distinguish the relationship within the church from that beyond the church.

Within the church we all have the inclination to condemn the standpoint that is opposed to us as that of the "weak." For the progressive, the integralist is the weak one because he is backward and clings to the letter of the scripture and ecclesiastical definitions and affirmations taken literally. For the traditional believer the progressive is the weak one, because his faith is still only partially identified with the fullness of the Christian truth and threatens to fall either into a heathen gnosis or into a Judaizing Christianity of works, or, as is often the case, into both combined (Jewish utopianism both as gnosis and as *orthopraxis*). The law according to which Christianity is established directs us—no matter who the weak or the strong may be here—to the transcending law of love, but now of course not a purely human love, but the love of the crucified eucharistic Lord who, precisely as that, is the measure and criterion of all horizontal-social inner-church love. It should be impossible to call oneself Christian and to claim a place in the church and at the eucharistic table without subjecting oneself to the claim of this criterion as Paul expounded it. At the limit it would be possible, as Christian, to set the human as the final dialogue-horizon in the church because our cohuman, Christ, has expanded it in such an exemplary way that he remains decisively characterized by it. Many today take this *via media* between a merely human and a decidedly Christian horizon which would have to include explicitly cross, Eucharist, and resurrection; they consciously place the human under an ideal which, in order to be effective in bringing about change as they hope, needs a power which they no longer dare to give to it. That will turn out, in the long run, to be the powerlessness of their own position.

But the brother or sister for whom Christ died stands just as much outside the church whose boundaries with the world today have become completely untraceable. These range from the countless "marginal dwellers" within the church who can or will only "partially identify" with it (with what and with whom in it?), to the "separated ones" of all shadings who get gradually lost so to speak in the camps of the humanists, likewise of all shadings—those who allow the Christian impulse to be effective on non-Christian ground, and those who develop antichurch/anti-Christian programs in which just as much Christian substance, perhaps forgotten by the church, and neglected tasks are at work—to the margins of humanity where those who despair of all meaning in existence and the hardened deniers, haters, and destructive types live.

It is not enough to see them all as actual dialogue partners and potential members of the true church; they are above all the brothers and sisters for whom Christ died. They therefore already lay within the great mantle which God's poured-out love has thrown around all. Christians and non-Christians together protest noisily that nobody notices or gets anything from such a love. That through it we would be relieved neither of dialogue nor of *orthopraxis*, but that it would only be made easier. That, where it does so happen in the world, such "mysteries of Christendom" should be taken only as an amusing answer and either brought under control (the Great Inquisitor!) or liquidated. That God has become poor for our sakes may well be, but that we would be enriched through his poverty (2 Cor 8:9), nobody sees. At most, the church has become rich through the centuries at God's cost.

So they talk, and so they will continue to talk. In a disaster area humanity will plan, with and against one another, all kinds of purposeful rescue missions. That it should do, and preferably with than against one another. But the terrible question, what is all this for, will grow louder and louder the more this little ball on which we stand imprisoned overflows with teeming masses, and marvelous inventions give them power over their own being and nonbeing and over the being and nonbeing of the ball. Ultimately the dialogue of human beings with one another can take place only within the prison cell in the *humanum*. Then the idea that the "others" are hell will be replaced by the experience that we are all mutually, and thus each one individually, our own hell. That is what no one can get away from, unless by means of spite and cynicism. Humanity is then collective egoism, and love, of course, is sex. And the rotating waltz of the general dialogue stands still because everybody already knows what can possibly be said, from Lao to Mao, and the boldest head-lines no longer catch the eye. Everybody will be an enemy to every-body else because no one any longer can be a friend to himself or herself. Whether, in one's flight from the enemy within oneself, one reaches for drugs or for one's neighbor, is immaterial; a vigilance about oneself is unavoidable, whether one in loneliness now finds oneself again, or, what is perhaps worse, the finding is in the mirror of the you to which one fled to escape oneself.

Are we making God once again into a stopgap? Hardly, so long as we are not talking about filling holes which human beings themselves in time could learn to fill. No, human beings are themselves the hole and the abyss. They themselves are the hopelessly broken communi-cation, they themselves are, behind the deafening noise of the dia-logue which they shout, the silence of death. The whole question is, whether anyone here in this icy silence beneath the noise even knows one word—a word that echoes through the vacuum of hell. What cross and Eucharist and journey through hell and resurrection mean (it is all this together and all one single word of "love to the end": Jn 13:1) first becomes audible and understandable when human beings have understood that they no longer understand, thus have nothing more to say, and so are forced, finally, to be quiet.

THE CHURCH

· 47 ·

Only those who follow the church have a sure guarantee for the fact that, in their obedience to Christ, they have not really followed just their own know-it-all wisdom.

Origin and Original Figures
of the Church

48 · People around Jesus

Every human being stands in an interhuman constellation; one single human being would be an intrinsic contradiction. Such a single human being cannot even be abstractly conceived, because being-human signifies being-with. No exception from this may be made with regard to the God-man Jesus Christ. Only in his relationship to the Father is he, both as God *and as human,* in the unity of the holy divine Spirit.

Precisely for this reason his being human with us cannot be confined exclusively to his human nature: as an undivisible totality he stands in a constellation of fellow humanity. This constellation determines him inwardly, is relevant for his divinity-humanity, is not secondary but primordial to his essence and function. To take him from this constitutive human group is impossible, even if this assessment in no way impugns his sovereign position. Should he (and the doctrine about him, christology) be abstracted from this, his figure, even if its trinitarian context remains intact, becomes hopelessly abstract. This clearly holds not just for Protestant, but, in a more latent way, also for Catholic theology, to the extent that the forms (*Gestalten*) that essentially belong to him are assigned to different theological tracts, if a place is found for them anywhere at all in dogmatics.

Let us mention right at the beginning the most important of these persons who, in the view of the New Testament, belong to this constellation. The selection is not easy because beyond those listed here are others with significant theological positions and tasks who need to be considered, such as the foster father Joseph, the witness of the resurrection, Mary Magdalen, the "friends" of Jesus, Martha and Mary from Bethany, the Jews who stand by him, Simeon, Nicodemus, and Joseph of Arimathea, and, above all Judas Iscariot, whom he chose in the knowledge that he would bring his own journey to completion through his betrayal. And behind the Baptist, the principal representatives of the first covenant make a bodily appearance at the transfiguration of Jesus: Moses and Elias who also play a major role in Jesus' controversies with the Jews, and certainly in his understanding of his own mission. But the following are the ones who stand in a theologically more significant proximity: The Baptist—his Mother—the Twelve, among whom there is Peter on the one hand and John on the other—finally the "miscarriage" Paul.

The chronological sequence is, theologically, not totally without significance. At the origin, at the center of the event of the incarnation, stands Mary, the perfect maid who allowed it to happen that she enters a relationship of physical and spiritual motherhood to the person and thus also to the whole work of her Son, which, with the maturing of Jesus into a personality independently making his own decisions, can be altered at most but never extinguished. Even the choosing of the Twelve, with Peter at their head, can never be independent of this prior comprehensive relationship; in it it has its situation, place. But between these two events the mysterious, in human terms scarcely comprehensible, and yet theologically profoundly significant relationship between the Baptist and Jesus finds its place. The gospels and the Acts of the Apostles approach him only in fragmentary accounts difficult to bring into full harmony, but even so are in full agreement in attributing decisive significance to him for situating the mission of Jesus. John's eschatological preaching of repentance and the baptism of repentance are doubtless historical, as in Jesus' baptism by·him. Quite clear is the Baptist's pointing to the approaching last things, even if he does not know in advance and later becomes unsure again whether Jesus is this one who is to come. Certain is the dissolution of the mission, the transfer of the disciples of the Baptist to Jesus, the pointing of Jesus to the extraordinary figure of the Baptist and his role in closing the Old Covenant. It is probable that Jesus stood for a time in a disciple relationship to the Baptist and that his own mission thereby came in human terms to its own final maturity. The inmost personal relationship of the two is not accessible to us; we can only see the objectivity of the relation between the Old Covenant personally epitomized in the Baptist and pointing beyond him, and the kingdom of God beginning and approaching in Jesus. But in all the objectivity of commissioned representation, humanly subjective relations exist between the bearers of mission. They are here—in the objective, respectful mutual deference to one another—of an inaccessible tenderness. They are the two decisive rings which, welded together, make the chain of God's historical plan of salvation unbreakable. Thus the disciple John, who we are quite sure went to Jesus at the behest of the Baptist (Jn 1:35–37), dared to put the spontaneous remark about the "friend of the bridegroom" (Jn 3:29) on the lips of the Baptist, which none of the Twelve would have dared claim for themselves, since the greeting "friend" is first found in the mouth of Jesus at the hour of the Eucharist (Jn 15:14–15). Thus it is theologically correct that medieval pictures of the judgment place beside the judging Lord, as the two great intercessory mediators, not Mary and Peter, but Mary and the Baptist, because he embodies in his person the fullness of the Old Covenant, of the already-begun saving action of the Father, and because in the interconnection of their missions and in personal intimacy he is the closest to Jesus after his mother, Mary. And just as Mary, the beginning of the New Covenant, is, on the occasion of the visit from Jesus' relatives (Mk 3:31–33), placed back together with the "brothers" in the abandoned Old Covenant, which is now to be superseded, so John, who himself remains standing at the border of the Old Covenant, is lifted over this border into the New as the "Elias who is come," as "more than a prophet," as the "greatest to be born of woman" (Mt 11:15, 9, 11), as the one who in his own "being-as-self-giving" (Mk 1:14) gives the signal for the entrance of Jesus into his own self-giving. Such a person will not be left behind and forgotten in the work which Jesus will found; as the earthly starter of the mission of Jesus, he enters into it along with him. His feast day, up to now still with vigil, is celebrated shortly before Peter and Paul. In the theology of the church, however, he is forgotten.

Only now does the choosing of the Twelve take place, according to Mark one of the first acts in the public life of Jesus, no doubt primarily referred ahead, as the symbolic solemn founding of the new Israel, but at the same time still looking back to what was embodied by the Baptist. Long since dissolved, and still in existence only as a fiction, the twelve tribes attain a new concrete present. In the (pre-) lukan version of the bestowing of the kingdom—"As my Father appointed a kingdom for me, so do I appoint for you that you may eat and drink at my table in my kingdom, and sit on thrones judging the twelve tribes of Israel" (Lk 22:29–30)—is a promise not just meant for the final judgment. "In Luke sovereignty is a legal fact already established in the present by Christ in a unique act," in which "one can talk only of a juridical transferral if this is to remain a reality." Intended is "a real future exercise of dominion which is already conveyed in the present," and the reference of Jesus to his own authority received from the Father "indicates at the same time the juridical origin of delegated authority being exercized" (H. Schürmann). In the lukan composition this present-future transferral of the authority of the kingdom is connected with the themes of the eucharistic meal, the betrayal, service as criterion of rank, and the special prayer for Peter. The connection was thus rightly understood where, in what followed, this legal function was interpreted as valid for the time of the church and the "thrones" or "chairs" interpreted as episcopal chairs occupied by the Twelve and their successors. The royal consciousness of Jesus, which he already possessed on earth, is expressed in this "bequeathing" of the kingdom handed over to himself from God; and what at the end is shown as a kind of "testamentary" action has its beginning in the sovereign calling of those whom "he desired" and whom he "appointed to be twelve" (Mk 3:14, 16), whom he has with him, instructs, sends out to preach, and supplies "with authority" (Mk 3:15). A glance at Christ suffices to understand that for him "authority unites in a fully natural and unforced way the majesty of the consciousness of his mission with the humility of 'service,' yes with the giving up of his own life for those served" (cf. Mk 10:42–45; Lk 22:25–30; Jn 13:13–17). His education of the Twelve—as the core of the wider throng of disciples surrounding him—tends tirelessly toward their comprehending him in his *essence*—not just in the doctrines he teaches, in deeds that can be imitated—that is the meaning of the first reason given for the call of the Twelve: "that they might be with him together." Sharing in his attitude, his mission, his authority, his zeal, and his self-giving, and finally in the upper room, in his flesh and blood and, in his departing discourses, in his trinitarian love: all that is one. Therefore the commission to speak (Mk 3:14; 6:12) and the authority to act (namely, "to drive out demons" [Mk 3:15; 6:7, 12], and "to heal the sick" [Mk 6:13; cf. Mt 10:1; Lk 9:1–2, 6]) are simply one. The authority can be related just as well to proclamation and the mission to action, for in Jesus, the incarnate, active word, both are the same. He portrays his mandate according to the prophetic words of Isaiah (61:1–2; 58:6; cf. Lk 4:18–20) as a proclamation to the poor, imprisoned, blind, oppressed, and as their active liberation: both together are the *euangelisasthai*, the announcement of the "good news" and the "Lord's year of grace." And if at the beginning of Mark (1:1, 14), in Paul, and in the Acts of the Apostles, there is talk about the "gospel" and about service to it (Rom 1:9), what is meant here is always this whole and indivisible reality.

Within this community of life, mission, and authority of the Twelve with Jesus, Peter and John stand out. Peter with such unforgettable texts in all four gospels that anyone who appeals to the "pure gospel" must, whether willingly or not, also swallow the fishhook of these texts. (We will return to this.) In the meantime, just two remarks: the first is that Peter's special share in the authority and responsibility of Jesus also imposes on him a special participation in his attitude of service and readiness for suffering (Mt 16:23–25; Jn 13:6–8; 13:36; 21:18f). The second is that the gospel of the Beloved Disciple, in which his special mission to depict the love of the Lord and for the Lord is carried out, places the primacy of Peter at the beginning (Jn 1:42; cf. Mk 3:16) and makes the whole peak in a subtly composed symbolic doctrine of the church (Jn 20:1–10; 21:1–25), in which the mandate to "office" (Peter) and the mandate to "love" (John) are so intertwined with each other that the "greater love" which is demanded of Peter (Jn 21:15) passes from John to him, but John nevertheless as "what remains and never ends" remains standing (uniting office and love together) beside Peter according to the sovereign will of the Lord of the church. Peter's perplexing question as to how this problem is to be solved is turned back with a repeated command to discipleship: "If it is my will . . . what is that to you? Follow me!" (Jn 21:22). More than ever it becomes visible here that in the mystery of the church the articulations are clearly set out and still inseparable from each other. Peter needs the johannine love in order to give the Lord the answer required according to his office, and he also obtains this love; hence, the johannine love has its place in Peter. But Jesus' missions do not disappear; John attains—in the deeper mystery of the good favor of Jesus—his own, different from that of Peter. It can neither be said that love disappears in office (or that office coopts love for itself), nor that office and love stand in opposition like two adequately separable structural elements, although we mean by this statement to be obligated in no way to the Donatist heresy that an official church rite carried out outside of love (in the state of grave sin) is invalid. Instead our attention is called clearly to the fact that the structure that emerges in the constellation surrounding Jesus can in no way be treated and analyzed according to a "structuralist" pattern. This is so because this constellation not only always has a personal side but because the person about whom these relationships crystallize is unique (because divine), and thus does not come under any common law. What johannine love is cannot be approached purely anthropologically; it is the unique divine-human love of Jesus within the church. And consequently what the petrine office is also cannot be analyzed purely sociologically: it is participation in the unique God-human authority of Christ in the church.

The bursting of all readily visible structures in the constellation with Jesus becomes, to the point of complete perplexity for human reason, to the point of apparent contradiction, evident in the vocation of Paul to an apostolate that is of the same rank as that of the Twelve. He must struggle for it, all the more because the vision of the risen

One which places him together with his mandate on the same level with the first witnesses is of a completely different type. He remains a supernumerary because his place is already occupied by the election of Matthias. And yet he is legitimate, even beside the "super-apostles," "even though I am nothing" (2 Cor 12:11). So much "nothing" that the heavenly Jerusalem remains built on the twelve foundation stones and no thirteenth pillar is provided (Rev 21:14). And yet the lion's share of the mystery of Christ falls to his apostolate and to his theological understanding; Luke and Mark are his companions, his deeds occupy the largest part of the Acts of the Apostles. He represents the "suffering of Christ" to the communities and for them so that he must be looked at as "type" just as he aligns himself according to the "type" of Christ. Not only is an unprecedented existential mediation introduced by this—the beginning of the great missions of the saints in the history of the church—but also an extraordinary clarification of what will be called office and authority in the church: again, both sides are inseparable from each other.

Paulinism is not only that part which Luther separated for himself as "doctrine" with the letters to Romans and Galatians, but also just as much that other part, the church rule of the letters to the Corinthians, which proceeds more authoritarianly than any successor of Peter would have dared to (how mild the letter of Clement sounds in contrast!) and which obviously possesses more than just antiquarian interest for the later church. This is how the Corinthian charismatic church, in reality and under the assistance of the Holy Spirit, was actually governed. But authority in the church whose most precise anatomy Paul has dissected for us here, theologically as well as pastorally—and for all times in the church—is just as uniquely stamped by the unique Christ-event as was, previously, the "structure" of Peter-John. It is authority which wants to proceed in harmony with the community, with all the means of love, a heartfelt but also official love; authority which, with reference to the immanence of the Spirit of Christ in the faithful (2 Cor 13:5), strives to build the *communio* and which threatens with "naked" authority as it were only in the instance of a —legitimate but regrettable—borderline case, in case the apostle did not find in the community the proper, loving obedience of faith.

Just as Peter relies on John and John is in Peter (and next to him), so too the petrine element appears perhaps nowhere more purely than in Paul; just as, on the other hand, the pauline element is unmistakable in the petrine letters which still, on the other hand, intend to provide thoroughly petrine tradition. Again two marked figures, obviously not merging into one with specific theological and ecclesiological valences, stand in *perichōrēsis*—just as in the living "body of Christ" nothing else is possible between its members.

But not every member communicates in the same way with the other. Within the structure we have pointed out (which we explicitly characterized as not clearly delimitable) there are delicate lines of connection which are drawn and expounded most clearly by Luke and John. Luke establishes a familial relationship between Mary and the Baptist and, as companion of Paul, builds a discreet bridge between him and the gospel tradition. Together with him John is the discloser of the hidden mariological depth-dimension. In the episode under the cross, told only by John, he, the one whom the beginning of the Acts of the Apostles always mentions together with Peter, becomes the "son" and protector of the mother: he slides thereby into an unemphasized but fully indispensable mediating center (between Peter and Mary, church of office and of men, and church of women), which points out to both dimensions of the mystery of the church their place and their proportion. Only when these proportions are seen and recognized in the light of faith, in meditation upon the concrete revelation, can one profitably speak in the church of petrine office which, in addition, can never be separated from its most intimate context within the college of the Twelve, each of whom has been called expressly by name.

49 · Origin of the Church in the Marian Consent

Is not the synthesis of Christ as *Alpha* and *Omega* so unique that a participation in its catholicity is excluded from the outset? Yet what is Christ, what is the New Covenant? *Verbum Caro!* No more the old opposition, *Omnis caro foenum. . . . Verbum autem Domini manet in aeternum* (Is 42:6, 8), no more a word that only speaks at the human being, but Word-flesh. And therefore also faith-flesh. Flesh now has the Word. It is not the Spirit alone that makes that act of faith which puts God first and hopes in him, but the whole human being down to the foundation of its matter.

Flesh says unhesitatingly man and woman, wedding, mother, father, and child. Otherwise the reality of flesh is not present. Whoever wishes to think about the incarnation of the Word of God must look carefully for the woman. We are now talking about the fundamental act which is not only faith in a Word, hope in a promise, but love for the lovingly self-effacing origin: the agreement of the whole human being to the bottom-most fibers of its flesh. If these were not in whole-hearted readiness, how could the Word become flesh? If it becomes flesh it must rise from the bottom-most foundation of life. And this bottom-most foundation must receive it not like an empty abyss, in pure passivity, but with the active readiness with which a female womb receives the male seed.

The fundamental act is the preference of the absolute; for this is right, no matter what, and one simply lets it come through. Today there is a silly argument going on over the primacy of orthodoxy or *orthopraxis*. What stands at the beginning, what decides? Let us say calmly, neither of the two. Neither *doxy* nor *praxis*, neither a mere holding-to-be-true nor a bounding forward into action. At the beginning is God's Word that will become flesh: God's is the *praxis*, mine is the letting God's will be done in me, the agreement, the consent down to my fingernails. That of course is deed, but deed as answer to God's doing, and of course faith, but not in a proposition but in God's personal action in me. And if this consent of the unconscious were not free, totally free, it would not be an act of human consent. But where would the human being get so free a consent without spot or wrinkle, without the slightest unconscious reservation? Where, if not as gift from the hand of God?

But are there not two different acts, the bestowal of the freedom by God (perhaps into a pure passiviity?) and then the appropriating and activating of this freedom? This is somewhat like the way Protestants distinguish justification and sanctification: there God (in Christ) acts on me in a sovereign way, here God's action (in the Holy Spirit) penetrates within me. Such may well be the case with the sinner, but not with the original incarnation. Here God needs from the outset, in order to let his Word become flesh, the consent that allows all.

And it really is *someone* who in perfect creaturely freedom becomes womb and bride and mother of the incarnating God: this fundamental act is neither—in a Buddhist way—a surrender of the unfree being oneself into the abyss of the absolute, nor—in a Marxist way—a self-endowing with freedom so that the human being can become its own creator, but a being gifted—by the unconditionally self-giving God—with the freedom to receive God unconditionally.

In this fundamental act in the room at Nazareth, in this alone the church of Christ is founded as Catholic. Its catholicity is the unconditional character of the Ecce Ancilla (*"behold the handmaid"*) *whose offer of infinite accommodation is the creaturely counterpart to the infinitely self-bestowing love of God.*

Whoever posits the church's beginning later, say, with the calling of the Twelve or the bestowal of authority on Peter, has already missed what is essential; such a person always will only be able to reach an empirical-sociological reality which cannot be distinguished *qualitatively* from the synagogue. Even the "infallibility" of office then dangles exposed in the air because it cannot be given root in any other way than in the fallibility of the human being bearing it.

Where is she now, this "bride without spot or wrinkle" (Eph 5:27), this "pure virgin" who is supposed to be betrothed to Christ (2 Cor 11:2), if the universal Catholic consent that must be expected of her is not real somewhere, and not merely ideally and approximately (like all our consents) or eschatologically (so that the church would only become truly Catholic in eternity)? Where would it emerge, the Catholica, if it were not created in its innermost reality from the first moment of the New Covenant, as the child's mother who has to be virginal in flesh and spirit to enable her to be the incarnate catholic agreement with the unconditioned thrust of the divine Word into flesh?

50 · Origin of the Church in the Event of the Cross

That the cross is solidarity, the ancient church has always seen in the figure of the cross itself: stretching out to all dimensions of the world, stretched-out arms that want to embrace everything. The cross is, according to the *Didache, sēmeion epektaseōs* (sign of stretching out), and only God can achieve so wide a stretching: "God has stretched out his hands on the cross in order to encompass the limits of the earth" (Cyril of Jerusalem); "God so stretched out his arms in his passion and embraced the earth in order to presignify that from the rising of the sun to its setting a future people would be gathered under his wings" (Lactantius); "O blessed wood on which God was stretched out!" But God can nevertheless do this only as a human being whose form is distinguished from that of the beasts "in that he stands upright and can stretch out his hands" (Justin), and thus he reaches out to both nations which are represented by the malefactors and tears down the veil that separates them (Athanasius). The cross is, according to its external form, already inclusive.

But the opened heart out of which the last of the substance of Jesus is given points out the inner inclusion: blood and water, the sacraments of the church. In biblical terms and in overall human terms (philosophically), the heart is considered as the real center of the spiritual-bodily human being, and the analogy to this is the heart considered as the center of God's self-opening to human beings (1 Sam 13:14). If in the Old Testament "heart" is more the seat of intellectual power and orientation (while womb, *rachamim*, *splanchna*, expresses more the seat of the feelings), in the New Testament both flow together into the concept of heart: the "wholeness of heart" toward God is the opening of the whole human being to God (Acts 8:37; Mt 22:37). Thus the heart that was hardened (Mk 10:5, with many OT parallels) must be renewed: from a heart of stone to one of flesh (Ezek 11:19, etc.; cf. 2 Cor 3:3). And if Greek philosophy following Homer saw in the heart the center of the soulful-spiritual life (for the Stoa it is the seat of the *hēgemonikon*), New Testament theology introduces beyond this on the one hand an incarnational moment (soul completely embodied in the heart, body in the heart as the whole sphere of expression of the soul), and on the other hand a personal moment (only the Christian, body-soul human being is, in God's calling, a unique person, and God turns with his heart to his unique being).

The account of the piercing of the lance and the outpouring of blood and water have to be read in the continuity of the johannine water-spirit-blood symbolism to which the key word "thirst" also belongs: earthly water results again in thirst while Jesus' water quenches thirst forever (Jn 4:13f); "if anyone thirsts, let him come to me and drink, as one who believes in me" (Jn 7:37f), thus the thirst of the believer will be forever quenched (6:35). Connected with this is the extravagant promise that his water in being drunk will become a source springing into eternal life (Jn 4:14); as scripture says, "Streams of living water will gush forth from his *koilia* (innards, bowels, heart: Jn 7:38). That Jesus, as the absolute thirster, is himself made to flow in an eternal fountain, we have already seen. The scriptural saying is connected either with the ever-present analogy of water and Word-Spirit (Jesus' words are indeed "spirit and life"), or better with the fountains in the new temple of Ezekiel (Ezek 47; cf. Zech 13:1), with which Jesus compared his body (Jn 2:21). That John saw the institution of the sacraments of Eucharist and baptism in the flowing forth of water and blood cannot be doubted in the context of his general symbolism (cf. Cana, 2:1–11; the unity of water and Spirit, 3:5; of water, Spirit, and blood, 1 Jn 5:6, with explicit reference to "Jesus Christ: he it is who has come through water and blood"). The opening of the heart is a surrendering of what is most intimate and personal to public use; the open, emptied space is accessible to all. In addition, official proof must be provided that the separation of flesh and blood (as presupposition for the shape of the eucharistic meal) was carried out to the end. The (new) temple just like the newly opened drinkable fountain point to community: the body given is the place of the new institution of the covenant, of the new gathering of the community: room, altar, sacrifice, meal, community, and its Spirit all at once.

* * *

The origin of the church on the cross is such a many-faceted *theologoumenon* that it cannot be treated here even in a sketchy fashion. In it the line which begins a completely new creation of the covenant people out of the one completely valid representative of this covenant on earth (this is where the favorite patristic image of the birth of the new Eve from the side of the new Adam slumbering in death belongs), comes together with the other line that the old nation will be brought to perfection beyond itself in the "holy remnant" so that in this grace-filled, creative transmutation from the Old Covenant, something like a prechurch (represented in Mary, John, and the faithful women) must be presupposed. Nothing of course prevents our assuming that even pre-Christian faith already took its life from the grace of the cross (Heb 11:26; 1 Pet 1:11; Jn 8:56, etc.). This means then that Mary especially must be characterized as (through Christ's sacrifice) prere-deemed. Further, the theology of the covenant being brought to com-pletion as a two-sided contract between God and human beings comes together here with the completion of the one-sided promise prior to this concept of the covenant: in as much as God in heaven and God on earth is the unity of the covenant ("But God is only one, *eis*": Gal 3:20), all men and women are at the same time in the unity of Christ included in this covenant ("you are all one, *eis*, in Christ Jesus": Gal 3:28), because Christ is human, and indeed human for the sake of all human beings. And from this second encounter is disclosed still another: the one-sided/two-sided contract between God and peo-ple in the Old Covenant was always compared with a marriage covenant, which said something about the holiness of its founding and the loving fidelity thus demanded. But now, since the Word has become flesh and his loving fidelity humanly speaking has been proven unto the end, the marriage simile is also incarnated, and the theology of the Song of Songs fulfilled along with it. And this is indeed done (according to the second, necessarily required conv-ergence depicted above) in that two-sidedness which requires the church to be simultaneously both: that is, the very body of Jesus Christ (through his Eucharist: 1 Cor 10:16; as participation in his flesh and blood given up to death: 1 Cor 11:26; Jn 6) and precisely *in* this being a body, also his virginal bride (2 Cor 11:2). But the possibil-ity of this "simultaneous" is mirrored through the paradisal account of the origin of woman out of man (Eph 5:30–33; in an indissoluble mutality: 1 Cor 11:7–12; to the extent that Christ too, from whom the church comes, "was born of a woman": Gal 4:4). Now this really implies that one must simultaneously fix upon the following: The absolute sovereignty of God who in Jesus Christ alone establishes his New and eternal Covenant with man and woman, *and* the shared acceptance of the letting-it-happen consent of the humanity repre-sented at the cross, which had to be made by Mary at the incarnation (and for all its implications) *loco totius humanae naturae*—in place of the whole of human nature—especially as kernel of the new church. In so far as Christ's vicarious suffering is not exclusive but inclusive, his including gesture can only be one of allowing-to-suffer-with. From this point it becomes definitively clear that the indicated approximations of divine abandonment from the Old and New Testament cannot be understood "psychologically" or "ethically" but, where genuine, only christologically. Indeed they must be postulated as christological. Such allowing-to-suffer-with becomes especially clear in John where Jesus allows the "one he loves" (Jn 11:3) to die, sends the worrying sisters no message, but leaves them in a dark night of apparent forgottenness, and then himself overwhelmed by this—imposed by him—night (Jn 11:33–38), and thus eucharistically distributes in advance his God-forsakenness. It is also this *com-passio* then, that belongs to his essential legacy to his church, and that makes it possible for the church to last through the hiatus of the day in which "God is dead."

Here lie the biblical-theological implications in utmost rigor and, at the same time, very close to each other, and only a completely coherent thinking through of the achieved synthesis from the point of view of the "promises" can keep them all in view at the same time. The synthesis is not constructable or surveyable in human logic, but is disclosed only in the ultimate horizon of trinitarian faith. Its foundation however is laid so broadly and so richly that none of the elements that are used in it may be left out in the believing overview.

The church is—as born of the utmost love of God for the world—itself essentially love. What it is, is also what it should be: its essence is its single commandment (Jn 15:12). It is significant in this regard that the love of the disciples for Christ (in John ten times) is rendered with *philein*, which is the word used for emphatically interhuman love, while the love of Christians for each other is designated without exception with *agapan*, which is the word used for emphatically divine love. What joins the Christians to Christ is the friendship instituted by him, to prove which he "lays down his life for his friends" (Jn 15:13, 15); what conversely joins them to each other is that all are brothers and sisters under the same Master (Mt 23:8), all members under the same superior head, and, according to the law of love of that head, must really care about one another.

51 · Mary—Exemplar of the Church

Where the church is "holy and blameless," according to its original election (Eph 1:4), where it is the "bride in splendor without spot or wrinkle or any such thing," "holy and without blemish" (Eph 5:27), there it professes itself, in full accord with the Son's law of incarnation, as "handmaid of the Lord" (Lk 1:38). This does not really express a consent demanded by God as a "free partner" distinct from him, for with the incarnation the time of such a two-sided covenant is past (Gal 3:20). Mary's freedom allows God to make use of her, hence the categorical *future*: "you *will* bear, *will* give him the name Jesus," etc. (Lk 1;31–35). God's salvific will comes upon her as something already set, established, and institutionalized from all eternity. And yet her consent is existential to the ultimate degree; it embraces not only the spiritual but also the bodily faith of the one being made use of—and this bodily faith will from now on be called fertile virginity— for otherwise than in such a faith, through it, and with it together, the Word of God would not be flesh. This mother's body, which was already (in the overshadowing of the Spirit) a bride's body, is proleptically the church body from which and for which everything will be formed unto Christ, which will later be called church. The ecclesiastical-marian obedience to the Son is a perfect and thus completely low-keyed one; it has the naturalness of love and of a mother-child relationship. It is an unconditional obedience because it is concerned with making the church similar in form to the trinitarian obedience of the cross. Thus the mother is "purified" just as the boy is circumcised, although neither of them "needed" it and thus (in their literal, incarnated obedience to "the law of the Lord" and "of Moses": Lk 2:22–24) these appear in a false light. Then Mary as "flesh and blood" is placed with the unbelieving relatives and not allowed in; she serves her Son as illustrative material for what he has left behind: family relationships, the Old Covenant (Mk 3:31–35). Finally she is taken with him especially to the cross in order to share there in his God-foresakenness, for as the Father abandons the Son, so the Son abandons his mother and thrusts upon her, the church, another "son" (Jn 19:25–27). In all this she is "blessed" because her existence is filled with "hearing the word of God and keeping it" (Lk 11:28; 2:19–51), in the johannine sense, "abiding" in it. In this primitive cell of the church the trinitarian loving obedience of the incarnate one can be imprinted without resistance, this is possible because she in no way at all plays "personality," which by a more or less heroic act renounces oneself in order to devote oneself to the service of God; but simply as "lowly handmaid" is struck by the glance of "his mercy," of the God who "exalts those of lowly degree, fills the hungry with good things, and sends the rich away empty" (Lk 1:48–53). Stripped by this *anawim*-poverty of every possible counterdefense (with "good things" from one's own argument or objections and "responsibilities"), the primordial act of the church can be the allowing-God-to-have-disposition-over oneself, an act into which the mature faith-experience of Israel—that God is with the powerless and those deprived of rights, and that God's saving action singles out and redeems especially them—enters and expands. Obedience is almost too special a concept for this allowing-God-to-dispose, for this precedes obedience in an analogous, transcendent way, like the way in which the kenotic obediential will of the Son preceded his earthly servile obedience as its transcendent presupposition.

52 · Peter—First Bearer of the Office of Unity

Simon Peter with his double name ("You *are* Simon, the Son of John; you *shall* be called Cephas, which means rock": Jn 1:42) is from the outset a double, a someone living in transition. He came to Cephas-being only after the resurrection, but even then he can still make mistakes which give Paul the right to "oppose him to his face" (Gal 2:11–14). The consciousness of the office communicated to him nevertheless already resides in him before, as when he, in living, but insufficient faith, climbs from the boat to be with Jesus, or when he wishes to distinguish himself as the one who will not betray the master, or when at the Lord's Supper he thinks he has to know who is the betrayer, or when he has the courage to draw the sword against an armed gang in order to defend the Master, or when, finally, out of a sense of responsibility, he goes into the court of the praetorium in order to know what is happening to his master. All these gestures, whose outcome is negative, proceed without doubt from his prerogative, whenever or in whatever form they may have been conveyed to him by the pre-Easter Lord. Even the words with which he warns Jesus against the passion or seeks to protect him from it, and which bring upon him the sharpest reproach of being a tempter and devil, can be dictated by his still-misunderstood awareness of responsibility.

Otherwise Jesus' words of reproach are mild and patient: he sees in Peter, and at the same time makes allowances for, the still-unavoidable discrepancy between willingness and ability. The betrayal is taken into account and is unavoidable, but he sees beyond that: " 'Simon, Simon, behold, Satan demanded to have you, that he might sift you like wheat, but I have prayed for you that your faith may not fail; and when you have turned again, strengthen your brethren.' And he said to him 'Lord, I am ready to go with you to prison and to death.' He said, 'I tell you Peter, the cock will not crow this day, until you three times deny that you know me' " (Lk 22:31–34). It is unusual that the Lord prays for "Simon," for him as a person in danger, but that in the prophecy of the denial he addresses him as "Peter," the one who fails in his office. There is the same kind of seeing and going beyond what is seen in John 13:36: "Simon Peter said to him:

'Lord, where are you going?' Jesus answered, 'Where I am going you *cannot* follow me now; but you *shall* follow afterward.'" The same twilight is found in the johannine parallel to Peter's messianic confession, except that Peter appears not only as the one making a personal profession of faith but also as connected more profoundly with the college of the Twelve: "Will *you* also go away?" Jesus asks the Twelve, just as in Mark 8:27–29 (par) he asks the "disciples": "Who do you say that I am?" Peter (in John already illumined by post-Easter light) answers for all: "Lord, to whom shall we go? You have the words of eternal life, and *we* have believed, and have come to know, that you are the Holy One of God."

But here there does not follow, as in the synoptics, the reproach to Peter for wanting to hinder the passion, but the reference to Judas, the even more profound shame of the church: "Did I not choose you, the twelve, and one of you is a devil?" (Jn 6:67–69). In the "we" of Peter, whose answer speaks in a collegial-representative way, lies the point of connection for the reference to him who breaks out of the college and cannot be covered by Peter's word. Even the exchange between Jesus and Peter at the washing of the feet is also introduced (Jn 13:2) and concluded (13:11) with a reference to Judas. The shocked question of Peter, "Lord, do you wash my feet?" which Jesus answers with his "now you are unable to understand, but later you will," and which brings about the outcry, "You shall never wash my feet!" results less from the disciple's awareness of office and much more (like Lk 5:8: "Depart from me, for I am a sinful man, O Lord") from the apalling consternation of being drawn into something larger than life, something even that upsets all order. (Somewhat the same holds for Peter's words about the "three booths" at the transfiguration: Mk 9:5 par.) With the calmness of one who has already made his choice, the Lord passes over this shrinking-back in order to bring the disciple into his own office ("Henceforth you will be catching men": Lk 5:10) and thereby into his own nature ("If I do not wash you, you have no part in me": Jn 13:8).

Three things in Peter must be viewed together. First, he was chosen for his office even before the capacity, that is, the Holy Spirit, for performing it on his own was bestowed. But with this being-chosen, the disciple's fundamental decision was already made: "When they had brought their boats to land, they left everything and followed him" (Lk 5:11); "Then Peter said in reply, 'Lo, we have left everything and followed you'" (Mt 19:27); from this decision is explained the (relative) openness of the disciples for their growing comprehension of what Jesus truly is. For "Christ did not make his appearance in Judea with the cry: I am the Son of the living God. This cry also would not have had the least effect. He waited until, through life with him and the acceptance of his life into that of his disciples, higher intuitions had come to life in them, intuitions whose natural expression at the first opportunity was naturally: 'You are the Son of the living God' " (J. A. Möhler).

Thus, what grows in them is not just human good will (which with Peter, of course, mostly misses the mark), is "not flesh and blood" which reveals the truth to them "but my Father who is in heaven" (Mt 16:17). And even if one would transfer to the period after Easter the following great promise of the Lord to Peter as the rock of the church, the messianic confession itself (Mk 8:29; Lk 9:20) is doubtless pre-Easter and hits upon something centrally right, even if it must immediately be corrected and amplified by Jesus in the direction of the suffering servant of God. Peter's decision knows no turning back ("To whom shall we go?"). With this he gives, as far as it is possible before the guidance of the Spirit, an inchoatively correct answer.

It is unbiblical to say that Peter the sinner, the purely natural human being ("flesh and blood"), did everything wrong and only the grace of office gives him the capacity for correct action. Also no impulse of arrogance on the basis of his priority in rank can be found in the pre-Easter Peter—he is not the one who desires to sit at the right hand of the Son of man, but the two brothers, the sons of thunder (Mk 10:36). Instead there are sure signs of a genuine humility. He has to accept many hard things said to him by Jesus. From here to his being the first of the line of popes in the community of his "fellow presbyters" (1 Pet 5:1) is not a long distance.

The second point, which comes from the situation in the New Testament, is the human Peter's being totally overwhelmed by the office thrust upon him. How should a "sinful man" control the "keys of the kingdom of heaven" so that his earthly opening and closing has eternal consequences; how should he be able to "feed" the "sheep and lambs" of Jesus, the single Good Shepherd (who in this represents God himself: Ezek 3:11–16), especially since he is reminded of his triple denial in the conferral of his pastoral authority; how is it possible for him, as he walks over such waves, not to sink? How should he, in the panic of that "hour of darkness," not take up the best weapon within reach with which he, both as a human being and as one of the Old Testament, is familiar, and which perhaps Jesus himself had recommended that he take along (Lk 22:36, 38)? How is he, in the same hour in which his Master, in accord with God's most hidden decree, is stripped of all power and led to the point of God-forsakenness, supposed to stand as the representative, both of a humanity whose guilt is now being suffered for, and of a church which is also supposed to share in the humiliation of its Lord? How is he supposed to be able to stand as the great, unimpeachable confessor of all this? In this hour of inexorable truth, there must enter into the light of pure objectivity just what a church would be, and indeed is, if one prescinds from the fruit of the suffering of its head. The theological precision of the passion scenes in which the Christians—betrayers, deniers, deserters—appear more shamefully than Jews and pagans, is so striking that, in the picture of Peter denying with curses and then bitterly weeping, every Christian can recognize in this primate only his own portrait. And directly into this bitter shame is spoken the inconceivably healing and comforting word of the promise of martyrdom for him who as shepherd should feed the flock of the incomparable shepherd: "'. . . but when you are old, you will stretch out your hands, and another will gird you and carry you where you do not wish to go.' (This he said to show by what death he was to glorify God.) And after this he said to him, 'Follow me'" (Jn 21:18–19). The chasm of demanding too much which yawns between the man and his mandate, between the sinner and denier and his mission to feed the flock *properly* in the manner of the Good Shepherd, is bridged by the grace of the Lord. What seemed impossible, an imitation of the one person who can be priest and sacrifice at the same time, is granted. According to tradition Peter was crucified with his head down, different, but in this reversal, still in the same form. But one must pay attention to this "where you do not wish": this identity of form with Christ is so completely pure grace that it takes place within a movement of resistance against it. But this resistance in world history will never be strong enough to cripple the grace of being in the same form with Christ. Jesus' prayer has overcome the "desire of Satan" (Lk 22:31). "The gates of hell will not overcome" (Mt 16:18) what has been founded on Peter.

The third point, which becomes visible even in the Acts of the Apostles, is the matter-of-factness with which Peter perceives his position of leadership at the beginning, until his imprisonment by Herod forces him to go "to another place" (Acts 12:17), and leave the direction of the Jerusalem community to James, the brother of the Lord. His sense for Catholic universalism, explicitly grounded in his vision at Joppa and openly proclaimed at the "apostolic council" (Acts 15:7–11), places him intellectually close to the view of Paul.

It is therefore internally consistent that he, like Paul, changed his main emphasis from the direction of an individual community to missionary activity, even though, in relation to the delicate and (at the moment) practically insoluble problems between Jewish- and heathen-Christians, this must have brought him—as one of the Twelve he stood much closer to Jerusalem than Paul—into much more severe internal conflicts than Paul.

Precisely because Peter stood much closer to the universalistic views of Paul than to the party of James—with whom he remained connected as one of the Twelve and on the basis of the division of the mission territory (Gal 2:7–10), without on this account having to speak about a dependency, not to speak of "subordination"—one can give credence to the supposition that, in relation to the Jerusalem party, Peter "had a much more difficult position than the independent Paul and that this conflict (about the food regulations in Antioch) must have put Peter . . . into a particularly painful dilemma that we can only surmise. . . . Mediators always have a particularly difficult position." The sword that cuts through Paul's whole existence—"To the Jews I became as a Jew . . . to those outside the law I became as one outside the law . . . to the weak I became weak. . . . I have become all things to all men . . . for the sake of the gospel" (1 Cor 9:20–27)—must, then, have even more painfully driven through the Peter who, although upbraided with "jealousy" (zēlos: Clem 5:4), kept quiet; and one would almost like to add, "that the (wicked) thoughts of many hearts may be revealed" (Lk 2:35) in this sign of contradiction.

Concerning the incident to Antioch, a few sentences of Ignatius Döllinger can be read with profit:

> The worst was thus averted (by the compromise of the 'Apostolic Council'), the Christian freedom of the gentile Christians rescued. But the principal difficulty still remained unsolved; it had quite intentionally not been touched at the Council. That the Jewish-Christians and the apostles themselves would continue to observe the law, was here silently presupposed. . . . Without doubt the view of the apostle was that the obligation of the ritual law would have to take a back seat over against the higher obligations of Christian brotherly love and the more important right of membership in the body of the Church.

Peter thus had "no hesitation 'to live as a gentile,' " to have table fellowship with the gentile Christians, until the party of James came and he withdraws from that table fellowship.

> This was no infraction of the decrees passed at the Council, for this whole relationship had there remained indeterminate and yet the person who dispensed with this part of the law was, in the eyes of all Jews, a despiser of the law. Peter might well think that he, forced to choose between two scandals, the one that would scandalize the Hellenizers or what would scandalize the Israelites, should decide for the lesser evil. He feared, said Paul, those of the circumcision. That was surely not a lack of moral courage; he had abundantly proven this [in Jerusalem]. . . . As the shepherd of the whole flock installed by Christ, he belonged to both [parties]; but till now he had been above all the apostle of Israel, and he did not yet want to relinquish his effectiveness in Jerusalem and Judaea . . . [although he] with the baptism of Cornelius had broken through the separating wall of the ritual law and asserted his right to do so against the misgivings of others.

This present decision of Peter was found by Paul,

> as the apostle of the gentiles and preacher of evangelical freedom, to be intolerable; he considered immediately how the party of the pharisaic zealots, who wanted to have the yoke of the whole law imposed on the gentile Christians, would misuse this example of the prince of the apostles. He reproved the conduct of Peter publicly and with sharp words. . . . He was acting out of mere human respect against his better persuasion, and this is *hypokrisis*, dissimulation. There is no account of how Peter answered this; in any case the misunderstanding was not a lasting one, for both apostles were of one mind in the matter itself. Paul himself never considered allowing the Jewish-Christians in general and in particular those living in Palestine complete freedom from the law . . . [indeed he] had no reservations even about himself obeying the law where it did not come into collision with the higher obligations of his apostolate and his position toward the gentile Christians.

This should be elucidated somewhat more completely so that the third aspect of the petrine reality is not restricted just to the moments of church leadership, mission, and martyrdom. In Peter's "being condemned" (Gal 2:11) in Antioch one might see a sequel to his pre-Easter failings of which we have indeed said that they went along with the "type," just as much as Peter's pre- and post-Easter sorrow for them (Mk 14:72 par; Jn 21:17). Nevertheless this "guilt" has a totally different value than something like a denial: it is now unconditionally a product of his pastoral concern to find the least damaging compromise solution to an objectively insoluble situation. How should such a "guilt" be left out of the characteristic type and real symbol of Peter?

The Essence of the Church

53 · Church—Community of Saints

The term "communion of saints" is found in the Apostles' Creed between "I believe in the Holy Spirit, the Holy Catholic Church" and "the forgiveness of sins, the resurrection of the body, and life everlasting" like a necessary link in the chain. The Holy Spirit is the foundation of all this: there would be no holy Catholic church without him.

Jesus has entrusted the building and extension of the church to the Spirit, just as he has entrusted himself eucharistically to the Spirit which develops from him who is the "head," the "body" as the fullness of Christ. If "communion of saints" is a closer, more intimate and secret description of the Catholic church, then this means that, in the first place, the communion of those who have been sanctified with the sanctity of Jesus by the Holy Spirit—they are the "saints"—is a communion of the gifted who all share commonly in something which of themselves they are not and could indeed never be. They do not become a communion of saints, if grace sanctifies them individually, on the basis of a universal human nature in which they already form a community; rather they became such a communion expressly through the community established by the Spirit (2 Cor 13:13), naturally on the basis of their call by the Father into the community of his Son Jesus Christ (1 Cor 1:9), as it is realized particularly in the eucharistic community (1 Cor 10:16ff.). But this common and community-creating fact of having been given a gift from God engenders of itself a horizontal community among themselves; the Holy Spirit, which founds the community, also fosters it among its members. The talk of "the encouragement of love, the community of the spirit, the deep sympathy and pity . . . the same love, being in full accord and of one mind" (Phil 2:1f.) points in the same direction. More and more over the centuries, as the church has reflected on its own nature, it has thought out and deepened this second horizontal element, without however detaching it from the first, in which it is perduringly founded; and it is indeed that which deserves particular thought, because in other descriptions and definitions of the church it is almost always given short measure.

The extent to which the saints—those who attempt to take seriously their sanctification by the holy triune God and to respond to it—are able in their community to be, to live, to work, and to suffer for one another can only begin to be realized when one has grasped the principle which welds them together into the unity of the community of the church: the unity of the triune God manifested in the self-giving of Christ and poured out in the Holy Spirit. For this unity is nothing other than pure being-for-one-another. If there were a definition of God, then one would have to put it in the form of unity as being-for-one-another. What, for want of a better word, we refer to as divine "persons," is the presupposition of there being such a pure being-for-one-another in God. These "persons" do not have a primary being for themselves which is only secondarily opened to others; that which we might speak of as their "being-for-themselves," their self-consciousness, they have in common as the one, indivisible God; but this One is integrated always from the beginning (and not subsequently) by the being-for-one-another. One cannot understand the Father except in his engendering giving of himself to the begotten Son, nor can one understand the Son except in his being for the Father. The self-giving of both to each other is once again a being-for-one-another which in the writings of the New Covenant is clearly distinguished as Holy Spirit both from the Father and from the Son; it is personified being-for-one-another in general and the absolute self-giving of God to human beings.

If one now reflects that this gift of God, which infuses the believers with the form of the divine being for one another, lays the basis for the essence of the church and so of the distinctively Christian form of community, then one can see clearly what a total reversal of human relationships and structures has taken place here. It is true that human beings form among themselves a physical whole whose mysterious ramifications run back from the material realm into the psychological (as, for example, C. G. Jung would claim to have described them in his theory of the collective unconscious) in a manner difficult to trace and to pin down. However that may be, it remains essential that these luminous spiritual apexes of consciousness, where everyone bears free responsibility and makes decisions, are distinct from one another, so that only on the basis of this distinction can they open to each other in dialogue. That this element of dialogue has a share in constituting the individual person and enables him to come into full possession and exercise of his personal freedom is not denied by this fact. But the form of the dialogue can indeed be very differently filled: with edifying, neutral and destructive contents.

The being-for-one-another which is bestowed upon the communion of saints by contrast opens the individual to the other precisely in departing from the personal apex. And this occurs with increasing intensity, the more deeply the believing person allows himself or herself to be determined, to be taken into and, as it were, dispossessed by this divine form of being-for-one-another. Whoever consents to this divine form of life, to a life in which from the outset one abandons all claim to possession in favor of the other; whoever offers for the other's disposal everything which belongs to him, including that which is most private and apparently most immediate, of such a person the God of love disposes in all truth and effectiveness for the benefit of his brothers and sisters.

It is here that the biblical concept of fruitfulness is introduced. This supersedes (but without destroying their restricted meaning) the concepts of wages and profits, which at first, as images taken from the world of human labor, presuppose a system of individuals distinct from one another in order to be able to stress the effective "being-for" of the saint (that is to say, of the truly believing, hoping, loving human being). The more "profitable" the being and behavior of a human being are—and he is not to be deprived of his profit—the more profitable he is for the community. And this by no means exclusively, or above all as a result of particular acts, like prayers or acts of renunciation, but because of his total bearing, his basic attitude, his will to understand himself as an expropriated being, as a being which may be given away. Of course such an attitude has its roots, in so far as it can by virtue of its divine origins take root in the world of human beings, in the Eucharist of the Son: he, as the one imbued with the spirit of the Eucharist, is the vine whose whole fruitfulness flows out of himself into the branches. The closest approximation of all to such an attitude is to be found in the maiden-saying of Mary by which she consents to her total dispossession in order to become the receptacle of the Holy Spirit. From Origen down to the middle ages one spoke of such a dispossessed soul as an *anima ecclesiastica*, as a soul bearing the form of the church. This soul has agreed to enter under the form of being-for-one-another, and this without imposing any conditions, without, for instance, demanding to receive back again as much as it itself gives.

This final point makes it clear that the communion of saints cannot be a closed circle of those who exchange their profits among themselves, in much the same manner in which firms amalgamate, in order to get a higher yield on their capital. The communion of saints can only be an open circle of those who "give without counting the cost," who let their light shine into the world without looking for its reflection. That alone is *agape, caritas;* only so did Christ pour himself out on the cross and in the Eucharist. And consequently, it is not possible to set limits to the comprehensiveness and effectiveness of this open circle. Only the person who is willing to lose can become a member. "A power went forth from him" (Mk 5:30; Lk 6:19; 8:46) is what is said of the miracles of Jesus. And he behaves as if he did not know into whom it has passed. It is of course true if one equates the communion of saints with the "Holy Catholic Church," then there will indeed be many profiteers whom one has to count among its number. And the transition from the "losers" to the "winners" is so gradual that it will not in practice be possible to draw any sharp dividing lines. Who, even among the true saints, does not profit from Mary's word of assent? She is the one who bears fruit, the virgin mother simply. We all take shelter under her cloak. But there are others within this cloak who themselves have smaller cloaks and they do not know who it is that finds shelter under them, for, at least on earth, only God knows what the extent and effect of the fruitfulness of the saints may be. Then by stages we come to those in whom sin grows and takes the upper hand but who nevertheless pour out a few drops of blood to the general circulation. Perhaps they take more than they give, but all the same they do give something. Serious sinners are those who absorb all grace for themselves without giving anything at all back. Here also there is a countermovement, but one cannot say that it simply outweighs the first. A rotten member in the body of the church can poison much in its vicinity. Evil is infectious. And yet it would not be proper to say that it has a kind of counterfruitfulness. It only has the possibility of impeding true fruitfulness. It is only what is good and selfless that bears fruit; evil itself is unfruitfulness. And yet one knows that evil causes the good to suffer and that the suffering of the good is deepened fruitfulness. In his Eucharist Jesus gained victory by anticipation over his enemies, even over his final enemy, death. And consequently the goal of the communion of saints is not properly the communal struggle against evil—as a corporation or club might set itself a common goal—but nothing other than the radiating out of the good; indeed not even that, for the good is radiated of itself; the aim is quite simply to hold oneself ready, the purpose is the abandonment of all one's own purposes, in order that God's aims may be fulfilled through his own people.

*   *   *

The image of blood circulation was sounded before. It is the old image used by Paul of the body of Christ in which the many members live and grow together in harmony and mutual care. In this picture the "Holy Catholic Church" and "the communion of saints" interpenetrate each other and are woven seamlessly together. For here the principle of the structure in its external, visible arrangement is linked with the principle of the inner, organic life by being set in relationship to an invisible, active center: "all made to drink of *one* spirit" (I Cor 12:13). And this spirit which circulates through the organism causes the members not only to care "horizontally" for one another but also (as Thomas Aquinas emphasized again and again) to love the whole more than themselves, the parts. And in the church or in the communion of saints the whole is Christ, in whom the fullness of the godhead dwells and who unfolds this fullness in his mystical body (Col 1:19; Eph 1:23). And so every member has its fullness, the principle of its fruitfulness from him—"from his fullness have we all received" (Jn 1:16)—and no one can pour forth such fullness (horizontally) without having received it, without owing it to the real source (vertically). Fruitfulness is always Eucharist, and Eucharist means thanksgiving to the source, to the "Father of lights from whom every good endowment and every perfect gift comes down" (Jas 1:17). The life which flows through the organism—as Holy Spirit or as eucharistic blood, for both belong indivisibly together—is that which gives every member its form and function and consequently at the same time relates it beyond itself to the whole. No member of the human body lives its own separate life; but it receives its vitality from the whole which transcends it, in order that it may in its turn serve the whole. And so Paul can move immediately from the organic level—leaving out the natural sociological level in which analogous and yet different laws obtain—to the level of the church, where the vital principle repeats itself, yet in a surprisingly new way, in the realm of the Spirit. Only now the all-embracing vital principle is no longer natural but supernatural. We must not overwork the image and attempt to get more from it than an image can give. The supernatural correspondence runs out into something for which we can provide no metaphors, precisely at the point where the visible, functional, and charismatically ordered Catholic church can no longer be equated without remainder with the invisibly functioning laws of the communion of saints. It is possible to observe and record a charism fairly extensively; but never the effects of spiritual fruitfulness.

There is perhaps no more comforting truth about the church than that in it there is a community, a communion of saints. For, on the one hand, this means that there is a continually overflowing richness on which all the poor may draw; it is also called the treasure of the church. It is precisely the same as the incalculable fruitfulness of those who offer themselves and all that they have to God to dispose of for the sake of the brotherhood and sisterhood. Real power goes forth from them; they are not spared by love (Rom 8:32) but are rigorously shared. Who knows to whom I owe which grace in my life? This excess which comes to us makes us poor and humble, for we sense precisely that we can only draw on such richness in the same spirit in which it has been given. We feel in this that we have already received much more that is not our own than we have ourselves given of our own, that perhaps, in so far as we have regarded and handled that which was not our own as our own, we have misappropriated the goods of others. The idea of the communion of saints inspires no little caution in us. On the other hand, it also exhorts us not to underestimate the fruitfulness which has been given us by God. There are many who in old age or in sickness or in imprisonment or in any of the other *cul-de-sacs* of existence imagine that they have nothing more to give. They seem to themselves to be useless and may be tempted to end their life. Such people should remember that only the one who is poor and precisely the one who is poor, who is conscious of having lost all that he or she owned, has been put in a position to give. The widow at the treasury gave more than all the rest, "she gave of her poverty." Those who are poor in spirit not only gain the kingdom of heaven itself, they open it to the others. Poor people have had the best knowledge of this mystery.

Misunderstood, abandoned even by her own husband she had buried six children but had not lost her natural readiness to help; regarded as strange by her sisters and sisters-in-law, a laughable person, who was stupid enough to work for others without reward, she had at the end of her life saved no possessions. A dirty white goat, a lame cat, rubber plants. . . .

We all lived alongside her and none of us understood that she was that righteous person without whom, as the proverb says, no village can live.

And no city.
And not our whole country.

(A. Solzhenitsyn: *Matriona's Farm*)

54 · Church—Bride of Christ (In Connection with Ephesians 5)

We would like to recall the well-known passage in the Epistle to the Ephesians where Paul places the performance of marriage under the exemplar of the performance of love between Christ and the church. Exemplar, not just model: Christ remains here, as always, both insurpassably superior—and still capable of being imitated. The end of the passage reads; *"This is a great mystery, and I take it to mean Christ and the church."* We can leave open what the apostle means by "mystery": the husband-wife or the Christ-church relationship, or the paradise story, brought in to make the point that Eve comes from Adam's rib as image for the origin of the church from Christ. Presumably the whole context is meant: ordered sexual relationship exists in Christian terms only in the encompassing space of the relationship of Christ-church, for which the original relationship of Adam-Eve remains an eloquent parable.

It does not need to be emphasized that Paul does not mean that the performance of marriage is the only or at least most effective manner of taking part in the Christ-church relationship. Like the Lord in the gospels, he elsewhere gives preference to the celibate life (1 Cor 7:7–8:32), which is dedicated immediately to the infinite and completely supernatural fruitfulness of this relationship. But a religion of the incarnation of God necessarily takes up and brings even the fundamental sexual relationship into the life of discipleship.

Paul begins powerfully: *"Be subject to one another in the fear of Christ."* A fear which, of course, means not dread but reverence for Christ and his mystery; a fear which places married people immediately under the ultimate norm of the behavior of Christ, and withdraws them from all self-invented norms. The passage explicitly says *"one another"* (as also in many other places: Gal 3:15; Phil 2:3, cf. 1 Pet 5:3), which of course prevents the exhortation from being related exclusively to women.

But now it becomes more difficult: *"Wives, be subject to your husbands, as to the Lord. For the husband is the head of the wife as Christ is the head of the church, his body, and is himself its Savior. As the church is subject to Christ, so let wives also be subject in everything to their husbands"* (Eph 5:22–24). Let us for the moment leave aside the irritating statement that the husband is the head of the wife; we will ask later whether and to what extent it is time-conditioned. Certainly not time-conditioned is the statement that Christ is the head of the church, and precisely insofar as he is its Savior, *sotēr*, so that the church as a whole, husbands and wives, have every reason to subject themselves to Christ. The image of Christ as the "head" stands in the foreground, so that the following will be evident: the church (as his "body") owes its existence as a whole to him who brought it forth out of his own fullness; only then can there be any talk of the church as "bride." Here the church is wholly female; it is conceiving, bearing, and giving birth to what she has received from Christ as his fruitfulness. She is the continuation and intensification of the relationship of Israel to Yahweh (since Israel was characterized often enough as the bride and spouse of her God). Thus, for the Christians of the first centuries and into the middle ages, the church was always perceived and represented as woman: *Mater Ecclesia, Sponsa Christi*, and this without prejudice to the fact that the hierarchy was entirely male. These men are the representatives of the bridegroom Christ within the encompassing femaleness of the church which among the fathers and in the middle ages was raised into even greater prominence because the church was often seen as a unity with the virgin mother Mary and often brought into a kind of identity with her.

The relationship we have described presupposes that *"Christ loved the church and gave himself up for her. . . ."* He wanted to *"present the church to himself in splendor, without spot or wrinkle or any such thing, that she might be holy and without blemish"* (Eph 5:25–27). If we ask where the church fully corresponds to this ideal, we are once again referred to the immaculate one, and we know that Mary gained this quality from the cross of her Son. Nevertheless, as mother, she exercised authority over her Son: *"He was subject to them"* (Lk 2:51). She brought him up into being human and into the religion of his fathers (in which he discovered his mission).

When one has recognized this role of the mother, one can approach the problem posed by Paul's maxim: *"Wives, be subject to your husbands, . . . for the husband is the head of the wife."* Time-conditioned? Does not Paul always require submission from the existentially subordinate members, from wives towards husbands, from children towards parents, from slaves towards masters (Eph 6:1–5; Col 3:18, 20, 22)? Does he not presuppose in this the ancient social order which put the responsibility for the upbringing of children on the fathers, not the mothers? Is there not also at work in the background the old idea, that lasted into scholasticism, that only the man was active in conception and the woman was passive, and that she was thus to be characterized as something deficient (*mas occasionatum*)?

But the first of these ideas was broken through by Christianity itself, and the second is definitively and fundamentally contradicted by modern biology which has seen that the female organism is just as active in conception as the male, and indeed, through the long pregnancy, the birth, the early feeding, and motherly care of the child, significantly more active than the man. Further, competent genetic researchers have expressed the opinion that the basic structure of the embryonic composition of living beings, including human beings, is primarily female, and the subsequent differentiation of the male is attributable to a tendency to extreme forms while the development towards becoming a woman indicates a perseverence in the original center. If this is correct—and it does correspond to an instinctive feeling that the womb of the *natura naturans* is feminine—one would have to turn the scholastic axiom of woman as *mas occasionatum* completely around and describe man as a *femina occasionata*. Be that as it may, it is certain that the active potency of the bearing, giving birth, and nourishing female organism (now viewed with the eyes of contemporary biology) makes the creature as such appear essentially female over against the creating God. For matter does have need of an initial bestowal by God of such active potency in order to bring forth from itself all the living, upward-developing forms. And in this view the relationship of the church to Christ would be a final concretization of the general relationship of the creature to God. For God has set the creature outside himself with the inner capacity to carry conceived embryos and bring them into being. With that in mind, what is to be said of the time-conditioned aspect of Paul's writing?

One must first say that the relationship of husband and wife in marriage is an image for the Christ-to-church relationship and must be regulated according to this norm. The decisive norm for the attitude of the husband towards his wife is thus a *theological* norm, not one that results from the general customs of a time. That is emphasized very clearly: *"Husbands, love your wives, as Christ loved the church and gave himself up for her."* And again summing it all up at the end: *"Let each one of you love his wife as himself,"* namely as *his own body,* corresponding to the way in which Christ loved his body, the church. And yet there still remains a second point which results from a comparison of sexual relationship with the far superior exemplar Christ-church. Christ does what the man on his own level can in no way do: he releases the church from himself as his fullness, as his body, finally as his bride. In his self-giving he bestows on it the desired form and structure, the life of the Holy Spirit that corresponds to him. The husband, on the other hand, finds his wife apart from himself, with her own freedom and giving nature, which he does not create, and further, as we saw, with a feminine fecundity that comes even less from him.

To underline that, Paul continues: *"Even so husbands should love their wives as their own bodies. . . . For no man ever hates his own flesh, but nourishes it and cherishes it, as Christ does the church"* (Eph 5:28–29). And there is a flashback to the Genesis passage which reads, *" 'For this reason a man shall leave his father and mother and be joined to his wife, and the two shall become one' "* (Eph 5:31; Gen 2:24). For Christ, this means that on the cross and in the Eucharist he gives his flesh and blood so unreservedly that in what comes from this, that is, in the concreteness of the church, he discovers himself. This would not be possible if he had only half given himself and half held himself back.

55 · Church of Jews and Gentiles

The church can become vivid in its fullness only when it is considered in its social composition as a "people" out of "peoples," concretely as the "people of God" made up of Jews and gentiles. When the people of the Jews is looked at first in its particularity, then the additional element the heathens bring is the breaking out of this particularity toward the unrestricted totality of humanity. This corresponds to the theological statement that the Word of God till now directed at Israel became "flesh," that is, human, and thus takes on the form and expressive power of a human being as such. One can, of course, rightly raise the objection that Israel itself from the beginning (since the promise to Abraham that all the nations of the earth would be blessed in him and his progeny) was a self-transcending nation directed to humanity as a whole, so that the tension between individual form and universality did not hold true first for the church of Christ but already for Israel, whose heritage the church claimed. The question arises whether the church's claim to catholicity can pretend to any novelty and originality relative to Israel.

But in this way the spotlight is directed on that point of the theological stage of the world which serves both as the center of the tragedy of God with humanity—Israel's No to what in the Christian view had to have been its fulfillment—and the birthplace of the church in so far as the church, coming from Israel, is distinguished from it. It is not the ("formal") opening of Israel to the totality of the nations and the world mission of the Christian church that form the real point of difference between the two, but the tragedy narrated in the gospel and in the Acts of the Apostles that "his own received him not" (Jn 1:11), in which "his own" is to be understood first ethnically and not individually. The origin of the church is thus due to a tragedy—one can say, the theologically and world-historically central tragedy—whose last act however has not been played, so that the nature of the "person" and "role" church remains in an odd state of suspense. In case Israel's No were not the final word, would then—and if so how—the shape of the church change?

This question is all the more mysterious in that the ethnic, as a specific characteristic of Israel, seems to be something it cannot give up; it is hard to see how it (ethnicity) could be preserved in the originating principle of the church which is a "rebirth" from above, from Spirit-water (Jn 3:3–5). We will leave the core of this question aside for a while and take up now the statement that the church of Christ, with regard both to the Jews and gentile peoples, can be called "people" only in an improper sense. There are no roots for the line of generation into which other, secondary shoots could perhaps be grafted. The principle is from the outset a supernatural one, even if not a purely spiritual one, since the body of Christ serves as the enfolding reality and the members as that which come from it. The characterizations of the church as "people of God" in the New Testament are obvious quotes from the Old Testament. This demonstrates the continuity between the testaments, but also does not allow the essential difference to be forgotten. As relatively open for the addition of strangers as Israel in its origins wanted to be, the complete incorporation of proselytes into its ethnic sphere became manifestly more difficult, while belonging to the church rests from the outset on the free decision of individuals, no matter from where they should come (Acts 2:9–11, 41): baptism and Eucharist insert members into the community.

On the other hand, beside the phrase "his own received him not" stands the following "but to all who received him. . . ." There is then a receiving Israel as well—one could, like Paul who counts himself among them, call it the "remnant" announced by the prophets—so that Israel really does go into the "synthesis" which was accomplished in Christ by the elimination of the dividing wall of hostility (Eph 2:14) and which, as a result, also continues in the church. But since everything valid in Israel is included in this remnant, and since not only the true "fleshliness" but also, on the other hand, full transcendence toward the whole of humanity pertain to what is thus valid, the question we have mentioned can be raised as to what new thing Christianity has provided above and beyond Israel, or whether a "synthesis" has really taken place at all. A glance into the Bible of the Old Covenant finds there not only the whole conceptual vocabulary of which the New Covenant makes use, but also an intellectual preunderstanding for everything here proclaimed and lived as apparently new. One could object that such a reading of the Old Covenant is possible only when one reflects back on it the light of the New, so that what was present in a hidden way in the Old comes to light for the first time (*Novum in Vetere latet, Vetus in Novo patet*). But if it really is present there (and not projected into it), could it not also be found by an impartial observer? But let us recall two central things: for one, election is a pure act of grace, salvation, and redemption not only from external slavery but utterly from guilt too, as forgiveness of sins, especially when they are confessed in repentence, so that the baptizer can baptize "unto the forgiveness of sins." Further, faith is the fundamental attitude, the central position of the command of God's love, surmounting the external sacrificial rites (which in the beginning were not even required: Am 5:21; Jer 7:22) by inner conversion (Ps 51) and covenant faithfulness (Hos 6:6) so that in Qumran the temple cult is already superseded; the perduring consciousness of the special presence of God in the people, of the priestly service of the whole people for God in the world which (as many late texts say) was created for Israel's sake and continues to exist through Israel's service and prayer; the vicarious redemption and atonement, manifold mediation of salvation, being a stranger among the nations and (at least for the later time) on earth in general (apocalyptics, Philo), the concept of corporate personality (the "great-I") from which the church as "Body of Christ" can be explained. In the final period of the Old Covenant the great promises were already claimed in the present: Qumran understands itself as the New Covenant, in which hearts have been circumcised, the Spirit poured out over the whole people. The idea of the resurrection of the dead comes ever more strongly into view (cf. Rev 23:6), but also the idea of the creational mediation of Israel which in any case was the "first thought" of the creator and on which the rest of the cosmos rests (just as later Christ will appear as the mediator of creation and recapitulation of the universe). Even in the exile the universalistic tendencies had broken through: the nations are to be built into (or built upon) Israel (Jer 12:16), and on the other hand, the religion of the "poor in spirit" with which Jesus begins his program of preaching was germinated. The concepts Israel developed successively or even simultaneously in the course of time are all clear preunderstandings of the church. Thus many of them could talk even of an "identity" between "synagogue" and "church" which represented "the same reality" because they are together the "one and indivisible people of God." In the light of such statements one could also recall all that the fathers have said about the unity of the (Augustinian) city of God "since Abel": say, Irenaeus's idea that in the Old Covenant the Logos "accustomed himself to live among humans," or the idea in Origen's and Gregory of Nyssa's interpretation of the Song of Songs that before Christ the Logos comes "bounding over the hills" towards the impatiently waiting bride.

And yet the fathers—including those mentioned here—are far from expounding a univocity between the old and new people of God, no more than do the gospel and Paul, despite recourse to the justifying faith of Abraham and to being children of Abraham, propound such an identity. With all the good things possessed by Paul's ethnic relatives (Rom 9:4–5), they lack the decisive "cornerstone" (Eph 2:20), so terrible a lack that Paul "could wish that I myself were accursed and cut off from Christ for the sake of my brethren, my kinsmen by race" (Rom 9:3), or that Augustine, despite his vision of the unity of the "city of God," places Israel on the side of the *civitas terrena*, or Origen sees the Old Covenant as the mold which is put together for the pouring of the bronze image (of the New) and afterward is broken apart.

This leads irrefutably back to the point where the one people of God is split in that "primitive rupture" (E. Przywara), which takes place at the birth of the Christian church and which makes both of the following points true: that Israel refuses to step over the threshold toward which its paths, in the Christian view, internally lead (which is why New Testament thought and speech continually uses and presupposes these ways), and that Israel as its own "remnant" nevertheless does cross over it and therefore, beyond the threshold, is no longer simply one with what has gone before but truly enters into a "synthesis." A wall of separation is torn down which can be no other than that particularity of Israel which prevented—despite its universalistic tendencies—the "nations" from being able to become a homogeneous whole together with it.

This is why the question of the missions to the "nations" by Christianity is completely different from that of an understanding between Christians and Jews. The former might well contain serious problems; above all problems of the critical assimilation of existing images of the divine in the context of Christian revelation, in the measure in which such images are supposed to become a valid expression for the "only name under heaven by which we must be saved" (Acts 4:12). But this understanding must always keep in mind that Christ himself as human being is due to the salvation-history tradition of his people—"Salvation comes from the Jews" (Jn 4:22)—even if, in the

Christian view, the Jews are and remain totally directed toward this salvation, and the one question of consequence is whether they find their salvation in Christ or whether they want to wait for a different Messiah who (according to the sermons of Peter: Acts 2:38–39; 3:17–26) will still be the same.

For Christian theology, which is all that we are doing here, the relationship of Old and New Covenant remains a dialectical one under every aspect since it can be ignored neither as a mere "identity" of people of God and history of revelation (in which Christ in some way or other is built in as a moment in the whole process), nor as a mere (Marcionite) opposition of synagogue and church, as *sarx* (*gramma*) versus *pneuma*. The salvation-historical monisms in the early and high middle ages and in Byzantium have led to the situation in which the books of Joshua and Judges were made into foundational books of the holy war; kings were supposed to become literally new Davids and new Josiahs, the priesthood itself was supposed to make use of the sword, etc. Today the same monism lives on in "liberation theology." But salvation-historical dualisms separate what is Christian from the trunk of the "cultivated olive tree" (Rom 11:24) and let it degenerate into anti-Semitism.

The problematic of this dialectic leads to the final question: is it solvable at all? And I mean not only on the basis of human-dialogic efforts including all the confessions of guilt and humiliations required for this, but also on the divine level so to speak, on the level of the economy of salvation itself? Two theological viewpoints are in opposition here: Charles Journet (who relies for this partly on Léon Bloy, partly on Jacques Maritain) and H. M. Feret, O.P., would classify the conversion "of all Israel" expected by Paul (Rom 11:26) as an innerhistorical event. Against this, for E. Peterson, Karl Barth, G. Fessard, it can only be a strictly eschatological event.

For Peterson, the "transcending of the (Jewish) concept of election . . ." can "take place only in the eschatological time; . . . in the time of the world Israel alone is and remains the chosen people, and none of the gentile nations can ever be taken up into the people of God or even make the attempt to play the role of the chosen people once again. But the time of the church is the eschatological time which has broken in, irrupted with the calling of the gentiles to the people of God." Israel and the church thus live in different times; in the innerworldly time, "no power of the world will be able to root out Judaism"; but because God's promises are without limit, "no definitive decision has yet been given by the separation of the synagogue and the church." Both "belong instead together until the last day." In view of this dualism of times, it must be asked whether and how for Israel a transcendence from the worldly into the eschatological time could even have taken place? In other words, in what sense can the remnant which has gone over to the church be "the Israel of God" (Gal 6:16) when it leaves the "worldly Israel *kata sarka*" (1 Cor 10:18) behind?

Karl Barth stresses in the strongest terms: "The community of God . . . exists according to God's eternal decree as the people of Israel (in the whole extension of its history in past and future *ante et post Christum natum!*) and at the same time as the church of Jews and gentiles," but not divided into two different aeons but as "representations" of the irrelinquishable two-sidedness of the event of the cross which is God's judgment and mercy together. Thus Israel, before the whole of world history, would be the representation of "the unwillingness, inability, and unworthiness of human beings in relation to the love of God bestowed on them." The church would be the representation of "the willingness, readiness, and honor of God toward sinful human beings." But both sides belong inseparably together, not only insofar as Israel is "the hidden origin of the church," which therefore represents "the revealed destination of Israel," but also more internally: "But the church only knows about human misery, insofar as also Israel—as mirror of the divine judgment—lives in it." (Must not at least the reciprocal also be stated here, that hidden in the judgment-suffering of Israel the messianic soteriological suffering is present?) This idea of world-historical symbolic "representation" of the two aspects of the cross leaves Israel no choice, or the choice is for Barth already and permanently drawn into a necessity belonging to divine revelation.

With G. Fessard, Israel (as the reprobated) and the church (as the converted gentiles corresponding to Rom 11) turn completely into insurpassable "existentials" of theological world history, both on the national and on the individual level, universal modes of conduct which come to light in exemplary fashion in the polarity of (pre-Christian) Jew and gentile and (post-Christian) converted gentile and stubborn Jew.

L. Bouyer puts his finger on the fact that the church which emerged from the Jews in its second generation became wholly the gentile church instead of remaining further a church of Jews and gentiles: it failed in its mission to the Jews just as Jesus had failed in his; but "one may assume that the church will only attain to its final form when it will have found that [the Jewish-Christian church] again." In respect to these remarks the question to be asked is whether such a synthesis, as Bouyer proposes, is even possible.

All these attempts, different as they are, agree in attributing to the existence of Israel in post-Christian time a recognizable role within Christian revelation and theology, and indeed—in opposition to Journet and those like him—one that remains for this worldly time. In view of these attempts it can be asked whether the opposing opinion of those who postulate or hope for an entrance of Israel into the church within time does not—when one pays heed to the total structure of Israel—betray a certain naiveté. Against them Fessard contends that in this position the whole pauline dialectical theology of history has no truth that is valid for the whole time of the church. Karl Barth would object that even the cross of Christ would lose its historically manifest form.

In Pascal's *Pensées* is found an odd proverb: "If the Jews had all been converted by Christ, we would have had only suspect witnesses. And if they had been annihilated, we would have had none at all." And he adds, "Those who have difficulty believing look for a reason in the unbelief of the Jews: [If the matter were so clear], one says [why then do they not believe?] And so their refusal is precisely the basis of our faith." Pascal's final message is that "this people is divided at the time of the Messiah. The spiritual join the Messiah, the coarse-minded remain behind to serve as witnesses to him." Augustine had said essentially the same thing: "They were not done away with but dispersed so that they, although deprived of saving faith, would still keep in their memories that with which they could help us: with their books our advocates. . . ." But the Old Covenant was already for him, as we saw, a (special, to be sure) part of the *civitas terrena*, a part which indeed symbolizes, but does not grant, heavenly citizenship. Thus he can describe Hagar-Ishmael (according to Gal 4:21) as *imago imaginis*, as symbol for the symbolizing "Israel according to the flesh."

56 · Church as Catholica (I): Demonstration of Its Catholicity to the Religions and World Views

We are asking not in the abstract about world views still possible today, but in the light of the now concretely existing theoretical-practical interrelationship of the human being and nature. This circle in which the serpent bites its own tail, the conditioned human being, who seeks to get a hold of the conditions of his possibility, is reality; and not just one reality among others, but its determining human model. How can one deal with this?

THE ASIATIC OUTBREAK

For the non-biblical person, *elpis* (hope) was always ambiguous; Prometheus, the crafty one in relation to God, remains nailed to the Caucasian rock for aeons. For Parmenides, Plato, Plotinus, there was an escape from the vicious circle of worldly illusion only in philosophy's vertical ascent perpendicular to the horizontal. The Far East has offered this solution as constantly relevant, even after the fall of Platonism, as in Brahmanism and Buddhism, and even more relevant than ever since the vicious circle of the *Sansara*, the meaninglessly turning wheel of fallen human existence, has taken on the acute form of the idealist-Marxist self-generation of human beings. Is not the social process of labor that continual rebirth of need and satisfaction of need, thus of that "thirst" (*tṛṣna*), from whose demon the Buddha recommended flight? Western pagan thought also (according to Goethe) knows nothing better than the desperate Nietzschean dialectic between Promethean "charge!" (to the "superman") and forced affirmation of the turning wheel ("eternal return"). This contradiction can be overcome only by distance, or even evasion. There is freedom only in the leap out of the circle, in the negation of surrender to "needs," in denying that the differences are anything but illusion.

Schopenhauer in the nineteenth century, next to Hegel and Marx, was the third great power in the field of world views. Today technology itself is required to pay its tribute on the road of evasion: the "deepening" attainable by great psychological effort finds its cheap substitute in drugs (which were always predominantly at home in Asia and were winning over the European intelligentsia as far back as the nineteenth century). The equivalence between Buddhist-Eckhartian and drug-induced mysticism is seriously discussed, and even its manipulability (ectasy which I hold in my hand and regulate), with which it openly shows a bold front to the Marxist ethos of achievement, is considered. The same is done by an antitechnological youth movement which is made to turn contemptuously leftward by the offerings of the consumer society. That such a schizophrenia of two societies existing side by side is going to make the globe uninhabitable has long been recognized: antitechnology ultimately must be brought together with the explosive forces inherent in technology, or rebellion against forced socialization will end in anarchy.

THE JEWISH-UTOPIAN BREAKTHROUGH

If evasion is impossible and, in addition, a betrayal of humanity's vocation to take possession of the world, then a ray of hope must *prophetically* pierce through the tragic law which says that humanity is to come to itself only by self-emptying into nature, but can never avoid this self-emptying: the hope that the round circle between humanity and world—the messianic breakthrough into the realm of freedom—will succeed in spite of all. The Old Testament dualism between Law (a morality externally imposed on me as servant by a

Lord-God) and prophecy (which thrusts this alienation to the forefront and promises identity between spontaneity of heart and "fulfilled Law": Jer 31:33), this dualism at which Kafka chafes, is supposed to be overcome in Marx, since he, forestalling all tragic history,
describes the human being on the basis of "Naturalism or Humanism" and thrusts this definition, as (messianic) ideal, to the forefront
where, by means of the historical processes to be gone through, it will
come to realization. In the model of Hegel's absolute *knowledge* (as of
a closed circle), Marx reads the necessary success of the absolute
action conceived by him. In order to arrive at a release of complete
freedom (where the mutual emptying of the human being and nature
must be fulfillment, love), all the severities of the historical dialectic
are accepted: the required lack of presuppositions will lead to, at first
unintended, materialism; the knowledge (not hope!) of the goal to be
reached, to economic determinism; the ever stronger manipulation
and technologization of human labor will at first lead ever farther
from the hoped-for humanization (as the Frankfurt School has established with horror), and the power to make the prophecy come true
requires the whole to strive to make its appearance as political party.

All these provisional stages become hardened and delay the leap
into the kingdom of freedom as much as they do the arrival of the
Messiah for Israel: and thus the ideal sought within the circle as
"positive humanism" takes on a more and more openly utopian
character: its reality lies ever more clearly in the "hope against all
hope" of the prophetic human being, which becomes the "principle of
hope" for the most genuine of them (*Prinzip Hoffnung:* E. Bloch).
Elemental "urge" (*Drang:* Scheler), which possesses the preponderance of reality against all idealities; primordial instinctual energy
(Freud), which reserves laws of censorship to itself in order to analyze
and criticize it; vital power which is crystallized in figures, in order
to constantly go beyond them (Bergson, Simmel); finally national
power, which pushes toward the occupation of specific land (Zion-
ism), and really wants to be understood in its fundamental form not
precisely as individual nation but as model of the true, manifest
human being (from Mendelsohn through Marx, who did not want to
be a Jew, to Rosenzweig and Buber). No matter how one might look
upon the dichotomy between Law and prophecy, between estrangement and its surmounting, between the particular nation and the
total human promise, the split which Hegel (following Luther) had
expounded as the tragic essence of Israel, it supports the correctness
of J. Taubes's diagnosis: "Israel is the restless element in world
history, the ferment which really begins to make history." From
philosophical idealism and scientific evolutionism Israel, by virtue of
its prophetic essence, has made an inexorably forward-driving prag-

matism. It did this in that it had unmasked Hegelianism as the last decadent form of a Christianity that has been proven incapable of changing the world and carrying out the world mission of humankind. Israel wrested from it its principle of "love of neighbor" in order, in compassion with the despised and anger toward the oppressor, to take it seriously.

THE IRRUPTION OF SALVATION IN CHRIST

Buddhism and neo-Judaism allow human beings to liberate themselves. That is why they also come into contact so often: in gnosticism and the *cabala* which assume that the human being's true core of freedom is imprisoned in matter, and it is important to free it therefrom (G. Scholem, H. Jonas, also Chagall's art); and let us not forget Schönberg's *Moses and Aaron;* nor the unspeakable remainder that is not left in Wittgenstein nor the pictures of the kingdom which, crossing through horizontal history, are magically evoked in Karl Löwith and still more in Walter Benjamin; nor finally may we forget that, after Auschwitz, the Germans were struck dumb, and fragments of the true speech of Yahweh were put in the mouths of a Celan, of a Nelly Sachs; nor also forget that the titanic attempt of the structuralists (Levi-Strauss) to catch all reality in the texture of the self-articulating word is of biblical origin: In the beginning was the Word, through which everything was created. Such cross connections do exist, which only says all the more clearly how much Christianity is today challenged by this one partner which must be taken seriously. With anti-Semitism nothing more can be done against this partner. The challenge must be accepted and sincerely carried through.

For Christianity, two things are clear: a faith that rests on the incarnation is barred from every flight from the world; but a faith that is wholly received from God's initiative, is forbidden every attempt to "force" salvation to come by one's own power. That is initially confusing: the prohibition against flight from the world seems to point toward the temporal future, but the prohibition against trying to build the kingdom of God into the future seems to redirect one's view (in an escapist way) toward a beyond. The Christian must accept humanity's world mission without succumbing to the Promethean temptation. Still more, the Christian must cooperate in a saving work for the world and humanity in the knowledge that in this world it can never be completed. In the present situation, Christians also take on the additional knowledge that the human being who is now set free in history can no longer count on any natural encompassing (Stoic) providence which, for example, would so direct the fate of nations that the atom bombs would not explode. Humanity must take care of that itself. "Providence" has withdrawn, so to speak, one step higher or deeper: it is providence in Jesus Christ who wraps his event of cross and resurrection around the world and world history as the ultimately decisive event. But this is the most real of all events: its power is, according to a New Testament understanding, ever present; sharing in it through faith, hope, and love, Christians master their task to order the world not only according to its needs and with its powers, but also in accordance with God's salvation. They do this with a power that surpasses their natural power, from a hope which stands "against the hope" of this age (Rom 4:18), because it is hope stemming from the resurrection of the dead and from eternal life as opposed to earthly hope which is crippled by the death of each individual and by the "vanity" of the whole. Christian hope is, at this point, clearly set apart from Jewish hope: it does not wish with prophetic-Promethean force to change the alienating Law, that is, the structure of existence and society, but, insofar as temporal life can reach, to fill this structure with the spontaneity of Christian love which the Holy Spirit pours into our heart (Rom 5:5). Even in the age of anthropology human beings can, in that which is most proper to them, only be indebted beings without ever arriving at a reflexive and technical comprehension of their creaturely origin from God, to say nothing of their graced "birth from God" (Jn 1:13). Their freedom too, together with its spark of absoluteness which is also bestowed on them from the absolute freedom, must be acknowledged as indebted. Hence, this mystery and venture of a setting-free of the creature can only be realized in an idea of God in which God himself (in the threefold character of his Spirit-life) bestows absolute freedom. For this reason the creature as set-free is not totally overwhelmed and coerced when God himself freely accompanies it into its extreme sinful impotence and loneliness.

The world, of course, when viewed in a Christian way, is not capable of perfection on the natural plane. The human being which has no choice but to try to make a go of it in the world, and which grows in struggle, can attain its full form only in failure. Man and woman together with their world—as Christian tradition in its best proponents has always known—are from the outset projected beyond the world toward God, and not just by way of a subsequent "elevation into the state of grace." Plato and Buddha had a correct inkling of this. Henri de Lubac has irrefutably described it in his great work *The Freedom of Grace.* Consequently, we construct not only ourselves, individually, but also our social world ultimately beyond the world toward God. We must plan as best we can, but the fulfillment of the plan is not given to us: there never will be room for the kingdom of God in the narrowness of this world. Nevertheless we cannot leave the responsibility for the kingdom just to God; we must responsibly use the freedom we gratefully receive and double the talents loaned us.

The mystery of human existence is that we can pour the eternal Spirit into earthen vessels in advance: not by violently breaking or stretching them with prophetic-anarchic force, but by transforming, liberating, and elevating the "alienated" Law from within by the spontaneity of love. Here we are in the tightest struggle with our Jewish brother and sister. We can concede no ascendancy in responsibility for the poor and the humbled, for the future of humankind. We should make sure that our anger over the oppressors and compassion with the oppressed is maintained in the contemporary world. And the Christian can draw strength from today and needs not console anyone with thoughts of tomorrow. Inasmuch as we demonstrate the present-day power of love, of conversion, of commitment, we are already beginning to change the world today, we are today already bringing direction and flow into its course—which is empirically always being disclosed as a kind of circulation. Direction and flow are mysterious, not statistically measurable (externally, everything just becomes more and more apocalyptical). But this is the mystery of Christian hope: right at the point where it is really alive, a vortex in the depths emerges. And thus, in the participation of the believer in the encompassing providence which we described as the event of Christ, the one who loves, intercedes, and vicariously suffers can in a hidden way share in influencing the course of the world. In Christian reality, the cross is the highest action, active where nothing else is of any further use.

Christian hope brings pagan and Jewish hope to meet each other at a point which is unattainable for both of them; it justifies both at a point beyond themselves, just as indeed it realizes that it itself has been gifted and empowered from a point beyond itself.

* * *

Buddhist-Platonic transcendence is unequivocally oriented to the *past*. It is the movement of re-ligion, of reconnecting with the lost origin. All forms of this transcendence have to do with "re-membering" (*Er-innerung*). The truth in the soul is buried in rubble, but the religious person recognizes the possibility of digging out from under the debris of the worldly and the sensual. The slave Meno is familiar with the principles of arithmetic without having learned them. The guru can recall his prenatal existences, can spiritually approach the point where the falling from the absolute, individuation, has taken place. Against the unsalutary dispersion of existence, only gathering into oneself is of help; the mysterious way leads inwards, into the depths, into the "essence" (*Wesen*) that always is as a "having-been" (*Ge-Wesen*).

Jewish transcendence moves unequivocally towards the *future*. When Israel recalls the great deeds of Yahweh, it does not do so to rehearse what has been, but to regain from them the thrust of its slackening hope. The messianic kingdom lies ahead, that which is to come is the open fourth wall which permits the person imprisoned in the Law to breathe: "Remember not the former things, nor consider the things of old. Behold, I am doing a new thing; now it springs forth, do you not perceive it? I will make a way in the wilderness and rivers in the desert" (Is 43:18–19). Every road back is concentrated in the suffering of the present; there is only the hope that God is turning the fate of Israel and is finally fulfilling his promise. And wherever this God would be no longer a living God, human beings must open themselves to the future in order to concern themselves with fulfillment.

And so for Christianity there remains only the *present*. And herein lies its whole strength. Evaluated from this standpoint, the other ways are ultimately only flight. For both of them, the present is untruth. Existence as it is lived in fact cannot be right. It is estranged from itself. It can only see enough of the truth to determine that. And the beginning of wisdom is the negation of what now is. Only Christianity has the courage to affirm the now because God has affirmed it. God has become a human being like us. He has lived in our alienation and died in our God-forsakenness. He has inserted the "fullness of grace and truth" (Jn 1:17) into our present. He has filled it with his presence. Because, however, divine presence includes all "past" and all "future" in itself, God has opened for us all dimensions of time from this presence. The Word that has become flesh is the "Word in the beginning"; in it we are "chosen from before the foundation of the world." And it is the "Word at the end" in which everything in heaven and on earth is to be brought together: *Alpha* and *Omega*.

Only in Christianity are these contradictory world views reconcilable. Both are encompassed by the real presence of God in the Eucharist: the *memoria* (remembering) as well as the *spes* (hope). We gather around the table of the Lord to celebrate the memory of his passion, but in expectation of a future (1 Cor 11:26). But when we in the Christian *memoria* become immersed in the great deeds of God for us, we do not sink in Buddhist or Platonic fashion into the preworldly-timeless, but into the grace of God who from time immemorial was always for us much more decisively than we can ever grasp or comprehend. Thus this grace is also opened before us as unforeseeable future. Because Paul understands that he has always "been part of Jesus Christ," he can say, "I forget what lies behind and strain forward to what lies ahead" (Phil 3:12–14). Not a possessing but a being possessed gives wing to Christian hope. It gets its vitality in the idea that the earth should respond to heaven just as heaven has addressed the earth. Not with their own power do Christians want to change the earth, but with the empowering grace of him who, changing everything, has taken the initiative in its behalf.

Because Christians are not left to their own devices in order to find themselves, but are set up and found by God, they can lose themselves neither in the past nor in the future: "All things are yours, whether . . . the world or life or death or the present or the future, all are yours; and you are Christ's; and Christ is God's" (1 Cor 3:21–23).

57 · Church as Catholica (II): Demonstration of Its Catholicity to the Churches of Orthodoxy and the Reformation

The establishment of a lack of culpability in its coming-to-be precedes all question of a culpable deficiency of the Catholica. The great missionary command assumes such a coming-to-be of the church through all space and time "to the close of the age" (Mt 28:20), and Paul does no less when, by way of contrast, he describes the fullness of the mature manhood of Christ attainable only at the end of time (Eph 4:13). This coming-to-be of every individual member through life on earth, and the succession of human generations, is not however opposed to the living structure of the Catholica's being constituted once-and-for-all (by the end of the apostolic age at the latest) as a result of the "body"-producing "fullness" of its head, the risen Lord.

Consequently, in the catholicity of the church, two moments need to be distinguished from the outset: 1. The Christ-effected *prior gift* of fullness which Paul describes almost plerophorically in Ephesians 4:4–6: "*One* body and *one* Spirit, just as you were called to the *one* hope that belongs to your call, *one* Lord, *one* faith, *one* baptism, *one* God and Father of us all, who is above all and through all and in all." 2. This unity is consequently described not as uniformity but, corresponding to the "manifold wisdom of God" (Eph 3:10), as a reality being unfolded in organic multiplicity and reciprocity (4:7–16), not only in order to be this unity but also to live it and even, in living it, to cooperate in generating it. Thus the prior gift becomes an *entrusting* and, thereby, a *demand*. In this once again doubled articulation is entailed the problem that will occupy us in what follows: the entrusting can even take place in such a way that the demand is fulfilled:

when that happens and to the extent that it does, catholicity is not deficient. But the entrusting can also take place so that the demand remains open; if it is not met, catholicity remains deficient. And this latter, it must be admitted, is the case wherever sinful persons do not fully manifest the perfection of the prior giving and entrusting to them of the fullness of Christ. As long as the church is made up of sinners it can never point to its catholicity in any way other than the indicative implied in the real prior gift of the fullness of Christ. But it can never point to the synthesis of this indicative with the imperative therein directed to it brought about by itself.

Unless . . .

Unless there are certain points in it in which the prior gift is so entrusted to the receiver that the demand is met in the entrusting itself, so that a response of the fullness on the part of the body or of the bride to the address of fullness from the head and bridegroom takes place. It is Catholic teaching that there are two such (structurally quite different) points in the Catholica. According to this teaching, the church without these two points at which not just a tentative, approximate but an adequate answer is given to the fullness offered (and entrusted) would not be Catholic at all, but would not go beyond the level of the synagogue. The first point is that of the *ecclesia sancta et immaculata*, "the church holy and without blemish, without spot or wrinkle or any such thing" (Eph 5:27); and Catholic reflection (since Irenaeus) has discovered that it really required such an unconditional answer of loving and hoping faith so that the Word of God can become man, flesh, child. This does not prevent this perfect answer, the exemplar of every church answer, from being brought about in advance by the blood-bath of the cross. If the holiness of the divine word had never been fully accepted and answered, the Word would never have become flesh; but if it has become flesh, then there also exists along with it the *ecclesia sancta et immaculata*.

The second point is of another kind, but it follows from the first, if the church, in correspondence with the visibility and bodiliness of its head, is itself supposed to be a visible and unified organism. Hence the organ of unity gets instituted for it, in the two-in-one form of a college responsible for the unity of the fullness of Christ (the apostles and their successors) and of that member of the college (Peter and his successor), which is responsible for the unity of the college and thus of the whole church, and represents this unity. The unity, which for its inner holiness is taken for granted, is so by no means for the external representation (which is quite clearly shown to be fallible in the *person* of Peter): for the office of the college, and furthermore within that for the office of the one representing the unity, there is the assurance of an infallibility which (in spite of all its capacity for self-expanding positivity) is a negative limit, a sort of instinct for the right direction that the historical church, despite all kinds of mistakes in individual matters, can never completely lose its course. That is implicit in Matthew 16:18. Just as the moment of holiness is personally centered in the unity of the church (in Mary), so the official function of unity is and remains personal (in Peter in the midst of the college) and thus demands personal apostolic succession.

What is distinctively Catholic, in contrast to the other Christian communities, lies therefore in both these related and mutually interdependent points which are attacked with varying intensity and constantly under the pretext that the prior gift of the fullness of Christ is here taken over by (usurping) human beings. When this occurs the moment of the entrusting or transmission of the prior gift is overlooked.

It is not the (collegial) apostolicity but only the full petrine character that is rejected by the Orthodox church, a situation which allows a still quite authentic even if imperfect unity of the Catholica (with possible intercommunion) to be maintained. The churches of the reformation, in contrast, go to the point of also rejecting apostolicity (as personal succession). This forces them to confine everything to the prior gift (without genuine entrusting). The distance between the two deficient forms is illustrated by the preservation of the marian element in Orthodoxy (in the cult of the *panhagia*) and in the rejection of this unique entrusting in the churches of the reform (even though they may in individual cases keep marian veneration).

The doctrine of justification considered to be foundational in the Protestant churches attests positively that the sinner is both justified and sanctified in Christ (as the previously given fullness), while on the negative side it denies that this fullness can ever be transmitted in any way to the church. On this basis therefore the idea must have developed that Christian persons have their truth not in themselves but in something other than themselves and thus require a homecoming from such alienation.

In the Catholic church, on the other hand, all becoming-Catholic—with which the church of sinners, as we said, will never be finished—is possible only on the basis of a fundamental being-Catholic. But we also suggested that the two poles which form this basis within the church are not unmediated. Mary cannot be the mother of the head without also being the mother of the body constituted by the head whose member she is besides as a believer, so that she does not escape the apostolic, petrine unity. But Peter, with all the official nature of his function, must also be steward over the holiness of the church, which is why he is asked at his installation about his "greater love" and also receives the assurance of a witness's death (which is a death of love: Jn 21:15, 18f). Without this joining of office and personal love he would be unable to feed the flock of the Good Shepherd whose office is identical with that of loving self-giving. Clearly Mary and Peter are finally "mediated" to each other in the form of John the disciple of love, since at the cross he took the mother "to his own home"; on the other hand, in the beginnings of the post-Easter church, he always appears representatively together with Peter.

The interrelationship of both poles of unity transmitted in advance to the church is, finally, the diacritical place of becoming-Catholic or of the visibility of catholicity, the place where this is more than just a title. It is the place where external obedience and inner disponibility toward God together show forth the "freedom of the Christian person." Expressed in a Catholic way, it is the freedom to follow unto death the Son of God in his free obedient love for the Father and for his saving will.

Looked at ecclesiologically, the *interrelationship* of the two instituted poles of unity is the true place of living coming-to-be in contrast to a distorting absolutizing of the one pole and to a one-sided orientation to it of being-Catholic. That is where the veneration of Mary gets distorted into mariolatry which gets disruptively mixed in with christocentrism and theocentrism; or where one finds the distortion of the official function of unity into ultra-Montanism and "popolatry." Then one forgets that both principles point beyond themselves to a higher, founding center: Mary is only the handmaid, Peter only the servant of the servants. The unity of the Catholica then lies ultimately in the vitally lived interrelationship of two poles which as such guarantee the real indwelling of the unity-founding head in his body: the "in" of the "over."

The dynamic of becoming-Catholic within a being-Catholic can be illustrated with the dynamic of the life of Paul: "Not that I am already perfect; but I press on to make it my own, because Christ Jesus has made me his own": in the being-made-his-own lies the surrendering; in the pressing-on lies the demand to be met in it. Paul insists, "Brethren, I do not consider that I have made it my own; but one thing I do, forgetting what lies behind and straining forward to what lies ahead"; but after this emphasis on the purely being-moved, he can once again dwell on being-taken-over from above: "Let all those of us who are mature be thus minded . . ." (Phil 3:12–16). In the final substantive (i.e., the being-taken over from above) it becomes clear that Catholics can claim for themselves the title of *being* Catholic only under the condition that they are minded like Paul and do not kid themselves and others that they have comprehended it. This could be the starting point of a whole Catholic ethics and ascetics, but we cannot go into that now.

Instead we must draw from what we have said two conclusions which belong to our theme in the stricter sense. The first concerns divisions in the church, the second concerns the relationship of the church to the world religions, world cultures, and all the impulses that come to it from outside.

1. An immediate cause of schisms has always been the fact that the catholicity of the church is simply assumed as given, but no longer vitally striven for. But because even where the church is strivingly on the way to itself, anything more than only a relative and defective catholicity can never be at hand, there will also always be occasion for taking scandal. No one has stressed more strongly than Augustine that "the whole church must say, 'Forgive us our trespasses.' It then has spots and wrinkles. . . . The church stands praying in order to be purified by confession, and as long as one lives here, it will stand so." In what has been surrendered to her by the Lord, she is a pure bride; in her sinful members she remains a whore, *casta meretrix* (Ambrose). But for the person who knows about the bestowal of catholicity, even taking scandal is something culpable; such a person can do nothing but appeal to the Lord whose fullness of holiness would reside in himself alone and would not be bestowed on the Catholica. But then he or she would have no foundation on which to build a better and more pure church. Only in itself is the Catholica *semper reformanda* (always needing reform). Where schisms actually do arise, the guilt lies on both sides, but the most humble confession of guilt and the most zealous desire of the Catholica to listen to complaints raised against it do not free it of the obligation to belong to/espouse the catholicity founded in it.

2. In so far as the church has the fullness of Christ not only above itself but also in itself—although as empirical church of sinners it can always only strive after this fullness—it does not have to look for this fullness outside itself or expect it to come from external growth. This principle creates delicate problems for Catholic Christians. For, on the one hand, with their createdly-limited and beyond that sinfully-forgetful consciousness, they are beings which can and also must receive impulses and additions from without, from alien religions and cultures and even ideologies, because their empirical consciousness is naturally never a pure mirror of their catholicity. On the other hand they must tell themselves that already integrated into the fullness of Christ are all *logoi spermatikoi* which in their nonintegrated form always bear a more or less distorted character. This is because they become absolutized when detached from the fullness. Thus empirical impulses from without—from Eastern meditation to take but one example—are in the end always to be accepted as admonitions to a deeper *anamnēsis* of the church's endowed Catholic character from

which these impulses first get their practical Christian form. Often enough they are reminders not only of something still undiscovered in the fullness of Christ, but also of something already familiar that existed in the Christian tradition, but was forgotten. Is there anyone, among those who today apply themselves to Eastern meditation, who is still aware of the great treasures of Christian meditation in the Eastern and Western churches and the already extensive Christianization of other methods of meditation which has been achieved there? Often a deep transformation must be undertaken in which the full power of the admonition must remain intact, as when the ancestor worship of earlier cultures or primitive tribes must be translated into dimensions of the *communio sanctorum* (communion of saints) or magic ritualism into Catholic sacramental realism.

To be sure, Christian Word-revelation is hidden in finite vessels of speech and thought, and so we are often quick to talk about the limitation of Semitic and, even more, hellenistic thought forms. A great deal of caution is needed here. Christ himself is an individual, a temporally, spatially, and ethnically limited man, which does not keep him from containing "the fullness of God in his body" and thus also from having room for the fullness of being human. Translations of the Bible into other language forms could always only be bringing to light what already lay in the authentic language-body of the word of God, and all new-sounding variations must take their bearings from the fundamental theme and be guided by it.

58 · Visible Church as Church of Christ

For Catholic Christians the visible, hierarchical church, of which they are members, is a mother with whom it is often hard to get along. The motherhood of the church often appears to be only a merely transmitted word which, especially for the present age, seems to have lost all helpful meaning. Baptism is not personally requested of such a one. The bread of the Word in its shop is bad. People buy it elsewhere or bake it themselves; and many go from there even to getting their eucharistic bread elsewhere. And what comes from Rome seems to be so antiquated that there seems to be no fatherly or motherly quality left in it.

It is really high time here to remind ourselves that there are not two churches; an ideal one—the church of saints—and a real one, the sinful church we have just described. There is not an infallible and a fallible church. Nor is there an invisible church which would be the true Catholic church permeating all confessions, and a visible church which is just one of the many variants of being Christian. To hold the latter is one of the consequences of a superficial ecumenism. There are already many people who have no willingness to get beyond this, even though it is nothing more than a false conclusion from certain correct premises. This idea that is so hard for us, that there are not two churches, can become more acceptable by remembering that the real, empirical church always was and still is to this day the church of the saints. In both senses of the word: it was and is the church for which the saints stood and because of which they suffered, and the church which, in an extraordinary sense, was constituted by the saints.

One realizes the tension was there from the beginning. The same Paul who addresses a community as the communion of saints and praises their faith, their zeal, and their love can, in almost the same breath, scold them for their unholiness. To his astonishment it was reported to him by Chloe's people "that there are divisions among you" (1 Cor 1:11), and even worse "quarelling, jealousy, anger, selfishness, slander, gossip, conceit, and disorder" (2 Cor 12:20). He undertakes excommunications, humbles the arrogance of the pneumatics, reproaches the inconsiderateness of the progressive "strong" toward their weak brothers and sisters for whom Christ died as much as for anyone, castigates the scandalous separation of poor and rich even in the celebration of the Eucharist. But at the end of each letter he brings them all together: "All the brethren send greetings. Greet one another with a holy kiss, . . . my love be with you all in Christ Jesus" (1 Cor 16:20, 24); "Finally, brethren, farewell. Mend your ways, heed my appeal, agree with one another, live in peace, and the God of love and peace will be with you. . . . The grace of the Lord Jesus Christ and the love of God and the fellowship of the Holy Spirit be with you all" (2 Cor 13:11, 14). First the gnostics, the Montanists, and Donatists, and finally all sectarians assumed two churches, an external, fallible one, and the pure, true one, *their* church.

For the church fathers the paradox of the church which was simultaneously both the spotless bride of Christ, which was the holy mother church, and that imperfect reality in which so much remained to criticize and correct, was a painful mystery that could in no way be avoided. Origen for example, who expressed his absolute loyalty to the church in such moving words, also described, almost in tears, the decadence of the clergy of his time. Augustine, whose Platonic origins suggested to him the distinction between a true church in the superworldly world of truth and a "mixed" church in the earthly world of illusoriness and unreality, heroically withstood—precisely as opponent of the Donatists—the temptation to cut through the threads between the two and, as bishop and saint, was a proponent of the organic unity of these two aspects seemingly so foreign to one another. Not once did he give into the temptation to describe the true church as the city of God with its home in heaven, consisting of angels and holy people, and the sinful church as that part of the *civitas Dei* fallen from heaven and now laboriously trying to find its way home. He does not do what the gnostics before him did, but looks upon even the earthly, pilgrim church as one made up of saints and nonsaints. We need not delve into his more detailed explanations of the paradox here, but it is important that for him the truly holy part of the church, in which it is "bride without spot and wrinkle," is seen as most intimately connected with the redeeming function of the bridegroom Jesus Christ. When a sinner is reconciled with the church through the bishop (we would say, when absolution is administered in sacramental confession), then it is the *columba*, the "one dove" of the Song of Songs, the holy bride of Christ which forgives with him and takes the sinner again into the unity of love. She it is therefore who has to pull the members of the lower and outer circles into the highest and innermost circle. This notion was already current among the earlier fathers, and indeed actually goes back to Paul himself, since already in his writings the weak members had been placed under the protection of the strong within the same organism. Whoever takes part in a more intimate way in the essence of the holy church, according to Augustine, is thereby given more responsibility for those who stand farther away. What we today call "partial identification" with the church and with dogma, for Augustine would have been the unequivocal sign of Christian imperfection. For Origen too it would have been a symptom of the fact that a Christian had not yet been transformed into an *anima ecclesiastica* (ecclesiastical soul).

We could generalize here on all church history and say that in the domain of the Catholic church, this principle holds: the holier the Christians, the more they identify their existence and fate with the existence and fate of the church. They do this in such a way that they know that the holy church existed long before them, that they owe their union with Christ as Christians to it. To it belong the gifts of God: baptism, Eucharist, reconciliation, holy scripture, the proclamation, the education and guidance, the community of familial love. All that is irretrievably prior to them, and is always the reality in the church from the beginning, even if it has never been more than an unfulfilled or half-fulfilled demand in the weaker members.

59 · Church as Institution

What institution originally is for Jesus we can see in his institution of the Eucharist: "This is my flesh, my blood poured out for you; *do this* in memory of me."

He gives himself, in a more bodily manner than we can imagine, and seals the gift in a form which keeps it alive for all future time. And Eucharist is only the innermost core of the whole institution which we call the church of Christ, to which a great deal that is just as essential also belongs that, individually considered, could seem mere shell, alienation, calcification, but which, assessed from the viewpoint of Jesus, is what makes possible and mediates his immediate presence. Among such things are especially office, scripture, tradition, and also church law, obvious things which one is accustomed with Hegel to designate philosophically as "objective spirit," but which, for the Christian, are always just modes of the presence of Christ.

Office, first of all, an authority, conferred by Jesus, to teach, to bless, to exercise pastoral care, which—thank God!—possesses an ultimate independence from the worthiness or unworthiness of the person exercising it. If it were the way the Montanists, Messalians, Donatists, Spirituals, and many contemporary Pentecostalists suppose, that only those who have the Holy Spirit can confer it, and all the more the more they have it, then the presence of Jesus would be linked to the degree of holiness of human beings and we would be deprived of any kind of certainty that this presence was mediated to us whole and entire. Where could a supposedly Spirit-filled person get the power to convey to me the crucified Lord's forgiveness of sins unless he or she had been officially endowed with this power? And unless this were done in such a way that the event of the cross by which God in Christ reconciles the world to himself became reality for me here and now?

In such a manner that the priest not only refers me to something that always and ever is true—I could relate myself to such a reality all by myself; but that in virtue of his office, the reality becomes present for me. Just as present as when, by means of the office, the eucharistic presence of Jesus, "humanity and divinity, body and soul, flesh and blood" becomes present for the believing community. The faithful are well aware that they cannot themselves bring about the sacramental presence of Jesus—for what we have said holds not just for confession and Eucharist but for all the sacraments of the church. The cookbook says, "Take two. . . ." In the church no one "takes"; it is given to one. That is also true, and in a special way, for the priest. No one takes this office. It is conferred so that the one on whom it is conferred will have the authority to hand it on. On the office is posted a "hands off": it is the Lord alone who gives himself but, because there is office, gives infallibly.

* * *

To office belongs the objectivized word of Christ and about Christ, the holy scripture. Letter and book constitute a form of institution on the basis of many conventions: on the meaning of the letters, the words, the sentences, of one or more languages; also conventions on printing, marketing, preservation in libraries, etc. The absolutely unique Word of God enters into this institution in order to be there for all, unfalsified and unchanging. It is of course inseparably connected with the free breath of the Spirit which is always interpreting the words anew and making them arise in an endless variety and fullness for every hearer and reader like a ripening field of grain.

"My words are spirit and life," says the Lord. That remains eternally true. But for it to be able to remain true there must be the scripture as institution, fixed and unchanging through all the generations, through all the exegesis that will come and go past it: "Heaven and earth will pass away; my words will never pass away." Paul may speak of the tablets of the heart on which he writes his letter, in contrast to the stone tablets of Moses, but he nonetheless wrote on parchment so that his words touched not only the hearts of the Corinthians but also still touch our hearts today. And when John in his third letter says, "I had much to write to you, but I would rather not write with pen and ink; I hope to see you soon, and we will talk together face to face" (3 Jn 13–14), he had ultimately to set this sentence on paper with ink, for our benefit, so that we too will know today that in the church, in conversation among the faithful, in prayer between ourselves and God, there is much that needs not to be written, perhaps should not be written because it is too personal and intimate. And it is all right this way because it is provided for us and authenticated through the institution of the holy scripture.

* * *

But, however immediately the scripture makes the word of Jesus and about Jesus present to us, it is itself still mediated by the institution of the primitive church, through the different traditions about Jesus that came to the evangelists and set them to work on material that was already formed, before their words themselves created tradition within their communities and finally merged into the great lasting form of the canon of the New Testament attached to the already existing canon of the Old. One could at first think that this fluid element of tradition in which the scripture came into being in order to reinfluence the tradition is just the opposite of an institution. But it isn't. That is well known by those of our contemporaries who complain about the constricting corset of ecclesiastical institution and long for a free immediate access to the original phenomenon of Jesus, for a so-called contemporaneity with him. But is there such a contemporaneity, if it is true that those who went about with him on earth did not understand him, or did so only just barely, and that the meaning of his life, words, and deeds dawned on them only afterward from the resurrection and from Pentecost? And if Paul, his most profound interpreter, was never contemporaneous with him at all but relies on ecclesiastical tradition in order to interpret him authentically? And in a certain way this authentic interpretation continues on throughout church history.

With regard to deviations and derailments the teaching office of the church, itself looking to scripture and tradition, again and again has had to declare and establish the true meaning of the revelation of Christ and thus make the original event present again, whenever an historical stream wanted to distance itself from it. And this is true not only of the solemn definitions of councils and popes; it is true analogously of the endless efforts of theologians and saints who are concerned in their lives and preaching and writing with the understanding of the original event and have contributed their share to the tradition. Apparently that is a dangerous enrichment of crust and skin around a living core which is in danger of suffocating inside; but we have here a kind of self-regulation by the Holy Spirit of the living Christ: the superficial falls by itself while the essential that gets formulated is changed into genuine life. According to Irenaeus' profound saying, the Holy Spirit continually rejuvenates the churchly vessel which contains the eternally young presence of Christ.

* * *

The same can be shown from canon law which is a particular thorn in the flesh of many outsiders (and of people in the church too): the ossification of what should really never be more than charismatic event, falling into a Jewish absolutizing of the Law which has indeed been transcended and relativized by Jesus and Paul. But what else does this element that brings order and structure to the church community want than to keep it living and ready for the presence of the one lawgiver who has introduced a law of love, grace, and mercy which is a most elevated form of righteousness? "Whose sins you shall retain, they are retained": even an ecclesiastical law of punishment and penance is still a part and function of this law of grace in which the law must both protect and mediate grace.

Church office, sacrament, scripture, tradition, canon law, all concern the same thing: that the living content takes form is the guarantee that the content remains alive; expressed in ecclesial terms, the institution is the condition of the possibility of the undistorted, personal presence of Christ.

On a higher, supernatural plane, then, the basic law of all living things from plants to animals to humans is repeated: only in an articulated organism can a principle of life, a soul, flourish and express itself. And so, to the humorless bores who go around grumbling against the ecclesiastical institution presumably so that, after tearing it down to its living core, they can find immediate contact with Jesus, one can respond as Goethe in his answer to the Philistine:

Natur hat weder Kern noch Schale,
Alles ist sie mit einem Male.
Dich prüfe du nur allermeist,
Ob du Kern oder Schale seist.

Nature has no core nor skin,
It's everything together.
Just ask yourself now whether
you yourself are core or skin.

What Goethe says of nature, we say of the church; his demand can be applied just as well to it: "Thus seize without delay/The holy public mystery."

* * *

From what has been said there are still a few essential conclusions to be drawn.

1. Institution in the church is similar in some respects to institution in the purely human sphere, and dissimilar in others. Whenever free human persons live together, something like institution, a valid legal system, is necessary for the protection of their freedom. Not in anarchy, but only in order, can the free personality develop. To deny this aspect of the church is possible only for one who sees in it no divinely willed organic community but an empty formal framework for purely private religious activity, which of course directly contradicts the gospel as well as the picture of the church of the first and all later communities.

But, if this human foundation of institution in the church is completely valid, it is by no means its own justification. For believers, according to Paul's teaching, the ordered community is for the faithful the "body" of the present Christ who makes himself present first in his instituted sacraments, and then allows all who, believing, take part in them, to share in his presence; so much so that according to Paul, the individuals become members of his (mystical) body, each one according to his or her *charism* or particular mission, just as the members of a body complement one another and are differentiated from the whole. This is where talk about the church as the primordial sacrament in the midst of the world, as *sacramentum mundi* gets its validity. The external organization of the church at which so many take offense is really nothing other than the representation of the vitality and capacity for life of that great organic body possessed and animated by the present Christ. This can be seen from the incessant circulation which prevails between Eucharist and church. The eucharistic body of Christ which becomes present in the liturgy of the community encloses the participating faithful within Christ's reality: "The bread which we break, is it not a participation in the body of Christ? Because there is one bread, we who are many are one body" (1 Cor 10:16 17). But on the other hand it is always the church, as the proleptically existing body of Christ, which through the office given it renews the eucharistic presence of its Lord: "The Eucharist makes the church, the church makes the Eucharist" (de Lubac).

2. Institution, let us say, comes into existence to make possible the freedom of persons. The more differentiated an organ is—for example the human hand—the more the soul can do with it. The whole body certainly imposes on the individual person the limitation of being this particular time-bound and place-bound human being; but at the same time it grants the freedom to be able to put oneself in contact with all places and times, present, past, and future. This connectedness is at the same time the condition of the possibility of a liberality which allows the spiritual soul to be effective far beyond itself. In a much higher sense this is true of the church as presence of Christ. Because Christ is present in the mysterious organism of the church, he is not absent to the other places in the world. Talk about the church as *sacramentum mundi* means the opposite: from his bodily presence in the church Christ permeates all world history as well as the existence of each human being—which however precisely does not mean that he (as the risen One) is free without this (bodily presence) to exist and be effective everywhere, wherever he wishes, so that his presence in the church would be something completely relative or superfluous. For the law of the incarnation is not superseded by the resurrection. It issues in the faith-witness of determinate people, in their common life as loving community which heeds the scripture, and the sacrament, and the ecclesiastical regulations by which the church stands in the midst of humanity as an unmistakably unique reality. But the church's privilege is also the source of a very serious demand placed on it; as the body of Christ it has the unconditional obligation of giving witness, by its example, to the world of this presence in it.

It should be the example of the love of Christians for one another and for all people, particularly in the unity of Christ, which once again is made visible and held together properly in the organizational unity of the community with its pastor, the diocese with its bishop, and the whole church with its pope. The purely external, organizational unity would not be an adequate witness; it must be an expression of the inner unity of faith and love in order to become a believable motive of witness. On the other hand, loving faith has no difficulty being inserted into the external form of unity whose whole *raison d'être* is to explode the subjectivity of the closed sect into the objectivity of a community which does not offer primarily a satisfaction of religious desires but the presence of so high a Lord that one must worshipfully subject oneself above all to *his* will and saving plan for the world. Thus Christians owe the world the witness of mutual love in Christ as the only effective apologetic for the truth of Christianity. Everyone, even the most uneducated, can contribute to this: "You should be one," prays the Lord, "as we (the Son and the Father) are one, so that the world may know that you have sent me and have loved them as myself."

3. In addition it must be properly emphasized that ecclesiastical institution as presence of Christ creates every desirable space for freedom for the individual Christian. We are not trying to say that the individual Christian can find Christ only where something is expressly organized. Take again the example of the human body: the eye is a most subtle arrangement, but it looks, without reflecting on itself, freely into the wide world; its glance is everywhere except on itself.

Whereas the German citizen needs a visa for many countries, the eye needs no visa to travel wherever it wishes; space is open for it to the stars. So too with Christians: the Christian can encounter God and Christ everywhere, in the quiet of immediate prayer without any liturgy, in encounter with the neighbor who is an image of God and a real or potential temple of the Holy Spirit, in the midst of the noise of a large city. Or when the Christian opens the scripture: by means of the letters, the contemplating spirit can dive into the depths of the Godhead. The form is the starting point for the Christian: it is at the same time an indication for starting in the right direction: "The truth will make you free." This is how it looks when contemplated from within by the person who lives the institution as the presence of Christ, whereas when seen from without, it looks like a cage. This brings us to the fourth and final point.

4. The institution of the church, which from inside is the presence of Christ and liberating space, strikes the world as a scandal. And precisely this scandal is indispensable if the scandal of the incarnation of God and especially his crucifixion is not to be dissolved in idealistic fog and superficial morality. The church in its tough structure will always be a "stone of contradiction" for human beings. The phrase comes from Isaiah, from the Old Testament, and in a certain way it can be applied also to the ever-present Judaism in world his-

tory. Israel and the church belong together in a very mysterious way we might even call tragic, like the front and back of a coin. Together they testify to the fidelity of God to his promise, the church, especially, the fidelity of Christ to his own: to be with us all days unto the end.

The attempt has been made to eliminate Judaism. That is impossible. The attempt might be made, perhaps with success, to decimate the church, but it will not be completely annihilated. One can observe today an "attack of the world religions on Christianity" (G. Vicedom). Why? What can apparently be assimilated has been sucked out of it, and the undigestible, tiresome institution is left over; it must disappear. But it is well-known that it is precisely the skin of a fruit that holds the most vitamins. It is precisely in the living form that life is found. Once again Goethe speaks to our point, "And no time and no power disintegrates the characteristic form, which develops in a living way." But with the form of the church it is not a matter of an end in itself but of the *forma Christi* which wills to be present in the world and world history and, working from there, to have its effect on the whole. *He* is the form, not we. We only take part in it, through grace, as servants in his cause. Human beings can add peripheral things to the institution of Christ, ballast perhaps, which time eventually hollows and washes away. But the living organism will never become ballast; only the lifeless corpse would be a naked institution which must then of course be buried or burned as quickly as possible. But there is still a long time until then, for this body about which we are talking is animated by an immortal soul, the risen Lord who does not allow his body, the church, to die, but will take it with him in the resurrection of the flesh. Not as if in eternal life there were still any need of the veiling sacraments, or the letter of scripture, or canon law; all this however will not be eradicated but transformed into personal life lived in the body. The world will not disappear into God; instead there will be the end-sacrament: the whole triune God revealed in the whole of transfigured creation.

60 · Sinful Church

The New Testament never talks about the assurances given to the church of Christ without mentioning in the same breath the threat of abuse, the possibility of defection. Nowhere is the spotlessness of the bride a *fait accompli* which the bride need only to accept and worry about no longer. Precisely the relevant saying of Paul shows this quite clearly: "I feel a divine jealousy for you, for I betrothed you to Christ to present you as a pure bride to her one husband. But I am afraid that as the serpent deceived Eve by his cunning, your thoughts will be led astray from a sincere and pure devotion to Christ. For if someone comes and preaches another Jesus than the one we preached, or if you receive a different spirit from the one you received, or if you accept a different gospel from the one you accepted, you submit to it readily enough" (2 Cor 11:2–4). Where does it come from, this susceptibility of the bride of Christ, her curiosity and greediness to listen to anyone who comes along and to turn her head instead of allowing herself to be led by the apostle to her one and only lover? This fear vibrates through all the letters of the apostle. Defection and relapse are always possible, and no sacrament, no reception of the word and Spirit definitively assures salvation (Heb 6:4f). Nevertheless something has changed. The terrible thing is not so much that the Christians themselves go astray, but that they "despise the Sovereignty" (2 Pet 2:10; Jud 8), the lordship which the God-man embodies on the cross, that they thus "crucify the Son of God on their own account and hold him up to contempt" (Heb 6:6); for "if we sin deliberately after receiving the knowledge of the truth," that is, resist the cross to its face, "there no longer remains a sacrifice for sins" (Heb 10:26). Because with the cross we stand at the end of all the paths of God, there no longer is, as there is for the whore of Jerusalem, a final promise superseding all disgrace. This promise has already been fulfilled on the cross, and thus the cross actually stands, mysteriously, in an unimaginable place beyond all the sins, no matter how great, of the old and new bride. Whoever pushes beyond this absolute end does not leave well enough alone. "Whoever spurns the Son of God, and profanes the blood of the covenant by which he was sanctified, and outrages the Spirit of grace," is cast into a quite different gulf of fire than Korah and his followers: the "hands of the living God" (Heb 10:29–30). The Old Testament mystery of the whore is in this way surpassed in the all-fulfilling mystery of the cross, just as the disgrace of the daughter of Sion in the Old Testament (as in Hosea especially) had already fallen back on the dishonored divine bridegroom (God as cuckold). And if in Ezekiel Sion is summoned to feel the deepest shame right in its final bestowal of grace, then it is already something like sharing in bearing the shame of God which is definitively taken over on the cross and incredibly carried out for the redeemed church and humanity. As a result the church basically can get a more real feeling for her own disgrace nowhere else than in her crucified Lord and in that share of the cross which the Lord will allow her to feel with him as an immeasurable grace. In its innermost, purest core, the whoredom of the new daughter of Sion is immersed in the absolute "folly of the cross" (1 Cor 1:18), in the "foolish for the world," the "shameful for the world," the "despicable for the world," the "not even to be considered" and "not even existing things" (1 Cor 1:27–28) which God has claimed for himself. The being despised and humiliated to the point of *mē-on*, however, stems from the Old Testament: it is already contained in the names of the whoresons of Hosea; Paul expressly quotes the passage (Rom 9:25–26), and Peter likewise (1 Pet 2:10). This is what God, superseding every possible insult, every disdain, from then on took on himself in order to put to shame the wisdom of the Greeks and the Jews' search for miracles, and whose seal he imprints on the world from the pure grace of the cross (1 Cor 1:26–28). The Jerusalem, around which the kings of the earth lurk, robbed by them of its garments and all its adornments, whose shame is made plain with contempt and finally hacked to pieces and cast into the fire, is no longer other than on the cross. That is why the Christians are likewise called to take to themselves the shame of Jesus by leaving the old Jerusalem (Heb 13:13).

Can a Christian thus settle down once and for all beyond the cross? Only if he himself could be conceded "perfect love" which "casts out fear" (1 Jn 4:18), full eschatological "confidence for the day of judgment." But he or she is a liar if he or she claims to have no sin (1 Jn 1:9), does not again and again step from the Old Testament toward the promise and hope of the cross, does not again and again, with all the sinners who encounter Jesus, go to him and recognize him as Savior once again, as if for the first time. With what urgency the apostolic church, to which we like to attribute a somewhat naive certainty of salvation, is summoned by the apostles to be mindful of its origin, to make sure not to forget it and face to face with its former shame to persevere in the behavior of Magdalene, in her confessing, adoring gratitude: "Formerly, you were . . .!" (Gal 1:13, 4:18; Phil 3:4f; Eph 2:11–12; 4:17–24; Tit 3:3; 1 Pet 1:14, 18; 4:3–4, etc.). Who could presume to characterize the real church, which is just as real, just as varied in bodily color as the old Jerusalem, with that purely eschatological stature which would stand once and for all beyond all dangers, all pauline shipwrecks (Acts 27)—in which the fathers could read a symbol for the historical church? Who would presume to confine it solely to the structures given and guaranteed it from above and thus dissociate it from all genuine historicity, all (only through danger "heroic") faith, hope, and love? The "subject" that could be equated with a fateless, guaranteed certainty is found neither "in the church" nor "as church." For church cannot be seen as saved and guaranteed except in the cross of its Lord (and not in itself). And if it is known as the fruit of the cross (and every Christian in it knows himself as such), then never in any other way than at the same time walking toward this cross in penance and conversion. This is how the church understands herself before God in her liturgy which is her surest *lex credendi:* "O Lord, protect, we pray, your church with eternally forgiving grace; and since human mortality goes astray without you, may it always by your help be drawn away from what is harmful and directed to what is good" (Oration, 14th Sunday after Pentecost). "May unceasing mercy, O Lord, *purify* and protect your church, and since it cannot remain safe without you, may it always be governed by your grace" (Oration, 15th Sunday after Pentecost; cf. Oration, 1st Sunday of Lent*). Here and everywhere the church prays for itself, and not just for its children with whom it identified itself in a motherly "as-if." All of these, praying together, are the church of Christ which is praying for its purifying, sanctifying, protecting grace.

Structures of the Church

61 · Holy Scripture— Witness of the Word of God

The scriptures are in no sense what they appear to earthly eyes to be—that is to say, a document which is hopelessly located in and tied to a particular stage in history, but rather a witness given to the church (as it believes, hopes, and suffers with its Lord), his real and spiritual presence, to accompany it on its way through history, a document which consequently possesses unconditionally the properties of a persistent actuality and accessibility, a document which instructs and illumines, which gives powerful comfort. In it the spirit has the upper hand over the letter, the immediate intelligibility primacy over the need for interpretation; the Bible remains a word for the poor in spirit. One can see its spiritual character already in the fact that the picture of Jesus which is given to us (by means of the four gospels) is given in such three-dimensional clarity that no attempt to reduce it to the level of the two-dimensional (of a photograph) will ever succeed.

There is no avoiding the work which must be done on this document, and which today is pursued more fiercely than ever, because it

---

* The old cycle of the Roman Missal.

is indeed a historical and highly complex structure which makes its claim to bear witness to that which is unique, unsurpassable. And such work is also very fruitful because the uncovering of its interrelationships with contemporary history and literature, of the successive phases of its redaction and of the utterances which thereby have been introduced at successive stages, each of them seeing things in a different and new way, has allowed the text to speak to us, to reveal itself to us, in a manner not previously known. This work must be pursued and made fruitful for the belief of the church. The belief of the primitive church—which is substantially the same as our own—had a part in forming the document; it would therefore be uncritical to attempt to put brackets round it in our research on the documents, or to attempt to get behind it.

It is the adequate eschatological answer to the eschatological testament of God. Both appear simultaneously or not at all. Both either are of equally pressing importance today as they were then, or else they never possessed the importance at all which they once claimed. And so one cannot possibly insist on the validity of the original literary witness (viewing all subsequent developments as a decline from that) without affirming at the same time the validity for all time of that to which witness is borne, of which the living witness of faith is itself a part; for otherwise everything slips away into the realm of unreality: only the written document itself still retains the full gravity of the eschatological reality; historical reality is measured against the original witness preserved in the sacred shrine, by its verbal correspondence to it, and is found wanting. But, equally, we should not simply assume the authenticity of the faith as we have it today, no more than we should abandon, as of no importance, the orientation of such faith toward the reality witnessed to in this document. Such faith would be necessarily abstract, that is to say, drawn away, removed from the concrete eschatological saving deed of God, which can only have meaning for us in the present, as a deed incarnated and sealed by Jesus' death on the cross and his resurrection.

Consequently, if one scrapes away layer after layer of the witness—like onion skins—rejecting them as conditioned by their own particular times, in order to get back to a "supratemporal," enduring (demythologized) kernel, then one has quite certainly understood the witness in a manner in which it itself does not intend to be understood. By analysis one has unmasked the central synthesis, which stands at the center of all the New Testament witnesses, as a derivative, hybrid product of unpermissible conflations and overlayers, whose historical truth for critical reason can only lie in the elements which precede the synthesis. Both positions—the practical identification of the eschatological event witnessed to with the testifying historical document and which bears witness to it, and the practical identification of present-day faith with the eschatological event, bypassing the document itself—tend mutually to promote each other. But both fail to recognize that everything hangs on the ever relevant entrusting from time to time (tradition) of the highest that God has and is to us who through all ages always persist in receiving in the same manner the same gift. And in the tradition of the church we pass on this faith which, if it is to remain intact, concrete, and undiminished in accordance with its origin, must continually take its bearings by the original witness. In the chain of tradition all receivers and answerers must check among themselves and for themselves whether they have received and answered with understanding the gift of God at its eschatological maximum, whether in eating and drinking they "discern the body of the Lord," for otherwise—as they step out of line and isolate themselves because of their superior knowledge—they could eat and drink to themselves judgement instead of salvation; "that is why so many of you are weak and ill, and why so many have died" (1 Cor 11:30).

History for the church is also a process of living change. But this is not change in the sense of a growing apart from its origin. Within the world all historical development brings with it a loss of intensity, a process of aging. In so far as the church travels a truly historical course, it is also familiar with this law: no stage which it reaches is absolute, that which has fallen below standard must be reformed in accordance with its origin, and the permanent effort to be true to its origin belongs, like change itself, positively to the phenomenon of its living tradition. Change means to become different, to alter, but believing change is a change within the context of an alteration which has been realized once and for all, which is the deed of God: in the transformation from death to life as it is hidden and constantly present in the transformation of the Eucharist.

This should make it clear why "scripture and tradition" are not two principles which can be set against each other but aspects of a larger occurrence which is exhausted by neither of them, which in its very nature is historically unique and (as a consequence) of universal historical significance. It is unique because in the Christ-event the whole fullness of God's self-giving is contained. There is no development beyond it or away from it. It is of universal significance because the ever-new realization of this fullness in the church, in its faith, prayer, suffering, and hidden victories, belongs internally to the being and activity of Christ. There is no head without a body, no child without a mother, no bridegroom without a bride. The church and its history are the "fullness of him who fills all in all" (Eph 1:23), and but for this fulfilled fullness there would also be no fulfiller.

62 · Holy Scripture—
Interpreted Historically and Theologically

Our starting point is the "immediacy" of God's word as it encounters and meets us in holy scripture. It could reasonably be objected that what is most immediate is not the word of scripture but the word received in its living proclamation which as such is essentially continuous with the Word to which the word of scripture is but a pointer, the Word Jesus Christ who endowed the apostles with the office and charismatic authority of preaching. This is true enough: yet, because the scriptural word has as its function to bear witness, under the inspiration of God, to the word of life, to the total Christ, both head and body, and because as a whole it is word, in the human and focal sense (whereas that to which it bears witness can only be so designated in a deeper and not directly intelligible sense), it needs a methodical and objective introduction. Scripture is one book among many, or rather a collection of books of the most diverse kinds; hence as a book (as one of extreme complexity, posing more scientific problems than any other in world literature) it must be subjected to all the methods of an exact philology. We can no longer agree with Origen (himself a great philologist!) when he occasionally compares this to the subjection of the letter to the retorts and torture-machines of the philological method, and almost equates it with the subjection of the incarnate Word to his torturers. This implied identification of the scriptural word with the Word which the Son is, this interpretation of scripture as an incarnation of the Logos, is too undifferentiated not to lead to numerous false conclusions. Insofar as it implies a suspicion of anything to do with natural philology this ingenious theory is really an expression of the Alexandrian tendency toward the doctrine of one nature.

Nonetheless, after allowing due scope for the science of the word, we must acknowledge what is correct in Origen's view. Holy scripture, as the uniquely privileged witness to a unique event, is so intimately bound to it that, apart from the event—understood in the sense in which it is witnessed in scripture, or witnesses itself in scripture—it cannot be interpreted at all. Philology can help toward this understanding but it can neither compel nor replace it. To understand the scriptural text according to its own defined mission (and to do otherwise would be to mistake its whole tenor) means accepting it in faith as the witness of the Holy Spirit (through the instrumentality of humans) to Yahweh's dealings with his chosen people of the covenant, and most of all to the fulfilling of this covenant in the divine-human person of Jesus. It is true of course that in every genuine, concrete, human statement there is a tension between intention and intended, the word holding them apart as well as conjoining them. Yet it is never the case that the uniqueness of a word should and could correspond with the uniqueness of what is meant, for the very reason that no event in the world can claim absolute uniqueness, and its comparability with other things remains a reason for its communicability. Consequently, however personal and relatively original a given utterance may be, it always contains an element of general accessibility and formality, bringing it within the purview of linguistics, grammar, syntax, poetics, comparative philology, and so forth. The event to which scripture bears witness is, on the one hand, a genuine part of human history, and thus something which can be genuinely expressed in human words. But it is also an event of such qualitative uniqueness that there is an absolute limit fixed to its comparability with other events in which the limit of the witnessing word in relation to general philology is also clearly set. If what is intended is wholly unique then so too is the relation of the propositional intention connected with it not merely incidentally but centrally governed by the identical uniqueness. In other words this testifying word necessarily implies this content; and, if scripture must be understood as essentially the word authorized by the Holy Spirit (since only God can speak adequately of God, only God can say what he means by his revelation), then it must be seen as the Spirit's word about the Word that is the Son; and this, its sublimest aspect, implies a relation to the Trinity.

This spotlights the partial truth of what Origen says, namely that there can only be an inadequate distinction between the testifying word and the word testified. Large tracts of scripture do not merely relate the revelation made by Yahweh to his people through the mediation of Moses, the kings, the prophets, even the pagans, and finally in the Word that is Christ. They are rather revelation themselves. In the prayers of the psalmist the Spirit reveals what prayer means for God; in the words of the prophets there is not only reference to a particular historical background, but there is reported the core of what God willed to speak into this actual situation through the prophets. The sapiential books no longer refer to any historical background but are themselves a tranquil contemplation of the historical revelation, and not only in an inspired way, but in a revelational form and tone, an uncovering of the goods therein contained. In the New Testament the mutual interpenetration is still more evident. This alone imparts to the words of scripture not only a unique ontological value in themselves but also that unique resonance that causes every human generation to pay heed and fosters a great turbulence in the sea of human words. Something of the uniqueness of the object testified to resides inseparably in the word that testifies, imparting to its inner credibility as witness—precisely and exclusively of this reality. Something of the logic of the object testified to, above all the cross and the resurrection of Christ, colors the logic of the statement. This has been often noted, but at the same time seems never to have been adequately treated.

63 · The Preaching of the Gospel

The apostles and the other disciples receive the charge to preach to the world what God brought about in the cross and resurrection. This joyful news (*euangelion*) is in its structure something quite different from the dissemination of a teaching. It is the making known of something done, a *factum* (fact, from *facio*). That this announcement takes the form of witnessing is certainly characteristic and quite important—since such a fact really can't be made known in any other way than by those who have experienced it, and have put their existence on the line—but again, compared with the weight of the fact itself, quite unimportant. The weight of the (life-)witness that is thrown into the balance by the apostle is small when measured against that before which his witness stands. In other words, the question of the believability of the witnesses stands on a deeper level than the question of the believability of the event. The witness is a word of the church, but that is "word about word"; the fact is that silent super-word of God which brings together in itself and supersedes all the words of the Old Covenant leading to it. The announcing word of the church is by nature transient, only an indicator of the deed which is made thoroughly visible and present through this word of the church and in this way arises with its own evidence behind and above the word of the church.

This is true despite the idea that the apostles (and their representatives and followers) are sent by Christ on the mission to preach in his authority and thus also with his power, especially when in Christian obedience they give witness by their lives, which as such makes present and confirms something of the fact of Christ. Paul repeatedly laid great emphasis on the different aspects of this apostolic witness. For one thing, he emphasized the fact that his message came "not only in word, but also in power and in the Holy Spirit" (1 Thess 1:5), so that his word could be taken and become "effective" in the faithful "not as the word of men but as what it really is, the word of God" (1 Thess 2:13). In addition, it is preaching with the emphasis of the example, frankly on symbolizing Christ's crucifixion-event (1 Cor 4; 2 Cor 4:8–9; 13:3–4). Yet even this whole—by Paul almost indiscretely emphasized—symbolizing and incarnation of the word realized by him must move completely into the background ("we do not preach ourselves"), in order to let "the light of the joyful good news of the *glory* of Christ, who is the likeness of God" (2 Cor 4:4–5) shine forth. So if, on the occasion of the witnessing word of the disciple, this picture shines forth, enough power is given it, through the (withdrawing) word of the church, to be witnessed, attested, and made evident in its truth. And this is true with its whole, perduring, mysterious character as super-word, as a God-posited fact that is not inserted into any conceivable "essential connection," unless into the paths which lead to him and come from him.

And certainly, the most important part of the path toward that event is constituted by all that Jesus himself said, taught, and did in the time of his public life. It was word pointed to the cross. The disciples decisively understood this word pointing to the cross from the perspective of the cross itself, and recorded their portrait and preached according to this understanding. Basically it doesn't make much difference how the prospective scheme and retrospective scheme are interrelated and delimited. As long as the prospective scheme must have been in the intention of Jesus and still not even have come close to being properly understood by the listeners, the understanding from the perspective of the cross and resurrection must be an adequate expression for the church and the world of what Jesus said and did in heading in the direction of the cross. In no case can and should this prospective word be separated from its *telos* and misinterpreted as something that stands by itself. For it would then sink to the level of an ordinary teaching lecture and basically be interpreted on the same level as the word of the church. In doing that Christianity would be changed from a belief in the deed of God to a religion (or gnosis) of divine and human truths. A certain inclination in this direction can easily be found even in the New Testament writings, if one, for instance, notes the growing use of the word *doctrina* (increasingly in the sense of completed doctrine, and no longer, as before, in that of proclamation, counsel, and sermon) in the deutero-pauline letters. Now the event naturally provides an infinite, ever more prolific occasion for interpretation and formulation, and this process is quite legitimate. Yes, it is even a dimension of God's deed itself which is especially reserved for the Holy Spirit (Jn 16:13–15). But the Spirit will "speak what he hears, take what is mine, glorify me": that is, the whole interpretation of the thought and word is always done *in view of* the event that Paul previously characterized as the "glory of Christ" and "image of God." In all the ramifications of ecclesiastical, theological, and pastoral interpretation the Spirit has not the least occasion of separating himself even for an instant from the center of the event in order to indulge in its own trains of thought; what meaning the Spirit draws from the glory and the image, is exactly what he reads into their depths; it has been indeed already shown that the subsisting convenant conclusion on the cross between God and his world underpins, grounds, and makes possible all truth between God and humans, ultimately all the truth of creation too.

The absolute scope and resonance of the event, however, determines proclamation in still another way. If this proclamation is the message of the happy event—and the hearer can know about this in no other way than through this message (Rom 10:14)—then the event as such always hurries ahead of the proclamation. It has already reached the hearer of the preaching, and only this reality that is already there can be proclaimed to the hearer. But that it is already present for the hearer means that it has already struck, seized, and taken possession of him or her, because when the hearer was still an unknowing sinner Christ has already borne his or her sins on the cross in advance (Rom 5:8). The faith that the preaching requires of the hearer is thus a dependency not on the preached word but on the incarnate, crucified, risen Word of God which makes the mysterious dictum of Deuteronomy come true in a superabundant way: "The word is very near to you; it is in your mouth and in your heart" (Dt 30:14; cf. Rom 10:8). In a true sense, then, every word proclaiming the event is already superseded, even though this ecclesiastical dimension remains indispensable in the spatial-temporal, empirically structured human world. The doctrinal truth of the church is true in a Christian way only when it is made radiant by the event of the glory of God in the crucified and risen Lord.

64 · Office in the Church

The church is nothing, unless it is Christ; all must subject themselves obediently not just to the transcendental law of unity, which is Christ, but also to his God-given mission. Now the question arises whether the transcendental unity—Christ—has need of a reminding and concretizing representation and whether Christ actually instituted something like that for the visible church community. Without being able to now go into the details of the founding and structure of ecclesiastical office, the question raised requires an affirmative answer. Office in the (Catholic) church is that special *charisma* whose purpose is the coordination of the individual *charisms* by pointing to the unity, by drawing close to it, by admonition to be limited to it, and which lets the transcendent unity of the church become ineluctably concrete. If all members of the church were totally obedient to their own *charism* (and its limitations by love), there would be no need for such an ordering function. But how could a Christian who remains ever a sinner have the confidence to guarantee his or her complete ecclesiastical obedience on the basis of purely charismatic order, an obedience which, according to its fundamental christological form, can in a crisis run against *another's* will just as sharply as did the will of Christ in the Garden of Olives against the will of the Father, and still be really resigned to it?

The objection, of course, immediately arises: how can an individual human will represent transcendent incarnate and trinitarian reality even approximately? The first answer which merits attention is that it does so by the guiding recollection that the unity of Christ not only exists, but that it is also the most real and demanding unity of the church. The presence of office exercises this remembering function on three levels. It reminds the individual that through his or her faith the individual is taken into a more difficult obedience than he or she would like to admit, an obedience not to one's own so-called "conscience," but to the Lord of the church and to the "talent" personally entrusted to that conscience by him (Mt 25:14–30). Moreover, it reminds the community that its unity does not lie in the mere harmonic interplay of personal *charisms*, or in a self-contained, self-satisfying innerworldly order (like in a work of art), but that this harmony itself must be obedient to the crucified and risen Lord. Nowhere does the church grow for itself; when it grows inwardly, it encounters the "inner man, the Christ dwelling in your hearts through faith" (Eph 3:16–17); when it grows outwardly and historically, then it does so in a bridal way toward "the perfect man, the mature Christ" (Eph 4:13). In this instructive remembering the official church can ultimately, on a third level, attain from the unity of Christ the authority to feed the sheep and lambs of Christ, to strengthen the brethren, to make decisions which hold also in heaven. Then the office is not just a sign but an effective, confirmed, sacramental sign. And whoever administers it is not only a teacher, but in an official-personal way—spiritually and bodily—the one injector of the unity of Christ into the community. The community can have many teachers, because being a teacher is a single *charism*, but not many "fathers" (1 Cor 4:15). The teacher, whether catechist or theologian, investigates and expounds the single aspects of revelation and shows their relationship; the bearer of the office of unity embodies that unwritten and never definitively formulable in letters *regula fidei*, which is the living, pneumatic quintessence of the faith of the church, as long as this faith has its unity and trinitarian-simple truth in Christ. As opposed to the single *charisms* which, obeying their special law (*quaerunt quae sua sunt*), pursue their perhaps very social and very altruistic interests, the office-holder, when he understands and lives his office, considers *ea quae sunt Jesu Christi*, who is the transcending unity of love (Phil 2:21).

The fact that in this representation of unity—in individuals who should perpetually be going beyond themselves in their faith and mission, in the community which should be borne in the love of Christ even through the greatest of contradictions, in the church to the extent that it should realize it is founded and sheltered only *en Christō*—indeed, that humanly speaking one can be talking merely about an achievement in service that can only be exercised in abiding weakness and frequent failure, only about an approximation toward a never-attainable ideal, is obvious. Official church (Peter) and church of love (John) have come together only once, in the founder, who on account of his transcendence as God-man, could be at once officiating priest and sacrifice of love, sacrificed lamb. But the theology of the church in John 20–21 shows us not only that John takes his place behind Peter (20:5), that Peter officiates for John (20:6–8), but that John "relinquishes" his (private) love to Peter, in other words, he lets it be taken into the anonymous unity of ecclesiastical love represented by Peter (21:15), while Peter obtains the unprecedented promise of being able to seal his office by his loving death as a martyr in the same way as his Lord (21:18–19). He, however, clearly remains the Lord over against the servant because solely from the head is there any disposition over the abode of the church of love in (as well as occasionally outside) the official church (21:10–23). All this demonstrates the continual tension in the body of Christ between "office" and "love," although this tension in Christ himself has always been resolved and remains resolvable by him. And Christians of all *charisms* are most urgently invited by John as well as by Paul to have a concern for this resolution.

They should therefore think not of the tension or even of the rupture in the church as a (psychological or sociological) "accomplished fact." The "fact" of the tension is there and will always be there, but it is by no means an "accomplished," but an ever-new (in love), superseded, and supersedable fact. The church will not be sundered only by schisms but already by the kind of Christians who play off their personal-charismatic mandate against the official church; for their obedience to their mandate is not something private or relating only to a group, but is also something represented by the office; it must *ultimately*, in obedience to *ecclesial unity*—which is not the office but Christ who is, of course, represented by the office—be preserved as Christian mandate.

65 · The Petrine Office in the Church

So evident is it that the church is presented to the world as a kind of organized society which has a kind of constitution and a kind of "leadership," it is also just as evident that it understands itself as a mystery (cf. Vatican II: *Lumen Gentium*, chap. 1) which, to the extent that it is ontologically connected with the mystery of Christ and thus with the Trinity (chap. 1:2–4), cannot be utterly comprehensible even to itself. True as it is, as Henri de Lubac continually emphasizes, that the Christian in the church can believe only "in" God (Father, Son, and Spirit) but not "in" the church, but can believe instead only "the" (existence of the) church, it is also true on the other hand that this existence, right down to its apparent structure, is not simply something available or even manipulable, but—as "body" and "bride" of Christ—an aspect of his mystery.

In the Catholic understanding of this aspect, it can be properly classified only from the total mystery of Christ, his self-giving and transmission to humanity. It can thus be classified neither sociologically (since the Easter-event is unique), nor (for the same reason) according to the history of religions, nor from a principle which is foreign to catholicism either, such as *sola scriptura* in the reformational sense, because the scripture can be interpreted in its proper meaning only within the church and for the church and its *traditio*. The hermeneutical locus from which the continuing existence of the petrine office and its form today and tomorrow can be judged is none other than the self-understanding of the Catholica in its faith-filled gazing on the form and will of its founder. From outside it can receive advice (useful perhaps and worthy of gratitude) at most which it will examine in relation to itself, but no prescriptions. As little as Mormons could pass judgment on whether or not Tibetans should do away with the Dalai Lama, can non-Catholics pass judgment on the existence or even the conduct of the pope. The same can be said of those "catholic" theologians in whom an anti-Roman feeling or some other kind of *ressentiment* against "structures" (at the mere mention of which they see red) has blinded them to the objective.

The papacy has always—from the petrine texts of the New Testament on—had to exercise the function of unity in the church and, indeed, of visible unity in the visible church which, considered realistically, is made up of sinners—egoists and separatists. This means that the function of perserving unity cannot be: 1. a mere honorary office without geniune decision-making power; 2. a mere expression of a unity already otherwise existing in the visible church (as between bishops, as Cyprian thought, or between the faithful who "love one another," no matter what they might hold to be true in dogma); or 3. a merely transitory function which could disappear after the fixing of the canon or be applied only from case to case or one day be totally abolished. Instead, this function of the preservation of unity is a constitutive function and is exercisable only under the condition that its bearer is given the powers that belong to him in the limits of his office. This presupposes from the other members of the church (bishops, priests, laity) a docility and reverence toward this *pneumatic* office.

Two remarks must be added right away. First, the church has not arbitrarily given itself this function; instead it has organically unfolded from the New Testament petrine texts which cannot be eliminated. A careful and moderate evangelical (Swiss Reformed) theologian like J.J. von Allmen is convinced that the primacy of Peter cannot be limited to Peter personally; it is "biblically solidly grounded"! "Perhaps this kind of horror, that seizes all us reformed theologians when we see that we are not getting around the problem of succession, comes from the fact that consciously and unconsciously we have the following feeling: if there is an apostolic succession, there is doubtless also a specifically petrine succession" (*Irénikon* [1970], p. 529). At any rate, the extreme difficulty of upholding church unity without the office of unity—just think of the continual tensions among the Orthodox, or of the fate of the Leuenberg Concord—can make the Catholic office of unity more plausible in its necessity.

Second, the papal function of unity is by no means the only function of unity in the Catholica; it is only one of the indispensable ones. The church is not a pyramid with Rome as its peak. (I have discussed that clearly in my book *The Anti-Roman Feeling* [Freiburg 1974].) The church has of course its deepest unity only in Christ (and thus in the triune God). As long as it lives according to the directives of Christ in love, the unity which comes from this is found in the mutual love of Christians. This love is, even for those outside, the effective proof for the truth of their belief in Christ. If the church as a whole had been only a holy, loving church, there would never have been need for the petrine office of unity. This makes its appearance only in the third place where the concern is, first, to preserve the faith in its purity and genuineness (cf. already as early as the Pastoral Letters) and then, as far as possible, to hold fast to the congruence between this one faith and the unity of love, and continually bring it about ever anew (along the path of exhortation, correction, decision as well: cf. the *Letter of Clement*).

66 · Official Church and Church of Love (According to the Gospel of John)

There is in John an extensive allegory on the relationship between *official church* (Peter) and *church of love* (John, or "the disciple whom Jesus loved"). Only those who see the two as real symbols of these two sides of the church of Christ understand the intention of the evangelist. As traditional material for his allegory there must surely have been available a Galilean tradition for the appendix chapter (Jn 21), quite likely with a confession of guilt and a calling of Peter (cf. the reflection in Lk 5). Whether Luke 24:12 is to be seen as a basis for John 20:3–10 (which is usually denied), or whether a historical core can be found in the story (did this story take place between the report of the women and the departure of the disciples for Galilee, in case they were even still in Jerusalem?) must be left unanswered.

That both disciples run "together" (*homou*) is an initial and abiding observation that is not superseded by what follows: the love, less encumbered, "runs ahead"; the office, with many things to consider, reaches the goal later. Love sees well what can be seen (from outside) but gives precedence to office, which takes everything into view (including what is not visible from outside), and from the arrangement of the head cloth reaches a sort of *nihil obstat* which allows love to approach so that it (by seeing the signs? by seeing what Peter had discovered?) comes to faith—a thoroughly wavering faith, "for they had not yet understood that he must rise from the dead" (Jn 20:9; the addition, "the scripture," is to be deleted). This first episode results in a two-peaked church, official church and church of love, in harmonious tension: office working for love, love respectfully giving precedence to office.

The appendix chapter continues the symbolism: Peter has the initiative in the first departure of the ship of the church without the Lord. It remains unsuccessful: effort and harvest are never proportional. There is conversation with the hidden Lord and obedience of the church to his signal, even without recognizing him. At the miracle, love recognizes the Lord, but tells it immediately to office which knows the right thing to do, and is in the right clothing to be with the Lord as soon as possible. Now a succession of pictures follow: the Lord with Peter on the shore (symbol of eternity, of the "infallible" solid ground); the others bringing the catch to both of them; Peter, who as the one in charge overall, boards the boat and brings in the whole overflowing net to the Lord; the meal together; finally, the conferral of office: the, for Peter the denier, unanswerable question: "Do you love me more than these?" There is no other solution for

Peter than (in the communism of the "Community of Saints") to borrow the greater love from John and thus provide the absolutely required answer. Peter's primacy is erected on John's renunciation of a "private" love for the Lord; with the command to pasture the flock, Peter is also promised a martyr's death for the sheep in imitation of the Lord: the unity of love and office is thereby sealed in him. The gospel of love thus ends in an *apotheosis* of office into which particular love is surrendered. Still, there remains something that does not disappear (Jn 21:20–25): Peter sees the Beloved Disciple (who really should have disappeared into him) still standing there and remembers his mediating role between the official church and the Lord (Jn 13:23f; cf. 18:15f; 21:7). He does not understand this, but feels in himself the official obligation to understand and thus to ask, "Lord, what about this man?" The question is understandable from the point of view of office, even justified, but the answer remains veiled because it rests wholly in the freedom of the Lord of the church. Peter has his mandate, as servant, and the rest does not concern him, namely where on earth run the exact boundaries between the official church and the church of love. This church of love will "remain" until the Lord comes again, but how and where, only the Lord knows. Peter *should* love; he should thus, as far as he can manage, be the church of love. This is the spirit in which he should pasture; he can in no way afford the opinion that any religion is as good as another if one only has love, that love which Christ by his death for all also merited for all and as supernatural holds in readiness. Why should that not be enough? But no more can he be hardened in the opposite opinion that only those who are contained in his visible sheepfold have the guarantee of true love and thus of eternal salvation. Between these two impossible ecclesiologies the Gospel of John leaves and dismisses us in a suspended middle-point whose foundation lies solely with the Lord. The last thing said to the servant, Peter, the last word of the Lord in the gospel, is the admonition (for the church and theology of all times), "What is that to you?"

67 · Baptism—Incorporation into the Church

The turning of the human person in pure faith to God has its necessary complement in the turning of the individual to the community of the Christian church. This church represents the place of the realized love of Jesus Christ on earth; it receives as one of its own each one who professes a believing love for Christ. Thus the sacrament of entry, baptism, is two things in one: letting-oneself-be-given the form of the death and resurrection of Christ for the life of the world as one's own affirmed form of existence (Rom 6:3–12; Col 2:12), and letting-onself-be-given the existential form of love and membership in the body of the Lord (Eph 4:4–5). In Christ himself "baptism" was both ritual (Mk 1:9 par) and existential (Lk 12:50: baptism of the cross), and he administers it to his own in the same twofold meaning (Mt 28:19; Mk 10:38f). Already in John the Baptist's view, Christian baptism moves beyond the water ritual to "Spirit and fire" (Mt 3:11). One must be made aware of the totally paradoxical character of a "sacramental conferral of the Spirit" (Acts 1:5; 11:16) in order to see the New Testament inseparability both of objective bestowal and subjective affirmation, and also of turning to God and turning to community.

68 · Personal Confession

There is no collective guilt. You can make clear to me that Western capitalism is responsible for the fact that in Brazilian plantations and Peruvian mines the natives are underpaid; but if I, after learning that, do what I in my situation can do to rectify this injustice (and there are some things that I really can do), it is meaningless then to accuse myself of the sin that I as a capitalist am guilty of the subhuman living conditions of Latin America. I could become culpable by deliberately avoiding every explanation of the interconnections of the world economic system under the pretext that I still can do nothing about it; some form of help is, in modest compass, possible to everyone. I have to wander not very far at all for there is my narrower or broader circle of acquaintances which I can essentially influence through my behavior and my existence and for which I am humanly responsible. This is true in the Christian even more than in the human sense; for in the general human sphere many laws of forbearance hold: "Live and let live," "Each one for himself," etc. The behavior of the milieu can be an excuse; you ought to be adaptable, you don't have to stick your head out. On the contrary, in Christian life every believer is personally placed before the demand of the gospel which separates "father and son, daughter and mother, daughter-in-law and mother-in-law" to the point that "the members of the household of each and every Christian" are "enemies." The "they" has no importance in the Christian world, but the "I" and the "we" of Christians have every importance. The family of Christians is formed of real persons who are responsible to Christ.

That is clearly visible in the gospels. Jesus always deals with sin personally. And in order to handle the sin of persons which is a hindrance to their proper relationship to him, he draws their personal, precisely outlined sin relentlessly into the light. That is quite clear in the scene at Jacob's Well where the woman stubbornly and thick-headedly declines his offer of spiritual water because there is a sin hidden in her which makes understanding impossible. So Jesus stops the instruction and tells her to get her husband: "I have no husband." "You have spoken the truth there; you have had five, and the one you now have is not your husband." After the abscess has been pierced and the sinner "gone to confession," the light immediately penetrates her soul and the conversation about prayer, the true God, the Messiah, becomes possible. With his disciples the Lord proceeds in the same manner. If one of them has personally said or done something wrong, he is "taken to task" in front of all the others: Peter again and again, mercilessly, but also the sons of thunder when they call down fire on Samaria, or Thomas when he does not want to believe the witnesses of the resurrection, or Philip when he still has not understood that in the Son one sees the father. The Pharisees and scribes are not simply condemned without distinction; there are some whose insight is praised: "You are not far from the kingdom of God." Conversely, the disciples have not yet energetically enough driven the "leaven of the Pharisees" from their hearts. Even on the cross the two malefactors are handled differently, according to Luke: one of them confesses his depravity, for which he is promised paradise on the same day; the other continues blaspheming and remains turned away. In the seven letters of the Book of Revelation, the exalted Lord journeys forth from heaven in order to "hear the confession" of his church in this wholly personal way. Each of the seven communities has something different on the "tally sheet." With most the Lord recognizes the good they have done in order then to highlight what displeases him. With some it is not much, with others it is so predominant that they are in danger of being repudiated for their deadly lukewarmness. (It can be seen in the letter to Laodicea that the Lord does not hesitate, with the shock of a massive "imperfect repentence," to threaten final rejection, and only after this drastic cure to add; "All those whom I love, I reprove and chasten; so be zealous and repent.") In any case, the manner in which he, during his earthly life and as glorified Lord, treats Christian sinners is far from a wholesale leveling process, as if all together were sinners (a little bit more or less makes no difference) and all together reconciled with God through the blood of Christ: *simul peccator et justus*. One can of course draw a good meaning from this Lutheran formula and approximate it to certain formulas of Paul. But, if one does not want to completely forget the conduct of Jesus towards sinners, one should do it in such a way as to not simply bury the personal in a general sociological process of salvation.

The church has tried to imitate the conduct of Jesus from the beginning, and indeed at his behest to discern the spirits and to forgive or (provisionally) retain sins with his authority. There were in those days a number of sins (not just three, as we are often told: murder, adultery, and apostasy), which excluded the sinner from the eucharistic celebration of the community and required a personal confession (before the bishop) and a personal penance (before the community). Whether this personal confession was made, as in the beginning, quite openly in public, or later more in secret (but even then with an imposition of penance which was at least visible), plays at the moment a minor role; what is important is that someone who in thoughts, words, or deeds has offended seriously against the Spirit of the holy church of Christ must personally come forward and responsibly confess. That is in no way "time-conditioned" and surpassable; it is connected with the innermost structure of the human essence, as it was recognized by the Son of the creator and brought to its perfection.

If anywhere, the human and Christian need of the grievously guilty person to be rid of his or her guilt must be incarnated in an external deed, in an encounter with a fellow human being which secures punishment and forgiving reincorporation into the community—both at the same time. A mere interior reconciliation with God by regret and personal acts of penance will not restore peace to seriously delinquent persons who have preserved their moral sensitivity. And the (visible) church, in which the Christian delinquent is incorporated as a visible member and against whose fundamental law he or she has offended, is not only one human community among others, but the community founded by God for the world and filled with divine character and saturated with divine life. Therefore serious internal sins which have not yet developed into external action also offend against its fundamental law. The person with mortal hatred is a real murderer in his or her heart. Therefore, reconciliation with this communion requires a genuine, personal, incarnated act which is provided for by Jesus as a normal ecclesiastical act in the authorization of the disciples.

The less personal confession is practiced in the church, the greater will be the pressure on the office hours of the psychologists where the need for doing away with personal guilt feelings and situations of guilt is met in a different way. Here too personal encounter takes place, something like a speaking out of one's guilt, something like reintegration into the community through something like "judgment" and "punishment" (the uncomfortableness of self-knowledge, the turnabout on the road of life), and something like "forgiveness" (the sympathetic dissolution of psychic entanglements, etc.). Everything is transposed to a different level, though, one that is possibly also important, but which remains confused with that moral guilt, and the psychologist has no power to absolve from this.

Against common penitential devotions of a gathered community with an officially administered absolution there is as little to object as there is against the daily common *confiteor* in the holy mass in which each of the faithful with all the others gathered there confesses his or her sinfulness and commits it to God's mercy. Well-conducted penance services can in addition uncover and bring to awareness many aspects of personal guilt which often escape those who are left just to their own examinations of conscience. The personal confessions can in this way become deeper, more genuine, more lasting in their effects. But these will always remain the central point of the sacrament of confession, because in the gospel each individual is called upon and must step forward in his or her lonely responsibility before God and human beings. It is this way already in the penitential preaching of the Baptist at the Jordan: the crowd listens to the exhortation, then each one confesses her or his sins. There is always the aspect of common guilt; it was there in the Old Testament where, in the order of the day, the people of Israel represented a kind of "large-I," a collective (cf., e.g., Neh 9). But already in Israel there is, besides the communal, quite clearly also the personal confession of sins (David!); many Psalms are obviously individual confessions of sins. How much more is the accent laid on the personal in the New Covenant!

In closing, of course, one thing must again be noted. Personal confession is not, any more than it ever was, something private in the church. I have personally sinned, yes indeed; and when I accuse myself I mean myself and no one else. But can I clearly separate my sins from those of everyone else? Or do I not by my behavior share in the guilt for much that goes on around me, and that would be quite different if I were different? My sin has a social echo that I cannot measure. And I must, without being able to view them, include all the consequences of my sin in my confession. In me the whole church confesses my solidarity with the sins of many, with the sins of all— just as in me the whole church also goes to communion. That is not a lessening but an increase of personal responsibility. The sin of the world is not divided by the number of sinners; it is in a mysterious and inexplicable way everywhere where sin is, indivisibly present. And so it is that personal confession is always something having to do with others, far and near.

Personal confession is simply required where a sinner has estranged himself or herself from the fundamental law of the church as Communion of Saints. But beyond this it is advisable wherever a person in a healthy (not scrupulous, ego-centered) way would like to do a more serious job of being a Christian. Then the confession of sin is joined with a conversation about one's entire life situation, so that a plan for the reform of one's existence can be made. Religious sensitivity has caused such personal exchange to arise outside of Christianity too (for example in Buddhism). If that can take place in a religion in which the divinity is thought of impersonally, how much more fitting will it be for Christians who in conversation with their redeemer want to make progress on the way which he is.

69 · The Eucharistic Self-Giving of Jesus

Jesus' life is oriented to that hour in which he will no longer have disposition over himself (in the passion); but (in the Eucharist) he can have control in advance precisely over this being a passive object of another's disposition (i.e., in the sense of the divinely willed pouring forth of himself). Toward this his whole anxious (Lk 12:50) longing (Lk 22:15) is directed. Even the simple formula of the words of institution shows the coincidence of disposing and being disposed: "This is my body which is given for you" (Lk 22:19), "this is my blood, . . . which is poured out for you" (Mk 14:24). The "being given" points, as the "being poured out" shows even more clearly, to the passion and the crucifixion. If the primitive church and Paul with it will conclude from the fact of the resurrection of Jesus to the universal salvific significance of the cross (which had to remain unrecognizable in the process itself)—"for our trespasses he was put to death and raised for our justification" (Rom 4:25)—it was because this truth as "sacred-public mystery" was already evident in the gestures with which Jesus at table shared his flesh and blood as given and poured. The gesture of self-giving lies temporally ahead of the violent events of the passion and thereby shows that it is also the ontological reason why the gruesome events following could gain universal saving significance. But the free self-giving wishes to go "to the end" (Jn 13:1), and the "end" can only be that the disposing of oneself turns into a pure *allowing* oneself to be and *being* disposed. Everything passive in the passion, binding, mockery, scourging, nailing, piercing, is an expression of the active will to give which itself necessarily goes beyond the bounds of being able to determine oneself, into the boundlessness of a pure letting oneself be determined. Such a will to give which, in the eucharistic gestures of self-sharing, transcends in advance all limits of human finitude, would have to appear as promethean hubris, if it were not itself already an expression of a previous being determined and disposed. The whole New Testament sees this clearly when it depicts the whole self-giving of Jesus to his own and to the world ("for you and for many") as the incarnation of the divine Word and fulfillment of the divine promise, the final deed of the God who, out of love for the world he created and in fidelity to the covenant he has entered into with it, gives what is most precious to him (Rom 8:32, Jn 3:16). And because the divine plan of salvation had the interrelatedness of Jesus and the world (with the church as core) in view right from the start, there can hover over this interrelatedness also the subjective-objective Spirit which Jesus obeys, which drives and inspires him, which overshadows Mary in the beginning, and after the completion of the passion is breathed by Jesus into the church.

The humanity of Jesus—his "flesh and blood" or his "life" (Jn 10:15)—is thus, even from the incarnation, eucharistically determined, inasmuch as it is the bodily gift of God to the world. The realization of this giving in the Last Supper, passion, and resurrection is only the execution of this gift long since intended and really established and begun. And inasmuch as love's "going to the end" has a soteriological intent, it must by suffering "take away" (Jn 1:29) the refusals of sin, take them on itself and represent them before God for condemnation (2 Cor 5:14, 21; Gal 3:13; Eph 2:14–16). The "for us" is by no means intended just in a juridical sense of moral satisfaction, but beyond that, really, and in a certain manner "physically"; it is my God-forsakenness which attaches to my sins, my dying, in my being estranged from God, to the point of the darkness of eternal death that Christ in his "being handed over" experiences, and indeed necessarily more deeply and more definitively than any mere creature could experience such things. Insofar as he is the only one to come "from above" (Jn 8:23) and even his coming into existence is an act of letting himself be disposed of (Jn 6:38; Heb 10:5–10), he takes on with his incomparable hypostatic suffering every possible temporal or eternal suffering of a created human being. And so it is that after he has plumbed the depths of death and won the entire breadth of the risen life he holds "the keys of Death and Hades" (Rev. 1:18). Precisely by the withdrawal of his most intimate "food" from God (Jn 4:34)—and perhaps there really is hidden behind Mark 14:25 a eucharistic fast of Jesus—God makes him to be food for the whole world. In the passion his whole human substance is "made to flow" so as to be able to enter those who receive him, and indeed in such a way that he dissolves along with it the clots of sin which rise against the fluidity of divine love, and melts them in the experienced God-forsakenness of which they essentially consist.

And now we can draw the conclusion. The eucharistic gesture of Jesus' self-distribution is a definitive, eschatological, and thus irreversible gesture. The Word of God that has become flesh in order to be distributed has been definitively distributed by God and will never again be taken from this condition of having been given. Neither the resurrection from the dead nor the ascension as "return to the Father" (Jn 16:18) is a movement contrary to incarnation, passion, and Eucharist. The farewell discourses speak here clearly enough: "I go away and I will come to you" (Jn 14:28); "You see me because I live, and you also will live" (Jn 14:19). When Jesus says he is giving his life in order to take it back again, that he is giving it of his own accord, has the power to give it and the power to take it back again (Jn 10:18), the continuation of the speech, "And I give them eternal life" (10:28) shows that he could not possibly be talking about a taking back either of what was once given or of the action and condition of giving and being given. The "flowing" of the earthly substance of Jesus into a eucharistic substance is irreversible; it lasts not only—like an "instrument/tool"—until the "end" of the world, it is the glowing core about which (according to the early vision of Teilhard de Chardin) the cosmos crystallizes, or better, from which it radiates. One must be clear about the profound theological significance of what is being expressed by the risen Lord showing his wounds; that the condition of self-donation during the passion is ending and will be subsumed into the henceforth eternal condition of Jesus Christ, and that consequently no difference can be posited between his heavenly and his eucharistic condition. After his distribution at the Last Supper, since in the "hour of darkness" he left his fate and the meaning and form of his redemptive work to the discretion of the Father and the interpretation of the Holy Spirit which will continue it in the church, Jesus' total giving of himself is so definitive that there is no way that it could be taken back again into an attitude of self-disposition. The activity which from the beginning depended on his readiness is not thereby taken back; one can say that it not only continues but, seen from this point of view, only now comes to fulfillment. Of course, after the passion Jesus is no longer the one overwhelmed in suffering, whose human power is insufficient for what is laid on him ("all things are possible to thee; remove this cup from me": Mk 14:36), he is through this overwhelming also the one who in his humanity is expanded to the dimensions of the divine salvific will and is thereby "made both Lord and Messiah" (Acts 2:36), "elevated to Lord" (Phil 2:11). But he is "the lion" (Rev. 5:5) and yet only as long as he is for all eternity "the Lamb as though slain" (Rev 5:5) which stands on God's throne. That means much more than that he, merely on the basis of the merits he has won, functions as intercessor before the Father (Rom 8:34; Heb 7:25, 9:24; 1 Jn 2:1); he stands, as the continuation of the johannine letter says, in this office as "expiation [or "sin-offering": *hilasmos*] for our sins, and not for ours only but also for the sins of the whole world" (1 Jn

2:2; cf. Heb 2:17). This is expressed in another image in the Letter to the Hebrews when it proclaims Jesus as the high priest who "entered once for all into the Holy Place with his own blood" (9:12) since he "through the eternal Spirit offered himself without blemish to God" (9:14). In this mysterious change the Spirit leading him to his self-sacrifice is just as eternal and definitive as the Spirit in which he is raised from the dead (1 Pet 3:18) and which is called down on the eucharistic forms at the *epiclesis.*

70 · The Mass as Meal and Sacrifice

The best entry into the eucharistic thought of John is the episode of the washing of the feet: it gives so to speak an anatomy of the Eucharist from the johannine point of view, and it is not possible that it is an accident that this episode in the fourth gospel stands in the place of the account of institution of the three others. Cullmann is certainly right on this point when he highlights the tendency of the fourth gospel to speak *indirectly* of the sacraments, for example, about the miracle at Cana and about the multiplication of the loaves to point ahead to the Eucharist; but also in the discourse of promise to make the clearest statements about them, while the fulfillment remains covered with a concealing veil. Without calling this into question, we would add that it is above all John who also makes a point of explaining the sacraments *existentially,* namely showing the attitude of Jesus, whose representations and creations they are, and correspondingly the sentiment of the community of the disciples which had to answer to the attitude of Jesus. One could understand the whole last discourse as giving a glimpse into the eucharistic heart of Jesus, but would not make a mistake by interpreting especially the action of the footwashing as being immediately transparent to the eucharistic event.

This transparency is at times seen, but it is also often mistaken in so far as the footwashing is interpreted all too materially in reference to a particular sacramental individual situation of the church. It is also not enough to understand it only "as 'image' of the saving death of Jesus insofar as he is the perfection of love. This 'perfection of love' is also characterized by this event in the special way that it is the utmost abasement of one who knows of his divine power. The washing of the feet as typical task of a slave is an image of the death on the cross, which is the death of a slave" (W. Thüsing). That is true, but it overlooks the fact that the scene takes place during the eucharistic meal and in the first (13:6–11) as well as second (13:13–17) interpretation looks beyond in typical johannine fashion to the Eucharist.

The first interpretation is decisive, the second has primarily consequential significance. The preparation for the act of washing is the Lord's stripping himself for the task of a servant, as Augustine depicts it in view of the Eucharist: *Posuit autem vestimenta sua qui cum in forma Dei esset, semetipsum exinanivit, . . . praecinxit se linteo qui formam servi accepit, misit aquam in pelvim unde lavaret pedes discipulorum qui in terram sanguinem fudit quo immunditiam dilueret peccatorum* ("He put aside his garments, although he was in the form of God, and emptied himself; he girded himself with a cloth, he who took the form of a slave, and poured water into a basin from which to wash the feet of the disciples, he who poured blood into the earth by which to wash out the uncleanness of sins").

But what is central is the conversation with Peter. It begins with his most profound shock: "Lord, do you wash my feet?" (13:6). It is the absolutely inappropriate, the reversal of every human sense of rank, to the nth degree, because washing feet could not even be demanded of a free Israelite, let alone the "Lord and Master" (13:13f), but only of a slave (1 Sam 25:41). Jesus' answer gives no explanation—a certain explanation comes only with the second answer—but only a confirmation of its incomprehensibility for now: "What I am doing you do not know now, but afterward you will understand," after the resurrection and the mission of the interpreting Spirit. The consent of Peter *in persona Ecclesiae* must result in incomprehension, in pure obedience, yes, even more, in the devastation of his elemental recoiling horror. This horror is expressed in Peter's second word: "You shall never wash my feet"; this is something that I can under no circumstances permit. Why? Because in this the whole religious hierarchy of values of the natural human being crumbles. God is above, the human being is below. The saint is above, the sinner is below. It is not an adequate response to accuse Peter here of obstinacy and blindness; the *homo religiosus* speaks or screams from him. The answer is, "If I do not wash you, you have no part in me" (13:8). There the order of the world, here companionship with Jesus. This sharing (*meros*) alludes to the eucharistic word *koinōnia*. But only one thing is important now, letting it happen in horror and incomprehension is a *conditio sine qua non*. That is why Jesus here forces a consent from Peter. The freedom to say no is for the believer, or lover, purely abstract; if he wants love, that is, fellowship or community, companionship with Jesus, then he must *will* what *he* in no way wants: the reversal of the world's order, the Lord's being a slave. Worse still, because it concerns the filth on the feet of Peter, the taking over of sin by the One most pure. What one is supposed to understand here according to John is that this Yes that is wrung from Peter is for him distressing. The jump over his own shadow, so often demanded of Peter, is accomplished once again in a kind of desperation of love which has no other choice: "Then Lord, not my feet only but also my hands and my head!" (13:9). The mystery that lies in Jesus' answer need not be aired here; on the whole it can only mean that the once-for-all of the loving allowing-it-to-happen is just as indivisible as the once-for-all of the passion of Jesus. But what Peter (in his not-understanding) must choose is the fact that the Master he loves above all suffers for him (it is indeed the situation of foot-washing).

Every true lover when given the choice of suffering oneself or letting one's beloved suffer, would spontaneously choose the former. And John presumes here that Peter, whatever torments he may undergo, is a true lover, nay more, that he represents the perfectly loving church. That, as the rest of Peter's story shows, might at first be utopia, but it remains nonetheless a johannine postulate. No matter what the personal sinfulness of Peter, he *must* represent the loving church, he *must* "love" Jesus "more" than all others (Jn 21:15). But to this absolute love, the creature, above all the sinner, can be raised only in an act of perfect "blind" obedience to which the divine love relentlessly, apparently cruelly, presses. This same pressure was already there in the eucharistic discourse of promise, since everyone who does not eat the flesh of the Son of Man and drink his blood does not have life in him (Jn 6:53). The person who wants eternal life is left no choice at all, and can at most relinquish it all: "Do you take offense at this? Will you also go away?" (Jn 6:62, 67). Peter's counterquestion, "Lord, to whom shall we go?" shows him still to be the prisoner of the demands of love which has outplayed any freedom in him. True freedom, that of divine love, lies incomparably higher than where the person can make its "free" choice. Thus those who have entrusted themselves to God unconditionally ("To whom shall we go? You have the words of everlasting life") are forced from their own level up to the level of God; they must choose the ultimate thing that they would choose by themselves. But it isn't really in this demanding self-transcendence that lies the "sacrifice" that human beings must offer, but in the renunciation of God which awaits them after this self-renunciation, which they are supposed to affirm, and which becomes visible in the eucharistic mystery of the cross, in the flesh torn and blood shed.

The humiliation of the Son of God in his redemptive work is a self-humiliation: *humiliavit seipsum.* Even if he is thus found in a total obedience to the Father and to the mission received from the Father, at the origin of this obedience there still resides the most perfect divine freedom which is of the same nature and substance as the freedom of the Father and the Holy Spirit. Nowhere in the worldly realm is any requirement made of the Son, not even from the existing prophecies which ultimately are there for him and through him. No creature can enter with him into this self-defense of the Son of God.

Instead, unity can be brought about only in such a way that we are *forced* by him into humiliation, on the basis, to be sure, of a once freely given consent of faith, but then in a being overwhelmed by *his* will to self-humiliation in obedience to the Father. This is in no way our own will; hence the elementary No of Peter before whom the humiliated Lord kneels: "You will never wash my feet." Christ obeys his Father in pure love, but we obey the Son's will to obey. This is where the real *subalternatio* lies, already *in actu primo redemptionis*, and johannine theology is concerned to make it clear to us from all directions. While the Lord goes into his passion in a royal freedom which is one with his obedience to the Father, the disciple who wishes to be there with him is left no choice but to will what he or she does not want, but to which the will of the Lord and love for the Lord compels him or her. This decisive corrective must be brought in against the platonizing interpretation of the pauline *homoiōma* by way of mystery-theology.

One can well say that the sacrifice of redemption is *in actu primo* a common one. For the cross this has just been shown; for the Last Supper, with which the self-giving of the Son arises, it lies, crudely expressed, in the fact that whoever wishes to have himself "consumed" by human beings needs a mouth to eat and drink him. The community of the disciples, and then the church, must do him this service. And must do so not primarily as representative of the sinners out for the kill, but in an attitude of serving agreement with his self-giving. In this the consuming mouth is an essential component of the sacrifice of the Lord. He acts in the upper room not as a soloist before an attentive audience, as an actor on the stage before onlookers in the orchestra, He always acts in such a way that he includes his followers in what he does.

States of Life in the Church

71 · The Layperson in the Church

Are there lay people in the church? Of course there are, and their name has found its place throughout the entire history of the church. The special constitutional law in the CIC (Code of Canon Law) is divided into the parts "Of Clerics," "Of Religious," "Of the Laity."

Thus it cannot be a question of working up a storm against a long-standing concept rooted deeply in Christianity, but at most of reflecting on its meaning and eventual limits, which can of course turn out to be consequential enough. The limits are obviously visible: they are found in those places in the church where the cleric and religious seem to have something more than the layperson: an official ordination which confers authority inaccessible to the layperson, or a religious consecration into a form of life opened to personal imitation of Christ which is likewise closed to the layperson. Thus, although the name "lay" may indeed be derived from *laos* (church-)people and to that extent means something positive—and here one must immediately emphasize that whoever belongs to this people, clerics and religious then too, is basically lay!—still, in the average use of the word, the negative predominates: the layperson is a Christian believer who possesses neither the privileges of the clerical office nor those of the religious. The layperson is, as the secular German word says, the nonexpert. The adjective *laikos* already had this negative meaning in pagan antiquity; in the Jewish sphere it signified a believer who was neither priest nor levite.

This negative moment which excludes from a certain sacral area necessarily places the layperson in a relationship to profaneness, to the "secular world"; and the more this is given a positive characterization (for the most varied of reasons) in church history, the greater, apparently, will be the chances for the layperson too to receive an ecclesiastically positive role and mission in the division of labor within the church, even while the negative aspect we have mentioned does not entirely disappear. Adding to this problematic is the difficulty inherent in the triple division of the "states" (*status, ordines, vitae*), that the priest-layperson axis is cut directly across by the religious-layperson axis (as "Christian in the world"); and this difficulty is doubled again by members of the worldly communities ("secular institutes") who wish to belong simultaneously to the state of the evangelical counsels (which religious take vows to follow) and to the lay state.

Only some reflections on the essence of ecclesiastical existence, and indeed of the church itself, lead out of this complex of problems however risky such considerations might be. But they will be clearly covered by the simple truth that every Christian in the church is called and is underway to the same perfection of love of God and neighbor, or—what comes to the same thing—that there are in the church many kinds of gifts of grace, offices, and modes of working, but only one Spirit, one Lord, one God (1 Cor 12:4–6).

When with Jesus the kingdom of God approaches from heaven towards earth, that eschatological reality in which the beatitudes and the apparently utopian directives of the Sermon on the Mount are in effect, and the call goes forth to repent and believe in the message of salvation (Mk 1:5), we are at that point still far removed from an ecclesiastical structure. And if it is also true that in God's plan of salvation his beloved Son will be delivered into the hands of sinners and will die for them, he still does not begin at all with the proclamation of the final phase of his fate but with the open, one might even say paradisically naive offer of the attitude of his heavenly Father: Be perfect, be merciful as your Father in heaven is perfect and merciful (Mt 5:48; Lk 6:36). His heart is nonviolent—"turn the other cheek"—it does not insist on its own way—"does not care for the morrow"—it bears no grudges—"as we also forgive our debtors." Will this kingdom with its heavenly mode of behavior be able to get established on earth? Jesus doesn't dissolve the Law, but in the same breath he demands an attitude that "is much more perfect than that of the Scribes and Pharisees," something that already lies formally above the Law (as it was understood in the Old Covenant), because the law is there only for the lawless and disobedient (1 Tim 1:9), while the lover after the fashion of the kingdom of heaven fulfills all laws without even thinking about it (Rom 13:8–10). Who can live this way? But even before his programmatic sermon Jesus called to himself a limited group of well-known individuals from whom he demands that they place their whole reliance on him alone ("leave everything and follow") and into whose mouth he puts the message of the kingdom, even gives them "power" to drive back the evil spirit before approaching the Holy Spirit (Mk 3:13–15). The kingdom of heaven, which with Jesus takes its place on earth, does this in such a way that a core of community immediately comes into being along with it: it is to this that the Sermon on the Mount is directed, while the crowd listens.

We are at this point still far removed from the founding of a hierarchy. But there are two things here: first the demand (and its fulfillment) of radical discipleship in existence for the kingdom and according to the ethos of the kingdom, and then together with Jesus the authorization, and soon thereafter the sending forth, to proclaim it and bring it in. From this kernel everything will unfold: later the specified powers of office, still later the organization of a special lifestyle of "leaving everything" (but this with a withdrawal from the world which preserves only half of what was present in the original kernel), and above all that spiritual radicalism (of striking root in the kingdom of heaven), which will be demanded of every Christian from his or her entrance into the church, but which appears here as an "incarnated" abandonment of everything (the word "literal" would be right except that it is too narrow, since we are preeminently concerned here with the Spirit). If one wanted to search in the church's later development for a form of life which comes closest to this origin, one could think of the "communities in the world" which try to live the radicalism of the counsels but unseparated from the world, and in which the members can be priests as well as nonpriests. But even these communities have a church-canonical institution which is still lacking in this indeterminateness of the beginning. This beginning situation should in no way be restricted to a state not accessible to women, for we specifically see also women serving and accompanying the Lord.

Of greatest importance is the insight that the kingdom from the Father which has come near to us in the person of Jesus cannot from the outset seem to be forced into forms which are suited to a human society hostile to God, whether these forms be profane or sacred. Just as the risen Lord (as a bodily being) goes through closed doors, so does the embodiment of the kingdom, at least at first, go through closed organizations. Again and again there have been attempts to get back to this origin which, although belonging to the first phase of the incarnation of the divine, still remains so to speak "u-topian" ("the Son of Man has nowhere to . . ." *ouk echei pou:* Mt 8:20). This placelessness of Jesus in his beginning has been compared with that of a Saint Francis whose ideal stands above every earthly livable rule and must first "die" into a form or into diverse forms through which it is possible to work towards it. Also, what Ignatius originally had in mind—before the Inquisition forced him to the study of theology—belongs here.

Now it can be said of those Christians who, by the negative qualification as we said at the outset, are usually called "lay," that neither the official priesthood nor the incarnated life of the counsels is for them, although they—the positive qualification—are fully qualified members of the church community.

This demands a fuller explanation straightaway. Both in the relationship of the layperson to the office-holder and in the relationship of the layperson to those in the life of the counsels, what dominates is not a Yes and No but an analogy which, as such, rests on an identity of the state of being called to the church and to the radicalism of (christological) love.

The analogy between the layperson and the office-holder lies in the variously characterized relationship of both of these to the "universal priesthood" of all Christians, since the whole Christ, head and body, offers to God that total self-offering of himself which as the true spiritual sacrifice is pleasing to God and reconciles him with the sinful world (cf. Augustine, *City of God*, X6). Just as all baptized persons give themselves into the death of Christ along with him, so too do those who celebrate the Eucharist together, inasmuch as they are ready to offer themselves together with Christ at the offertory in the gifts of the church, bread and wine. If they have already decided to give (to offer) what is most precious to them—their Lord and redeemer—for the salvation of the world, how much then are they ready to offer themselves who, over against this most precious reality, count as nothing! *Meum ac vestrum sacrificium*, "your sacrifice and mine," says the priest to the community; but the analogy that really holds here is rooted in a common *nostrum* (our) which is inseparably bound with the self-offering of Christ. The same analogy is also visible in the differing relationship to the preaching office: if it is the priests who primarily have the assignment of proclaiming the gospel to the faithful, interpreting it, and (here the pastoral office also comes into play) witnessing to it through their whole lives, it is the laypersons who extend this proclamation into the world by passing on to the world outside, to the non-Christian sphere, by their example and the account they give of their faith, this witness of the truth received in the church. The idea that mission is above all an affair of the clergy and not equally an affair of the laity must be quite seriously relativized, both because of scripture and church history and above all the present situation of Christianity—just think of Péguy's proclamation, "We are all standing at the front" (*Laudet* 82–86). As far as the pastoral office of the church is concerned, it is primarily a function within the church in the service of all the people of the church (not least of its unity in mind and belief); and only by means of this primary aspect and the use made of it by the Christians is it a Christian witness to the world outside. If Christians as a whole do not give the witness of unity, which the papacy as a function is destined to promote, this function exists in vain. At this point also is visible the inner analogy by which the delicate problem of the acceptance of hierarchical decisions (reception) can remain prescinded.

The analogy between laypersons and persons in the state of the counsels has already been treated where we spoke of the freedom of Christ to call "those whom he wished" (Mk 3:13), both men and women, to his closer discipleship. No one who does not hear this call can complain about being pushed aside by the Lord to the second level. This is the time to remember that the call of the disciples in the gospel took place during the first phase of the proclamation of the kingdom, at a time when no distinction between "states" in the church had yet been made, and all were called to entry into the sphere of the kingdom; but that meant into the perfect attitude of love of the divine Father which was now to take its place on earth. The call to the kingdom is the comprehensive radicalism of all forms of Christian life. It would not be good to characterize the life of the religious and that of the laity respectively by "state of the counsels" and "state of the commandments," because the Old Testament commandments all transcend into the sphere of the "counsel," of the spontaneous doing-more, because the God now being revealed is the God of the "always-more."

As seen from this point of origin all Christians are, first, simply Christians, and all must strive continually for the "more" of the new love. This picture is transmitted by things like the letters of John where there is never any mention of the states or forms of life. But one finds the same thing even in the pauline letters in which the figure of the apostle stands out so strongly as that of the distinguished hierarch and fulfiller of the life of the counsels. The community is continually challenged to participation in all that the apostle does, suffers, plans; the I is changed unarbitrarily into a We; indeed the I is understood ultimately only as the servant to the Your.

A brief word about matrimony which is a possible (not necessary) form of life of laypersons, while it contradicts the life of the counsels and is forbidden to the office-holders of the Western church (because of the convergence we have mentioned between office and special election). Although marriage does not go beyond the threshold of the eschatological kingdom (Mt 22:30), and whoever wishes to live an eschatological existence should, if possible, give up marriage (1 Cor 7:8f), marriage, instituted as it is by God from the beginning (Mk 10:6; Eph 5:31), may not be dismissed as un-Christian and simply outmoded (1 Tim 4:3). In many situations it is strongly encouraged (1 Tim 5:14; 1 Cor 7:9). But in the New Testament its whole ideality lies not in itself but in the supra-sexual relationship between Christ and the church: aligning itself with this "great mystery," striving toward and being formed by it, marriage—as sacrament—shares in it (Eph 5:32). If (as Augustine expressly says) the virginal person is not by that mere fact more perfect than the married person, virginity is still, as such, more perfect than married life. In virginity vowed for the love of Christ, the "form" is perfect and the life must as far as possible be shaped accordingly. In marriage, the "form" is rooted in the old aeon and it requires a tremendous effort to purify earthly *eros* into a pure expression of heavenly *agape*. This effort can by the grace of Christ and by sacramental grace in particular lead to the goal only with all kinds of abnegation which thus leads from the sphere of the proclamation of the kingdom into that of the cross.

In conclusion it must be noted that everything in the church which has the character of a special qualitative election (office or the life of the counsels) is subject to the dialectic of the "last place" so forcefully demonstrated by Christ. If he, whom we rightly call Lord and Master chooses this place (Jn 13:13), how much more must this be done by the "servants" and "those who are sent." Everything that is structured in the church is service, so that ultimately what is not (qualitatively) structured stands in the—not undangerous! (1 Cor 4:8)—first place: "For all things are yours, whether Paul or Apollos or Cephas or the world of life or death or the present or the future, all are yours; and you are Christ's; and Christ is God's" (1 Cor 3:21b–23). The Christians of the community form the center of the church for which office does service, and the life of the counsels is the "fertilizer" (Augustine). Seen this way the negative aspect of the characterization "lay" completely disappears and the word can be avoided and completely replaced by "Christian." If the office holder is an ever-new "emissary" from Christ to the community (2 Cor 5:20), the administrator of his mysteries (1 Cor 4:1), then this intraecclesial sending is directed to the sending of the whole church and of the concrete community and each individual into the world. In that way the Christian, receiver of a Christ who was sent, also steps into the role of one sent, equipped with a personal *charism* that is never a goal and purpose unto itself but always the means for a service to be provided. Because of this *charism*, which should not be equated (in quantitative conversions) with the apostolic office (so that the community itself could be in charge of the office), all become one body with many members: "You have one master, and you are all brethren" (Mt 23:8).

72 · The Election to Qualified Succession

The *qualified vocation* is, like the general vocation to the church, clearly a calling out, not out of the "world" outside the church, but out of the world inside the church. The consequence of this vocation is always invariably the same: "And when they had brought their boats to land, they left everything and followed him" (Lk 5:11); "Immediately they left their nets and followed him" (Mt 4:22); "And they left their father Zebedee in the boat with the hired servants, and followed him" (Mk 1:20); "He said to him, 'Follow me.' And he rose and followed him" (Mt 9:9); "And he left everything, and rose and followed him" (Lk 5:28). The "leaving everything" is the unequivocal condition of discipleship; it is required by the call itself which is so demanding and so clear that whoever hears it can hear it only in this way. For those who would like to reduce the force of this, it is made even more clear: "For which of you, desiring to build a tower, does not first sit down and count the cost, whether he has enough to complete it?. . . . So therefore, whoever of you does not renounce all that he has cannot be my disciple" (Lk 14:28, 33). And all of this goes together, indivisibly.

It is not just the leaving of those living but also of the dead (Mt

8:21–22). It is such a fundamental abandonment that it even leads out of "den" and "nest" to being completely outside every "place in which to lay his head" (Mt 8:20); it leads thus to being outside all human security in the world at a place that is not even definable in worldly terms because it is not a place within the world of natural orders and calculable possibilities, not a place provided for in creation, but which can be characterized in the world's view only as nonplace (*ouk echei pou*). It is the outside, pure and simple (*exō:* Heb 13:12–13). And those who have taken the step are aware of its indivisibility. They do not count what they have left behind; they know that their leaving includes everything: "Lo, we have left everything and followed you" (Mt 19:27). They have performed and perceived this as one single act even if they have to repeat it day by day and work out that one act day by day in little acts of abnegation. Nonetheless it is everything. And so they stand there: the everything of the world behind them, and ahead of them nothing but the following of him who calls himself the way. Where he leads cannot be seen from the world. Thus, the question may be asked, "What then shall we have?" (Mt 19:27).

For if one really takes this "everything" seriously, a mere continuation of one's former existence in the world is no longer conceivable. Human beings need goods and means in the world in order to keep body and soul together. And because these goods since the Fall are scarce and subject to dispute, they must be concerned about getting possession of them. The being outside and "not-of-this-world" (Jn 18:36) into which those who are called are led cannot, on the other hand, be a worldlessness: they must "be in the world" (Jn 17:11) and live in it even when they, inwardly, "are not of this world" (Jn 17:14). Thus their position is for the world an incomprehensible and mystifying stance beyond earthly laws and orders from which, nevertheless, they are not removed or exempt. This position, impossible for the world, is something to be perceived and assumed only in the faith which blindly follows. It *is* the place of faith and discipleship itself: "If anyone serves me, he must follow me; and where I am, there shall my servant be also" (Jn 12:26); but the "where" of Jesus is, especially on the cross, precisely this "outside" (Heb 13:12), "without place," "not of this world." But it is, for that reason, the place which is created by his mission. The "where" of the redeemer *is* the sending of the Father and thus the "where" of the called is the sending of the Son: "As the Father has sent me, so I send you" (Jn 20:21).

To be able to stand at the place of the sending is thus first conditioned by the radicalism of leaving everything. Every security which is tied to the world threatens not only a part but the whole of that stance. For the sake of the hidden treasure "all that he has" must be sold, and similarly for the sake of the precious pearl of the kingdom of heaven (Mt 13:44–46). Every looking back, even if only to say fare-well, is a betrayal of everything: " 'I will follow you, Lord; but let me first say farewell to those at my home.' Jesus said to him, "No one who puts his hand to the plow and looks back is fit for the kingdom of God' " (Lk 9:61–62). The attempt to hold to something that one intended to give up is deadly (Acts 5:1–11). Whether one possesses little, like the disciples, or much, like the rich young man who desired perfection, is, once the call has gone out, all the same; for the demand is also made of the rich young man: "Sell all that you have and distribute to the poor, . . . then come, follow me" (Lk 18:22). We are talking about an abandonment of external material goods which is so real that a symbolic interpretation here would be ridiculous; but we are talking just as much about an inner abandonment, a giving up of every worldly dependence: "If anyone comes to me and does not hate his own father and mother and wife and children and brothers and sisters, yes, and even his own life, he cannot be my disciple" (Lk 14:26). Hate for oneself is extended into a hate of the whole of earthly life (Jn 12:25), and not at all with the secret thought of keeping it, but with the certitude of the loss of this earthly life (Lk 17:33).

73 · The Religious State

In the meaning they have here, neither the word "(religious) order" nor the word "state" come from the Bible, although on the one hand the principles of distinguishing between the different forms of life in the people of God ("election," "calling," *"charism"*), and on the other hand the reality itself (cf. Old Testament states of priests and levites, prophetism as form of life in the early monarchy, later groups similar to orders like Qumran, New Testament apostolate, etc.) were already there. In terms of church history, no matter how variable the classification and differentiation of ecclesiastical states may be, the constant lies—and we are talking just about the New Testament—in Jesus' calling of the apostles. It is first of all a free act of choice by the Lord (Mk 3:13) proceeding immediately from his prayer (Lk 6:12; cf. 22:31f). Secondly, it contains the requirement of leaving everything, even one's family (Mt 8:22; 19:27ff) in order, thirdly, to be perfectly instrumentally (Acts 9:15) disponible for the mandates of Jesus (Mk 6:7; cf. 6:30) and the affairs of the kingdom of God (Mt 10:5ff; 28:18–20). Not everyone who would like to enter into this state is admitted (Mk 5:19), nor does everyone who is invited find the internal courage and power for it (Mk 10:17ff). It is quite contrary to the New Testament text if one structurally identifies the general vocation to church membership (Rom 1:6) with what is described as personal vocation (Rom 1:1: "Paul, a servant of Jesus Christ, called to be an apostle, set apart for the gospel of God . . ."); or if, correlatively, one wanted to speak of a "call" to Christian marriage or to a *charism* of service in the church or even to a secular vocation which a Christian practices, in the same univocal sense as of the special calling which, in one way or another, represents the exclusive service of Christ to the church and through it to humanity. That remains true despite the fact that Luke has the saying about leaving everything (as the fundamental condition of discipleship) be directed to great crowds (Lk 14:33); for a thoroughgoing analogy of course connects every Christian calling (general or special) to one, single, common ethic, since in baptism all have already died to the world and been buried with Christ and raised to a new being and life in him.

But a rather profound question emerges when we notice that the apostles—as especially called to discipleship and abandoning everything—are the prototypes both of the presbyterate and of the religious state or, in a better and more general sense, the state of the counsels. But the *presbyterate* had from the beginning a double aspect. It is on the one hand office, "function," and on the other hand it is a "life" which has to be an "example for the flock" (1 Pet 5:3; 1 Tim 4:12). Such a "life" is necessarily related to the "counsels," and all through the history of the church both sides of the presbyterate have been struggling for a harmonious balance (obedience to the bishop is inwardly necessary; celibacy is extremely appropriate; poverty in the form of generosity, an open house, not clutching to one's own possession must characterize every priest or bishop [1 Tim 3:3; 3:8; 5:3; 6:8f; Tit 1:7f]). If we are not wholly mistaken, the near future will try to split apart the synthesis toward which the presbyterate is constantly striving. Some will place a one-sided emphasis on office and function (consistent with the present-day inclination to functionalize the living human being) and see in office nothing more than one functional *charism* among others in the people of God, compatible with marriage and with secular vocations and to be exercised according to the need of the community. These will lose sight of the connection to the special calling found in the gospel and have a tendency to deny its existence. Others will hearken to the call to imitate the poor, obedient and, for the sake of God's kingdom, unmarried Christ, and see their entrance into office under the sign of a dedication of their lives for the brethren. They (and they alone!) will in the existential sense also be successors to the apostles who themselves would be able to become in Paul and Peter (Jn 21:18f) successors of the Lord unto the end.

This total dedication thus brings the presbyterate, understood this way, together with the religious state in the strict sense and the secular institutes into an existential unity; to the state of those people who dedicate their existence—spirit, body, and possessions—to the service of the kingdom of God, no matter where the Holy Spirit may subsequently point out their place to them in church and world.

One final, serious note: there have always been people, and they are now more numerous than ever, who avoid and run from a clear (!) vocation in the strict sense, who do not want to perceive it, and deny it. They become those clearly recognizable "forced lay persons" who propagate secularism with *ressentiment* and make fun of that form of life-dedication which we have summed under the loose concept "life of the counsels." For a Christian with spiritual power of discernment, they are easily distinguishable from the true, zealous lay apostle. They cause the greatest damage to the church. *Hos devita!* ("Avoid such people": 2 Tim 3:5).

In order to speak of the *religious state* in the strict sense, one must above all have a sense for the Christian hierarchy of values which is fundamentally distinguished from the purely natural one, especially that of today which sociologically turns profitability and measureable success into the principal criterion even for church structures. Not utility but *fruitfulness* (for the kingdom of God which for the present remains invisible) is the decisive category. From a life which puts itself in humble love totally at God's disposition, completely, once and for all, and ever anew day by day, from such a life God can make something; what is disponible for everything can be formed by God to anything. With those who are following their own programs without being more directable and available, he cannot start anything in the deeper sense. This dedication of the person in the religious state is God-directed: aimed at engaging that person's life in the work of salvation for the benefit of the whole world of fellow human beings. None of those who think in a Christian way enter an order to make themselves perfect but, together with Christ, to be of more help to the brethren. This love is indeed that "perfection" which is one with the loving renunciation of possessions and is not preoccupied with itself.

The hardest renunciation of those who enter, but also the most fruitful, is giving control over the fruit God will draw from their dedication. The "rule" into which they insert themselves has three interlocking dimensions. It has as its *content* life according to the gospel and thus, on the one hand, life as "praise of the glorious grace of God" (Eph 1:6, 12, 14), and on the other hand, life in a brotherly or sisterly love which should be a model for church and world. As *form* however, it is a life that lifts individuals out of themselves and helps them toward Christian self-transcendence, a form of life which, like a trellis to which they are tied, keeps them from falling back on themselves in times of fatigue, etc. Finally the rule *demands* (what it cannot, of course, force) that this form never turn into formalism but that it remain transfused with its content, evangelical love. Since human beings remain sinners, they will never perfectly, and at times not at all, fulfill this demand, which then gives an outsider the chance to pass derogatory judgment on monastic life. That is for the most part oversimplified and unjust because these critics have no eye for the invisible value of the renunciation which was dared once and for all: "Christ has made the world to be crucified for me and me to be crucified for the world" (Gal 6:14).

It is of the essence of the religious state that the human person is made free for God: *vacare Deo*. This can take different forms. It can be the pure "praise of God" of the divine office, devoid of human utility, as Israel always practiced it; it can be the personal meditation on the word of God in the listening heart, such as Jesus praised as the "best part" in Mary of Bethany—who serves so to speak as the mother and patronness of every contemplative cloister—and which, when carried out in the right love is, according to Thérèse to Lisieux, the real motivating flywheel of all external church activity; it can also become the (indispensable) starting pont for being sent from the stance of total disponibility to the most varied of individual tasks and activities in the service of the church and the world, together with the responsibility which the individual in assuming such a task also assumes along with it. In this there is no essential difference between a Benedictine who teaches school, a Dominican who preaches or teaches, a Jesuit who performs some missionary activity, and a member of a secular community who works at a secular vocation. At the innermost ground stands everywhere an unrestricted disponibility for God and for church which allows one to be sent as Christ allowed himself to be sent by the Father and thereby, in his own responsible engagement, threw onto the balance what was best and most personal.

Today, in order to guard against abuses, it is less a question of lessening the disponibility of those sent than it is of heightening the responsibility of those sending who must stand by their act of sending just as God the Father stands by the sending of his Son, accompanies him in the Holy Spirit, and does not "think better of it" in the Garden of Olives or on the cross. If all that is taken seriously, both theologically and in fraternal Christian love, there is no reason to consider older forms of religious life as fundamentally outmoded as such (which of course Vatican II in its decree on religious does not do either, and indeed completely rejects). It is also in no way true that a certain historical development of the religious state to an ever greater "opening to the world" would in each case push aside older forms as outmoded and not up-to-date.

For foundations which are made in the Holy Spirit have a certain share in the timelessness and abiding regenerative power of the church, and there are also always contrary movements, as, for example, the Carmel of early modern times or Charles de Foucauld show. Young people making a vocational choice should keep this above all in view, and guard against blindly following after the most modern. But the religious orders themselves must also pay attention to this (and perhaps most of all the congregations from the nineteenth and beginning of the twentieth century) when they carry out their obligatory *aggiornamento*. How many necessary and extremely valuable things are not, as the consequence of a superficial and nervous urge for reform, blindly thrown overboard ("perpetual adoration," for example) by poorly advised and unadvised nuns or brothers who do not know what they are doing! It is not as if there were nothing to reform in the orders and congregations; indeed it could well be that here and there in more recent foundings one will have to go some distance back beyond the immediate purpose of the founding, or even the intellectual-theological horizon of the founder and foundress, in the direction of the full, open gospel.

But one thing is sure, one does not come closer to the gospel with a mere loosening of bonds or mere democratization, but only to the extent that one fulfills the most serious demands of the following of Christ which not infrequently can appear to be pushing beyond the limits of the purely natural human being. And if everything is to take place in the love of Christ, and this—as we said—is the true content of the "rule" as form, it must still never be forgotten what a stone-hard face this love had to assume for Christ himself in the deadly gravity of the Garden of Olives and the cross.

All orders have their source in the cross: from that point where Jesus breathes out his spirit to the Father (so that he could breathe it out on the church at Easter), arises all grace of unconditional following. All orders must therefore continually reform themselves anew by looking directly to the crucified. And if the cross is not superseded by any post-Easter time because (according to Paul and John and the whole New Testament) the exalted One is the same as the crucified and the crucified the same as the exalted, then too, that life of following which is expressed in the call to a total dedication of one's existence and in answering it, is never superseded, whether it is expressed in priesthood, in religious life or—in secular communities—in ordinary life in the world.

74 · Life on the Edge: the Secular Institutes

The movement which, in 1947 with the apostolic constitution *Provida Mater*, led to ecclesiastical recognition of the new "secular institutes" (*Instituta Saecularia*), came from below. After early successful (Ursulines) or unsuccessful (Mary Ward) attempts to live a life of radical following of Christ in the world free from the canonical restrictions, it was significantly the pressures of the French Revolution with its dissolutions of monasteries which provided the occasion for the connection between life in the midst of the world and the evangelical counsels. At the beginning of our century the attempts spontaneously increased, although their paradoxical unification of what previously did not seem to be unifiable still aroused mistrust and rejection until the formal recognition we have mentioned was given.

But this recognition can at most approve the paradox; it cannot remove it. A life such as is lived in the secular communities will, even within the church, find misgiving and disparagement, to say nothing of the complete misunderstanding it will almost always encounter outside the church. How can someone who seriously and with full responsibility wishes to be in charge of secular things—professionally, financially, politically, etc.—at the same time live "in obedience"? And how can someone who seriously wants to share all the worries and burdens of the existence of fellow human beings, wish for Christ's sake to remain unmarried and thus refuse to experience one of the most important spheres of human existence? Is the combination of existence in the midst of the world and at the same time in the evangelical counsels not a wooden sword with which, because of the attempt at an impossible amalgamation, the clear witness and the effect of both Christian forms of life gets lost? The objections have weight.

But we can also look at the matter from the other side. Are not all Christians called to be "in the world but not of the world," "to use" the things of the world "as if they were not using them"? Does not the saying, which comes from this general Christian paradox, also apply here, that "he who has ears to hear, let him hear"? Isn't it too easy a solution if some (the "ordinary" lay persons) specialize in the use of things while others, members of orders and congregations and celibate priests, become, by their state of life, representatives of the final clause: "as if they were not using them"? The paradox that baptism brings to every Christian path must be lived as an example by all clearly and unambiguously. The "secular communities" consciously take their stand at that exact point where the two demands join, where the seam must be sewn together—once and for all and anew every day—regardless of whether or not they in doing so make themselves unpopular as disturbers of the peace in church and world.

Yet another point: the secular communities had quite quietly and decisively recognized as their task the necessity of living the Christian paradox in this way long before the nervous trend set in after the Council away from contemplative and active orders and from the forms of traditional priesthood. They do not need to strive after the world, they are already in it. But even in their secularity they do not betray their special election to the evangelical counsels, for in that has always resided their justification for existence. This is "the following of Jesus Christ in the midst of this world," discipleship understood in the radical sense as in the way the apostles were called, to leave everything and to stake their whole existence upon the person of Jesus and his directives. The whole Christian paradox receives its highest visibility and its sharpest precision in the secular communities.

Seen from without, the ideal of the secular communities remains abstract (which is to say, not livable in the concrete, a compromise). Those who criticize them have an easy job, at all levels. Their answer to this criticism is hesitant and labored; when they talk about it they lose credibility. Let us be frank: the existence of the secular communities is and remains difficult. It is above all an ever new and inexorable demand: "It *must* work!"; it is not a stable, achieved possession. It is always a question of balancing the two equal claims: independent responsibility and open readiness to be made use of more and more. Stewardship of possessions without being interiorly attached to them, genuine love of neighbor to the point of giving one's life without entering into the kind of exclusive relationship which is the foundation of marriage. But did not Jesus live all that before us? Is not the existence of Paul a complete book of grammar in which this language can be learned? Does not even an elementary Christian reflection tell us that when persons consecrate themselves completely to the absolute, personal, and universal love of God, they are simultaneously committed along with that to the work of God for the world—which leads to death on the cross? If there are some who think they are going to find in the secular communities an easier way (than, for example, in Carmel), perhaps a "modern" way, or that they can here "kill two birds with one stone," they are sadly mistaken and should not even give it a try. In addition to the continual inner effort that is required here if the salt of the earth is not to lose its savor, there is required at least as much generosity, as much abnegation—which counts not the cost—as much total inner readiness and disponibility as for life in any active or contemplative order.

The secular communities are an approved and desired *form* of life in the church. By form is meant that they are not just associations according to the preferences of the members, but fit into a structure, existing, even if in a very loose and hardly visible way, within the church. Theologically this means that the dedication of the individual to God and his work in the world is directed into an ecclesiastically approved structure of community which is established to accept this dedication and give it the character of a definitive *consecration* of one's whole existence. Thus the dedication is from the outset withdrawn from the sphere of my preferences. The idea, so popular today, that one cannot honestly bind oneself for a lifetime, that (in marriage, priesthood, religious life) the door must always remain open to go back, most intrinsically contradicts the definitive character of what God has done for us and our answer to him. Secular communities can rightly impose a long time of probation before they admit one to a definitive commitment: this is required by their exposed form of existence. But what is intended from the beginning and through everything is a total life dedication.

The secular communities are young. They are still experimenting a great deal and thus discovering that many things need revision or better protection. All of them have difficulties with the problems of a solid religious formation which must take place along with the professional, and the problems of a community life which, even when many members live alone or in quite small groups, must still be successful to the extent that the consciousness of community is not stunted and the incessant promotion that comes from community does not suffer. While hiking along the sharp ridge between the kingdom of God and the kingdom of this world, it is not just individual persons but whole institutes that can be affected by dizziness and be in danger of falling into the gulf either of a one-sided spirituality or an excessive secularity. They exist and remain alive only in a daily "watching and praying," a continual discernment of spirits. Whoever is looking for a secure barn has to look elsewhere.

But perhaps this constant inner danger is today the best recommendation. Many are crowding, as we said above, to the place where the secular communities stand 'without being called to them: in general a transformation of existing orders and congregations into secular communities is inadvisable: "Let each remain in whatever state each was called" (1 Cor 7:24). On the other hand, we do not know how long we will still have orders and congregations, or whether they will not, as in many Eastern countries, be restricted to small, "undangerous" fields of action. What then? In the East there remain only (secret) secular communities which stand on the firing line as effective church groups. Perhaps the decisive hour for this new form of life is still to strike in the church, and it should until then make good use of the time to make itself ready by various tests of its possibilities.

The great predominance of female over male communities is abnormal. Ways must be found to make this way seem more accessible and more attractive to men in secular occupations. There are also approved secular communities of priests which are making a significant contribution to the contemporary church. That they actually bear the name "secular communities" is criticized from the theological side, but it can perhaps be justified from the fact that these priests, taking their following of Christ very seriously, strive for the greatest possible nearness to people and through that to the things of this world to be ordered according to the mind of Christ. But it is certain that all lay communities are dependent on priests who understand their special ideal, and many communities sensibly contain male, female, and priestly branches which, as circumstances permit, work together.

The paradox remains: wholly for God and wholly for the world—in one ecclesiastical community. It can be lived because the whole God has involved himself in Christ for the entire world, and because the place where he does this ever anew, is the church of Christ, the "sacrament of the world."

The Church Today

75 · The Credibility of the Church Today

The world of today, when faced with the Christian church, is filled with a sense of profound mistrust. Strangely enough, this lack of trust has increased rather than decreased since the last Council which stressed the very intimate relevance of the church to the world and summoned it to involve itself wholeheartedly with the world. The reason for this lack of trust, however, is probably that people are no longer making any headway with humanistically inspired plans of action—there are enough of these to be found in political movements of all kinds. People are more prone to put their faith in the kind of involvement that effectively changes the world, whatever the ideological background of this may be. If the Christian church were of the opinion that only the Christian religion were able to inspire a meaningfully planned involvement of this sort, then it would be relevant to speak of a hidden presence of "grace," to be discerned wherever such a commitment can be observed, and to describe someone engaged in such activities as an "anonymous Christian." God's purpose after all was not to liberate the church but the world; the grace which he has bestowed upon the world in Jesus Christ must of necessity flood over the boundaries of the visible church even though the church continues to be seen as focal point of grace, the *sacramentum mundi*, as the Council called it. There is nothing new, of course, in this point of view. For centuries now, theology has spoken of a "baptism by desire" (*in voto*), that is, a baptism received by those who according to their limited insights have resolutely involved themselves to contribute as best they can to the welfare of their fellow human beings and of the world as a whole. They are received and sustained by God's grace and made invisible members of the visible church.

Such a view is no doubt liberating for many, and it is certainly not our intention here to call it in question, or to return to an earlier and narrower interpretation of the principle, "Outside the church there is no salvation." We support the new and more generous interpretation that God bestows his graces in every part of the world because of the presence of the "whole Christ" in the world, the Christ who is eternally and inseparably both head and body, the man from Nazareth raised to the dignity of Lord, and the community which draws its life from him, his church in so far as she possesses his Spirit and follows his example.

Such an interpretation, however, has its hazards. It does indeed point to the opening of the church to the world. But it also creates the impression, particularly for those outside the church, that the visible church is nothing more than an institution with a heap of rules, laws, and precepts as to what is to be believed and how life is to be conducted, while the substance of the life of this institution can equally well be found outside it, scattered over all the world. And the driving forces of the institutional church (for example, its hierarchical organization, its rules about Sunday worship and the reception of the sacraments, and more incisively, the rules regulating married life), if taken in isolation, appear lacking in credibility, superfluous, disturbing and even directly opposed to the life and example of Christ. In fact if the authentic substance of Christianity is disseminated throughout the entire human race, then the "church of Christ" is left with but the form or carcass of Christianity as its distinguishing feature. Once this point of view has become prevalent—and it has to a great extent—then the church is going to be hard put to escape being classified in this way; it will see itself as essentially an "organization" whose function is merely to organize the transmission of the light of Christianity, which issues from it and floods into the world. This was certainly the guiding image in the movement known as Catholic Action, launched over fifty years ago, though it has now ceased to exist in most countries and in others is destined for extinction.

But how otherwise then is the church to see itself, once the theory of "anonymous Christianity" is accepted, the theory, that is to say, that all who struggle for the salvation and advancement of the human race in the spirit of self-sacrificing engagement are united together in a living, quasi-religious union? Does the church still have a function to fulfill at all more than that of being a mere functionary in this process? There are indeed quite enough Bibles printed for all who have the inclination to acquaint themselves with the life and work of Jesus and his disciples, without a particular social organization announcing that it has exclusive monopoly over the contents of the book. Today at face value at least, in any case in the West, that is the dilemma, and the questions this raises are not easy to answer. For the more liberally the church is opened to the world and accepts its values, bathing them in a Christian light, the more it seems that all that is left to the church is the purely formal which robs it of its credibility. From all sides, therefore, her outward structure is attacked, even in places where Christian values are still, to a certain extent, accepted.

It is possible, however, that this dilemma which looms so large in our immediate relationship with the church is not so inexorable as it first appears. We have only to look East, to men and women such as the great Christian writers of Russia—Solzhenitsyn, Daniel Sinjawski, Michael Bulgakov, and others—or to the Baptist movement in Russia, to see something quite new. Practically the alternatives take on quite a different cast. Here there are still some traces remaining of the hierarchical and liturgical life of the church, which is constantly under threat, though tolerated to a certain extent. The opponents of Christianity do not direct the main force of their attack against this, but rather against persons and groups who are living a distinctively Christian life; living it more than preaching it in words. It is indeed strange that in the writings of Solzhenitsyn, self-confessed Christians are basically peripheral characters and apparently play no decisive part in the plot. On the other hand, for the most part the fearsome and tragic landscape of humanity he spreads before us is lit by a glow of reconciliation which one cannot specifically designate as "Christian," but which in an almost inexplicable manner brings this estranged world back to its truth. The ideological masks behind which people hide fall like scales to leave their true faces unmasked (as in the novel *Cancer Ward*), the harsh glare of the searchlights is extinguished, and things appear once more as they fundamentally are, without any attempt at pretense. In this, the contradiction that we still note between life and institution has been transcended. For it is precisely this "anonymous light" of Christianity which lights all places and all characters—unique, unparalleled, penetrating—which irritates the ideologists and stirs them to persecute and fight for its extermination. Can anyone forbid this light to shine? Is it possible that Pontius Pilate could sentence the risen Christ to death a second time, Christ who has had the impertinence to go on living? He is indeed no mere phantom: "Touch me and see," he says, "for a spirit has not flesh and bones as you see me have"; but in spite of this, he himself cannot be crucified afresh, nor can he be beaten with rods.

The disciples of this Jesus, however, who can indeed be beaten with rods, have nonetheless inherited something of this mystery. They are, it is true, "organized" insofar as they are organically linked together and constitute a church; but whoever directs an attack at their organization will not, in fact, touch them. For they are brothers and sisters to all those who in this world are involved in the struggle for human rights, but those who claim that they are simply a particular kind of humanist (or "anonymous Christians") have once more failed to do them justice. They have a clear and irritating style of visibility (for why otherwise would Solzhenitsyn or Sinjawski be persecuted in such a way?), which is not simply to be identified with membership in a religious association. They, and many others of their kind who are less conspicuous, radiate something outward; and the sense of the pages which follow is to ask ourselves this question: What is this power or this brilliant light, where does it come from, and what is the connection between the source of power which nourishes Christians and their involvement with humanity?

One thing we can say in advance: from the true Christian there radiates the kind of freedom that is always the first thing to be sought after by the non-Christian. In modern times, human freedom is a theme which preoccupies both Christian and non-Christian, and there is a kind of competition as to who can understand this freedom more profoundly, who more effectively put it into practice. Atheism is wholly preoccupied with this theme: the freeing of reason from the fetters of faith (the Enlightenment); the freeing of the economically enslaved for humanly worthy work (Marx); the freeing of the individual from the chains of an unmastered past (Freud); the freeing of all humanity from the nightmare of a concept, namely God, which is no longer believed and which has been dragged like a corpse through world history (Nietzsche). Everywhere at the very portals of freedom the human being seems to be chained to some past, to a traditional custom, to a moment in history made absolute, or to some forbidden totem in the realm of nature or culture. And yet human beings only become truly human when they have chosen and actuated themselves in freedom; when the "nature" in them has been totally and freely appropriated and responsibly worked through. So long as Christianity appears to be principally a matter of traditions and institutions, the emancipatory movements of modernity will have an easy time of it.

The competition will only begin in earnest when the Christian undertakes to show in theory that God's free opening of himself in

Jesus Christ is an invitation into the realm of an absolute and divine freedom, in which alone human freedom can be fully realized. Nor is this just an invitation, but through God's becoming human in Jesus Christ, which is an exemplary fulfillment for all, there is a break-through and entry into the sphere of precisely that kind of freedom which is so feverishly sought by the moderns but which, without the opening of God, they cannot find. As opposed to that searching free-dom which is always coming up empty, Christians will present the message of freedom accomplished and accomplishable by us. Not-withstanding, they must be careful not to overlook a weighty objec-tion which is leveled against their standpoint as it is against the position of a well-founded kind of modern evolutionism.

We live in a world, it is said, which from time immemorial has advanced by means of the aggressiveness of the strong and the de-struction of the weak, whose every "good" movement is founded on the principle of "exploitation" and "suppression" on the part of the "so-called evil" (O. Lorenz). How can such a world advance toward freedom at all? How is even the merest preliminary sketch of freedom thinkable? At all events, this world view, which can scarcely be dis-missed as unscientific, resists all these, be they Marxist or Christian, which dream of the erection of a kingdom of peace on earth, in the name of Lenin or Christ. Did capitalism and exploitation exist in the world before the human being made its appearance? Many biologists who were unwilling to renounce this view were sent to Siberia after the communists had seized power. But is not a world based on such principles quite unacceptable for us Christians also as a basis for Christian teaching? Is a world like this the work of a good God, is it capable of being transformed and explained, or will whoever opposes this world in the name of Christ and freedom not in fact be destined to be sold ruthlessly to destruction? Are perhaps Christians and com-munists alike utopian in their efforts to find freedom? Have perhaps the Christians only this advantage, that, nourished by a source which lies beyond the limits of this world, they can, with their utopian hope, reach out toward a goal which lies beyond the boundaries of time? And that this movement of theirs within a cosmos of murder and senselessness provide the one glimmer of freedom?

76 · Tearing Down the Ramparts

Most of the criticisms made against the church are directed against what, until recently, used to be called "the hierarchy," but what we now call more simply the official ministry. In view of the fact that the ministerial officers of the church have been given special responsibility to guide the faithful, and to this end have been appointed as "apostles, prophets, evangelists, pastors, and teachers" (Eph 4:11) for the "equipment of the saints, for the work of the ministry, for building up the body of Christ" (Eph 4:12), they ought therefore to resign themselves to the fact that the buck will be passed to them. To give it its proper due, this ministry is nothing less than a "foreign ministry" of the church. One might well compare it to the skeleton which enables a living organism to walk upright, and though rigid itself, gives flexibility to the rest and is wholly concealed within the living body. It is quite possible that this unseen and thus more effective role in the life of the church will gradually be returned to the ministry, thus enabling the church of the faithful, the living small communities which have always constituted the "outer skin" of the church, where the church brushes against the world around her, to resume their place in the front rank, and one could even say, in the line of fire. For the church will in the future be as credible as are those who represent her in the world.

But those who represent the church are already, because they are so different and scattered, rather hard to identify. It is impossible to classify them under one heading or supply them with one single label. The only thing really that can sum up and characterize them is the faith which they confess and which in turn demands a lived witness of them. If this is so, then the church will no longer be judged according to her credal formulae, still less according to its theologians, but according to what this *credo*, through and beyond all its formulations, means at its core; what it promises of God's grace and demands of human commitment. Those theologians and other Christians who refurbish this creed in order to present it in a more modern and acceptable form will, as a matter of course, no longer hold the limelight. We are slowly returning to the realization that those faithful who most clearly live the *credo* of the Christians, who used to be called "saints" (whether canonized or not), are the people in whose hands lie the validity and destiny of the church of today and tomorrow.

It is by no means necessary that these "saints" should be exceptional figures. Some have such a calling, but they are few and far between. And these are often only the starting point for the formation of smaller or larger groups to do the work of spreading the newly given light in the dispersion of the world. The members of such groups may devote themselves especially to prayer and devoted service for the world within the context of a religious order, in which case their light will automatically be almost hidden from the eyes of their fellow humans. They may, alternatively, make their way into the non-Christian world, having formed themselves into loosely knit groups or associations, thus living "close to the earth" (which is what humility actually means) and will therefore always be ready to sink like "a grain of mustard seed" or "grain of wheat," wherever the earth should open to let them in. This often happens so unobstrusively that afterward people are amazed when the "full harvest" comes or "the greatest of all trees in the garden" grows, for they are unable to trace either of these to their origins. But only because something authentically Christian has risen can one conclude that here something authentically Christian must have once sunk into the earth. And such authentic Christianity will give the world a great deal more to worry about than the towering edifices of the hierarchy.

We will plead, therefore, "for a poor and servant church" because it alone can be sure of making contact with the world of today, not because of a desire for success, but because of its mandate. That is the church which, so long as it can be effective in the world, cooperates with it, yet which is certain from the fate of Jesus that where visible, active effectiveness ends and where suffering, sickness, and evident failure begin, its work does not cease, but rather begins in earnest. Such a church has torn down its ramparts which protect it from the world. It sees itself no longer as a "mighty fortress" but rather as a model for God's greater purposes; for God's concern is, through its mediation, with the world. Perhaps God allows only as much of the church to survive as he needs in order to have new yeast to mix with the dough, or new corn whose only purpose is to fall into the earth and die that it may be raised as something else. This affords a totally different dynamic understanding of tradition than as a mere unchanged handing on of what always was. For in a living tradition, at every moment the original *traditio* (that is, the surrender of the Son by the Father for the salvation of the world) is repeated. And in an imitating self-surrender (as we see in St. Paul's leave-taking from his apostolate: Acts 20:17–38; Phil 2:17ff; 2 Tim) the church lives in a perpetual process of death and resurrection within the living source of the tradition.

What we have said of today's church—that it is growing closer to the earth and that its former outer structures are becoming a feature of its interior life—lets it appear as a small flock wherever it does concretely and genuinely make an appearance. It lives in small centers of influence which are scattered over the world like tiny lights in the night. It is in these centers that one experiences the love of God in Christ: sacramentally and existentially, in prayer and the selfless exchange of love; and the kind of life experienced by this small community can thence be carried by its members as individuals and by the community as a whole into the world of non-Christians. But in doing this, the Christian will have the confusing new experience of discovering that most of what she or he brings to the world is in some way or another already there, presumably not in its entirety but in fragments, not as a known but as something subconscious or presupposed, not as welcomed but as something rejected from the outset, at least in the caricatures in which it has become known. For the images of God and of the church of Christ that circulate in the world are so incredibly grotesque that one need not wonder about atheism and hostility toward the church.

Jesus himself, of course, on several occasions had this experience of coming upon something already there, for example, when he met the Syro-phoenician woman (Mk 7:24ff), or the pagan centurion (Mt 8:5ff): "I have not found so great faith, no not in Israel." Only the foreigner, a Samaritan, thanks Jesus for having healed him (Lk 17:16); it is another Samaritan who becomes the example of Christian love for one's neighbor (Lk 10:25ff); and a foreign woman from Samaria becomes the occasion of his first genuine wave of conversions (Jn 4:39ff). For the most part, it is the Gentiles who are not closely associated with him rather than the Jews who are closely related to him who accept the gospel message, and this is often foretold in the sayings of Jesus and confirmed in the Acts of the Apostles. It is almost as if the longing and the hunger of those who had to go without more is a better preparation for the unexpected than the hopes of those who have already formed for themselves on the basis of the promises a firm picture of that which is to come. For this picture distorts the place of God's arrival whereas the pagan emptiness is able to receive him.

And then, throughout the centuries of the church's history, there is a diffused dissemination—I do not say of the grace of God among all people, for we have no overview nor experiential data for this—of Christian teaching, which has been spread in innumerable ways, both open and concealed, and has infiltrated some world views quite foreign to itself. One has only to think of how much biblical material has been propagated through the Koran, and also how Indian ethics have been transformed through its contact—scarcely conscious to itself—with Christianity. This is to leave unmentioned all the innumerable sects and denominations which exist like so many distant suburbs of an urban center. Yet who knows how much of the spirit from the center they have carried with them to the edges? In contemplating this worldwide phenomenon, we can see in a new way how God's grain of wheat falls into the earth and dies, but can also, indiscernibly, rise and live under a different form. From God's point of view, this strange growth from his seed is often more vigorous than another growth which calls itself Christian but deliberately turns and moves away from the authentic center.

This can give new heart to the little flock. Not only is God for it, and who then could be against it? (Rom 8:31), but God has also prepared for it many confederates where it thought it had been left entirely alone. In the gospel, Jesus sends his disciples to places where he himself will follow afterwards. In the history of the church, however, he hastens on in front of them, and they often find him already there in some way when they arrive. But this should not make them nonchalant. They are needed; for we, who have been freed, are to share in bringing God's freedom to fulfillment. And what is Christian must always, even historically, flow into the world from a living and glowing center—there is already enough cooled-off lava lying around.

Liberalized, dedogmatized Christianity is still at times a remote ray from the center, but does not have its original generating power. Only that inner circle that centers its life on God's initiative in the Christ-event has this power. For this inner circle is the community of those for whom the Word had not grown cold and become just abstract doctrine, but is the living personal presence of the Trinity, articulated in their life of brother-sister love and a communion which is both sacramental and existential. Wherever in the world such a community exists is where the liberation of the world is beginning to take place. That is also where fear of the challenge that comes from atheistic emancipatory projects is done away with. For ultimately they all stand, together with the Christians, under the same challenge from the stark reality of the world itself, and they can meet it only with some utopia which transcends this reality. Never will the master-servant relationship be fully superseded in this world (Marx); never will the human being completely integrate and appropriate its origin (Freud); never will he as "super-man" be the complete giver indebted to no one (Nietzsche); never in this world will the human being be able to conjure from itself the truly free *homo absconditus* (Bloch) or an aggressionless nature (Marcuse). The Christian design for freedom is much broader than any of those schemes because it not only includes freedom unto death (with the Stoics and Buddhists), but transcends it in the free faith of Christ that God will lift him, the whole human being—with his brothers, with his sisters, with history and the cosmos—into salvation "on the third day."

77 · Divided Church—Ecumenical Concerns

The division of the church, caused by sin, is made even easier by the fact that opportunity for it is continually provided in the distribution of the various *charisms* and offices. This is where the community needs to be especially warned against envy and jealousy. The gift that someone else has received, and I do not have, is administered within the body for the good of the whole, of which I am a part: The eye sees for the whole body, etc. (1 Cor 12). The administration of the *charisms* presupposes selfless love in all (1 Cor 13). Yet only a slight shifting of perspective is needed in order to make the special, perhaps striking and attractive quality of a *charism* seem so significant that its value surpasses that of the organic unity of the church. This results, often without fault of the bearer of the *charism*, in biased partisanship. Hence the exhortation of Paul: "Let no divisions arise among you, but be united in the same mind and the same judgment. For it has been reported to me . . . that there is quarreling among you, my brethren. What I mean is that each one of you says, 'I belong to Paul,' or 'I belong to Apollos,' or 'I belong to Cephas.' . . . Is Christ divided? Was Paul crucified for you?" (1 Cor 10:10–13).

There is of course a difference between these schisms within the church and the definitive schism which separates from the unity of the institutional church. But, without fail, the former were the cause whenever the latter came about. Sin within the church is the origin of the equally sinful separation of the churches. The process within the church can last for centuries—just think of the long prehistory both of the Eastern schism and that of the reformation—and it is also always something that can be documented in one way or another, which does not in any way justify the final break. Falling away from the love which protects and builds the catholicity of the church is the perhaps very hidden beginning of every division in the church: *ubi peccata, ibi multitudo.*

Then the rather difficult question arises whether and when the internally and often externally divided church ceases to be a single person in the salvation-event. Two points of view have to be determinative here. One of them is that the church is conceived and equipped both as community of saints and as an institution for the support and rescue of the sinners living in it, that it is a *corpus permixtum* and may not set itself apart as "church of the pure," "elect," or "predestined." And so it must continually endure the internal tension between its ideas and its fallen reality, and continually endeavor to educate its peripheral members towards its center. So too must it support the encompassing unity (the "net") as that kind of principle by which it can keep in the fold even those who have fallen away, so long as they do not decisively break away. But at this boundary the other principle is in force: theologically speaking, there is no way in which there can be several churches of Christ, and if such a plurality exists in the empirical sphere, these numerous churches of Christ could not represent theological "persons." Thus it is also not possible to derive the all-encompassing concept of one church by the abstracting of what is somehow common from this historical plurality, for its unity is not generic, but a concrete and individually unique unity, corresponding to its founding by the unique Christ.

Listen to Karl Barth at this point: "One should not try to explain the multiplicity of churches . . . as a divinely willed and thus normal unfolding of the richness of the grace bestowed on humanity in Jesus Christ," nor "as a necessary characteristic of the visible empirical church in contrast to the invisible, ideal, essential church. One should not do this because this whole distinction is foreign to the New Testament, because the church of Jesus Christ even from this point of view is only one: invisible according to the grace of the Word of God and the Holy Spirit, . . . but symbolically visible in the crowd of those who profess loyalty to it, visible as community and community office, visible as service to word and sacrament. . . . There is no escape from the visible to the invisible church." If one attempts to produce such an ecumenical reality, then "one is doing, no matter how beautiful it might sound, historical and social philosophy and not theology; that is, in order to eliminate the question of the unity of the church, one produces one's own ideas instead of staying with the question put to us by Christ. . . . If we listen to Christ, . . . we do not exist above the differences separating the church but in them. . . . One should not want to explain the multiplicity of the church at all. One should deal with it as one deals with one's own and others' sins. . . . One should understand it as guilt." Thus it is also pointless to seek in the New Testament for guidelines as to how separated churches should get along with each other; the most one will find are indications on how to avoid divisions.

Thus, in the Christian communities that have set themselves apart with full awareness from the institution of the Catholica, it is of course possible, along with Vatican II, to discover "some, even very many, of the most significant elements or endowments which together go to build and give life to the Church," above all to recognize that "whoever believes in Christ and has been properly baptized is brought into a certain, though imperfect, communion with the Catholic church" [Decree on Ecumenism, Nr. 3]. Nevertheless, that does not say that such communities form theological persons of their own over against the Catholica. In the relationship between the Roman Catholic and the Orthodox churches the question may be put whether the mutual alienation has gone so far that one must really speak of two "churches," or whether an objective historical investigation does not show that the unity "deep down has never ceased to exist."

The attempt has also been made to explain the theological "necessity" of schisms from the Old Testament schism between the Northern and Southern kingdoms or from the "primitive breach" between

Jewish and gentile Christianity at the founding of the church. But as
far as this first schism goes, the tribes of Israel were never a unity
comparable with the "Body of Christ," but a "confederation of different tribal groups" which only shortly before had been brought together "into personal union" by a monarch. As far as the second is
concerned, one would have to stretch things pretty far in order to
make a recalcitrant Israel responsible for the interchurch quarrels
among Christians which, according to Paul, must be at one (or
united) from a totally other principle of unity than the Jewish "sects"
(to one of which Paul too had belonged).

But precisely because this principle of unity—the Eucharist of the
pneumatic Lord—is a completely new and incomparable one, the
division which is pushed to full schism becomes quasi-unhealable.
The "ecumenical movement" must, on the basis of elementary Christian obligation, be unceasingly concerned for the reunification of
separated "churches" and in so doing can doubtless achieve many
partial successes—the elimination of mutual lack of understanding,
suspicions, disparagements, etc.—but since the group separated from
the Catholica has necessarily separated itself from the visible symbol
of unity, the papacy, there does not exist in the dialogue partner (not
even when it is orthodoxy) any authority, which, as recognized by all
the faithful, can officially represent them. One has to deal in each
instance with individual groups or bishops who, when union with the
Catholica is being weighed, regularly divide into an agreeing and a
rejecting party, or possibly make the offer of an abstract Catholicity
achievable by prescinding from the real differences. We described
this above as unacceptable.

Over and above all possible mutual fertilization and instruction of
the "church," there is for the Catholica only *one* path of meaningful
ecumenical activity: the representation of its own principle in exemplarily lived holiness. This will, as is the case with the great saints,
show ecclesiastical obedience in the Catholic sense as not only able to
be integrated in Christian *agape* but also specifically demonstrate it
as an unrenounceable element of this *agape* and of the discipleship of
Christ.

78 · Identification and Criticism

How can one manage a halfway decent attitude with regard to such
a multileveled phenomenon as the empirical church, especially
when one is sure of the need to criticize certain aspects of it (it does
not matter for the moment which), and on the other hand would not
want simply to turn one's back on it, but discovers a number of

vitally important values in it which one affirms for oneself and in which one wants to have a share.

It is not our intention here to enter into the very complicated problems of partial identification with the (or an) empirical church and of criticism of the church. We only observe that criticism of the church can be meaningful and creative only when one is identified not (partially) with some aspect or other of the church but with its core. By this is meant not a merely invisible, ideal church, but a church which, while remaining empirical, is one that stems from Christ and is endowed from the beginning with an office. The core, the essence with which I identify myself, allows me if necessary a critical attitude toward peripheral aspects. But the core is not a (unfulfilled) postulate but a reality flowing out of the work of God in Christ: something given in the strongest sense of the word, something bestowed by way of grace, something that is already there and to take part in which I too am invited and, if I wish, is given to me. And because this core is the fruit of Christ's love and *is* itself love—and by very definition as participation in absolute love—nothing in me which is need for, and active attempt at, love can be foreign to this core. Therefore I must, to the extent that I have understood what church at its core is, love the church, and not just as something "other" that stands over against me, but as the already given reality of what in me is longing, inclination, possibility, as the fullness of what in me is in any case only partially and one-sidedly present. Hence, when one is talking about the essence and core of the church, the formula of partial identification is exactly reversed: I, the partial one, come to total identification with myself only through a total identification with the church.

But since it is already given to me—not only as idea but as reality—I cannot sketch out according to my own predilection how it should be, in order then to love my own fantasy, but I *am allowed* to accept it as the best possible plan of God's love in the world because it is conceived and "produced" by God (Eph 5:26). Everything in it which is not suited to this core—whether it is struggling toward it or even turned aside and moving away from it—can be criticized from the center and toward the center, as well as from love and toward love, and not from the self-distancing periphery. That means, furthermore, that we can criticize the church only from the center of its love, not so much then in a love *for* it as in its love itself. In our love for it we objectify it and distinguish between its love and our love. But here it really is true: *il n'y a pas deux amours*. And it would also be true only in such a way that I attempt to direct my love, which of course can never equal the fullness of love glowing in the core of the church, intentionally according to the church's love, and likewise seek to consider and evaluate intentionally with the eyes of the holy church its own holiness (to which I belong). The look from the innermost to the peripheral levels can be respectively a look of anger, of hard demands, or of forebearance and forgiveness. Both can be found in Jesus Christ, but certainly the first not without (at least hidden) the second. And if the forebearance, as for example toward an individual sinner, is what predominates, it will inexorably change into the demand: "Go, and sin no more."

For individual Christians, the relationship between severity and forebearance is not a matter of free choice. They will be reminded instead of the parable of the unmerciful servant: "You wicked servant! I forgave you all that debt . . . should not you have had mercy on your fellow servant, as I had mercy on you?" (Mt 18:32f). That also holds when they are upset about individual persons or circumstances which harm others more than themselves. They will have the words to the sons of thunder addressed to themselves: "You do not know of what manner of spirit you are" (Lk 9:55). They would have not had the Spirit of Christ if they took it as self-evident that they had it and that they, from the perspective of the head, were sitting in judgment over the church as his very imperfect body; they would not even have had it if they had been sitting with the same self-evident attitude on one of the twelve chairs which Jesus was assigning to his disciples as he "made over the kingdom" (Lk 22:29) to them. Only the head itself has the standpoint of the head and the representation of the head can only be overtaken by the one to whom an official mandate was given for that purpose. Certainly all should come to know from the words of the Lord—even the severe ones—the Spirit of the Lord and seek to appropriate it, but their standpoint remains within that church which has received in the gospel a wealth of clear directives, what its rank and place is and what it should not measure against itself. That means within the church, neither above it nor outside it nor in the place of the church itself. For here the thought again returns that all members of the church are in debt to the church and they cannot outgrow this position of indebtedness towards it even when they come to Christian maturity. The member of the church is a Christian not through an abstract Christ but through the Bridegroom united with the bride—the *una columba immaculata* (one taintless dove)— through the unity of head and body. No Christian can grow out of the love of a child toward its mother the church.

Christians can at best develop in their Christian love by overcoming more and more the initial appearance of an opposition between Christian and church, or of seeing the church as object, in order to be identified with the mind of the church at its core. This would precisely not mean that they grow out of seeing the church as a falsely objectified entity and into a purely personal relationship of love to Christ and the brethren, but that they grow into the church in such a way that they, as church, in its spirit and in its form, cooperate in carrying out the acts of churchly love for Christ and for the brethren—not privately, but in circumincession with all *animae ecclesiasticae* (churchly souls). Everyone can recognize in the saints that this is possible, how it takes place, and how little it levels the particular personality of an individual. It is characteristic of the saints that they do not place ecclesiastical pneuma and ecclesiastical institution in opposition, but recognize the unity of both as a consequence of the incarnation of God. Even where they have to criticize the institutional, because the inclination and inertia of human beings caused by original sin repeatedly misuses it, they do it from the true unity of pneuma and institution. For the world of the sacraments out of reverence for their holiness, for the sphere of office from a fundamental readiness to obey, which in certain places can be in opposition, even conflict, in order to restore again the pure relationship of obedience. For in the undivided ecclesiastical unity of pneuma and institution, the saints love the Spirit of Jesus Christ who assumed the form of a servant, humbled himself, and became obedient unto death, even to death on the cross.

LIFE
IN FAITH

· 79 ·

When our chords are taut, God plays on our soul by himself. And more than this we should not attempt at all: to be taut toward God.

Faith as Agreement with God

80 · The Fundamental Act:
Indifference as Agreement with God's Action

The determinacy of the divine love first becomes knowable at the end of the biblical revelation in Jesus Christ. In the Old Testament a determinacy was of course also manifest, but in such a way that an inner participation in his essence as distinct from the created world was only possible at a certain distance: One lived in God's care, under his view, in his country set apart for the use of his chosen ones, etc. In older religions which reflectively reduce anthropomorphic images of God back to some One, which stands indifferent within and above all worldly differences, a participation in this One may only be conceived by delimitation and removal of every uniqueness.

That the eternal destiny of humanity can, in God, be more than an eternal "over against" (as in the Old Testament), namely an inward share in the life of God himself, and thereby no "getting lost" in this life (as in the speculative religions), but a being bestowed with the divine freedom inside one's own freedom: this can only be understood in New Testament terms, where the inward life-process of God (*theologia*) is opened to the world in Christ (*oikonomia*), in order thereby to imbed the world within the divine process.

Now this has already begun to take place wholly within the realm of earthly existence in the life of faith, hope, and love, and to such an extent that the transformation of this temporal mode of participating in God into the eternal mode is more the unveiling of something already existent than the new creation of something still outstanding.

What can already exist anticipatorily in the life of faith, hope, and love—in various degrees of perfection—is the mystery of the homecoming of one's own freedom to the freedom of God, as the start of Ignatius's prayer of self-giving formulates it: "Take and receive, O

Lord, my liberty; take all my will, my mind, my memory." Even if this coming-home of freedom to God is striven for in most religions, it nevertheless becomes fully possible only in Christianity. For, on the one hand, here the universal speculative idea remains in full force: that God in any case is the absolute, and thus also absolute truth, justice, goodness; that therefore each act of God's will that comes to be known is right in each case and is to be accepted by human beings for their salvation and so also for their greater freedom. On the other hand, this idea becomes infinitely concretized by the fact that the intradivine relation of the Son's self-giving to the Father (and, presupposed in this, not only the self-giving of the Father but also the Spirit of the self-giving of both) become known in the subjection of the human will of Jesus Christ to the will of the Father—"Not as I will, but as you will" (Lk 22:24). In this simple, if often very difficult, preferring of the divine will, an allowing of God's way to be in our lives, there is actuated already in mortal life the central feature that marks the essence of the eternal, and indeed far more central than would be attainable, say, in exercises in self-dissolution under one's own power (which God does not at all require) or in supposed experiences of union with God. Such techniques and methods are always secretly fed by the idea that creaturely limits (even of consciousness) are an obstacle for God, while actually, in Christianity and its mystery of the incarnation, God walks precisely the path of limitation in order to reconcile the world to himself.

What Christian theology calls the "theological virtues" of faith, hope, and love (1 Cor 13:13) are ways of appropriating one's own freedom in the freedom of God: in his truth (faith), his fidelity to his promise (hope), his self-giving (love). They have been called "theological," because human possibilities of faith, of hopeful trust, and love have been transfused by the "Holy Spirit, poured forth in our hearts" (Rom 5:5), who precisely in this manner brings the inner attitude of the triune God into us and in this way qualifies us on two sides: to respond to God's call and gift in a manner worthy of God, and to impart the divine attitude into our relations with our fellows (cf. 1 Cor 13).

81 · Indifference in the Gospel of John

The johannine mystery of being in agreement with the sacrifice of the Lord is in its center a feminine mystery. Adrienne von Speyr saw this in its entirety for the first time in her meditations on the Gospel of John. She unveils it as the "mystery of the three Marys": the Mary of Bethany (12:1–8), the mother Mary (19: 25–27), and Mary Magdalene (20:11–18). In all three there is a single stance which is demanded, and each time this gets specified and shaped by the sacrificial stance of the Lord alone.

In Mary of Bethany, the "contemplative" (Lk 10:38–42), it is the pure, open consenting of a love that accepts all that is to be in the gesture of self-lavishing, whose aroma fills the house. For this reason she does not need to know what she is doing when she anoints Jesus, and it is not to her but to the companions at table that it is explained: "She has anointed me for my burial." The yes of Mary of Bethany is a yes to death on the cross: it is an anointing of the suffering Messiah-servant of God to his decisive office, an anointing not by God—which he always had anyway—but by the "church," and indeed by the church listening expectantly to, believing in, and loving God's Word, whose gesture is an expression of its faith and its love. This consent of the loving church was obviously needed by the Messiah to be able to enter upon his solitary, incomparable office. It is a yes which is fundamentally open in an *a priori* fashion, which disposes of nothing on its own, and which holds itself ready and allows itself to be formed; from it the masculine mission of the Son of God can shape everything that is needed for his mission. This setting no limits to and thus nonemphasis on the sacrifice stands in contrast to the masculine difficulties of Peter, who wants to understand, know, determine, and set limits before hand. This feminine setting-of-no-limits becomes the pure medium in which the sacrifice, Christ, is actuated and the element with which it is made visible. It is sacrifice as pure not-standing-in-the-way, pure allowing-oneself-to-be-drawn, and precisely therein, the hardest sacrifice for the one who loves.

At the other end of the *Triduum Mortis*, Magdalene stands at the grave: as representative of the sinners redeemed by the cross, she is pure, ennobled eros for the "blood-groom" whom she seeks blindly in tears and in the yawning emptiness of the tomb. To her comes a share of the grace of Easter in a flash of fulfilling encounter: "Mary!" "Master!" And straightaway in the midst of this fulfillment, this mutual commotion, comes the order: "Do not hold on to me, for I have not yet gone to the Father, go instead to my brethren. . . ." The paschal mutuality is held open so widely that there is room for absolute love in it: a sacrifice of being drawn to the Father, a state of agreement with the movement of the resurrection itself, with the coming from the realm of death and the rising up to the heavenly kingdom, the unique, solitary movement of Christ, which however will yet be accompanied by the agreement of the saved lover: *personam ecclesiae gerens*. It is the post-Easter, transfigured form of sacrifice which really allows only the empty shell of suffering to be seen, while the required renunciation immediately gets overwhelmingly filled with a new, indeed more greatly fulfilling, content of love: with the going forth to the brethren and the proclamation "that I am ascending to my Father and your Father, to my God and your God"; with the proclamation of the great saving synthesis between earth and heaven, Christ and the brethren, God and humanity. And this proclamation is bestowed upon the church as its most proper Easter joy (inside its "renunciation," its "accepting all that is to be").

Between the two Marys is a higher midpoint: the mother of the Son on the cross. She does nothing and says nothing; she is only there. And the dying Son disposes of her—so thoroughly that he places another son under her care, and gives her to him as mother. She is not asked; her agreement is presupposed, as has been the case right from the conception (Lk 1:26–28), where Mary spoke her comprehensive yes to all that can be in God's will and word, while at the same time not really answering a question. The announcement of the angel talks about an inevitable future: "You *shall* conceive, *shall* bear a son, *shall* give him the name Jesus, he *shall* be great and *shall* be called son of the most high, and God the Lord *shall* give him the throne of David his father, and he *shall* rule over the house of Jacob, and of his kingdom there *shall* be no end." It does not happen the way a wedding between husband and wife does, where a mutual agreement is requested and granted. But Mary's agreement is presupposed from the beginning, in utter silence, as when something is taken for granted, about which use can be made without question.

The question she puts to the angel regards the rightness of her conduct: what must I do to prepare myself for all of this to happen? The response however does not tell what she must do, but what God will do and accomplish with her: "The Holy Spirit will come down upon you." Here, too, is only agreement and acceptance of whatever may happen, without limit and condition. The rest of the marian scenes give shape to this accepting from God whatever may come: birth at a bad time, not understanding the apparent disobedience of the boy and releasing him to "what belongs to his Father," being drawn into the public mission without being drawn into the plan, and anxiety. There is rejection in Cana, rejection on the occasion of the visit with the relatives, being put aside until such time as she is needed once again: at the cross she is officially and definitively put aside. Here the relationship of this mother and this Son, of this bride and bridegroom, of this maiden and this Lord achieves its final form: she has to let him be pulled away, not only in bodily death, but in abandonment by God, to the point where any communion, any form of help is rendered impossible. And she has to let him be drawn away, not out of her own resolve, or in virtue of her own contribution to his sacrifice, but simply because *he* goes away, leaves her standing, sends her away, settles her someplace else. That she thus becomes most nearly conformed to him, because he too is the one sent away and abandoned by the Father, she can neither see nor (in case she could see) understand. She allows herself to be used for his purposes, veiled over in the darkest night. Just as between Father and Son, so there presides between Son and mother the oneness of being abandoned. "Just as the Father has left me, so do I leave you," expresses the situation if put into words. That is the "sword through the middle of the heart," to which her heart had constantly opened itself during the course of a lifetime, from the beginning and ever anew, up to the moment of the piercing of the divine-human heart on the cross.

Turning to God in Prayer

82 · The Irreplaceability of Prayer

The Christian stands and falls with prayer; faith has only one content: that God has loved and continues to love him, her, and everyone—not just everyone anonymously but also him or her as a particular individual. Israel's election was the beginning: you and no other shall be my you, said God to the people, and not because you are beautiful or great or powerful, but because I in my unsearchable freedom have chosen you to love, to mutual love with me. A terrifying fate, thus to stand face to face before God. Israel would like to look away, but its sideways glances are unmasked as the prostitute's leer. Israel is transfixed by a word which has its origins in a groundless freedom: the instruction and wisdom of the Lord. And God swears that his word will not return to him from the earth without the fruit of Israel's answer (Is 55:10f). The people achieved the answer of the liturgical psalms: the song of praise, of thanksgiving, of supplication, of hiding oneself under God's wings. That is good and will and must remain in this way. But in Christ, the human being, the God who elects does not come globally to a whole people but—more urgently than in the prophetic calls—to individuals: you, follow me. The force of my hand is laid on you, choosing, challenging, and pressing you into service.

The one called drops everything and follows: there is nothing on which to fall back, no reserve in case things go wrong. If freedom is offered there is only "Lord, to whom shall we go? You have the words of eternal life." I have staked my life on your words which ring out to me from eternity; how then can I deny you your reply? A reply not by deeds of great fecundity, appropriate as such to Christ's commission, and for humans and the world, but a direct reply in which the heart, which has heard itself addressed from eternity as you, pulls itself together to speak, in formed or soundless words, a you! to the eternal love which chooses it. All the work which the apostles carried out in the world was but the echo spreading from this most original you in the heart of those sent. Where is there more personal prayer than in the letters of Paul? Often he takes the liturgical prayer of the community and blends it into a prayer of his own heart. And not because he has retained prayer customs from his earlier life as a Pharisee. But the Lord whom he serves is the Word of God the Father, the Word which was not first spoken into the world at large by the Father's mouth, but the eternally subsisting Word which was always from the beginning the praising, grateful answer to the Father, *eucharistia*. Notably in Luke, Jesus prays continually, withdraws to solitary places for personal prayer; his baptism, his transfiguration, the beginning of his passion occur during his prayer (3:21; 5:16; 6:12; 9:18–21; 11:1). In John, Jesus summarizes his whole mission in the "high-priestly prayer" (ch. 17) in which he commends all his work, from his going forth from the Father to his return to him, into his Father's hands. Even in his dying words he is still in dialogue with God.

Christians of all ages, including now, are drawn into this prayer. There is no excuse; no evasion will be permitted. Nor may refuge be sought in mere action, nor simply in the liturgy, nor in solidarity with all those who can no longer pray or who no longer know anything about prayer.

Not in action. Of course it is true that in earlier ages many a Christian took flight from the efforts of action in the enjoyment of contemplation as a foretaste of heaven, or simply as the easier way of buying God off. (Yet people like John of the Cross or de Foucauld can teach us what an enormous effort and overtaxing of one's total existence is the true Christian way of contemplation.) It is possible too that the apostles and many of their successors underestimated the active effort which was demanded of them when they remained gathered in prayer in Jerusalem and only undertook minor apostolic excursions into the surrounding country: Paul had to show them what was really true, world-transforming apostolate.

The fact that today young Christians demand above all a Christian witness through deeds, and indeed deeds which truly change and revolutionize the structures of society, is intelligible and justified when one sees the terrible state of affairs in the world and with what paralysis and lack of imagination we Christians gaze at all the horror and the anguish. Enough of saying "Lord, Lord": the time has come to do the will of God, to put one's hand to the plough. Enough of walking past the beaten and bleeding person, piously saying one's rosary and breviary; the time has come to get down from one's saddle like the Samaritan—to do for the least of the brothers and sisters in the underdeveloped countries that which Christ reckoned as being done to him. In spite of this—and this is said to Christians who realize what is going on—*Christian* action must, if it wants to deserve this name and be distinguished from secular action, come from much more than simply human compassion; it must come from the knowledge of and gratitude for God's compassion on the cross, and it must be prepared to go even farther: to the point of suffering, of participating in the cross. Christian action is a mediating link between the offering of oneself in prayer and the giving of oneself to be disposed of entirely according to God's will.

Not in the liturgy. For good reasons the people of the middle ages built their cathedrals larger than a liturgy could fill. Only in an age when one gives up personal prayer in order to be simply a communal animal in the church can one design churches which are determined purely functionally by the services of the congregation. The restoration of the genuine liturgical congregation by radical reforms in language, text, homily, and dialogue, as well as by the appropriate arrangement of old and new buildings for this event, was both right and important. But, alas, what a welcome alibi it provides for a new clerical dirigism, for forms of clerical busy-work which never stop moving the altar around, fumigating churches, buying new vestments for the servers and a thousand other odds and ends, and again puts the emphases in the wrong place. As if a break of two minutes after the sermon or after the communion could satisfy our elementary need for silence in God, of communion from the heart with him! And who can, as he swallows the host, "realize" what holy communion means? Does he not need for that the unfunctional, silent "adoration of the Blessed Sacrament," or silent, personal meditation on the holy scriptures? The clergy, whether old or young, should make no mistake about it: no matter how far the sermon has been prepared by the standards of modern exegesis and of pastoral sociology (in case they still find time for this), if it has not been achieved in personal prayer the congregation is fed stones instead of bread. And the faithful have a very fine sense for whether the preacher's words come from the depths of personal prayer or ultimately are as flat and as vain as anything they might read in a newspaper. When they want a "new image" for priests, the clergy would do better to ask themselves what the congregation asks of them and holds up to them as its ideal of a priest, rather than what the most modern fare is that they can set before the congregation.

Two things in the Old Testament were superseded by Christ: servitude to the law and the liturgy of the temple. The first was expounded by Paul, the second by the Epistle to the Hebrews. Today everyone welcomes the first, to the point of reaching a kind of Manichaean dualism between law and gospel, which comes however not from the gospel itself but from Luther and was mocked by Kierkegaard: there's so much "gospel" and "spirit" that there is nothing left of the fulfilling of the law by the gospel! But the second point, namely that the liturgy of the temple has equally been outmoded, is hardly something you would notice in our present liturgical spring. The very act of hammering out new forms makes one both "pious" and modern at the same time. And yet how uncreative in word and gesture is our age. Thus everything gets quickly out of date again, and everyone is in danger of getting fed up with all this liturgical magic. Then, presumably, no prayer of any sort will be left but only political action, so long as the government allows it. Liturgical prayer that is Christian must be grounded in personal prayer and find its originating source there. At the core of the liturgical event Christ prays, the communion of the true saints prays, and they are always people of prayer.

Finally: *not a flight into solidarity* with those who do not pray. The latter have established far-reaching theories why "Modern Man" (always written with capitals) can no longer pray, theories which are regarded with admiration by many Christians. Because God is dead—that is the simplest way of looking at it; there is no point in talking with corpses. Because God is unobjectifiable, uncategorical, and because one should not think of him naively as a you standing in front of us, as someone to be spoken to (no wonder, then, if he remains silent). Or more mildly, because God's will is done no matter what (for he is absolute will and it is childish to wish to interfere and to alter that will). Others maintain that they have honestly made the attempt to pray, but have only prayed into a void, to a wall; they have not received the slightest trace of an answer, only the eerie echo of their own voice. Eclipse of the sun; epochal remoteness from God and absence of God. That, so it is said, is the experience of the majority of our brothers and sisters: and do we want to be better off than they, to experience the "consolations of prayer"? But is it really a question of "consolations"?

Or is it not, rather, the assumption of responsibilities? Could any Christian want to pray merely for himself or herself without also including his or her nonpraying brethren in his or her prayer before

God? Since Christ prayed and suffered for all, prayer can still only be catholic, universal, can only become a living mouthpiece for all those who are silent before God, can only offer itself to bear the burdens of all those who are a burden to themselves and perhaps also to God. And if one does this seriously, who knows how seriously he or she may then be taken by God. What good is it to those who are fumbling in the dark if I choose to fumble with them instead of switching on the flashlight I am carrying, instead of "shining like the stars in the universe" (Phil 2:15) from the tiny point which I occupy? If many, indeed all Christians together, would shine as best they could, then we would somehow find our way through this moonless night. The only ones who show true solidarity are those who contribute for the benefit of all that they have (received as a gift). Such persons will pray out of gratitude to God and from responsibility for their fellow human beings. They will not worry a great deal about what they do or do not feel, or the extent to which they experience God's presence or absence. Perhaps they will be allowed to feel the absent God of those who do not pray, in order that the latter may catch an intimation of the God who is present. Such things happen in the *communio sanctorum* which in the widest sense is the community of all those for whom God on the cross has suffered total abandonment. And that indeed includes everyone.

83 · Liturgy—Celebration of God's Praise

What liturgy on the part of human beings would be worthy of the object of its reverence, before which even in heaven every being casts itself upon its face, removes its wreaths and crowns, and places them in a gesture of worship before the throne of God: "You alone, O Lord, our God, are worthy of praise, honor and power" (Rev 4:11)? This heavenly giving back of every good received by creatures to the one "who has made everything by his will" can compel an earthly community made up of sinners on its knees from the start to a *Domine, non sum dignus.* If this community gathered for praise and honor were to have in mind anything but an act of complete worship and self-giving—for instance their own edification or any other undertaking in which they themselves should become the theme of the liturgy along with the Lord who is supposed to be the one to be honored—that would be an alienating, if ever so naive, self-deception.

In a purely monotheistic religion the gesture of *proskynesis* (kneeling and bowing) is the most perfect expression of the giving over of the entire person, even in a great assembly. What Christian cannot be deeply struck at contemplating the silently worshipping crowd in a mosque! In the religion of the covenant, the hearing of the word of God, the Torah, stands in the middle: God speaks, the human beings receive in obedience, seeking in their hearts how they might rightly respond. And symbolic rites can also have a part, such as eating the Passover meal, the final nourishment before setting out into the desert under God's guidance, while standing, ready to depart.

But then, in the trinitarian religion, an unheard-of transformation occurs: from the arbitrary lamb eaten in the family circle into "the Lamb slaughtered from the beginning of the world" "which takes away the sins of the world" and gives his flesh and blood as "true food and true drink." One can understand those heretics (even if one likewise understands their condemnation) who shrank before the excess of this divine mystery and charged the faithful not to make common what is ineffable and worthy of fear, bearing in mind Paul's saying, "Whoever eats the bread or drinks the cup of the Lord unworthily, will be guilty of profaning the body and blood of the Lord. Hence, a person must examine himself," in order not to "eat and drink judgment" upon himself (1 Cor 11:27–29). We are constrained by God, indeed compelled, if we want to gain eternal life "to eat the flesh of the Son of man and to drink his blood" (Jn 6:53). But we can only do this insofar as we keep in mind the terrible exchange between our guilt, which he bears, and his innocence, which he gives to us on the cross. Inasmuch as we receive him into ourselves, we remember that in his passion he has received us into himself; that, as Augustine repeatedly tells us, we receive the doctor who heals us in our very act of having put him to death: "As often as you eat this bread and drink this cup, you proclaim the death of the Lord, until he comes again" (1 Cor 11:26). And yet we are not supposed to approach embarrassed and downcast, for the Lord who wants to come to us calls us his friends (for whom he died: Jn 15:13); he does not want us to feel strange (like the disciples at the meal at the Sea of Tiberias: Jn 21:12), but to open wide our souls for the gift of the Father. For our gaze at the celebration is not narrowed to Jesus, but raised to the One from whom the highest of all goods ultimately comes, to the Father; nor are we ourselves the ones to bring about this opening and raising, but the Holy Spirit of the Father and the Son, who is poured out into our hearts. The worshipping community, which celebrates God's generosity and liberality, is gathered for the triune God and nothing else.

The glory of God, the majesty of his dominion, approaches us with its precious gifts, we who have to "praise the glory of his grace" (Eph 1:6). This last demand brings forth the norm and measure for the shaping of our worship. It would be laughable and blasphemous to desire to respond to God's gracious glory with a counter-glory made up from our own created reserves, in contrast to the heavenly liturgies the Book of Revelation portrays for us as completely over-whelmed and penetrated with the glory of God. No matter how the shape of the response of our liturgy might look, it can only be an expression of the purest possible and most selfless reception of the divine majesty of grace; even though reception implies nothing passive, but rather the most active deed of which the creature is capable.

What can such active reception not imply? Let that be our first question. What form can it take? Let that be our second. Neither question is, as we shall see, cleanly separable, because forms that for some people are a matter of purest receptivity, for others can be a matter of self-mirroring and worldly pleasure.

Surely excluded is everything which directs the community away from attention to God and his coming and turns its gaze back upon itself—unless it be at the moment of the examination of conscience, of confession of guilt, and of *Domine, non sum dignus.* Everything in the celebration which does not guide the hearts and thoughts toward the One being celebrated is evil; and all the more so, the more the quality of festivity is separated from its objective and itself becomes the center. We are already involved with the ambiguity, for which still more extensive examples may be supplied: That the praise of glory which is reserved for God alone gets turned back toward the one doing the praising, so that a part of the whole falls back on the praiser. It often happens—and the danger seems greater today than in earlier times—that a liturgical community measures the achievement of a celebration against its own edification, according to the measure of how much the participants take part in it and are caught up in it, instead of being captured by God and his gifts and letting him take part. There are communities which, perhaps unconsciously, celebrate themselves more than God; this is true of the liturgies of traditional as of progressively structured, of old, well-established as of freely formed parishes such as the young people love. This means that even the criterion of "vitality" of a worship service remains quite highly ambiguous; the question is always raised as to whether it brings about a living opening and conversion of the heart or the self-enjoyment of one's own vitality. Of course this ambiguity comes to light in an especially acute manner in regard to the homily or sermon, which should be aimed at only one thing: directing the attention of everyone (including even the preacher) to the mystery celebrated in its inexhaustibly manifold aspects and, in so doing, allowing no reflection from the divine brilliance to fall back upon the speaker and the spoken word.

The inclination of a community to celebrate itself instead of God will go unobserved or rather even arise necessarily if its faith in the reality of the eucharistic event fades. If a, so to speak, rudimentary church, gathered to await its Lord and to have itself be filled by him, is considered beforehand as that which is already present, to which nothing more can be added, then the eucharistic celebration will degenerate into sheer symbolism, and the community will be celebrating nothing other than its own divine blessedness which was already there and now feels itself strengthened by the renewed gathering: phariseeism is near. But if, on the contrary, the gathered people feel in their inmost selves how much in need they are of the arrival of the Lord among them and in them, in order to grow together into a real church and for each one to be filled with an ecclesial attitude, then a subjectively responding event will correspond to what occurs objectively. With the awareness of one's own unworthiness, the worthiness of the liturgy grows. This cannot be manipulated in any way or brought about by techniques: if the Christian attitude of the (majority of the) community and of the priest is genuine, then the celebration is worthy.

Here, however, one can observe—and so without a noticeable transition we come to our second question—a rare phenomenon. There are objectively worthy forms of liturgical prayer, which could have been formed naturally only in epochs of genuine subjective attitudes of prayer, forms such as our treasured canons, collects, and prayers at mass, which by reason of centuries of being prayed subjectively have taken on something like a new emphasis in worthiness. But many think that just because they allow themselves to be carried along by these forms and entrust themselves to these centuries of people praying along with them this constitutes a guarantee of the rightness of their subjective attitude. They are deceiving themselves in this regard. For these persons the worthiness of the form—a perhaps marvelously polished aesthetic worthiness—is more important than the ever new and never objectifiable value of the divine event. The awareness of present glory has given to the great ecclesial tradition the inspiration for works of incomparable worldly beauty; but these works become usable for present-day liturgy only if, through the beauty, those taking part in the celebration are not only aroused to sensations of an aesthetic nature but also come to encounter that glory of God to which the creators of such works wished to lead them.

To the realm of these works belongs not only the Gregorian chant, the world surrounding Palestrina, a great portion of the older German church hymnody (including that of the Protestants); but also the high masses by Bach, Haydn's masses, Mozart's litanies, and—what is a highpoint in the musical expression of the faith—the unfinished *Credo* of Schubert's Mass in C-Minor and the *Kyrie* of his Mass in E-flat Major. If all these and similar works should really be prayed by the singers, they would, to human beings who possess a sensorium not only for the beautiful, but for the sacred, for the divinely glorious, be capable of mediating something of the true original inspiration. Whoever listens only for the beautiful, or is only gripped by the beauty, can have a fake religious experience—like the many people who listen to the St. Matthew Passion on Good Friday; but they remain caught in a deception with respect to the true meaning of what they have heard.

Whether beautiful liturgy (which, in order to be beautiful, certainly does not need Latin, which is unintelligible for most people) is only beautiful for certain generations, while successive generations can no longer perceive its beauty, can remain an open question. Even the beautiful must die, and embalmings do not become it. But in no case should it be replaced by something ugly or vulgar, trivial or without content, but rather and at best by something simple which does not need to make way for something grander in dignity that is unintelligible to the world. "Blessed are the poor in spirit," if they only admit their poverty and do not seek to clothe it over for their own sakes. If a people were to be incapable of creating genuine religious images or statues for the churches, it should not say that empty walls concentrate the spirit more effectively upon what is essential. If we have become small people, we should not seek to reduce the mystery we celebrate to our dimensions.

Each person, by reason of one's own seriousness and readiness for prayer, is co-responsible for achieving a worthy liturgy. The texts of the first Christian centuries witness unequivocally to this. The unique quality of a Christian assembly in its celebration of the Eucharist is a guarantee for the fact that it is possible "to give thanks in truth worthily and rightly" to the eternal Father for having demonstrated by the giving of his Son to the world and to each person in it, how much he "is love."

84 · Meditation (I): Differences between Eastern and Christian Meditation

Before speaking about the Eastern and Western methods of meditation, a prior observation is in order. It is a striking fact that nowhere in the Holy Scriptures of the Old and New Testaments is there even the least trace of technical advice about meditating. One can merely say that a space for contemplation—in a broad and indeterminate sense—is made free, perhaps in the enjoining of the "principal commandment": "Hear, O Israel, the Lord, our God, is one lord, and you shall love the Lord, your God, with your whole heart, with your whole soul and with all your strength . . ., and these words shall be engraved on your heart, and you should inculcate them to your children, and should speak of them when you sit in your house and when you travel on the paths, when you lie down and when you get up; you should tie something to help you remember on your hand and bear it as a sign upon your brow."

The intensity, but also the externality of this prescription is deepened somewhat in what the Psalms call "contemplating" and what a softly murmuring, repetitive recitation of a passage from the scripture bespeaks, something that continues on in the Jesus-prayer of the Byzantine *hesychasm* and in the stories of the Russian pilgrim. (The Byzantines are also familiar with prayer in accord with the rhythm of one's breathing, and this form of prayer is contained even in the *Spiritual Exercises* of Ignatius Loyola, nos. 258ff.)

Nowhere did Jesus perform meditative exercises with his disciples; he taught them a simple oral prayer. How he prayed in his solitary hours of prayer we do not know. Paul speaks in many passages of the "ceaseless prayer" (and from him Luke probably introduced the notion into his gospel: Lk 18:1). The directive has been given the most diverse interpretations. Biblical revelation of itself requires one to take time for the God who has proven himself so marvelous and incomprehensible in Jesus Christ: for the wonderment and gratitude that the sublimity of God comes down so low for the act of response that is so necessary in relation to this ever greater God of foolish love. Throughout the centuries, the directions have accumulated on how one should expose oneself to this love of God and respond to it. But none of these directions has even been fixed as the obligatory method for each individual.

* * *

In the East there stands out most clearly and most representively for contemporary men and women what was once the common fund of all peoples: the religious as the characteristic of the human. It has a point of departure, a route, and a goal. If this religious element remains referred to its own sources of support, it thus has a tendency in its quest for the absolute to confer an absolute character on the circumstances of this quest.

1. The *point of departure* is the basic religious experience that the world of appearance surrounding us and of which our empirical "I," our character, and our everyday business are a part cannot possibly be the ultimate, absolute reality. The primordial religious experience is that of a cleavage between the primordial ground and ourselves, of a dissociation of that which is fundamentally one, of an alienation (according to Plato and Plotinus we dwell in a *regio dissimilitudinis*, a domain of dissimilarity). Alienation also means lack of freedom, being confined. Were one to posit this overarching experience absolutely, then the world of appearance becomes a mere illusion (*maya*),

the confinement a misfortune, and the eternity of sheer becoming a detour without a way out (*samsara*).

2. Hence the outbreak of religious desire, of the restless heart, wherever possible in the footsteps of a wise person who has found a way into the clear and can mediate it to others. There is a *methodos*, a pursuit (*meta*) along a path (*hodos*), which is a "path of clear direction" (*dhamma-pada*). The path is—absolutized in its own terms—radical: it leads from the outward to the inward, out of the din of multiplicity into the silence of the one; it digs out the rubbish that has filled it so the primordial spring flows once again. Persons who take the initiative for this have to train themselves, especially by abstinence (*askēsis* means simply training).

3. The goal can be only the being touched by, the encounter with, the entry into, the sphere of the absolute, the origin, the not alien, the home; it can only be the elimination of division. As absolutized in Shankara's Vedantism of the *advaitya:* the goal of undividedness, or in another (naturally constantly somehow probing) formula, of the congruence of what is most inward in a human being (whether it be characterized as *Atman* or *Purusha* or whatever) with what is the ultimately encompassing reality (*Brahman*).

The absolute can carry personal characteristics into the foreground—in this foreground still-individual persons can pray to an individual divine person, and entrust themselves to it, etc. But since "religion" as outbreak from the side of the human conceives of person with the properties of human limitations as well, these personal traits and modes of conduct fade away at the final stages of a depersonalized experience. Consequently, in this context one can only speak of a guilt (which somehow stands at the root of the alienation and gets overcome along with it in a step-by-step fashion), but never about sin in relation to a God who is ultimately personal.

* * *

Biblical revelation is not a variation on religion as a foundation of anthropology as has just been depicted, but rather it is an answer to it *from above*. Everything starts with the free initiative of God, and everything (even the world and I) have been established by it. Hence guilt appears in its true guise as sin; but then, too, the self-disclosure of God appears as free grace.

1. The God of Abraham, Moses, and Christ is the free creator of the world, which has been affirmed by him—no matter how it might appear to us—as very good. Its otherness from God is thus not alienation or impropriety, at least not at the outset. Behind the specificity of the creature, as well as of the I, stands a will, who affirms the creature, this I and You, and confirms it in its specific character. For God, this creature, this I and You, is valuable and worthy of love just

as it is. This means two things for the creature. First, that in its condition as creature it has to be grateful to this eternal will whose motive for creation can ultimately be love alone.

For the sake of clarification, let us insert here a meditation of Fénelon, for which, since Augustine, there have been numerous parallels in the Christian tradition:

> There was nothing in me that preceded all his gifts and could serve as a container to receive them. The first of his gifts, which lies at the basis of all the rest, is that which I call my own I; God gave me this I, so I owe him not merely all that I have, but all that I am. O unheard-of gift, which is quickly expressed in our weak language but which the human mind never comprehends in its entire depth! . . . Without God I would not exist; neither would I have the I which I could love, nor the love with which I love this I, nor the will which loves it, nor the thought by which I know myself. All is gift, and the one who receives the gifts is itself the first gift attained.

But then it is true that the I knows itself as affirmed and loved by an eternal I, and has to affirm itself ultimately as that to which God says You, in an absolutely personal relationship, which is not exchangeable with any relationship I may have with another human being. The ever-unique God calls me by my unique name that does not exist twice. But that means that the biblical God is a creator in order to reveal himself; creation is the foundation for his self-communication. And the quest for God (transcendence) on the part of human beings is the presupposition built into creation, so that God can come to humankind, and be understood and accepted. If this is the way it is, then the true outbreak of human beings towards God is not a denial or stripping away of their finitude, but a making themselves free and ready to be gripped entirely by God and taken into his possession.

This entails of course an active doing (in this respect comparable with religious "method"), but a doing of the sort that has to become ever more deeply aware inwardly of the freedom of the approaching God who belongs to his very essence. Hence it pertains ineluctably to the biblical-Christian method, a person becomes used within it to experiencing that the coming of God cannot be coerced or created by any exercise or form of readiness. Consequently, the Christian path to God must include the experience of *desolatio*, of the nonexperiencing of God's coming. The degree of inward purity and readiness can be the same at two different times: one time I can share in God's turning towards me and nearness; another time, not at all. In the parables of Jesus one has simply to watch, without knowing when the Lord or the bridegroom is coming.

2. Since God as the free creator and revealer is personal, guilt,

which now appears as sin (over against his absolute love), plays a completely different role. Alienation is no mere matter of nonidentity, but the turning away from absolute love—by egoism, by making an idol of a creature, by not following out a divine command, etc. This turning away is a loss of the divine love, which is not available to me as a possibility of my own, so that as I can just turn back toward God. To be sure, the prodigal son breaks away to return to the father, but only because there resides in him like a foreign treasure the unloseable knowledge of the fatherliness of the father. Conversion is not a technique, but rather an act which as a whole is due to the all-embracing initiative of the divine love—and it also realizes this need to give thanks.

3. Grace is God's turning himself towards us, not just to display himself as in a drama, but to grant a share in himself. From the Christian point of view this act of sharing proceeds within the sphere of the divine to the point of a rebirth out of the womb of the fatherly Godhead and a filiation to God the Father which far exceeds mere creatureliness—and yet which does not swallow it up. Otherwise I would no longer be myself. On the irremoveable foundation of the ever greater dissimilarity there is raised up a similarity that evokes an exchange. No objectification of God is possible; he is ever the You of our I and We, a limitless "Over-You" which as the ever greater One above us demands eternal worship. Worship is not a becoming identical: this is clear to us from the perspectives on eternal blessedness, secret revelation at the close of the Bible. But in the midst of the worship there is talk about the "marriage of the Lamb," of a wedding between heaven and earth, of God and creature which signifies the complete arrival of God into the world. In the closing symbols all the waters of salvation flow from his throne, all the fruits of immortality grow on these waters; God is the unique light, the uniquely holy One; his face is completely unveiled; his name stands upon the foreheads of those who have entered into salvation—images intended to bring home to us that the constant worship at a distance guarantees the mystery of union all the more profoundly and perfectly.

85 · Meditation (II):
Attempt at an Integration
of Eastern and Western Meditation

According to the Asiatic image of human being, the created person would be endowed with a basic tendency to break out towards the absolute ("to seek God, and, it might be, touch and find him": Acts 17:26f), so that when God, for his part, breaks out toward humankind in order to give it his grace, he should not find people indifferent, unreceptive. In revelational religion, natural religion is thus presupposed as a basis and raised along with human beings. Human spontaneity toward God has a part to play. It is only that it can no longer be actuated according to its own plans, but receives its norm from the grace that freely approaches it, and so it is protected from any self-absolutizing and from self-aggrandizing methods. This impoverishment of the human being's methodical capability and knowledge, of any self-developed acrobatics of the spirit, is an enrichment in the sense of the gospel's "Blessed are the poor in spirit." Can one who has actually mastered the eight levels of Yoga really be called poor in spirit, even when this involved one ever so much in becoming inwardly open? Christian training cannot be anything other than placing oneself ever more completely at the disposal of God and his gracious will. Thus, in what follows, it will be evident that an (apparent) commonality of Eastern and Western ways of meditating does indeed exist: the ways, methods, and practices look enough alike to be mistaken for each other, and can even be in material agreement (the religious element is not abolished in the religion of revelation, but fulfilled). But the more the particularly Christian element moves into the foreground, the more the particular component of human participation is displayed; and this particularity—as one only now fully recognizes—is effective all the way back to the initial, apparently common steps.

1. A common element is surely the initiation of the training for the sake of the essential freedom for the absolute: purification of external and internal dependencies; the severing of the bonds of passion which fasten us to external things; the gaining of distance from the fascination of worldly things; mastery of the tongue, but also of the imagination, of our wandering thoughts; the giving up of centeredness upon one's own interests; the gathering together of the soul's powers into one's inward heart (*redire ad cor:* Augustine) where stillness reigns, the first step towards truly spiritual watching and listening. The book of the *Exercises* also requires such a progressive departure from oneself in order to make oneself ready to touch God and participate in his grace. But right here we can also immediately show a twofold difference:

a. For the Eastern practitioner of meditation (as well as many Christian monks influenced by them, like Evagrius Ponticus) the practice of love of neighbor (*prakitikē*)—as a training in selflessness—as a part of this prior purification is *a means to the end* of a higher vision, whereas in an authentically Christian way it can never be demoted to a mere preparatory stage.

b. The Eastern practitioner of meditation will be concerned from the outset to reach a simplicity of inner constitution by means of abstraction from all thoughts and ideas of objects, etc., whereas Christian meditators must apprehend the gracious word of God for which they prepare themselves never *only* as an inner reality, but always also as one that has become incarnate and encounters one in history. Hence, over against the first, the Christian seems to be at a disadvantage; but only if one does not understand Christian contemplation the way it is seen by God, as a training by means of external life, example, and the sacramental efficacy of Christ into the inward knowledge and faith-experience of that which God is: for us and in himself. The apparently purely objective nature of a contemplation of the life of Jesus, if it is going to be meaningful in a Christian way, has to lead from the outset beyond this positing of objects, since it is meant to make clear how the absolute, how God *is*, for whose coming into our entire (and thus especially into our truest) being we are preparing ourselves. According to the *Exercises* we should also, through the movement of an outward scene, become more sensible to "the infinite fragrance and the infinite sweetness of divinity," that is made known within it. (It is known that even for the Buddhists, *nirvana* is "pervasively fragrant.") For the Christian abstraction from the outward turmoil, the gathering inward, is only a means toward the ordering of the *whole* person, never a goal; for just as the God of the Bible wills to come as incarnate, and not just in his most inward self, into the *whole* human being, so too the person's preparatory, purifying ingathering ought to have an effect upon one's entire bodily and everyday existence.

2. In the Christian mode purification is above all conversion to love. This is not solely or even preferably attained by the practice of method but rather by the acceptance and handing on of forgiveness received from God. Its reception does not require the state of a reflection-free absorption, but rather that of a recollected awareness which awakens true repentance, which can also restore order to the disorder between me and my neighbor. Reconciliation with the estranged brother, according to the Sermon on the Mount, is a presupposition for being capable of bringing the (self-) sacrifice of the person into the (inner) temple. To be sure, the Buddhist, too, knows a lot about the ethical stance of selflessness demanded of one who lives a life of contemplation. Only it remains conditioned by a theoretical knowledge that I and You (just as I and the absolute) are not ultimate objects, so that this ethical selflessness remains only an aspect of the metaphysical selflessness of the meditator. It should not be denied here that there are real "passive purifications" of the soul (as John of the Cross depicts them), but certainly never without being preceded by active purification in the ordinary state of awareness, and not as a way for people to follow methodically.

3. The gathering of one's powers towards a simple ground of the

soul can generate in East and West a similar awareness of having surmounted the dichotomy of subject-object. But this experience can still be nothing more than a stage preparatory to the real openness for the absolute, for God. It can be a reflexive intuition of the subject, or the intuition of the conditions of the possibility of objective intuition, or the intuition of a cosmically expanded consciousness, or the intuition of one's being made in God's image or of one's open yearning for the absolute. Here one would need to query Rhineland mysticism as to what it ultimately intends by its ideal of the sheer being of the soul: is it a deobjectification in the sense of Eastern meditation (which from a Christian standpoint does not present a supreme value), or is it a clearing away of all human resistances towards God, a complete, humble transparency (only this is of supreme value to the Christian)? For such a person the emptying that overwhelms the total existence of the Christian, the practice of a deobjectifying meditation, can contribute as a means, but it is neither to be confused with nor equated with it. There are indeed paths that God can take with people or which persons can take in their relationship to God, which take different routes to the same goal. The most perfect human Yes—"Behold, I am the handmaid of the Lord, let it be to me according to your word"—in all probability, since the speaker was a Jewish woman, did not come to maturity by way of deobjectifying meditation.

Let us say in conclusion then that the ambiguity of the word "selflessness"—in its Eastern and Western-Christian emphasis—promotes a commonality of the first steps, and indeed it does so both in its ethical and in its psychological understanding. Just as the Buddhist has to dissolve the illusion of his I as a substantial center in order to catch sight of the absolute, so, too, does the Christian have to dissolve the geocentricity of his self-awareness, in which everything revolves about his psychological ego in favor of a heliocentric, i.e., theocentric worldview, in which the created and graced I is both received purely from the central sun of divine grace and allows itself to be determined by it. So much is this divine center the absolute that the word "objective" in the worldly sense is not applicable to it. It is, according to Augustine, at once "more inward than I am to myself and more sublimely superior to me," and for this reason coming to me from within as well as from above-without. But in this coming the finite I is posited, affirmed, loved; and indeed not only my I, but that of all persons who in their essential uniqueness and irreplaceability are a radiation of the one God, and indeed become that more the closer they all come to God. Here the particularity of Christian in contrast to Eastern meditation becomes completely evident.

* * *

Generally speaking the degree to which the Christian practice of meditation exceeds the Eastern becomes clear from the fact that the historical self-disclosure of God in the history of salvation that reaches its peak with Christ can never, in the divine encounter with humans, be relativized, superceded, and placed in brackets. Here God wanted to lay bare his inmost heart, since he loved the world so much that he gave up his only begotten Son for it. Into this salvation history Christians are objectively invited and integrated, whether they are aware of this—for example, in a state of absorption—or not. For this history they are needed. Let's consider three aspects, which all inherently belong together, of the way the Christian practice exceeds the Eastern.

1. The creaturely, free I as posited by God is something definitively treasured, willed, and loved by him; it is for God a You. This free You is solid enough on the basis of its creation to receive God, since he wills *to become human* in his Son. The image and likeness of God that is the human being becomes in the Son completely transparent towards its archetype: "Whoever sees me, sees the Father." Hence, as already mentioned, true Christian contemplation is not just categorical, but transcendental, or better—since these categories are not adequately applicable here—sacramental. In Jesus the good shepherd one sees God the good shepherd: Jesus is the authentic and unsurpassable interpretation of God. In the apparently finite medium of his deeds, sufferings, and attitudes the ever-greater of the infinite God is made known. One notes here the role of negative theology within the Christian domain. It does not have the job of negating any proposition about God, because any concept is always determined in its contents, while the absolute, on the other hand, can only be the complete emptiness of all determinacy; it has rather the job of indicating the fullness of being disclosed and hidden in the finite sacrament. For that fullness escapes every idea and is ever-greater than what, even in virtue of removing ever more restrictions upon myself, I am capable of grasping. A necessary reflection of this Christian negativity is already present in the Christian I-You relationship between persons: in genuine love the You is loved for its own sake, and, in its freedom, this self is always something that is beyond the forms of its appearance as well as of any concept I might have of it.

Furthermore, the Son-become-man is the one who in the most absolute manner constantly receives his self from the Father and is indebted to the Father. As a result, the Son will eternally say, "The Father is greater than I." It does not occur to him, therefore, to want to identify himself with the Father, because he is prefigured in the

Father as in his source in such a way that in him he could apprehend his exemplary identity. In the Son's becoming human there is portrayed not merely the exemplary attitude of the creature towards God, but a paradigmatic attitude in God himself: to be received and to be indebted is itself divine and hence definitive.

2. Just like the Buddhist, the Christian bears in mind the horrible burden of suffering in the world, behind which stands the burden of guilt. But for the Christian, this burden cannot be eliminated by means of meditation (as exoneration); not even by means of the famous compassion of the one who has become Buddha and who renounces his entry into *nirvana* as long as any being in the world is suffering. The event of Golgotha is something completely different. It is a vicarious bearing of the world's guilt, solidarity in the state of God-forsakenness, but out of love for those who have turned from God, and thus their atonement. (We cannot and need not elucidate here the entire depths of the theology of the cross.) One thing becomes evident in this: for Christians there is no path to God—be this way mystical or of any other sort—which would not bear the imprint of the event of the cross. One hears practically nothing about this in the countless Christian books about Zen meditation. Paul, who was taken away to the third heaven, bears on himself the marks of Christ's suffering. The dark nights of the mystics, where they are Christian and genuine, are by no means just anthropological purifications of the depths of the soul in order to have a better share of the divine light, but a sharing in the passion of Christ. Paul "makes up what is still lacking in the suffering of Christ." He does not live from this world for the sake of a superworldly God, but he lives in God's initiative for the world—and this initiative is called the cross. He lets himself be placed by God together with Christ in the last place for sinners, for the church and, if God would will it, "be cursed by Christ" for the sake of his brothers and sisters. The highpoint of Jesus' existence on earth is not the light of Mt. Tabor, but the great darkness on the cross and his cry of abandonment. (Here the little Thérèse actually realized something more than even John of the Cross.)

3. In conclusion, for Christians the highest value is not the experience of transcendence but persevering through the grayness of everyday in faith, hope, and love. We stated it at the outset: the counterpart of the oriental Yogi or Zen master (who has attained the peak of human capability) is not the Christian mystic, but the Christian saint, whether mystic or not. This saint is acquainted with asceticism as training in a continual being in the presence of God: "Speak, Lord, for your servant is listening." Like the Eastern practitioners of meditation, Christians too have to collect themselves from worldly fragmentation and alienation, to excavate themselves from the

worldly rubble. What they then receive, conveyed to them in their recollection, is their *mission*, which for them is what God has provided: their mission is exactly congruent with their intelligible I. Mission, however, releases me from God to world and neighbor (perhaps to a determinate action, perhaps to a co-suffering of the Son's suffering on the cross. For what one calls the contemplative order has its special home here).

Mission, especially qualitative, great mission, is decided eye-to-eye with God; in solitude, therefore, sometimes in being enraptured (as for instance is shown in the callings of an Isaiah or a Jeremiah). And if the mission is to be successful, it requires in this solitary encounter the greatest possible selflessness, indifferent readiness to everything God wills. In this total disponibility lies the true Christian analogue to the Eastern elimination-of-self by meditation. And the indifference must also persevere throughout the entire mission of everyday and continue to be effective through all the intellectual capacity of the one sent: memory, understanding, and will are given back to God, delivered over as the Ignatian prayer of self-giving puts it—so that God alone disposes of them.

But God always disposes for the good of his world—that is why Christianity is the only religion really oriented toward the world—and in this initiative of God with the world lies also the self-demonstration of his glory.

86 · Experience and Faith

If God were not incomprehensible, then he would not be God but an ideological superstructure of the human spirit. If everyone could have an immediate insight into the divine sonship of Jesus of Nazareth, prove it, explain it to others the way one demonstrates any historical fact, then he surely would not be the appearance in the world of the essentially incomprehensible God, but just another link in the chain of historical events. At least this is the view of Jesus himself when he says, "No one knows the Son except the Father, and no one knows the Father except the Son and he to whom the Son wills to reveal it" (Mt 11:27). Shortly before, Jesus says too who will share this revelation: not the wise and the clever people (for these it stays concealed), but to the simple, or literally, those not yet of age. What holds true of God and of his revealer in the world, necessarily has to hold true of that structure which Paul calls "the plenitude," the "body," the "bride" of Christ, which John addresses as *kyria* (since it clearly shares in the hidden lordship of Jesus). Who and what this church as the presence of Jesus (and of God in Jesus) in the midst of world history really is, can be construed just as little on the basis of its external form, its official, cultic, and sociological visibility as can the divine quality of Jesus on the basis of his human body.

People who demand a logically incontrovertible proof for the church's claim of being the presence of God in Jesus Christ—whether they do it now for the sake of assuring themselves of more easily refuting that claim—will in all probability approach Jesus with the same demand ("If he is the king of Israel, let him now get down from the cross, and we will believe him"); and they will finally even make their faith in God as well dependent upon his being able ultimately to prove his existence swiftly and clearly. If such desires of wanting to be assured by some sign and miracle or by means of learnable techniques of religious experiences of God have been expressed by people of every time, they are obviously even more prevalent among modern people who will accept as true only what they get demonstrated with $a + b$ or what they can experience with their own senses. That this is practically equivalent to a naive, perhaps totally innocent atheism is something of which these modern persons are not even aware, because they hold the physical demonstrability of all truth in their blood like a dogma. That today inside the church as well the demand for "experienceability" (precisely of the church in its character as the presence of Christ) is raised with an unprecedented stubbornness, and that the existence or nonexistence of a genuine church gets measured according to the success or failure of such experiences—these are an unconscious submission to the *Zeitgeist* (climate of opinion, spirit of the times), whether one wants to prove for oneself or others that one is right in seeking access to Christ and to God in the church.

But whether one strives for the experience of the divine as a means of inner psychic assurance, or whether one uses precisely this experienceability to reduce religious experience to a sheerly psychological matter and so to subject it to a profane science, one thing is certain: if one is really supposed to be dealing with the relation of human beings to God their creator and the origin of every being in the world, then there can be no talk about a direct experience. *Si comprehendis, non est Deus:* "if you think you have comprehended, then it is certainly not God." Whenever the relationship of the finite and infinite, of the relative and the absolute, of the worldly and the divine, has been thought through in a way that is at all pure and consequent, one will constantly come across a dialectical formula, an approximation to a knowledge of the divine by way of a negation and cancelling of immediate experience: in place of a grasping, a letting-go of any desire to grasp for the sake of letting oneself be grasped; in place of a hand which closes and grasps, an opening to become gripped (which, however, does not imply any psychological possession). With each step of thought by which one intends to approach the absolute, there is the mounting certainty that this means derailing every logical operation. This on the basis of the simple conviction that human beings and God are never capable of confronting one another as separate entities, because God is "everything" (Sir 43:27), and human beings, who are "something" at best, can never exalt themselves before the All. In order to enter into relationship with it, human beings have to let the All be in them that which it is: not something, but everything. Religious-philosophical reflection can reach this point, only to be then struck dumb before the obvious paradox: how then can something like the world or the human being get room to exist at all next to or beneath or within the All of God: whether perhaps it (the world and the human) is indeed not something, but nothing (because God is All) or whether perhaps God is after all not All but is in need of the world in order to become All (because humankind is something).

87 · Action and Contemplation

When human beings receive in faith the joyous good news, they find themselves in a strange predicament. On the one hand they learn that God's greater love has overcome the world (Jn 16:33), and that even the last enemy, death, has had its sting withdrawn (1 Cor 15:55). This involvement of God precedes everything that a human being can be or do or answer. Under this involvement everything is set just right, including the person on the receiving end. They can thus do nothing better than to surrender themselves in childlike trust to this source in whom all truth reposes. They determine once and for all to know no other "except Jesus Christ and him crucified" and abandoned by God (1 Cor 2:2), lest the cross of Christ, the source of all power, "should be emptied of its power" (1 Cor 1:17). Were they to resort to relying on their own efforts and to turn away from the pure unmerited gifts which flow from this source, then "the scandal of the Cross would be no more" (Gal 5:11).

On the other hand, however, this source does not allow us to rest in it as an established fact or to regard it as an abstract truth or a beautiful picture to be satisfied with only a word of thanks. For the source is not a brute fact, nor a truth nor a picture but God himself in his eternal involvement for my sake and for the sake of the whole world. I myself cannot, in the face of this, stand by as a mere spectator. I am involved, only in so far as I involve myself. To put this less concisely, in the process of God's involving himself for my sake, I am already affected by his involvement. But it is not just the result of

God's efforts that benefits me; through becoming involved, I have inevitably entered into partnership with that eternal love which is manifested as such in all the tremendous work that love does in the world. Hence, what we call the gift to the world of the free, unmerited grace of God is in fact his involvement on behalf of the world, in which, however, the world itself is already and eternally involved.

In a strange way, this displaces the dualism between prayer and works, between contemplation and action. One usually imagines that for a Christian (as for every somewhat religious person) action flows from contemplation in such a way that contemplation can and should continue throughout the action and fertilize it. This is not false to the extent that in Christianity (as in every religion) God as the absolute enjoys the primacy that is due to him; that we must therefore, first of all, turn to him in order that we may know him and be able to proclaim him to others, that all our actions in the world should form an echo and correspond to this initial experience of God. God's grace is in any case prior to our active engagement: for God in the world and for the world for his sake.

But this first rule, to which there is no exception, takes on an essential modification in Christianity by the fact that the source of grace at which I as an individual must first drink is nothing less than the absolute involvement, the absolute action of God for the world. Were I not involved in this saving action of his, I would never learn that God is love, triune love. For I can never prescind from God's dramatic action in the incarnation, cross, and resurrection of Christ, in the attempt to contemplate "behind all this," a self-sufficient God, an everlastingly happy primordial "essence" of God. What we are looking at when we contemplate the love of God is "Christ, giving himself in love" and this impels us, because we are convinced that "one has died for all, therefore all have died" (2 Cor 5:14). In contemplating this, we suddenly realize that we have been made to take our part in the action as a whole and that we are therefore participants in this action. God's practice "compels us" into practice: For since he has laid down his life for us, we too ought to lay down our lives for the brothers and sisters (1 Jn 3:16). By means of contemplation, we are drawn deeper into the living source and also as it were forced from the source into our own channels of activity. If, however, we go about our practice in the right way, we shall also be penetrating ever more deeply into the source. For the freedom we want to find is in the last resort already given to us in the source.

We can neither simplify nor go beyond this argument, and must instead warn urgently against any over-simplification. Under no circumstances may we turn our back on the source of God's grace, as if it were something with which we had long since become overly familiar, like an object of knowledge or some valuable object which has come into our possession and which can now be put to use in the world or changed into ready money. The source is the mouth of God from which we must never take away our mouths. The source is the ever-present event through which we get into our own flowing truth and are enabled to abide in it. The basic johannine word "stay, abide" expresses this. "They went with him," the fourth gospel says, "and saw where he was staying and stayed with him that day" (Jn 1:39).

On the other hand, "They went out from us, but they were not of us, for if they had been of us, they would have stayed with us" (1 Jn 2:19). "To stay" means to persevere in receiving one's true self from the grace and involvement of God, in overwhelmed thankfulness, in adoration before the wonder of unconditional love. This is what St. Paul has in mind when he talks of "praying without ceasing" (1 Th 1:2; 2:13; 2 Th 1:3, 11; 2:13; 5:17; Rom 1:10; 1 Cor 1:4; Eph 5:20; Phil 1:4; Col. 1:3; Phlm 4; cf. Lk 18:1); and Origen provides a delightfully human explanation of how such prayer is in fact possible: To pray without ceasing, (he writes [*On Prayer* 12:2]) is to join one's prayer with one's daily work and to unite suitable actions to one's prayer; for even good works or the fulfilling of God's commandments are to be included as a part of prayer. We can only accept the command to "pray without ceasing" as practicable if we conceive of the whole life of the believer as one great unbroken prayer. A part of this great prayer is what we are accustomed to call prayer. The source is rich enough to fructify all our activity in this world *if* we keep it alive in us and never stray from it. It alone is true fruitfulness; and our fruitfulness will be all the greater as we internally form ourselves to it and let it, as origin of life, flow into our own origin and let its authentic action become the principle of all our action. The more we stand open to it like an immature child, in a receiving mode, the more will we be able to open ourselves to the world as mature adults in a giving mode.

Spiritual Stances and Ways of Carrying Out One's Life

88 · The Evangelical Counsels

In the midst of the radical exodus that for human beings takes on the guise of an unreal and unfulfillable demand, because it places them in pure emptiness, the command resounds: let go of everything to possess a blind trust, a naive lack of anxiety. "Care not, fear not," is the constantly recurring admonition of the Lord. Everything depends on a correct ordering of one's acts: not to seek first an earthly security in order then to let go and dedicate oneself, but a relinquishing of every earthly care and security, of any regard for what is possible or impossible, in pure dependence upon the obedience of the "Follow me," in the loss of all ground under one's feet while being put in that place where one will be able to live further only on the basis of faith. After the demand has sounded of not wanting to serve two masters, God and mammon, there come those urgent warnings and promises which try to touch the inmost heart of the person and turn it around: "Therefore I tell you, do not be anxious about your life, what you shall put on. For the Gentiles seek all these things; and your heavenly Father knows that you need them all. But seek first his kingdom and his righteousness, and all these things shall be yours as well. Therefore do not be anxious about tomorrow, for tomorrow will be anxious for itself" (Mt 6:25, 32–34): "Do not lay up for yourselves treasures on earth" (Mt 6:19), "for it is not in the abundance of possessions that one's life consists" (Lk 12:15). Without anxiety the believers should, in giving up all earthly things, receive the kingdom from the hands of the Father: "Fear not, little flock, for it is your Father's good pleasure to give you the kingdom. Sell your possessions and give alms" (Lk 12:32f).

The exhortation not to be anxious and not to fear would not be enough to make people take such a crazy step. Faith has to be blindly trusting. But to the generosity of this giving the Lord owes a response which surpasses by a hundredfold any human generosity. He has to erect a foundation in the midst of the pure outside of faithful discipleship on the basis of which the one following can stand as a human being as well. As long as Jesus prays, "Not that you should take them out of the world, but that you should keep them from the evil one" (Jn 17:15), he has to grant his own a state of life within the created world.

He must first literally fashion this state of life, found it as a guaranteed sociological possibility—as a possibility of course within a supernatural sociology, which will always get repeatedly called into question by every natural sociology—but for the faithful themselves a simple, indeed a hundred times tested and proven possibility of really being able to stand in the place to which they have been ordered. So the Lord decrees the great promise which has to hold good as the foundational proclamation of the new state of life:

> "And every one who has left houses or brothers or sisters or father or mother or children or lands, for my name's sake, will receive a hundredfold, and inherit eternal life." (Mt 19:29)

> "Truly, I say to you there is no one who has left house or brothers or sisters or mother or father or children or lands, for my sake and for the gospel, who will not receive a hundredfold now in this time, houses and brothers and sisters and mothers and children and lands, with persecutions, and in the age to come eternal life." (Mk 10:29–30)

> "Truly, I say to you, there is no one who has left house or wife or brothers or parents or children, for the sake of the kingdom of God, who will not receive manifold more in this time, and in the age to come eternal life." (Lk 18:29–30)

The simple law, as Matthew expresses it, gets specified more closely in different ways by Mark and Luke. On the one hand Mark paints in the hundredfold reward in this world in each instance: in place of house, houses; in place of mother, mothers. On the other hand, he places this hundredfold earthly reward corresponding to the rest of the Lord's prophecies in the framework of persecutions. Thus, in the midst of the insecurity of having left everything, which leads to hatred of the world and culminates in persecutions, there is enough room for a hundredfold reward already in this world. Luke adds as new and significant the leaving not only of sisters, of parents and children, but expressly the spouse too. This renunciation was of course already included in the leaving of house and lands and children, but by the explicit formulation he completes the picture which otherwise would have furnished an opportunity for insecurity and question at an important passage.

The solemnity of these texts reduces all doubt to silence. Just as the leaving is demanded and put before us, so also the promise is to be taken literally. It will not only be barely possible to exist in the new life-space, but this, from a worldly point of view, impossible state of life will have in the breadth of its staying power the hundredfold of the worldly state of life. It will be a standing "in the midst of persecutions"; a standing, then, which day by day will recall the radicality of the exodus from the world, and which will appear to the world more and more as a hanging in midair; a standing that is not allowed ever to get transformed into a secretly (but that's what the hundredfold is for) secured existence. In this way, after the exodus from Egypt, the people in the desert depended exclusively upon God's leadership, on the nourishment they received from heaven and on the drink they received from the rock. Or in the New Testament scene, at the moment the disciples no longer advanced in faith over the waves of this world, but rather, reflecting upon themselves, began to lose sight of the Lord, they would start to sink. Evangelical poverty is only possible on the basis of evangelical faith. If it changes unnoticed or even noticed into a mere moral virtue, into something that has to be cleverly adapted to worldly relationships, then it has lost its Christian brilliance and the guarantee of grace. Everything depends on the truth of total leaving. Only if this happens "for my name's sake," "for the sake of the gospel," "for the sake of the kingdom," does it have a claim to the reward promised. And this "for the sake of" is not only indivisible in the moment of the initial leaving, but remains so during the whole time of following Christ. The exodus from the world is final; even when it appears to the believer to be a desert journey, there is no return to the "flesh pots of Egypt." The receiving of the hundredfold reward is no turning back from the election into the exodus-state of life, but it is assured in the extent to which the discipleship perseveres in poverty, chastity, and obediences.

For in fact it is really a matter of the unity of these three. *Poverty* always gets put at the beginning with a certain breadth and urgency. Selling one's entire possession and dividing up one's savings as alms is such a striking demand not to be argued away by any subtlety, that it is set forth as the visible embodiment of leaving everything. It would not have made sense to want an approach to evangelical obedience to be fashioned without stepping through this entry gate. This is also why the promise is so clearly coupled with this act, as if the whole edifice of the state of life to be newly established were determined by poverty, as though virginity and obedience were only conclusions or forms of a more profound understanding of this first renunciation.

Virginity appears on the one hand (in Luke) as included in the law of poverty, since the leaving of the spouse was inserted in the middle of the leaving of the rest of the relatives and earthly goods. It appears on the other hand (in Matthew) to be in an exact parallel with poverty, in that the opening by the Lord of the possibility of poverty and virginity follows both times as a response to the disciples' perplexed astonishment. In the case of poverty, it is the disturbed question after the departure of the wealthy young man, "Then who can be saved?" (Lk 18:26), which serves as the introduction to the great promise. In the case of virginity it is the no less disturbed insight of the disciples: "If such is the case of a man with his wife, it is not expedient to marry" (Mt 19:10). Both times the person is led by the inexorableness of the Christian demand as if up against a stone wall with apparently no way of going farther, until the miracle of the establishment of the new state of life occurs, which opens a place right where none seemed possible.

That poverty gets put so unequivocally in first place and virginity at first takes a backseat in the promise, is based on the fact that the Lord calls his disciples out of the Israel of the Old Testament, in which the married state was a state of promise. He who came to fulfill the law and not to abolish it (Mt 5:17) did not want to build his church upon men who had not lived in the true messianic tradition. Hence, the unmarried state could at first only be the exception, an exception of course that was, right from the beginning—in the Baptist, then in John and Paul—so strongly highlighted that in these figures it could already become a rule for the succeeding generations born within the New Testament era. For out of the law of life of complete disponibility that the Lord sets up for the chosen disciples and that Paul lives out in purity as a kind of example for the eleven, it follows quite clearly that renunciation of one's spouse is no less required than that of house and land and bonds with relatives. Nonetheless, in the New Testament texts, virginity is characterized most clearly as a "counsel" (Mt 19:10–12: "He who is able to receive this, let him receive it"; 1 Cor 7:8, 25: "It is well for them to remain single as I do. . . . Now concerning the unmarried, I have no command of the Lord, but I give my opinion as one who by the Lord's mercy is trustworthy").

If poverty and virginity are the clearly indicated entry to the new state of life, then *obedience* is its midpoint. The detachment from all earthly goods and dependencies, in the way the Lord portrays it, is always only a means toward the end of complete discipleship, toward that outward as well as inward mobility which permits the disciple to follow the Master wherever he goes, even away from everything into the complete outside (Heb 13:11–13). Clearly, the two phases get separated: "If you would be perfect, go, sell what you possess and give to the poor . . . and come, follow me" (Mt 19:21). This following is going to be the content and the law of the life of the disciple. The obedience of the Son who has come not to be served but to serve, and to give his life as a ransom for many (Mk 10:45), gets portrayed as the example of a life of discipleship whose rank will henceforth be determined in accord with the perfection of his service (Mt 20:26–28).

Service to the Lord will be the exclusive content of the life of the disciples: they have to assume his thoughts; to let themselves be sent out by him with his assignments; to accept exact, almost minute directives concerning their food, clothing, equipment, meals on the way, conduct on the trip and in strange houses, wages and manual labor; they have to set out two by two and complete the assignment for the sake of which they have been sent (Mk 6:7–13; Mt 10:5–14; Lk 9:1–6), and upon returning they have to give an exact account of what they have done and left undone (Mk 6:30). They also have to execute particular orders: to set forth on a journey and cast forth the nets (Lk 5:3–4); or hold a boat ready for him (Mk 3:9); or, without any concern for the difficulties that might arise, to untie a young donkey and bring it to him (Mt 21:3, 6); or to prepare the paschal supper in accord with exact prescriptions (Lk 22:8–13).

89 · The Unmarried State as Eschatological Sign

One often speaks of Christian celibacy as an eschatological sign. That is beautiful and true, right up until the article "an." It is more: it is *the* sign, and hence it becomes indispensable. The new and eternal covenant, in comparison with the old, fully transvalues sexuality. In the Old Testament it was the sign of theological hope in the Messiah, as is clear, say, in the Book of Tobias. With Christ's birth from the virgin Mary, with his virginal life, with his death, his descent into hell, and his resurrection from the dead, theologically a new situation is created. Sexuality has reached an inner term; the further propagation of the race has taken on a certain theological unimportance which should not be outmanoeuvered and made unclear by an application of the idea of evolution to the history of the church. From this point of view it could seem as if the reduction in importance of the idea of propagation as the primary end of marriage and the preference of the reciprocal love of the married pair (even under express exclusion of propagation) has a justification in the New Testament: it would perhaps be a clearer symbol of the mutual love between Christ and his bridal church in the eucharistic giving over of his flesh and blood than celibacy. But such a theological inference overlooks the fact that the eucharistic love between Christ and the church quite essentially includes the *memoria passionis*, the complete and painful renunciation of the cross, in which alone God's love gets definitively revealed; and the image of which therefore has to be contained in all ecclesial love, which is supposed to be a symbolic or sacramental sign and copy of that love.

Mary's fruitfulness, the fruitfulness of the woman of the Apocalypse who throughout every age gives birth between heaven and earth to the Messiah and his members and brothers, is a fruitfulness in the suffering of the passion: the woman cries out in her birth pangs. This woman who afterwards (but what does this mean in temporal terms?) is taken into the desert is the exemplar of the church, its ontological pattern. And this is not established in any arbitrary fashion but is actually ontologically necessary, that this, its inmost reality, is also portrayed existentially through such things which the church must officially represent. Otherwise the ontological reality of the church will disappear behind a sociological form manipulated by human beings. Hence, that Protestant was right who admonished us that the regarding of marriage in the New Testament from the vantage of the encompassing form of virginity is an attempt to let sexual *eros* be taken up into the heaven-given *agape*—into *agape* as it was first lived exemplarily in the flesh by Christ. And if Christ is not to sink once again into an abstract principle without existential consequences, one has to regard it in Catholic fashion always in connection with human helpers, who together with him form his constellation and with whom his mission is indissolubly bound: with the certainly virginal precursor, John, with whom his destiny was so thought-provokingly coupled; with his mother, Mary, whose bodily and spiritual relationship to him can never be too closely or essentially apprehended; with the beloved disciple, who opened himself with a nearly wifelike dedication to his teachings and to his love; lastly, too, with Paul, the first, great, exemplary mission in the emergent church.

90 · Obedience in the State of Life of the Counsels

The total life of the counsels in the church corresponds to the wish, and still more to the vocation, of individual persons and groups in the church to understand the call of Jesus to discipleship more literally than is possible for most of their fellow Christians, to take seriously the identification of one's entire existence with the offer of Jesus to live in and out of his life. Life in accord with the counsels will thus by no means seek to establish a special church alongside the so-called "great church," but rather to seek to authenticate its nature as body of Christ.

The three evangelical counsels (whose historical articulation will not be dealt with here) are not three independent essences standing alongside one another, but rather the anthropologically necessary threefold unfolding of a stance of total disponibility for discipleship in the christological mission. As an ecclesial possibility this life is unfolded in the immediacy of each individual to the triune God, of the commonality of all members of Christ who serve and obey each other with their charisms, and of the subjection under an authority mediating this immediacy and commonality.

The counsel of obedience is apprehended on the basis of a particular, personal call to discipleship. Not everyone in the gospel is called to this narrower discipleship, as can be seen in the rejection of the request of the demoniac healed at Gerasa to be allowed to go along with the Lord and the disciples. This call is directed to the total existence of the one called "to leave everything," to put on, as Paul says, in a definitive and incarnational way the obediential form of Jesus. It is important that such a call always take place by name, in personal solitude, never in groups, even though for each person (even for the hermit) it is naturally a call into the ecclesial community. The giving of one's existence to Jesus and through him to the Father in the Spirit is unconditional, absolute, even though the choice of the means for living out this absoluteness, say of entering *this* order, is relative, which means precisely that it remains related to this absoluteness.

In this way the first aspect of the counsel of obedience becomes clear: the choice of a superior who is capable of training the one called through spiritual direction into absolute obedience to God. This superior is an expert of the spiritual journey and all its difficulties, a *pneumatikos*, about whom the first monks in the desert flocked, a *starets*. As soon, however, as the second essential dimension of obedience enters, the community (*koinōnia*) of mutual obedience in love, in which the one called has to be trained straightaway into a person of the church, the function of the pneumatic guide becomes simultaneously that of a director of the community who is chosen *by* the community not only because of the enlightened way of directing individuals, but just as much because of sagacity for the job of director in the community. Under certain circumstances, the functions in the order will be differentiated: here the master of novices and the so-called *pater spiritualis*, there the superior of the house, of the province, etc. Such a division of labor remains secondary and does not affect the counsel of obedience. Only note that no pneumatic person, even if called to found an order, can claim any ecclesial authority, something that has never been done by a founder approved by the church. (The *Regula Magistri* here constitutes a notable limit case.)

The first dimension of the counsel of obedience, a calling in one's personal immediacy to the obedience of Christ, can and should not overbalance the second, the maintenance of obedience in ecclesial mutuality, so that the exercise of *agape*—as is the case with Evagrius Ponticus—becomes a means to the end of a gnostic, solitary perfection of the individual. What Evagrius calls *praktikē* may never be diminished to a stage preparatory to (mystical) knowledge of God, since indeed in Paul's view, Christian *agape* is the goal and peak of all personal charisms. The cenobitic life is not a preparatory step for the eremetic life; the truly Catholic eremite, who has become complete in love of neighbor, goes even further in living in eminent fashion in and for the community of saints, as is clear from the Carmelite ideal. The opposite danger is prevalent in our day: that the community dimension of the counsel of obedience will outweigh the personal to the extent that the community democratically disposes of and votes on everything to be done and changed, whereby the fundamental christological and crucifying dimension often is either almost or completely lost. The chapter advises, but the abbot decides, after, of course, listening with utmost seriousness and most profound humility to the voice of all, even the youngest. Whenever the community as such appropriates the permanent, highest authority, the call of the individual gets frustrated and the field of the ecclesial life of the counsels is abandoned.

Just as little can the counsel of obedience ever outgrow the third dimension, ecclesial-hierarchial obedience: Francis of Assisi lay his rule at the feet of the Pope, Ignatius had the Pope be the highest superior of the Order. Juridical exemption means liberation from certain confining bonds (to the local bishop), in order to be thereby more immediately bound to the interests of the whole church; but today there is much discussion about whether or to what extent such liberation really serves these interests. Nevertheless the secular institutes are also set up in such a way that they should first receive episcopal approval, but the bishop cannot lay a hand upon them in order to take control of them for diocesan purposes.

No matter how many different shades of color the three-dimensional counsel of obedience can take on, it cannot forgo any of its dimensions if it wants to remain a way inside the Catholica. It can neither become onesidedly personal (religious life for the sake of personal fulfillment), nor onesidedly social or under the sway of group dynamics (as in certain Pentecostal groups), nor onesidedly functional for the hierarchy (as the Ignatian obedience gets portrayed in caricatures). If it must be reckoned as a whole in the realm of the charisms, one still has to be careful about Donatist tendencies today. The Donatist judges the priest or charismatic leader according to the measure of personal spiritual gifts and correspondingly obeys more or less, altogether or not at all; one obeys, then, ultimately one's own inspired judgment, which means no obedience at all.

In a time so influenced by the so-called history of freedom since the Enlightenment, such Donatism resides also in the blood of Christians; at best, one obeys another whose spiritual authority illumines one—

one who is an authority, not one who has it. Two things get forgotten: that all human authority in the church has a referential character— to God, to Christ, to the gospel, as well as to the ideality of the *Ecclesia immaculata infallibilis*—and that ecclesial authority is primarily instituted, not self-established, authority, no matter how much its bearer must be concerned to form his existence as far as possible into a witness for the authority entrusted. *A priori*, no history of freedom, however, can grow beyond the authority of Christ, and beyond the reference to it and the *exousia* (power) of representing it. For there is no greater freedom than that of God, even when the freedom of the Son in God consists in doing at all times the will of the Father out of fullness of divine love, and in revealing at all times not himself, but the love of the Father, and in understanding his own state of being filled with the Spirit as a gift of the Father so that he might obey him more humbly as a human being and that he might, together with the Father as God and as glorified God-man, breathe out this and no other spirit of freedom into the church and into the world.

Theology—a Ministry in the Church

91 · Contemplative—Kerygmatic —Dialogical Theology

The initially narrow pattern of Yahweh-Israel, which is supposed to be surmounted eschatologically in the promises of the Old Covenant, is so expanded in Christ, that he "to whom all power in heaven and on earth has been given," sends his messengers "to the ends of the earth" and accompanies their mission "till the end of the world." What was suggested in a shadowy fashion in the covenant with Noah, that God will conclude a covenant with the whole of creation, is fulfilled bodily in the death and resurrection of Christ, which proclaims the reconciliation of God with the entire world (2 Cor 5:19; Col 1:19f). We believe that the universality of Christianity, which is the form established in history (ultimately as the death and resurrection of Christ, wherein the destiny of the world is given a decisive turn), remains the irrevocable midpoint that as such holds sway over earth and universe as head, and yet is not dissolved into it. This structure successively unleashes from itself three distinct and yet inseparably connected theologies.

1. Meditation upon the pattern of revelation for the sake of attaining its actuation more profoundly and adequately by means of understanding, insight, *sapientia* (*fides quaerens intellectum*); a not exclusively, but predominantly contemplative theology that flourished from the time of Augustine via Anselm down to the twelfth century. It includes a steeping oneself in particular saving events in order to appraise their divine dimensions, a comparison of situations or words, in order to reach new perspectives (the *spiritualia spiritualibus comparantes:* 1 Cor 2:14) of Origen, a thinking above all about God, in order to praise and glorify the grandeur of his gracious self-disclosure. A form of theology that is indispensable for all succeeding forms and which tries to correspond responsibly to the most primordial reciprocity of God-man, but whose danger lay precisely at the point where it would close itself off from the others as a unique or highest form: the danger of a sheerly contemplative foretasting of the eternally blessed vision of God. And yet even in theology God is to be given honor first of all, not only with the lips or with the heart, but with the understanding which strives for his sake to understand with reverent thanks whatever he has granted us. From this *intellectus* the precisely monastic theology never separated its practice: existence as "praise of his glorious grace" (Eph 1:6, 12, 14). The whole person should and does want to respond by imitation to the gift the Father has made to us in his Son. This is why, in the letters of Paul, the practical (parenetic) parts are so very much steeped in the dogmatic parts that, if the theoretical sections were to be lost, one could reconstruct his theology from these alone. Hence, John simply equates practice and the understanding of that which God is: love (God) acknowledges only those who, in imitation of God, give their life for their brother. But with this, the first circle has externally already burst into the second: theology reflects on and gives the norm to the *kerygma* of those messengers and witnesses of the faith sent out into all the world.

2. Theology oriented toward proclamation presupposes that in the depths of things is the universal validity of the particular historical activity of God in Jesus Christ (along with his prehistory). The space in which this activity is unfolded and which it originally intends is coextensive with creation as a whole. The Holy Spirit effects this inner universalizing (as rising and exalted, Christ is already the "spirit-man") and directs in consequential fashion the ever-renewed transpositions of the articulation of salvation history into the kerygmatic forms and dimensions necessary for this universalizing. The already achieved Hellenization of the Bible (the Septuagint) had

accomplished the decisive preparatory labor. The requirement of translation implicit in the task of making it intelligible to all peoples is not free to make concessions ("teach them to hold *everything*"); the translation must then result ever anew from a view of the totality (of the first theologians), and must in a critical sifting make use of the thought forms of the nations. Because the definitive word of testimony about God's saving activity inspired by the Holy Spirit remains normative for preaching, while on the other hand it contains not naked facts, but a presentation of the facts already meditated upon theologically within the people of God—both are inseparable—the intrabiblical theology can never be simply relativized nor prescinded from by a *kerygma* of a later date, but, without suffering loss, must be taken into the work of translation. Something analogous holds true of the decisive directives of eccesiastical authority for the interpretation of the fundamental articulations of the faith. The need to take along and think through the heritage of the history of the intellectual labor of the people of God implies no narrowing constraint for the messenger of the faith of today, but it guarantees that by reason of this history the messenger stands in real identity of sentiment with the central event of salvation. Never has the *kerygma* for a new age achieved anything truly creative without a transforming assumption of the theology contained in scripture and tradition, even when it had to put through new propositional forms in a difficult struggle against what was handed on in an unreflected manner.

3. In this second form, however, the third already lies hidden. Preachers are not just supposed to address fellow human beings with some general considerations about their particular culture, but to authentically retrieve that culture, to integrate the foreign and incompatible standpoint into the event of the preaching of the faith. This is done very imperfectly by a so-called "apologetic theology," although even it has its legitimacy. The apologete presents the shape of revelation to an outsider in a form that makes it appear plausible, coherent, and acceptable to this person from his own standpoint. But the apologete is still set upon an essentially onesided discourse, at best in the direction of an anticipatory refutation of possible objections. Now according to the presuppositions implicit in the universality of the Christian saving event, every other person is fundamentally already affected by the grace of Christ (or at least by its offer). Each person, without exception, is the one for whom God "has made his Son into sin" and allowed to die in a state of abandonment by God. For this reason, much more credit is to be granted the fact of the hearer having been loved by God and being able to correspond to "the unknown God" than the apologete usually does. What is needed here is a "dialogical theology," in which the messenger of the faith takes the partner seriously as a brother or sister in Christ, so that

together they both encounter one another under their common Lord and judge. Christians, therefore, will have to allow things to be said which, to themselves or to the church in whose name they speak, appear unbelievable (for example, the divisions among the churches); they have to expose themselves to criticism in this dialogue, but in such a way that they neither relativize the truth of the Lord nor put it up for grabs. But Christians will be reminded that the saving event they preach deals with the total exposition of God—to the point of what is the opposite of God, to the most secular world, to abandonment by God, to malicious misunderstanding, to betrayal, etc., for the purpose of bringing in their resisting opponent by means of love and of opening them from within (by taking over their guilt). Dialogical theology is, in contradistinction to kerygmatic, no longer one that thinks from within outwards, but rather, in conversation with the other, leads from outside inward, but in the shape of a *theologia crucis* not merely in virtue of an intrinsic (formal-logical) paradox, but of an existential event especially in the Christian who can open up the final otherness in the being and thinking of the other no longer by words and arguments, but . . . by what indeed? Perhaps by a silent, accompanying testimony to the Lord. Naturally, with the portrayal of this third form a new theology is not supposed to be established, but rather the fuller dimensions of so-called "apologetics." Nor is any talk about an equal legitimacy of all religions or irreligions intended, for the Christian has come to know that God in Christ has acted not only once ("once for all"), but in a way that cannot be transcended (*id quo majus cogitari nequit*). Still, the Christian has to stay aware not just that there is also something true in other standpoints, but that the Christian truth is ever greater than can be taken in by thinking, preaching, or even living; that the Christian, then, precisely because of this realization, remains under the judgment of the word preached, and that this judgment can come from the other as well. Still less will he, beside the second, forget the first form of theology: the ever-new prayerful, worshipful absorption immediately into the primordial truth, beyond all kerygmatic and dialogical purposing, in order, in meditating through the incomprehensible mystery of God's love, to draw new power for preaching and encounter.

92 · Theology—a Science?

That theology is at all a science in a sense either identical with other sciences or just analogously has by no means always been an accepted fact. For the fathers it was the somehow conclusive gnosis, which brought to truth what the Greeks and other peoples characterized as philosophy (which always included a doctrine about God or the gods). In the early middle ages the existential moment was emphasized: theology stands higher than (sheerly theoretical) science. It is wisdom, *sapientia* (*sapere:* to taste, to appreciate experientially); God gives a share of himself in his self-disclosure from outside (in the history of salvation) and from inside (in the infused virtues of faith, hope, love). In the transition to high scholasticism and with the more precise apprehension of the notion of science on the part of the emergent Aristotelianism the problem became a more pressing one: Thomas produced a provisionally definitive solution that encompassed the many attempts of his precursors.

Sciences are not simply autonomous, but, from other sciences with which they together elaborate the overall interconnected total field of reality, they constantly need to take over (to "believe") certain propositions or results. Now there is a double science of God. One proceeds from the evidence of human principles of reason as bound with sensibility in order to think its way to the first cause of things—philosophy (or natural theology). The other proceeds "in the manner of the divine itself, so that this is apprehended in itself; for us on earth this is possible only imperfectly; nevertheless there is both a participation in and a similarity with the self-knowledge of God, if we [do justice to] adhere for its own sake to the primordial faith which has been granted us." Hence, Thomas establishes an analogy (not an identity) between the structure of natural reason (the sensibly given, elaborated by the light of pure reason, which corresponds with the basic structure of "being as a whole") and the structure of theological reason (the historically given—the Bible, summarized in the creeds, the *kerygma*—believed and progressively, understandingly worked out by the light of faith which implies a certain participation in the God's vision of himself and in the vision of God by the blessed). Since even in the second instance human reason is called upon to penetrate with its own power of thought (aided by grace) what has been presented to it for believing, to see connections, to draw conclusions, the work of theology has a quite genuinely scientific character.

Two things with this, even today noteworthy conception of theology seem to us not right: on the one hand, fixing the object of theology on the *sacra pagina*, the Holy Scripture (the formulation is sanctioned by the patristic tradition and gets radicalized again in the Reformation), or even on its short formulation in the articles of the creed, to which there accrued its secondary interpretations through the tradition as *sententiae* and finally the rational interrogations (*quaestiones*) of the *Magistri*. These are what actually characterized so to speak the real business of scholarship. Today in the epoch of historical mindedness we would designate the proper object not as standing *behind* the scriptures, but rather as documented and envisaged by the scriptures, the living history of God with the human race chosen by him as his partner. In this way, the second alien element would disappear as well, because then faith for us would not be related to the letter of scripture or to the article of faith or to dogmatic formulations, but rather—as in the event of the Old and New Covenants—only to the living God who of course nowhere reveals himself in his naked self-subsistence (were that even conceivable), but in his revelatory deeds, leadings, accompanyings, instructions and commands, promises and fulfillments for humankind, real events which, as befits the deepest nature of encounter, are repeatedly made available in word, and lastly of all in a form of word which—with the Spirit of God taking responsibility for it—testifies to his history with humankind and by the same Spirit makes it become present and active again and again through all the future.

Without the notion of analogy nothing could be done with the question of the scientific structure of theology for it cannot possibly be placed univocally alongside other sciences (which argue from first principles evident to reason). The faith in "what is presented for faith" (whether in propositions or historical events) remains the foundation and precondition for it; on the other hand, it can only then be called (analogously) a science, if what is accepted in faith can be appropriated intelligently in a genuine activity of reason. This implies two things: 1. It pertains to the essence of this and *only* this science, that its scientific objectivity rests upon the decision of faith. Therefore there can be (seen theologically) no neutral objectivity that deals with the object of faith without faith, or in other words, that prescinds from the issue of faith or lack of faith. The theory so favored towards the beginning of this century that considered objective science and subjective engagement as separable, is here, at any rate, inapplicable, even if it should be applicable elsewhere. 2. The apparently total isolation of theology from the rest of the sciences is being demolished in that the *Geisteswissenschaften* (human sciences—which only recently have become known in their true nature) are seen and accepted as the this-worldly proof of the analogy of the sciences. There is genuine science even of (relatively or completely) unique realities, even when these unique realities can be encompassed and expressed only with the instrumentality of a variety of analogies. Both a historical event and a great unique work of art can be the object of scientific inquiry and indeed of progressive knowledge, without implying that the object would ever actually be exhaustively worked out, since precisely the character of uniqueness (and to that degree, incomparability) pertains to its very essence. No computer will do justice to *The Magic Flute;* but perhaps the very uniqueness of a congenial interpreter can come closest to the totally other uniqueness of such an enchanting work; and I myself in my uniqueness may through the mediation of the uniqueness of a great teacher (and learning as it were to look at things through his eyes), glimpse the uniqueness of the work of art. Take away the analogy of the *Geisteswissenschaften* and the dialogue between the natural sciences and theology would be meaningless and impossible. The humanly-unique builds a bridge towards the understanding of what is biblically-Christianly-unique.

93 · Theology and Philosophy

The Christian history of ideas, in all its high points, has placed the biblical plus in knowledge of God critically before the metaphysical knowledge concerning the mystery of being. *Si comprehendis non est Deus* (If you comprehend it, it is not God), Augustine warns us along with the Greek fathers. Nor is it otherwise with Gregory the Great; nor with the tradition of Dionysius the Areopagite that was taken up again and again in the Latin middle ages right down to Nicholas of Cusa. That this was proper from a Christian point of view is shown by the guiding experiences of God of the great saints: of a Benedict, who places Christian existence under the characteristic form of humble reverence; of a Francis who, from the midst of a Christian experience of God far distant from any pantheism, picks up the traces of the presence of the God of love by way of the brotherly and sisterly creatures and encounters it there; of an Ignatius of Loyola who breaks open the contemplation of the Christian mysteries of salvation to include the cosmos (in the *Contemplation to Obtain Divine Love*) and experiences everything as epiphany, as gift of the God who communicates himself, as dwelling of the God who is immanent in all things, as accomplishment of the God concerned about all things, finally almost in Plotinian fashion, as the streaming light and water of God himself. But how did the theology of the Schools on the one hand, the pious mysticism and spirituality on the other, let themselves be critically judged by a court which apparently stood far below them?

Scholastic theology dissected the God who had revealed himself: spirituality forced to the heart the very God who as Father had sent the eternal Son and poured into the hearts of the faithful the eternal Spirit of love, that Spirit who searches the depths of the divinity and who is given to us, certainly so that we might search along with him (1 Cor 2:11–16). Who would want to block the way from Eriugena to Eckhart and Nicholas of Cusa, and thence to Hegel?—the way that, from the balance between a metaphysics which knows of the indisclosable mystery and a theology that still acknowledges the mystery, leads to that total metaphysics that built mystery into itself (in the philosophy of nature) as the ancient stage preparatory to an all-knowing, Christian-theologically-enpowered human reason. However, once this theological *a priori* of human thought is seen through, theological gnosis is discredited; faith gets relegated to its (theory-less, existential) boundaries, and reason, like a burned child, takes care not to let itself in for a similar adventure in the future but establishes its positions much more restrictedly and in a less exposed fashion than ancient philosophy had done.

This seems to put Christian proclamation in a precarious situation. If from the third until the nineteenth century it had adopted antiquity as an ally, this assistance is now, on the one hand, despoiled of its weapons—ancient thought about God is rejected as mythic and primitive by an enlightened reason—and on the other hand, theology, clogged with this sort of philosophism is told to demythologize itself in order to be up to date. Of course, a theology that has been dephilosophized in this way will no longer have anything to do with being as a whole, but essentially will be able to serve only as a consolation for the existential subject.

One can see how endlessly complicated the theoretic question is, but what brutally practical consequences it has! Right and wrong are almost indissolubly fused. The question *why* there is any being at all is for modern people still just as elementary and primary as for people of every earlier period, and no science (which, to be sure, always begins thinking from what is on hand) can take this question away from them. If modern persons do not ask it or (what amounts to the same) think they can refer it to a specialized science (say, about matter), they are charged with the same unforgivable sin and "darkening of the heart" (Rom 1:20–21) as were the contemporaries of Paul. The guilt shared by Christianity with its gnostic inside knowledge about God and his mysteries (and that means, with its naive oblivion of God) does not excuse the inexcusable. On the other hand, the alliance between theology and (ancient) philosophy is problematic, and indeed not just because Christianity took over the envisioning of the invisible by way of the visible, or briefly put, the insight into the *analogia entis* (analogy of being), but most of all because it did not perceive the limits of philosophy as disclosed in theology and hence took up a false position in regard to philosophy.

It is possible that by making good on these mistakes, Christianity could be led from its contemporary uncertainties and discouragements. But where does the boundary of philosophy lie? Not where nominalism or empiricism wants it to be, in the impossibility of moving from the individual entity in the basic act of metaphysics in the direction of the mystery of being. This path has been traveled not without justice from the pre-Socratics to Plotinus in that human style which Nicholas of Cusa calls "enigmatic" or "conjectural." To follow this path is thoroughly human and by no means specifically Christian. The boundary, however, does not lie where the same path gets tried subjectively (for it is basically the same path): i.e., as ascent or return from the finite to the infinite subject, from the empirical to the intelligible I, and whether this way be traveled in the manner of Plato or Marcus Aurelius or Augustine or Descartes or Fichte or Baader. And if Augustine speaks emphatically the *noverim te, noverim me* (that I might know you, that I might know myself), if the knowledge of God and soul between him and Newman is set up ever again as the quintessence of Christian inquiry, then it must be said that this emphasis can also be colored in a Platonic, Stoic, and modern-idealistic way.

This God-I relation would be decisively Christian (or in other words, biblical) only where God comes up against the I as infinitely personal freedom, where thus the definitive exaltation of God above the ancient *theion* of encompassing being would come about without thereby undermining the philosophically proven statements about the *theion*. The personal exaltation, as it is visible in Yahweh, is only an apparent condition of a—to be sure philosophically impossible—acosmic separation of God from the world; it guarantees instead a far more inward immanence and a far more intrinsic presence and indwelling of God than was even imaginable for ancient thought. The illusion of the distancing of God by personal exaltation has repeatedly aggravated the philosophers (e.g., Spinoza, Hegel) and set them against the Old Testament. God leaves it to the human being as thinking subject to see the exalted transcendence of the tri-personal God of majesty and glory as one with the never-denied and indeed intensified immanence of God in all things.

But this exalted transcendence of the free God first brings about his relation to the world *as creation*. It is clear then that thereby the question why there is being (world) at all becomes much more mysterious and irrational than for the wisdom-seeking Greeks. For the world of ideas is now useless for explaining existence. Indeed, it is no less useless for explaining the being such-and-such of essence. This tree is not a tree because there is an idea of the tree which it embodies. Instead the question is, Who has had this idea of the tree, to whom has it occurred? The abstraction seemed to help us take a step further, not only for classifying, but also for separating the initially essential from the unessential. But how does the matter stand in the case of human beings? Whence arises the distinction among individuals? It arises *rationi materiae* (by reason of matter). But in this way the far more terrible question is not yet raised: Whence comes about the distinction and the setting over against one another of subjects? Here precisely is the limit of all philosophy, for which one I can be distinguished only "accidentally" from another. Consequently it constantly speaks only of the I, of the subject, of consciousness in general, and right to the end excludes the question of how it is possible for an I-consciousness to encounter another I-consciousness. Questions concerning interhuman relations are never approached and solved in philosophical ethics except with the presupposition and the viewpoint of an identical human nature in all subjects. This has been the case from Plato and the Stoics down to the philosophy of human rights. And quite consistently, Kant takes the standard for treatment of the You from the I understood in its depths and dignity: *Persona est philosophice ineffabilis, immo incogitabilis* (person is, philosophically speaking, inexpressible, nay more, unthinkable); not person in itself, but this one-of-a-kind (but "of a kind" is already wrong) and thus irreplaceable person. Philosophy can only project a general anthropology, with a general psychology (as a doctrine of individual behavior) and a general sociology (as a doctrine of collective behavior), both of which can be all too easily dissolved into so-called scientific statistics wherein, on the one hand, the anonymous average instance, and on the other hand, controllability from below (chemical means, suggestion, propaganda, etc.) constitute the criterion and goal. That the single person can possess eternal and irreplaceable value cannot be philosophically grounded, neither in pre-Christian philosophy nor in post-Christian idealism, not to mention materialism and biological evolutionism. What is not I, is Non-I, which is projected for the sake of the I and gets mastered by the I. Hence the elemental horror of a Jean Paul in the face of Fichte, similar to the elemental horror of Herder in the face of Kant. For the distinctively Christian factor there is no philosophical substructure; it makes little difference whether one constructs philosophical anthropology in the manner of Plotinus, Thomas, Nicholas of Cusa, or Fichte (as do Maréchal and his followers). All this "the heathens do as well."

The Christian's distinctiveness begins and ends with the revelation that the infinite God loves the single human being infinitely; that is made known in the most exact fashion in the fact that he dies the redeemer's (i.e., the sinner's) death in human form for this beloved You. Who I am will not be made conscious for me out of a general *gnōthi sauton* (know yourself!) and *noverim me* (that I may know myself), but precisely on the rebound from the deed of Christ which at once says both things to me: how great a value I am for God and how far away from God I have fallen. And the deed of Christ is the making known of the eternal love of God, my Father, by reason of

the fact that a fellow *human being*, a You, took up my cause, redeemed me vicariously, and restored me to being a child of God. My I
is therefore the You of God and can only be an I, because God wants
to make himself my You. If this is the primitive meaning of being and
I nevertheless am not supposed to become a mere supplement of God
(i.e., to the beings of God himself) for the ultimate idea is ineluctable,
that God in himself must already be I and You eternally as well as the
vital unity of both, then, the mystery of the Trinity becomes the
unimpeachable presupposition for the fact that there is a world at all,
namely that *between* God and world the drama of love is played out
and that this drama *intrinsically* fulfills the encounter of I and You.

Such an encounter is not possible except insofar as it implies the
Christian fact (and in this, the entirety of Christian dogmatics). Any
such an encounter is an *anamnesis* of the deed of God in Christ and a
practical recapitulation of the Christian doctrine of God, christology,
ecclesiology, mariology, and even sacramental theology. If the encounter occurs only in the framework of what "the heathens do as
well," then it is the encounter of exemplars of a common nature. In
the framework of this nature, this is an agreement of customs (*ethos*),
of social agreement (social contract) which has, in brief, settled on a
compromise for all useful restraint of individual drives and egoisms
(as Hobbes so realistically portrays it). It is quite possible for this to
entail that, in case of necessity, the individual (in accord with the
model of the state made up of animals) may be sacrificed for the sake
of the common good, and that it is noble as well to carry out such a
sacrifice voluntarily (like many heroes in the tragedies of Euripedes).
Between this and the Christian fact is a gaping abyss. That one person, Jesus Christ, takes me so much as a spiritual person that he dies
for my eternal salvation and, dying, buries my lack of salvation with
himself in hell is what first arouses me to be a person: "By this we
know love, that he laid down his life for us; and we ought [*opheilo-
men*] to lay down our lives for the brethren" (1 Jn 3:16).

This, however is only possible, if I understand myself as one borne,
redeemed by Christ, and if I consider the You whom I encounter as
that which in truth it is, the eternally beloved of God, for which he
died and for which I likewise hold myself ready in the attitude of
dedicated living. If I am a Christian, I not only can, but *must*, in the
neighbor see Christ, and in the deed of Christ the eternal love of God.
Insofar as I, however, approach my neighbors with this kind of outlook and in this attitude of readiness, not only do they reveal Christ
and God to me, but I reveal Christ and God to them. And this is not
some rapturous achievement for the elect, but is the one and only
everyday command of Christ which compels us to encounter God
continually in the most real way possible, inasmuch as we encounter

in an incomprehensible way the other, the incomprehensible You who is loved by God in an incomprehensible way. In this most sublimely everyday living out of one's faith occurs not only the continual experience of God among Christians, but the continually real witnessing of such experience to non-Christians. And if the non-Christians complain that the cosmological mediation of God has become ineffective today—presumably because the cosmos is no longer ordered toward God, but toward humankind as its meaning and goal—then they need only to take seriously their neighbor in the manner in which they themselves are taken seriously as neighbor by (true) Christians, in order to have found the shortest, most compelling way to God.

Of course this path is, philosophically, not passable, because it is philosophically impossible seriously, and not just enthusiastically, to give an eternal significance to the intrinsically so threatened encounter of a finite, transient I with a finite, transient You. Therefore with the Christian factor one cannot make much of philosophy. The fact which the Christian factor places in the center is so trifling in comparison with the glorious systematic projections of transcendental and evolutionary anthropology, that it remains imperceptible even when sought through a philosophical microscope. For it depends upon the eternal love of God for me, a fact that I would never have happened on in a dream, unless God were to say it and to prove it to me. That the theological fact remains imperceptible philosophically is a sign that in revealing himself God has chosen the "little way," yes, the "last place." Revelation and cross are one and the same, and Christian theology is nothing but the reference to this little way, this last place, this foolishness of God. But from here radiates forth all glory (*kabod, doxa, gloria*, etc.), because every meaning which justifies being shines forth from the empty, for-nothing of the foolish love of God for the world.

Biblically it is already the case that God's glory in the universe gets seen, understood, and praised to the extent that God's glory in Zion gets acknowledged. In order to be really effective and to avoid the danger of turning the world into an idol, the cosmological mediation depends on that of the history of salvation. Thus, in our times of church history, the responsibility for the effectiveness of the cosmological mediations is also placed in the hands of the Christians. Whenever the saving sign of interhuman love shines forth, the hieroglyphics of the book of the universe may be unraveled somewhat toward God. The more transparent Christianity makes itself toward the cross, the more it allows its super-wise foolishness to radiate out into our so modest and so confused present—in deeds, not in words alone—the more theophanous will it make the world once again.

Responsibility of Christians for the World

94 · Changing of the Structures

Christians live with their involvement in the involvement of God for the freedom of the world. They know that each one has been chosen by God and called by name to assist in his work of liberation. In this work human beings are central, not the angels nor the subhuman things created for the sake of human beings to rule as God commanded and chose them to do. Christians must, first of all, learn to see fellow human beings and all created things through the eyes of God. This does not mean that the human being seen in this light, ceases to be a profound mystery. Just the opposite. If it is true that God has made the human being in his own image and likeness, then this ought rather to mean that something of the uniqueness and unfathomableness of God shines in the human person, so much more clearly to the beholder when God, in choosing him and acting in and for him, sheds upon him God's own mysterious light.

The human being in general—and each individual in particular—is a mystery. This being emerges from nature and transcends it. On the one hand, he looks to nature, which it is his task to render serviceable and to bring into order; on the other hand, he looks to God, whom he must seek after "in order to find him"—but his transcendence does not yet guarantee him the finding of his final goal. This must come to him in freedom. In himself, he constitutes the boundary between the world and God (as the Greeks already noted), and it is for him to order the things in this world with a view to his own transcendence. He must therefore relate the world to that which lies beyond him, without knowing himself the goal toward which he must orient himself. The shadows of contradiction are deepened by guilt and death. He can neither close himself into his own finitude and mortality which is his real life, and leave the future to an anonymous human race and an anonymous providence; nor can he behave as if his death counted for nothing, and simply busy himself with the general goals of humanity, with the technical administration of the world of things where death plays no role. The riddle is totally and incessantly exasperating.

Only the involvement of God in Jesus Christ takes the human being fully seriously, and not just the species as a whole but each individual. Everything depends on the infinite worth of the person chosen, but who is not chosen privately merely for his or her own sake, but for the sake of the brothers or sisters not yet chosen: "Go therefore and make disciples of all nations (Mt 28:19); "Go to my brethren and say to them, I am ascending to my Father and your Father" (Jn 20:17); "Go home to your own friends, and tell them how much the Lord has done for you, and how he has had mercy on you" (Mk 5:19). Election and choosing is a personalizing and at the same time a dispossessing of the person for the benefit of others, as Paul finally explains in his great theology of history on the relationship between Jew and Gentile (Rom 9:11). But only the involvement of God in Christ takes human finitude, guilt, and death seriously into account, and does not stand contemptuously aloof from this world and its tragic tasks in order to resettle the human being in a spiritual world on the other side; instead it gives the whole fiasco of life in this world a meaning beyond itself by making all human concern for the world into one of the presuppositions for the resurrection, for bringing the "marks of the wounds" into eternal life. Human sweat and blood were not in vain; God in his free involvement brings everything into the final, perfect form of the world. Hence in the "solution" that God offers to the human riddle, all the tensions remain and no aspect of the human being is suppressed. For God is great enough to embrace this endlessly open being in his own still more immense openness.

To look through God's eyes at the human world means enduring both the openness and contradictions of humans, not forcing them onto a dogmatic procrustean bed but bringing everything under the unity of God's plan. Whoever can see more truth than someone else when they look, is in the right. This means first that the human being exists centrally as a person: a person intended by God, loved by God, and for whom God dies in order to rescue and draw him to God. Hence all that has the status of a thing, all that is not personal in this world, has value only in so far as it serves the purposes of the person, and is harmful when it betrays the person into the hands of the impersonal, reducing him to slavery and to the status of a thing. This determines the Christian's attitude towards technology. Our battle with the universe will always remain something of a struggle and perhaps even a violent war, but such a war will be just and permissible only so long as its normative aim remains the humanization of the human being. But who that being is who is to be rendered human, in the final analysis, is known only to the Christian who knows about God's love for us, his dying for us, and his resurrection as the "first fruits of those who have fallen asleep" (1 Cor 15:20). This human being whom God loves is not one who lives for riches, power, sensual pleasure, or reputation; for the latter misunderstands himself or herself and all his or her ordering effect on the world.

One begins to realize how difficult it will be for Christians to pass from the total vision of reality given them by the gospel, into collaborating with others in the building of the human world when most of their co-workers do not share their vision, or even reject it.

In an ideal world, the structures of the subhuman creation and those which determine the way society is organized would be capable of being so deeply imbued with the spirit of Christianity, that they would enter completely into the service of interpersonal love and of Christian communion. It is clear, however, that such an imbuing of the world would imply the transfiguration of matter and would be the world after its final resurrection. In the real history of the world— past, present, and future—total redemption has only been accomplished *in spe* (Rom 8:24; 2 Cor 5:7). To think that Christian efforts could change the structures as such is chiliasm or unrealistic enthusiasm. The structures belong inseparably to our mortal existence, an existence which is constantly threatened by and actually affected by guilt. The desire to do away altogether with the present order of society and its indispensable organizational forces leads ultimately to anarchy and takes us not a step further toward the heavenly Jerusalem.

Theology has no direct competence in the realm of worldly structures; it simply sends Christians into the world with an image of the human whereby and according to which they are to organize its structures as responsibly and intelligently as they can. They must not overlook that they are structures of finitude and "futility" (Rom 8:20). They must not forget their contingency and, for example, casting all political considerations to the winds, demand out of Christian charity and communion complete disarmament or nonresistance or pacifism. Such ideals are indeed justifiable normative goals, but to want to put them directly into practice would betray a lack of a sense of responsibility.

But this does not mean resignation in the face of the world as it is now and ever shall be. The Christians' task is, as far as they can, to imbue the structures of the world with the boundless spirit of love and reconciliation, even though they will always encounter opposition throughout this imbuing. It will be necessary to reach compromises. To take a common example: A Christian architect is given the task of designing a modern hospital. His general plan will perhaps look quite different from that of an atheist because he has in mind the personal dignity of the sick. Central to his conception is this concern for the person rather than the frictionless apparatus in which the patient as an individual becomes submerged. He will be able to implement something of this emphasis, but then technical considerations will come into play; the fully "humanized" hospital will be impossible to build. Or a district attorney will, in dealing with the accused, attempt to exhibit a very high degree of Christian humaneness but still must protect the interests of the state and society. It would be a particular bit of luck if he were able to convince the convicted person that the punishment meted out to him also lay in his own better interests.

As a fellow human being, the Christian is of course committed to taking part in the total effort of humanity towards the humanizing of the world, the perduring problematic and indeed tragic nature of which we have already indicated. The Christian, however, has no clear-cut recipes or solutions to offer to this problem, and like others must wrestle with the deciphering of the riddles of nature and of history. In this pursuit Christians are at one with their fellows. But from their knowledge of God's involvement for the world, they have a wider horizon which embraces the problematic and tragic, without eliminating it, and from which there falls on the world the only light that is truly illuminating and helpful. They must bear witness to this light not just abstractly—by professions of faith—but concretely in their professional and human involvement. Under certain circumstances this witness can take the form of a protest, and does so when the encompassing and compliance-demanding secular schemes clearly decide to go against God's involvement for the sake of the world.

Yet this dilemma has always faced the Christian, from the time when the first Christian apologists made their declaration of loyalty to the Roman emperor; their appeals, however, resounded with the proviso that a greater obedience was owed to God the Father of their Lord Jesus Christ (cf. Acts 5:29), to the time when Russian Christians vowed loyalty to the Soviet regime—recognizing here achievements in the social sphere that "Christianity had not brought about by its own efforts, yet at the same time refusing to engage in dialogue about the contradiction between the fundamental positions of theism and atheism" (cf. the lectures of Nikodim [Rotov] given to the World Council of Churches at Uppsala). There is nothing, and indeed no one, who can liberate Christians from this dilemma in which they have been placed and must remain because of the attachment they have for God and his involvement for the world. The dilemma is not caused by the Christians but by the ambiguity of the world itself which oscillates between being a good creation and shutting itself up in hostility, against the love of God: constitutive and irremediable in this period of the world.

If this is so, the question then arises for Christians as to how it can ever be possible to take a clear position in a constantly changing atmosphere. When can they cooperate? When must they renounce cooperation and move to resistance and witness-giving? And should this question, because of the constant changing of the situation, never permit of a clear answer, must they not then remain uncertain in every involvement, and themselves begin to change their own position? But is not the consequence of this that the camps within the church become more and more estranged from one another: here the progressives with their plans for cooperating as fully as possible with the world; there the integralists or conservatives, who confessionally hold up to the world the church's exclusive plan, impressive in its indivisibility? But to divide these two necessary tendencies into two such radically opposed camps means foregoing hope of mastering any given concrete situation. The one camp is right, in that the Christian is not called to offer the world completed programs of action, but rather to get involved in working for and in the world with God in Jesus Christ. The other camp is right in that this involvement of the Christian must always persevere in the source-point of God's action, and be responsible to this source. To move progressively from the source into the world is an action specifically condemned in the New Testament ("anyone who goes ahead and does not abide in the doctrine of Christ does not have God": 2 John 9); but a clinging to the Alpha, by which it would turn into a mere past and not release us to stride toward the freedom of the Omega, the failure of co-involvement with God for the world, would be directly contrary to the whole idea of existence in mission which is the particular form of Christian existence (Jn 17:18; 20:21). Our way must somehow lead between both cliffs.

One must here above all remember the promising of the Holy Spirit, who will not only help Christians toward a profounder understanding of what the Lord has said to them or merely hinted (John 16:13ff) but will also give them the appropriate words to say in moments of difficulty and danger (Mt 10:18ff). Certainly, whoever wishes to receive this Spirit for a given situation must abide in the source where the Spirit blows: between the Father and the Son; thus in prayer, in self-denial, and in readiness for any mission, such persons will, in the Spirit, be able to recognize and do what is needed. In other words, by their behavior as Christians they will be able to bring some unambiguity to ambiguous situations. By decisiveness they will move others, who suffer under the opacity of the same situation, toward a right decision. The Spirit has a clarifying effect, through the Christians, even on the non-Christian world. This does not release Christians from the obligation of studying carefully the complexities of a situation, or of accepting them as such. They should not become one of those frightful over-simplifiers, nor should they, as we have already said, hack through the complexities of the profane disciplines from outside with the sword of a theological argument. The Holy Spirit works through Christians in a different way. It is characteristic of the Spirit to take the things of this earth and move them and make them clear from within (Rom 8:26ff).

In this process of clarification, however, the limits also become visible to which Christians can still responsibly go and beyond which they must say No. This No which classes the Christian as a confessor, and if necessary as a martyr, is nothing less than an authentic continuation of the original Yes to God's eschatological involvement for the world. If we look at it objectively, martyrdom is nothing less than pure triumphant joy that "the Son of God, the Christ Jesus that we proclaimed among you—I mean Silvanus and Timothy and I—was never Yes and No; with him it was always Yes. And however many the promises God made, the Yes to them all is in him. That is why it is 'through him' that we answer 'Amen' to the praise of God" (2 Cor 1:19ff). The Christian confession of faith in God's Yes is its witness to God's decisive commitment to the world; it is thus in itself not unrelated to the world, but neither is it the confession of a religious fanatic. It simply follows through on the single-mindedness of the commitment taken upon themselves by Christians as responsible fellow human beings for the whole world.

95 · Partisanship for Those Deprived of Their Rights

In the preparation for Christ in the Old Testament God appears very strongly as the protector of rights between one human being and another with the people. By grace God led the people out of Egypt and entered into a covenant with it. Gratitude for this grace is demanded on the first tablet of Moses and on the second stand the orders as to how human beings, out of the selfsame gratitude for the grace bestowed on them, are supposed to demonstrate it in a loving way toward their neighbor as well. Actually Jesus' parable of the unjust servant summarizes this best. One to whom so much has been forgiven has to forgive the neighbor the little bit that is owed. And if there is injustice within a people, if the poor, the widows and orphans, the day-laborers and immigrants are oppressed and cheated of their salaries, then almost in an act of partisanship, God makes himself the advocate of those deprived of their rights, who are unable to prosecute their claims. Whoever is guilty in this matter, will have to reckon with God himself. This is the way it is in the Old Testament. And as is well known the New Testament is summarized in Jesus' statement, "As you did it to one of the least of these my brethren, you did it to me." Here we see something new. We see that whoever is concerned with the struggle against injustice and the prosecution of rights in the world, does so in utter immediacy together with the God of revelation and of love and grace, whether realizing it or not. Why? Because God became man to take upon himself sin which does what is unjust, and to pay for it by suffering. Whoever is concerned about the demolition of injustice, lovelessness, and hard-heartedness in any shape or form—by helping the poor, by really taking up the cause of the rights of the proletariat (Marx was a Jew!), by fighting for the elimination of war, of nationalism, of racial hatred, or against whatever there is of unbearable injustice in the world—stands right at the place where one encounters God (in Jesus Christ) at the locus of injustice and of suffering in the world. To such a one are addressed the words of Christ at the last judgment in a special way. For it does not stand written, "Come, O blessed of my Father, inherit the kingdom which you have helped establish by civil administration, by building airplanes and power plants"; but it stands written, "Come . . . , for I was hungry and you gave me food, I was a stranger and you welcomed me, . . ." Does this mean that airplanes and turbines are dismissed as unimportant for the kingdom of God? No, for there is the commission given humanity at the creation. The attitude and work of those who carry it out in obedience to God will get integrated into the final outcome. But how much more immediately significant is the turning toward the suffering brother or sister. Here the human encounters the partisan character of the loving God, whose heart cannot but enter into solidarity with the poor and abandoned.

And this preoccupation of God is so urgent that he at times puts it ahead of everything else in order to promote it and carry it out. This occurs for instance when he calls upon a particular person to "drop everything and follow after me," to become a specialist, so to speak, in the special preoccupation of God. In such cases it is inevitably a matter of locating oneself at the place where injustice is occurring, and of meeting this with the "weapons of God," with "an obedience unto death, yes, even to death on the cross," by a freely willed taking upon oneself of suffering and renunciation and shame and persecution in the spirit and with the intention of Christ. Vicariously, Paul wishes on behalf of the rest to "suffer in [his] flesh what is lacking in Christ's afflictions" (Col 1:24). In the end, any special Christian calling (also, for example, one to a contemplative life in the cloister) is meant to be so. In addition to this fruitfulness of the inward, personal renunciation, then, there are all the other external initiatives such as are performed by Christian orders, congregations, and other works in great number: care for all the poor, weak, sick, immature in any form. And this special calling is obviously no hindrance to a sharing in the Christian action on the part of one who out of a spirit of responsibility for the sufferings of humankind becomes concerned with the alleviation of need in any way whatsoever. Because the most fruitful deed of all in this respect was the deed of Christ, the effects of which, however, are beyond all statistics, external success will thus also never be a valid standard for the meaningfulness of any Christian social initiative. At its core, everything Christian is beyond statistics. Not to remember this and, in keeping with the time, to want to measure everything according to profit and success amounts, in Christian terms, to suffering a relapse from the New Testament into the Judaism that misunderstands itself, namely, into a religion of works. Many today are succumbing to this temptation. To them Paul would cry out as he did to the Galations, "O you foolish ones! Who has bewitched you, before whose eyes Jesus Christ was publicly portrayed as crucified?" (Gal 3:1). Quite often in this day, these foolish ones are people who want to take the matter seriously and who would like to move beyond a merely apparently unfruitful faith to its realization in existence. In this seriousness they are completely right: a faith that is not lived is a contradiction in itself. But love, which is the core of faith, has to persevere in its sublimity. It should not offer works as an installment payment in its place, any more than the self-disclosure of the love of God can ever be exchanged for any world view or philosophy without suffering harm or loss. All philosophies are only human attempts to interpret the structure and the meaning of being; in his self-disclosure God says who he is and proves it as well. Both of these things do not get encroached upon and consequently neither do Christian faith and human thought. Conflicts only arise where one mixes up and wipes out the difference between the levels. And a person will do this too out of an understandable striving: i.e., to get an overview and to reduce as much as possible under one denominator. But it is indeed the case, and it must be so, that God cannot be reduced to the human denominator. Above God and God's word and deed there is no overview. The "over" always belongs to God. For human beings it is already a great deal if they are really "under" God and obedient to him, for then they are also "in" God by participation in his love.

Saints in the Church

96 · Holiness in the Church

That the church in its institution and tradition, its hierarchy, its sacraments, and states of life has preserved the promise of an objective holiness that is not to be overwhelmed by the gates of hell is a guarantee for its divine mission till the end of time. So little does it relieve it of the obligation to subjective personal, lived holiness, that rather everything institutional and objective is only there for the sake of such a life. The office of the priest is there for the community; the gracious fonts of the sacraments are there for the recipients; the word of God is there for the bearers. And the nearer persons stand to the church's objective sources of holiness, as priests or as members of an order or as trustees of a sacramental grace, the more they are obliged to make their lives like, and ready for, the objective holiness which they serve, which they protect.

But also the opposite holds true. If the subjective making holy of the members of the church is the goal of the ecclesiastical institution, then this goal cannot be attained except in the church. In the church and for the church, which itself is there for the world. For the church is the body of Christ for all; and this body is built by means of the attitude of the Spirit of Christ, of the Spirit of love toward God and toward humankind to the point of complete self-emptying that is being realized in all its members: "By this we know love, that he laid down his life for us; and we ought to lay down our lives for the brethren" (1 Jn 3:16). For no other reason is Christ "made holy," than "that they may also be consecrated in truth" (Jn 17:19). Subjectively, holiness is identical with that love which puts God and others before itself and which, therefore, lives for the community of the church. "Love does not insist on its own way" (1 Cor 13:5) and a holiness that insists on itself, that would want to make itself the goal, would be self-contradictory. But it is not left to individuals as members of the church to decide how they will give themselves for the whole. Otherwise there would arise in the body of the church a sort of chaos of love. Love itself acknowledges an inner order, and the Spirit of love who builds up the subjective holiness of the church in the framework of its own objectivity is at once the spirit who distributes the offices and charisms.

Now there are varieties of gifts, but the same spirit; and there are varieties of service, but the same Lord; and there are varieties of working, but it is the same God who inspires them all in every one. To each is given the manifestation of the Spirit for the common good. To one is given through the Spirit the utterance of wisdom, and to another the utterance of knowledge according to the same Spirit, to another faith by the same Spirit, to another gifts of healing by the one Spirit, to another the working of miracles, to another prophecy, to another the ability to distinguish between spirits, to another various types of tongues, to another the interpretation of tongues. All these are inspired by one and the same Spirit, who apportions to each one individually as he wills. (1 Cor 12:4–11)

In the mission which all individuals receive lies the essential foundation of the form of holiness given to them and demanded of them. For them, the carrying out of this mission is identical with the holiness adequate to and attainable by them. Hence, holiness is something essentially social and thus saved from the caprice of the individual. God has an idea of each Christian that assigns them their places within the ecclesiastical membership. There is no danger that this idea, which is unique and personal and embodies the holiness thought out for each individual, might be either not sublime or not broad enough for anyone. It participates in the divine infinity, and is so sublime that it has never been perfectly attained by anyone except Mary. To realize this idea which rests in God, to transpose into living this individual law which is an utterly supernatural law freely projected by God, is the highest goal of the Christian.

So it is that Thérèse prays, "I want to fulfill your will perfectly and to reach the stage of holiness which you have prepared for me in your Kingdom; in a word, I request that I be holy." The "fulfillment of the will of God" is neither the pursuit of a general, anonymous law which would be the same for all, nor the slavish copying of an individual model—the way a child sketches out a drawing in black and white; it is the realization in freedom of a loving plan of God, who takes freedom into consideration and, still more, bestows freedom. No one achieves a higher degree of self-realization than the saints who adapt themselves to the plan of God and make ready their whole being—body, soul, and spirit—for that plan.

In the sketch of his idea of holiness, God takes into account the nature, the strengths, and possibilities of the individual. But he proceeds with as much freedom as an artist with the colors of a palette. One cannot tell beforehand which colors an artist will prefer, which perhaps might be used, which, in contrast, might be hardly touched, which mixtures will be turned to most often, which overall effects will be tried. From a contemplation of the mere nature of a person one can never tell what God's grace has in store for him or her, or in what manner it will have to give itself up, or which idea of God's holiness it will have to fit into. But *that* this must be so is clear from the outset, since all love is renunciation of one's own. Each individual seeks to experience and to hear God's will concerning his or her holiness in prayer and contemplation, and no one can discover that personal kind of sanctity otherwise than in prayer. On this conception rests, among other things, the whole structure of the Ignatian *Exercises:* within them, meditating on the life of Christ, "we are supposed to seek out and prayerfully sense in what life or state of life the divine majesty wishes to make use of us; we are supposed to prepare ourselves to come to what is perfect in whatever life or state of life which God our Lord offers to us."

97 · The Saints as Theme of Theology

The missions bestowed immediately by God on the church all possess something of the property of God, that of being at once perfectly concrete and completely incomprehensible. Like the essense of God, they are the absolutely specific, inexchangeable, determinate, and realized, and yet at the same time possessed of an inner infinity and limitlessness of wealth which mocks any definitive determination and definition. Precisely for this reason they have an enkindling and stimulating effect upon the church, not only upon the broad ranges of the faithful, since all discover in them something for their own taste while still remaining in agreement about the nature and character of the saint, but also upon the investigation of the theologians and of all those who steep themselves in the phenomenon of some saint and quite rightly always uncover and describe new aspects about him or her. Those saints who do not belong to this group do not possess this paradoxical character or perhaps do so only in the measure that every Christian life does. They constitute an intensification of what is usual, examples for the perfection of one or many Christian virtues and they are thereby entrusted to the Christian people in another way: they grow out of these people and show them how far they can go under the same natural and supernatural conditions of life.

Still, the saints of the first group are popular favorites. Although they are far less directly imitable, the Christian people know instinctively they are the great gifts God makes to us, not only as "patrons," whom one can invoke in certain cases of need, but as the great consoling and warming lights which God has placed in the midst of the church. For the people they are above all a new form, given by the Holy Spirit, of following Christ in life, an illustration and exemplification of the gospel for everyday. For the theologians, in contrast, they are more a new interpretation of revelation, an enrichment of doctrine concerning new, until now little noticed features. Even when they were themselves not theologians or learned persons, their existence as a whole is a theological phenomenon, which contains a living contemporaneous and fruitful teaching bestowed by the Holy Spirit and is thus very worthy of attention. And since that teaching is directed to the entire church it is something that no one should inattentively pass over.

Of course, no one is obliged to honor any particular saint, to believe in a given miracle or private revelation, or to accept a word or teaching of a saint as an authentic interpretation of God's revelation. But it is not a matter here of the negative delimitation which safeguards the absoluteness and uniqueness of Christ's revelation. It is a matter of a vital and essential part of the tradition which these saints represent, of that ecclesial tradition which the Holy Spirit demonstrates in a living way throughout all ages *in interpreting* the revelation of Christ deposited in the scripture. This interpretation takes place indeed on the one hand through the apostolic office, the hierarchy, and on the other hand no less strikingly through the saints who are the living gospel. The objection that the Bible is enough is a quite superficial one, for who can measure the scope of the Word of God? Who can dispense with the vision of those interpreters introduced to the church by the Holy Spirit as the authentic representations of what is meant in scripture? From this emerges the need for an intimate as possible interaction between hierarchy and holiness, as well as between speculative-academic theology and the theology of the saints.

Only one who stands in the sphere of sanctity can understand and interpret God's Word. All the church's theology feeds on that epoch that extended from the apostles to the middle ages and in which the great theologians were saints. Here life and teaching, orthopraxis and orthodoxy mutually interpret one another, fertilize one another, and generate each other. In the modern age, theology and sanctity have grown apart, to the great harm of both. The saints are theologians only in rare cases, and hence they are no longer taken into account by theologians. Instead, they are relegated, together with their opinions, to the side wing of spirituality or, at best, to spiritual theology. Modern hagiography has made its own contribution to this breach inasmuch as it portrays the saints, their lives and work, almost entirely in purely historical and psychological terms and is rarely even aware of having also, and especially, a theological task. Such a task, however, requires a correspondingly modified method: not so much the biographical-psychological development from below as a kind of *supernatural phenomenology* of the great missions from above.

The most important thing about great saints is their mission, a new charism bestowed on the church by the Holy Spirit. The person who possesses it and bears it, is only the servant of the Spirit, a servant who is weak and unprofitable even to the point of the most sublime achievements in whom the luminous quality is not the person, but the testimony, the task, the office: "He himself was not the Light, but he came into the world only to bear witness to the Light." All saints, especially they, realize the deficiency in their service to the mission, and one should believe them in what they say so urgently. The chief thing about them is not the heroic personal achievement, but the resolute obedience with which they have given themselves over to being slaves to a mission and understand their entire existence only as a function of and protective covering for this mission. One should place in the limelight what they themselves want and have to put in the limelight: their mission, their interpretation of Christ and of the Holy Scripture. One should leave in the dark what they themselves want to and must leave in the dark: their paltry personalities. One should attempt, therefore, through their saintly existence, to read and to understand the mission of God to the church. One should try, just as far as one can, to distinguish the salutary and wholesome mission from its deficient realizations. Not in the sense of a separation, since this mission is indeed incarnated precisely in the life, in the deeds and sufferings of the saints, as well as in their persons, history, and psychology, and in all the little anecdotes and circumstances which accompany and surround the life of a saint. Hence, we must distinguish the mission not in an abstraction from what is living, in a conceptualization of what is concrete, in a depersonalization of the uniquely personal, but rather, after the pattern of the phenomenological method which studies the essence, the *gestalt*, the *intelligibile in sensibili*, as far as this is humanly attainable. Only here the *intelligibile* is something supernatural, and its envisioning presupposes a faith, yes, a sharing in the life of holiness.

98 · People of the Church (I): Irenaeus

The bloodiest persecutions of the young church represented little danger in comparison to the monstrous temptation of gnosis. Rooted in late paganism and luxuriating in incomprehensible secret teachings, the parasite usurped like a vampire the blossoming powers of Christianity. The simple word of the gospel—stark and unfathomable in virtue of its purity—was transformed under impure hands into a thousandfold scintillating and tempting secret science. Faith was supposed to become enlightened in magical knowledge, revelation in pungent speculation.

Everything that could attract curious and half-educated people was offered for sale at this carnival: from drastic sensual pleasure (since "to the pure everything is pure") to murderous asceticism, but especially a power-assuring knowledge: the timetable of every journey into the beyond of the soul, the outline of every world and star, the key to every puzzle of nature and history, the anatomy of deity itself. Shuddering, the adept gazed into the abysses of the eternities, and out of the eternally silent "unground" of absolute emptiness saw a swarming horde of powers, eons and divine effluences (emanations) arise, mix with one another, and bring forth new divine beings, among whom there even might be found—as one among the innumerable—the Christ. In this ghastly interrealm between the unground and our earthly world, tragic scenes are forthwith played out. One of the gods, forgetful of his origin, sets himself up as the world-creator (demiurge), creates out of his own power and against the will of the "Primordial Father" (*Propator*) the terrestrial world, the domain of ironclad destiny, of hard justice, of blind impulse, of bodiliness. But by means of a crafty strategem, one sent by the most high God breaks through the sphere of the antidivine demiurge to the earth and there, by means of initiation into the most sublime mysteries, redeems the elect. In a second tragic myth the daughter of God, Sophia (*Achamoth*) has strayed outside the divine plenitude and from her tears and anxieties emerges the material world. The Christ redeems her at last and together with her the higher spiritual souls.

The most pernicious form of this battle of the gods, because closest to Christianity and unburdened by extreme fantasy, was proclaimed by Marcion in equating the evil demiurge with the Yahweh of the Old Testament and the redeemer-god with the Jesus of the Christians. They stood opposed as principles of justice and of love, as representatives of the religion of works and of grace, of legalistic externality and conscientious interiority: the first form of theological antisemitism.

But this dichotomy pervades all the other systems of gnosis. It is reflected in the terrestrial world as the crude opposition of body and spirit, whereby the bodily stands for the antidivine element which the spiritual person strips away in order to become redeemed as a pure spirit through secret knowledge and to return into the supraworldly regions of the spirits whence he fell. It is reflected as a dualism of lower animal souls and of higher pneumatic souls of which the former, by nature incapable of the higher initiation, rush into perdition and the latter, by nature predetermined for gnosis, are sinless and walk along the path of redemption from matter.

From elements of ancient Greek tradition, oriental, and Egyptian doctrines of redemption, and reinterpreted episodes and words from the Bible was brewed what one must call "the myth of the second century." Myth means symbolic secret doctrine, a spiritual expression of a privileged race of higher human beings. The myth is essentially exclusive; it sets itself apart from the mass to which it can be offered at best in a primitive, coarsened form. The myth is essentially ideological; it aims at a "higher knowledge, higher people," separation from the ordinary existence of everyday, even when it acts as the myth of the earth, of the *chthonic*, of worldly love. The myth is ultimately tragic; at the basis of all its distorted images lies the burden of an irremovable dichotomy, and hence also an irremediable melancholy.

In all these characteristics this gnosis, so antiquated in some ways, is always modern in its effect. Jacob Böhme and Schelling live out of the spirit of gnosis; in Hegel it is vibrant. But also any thought that regards life and spirit, bios and ethos, nature and God as antagonists or even only as oppositions lives secretly out of the same gnostic sense of things. Orientations that are apparently foreign or inimical toward each other come together in the spirit of Marcion. The biologistical ressentiment against the Jewish God of the Old Testament feeds on this—and can it be accidental that Harnack even proposed a memorial in Marcion's honor? Gnosis springs up ever anew in all those places of Western intellectual development where human beings, wearying of existence in faith, foolishly seek to get control of this faith and, in place of salvation by God descending into "ordinariness," put the self-salvation of a humanity striving to climb up and out of "ordinariness."

For these reasons the encounter of the Word of God with the myth that took place for the first time in the second century of the Christian era and has been repeated ever since is the authentic core, the dramatic knot, of Western and indeed of world history. It is encounter as decisive challenge to battle. Myth intends the ascent of humanity; the Word of God intends the descent of God. Myth intends power; the Word of God intends the recognition of weakness. Myth intends knowledge; the Word of God intends faith. Myth is sudden flashing lightning between contradictions; the Word of God is gentle patience amid the unspeakable tensions of human existence. Myth rips God and world asunder in trying to bring them into magical unity; the Word of God unites God and world while sealing forever the distance of human beings from God. Hence myth breaks ultimately into the doublet of "being as God" and "tragic existence"; the Word of God saves from both, because the incarnate God in his earthly suffering frees human beings from their tragedy.

The Word of God unmasks the myth: it is the desperate pride of human beings who will not bend under God and thus forges their own paths to heaven. The final result of this attempt is just as grotesque as it is tragic: following upon the Icarus-flight beyond faith into the depths of God is the blinded crash into the subterrestrial and demonic. The deity that the myth-maker pretended to comprehend in its plenitude (*Plērōma*) is ultimately unveiled as silent emptiness and anonymity, as the empty depth of humanity itself from which rise—as the more recent forms of European thought show—the anxiety-filled swarm of its thoughts, fantasies, and addictions cast monstrously, demonically, and crazily against the wall of the Absolute. With this "astral body" humanity stands more lonely and unredeemed than ever before, for it has now conclusively posited its tragedy, its contradiction, and elevated it to divine status.

Paul and John introduced the struggle against gnosis. Then it was in its initial stages. The great and decisive battle was only possible when it expanded to its fullest extent at the end of the second century. About the year A.D. 180, Irenaeus, bishop of Lyons in Asia Minor, who in his childhood had known the elderly Polycarp, the disciple of John, composed his "Five Books of the Unmasking and Refutation of the Falsely So-Called Gnosis." Together with the "Demonstration of the Apostolic Preaching" and some fragments, this is the only work by him in our possession. It is enough to prove him the indisputably greatest theologian of his century, whose importance reaches far beyond his century and indeed bestows on him a unique position in the entire history of Christianity. For never again would the Word of God and myth look each other in the eye so sharply. Soon after him, with Tertullian and still more with the great Alexandrians, the spiritualistic temptation in the purer form of the platonic and neoplatonic myths take control of Christian theology and it will require long and confusing struggles before the poison that had crept into Christian thought could be eliminated.

Irenaeus stands as the only great thinker of Christian antiquity before this inner civil war. In him the front line is still sharp and clean. In him it is evident that this line is delineated in just the opposite way than one is accustomed to regard it today. Today Christianity is a "religion of the beyond"; paganism, of "this-worldly affirmation." For Irenaeus the gnosis of the pagan is the sworn enemy precisely because in its stubborn spiritualism it is in flight from the body and the world, and in place of the really existing, sinful but redeemable, and by Christ actually redeemed world it posits an imagined hinterworld. Christianity however demonstrates its truth and power by means of its full recognition of the terrestrial world. Against the separation of body and soul, spirit and flesh, pneumatic and animal existence it posits God's becoming human, yes, even flesh, in which the redeemability and factual redemption and resurrection of the entire terrestrial world is shown to be possible and actual. Against the separation of Old and New Covenant then, it posits the unity of the Testaments in Christ and their diversity as stages of a divine education of the human race. Against the cold flashing pretensions of gnosis then, it posits the patience of God, visible in Christ and his suffering, bestowed upon us as the grace of redemption in the form of faith, hope, and love by which we know how to preserve a patient and humble distance from the eternal and incomprehensible God. This stance is the great condition of all salvation; indeed it is redemption itself. Ever anew Irenaeus reduces every single question to the simple relationship of superior God and humbly bowing creature, of the eternal majesty of the triune, self-contained being and the eternal neediness and desire of fragmentary, ceaseless becoming.

But for Christians this relationship has lost the last shadow of the tragic. In Christ—from God's side, then, and not from that of humanity—the abyss is bridged. The person becomes God's vessel; the earth becomes God's dwelling place; bread and wine, the fruits of the earth, seal in their eucharistic transformation the redemption of the world and the thanks of the creature. With Irenaeus everything is radiantly warm joy, elevated, wise mildness. To be sure, his word of battle is as hard as steel and clear as water. A compromise, a synthesis of the Word of God and myth, does not even arise as a possibility of thought. But his battle is not dialectical. He refutes by unmasking and, still more profoundly, by setting forth the truth. He does not seek to persuade by the use of syllogism; he lets the truth like the sun do its lighting and its warming. He has the patience of maturity, and the two words, "patience" and "maturity," recur again and again in the most decisive passages. He is naive in the noblest sense of the word, just as the Word of God in human form was naive: In this sign he has "overcome the world."

99 · People of the Church (II): Origen

To overestimate Origen and his importance for the history of Christian thought is all but impossible. To place him beside Augustine and Thomas simply accords him his rightful place in this history. Anyone who has taken up patristic research for any length of time will have the same experience as the mountain climber. Slowly and constantly the peaks about him sink lower but even so still seem threatening, and behind them looms up majestically the till now hidden dominant middle of the massif. None of the great fathers, from the Cappadocians to Augustine, to Dionysius, Maximus, Scotus Eriugena, and

Eckhart, managed to elude the almost magical, radiating power of the "man of steel," as they called him. Some fell completely under his sway. Take away the Origenist brilliance from Eusebius, and all that would remain is a dubious half-Arian theologian and an industrious historian. Jerome continues to copy straight from Origen's pages when he comments on the scripture, even when he has in an outwardly tough and scornful way broken the chains and denied the bonds that linked him to the master. Basil and Gregory Nazianzen make a collection in enthusiastic wonder of the most fascinating passages from the virtually endless works of the one to whom they return all through their lives when their day-to-day struggles allow them a moment's rest. Gregory of Nyssa fell under his sway even more profoundly. The Cappadocian writings mediate him almost intact to Ambrose who also knows and copies from him firsthand. Many of the breviary readings from Ambrose (like those, of course, of Jerome and Bede) are practically word for word from Origen. Thus, flowing from several sides at once, the heritage of Origen, already in anonymous form, already become a universal resource of the church, pours over Augustine and through him into the middle ages. In the East, however, wave after wave of enthusiasm gets cast up; always wider than a stream, Origenism becomes even more shallow. It runs over into the hands of obscure monastic groups which tenaciously and without a clue defend the "letter" of the master—the exact opposite of what Origen himself would have desired. And the more the spirit of the master departed, leaving behind only the dull dregs of the system, the more distorted did it stand before the bar of church teaching. The ambiguity and suspicion that in the West had long ago been cast over the name of the Alexandrian by the embarrassing dispute of Jerome and Rufinus, fell upon it later, but more fundamentally, in the East. With the condemnation of the Emperor Justinian the power of official Origenism is basically broken.

But what was the point of making perfectly innocuous this already half-dessicated system of theses, of attacking the preexistence of souls, the angel-like incarnation of the Logos, the soul-existence of the celestial bodies, the spherical form of the resurrected bodies (which Origen actually never proposed), and finally the elimination of hell at the end of time, when from these impoverished remains of a brilliant whole—one is tempted to compare them to the wreckage from a crashed airplane—the spirit, the nerve, the charm had long since disappeared? But this was only the open occurrence of what had long since taken place unnoticed: while the vessel was breaking into a thousand pieces and the name of the master was being stoned and manhandled, the fragrance of the ointment was coming forth and "filled the whole house."

There is in the church no thinker who might have remained so invisibly all-present as Origen. He himself practically never wrote, but only spoke: almost day and night he spoke indefatigably, to an ever-new succession of scribes. Thus his works—the six thousand books mentioned by Epiphanius are surely legendary, but Eusebius and Jerome are actually aware of about two thousand—are nothing but the resonance of his voice, of a voice that penetrated directly through everything, always forward, without fanfare and without fatigue, almost, it seems, without an intended goal, with the possessed character almost of madness and yet with a cool, unapproachably intellectual reserve never again equalled. It is not the voice of a rhetorician (patristic literature already has enough of these that the difference is immediately obvious), indeed this voice does not in the least wish to convince. It is also not the inspired voice of a poet (although the images and parables take flight everywhere in swarms), for this it is too polished, too dry, and lacking in ornamentation to the point of poverty. Thus it is also not the voice of an enchanter: nothing of the captivating *chiaroscuro*, baroque finery of the Areopagite, nothing of the magic word-geometry of the bishop of Nazianzen. Everything here is unpremeditated, unforced, and expressed with an ever-disconcerting modesty; with small formulae of excuse, in case "something more clever" be "ventured" or with a smile and a "you might consider whether perhaps," thus leaving the solution to the reader. No trace of the Augustinian *pathos* that without asking any question breaks open the doors of the heart and that is accustomed like the doctor to examine it naked and to place it before God. But no less distant remains the prudent and, in the best sense, humanistic equilibrium of the great bishop Basil to whom leadership was innate and in whom moderation was second nature. The voice of the Alexandrian is much more like the glowing, rainless winds of the desert, that at times sweep over the Nile delta, with a thoroughly unromantic passionateness: pure, fiery gusts.

Two names come to mind in comparison: Heraclitus and Nietzsche. For their work too is, externally, ashes and contradiction, makes sense only in virtue of the soul of fire that forces their incompatible matter into a unity, and in an enormous consumption of fuel leaves behind a fiery track straight across the earth. The passionateness of those two stems from the Dionysian mystery of the world. But here in Origen the tongues of flame reach out and lick higher toward the mystery of the supraworldly Logos–Word that only fills the earthly globe in order to baptize it in his fire, to scorch it, and to transform it in the Spirit. Right down to its very form then, the thought of Origen shares in the completion of its unique object: of God who is voice, speech, word and nothing else but voice, which strikes the heart like a fiery sword; speech, which with other-worldly tenderness whispers abroad in the world one mystery of love after another; word which is the brilliance and radiance of the hidden beauty of the Father. Into the anonymity of this Word the voice of Origen has also been drawn, and in this form it has taken on that omnipresence in Christian thought of which we have been speaking.

100 · People of the Church (III): Augustine

It is one of the characteristic distortions of our time to esteem the way more highly than the goal, and the seeking more highly than the finding. In the sense of one who is superficially interested, this estimation may be correct; in the decisive sense of the truth it is false. Augustine, the greatest of all seekers, and finders, would be the last to have something to say to a complacent possession without any question. For him God is not only here below but eternally the one to be sought ever anew—even in having been found: "That one may seek him in order to find him, is he hidden; that one may seek him, when he has found him, is he immeasurable" (*In Joh* 63, 1). But the finding, about which we are speaking, nevertheless remains a genuine finding, yes, an ever more profound, an ever more unshakable, an ever more responsive finding. The seeking without finding is the outer courtyard that the *Confessions* describes as the slippery path to conversion. Entry into the church is the first, happy turning point of this dramatic existence. But a second, still less clearly delimitable road remained to be taken: from a mere recognition of the Catholic church to full existence growing from the church itself. This is the road stretching from the philosophic years of youth to theological maturity, from the speculative existence turned complacently inward upon itself to the preaching existence of priest and bishop living only for the church, and therewith the gradual but relentless shifting of the accent from a wrestling about "God and soul" in the soliloquies (*noverim me, noverim te!* [That I may know myself, that I may know thee!] 2, 1; 1), about the general problem of truth (in the Christian Platonism of the early works), to a struggle from the truth of the gospel with any heresy encroaching on this truth.

In this second and last turn Augustine first travels to the end the way of the great converts. This way begins of necessity with a preoccupation with the I, his "religious problematic," so as, just as necessarily, to lead on to a growing estrangement from itself, in the measure that the I and its narrowness give way and get submerged into the ever more deeply acknowledged and lived church.

The Catholic image of the world possesses three burning issues: God, Christ, the church. These three do not however stand side by side without relation to one another, rather they form an inseparable one. God is disclosed and accessible for us only in Christ; Christ is disclosed and accessible for us only through the church. This "God in Christ in the church" is however not to be understood in the sense of a chain let loose in an upward direction, as if thereby the church made itself superfluous, such that it would have mediated Christ to a soul, and then Christ made himself as a means superfluous inasmuch as he would conduct this soul to the Father. This ascending way, that as such is of course the "order of salvation," has for its most inward and most irrevocable form precisely the *descent* of God: descent of the eternal Word into definitive existence in the flesh; descent of the mediator become flesh as head of humanity in his body, the church. This direction of descent is the criterion of the genuineness of the soul's ascent to God. Therefore "religious existence" (as intercourse with God) has its genuineness in "Christian existence" (as transformation in Christ, the Way), and "Christian existence" has its genuineness in "ecclesial existence" (as the entry and submersion of all merely personal, private religion into the life of the church). This last is not only the only genuine entry into the attitude of Christ who divested himself of himself, emptied and annihilated himself in order to become obedient to the point of death, yes, even the death of the cross (Phil 2:7), and so the genuine "No longer do I live, but Christ lives in me" (Gal 2:20), but it is also the genuine entry into the inner life of God himself, since the possession of the Father in the Son is first completed in the possession of that Holy Spirit, who as such is the Spirit of the unity, of the community of the church. The Holy Spirit is the soul of the church, and Augustine is bold enough to say that the exact measure of our love for the Spirit and hence for God in general is given by the measure of our love for the church. So all Christian mysticism and all trinitarian mysticism has its measure, its place, its genuineness and fruitfulness in a "mysticism of the church."

Therefore Augustine, as mature man and bishop, is no longer anything but a man of the church, and all attempts to interpret his maturity in reverse order (back to the period of searching in his youth) or to abstract from the pathos of his ecclesial character toward any sort of universal-religious problematics consequently result not only in an incomplete but also in an essentially falsified picture. The church is the clear, unsurpassable horizon of the redemption of Christ—not a confining horizon, since it is the Catholica, the universal—just as Christ is God's horizon for us. Hence the entire effort of the mature Augustine goes exclusively and relentlessly toward the maintaining, establishing, and broadening of this ecclesial horizon, and in defending (taking up more than half his works) against any religious aspiration deviating from the Catholic as well as against any spirit of dividing up the unity of the visible Catholic church no matter under what pretense. The entire work of Christ is epitomized for him in the great commission: the testament of the Lord as he was departing from earth is the unity of the Catholica, and nothing other than this unity. The one unbearable thing is any undermining of the confines of the church: anyone who, even with the best and purest intentions of improvement, departs from the unity is, precisely for that reason, indiscussibly in the wrong.

One has to be clear about this matter: all the aspects and possibilities of "Augustinianism" that in the later course of church history have provided ever new pretexts for schisms and heresies—from medieval enthusiastic movements, through Luther, Jansenius, and Baius down to the most modern versions of Illuminism—are in Augustine himself only weapons and means for the defense of Catholic integrity. Although Luther and Jansenius may have had such profound insights into the augustinian doctrine of grace, they fall short precisely because they take their stand outside the burning intersection of the Catholica, which is essential in Augustine. An Augustine in sympathy with Luther or Jansenius is just as contradictory as an Augustine in sympathy with Pelagius or Donatus. For every other consideration fades in the face of the all-pervasive concern for the unity of the church. All that later appealed to Augustine against the form of the church took its life openly or hiddenly, from a resentment against this unity: resentment against the visibility of the church in general, against its worldliness, its bureaucratizing in particular, against any form of its being in the form of a slave (Phil 2:7). But if ever a person of the church was free of resentment against it, then it was Augustine. Perhaps no one has suffered more under its "form of a slave": under the wrongs, indeed the prevailing decline even in its inner life, but certainly no one, in the midst of almost unbearable pain over this form of the church, has spoken out his "and yet . . ." in a clearer, more luminous, and more knowledgeable way than he.

101 · People of the Church (IV): Maximus

We search for examples with a lantern; at any rate we do not like to look for them in the more distant past. Here is one that is uncannily modern. An intellectual citizen of the world who was engaged in the quietest of labors while the waves of the Sassanides, and then the still more threatening hordes of Islam drove him farther and farther from home. Ecclesiastical and political integralism captured him, gave him a hearing, tried to seduce him, then rejected and exiled him until he died as a martyr in the southern extremity of what would later be holy Russia.

Doubtless Maximus had read widely, but he built his intellectual house on just a few well chosen pillars which enabled him, beyond all spectacular dead horses and straw men, to recover the true shape of the living tradition. The genius of Maximus was that he had the ability to open up to each other five or six apparently no longer interconnected worlds of the mind, and that he understood how to draw from each a light that illuminated all the rest and set them in new constellations, thus giving rise to the most unexpected reflections and interconnections. He is a contemplative theologian of the Bible, a philosopher of the school of Aristotle, a mystic in the grand neoplatonic tradition of Nyssa and the Areopagite, an enthusiastic logologist in the discipleship of Origen, a strict monk of the Evagrian tradition, and finally and above all, an ecclesial champion and martyr of the orthodox christology of Chalcedon and a church centered in Rome.

The catchword of Chalcedon is the germ from which he could and had to develop his worldview: *asynchytōs*, "without mixture." Should not precisely the concluding christological formula, understood in its depths, be the sought-for world formula? For Maximus the synthesis of Christ becomes the theodicy of the world, not merely of its existence, but of the plenitude of its essential structures: all things are integrated into even more comprehensive syntheses, indeed they are themselves syntheses in view of the last, all-justifying synthesis of Christ. "Synthesis," not "mixture," is from the start the structure of all worldly being. It is only in the coming of Christ that it became indisputably clear that the creature is not the pure negative of God, and that it thus cannot be redeemed onesidedly by a mystical dissolution in God, but—even with its elevation to divine participation and its dying to this world—only in the explicit preservation and perfection of its nature. The great deed of Maximus remains the choice of the christological formula as the axial point of his world view.

The "inexpressible mode of the union" of both natures in Christ is ultimately opaque: "For who would know how God assumes flesh and still remains God? or how God, remaining truly God, is still truly human? This is understood by faith alone which silently reveres the Word of God." "This is the mystery that spans all eons and discloses the hyper-infinitely and infinitely incomprehensible great counsel of God existing before all eons. It is, to be sure, for the sake of Christ, or for the mystery of Christ, that all eons and all eonic natures have their beginning and their end. For that synthesis was figured out long before all eons: a synthesis of limit with the limitless, of measure with the unmeasured, of restriction with the unrestricted, of creator with the creature, of rest with movement. It is the synthesis which in the final age has become visible in Christ, bringing with it fulfillment to the plan of God." That Maximus, in the scholastic dispute (and in opposition to John Damascus), would have stood unhesitatingly on the side of Scotus is, according to this text, beyond doubt. Not redemption from sin but the unification of the world in itself and with God is the final motivation of God's becoming human. As such, it is the first, primordial thought of the creator prior to all creation.

Maximus cannot do enough to praise "all the various syntheses by Christ of the creatures set apart from one another." Inasmuch as the Redeemer conquers all the inimical forces of the air, he restores the relationships between heaven and earth and "demonstrates that the celestial and the terrestrial beings, in relation to the distribution of the divine gifts, form a single festive cohort." And "once Christ had finished his work for us in the history of salvation and together with the assumed body had ascended, he unified through himself heaven and earth, and joined the sensible things with the spiritual and so showed forth the unity of creation in the polarity of its parts."

In particular there are five great syntheses that lead to the unity. The first, the sexual, in a first inkling of the remote unity, overcomes the curse of the penalty for sin: "In Christ Jesus there is neither male nor female" (Gal 3:28). Here is rediscovered the generative power for that primordial fertility of the spirit that preceded sin.

Thus, this first synthesis already presupposes the completion of the second, to which Christ points in his words from the cross, "Today you will be with me in paradise" (Lk 23:43): The cursed earth and the original Eden have become one; "the whole earth is atoned for by his journey back through death into paradise." The unenterable land of desire has become an earthly reality, to the extent that the earth, in dying, crossed over into its sinless form. "Because for Christ the only reality that our earth still had was that of paradise, he appeared on it again to his disciples and involved himself with it after his resurrection and demonstrated how henceforth the earth was one and united with itself." In his eyes "the earth is no longer torn asunder into the diversity of its regions, but rather gathered together for him who would not suffer that any one of its regions be kept separate from the other." Then "he ascended into heaven" (Acts 1, 9–11), and thus united the spheres with the earth, by which was shown "that the entire sensible creation, taken in its universal conception, is a unity. But the characteristic of its separating difference moved into the background."

But the ascension does not stop at the sensible heaven, as "he ascended far above all the heavens" (Eph 4, 10) and conclusively united spirit and matter, inasmuch as he mixed a sensible body and a soul among the choirs of angels and thus brought together the whole of creation. But what was united in this way he, standing before the Father" in his own totality, offers to God: "Encompassing the universe in himself, he manifests the unity of the All as that of a single human person," the cosmic Adam. For as God he possesses "body and sensible feeling and soul like us, and spirit, in virtue of which parts he unites all parts among themselves into wholes and can unite these in turn in a supreme totality." And while Christ as all-human thus subjects himself to the Father, "he unites in love created nature with uncreated—O wonder of God's tender good will to us as humans!—and shows that through the relationship of grace both realms constitute just one single reality. The whole world interpenetrates and indwells (*perichōrēsis*) in totality the whole of God, and becomes everything that God is, except the divine nature itself, and receives in place of itself the wholeness of God."

The syntheses which Christ achieved provide the basic outline of those others which the world and every individual must carry out in virtue of the grace of Christ. Other texts show that Maximus understands love, *agapē*, as the synthetic power purely and simply. Love for God and for the world are not two different loves, but two aspects of the one, indivisible love. Through it is actuated the total synthesis of humanity into a single identity, whereby each exchanges his or her uniqueness with the other and all exchange theirs with God. Those united in the love of Christ, who is love and therefore unity, are the members of his body, one also among themselves to the point of mutual knowledge of hearts and minds, to the point of impossibility of being absent from one another, because in love they directly interpenetrate as one. There is hardly a letter of Maximus that does not start or close with such ideas: the evangelical love that has given up all its own power is the ultimate synthesizing power of his thought and life. The becoming-God of human beings comes about as God-Love, *dia to philotheon;* the becoming-human of God comes about as Humanity-Love *dia to philanthrōpon,* "for always and in everything the Logos of God, who is God, wants to bring about the mystery of his becoming man."

Under the threefold primacy of the philosophic Logos, of the biblical Christ, and of the Roman midpoint Maximus brings in the fullness of Asia; he knows that it is not viable without the religious pathos of Asia. How much of this impulse, this human thought-form can be assimilated by Christians, and in what fashion, without endangering what is Christian? And how strongly and sublimely must the idea of the christological synthesis be built; how much must it be brought into the center of creation-theodicy as well in order to make the dyad of God-world bearable for Asiatic thought? All these are endlessly urgent and subtle questions which we can handle even less today than ever. The mission to the Asiatic high religions grapples with them. Syntheses of East and West on the basis of the sheer relatedness of "spiritualities" or "mystiques" even then could not be constructed; how much less today! Hence we must also characterize as inadequate those attempts which would have India and Europe encounter one another halfway in Byzantine Hesychasm, in the practice of the Jesus prayer and certain body postures and breathing exercises (in which Eastern Christianity has become orientalized again after the great synthesis), not to mention all those which, bypassing all philosophic-theological clarification, would plant Indian and Far Eastern practices in the middle of the Christian church. Against such naiveties which never lead to the gain of the foreign, but rather to the loss of what is one's own, Maximus may be held as an example: the final and highest reconciliations are achieved only by way of the clear, discerning, and deciding Spirit. Maximus is *the* philosophic-theological thinker between East and West. In his humble serenity, but also in the unshakableness of his truly free spirit, he shows how and from where both go together.

102 · People of the Church (V): Ignatius Loyola

If the charisms of the Spirit, that in the course of the centuries have been bestowed on the church are actually new illuminations and interpretations of the gospel, they are always, besides their eminently practical and theological significance, of an essentially theological nature as well. They show the exact point to which the Holy Spirit would draw the attention of the church in a given epoch. Through Augustine to grace, through Bernard and Bonaventure to certain forms of incarnate love, through Francis to meekness and poverty, through Hildegard of Bingen to the grand interconnections of the economy of salvation and of the mystical body being exchanged between heaven and earth—each time it is a fundamental aspect of revelation that gets moved anew and as if for the first time into the light, a viewpoint that runs throughout the whole revelation; and hence theology as interpretation of revelation cannot be indifferent to it.

The church as established upon apostles and prophets, upon office and charism, upon objective and subjective holiness is fertilized by nothing more strongly than by the cooperative labor of theology and holiness that together can always provide a relevant interpretation and exposition of the objective revelation of God in Christ. In order to appropriate the synthesis that was so fruitful in the patristic period right down to the great scholastics, two things would be required: first of all a theological hagiography, that is the effort to dig out the theological content in the great and ecclesially significant missions of holiness, a content that can also be present in cases where the saints themselves were not explicitly theologians, as for instance Aloysius, Vincent de Paul, John Eudes, John Vianney, Thérèse of Lisieux. But then, to be consistent, a concern, present and future, for saints to be involved with the theological interpretation of scripture, and for theologians to be involved with the life and problems of the saints and of holiness, is also required.

This task extends over the whole life of grace in the church and in the mystical body of Christ. Such a renewed hagiography would mean an incomparable enrichment for the whole church, even in doctrine. Our school theology, which remains abstract and schematic wherever it is not casuistic, could gain a great deal from a deepened, not merely historically-descriptive but truly theologically-explanatory study of the saints.

This is probably true of no one more than of Ignatius Loyola, who, although surely no school theologian, carried out in his *Exercises* a real and outstanding "doctrinal mission" in the church. One would be deceived about its scope, were one to relegate it only to the realm of praxis and asceticism, a field with which the dogmatic theologians of the guild supposedly would not have to bother. This has been done long enough, for centuries actually, and so nowhere was there a serious theological study of the *Exercises*. The flood of literature on the *Exercises* remains almost entirely fixed on pastoral and ascetic themes; it occurred only to a very few that there should be important hints and inspirations here also for theoretical theologians.

The theological mission of Ignatius circles around the centers: "choice," "indifference," "obedience." The central point of the *Exercises* is the *election;* the central encounter with God is encounter with a choosing God. Not with the Augustinian God of the *requies* for the *cor inquietum*, not with the Thomist God of the *visio beatifica* for the *appetitus naturalis* and *supernaturalis visionis*, but with the God who, choosing in incomprehensible freedom, descends upon the one chosen in order, cutting across all unrest and all striving, to enlist him for his unforeseeable purposes. The substance of God's demand will be revealed with his proclamation in Christ to the "whole world without exception," which however is always a completely personal proclamation "to each individual in particular" (*Exercises*, no. 95), who has to choose the contents of this proclamation as the very substance of his or her life, and whose attitude then has to be, "Not to be deaf to his calling, but to be quick and ready to respond" (91), in order to be able to choose what God has chosen and to give up the independent, purely creaturely freedom that indeed has been emancipated from original sin ("Take and receive all my will [234]"), and so in grace to share in the freedom of God in the co-actuation of his choice. It is thus an image of God that has its center in a personal sovereignity of the once-and-for-all decision, as it has appeared and remains uniquely accessible in the once-and-for-all appearing, encountering, and election of Christ and his "Follow me." And it is an image of human being that has its center not in aspirations and desires of the heart that press on even to the point of absolute realization, but in praise-reverence-service of God (29) and in readiness (*disposición*) for a will of God which can never—neither as a whole nor in particular—be deduced from one's own nature or figured out in advance. Consequently, we have as the substance of Christian life the double aspect: choice of a state in life as a whole, i.e., the total form of life chosen by God for the individual (135), and which, through its dichotomy "worldly state-religious state," underlines the choice character of ecclesial existence in the sharpest way possible. (This points out the need for a theological doctrine on states of life in the church, which to this day has been constructed neither within ecclesiology nor outside it.) On the correctness of this basic choice depends the weal or woe of one's entire Christian existence, which then appears on the whole as misplayed, if it has tried to turn an erroneous and bad decision into a divine vocation (172), thus ultimately making the divine will conform to one's own will (169), or if, not deciding at all, it remains characterized by lack of decision. The basic choice or election of a state in life, however, is only the framework and hence point of departure of the ever-renewed personal choice of God in each moment of life: the *analogia electionis* must become the all-transforming form of the Christian life.

Behind this form of life stands, as we have shown, a distinctive image of God which is, however, immediately concretized in Christ and his relationship to the Father: Christ as Lord of the world and of each and every soul by reason of his complete obedience toward the Father. This obedience is ultimately trinitarian: just as the entire mysticism of Ignatius, when traced to its roots, is a trinitarian mysticism. Thus, in order to ground the theology of the *Exercises*, an image of the Trinity has to be projected in which the threefold life is described as the mutual choice and the mutual letting-be-chosen in love as the determinacy and indifference in the groundless personal freedom of God (without prejudice to the necessity of the processions). This image would be gained on the basis of the image of God revealed in Christ, just as he is our model; this would have the double advantage of having the trinitarian life of the revelation of God in the flesh become clear to us concretely, but the life of Christ become clear to us in detail in a trinitarian fashion.

The further key words, "indifference" and obedience" are virtually contained in the first, in "choice." *Indifference* is the existential (and thus also the moral-ascetic) presupposition for the making of the choice, that is, for performing that act which grounds Christian existence. For even objective-sacramental existence does not simply precede choice (since for the baptism of a child at least the faith-decision of the church is required) and is bestowed in view of it. Indifference is the fundamental act of the creature; the theology of the *potentia oboedientialis* is to be developed starting from it; it is the unique presupposition of the unique choice (of state in life), which, as form-giving of Christian life, is a conclusion, but even more a beginning, namely, the presupposition for a God-chosen life fruitful right down to its individual acts. As such it is a permanent attitude, that pervasively, in the *analogia electionis*, grants primacy to God's will over one's own. Precisely in this way is it the spring and form of faith, love, hope, for it is the basis for preferring the divine truth to one's own truth, the divine love to one's own love, the divine promise to one's own security.

Consequently it is also the source of the cardinal virtues understood in a Christian way which attain their meaning, form, and justification from faith, love, hope. In negative terms, then, indifference is the attained exclusion of all disturbances and hindrances that from the side of our nature affected by original sin could as "disordered inclination" mar the choice of the pure will of God. Ignatius unfolds the perfect accomplishment of indifference theologically understood in the "three degrees of humility," which one can also call degrees of readiness to let go of one's own disposing and to adjust to God's disposing (161–65). The first sums up the Old Testament world of the commandment and demands readiness "to obey the law of God our Lord in all things" in the still undifferentiated mode of an either-or of a for-God or against-God. The second stands as it were at the threshold between Old and New Covenant, since God has appeared personally, in other words with a personal plan and will, and *even before* he unfolds his plan demands absolute discipleship. This is the characteristic locus of indifference, since at this second degree is required "that I find myself at the point"—and it really is only a point!—"that I no longer incline toward having wealth rather than poverty, desiring honor rather than shame, wanting a long rather than a short life, where the service of God our Lord and the saving of my soul are the same." The living out of this attitude of readiness for the plan of the personal God thus provides protection in a differentiated form from a deviation from God's will, in other words from venial sins.

The third degree of humility gives only the structural development of the New Testament plan of salvation, the structural difference of the choice of God in Christ which there is called poverty, humiliation, folly of the cross. But Ignatius refrains from turning this structural determination straightaway into an individual determination of the divine will for the individual, unless this individual has really appropriated the Old Testamental levels of keeping the commandments and the level of the threshold between the Testaments, indifference. For the individual, the choice of the cross is subject to a twofold precondition: i.e., that the "first and second degrees are presupposed"; hence, not just a general habituation in keeping the commandments, but particularly also a habituation to perfect readiness; and that "the praise and glory of the divine majesty should be the same." The choice of the cross thus results not from a personal preference and enthusiastic offering of self, but in real knowledge of one's having been objectively chosen by God, just as theologically the New Covenant only goes beyond the Old as the fulfillment of its "jots and tittles" and just as the Old leads into the New only in the form of the elective decision of God. In Ignatius's teaching about indifference then lies in a germinal way a type of existential doctrine of the Testaments and of the economy of salvation, whose development could allow the ideas of the historicity of God, of Christianity and of Christian existence, for which are already grounded in the election, to become conscious.

For this reason everything centers in a theology of *obedience*: not primarily that of humanity but of Christ toward the Father and hence in the theology of a trinitarian obedience, corresponding to the trinitarian interpretation in the Greek fathers of the saying, "the Father is greater than I." This trinitarian obedience is shown and given to the world objectively in the obedience of Christ, and through Christ primarily to the bride of Christ, the church, which possesses its source and permanently fertile womb in Mary. Hence, the first contemplation of the life of Christ in Ignatius is explicitly marian; and the conclusion of his little book "Rules for Thinking with the Church" are implicitly marian, insofar as all ecclesial obedience is placed under the sign of the "bridal nature of the church" (363–65). The preferred form of prayer is also marian, insofar as it is subjectively arranged under the objective granting of grace from God through Christ through Mary (62–63). The obedience of the individual is thus trinitarian, christological, marian-ecclesial obedience, standing under the rules of feeling not merely for the general-universal, but also personal, every here-and-now self-revealing elective will of God, under the rules of personal intercourse between the Christian soul and God, as Ignatius sets them in the "Rules for the Discernment of Spirits," thereby picking up anew an essential, long interrupted aspect of patristic theology.

All of these are only indications, so brief that they will appear to many to be subject to misunderstanding. To clarify them would have to be the task of a theology of the *Exercises*, or better still of a theological interpretation of the mission of Saint Ignatius. Nothing could make the practice of the *Exercises* more fruitful than such a theological explication. And from few quarters could one hope for such a rich fertilization of theoretical theology than from such an enterprise. The solemn sanctioning of the *Exercises* by the hierarchy, their being recommended for clergy and religious, for all the faithful, shows that here the church sees far more than simply a mere practical means of spiritual renewal: an authentic genuine interpretation of its deposit of faith. A look at the flood of literature on the *Exercises* could lead one to believe everything has already been said, that the "truths of the *Exercises*" have all been delivered and one could justifiably turn to other spiritual food. But the quantity of what has been written is deceptive. If all, according to Ignatius's urgent wish, are free in the church to choose an ecclesial leader for themselves according to their own personal taste, it is on the other hand true that the extraction of the theological substance of this inexhaustible mine has only just begun.

103 · People of the Church (VI): Thérèse of Lisieux

In recent times we do not have so many great saints that we could afford to make it without them. One might perhaps object that the designation "great saint" does not exactly fit the "little" Teresa with her doctrine of the "little way," which was described by her explicitly and carefully as a way for all Christians, and precisely for "little souls." Now we do not wish to talk about the fact that Thérèse Martin really did have an idea of being a great saint, namely, one to whom a great mission in the church was given; it is enough to note that the fervor of veneration for her across the entire world has surely been fanned by the breath of the Holy Spirit and that one applies the expression "great saint" at best to those who have been borne toward canonization by the Holy Spirit itself (and especialy not by human interests), as for example the Curé of Ars or Don Bosco.

But already another objection takes shape: Did not this little Thérèse have her hour at the end of the nineteenth and the beginning of the twentieth century? Does she not stand and fall with a becalmed, perhaps even complacent bourgeois Catholicism to which the entire milieu of her family (compare the letters of which still more have been recently published) and even the supremely insignificant cloister in which she had to spend her few years of life bear living witness? Can we still put up with the flowery boarding-school style in which she wrote her memoirs, not to mention the sweet poems that today have become unreadable in their original language? And does not this level of becalmed conventionality cry out precisely for the spade of the psychoanalyst to break away the all-too-smooth facade and to lay bare behind it—just think of Thérèse's puzzling juvenile sickness!—a whole tangle of complexes? I.F. Görres has begun this labor, and François Six carries it on today far less inhibitedly. Someone has irreverently said that the Thérèse-boom is over for good.

Now great saints are not dependent upon advertising, but at most upon the love of the faithful, and this love arises wherever there is a feel for the special quality of their mission and for the suitability of its execution. Whoever might take the trouble to read in an unbiased way Thérèse's authentic writings—the three parts of her autobiography, her letters and poems (the "Last Words") in a critical selection and with care—will be astonished at the freshness and genuineness one immediately encounters, the indomitable temperament, the will to convince, to bring one along, the impatience with all tepidity, all resignation, all false humility, even when Thérèse must take cognizance of such traits in her priest friends.

Joan of Arc was not her favorite saint for nothing; she was the one with whom she competed in spirit, with whom she compared her mission, whose part she played so enthusiastically in a theatrical piece, as photos we still possess can attest.

Before we pass over to the more properly religious and Christian dimensions we must note that in recent times no canonized saint is known to me who possessed such a poetic capacity as Thérèse of Lisieux. The images really bubble forth from pen, always original, always striking home. They illustrate her teaching about the little way, that it thereby becomes still more colorful, intelligible, and attractive. To be sure, one must be able to prescind from time-bound expressions, but that is made easier for one by the surging fullness of insights (especially in the letters). Naturally the "great" Teresa is the greater poet, but she wrote her poetry as a mature, experienced woman, just as her entire work as a foundress of many cloisters took up a great deal more space, to speak in earthly terms, than that of the young woman, who, barely twenty-five years old, died of tuberculosis. And yet this young woman, with all due respect for the great Teresa, did not shy away from laying out a different path up Mount Carmel, laughing along the way, often a little bit maliciously, to supply a bit of corrective to the two great peaks of Carmelite reform—Teresa and John of the Cross. They are two "eagles" who have swung out in mystical flight over the clouds of everyday life, and who, by the description of their experiences, could perhaps mislead souls not called to such exalted flights into false desires, or even to an unsalutary training in mysticism. The little Thérèse realizes that the perfection that the gospel intends is accessible to all, even when striving for it requires the complete involvement of the person. Thus we have reached the point where the special character of the Thérèsian "little way" has to be at least summarily portrayed. Three aspects of her teaching should be emphasized.

1. The "little way" is so called, because it always undertakes to prescribe only the next step that needs to be taken right now. No high-flying plans for tomorrow, but the little bit that is required today, in this hour and minute.

Maybe we put up with an unpleasant person. Maybe we persevere in patience with some work, without stopping early. Maybe we go to the end of some prayer in which apparently nothing will come out right. Only today counts, even though the spirit would so much like to dream about tomorrow. To be sure, this today is transitory; Thérèse feels this urgently and longs for eternity with God. But for now God is nowhere else comprehensible than just in the now. Eternity, that to us seems to lie in the future, is in truth the hidden depth of the present moment. When I fill up this moment with Christian love, as much as I can, to the limit, then I am in contact with the eternal, divine love, which accompanies me from moment to moment. It makes no difference at all whether what I have to do now appears important or unimportant; what makes a difference is only how I do it. Here the name and symbol of Thérèse becomes significant: she is called Thérèse of the Child Jesus and of the Holy Face—both are essentially bound inseparably together. The child is—like the Lord in the gospel—the exemplar, because his moments are filled concretely as it trusts in each now, posits love without deviating into abstract theories, does not care about what tomorrow brings, does not hoard and store. But as in the gospel the example of the child is inseparable from the example of the passion: to have to so persevere in the moment, to be nailed fast to it, can itself already be passion and will genuinely become so when God fills the moment of the believer with traces of redemptive suffering. In the course of the years Thérèse's inner landscape becomes ever more precarious, more dark right down to experiences of complete dryness, of abandonment, and even of temptations against faith, which she, together with nonbelievers and to be in solidarity with them, needed to experience. And this always in a feeling of weakness. A child is not strong. It trusts that it will be carried through. The one suffering on the Mount of Olives is not strong either; when he says "Your will be done," he does so trusting that the will of the Father will lead him through what must humanly speaking appear unbearable.

2. In the "little way" there is no separation or opposition between love of God and love of neighbor. Such a distinction would never even have occurred to Thérèse; from her earliest youth, she sees both as the full Christian unity of life.

For her it is completely obvious that she loves God because he is love, love for all human beings, for all sinners, because he—as she says so many times—went to the point of madness in this love for humanity. For her, God and eternal life, in the abyss of the love of God, is the whole meaning of creation; this is why she wants to lead as many people as possible to this God, precisely because she loves human beings. She lives in Jesus Christ, who in her mind is inseparable from the self-giving of God to humanity and the mediating point of the self-giving of humanity to God. In her love for this radiant center of the love between God and humanity Thérèse discovers her own theological standpoint. In the famous conclusion to the second manuscript, she would like to encompass every particular charism in the church, in order to love God and the world out of all of them. But then she discovers—in the transition from the twelfth to the thirteenth chapter of First Corinthians—"that love [inseparably love of God and of neighbor] simultaneously contains and transcends all charisms in itself. . . . I grasped that the church has a heart and that this heart burns with love . . . that love includes within itself all vocations . . . at last have I found my vocation: it is love!"

That sounds overenthusiastic, but Thérèse converts the grand ideas into the small change of everyday: in the ever-now moment she distributes love to God and to the people she meets; a Sister, who was inwardly unsympathetic to her, says in amazement, "I do not know at all why Thérèse of the Child Jesus acted so specially to me." As a Carmelite, Thérèse understands that she cannot make her love known by outward works in the church: her "work" is the total self-giving of love, the "whole burnt offering," which she knows is the most efficacious, most fruitful action of the church. She compares herself to a small pendulum that sets all the great wheels of the ecclesial apostolate in motion. And the church has for its part acknowledged this insight of Thérèse by declaring her the patroness of the missions. She understands her works to be the product of a complete selflessness: she wants to do no good deeds and to collect no profits; but rather to radiate everything before her for the benefit of the world and the good of the church. And so much does she understand this action to be the definitive attitude of Christian love, that even in heaven she wants nothing but to be for God the "defoliated rose" whose petals are wafted down over the earth.

3. This greatest possible opening in the heart of the church affords us a presentiment of the third element that characterizes the theology of the saint: it is a theology of hope in that, emboldened with total love, she pushes on almost rashly toward a total hope; she dares to step into new territory, at least as far as the theology of the past centuries is concerned.

Without circumvention she says, "One never expects too much of God; one receives as much from him as one hopes for." And hence, "One demands of God exactly as much as one expects from him." But there is nothing which Thérèse would not expect of God's love. For her faith (that believes all God says), love (that seeks to respond unrestrictedly to his unrestricted self-giving) and hope (that hopes for everything from God's love) are coextensive. For herself, she lays claim to a "blind hope"; she also makes her own the pauline "hope against hope." And because the Son of God under the mandate of the Father died for all sinners and because Thérèse herself understands her mandate in this sense, to offer herself and to give herself for all sinners in the discipleship of Jesus, she does not see any reason why she should be heard only partially and not totally. These keen insights of Thérèse have in them nothing of a dry expertise about God, of a half-hearted notion that "everything will come to a good end." Just the opposite is the case: it is a glowing, if also always reverent falling head over heels for God, and it is simultaneously an attentive listening to the fundamental tone of the Bible, an understanding (without any knowledge of Hebrew) of the fact that God's justice is completely one with his love.

One has to break through superficial outer skins, and then one sees with astonishment: Thérèse has answers, yes, in large part *the* answers to questions and problems of the church in our time. The breakthrough that she signified for us in no way lies finished behind us. First she has the right answer to the slogan of orthopraxis: her little way is nothing else. But it really lives, as it would have to, as Christian, completely out of loving faith. She has the right answer to the problem falsely posed between love of God and love of neighbor, for she shows us that both in truth are one and each side always inevitably refers to the other. She has the right answer to the one-sided and overheated theology of hope, inasmuch as she points to its true object and offers herself for it with a total existential commitment.

In her life and thought Thérèse is far richer than these few strokes of the pen could sketch. If one takes her total work seriously, then one is staggered by the fullness and force of what was achieved in few years. To speak in medieval terms she is a mistress of life as much as of reading. She herself had educated novices and given and shown them lastingly practical wisdom, often almost the wisdom of the ages. She would not have any problem if we were to ask her now to take us into her school.

104 · People of the Church (VII):
Adrienne von Speyr

Adrienne von Speyr, who died in 1967, possessed in a special way a charism of theological insight. To the central insights bestowed on her belong the mysteries of Holy Saturday and hence of hell and of universal redemption as well. Concerning the range of these insights I shall not deal in this short text; for that, one would need to compose both a historical and a systematic treatise in theology about the themes of cross and hell. Nonetheless, even the lay person in theology will straightaway notice that doors open here, which until now had always been closed; opening into a period of the history of the church in which it has become evident that the preaching of the dogma of hell in the way that we have become used to is no longer possible; but that on the other hand (at least the more thoughtful see this) still less is accomplished by merely treating this important and not to be demythologized facet of biblical revelation with a deathly silence. Now there really have been, especially in earlier periods of theology, in the fathers of the church, numerous approaches that sought to do justice to the biblical statements, above all a theology, which later became superficialized or lost, of the *descensus Christi ad inferos*, which regarded this descent as the decisive act of the redeemer (cf. the Byzantine and Russian pictures of the journey to hell); and in so doing did not of course make the sharp Western separation between limbo and hell. There was the great systematic attempt by Origen and his many open or secret disciples especially in the East, but also in the West up to the middle ages, which doubtless retained decisive elements of revelation, but presented it in an oversimplifying, more Greek than biblical conceptual language, so that hell and purgatory practically coincided. There was the grandiose attempt of Dante to wander through hell existentially as a believer, but this existential character did not possess any adequate theological, salvation-historical support, and so it could not influence the theology of its day. There have been in modern philosophy mighty speculative attempts, such as, say, that of Schelling, to come to a definitive resolution of the profundity of the problem of hell, and this, too, with no possible profound effect upon the theology of the church. Still less was something like this to be expected of the descent into hell of the modern, for the most part "revolted" poets, from Rimbaud to Sartre.

These manifold attempts at beginning could not be brought into a convincing unity, and so the theology of Holy Saturday became emptier, ever more neglected and forgotten. And yet Holy Saturday stands as the mysterious middle between cross and resurrection, and consequently properly in the center of all revelation and theology. And here in the center like an unexplored, inexplicable blank spot on the map! But who was authorized to draw out lines here which only inceptively pointed toward an unreachable center? It is often the case that a time has to become ripe for a new perspective on the Bible, for a new grace of the Holy Spirit who casts his light upon a till-now little or not at all attended field of revelation. Has perhaps our time been made ready for this grace by the fact that the modern experience of the remoteness of God, of "God is dead," and even of the hellish dregs of human existence had to be undergone first before something like the charism of Adrienne von Speyr would be meaningful?

If hell is supposed to be a dogmatic truth, then it can have a meaningful and, in faith, intelligible place only within the framework of the doctrine of the Trinity, of christology, and of soteriology. This place will be here given to it for the first time in a serious way. The central point of the preceding propositions is the statement that Christ's experience of hell on Holy Saturday is a trinitarian as well as a soteriological experience that forms the necessary conclusion to the cross as well as the necessary presupposition of the resurrection. The mode in which this experience could be here realized charismatically and be evaluated in its whole fearfulness as well as its salvific significance, will save everyone from the judgment that the seriousness of this dogma is here rendered harmless. Nonetheless the reader will have to concede that the Holy Spirit has seldom bestowed on the church a greater and more redemptive vision than this one, which here too allows the application of the theological basic principle: Only love is credible. Those versed in the history of theology will be happy to see than none of the beginnings of solutions there mentioned is entirely missing, and that the apparently impossible has happened: the implanting of the Eastern (from Origen) doctrine of the redemption in a much deeper synthesis that rests entirely on its biblical basis. Also Dante's journey through hell—though for those suffering there utterly unawares—is retrieved and thereby transformed into a theologically viable truth. Even Schelling's speculation about hell is saved in its best insights, without the least need for the experiences depicted to have been the result of intellectual subtleties. But beyond everything traditional, one will not mistake the novelty of the central propositions; and only on the basis of these new propositions could there succeed something like an integration of the former fragments into a living, supremely fruitful whole.

105 · People of the Church (VIII): Madeleine Delbrel

Madeleine is so original not simply because as a Christian she labored unprotected in a Communist environment and with Communists; but because in spite of everything she bore within herself an unerring, radiant Christian faith, a faith as naive as it was deeply reflective, a faith which confirmed her ever anew in a breaking-through of all traditional forms, and which poured into her a love for the Catholic church that no painful disappointments could lead astray. She lived from its mysteries and drew from them her boundlessly loving involvement for her non-Christian brothers and sisters.

Madeleine Delbrel was born in 1904 in Mussidan (Dordogne) in the house of her maternal grandparents. Her father, a railroad official, was often transferred during the course of this career: Lorient, Nantes, Bordeaux, Châteauroux, finally Montluçon in 1913. This did not exactly favor the educational formation of the young girl. She was tutored privately, had contact with some pious priests who awakened in her a simple, vital faith. The picture changed as soon as the father was called to Paris in 1916 and Madeleine entered into agnostic and atheistic circles, under whose influence her Christian faith was extinguished: "If extraordinary people brought me the faith between the ages of seven and twelve, no less extraordinary people gave me the opposite formation in the succeeding years. By fifteen I was strictly atheist and found one world daily more absurd." "God in the twentieth century was absurd," she would later write, "incompatible with a sound mind, insufferable because unclassifiable." At the age of seventeen she composed, already in the lyrical prose that was later so characteristic—rhythmic, pithy, at once solemn and unacademic—a sort of nihilistic manifesto: "God is dead—long live death." If God is absurd, death is of course even more so, and the world and its history are exposed as "the most dismal farce imaginable": "At the age of twenty [in 1924], a violent conversion, followed by a rational religious search." Then, in 1927, she published a volume of poems. The conversion was in fact so "violent" that it lasted until her death (1964): God became for her the daily new miracle that she experienced as an inconceivable gift, as giving, as self-giving, and which she could respond to only with the indivisible double giving over of her self: to God in prayer, to fellow human beings inside or outside the church. At first she thought about entering the Carmelites, the fruitfulness of which, as one of the more lovely texts about Thérèse of Lisieux shows, she had clearly comprehended. But then she resolved to dedicate her life to God in the midst of the most secular world, for she knew about the mystery of the church, which is not an "institution," but the living body of Christ in which the members, no matter how alone they seem to be living in the world, are joined by a completely different bond than mere brotherhood: "One cannot live a realistic life in accord with the gospel in an abstract church." And even when we have to suffer on account of the church—and Madeleine, connected as she was with all the dramatic movements of the "mission of France" and the Worker Priests, had to suffer profoundly on account of it—this suffering is a sign that one is in the right place: "A realistic love for the church leads necessarily to receiving blows and bearing wounds. . . . In this way do we let God's love flood into the world. Nothing can lead us deeper into the ultimate reality of the church."

Together with two fellow pilgrims in the social service Madeleine resolves to go to work in Ivry. From 1933 on, for thirty years, this will be her headquarters. She works privately at first, and then in public service. In 1935 Maurice Thorey coins the slogan *Main tendue* to describe the hand extended in cooperative labor. A mixed committee of Christians and Communists for social aid (it was the period of great unemployment) "performs an enormous practical task." During the war—Ivry was bombarded twice—the work even doubled. After liberation Ivry remained Communist. Working in close and friendly cooperation with the leading figures of the Party, who would have gladly won her over to it, Madeleine experienced "her temptation to Marxism at a time, when it still would have been original to succumb to it." Although it never occurred to her to oppose her own efforts to the parish organizations, but rather continually worked along with them, there still there came about in 1944 a kind of second conversion, in which God took complete preponderance over everything, even if this "everything" came to include both the Christian and Communist concern for the welfare of humanity. "God was and remains for me the blinding miracle. For me it was and remains impossible, to put God on one side of the same scale and on the other all the goods of the world, my own and those of the whole human race." She did not reject the ideal of Communism, but heightened it and included it into the demands of the Sermon on the Mount, in the program of a church that nourishes from the inmost sources of faith, love, and hope and turns itself into God's gift to the world. She loved this church that had its concrete center in Rome, and continued to do so even when, between 1953 and 1960, it was the source of the blows which struck against the new apostolic attempts in France. She resolved to let no split come to pass: "The mission should not weaken the parish; it must force it to strengthen everything in it that is vital." Madeleine wanted to give a signal; to make a day's journey to Rome in order to pray alone there at the tomb of Peter. Objections were raised that that would be an expensive prayer. She conceded, unless she would unexpectedly be given the money for it. In the same week she was given a lottery ticket that won. Madeleine set forth: "Rome for me is a kind of sacrament of the Christ-church; and it seemed to me that certain graces one needs for the church can be gotten for it only in Rome." Early in the morning she went straight to Saint Peter's, prayed the entire day at the tomb of Peter and returned home by the nighttrain. She would travel many more times and make all kinds of connections. From Archbishop Montini she received an encouraging letter. She wrote briefs for bishops on the question of Christians and Communists living together and much of this will be helpful later at the Council. After years of illness (1954–58) she published, without great success, her book, *Marxist City as Mission Field*. On all sides she was asked for statements, papers, for an ecumenical meeting in Bossey, to Marseille, by students. Friends invited her to Poland; a group on the Ivory Coast, members of the team that had since grown up around her, invited her to Abidjian; she began to see the problems of the Third World. She, who her whole life long had felt death to be the sign of the disorder of the world, died suddenly on 13 October 1964. With the posthumous publication of numerous death-notices, her wide influence began.

CONSUMMATION

· 106 ·

Perfect hope must be grounded in love, that is, in a possible prescinding from the "fulfill-ment" of the relationship of love.

107 · The Catholicity of Hope

What hope and expectation fills the chuch and the Christian as they move beyond the confines of their own existence into the world of non-Christian humanity? This cannot be expressed by a single concept. The dimensions of Christian hope, measured against those of what is called world history, seem at once both greater and yet smaller than the latter. Think back to that broken figure of the saving event that bears the name Jesus Christ: a horizontal course of life up to death, into "hell," into solidarity with all those who have died in body and in spirit; then vertically, a being lifted from the "underworld" into the "world above" of God's eternity. Under this overarching figure Christian life and the church as a whole have been set. And the center of the figure expressly points toward the breaking of the power of death. St. Paul maintains that this breaking of the power of death constituted from the very beginning the ultimate meaning of Israel's faith (Rom 4:17–25; cf 1 Cor 15:4).

Now the earthly time of history is thoroughly determined by mortality. The subject of this time is not of course an abstract humanity which exists unassailed throughout the centuries, but rather the concrete number of human beings, of whom thousands die at every moment. History is concretely put together from innumerable finite moments; the deathless continuity we create by the exclusion of all real deaths is a secondary temporal phenomenon. What we call the progress of humanity, be it cultural, technical, or even moral, as many think, can at best be related to this secondary or artificial kind of time from which the primary phenomenon of dying has been excluded. In this respect, even the hope that the world in the historical future will get "better" than in the past and present, is, in the light of Christian hope, at best a secondary hope. For Christian hope is characterized by the involvement of Jesus Christ, by his victory over death through the resurrection. Even were one, in one's more utopian or foolish moments, to hold hopes that some day in the future a victory might be gained over human mortality, this would still not have accomplished anything at all for the whole of past and present history. Christian hope, however, is essentially related to all human generations past, present, and future; St. Paul tells us expressly that the last generation before Christ's second coming, which perhaps will not have to die, has no advantage over those who have fallen asleep (1 Thes 4:15). For the real object of Christian hope is the overcoming of the boundary of death which at every moment cuts straight across the (apparent) onward flow of history.

If we reflect on this quite soberly, God's involvement in world history on behalf of all dying human beings affords no ("theological") hope for the historical future. If it did, then God would be intervening in his work of creation to make corrections, and that would not be worthy of him. For when he put human beings on earth that they might increase and subdue the earth (Gen 1:28), when he "endowed them with strength, like his own" (Ecclus 17:3), but directed them to "seek after God, in the hope that they might feel after him and find him" (Acts 17:27), he endowed them from the beginning with a primordial freedom and responsibility. They were to enter on the future that opened before them with this manifold commission to accomplish, and inherent in this mandate of creation (and written into the very nature of this human being itself) is hope that it is fulfillable. Fulfillable precisely to the extent that the human being remains true to its created nature, tries to unfold it in freedom, and lives responsibly in accordance with it. All this of course has been shattered by social, personal, and indeed cosmic decline, by those laws, written into nature herself, of the will to power, to aggression, and to the overwhelming of the more noble by the vulgar, which constantly make all human effort seem ambiguous and in the end to be vain (Rom 8:19). And yet, this futility does not free the human being from his responsibility to shape the world and humanity; and in this responsibility is contained a hope which swims against the tide of futility.

Now we must emphasize that this form of hope, in so far as it is directed toward some earthly prospect is not resolved by Christian hope, because the latter has a different objective, namely the salvation of the whole world, and of the whole of history, past, present, and future, seeing it lifted into the eternal life of God himself. This cuts right across all possible objectives and circumstances that lie in the path of secular time. But it is precisely because there is a difference between secular and Christian hope that the latter can have a decisive significance for the world. Secular hope is essentially shattered every moment it is concretely smashed by death. Beyond my death, there is no hope for me in the world's future. Is there any for others? But then again, all others will have their own death before them. But how, if death is now no longer able to destroy hope because its sting has been withdrawn? The power of death, however, has already been fundamentally broken where death, drawn into the infinite consent and agreement of Jesus with his Father's loving will, itself would be the decisive expression of that loving will. And the power of death is yet more radically broken where, in Jesus' death, the guilt of the world was plumbed to its depths and suffered through in God-for-sakeness, where thus the very ground is swept from under the despair, hopelessness, and resignation of the human being in the face of fate.

For this reason, Christians enter upon their path through the world with a completely fresh hope truly drawn from its divine source. And if they stay close to the source and drink from it, they can also open the way to the source for others who thirst, and can even give to others to drink from the source through themselves (Jn 4:14; 7:37ff). They can realize about themselves a model of existence which is both personally and socially freed from the powers of the world and provides a foretaste of the risen life far beyond death in all its possible forms: a hidden existence indeed (Col 3:3), yet possessed of such effective force that it vitally permeates the texture of human society. Indirectly, very indirectly, the outer structures of this society can be touched by the inner change; and quite indirectly, one can conclude from such a change in structures to an agent of change in society. But here we come against an insuperable barrier. "The form [*schēma*] of this world is passing away" (1 Cor 7:31). A changed structure is no guarantee of a change in spirit, even if the changing spirit was the cause of the change in the structure.

It remains a significant sign that Christian involvement in its most resolute forms has always been initiated with a persistent and sometimes almost stubborn preference for places where, from the human and worldly point of view, there is no more hope, or the involvement no longer seems worthwhile. For example, in caring for the dying, for life grown old and worn out, for the incurably sick, the mentally ill, or the handicapped, where not even a smile of thanks is ever to be expected, we should not ask whether such undertakings make sense or are worthwhile, for they were undertaken as a challenge to the meaninglessness of this world, in the consciousness that, in an involvement of this sort, the Christian understanding of hope sometimes becomes visible in its pure form. Now the genius of Christianity both ought and could, with this same quietly challenging kind of freedom, move into all the other structures of human society, all of which indeed have something of the hopelessness of the dying, sick, and insane about them, and bring to their care and treatment that hope which lasts beyond death, even though it takes death into account. One will object that this is an activity and program for saints. This may well be; but from the beginning, Christian living has always first begun to be credible where at last a glimmer of true holiness has shone from it.

108 · The Judgment of the Son of Man

The biblical vision of world history and of individual life is to its very roots distinguished by the reality of sin as the free turning away—and consequently the fateful state of being turned away—of humankind from God. God's saving institutions in the Old Testament, reaching a highpoint in the atoning death of Jesus in the New Testament, are events whose inseparable aspects are called judgment and grace. The presence of injustice and of personal and social guilt in the world is too pressing for all religions not to have been concerned with a solution for this mess: i.e., through some form of judgment. This attempt becomes all the more necessary when it is of the essence of guilt—sin, a Christian would say—to blur the existence of truth, or, where possible, to completely obscure it. Sin is essentially untruth, a lie which, once it has become personally and socially objectivized, seeks to pass off a substitute form of secondary truth as the normal and obviously valid. The sun, now left behind as (bad) conscience, cannot effectively disperse this fog; it usually manages only to bring it about that the ersatz truth gets recognized and challenged as "superstructure," but only to have it be replaced by another form of secondary truth. The cycle of ideologies is the real veil of *maya* that cannot be penetrated by humanity. The "Not that way!" that it can cry out in the face of open injustice is much more decisive than the "But this way!" that it has to offer as the way out, because it is aware of a blocking out of the truth within itself. This hinders it from entering the scene as the undeceived standard of truth for others and for the conditions in the world: "Whether it is love or hate man does not know" (Eccl 9:1). The science of this awareness takes its authority from its pretention to explain psychologically or sociologically the presence or absence of a determinate standard of "right" action, and thus the criteria become ever more opaque.

That the pendulum movement within world history and individual life should be one of justice-creating equilibrium is unacceptable; the "pendulum theory" of history comes about within a horizon we have previously described as the cycle of ideologies. And as for individual breakthroughs into profundity, which one calls "conversions," they too need an ultimate standard of right, which is never clearly there: for example, how questionable is a "turning away from the world" in order to forge some kind of a direct "path of knowledge" to God, as long as it has not been demonstrated that such a turning does not arise from mere resignation or perhaps even from flight from the secular tasks that remain. The opposite course is even more obviously problematic: an activist, supposedly altruistic preferential laboring in the horizontal sphere that has long since either forgotten or given up any vertically supervening will of God.

Consequently the "good will" of human beings never remains its own criterion. It must instead be ready to let itself be measured by an impartial good. It must be moving toward this criterion which gives it direction, must attempt to let itself be determined by it even in the present, but it can never presume to want to be itself the material or formal (Kant's categorical imperative!) criterion of every good action.

The human being as individual and as race (for its deeds are all caught up in one another) must undergo a judgment. It is idle to speculate about the "point in time" of this judgment—say, about the interval between the particular judgment after the death of the individual and the general or last judgment after the end of history— since we can only do this from within intratemporal perspectives, whereas the judgment is located on the threshold of eternity or more exactly (as we shall see), on the threshold between the "Old" and the "New Eon," that can not be grasped with our chronological understanding of time. It is the happening-point at which the authentic and conclusive confrontation of the deteriorated and discarded truth of humanity with the standing and open truth of God takes place. There is nothing against the possibility that, within the terrestrial existence of a human person, such a conclusive confrontation already takes place by God's grace and that this person has gone through the judgment (Jn 3:20–21).

109 · The Judge and the Co-Judges

That there must be absolute truth by which relative truth and untruth gets judged and disentangled, is evident. In the Old Testament the judge is God himself, in his relatedness to the world, as partner in the Covenant to which all peoples stand in some relation. And one knows that his judgment on Israel in the end (after the many rigorous judgments of this world) will be predominantly one of righteousness in the sense of fidelity to the covenant. His judgment on the nations in the end (after their uses in this world for executing justice upon Israel) will be predominantly one of justice in the sense of rigor. "Predominantly," for there are also prophetic passages in which the peoples get included in the salvific area of Israel (e.g., Is 66:18–23). Furthermore, there are the passages in which the last judgment runs straight through Israel, in whose midst are found the godless mentioned in the Psalms.

God in his relatedness to the world in the New Testament becomes the Word of God which in Jesus Christ has become human, which was crucified, descended to hell, and by God—who justifies himself—was raised from the dead. This Word of God, which as such assumed the measure of the human being and experienced from within all the dimensions of the world as turned away from God even to the point of the condition of death and in so doing did not cease to stand in the most immediate obediential contact with the heavenly Father from now on becomes necessarily the judge of the world: "The Father judges no one [more]; but has given all judgment to the Son, that all may honor the Son even as they honor the Father" (Jn 5:22f): whereby "to honor" means both to appreciate rightly (namely as judge) and encounter with reverence (*Ehr-furcht:* honor-fear).

The gospels and epistles, on the basis of Jesus's own statements, look toward his "coming again" in judgment, or in other words to the moment of approaching his judgment seat (1 Cor 4:4–5; 2 Cor 5:10; cf. Rom 2:5 ff; 14:10f), as an event that breaks in "like a thief in the night" (Mt 24:42ff, 1 Thess 5:2; Rev 16:15) and makes visible the judgment in the glory of God (or of "his Father") (Mt 16:27 par; 19:28; 24:30 par). The question arises however how this "glory" is to be understood. Literally it is of course derived from the picture in Daniel (7:13ff) of the Son of man coming in the judgment; but theologically this glory is inseparable from the glorification of God through Jesus' work of obedience and from the glorification of Jesus precisely in this work of obedience (Jn 13:31–32). His form of glory is not to be separated from the wounds attained in his work of reconciliation, which he shows forth even as the risen One. For this reason John insists twice on the Old Testament source which now reaches its whole depth of meaning and which without reflection gets combined with the passage in Daniel: "Behold, he is coming with the clouds, and every eye will see him, every one who pierced him; and all tribes of the earth will wail on account of him" (Rev 1:7; Jn 19:37; after Zech 12:10).

This picture breaks through the usual picture of the glory of the judge in two ways: First, inasmuch as he appears before all the peoples as the pierced one, which means as the living, palpable proof of what the sin of the world has in reality done to God. This aspect was already anticipated in the promise that "the sign of the Son of Man" will "appear in heaven," which also shall be accompanied by the "mourning of all the tribes of the earth" (Mt 24:30). Then second, this lament is not for one's own peril, the anxiety of being repudiated, but rather is a lament for the pierced one himself, a lament that is already objectified and concerns the injured absolute and personified justice of God. In the original passage from the prophet Zechariah the lament at looking upon the pierced one is as profound as "it is the death of an only Son, of a firstborn"; and in connection with this lament there is talk about an "opened fountain" of salvation (Zech 12:10, 11; 13:1). The lament in the face of the judgment being passed is at once a lament about the injustice done to the judge, and a lament in the face of the fountain opened in this manner that flows from the pierced one as salvation in the judgment (Jn 19:34).

This means, first of all, that the judgment is present as realized in the judge himself. First as the judgment perpetrated on the judge by the sinful world: he is the one imprisoned by the world, condemned, spit upon, beat about the ears, crowned with thorns, crucified, and mocked in his impotence and abandonment by God. But behind this judgment of the world appears in him the free willingness with which he suffers everything as a Son in obedience to the will of the Father, and thus understands it as a being delivered over by the Father to the world: everything that has been reckoned in the counsel of the Father "before the foundation of the world" as God's own spontaneous deed: the giving over of the beloved Son out of love for the life of the world (Jn 3:16; Rom 8:32). He is the lamb slain from the beginning of the world (Rev 13:8).

The judge appears in his form of power (Rev 1:13–16), which, however, includes his form of weakness, not as a forgotten past, but as the permanent presupposition of his authority ("I died, and behold I am alive for evermore, and I have the keys of Death and Hades": Rev 1:18). This having experienced all the forms of sin and abandonment in his own body gives him the highest competence as judge, and in no way compels his majesty and freedom to pass sentence in a certain direction. Those who are to be judged by him can draw hope and grace from his form of weakness, his solidarity with sinners and the lost, but in no way can they derive the outcome of the judgment in advance. The more exactly the judge knows from within the situation of those to be judged—and here this inner knowledge is complete—that much more does the situation cut two ways for the guilty: it is just as possible for them to draw hope for gentle treatment as well as nurture fear that their behavior is unforgivable. They are the ones responsible for the judgment, for better or for worse. This two-sidedness of the situation of each one who comes to judgment is expressed in the action of separating the "sheep and goats" (Mt 25:33f) that is depicted in the parable as a final action, without possible synthesis. For the synthesis lies inaccessibly concealed in the freedom of the judge. He has borne in advance the guilt of each one whom he judges; the central event of the judgment of the world is his cross ("Now is the judgment of this world": Jn 12:31) at which he at first really represents everyone condemned in the unrelenting justice of God. The relentlessness of this judgment carried out on him necessarily becomes, "there where the sign of the Son of man appears in the clouds," co-present. This is the "iron scepter" with which he rules and can "break" the nations "in pieces like pottery" (Rev 2:27; 12:5); this is the "sickle," too, with which the "Son of man reaps the harvest" of the ripe earth (Rev 14:14–16). From the presence of this relentlessness of the cross the one judged cannot be spared, although even here the freedom of the judge intervenes, the freedom that decides in what manner and to what degree the individual should become aware of this character of judgment. And precisely at this point a new modifying moment makes its entry.

According to scripture the judge does not come to the judgment as an isolated person: "For the Son of man is to come with his angels in the glory of his Father, and then he will repay each one for what he has done" (Mt 16:27). Before the Sanhedrin Jesus says, "Hereafter you will see the Son of man seated at the right hand of power and coming on the clouds of heaven" (Mt 26:64 par). In the parable of the judgment of the world the Son of man comes "and all his angels" in order to receive "the throne of his glory" (Mt 25:31). These angels will be sent out by him to gather the elect from the four winds (Mt 24:31; cf. 13:49f). But added to this is the prophecy to the twelve elect: "When the Son of man shall sit on his glorious throne, you who have followed me will also sit on twelve thrones, judging the twelve tribes of Israel" (Mt 19:28). The Christ, who has shaped the church as body, will not be separated from it in the judgment, but—now in the representation symbolized by its twelve "foundation stones" (Rev 21:14)—will have it present to him. Concluding further from this point, Paul puts all who, as true members of Christ, have gone over to his side also beside him at the judgment: "Do you not know that the saints will judge the world? Do you not know that we are to judge [fallen] angels?" (1 Cor 6:2, 3). Thus the opinion is expressed that, whoever here below in virtue of a life lived in correspondence with baptism has already "died" and "risen," and indeed, "ascended into heaven" with Christ (Eph 2:6), comes to stand by Christ's side in judgment, inasmuch as by his grace he or she shares in his being as standard of the world. That holds true first of all for those who followed Christ in the sacrifice of their blood, which is why in Revelation it can be said, "Then I saw thrones, and seated on them were those to whom judgment was committed," those, then, who for the sake of witnessing to Jesus are immediately characterized as "beheaded." They are the ones who have refused the worship of the beast and its image (Rev 20:4). From this bodily sacrifice of life the Christian tradition concludes to an equivalent value of spiritual self-sacrifice that makes co-judges of the truly renouncing, the truly poor (Augustine, *City of God*, bk. 20, ch. 5; *Glossa ordinaria* on Mt 19:28: "Those who have left all things and followed God will be judges"; Thomas Aquinas, *Suppl.* q. 89, 2).

This idea—of the inseparability of Christ from his true church even in judgment—has self-imposed limitations; it cannot be a matter of a judgment assembly in which each individual as it were would be entitled to vote, and the verdict would be a result of a vote, but only a matter of a co-judging by consenting to the verdict of the one judge (Thomas, *op. cit.*). But this needs a further nuancing too. For on the one side there is over Christ the stark evangelical saying that he is not come "to destroy, but to save" (Lk 9:56); that "God did not send his Son into the world to judge the world, but so that the world might be saved by him" (Jn 3:17): "For I have not come to judge the world, but to save the world" (Jn 12:47). Next to these words that portray his mission and his deed, there stand nevertheless the words that explain the judgment as a process taking place with respect to him, but without him: "He who rejects me and does not receive my sayings has a judge; the word that I have spoken [not he!], will be his judge on the last day" (Jn 12:48; and with the same sense, 3:19: "And this is the judgment, that the light has come into the world, but human beings loved darkness rather than light"). This aspect of the situation, without it being able to limit the freedom of the judge, nevertheless shows that at his mere appearance before all beings, the spirits are separated. He and those with him have the effect of a catalyst.

This idea has to be expanded by a further one. Those who are to be judged do not stand over against either Jesus or his church as alien. He has become their brother, yes, much more: their advocate before God. He has borne their guilt: this is in him. Whatever has estranged them from God has become estranged from them by Jesus. By him they have been ontically changed in the most profound way, whether or not they acknowledge it or let it happen—this would be the essential part of their redemption—or whether or not they, if they are capable of it, refuse it and so harden themselves in their guilt as their own. And whatever holds true primarily for Jesus, holds good on another level, secondarily, for those who have followed him and now appear together with him at the judgment. Not one of these has saved himself on condition of the exclusion of all others. Each one has had the love that "seeks not its own" (1 Cor 13:5), that does not gather merits for itself, but rather in a Christian and christological sense radiates the grace received: to others, for others. The church in its pure core is co-advocate. It is not for itself, but there for the world. It mediates the Lord to it; by preaching, but much more by its self-renunciation, its selflessness, its whole being. Mary, the handmaid of the Lord, must be mentioned first here; she is the true core of the "church without wrinkle or stain" (Eph 5:27). Wherever she appears, the child in Elizabeth's womb stirs: grace and mission are mediated. Wherever she asks, water is changed into wine.

We are at the heart of the unfathomable mystery of the exchangeability of all spiritual goods in the household and circulatory system of the mystical body of Christ: "If one member suffers, all suffer together; if one member is honored, all rejoice together" (1 Cor 12:26). This is not only in an external sense of the relationship of independent elements standing alongside one another, but in that of a mutual being for one another and ability for one another before God. The penance of one can effect for another the grace of conversion, without that person's ever knowing—prior to the judgment—from where it comes to him. The fundamental reality of the mystical body of Christ is the fruitfulness of the theological virtues in the life of those sanctified by them: All those who let them work in them without obstruction, become through them, whether they intend it or not, vessels which let the divine life stream through them into the world. Even non–Christian religions have known about this mystery, although mostly in a limited sense. However, certain of the Christian confessions derivative from the Catholic church have almost entirely forgotten it out of pure concern for personal salvation. Yet in the midst of the Catholica lives the knowledge of this marvelous mystery, which, in its concrete effect, cannot be demonstrated in individual instances: that for one another we can "shine like the stars in the universe" (Phil 2:15).

What comes from this in the judgment of Christ? Who would want to describe it? In any case, the image of two fronts standing rigidly opposed to one another—the judge and the judged—is dissolved into a fluid transition. All are fundamentally in virtue of the mystery of the cross "in Christ," the judged judge. And out of all these there are some, yes, actually many, who have helped retrieve those who are to be judged from judgment into redemption. For the sake of another the judgment for one can be spared or lightened. The intercession of the saints with the judge is not, as it would have to be represented in old pictures, a purely external thing, whose success remains doubtful according to the incalculable whims of the judge; it is above all an inner weight which, laid upon the scale, can make it sink.

110 · Purgatory and Hell

The disposition of those who come into the judgment of Christ and are measured against him as standard differs to the point of the most extreme oppositions. From the parables and warnings of the Lord we know that not the number of "talents" received is decisive, but their use (Lk 19:16ff), especially not the storing up of religious values against the day of judgment: "Tax collectors and harlots will come into the kingdom of God before you" (Mt 21:31). "On that day many will say to me, 'Lord, Lord, did we not prophesy in your name, and cast out demons in your name, and do many mighty works in your name?' And then I will declare to them, 'I never knew you'" (Mt 7:22f). " 'Lord, Lord, open to us.' But he replied, 'Truly, I say to you, I do not know you'" (Mt 25:11f). Paul explains more closely the point of all this: God himself and the church have laid the foundation but "let each one take care how he builds upon it." The set, unshakable foundation is Jesus Christ, "if anyone builds on the foundation with gold, silver, precious stones, wood, hay, stubble—each person's work will become manifest; for the Day [of the Lord] will disclose it, because it will be revealed with fire, and the fire will test what sort of work each one has done. If the work which any one has built on the foundation survives, he will receive a reward. If any one's work is burned up, he will suffer loss, though he himself will be saved, but only as through fire" (1 Cor 3:11–15).

The fire of which Paul speaks here is the testing and purifying fire of the judgment of Christ. It is meaningless to distinguish here between "purificatory fire" and "eschatological fire." It is a matter of a single process, that of judgment, which for each person can have different depths and lengths. For in any case there is—without prejudice to what has been said above about ecclesial advocacy—an existential preparation of the individual to take on the attitude of the kingdom of God. The required attitude is that of complete selflessness, not in the loss of the I, but in its being penetrated by the radiance of the attitude of the divine triune process: "Person in this is unique through and for the exchange of all the realities of the divine essence. Fire draws one into this. The work of wood is what is erected to the honor of one's own I; this work has to be torn down to the ground, and the I, salutarily stripped of its work, must from the ground up learn blessed poverty in spirit. That can be a long and painstaking process, perhaps in the shape of the unfolding of scant initiatives in a life that has otherwise been completely egoistical. The fire destroys the I-saying and makes one practiced in You- and We-saying. And this not in a vibrant dialogue with others in the purification taking place, but as it were in solitary confinement, in which everything distracting and hesitating is gone and one's concentration upon the goal is complete. This goal is the absolute love of God for me, as it became reality on the cross of Christ: *Videbunt in quem transfixerunt* (they will look on whom they have pierced), each one has only to look upon him who died for him (2 Cor 5:14f; Rom 14.15; 1 Cor 8:11). One must become practiced at what is the ontological truth: If one (who is God) has died for me, then I have died: "I live, now not [longer] I, Christ lives in me" (Gal 2:20). The purification (so it has been said) is at an end at that point when the one who is fixed upon the pierced one would be ready to persevere in the fire as long as (not my own, but anyone's) sin brings about this pain in the God-man. Who causes it has become a matter of indifference in view of the fact that *he* suffers. Whoever has been brought this far can enter into the "communion of saints."

There is a final question that has been raised but, after all that has been said, cannot be answered. How does the judge proceed with those who enter before him as turned away, who appear in the gospel parables and other pronouncements of Jesus as the "unknown," the "turned away," the "outcasts" (Mt 22:13), the ones left out in the darkness? We do not know. We are permitted to attribute a part of the definitive separations (say, in Mt 25:31–46) to parenesis (cf. especially clearly Heb 6:4–12). And another part presumably to the typical form of eschatological black-and-white-painting that was common in the Old Testament. But even in doing so the disturbing remainder is not dissolved. It is only permissible to say so much: God even as redeemer respects the freedom which God has bestowed upon his creature and with which it is capable of resisting his love. This respecting means that God does not overrule, pressure, or coerce with the omnipotence of his absolute freedom the precarious freedom of the creature. In doing so he would contradict himself. It remains however to consider whether God is not free to encounter the sinner turned away from him in the form of weakness of the crucified brother abandoned by God, and indeed in such a way that it becomes clear to the one turned away: this (like me) God-forsaken one is so for my sake. In this situation one can no longer speak of any overpowering if, to the one who has chosen (maybe one should say: thinks he has chosen) the complete loneliness of being-only-for-oneself, God himself enters into his very loneliness as someone who is even more lonely. To get an insight into this one must recall what was said at the start according to which the world with all its destinies of freedom has been founded anticipatorily in the mystery of the sacrificed Son of God: this descent is a priori deeper than that to which one lost in the world can attain. Even what we call "hell" is, although it is the place of desolation, always still a christological place.

111 · Resurrection of the Flesh and Eternal Life

Eschatology has its center in the decision of God to bring into his own infinite, divine, and inner life the created world, when it comes to its end, together with humanity as its center. Just as the condition of humanity's coming to be and passing away and the constitution of its knowledge and its freedom is thus a provisional one oriented towards another final condition, so also is the structure of the total material spatio-temporal world in which, of course, our preview into the mode of being of the "new heaven and the new earth" is blocked by the barriers of death. For this reason we can speak only prophetically, in parables (like Paul in 1 Cor 15) or in the warding off of analogical conclusions (like Jesus in Mk 12:25). At the center of the Christian certainty of the resurrection, however, stands no speculation, but the fact of the resurrection of Jesus and of his re-encounters with his disciples, from which the entire turning of the present old eon to the coming new eon is illuminated in two ways: The personal identity not only of the spirit, but also of the body and hence of the whole earthly history belongs to this person. With his wounds, Jesus shows the disciples "I am he!" (Lk 24:39)—and nevertheless the transformation into a completely new condition in which the spirit is no longer dependent on matter, but, instead, matter is freely at the disposal of the spirit.

It is significant that this "beginning" of the Christian resurrection in the midst of the unfolding history of the world takes place as it were perpendicular to it, while the fragmentary beginnings of the Old Testament expectation of a resurrection were imagined either as messianic end-time immanent history or as an event at the end of historical time (Isa 26:19; esp. Deut 12:1ff; 1 Macc 7). This explains the total lack of comprehension of the disciples at the foretelling of the resurrection of Jesus "on the third day" and at the end itself when they met with it: even when they conjured up for themselves notions of the resurrection (Mk 9:10f, just as in a vague way even Herod and others do: Mk 6:14–16), still the category required to do this is in no way available to them. The resurrection of Jesus emerging vertically from the horizontal history, that for Paul and John is the promise and pledge of the resurrection and transformation of the world as a whole (1 Cor 15:17–23), no longer permits us to expect the breaking in of the new world in the chronological continuation of a historical time that has run to its end, but in a dimension that is incommensurable with this. And only the knowledge of the solidarity of all human destiny forces us to the idea that the incommensurable new world must stand in a relationship to the total world history (whose chronological conclusion is yet to come).

To the extent that the completedness of humankind as having passed over into the new eon (cf. the definition of Benedict XII on the full beatitude of those who have died and been purified in the course of history: DS 1000/1) must be compatible with something still to come, an expectation and hope, as was commonly assumed from Origen (*Hom in Lev.* 7, 1–2) to Bernard (*Sermo 3 in festo omn. Sanct.*), all the more compatible must it be since indeed Jesus himself, the one who certainly is resurrected bodily and enjoys full beatitude, can lay the kingdom at his Father's feet (1 Cor 15:24) only after the conclusion of world history, but who meanwhile must reign as king "till all enemies are laid beneath his feet" (1 Cor 15:25), and thus must ride with blood-drenched robe into the battle (Rev 19:13), suffers somewhat if his mystical body is persecuted ("Saul, why do you persecute me?": Acts 9:4 and Augustine's interpretation), is in agony until the end of the world (Pascal), can first subject the kingdom to the Father when all his members are subject to him (Ambrose, *De fide ad Gratianum*).

To this extent the position of the resurrected Christ, of the exemplar of his church assumed bodily into heaven (Mary), and of the saints dwelling "with him" (Phil 1:23) is identical: Unity of ultimacy and provisionality inasmuch as the entire new eon remains in a communion of innermost participation and involvement. The Father does not cease from delivering over his glorified Son in the form of the Eucharist for the life of the world, and the divine Spirit—as it were the inmost hinge between the eons—does not cease to groan from the bowels of the uncompleted world subject to transitoriness "with sighs too deep for words" for the "setting free from its bondage to decay" (Rom 8:26, 21). This "com-passion" of the whole heaven, which as such is blessedness with God, with the world, this "lying in travail" on the church's part between heaven and earth until the end of time, until the "other offspring" of the "woman" (Rev 12:17) have been brought to the world is surely mysterious, but not more mysterious than the mercy in the heart of the divine Father for his suffering creature; the Father himself is, according to Origen, not without "pathos" (*Hom in Ez* 6, 6).

For confirmation of what has been said, we can take a step back and try to take the belief in immortality of the soul, present in all religion in various degrees of intensity, and confront it with what has been said (extra-biblical belief in resurrection, is, where it comes up, more a sign of inability to abstract: What has been is supposed to remain or return again the way it was). One can best describe the relationship most simply by saying: Immortality is the outlook that is possible from the perspective of the independent selfhood of humanity; resurrection is that fulfillment that through the gift of God, the "acceptance into the children's place," becomes part of human expectation.

The completing factor, which in the resurrection from the dead that begun with Christ is added on, does not reside so much in the (philosophically) positive evaluation of matter or in the insight that the human soul needs the bodily senses in order to realize itself in consciousness in that it enters into relationship with other persons and things in the material world (which is all true); but rather in that the human being only becomes himself in his unique decisions within his bodily-mortal life. The earthly life given to him is not an arbitrary one out of a series of rebirths, and also not an arbitrary one within a great biological-cultural process of evolution, but his own unique life in which, in probation among beings similar to him and in his personal and social task, he confirms his freedom and plays his chance within his finite span: *les jeux sont faits*. This decision taking place in time is and remains the basis of his eternity: however much the grace and righteousness of the eternal judge may transform it and however great the change in state from the eon of mortality to that of eternal life may be. No one exhausts the depths of the intratemporal situation in which he decides about himself: in the resurrection of the dead this depth becomes manifest that in God's plan was already implicitly there.

This does not mean that the human being remains in eternity the captive so to speak of the four walls of his temporal life. Eternity, as it exists in the absolute freedom of God, and in which the creature is to receive a share, is on the contrary the opening of all possibilities, an unimaginable plenitude of dimensions into which free realization can occur. But the costliness of the temporal order does not go lost in it; this remains root and branch whence blossoms and fruit of the eternal first of all unfold. And in this there is certainly a genuine past of that which was the torment of the birth pangs: "The Lord of hosts . . . will swallow up death forever, and the Lord will wipe away tears from all faces, and the reproach of his people he will take away from all the earth" (Is 25:6–8); "for the first heaven and the first earth had passed away, and the sea was no more" (Rev 21:1); "death shall be no more, neither shall there be mourning nor crying nor pain anymore, for the former things have passed away. And he who sat upon the throne said, 'Behold, I make all things new' " (Rev 21:4–5). "Remember not the former things, nor consider the things of old. Behold, I am doing a new thing; now it springs forth, do you not perceive it?" (Is 43:18–19).

Recollection in Prayer

112 · Prayer for the Spirit

Deus qui diligentibus te
  bona invisibilia praeparasti:
Infunde cordibus nostris
  tui Amoris affectum,
ut te in omnibus
  et super omnia diligentes
promissiones tuas
  quae omne desiderium superant
  consequamur.
    (Collect for the Fifth Sunday after Pentecost)

"God, you have prepared in advance unseen good things for those who love you." God, with this name we must name you, though we would rather leave you unnamed: for as all names are conclusive, they point to a this which is not that and that. But when our heart, however refusing it may be, is moved toward you, it would like no longer to dash against any this or that the way water dashes against stones in a stream bed, but, tired and wounded by so many ob-jects cast up against it, to let itself flow into your infinity. Did not your angel, Lord, once ask, "Why do you inquire after my name? It is wonderful." Permit us to put down your name and at once to cross it out: we gaze through it as through a window at you, the Unnameable one, and we beg you that if your name should ever become for us a wounding stone and a possession that does not let us through, then flush it away and let us flow over it to the ocean of your boundlessness. Why do you permit names to be given to you, and even give yourself names as distinct from humanity? Certainly because you are the You and not the We and we may not exchange You for our We and our possibilities and desires and our ever higher climbing. No, we would not like this: in our striving toward you always to find ourselves again, to see in you nothing more than our own ideal that we project and then also somehow surpress, so as in the end to arrive back at ourselves and to look into our own mirror-image. Be therefore for us, as the first reality, our You, or at least our Not–I, and accept—beyond all our nameless desires—your divine name, which guarantees this for us. We would like to come to you, and if in the end we are unable to put off our I-existence, which often seems like a prison to us, then only in

such a way that we are for you an I, willed and affirmed by you, your You.

That we "love you" is something we say quite unemphatically, almost in embarrassment, because no other expression occurs to us to bring to your attention the flowing of our being, which, whether we want it or not, is flowing toward death and thus emptying into your endlessness. We cling to earthly life and are, nevertheless, already tired of it in advance. We love it as something that is taking its leave of us, which presses something already vanishing even faster to our hearts. We can manage, for moments, to cover over the margins of the past and look at the center of the picture and imagine ourselves in it completely. But only a picture of us is wedded to picture, and in the midst of the wedding, which is supposed to last, the self begins to flow again and reminds us that we only exist as flowing. And even at the point where both seem to be one, standing still and flowing, the stream of life goes on without us; beyond ourselves, the child lifts itself and walks away from us on its own legs. But in the end we can set ourselves up as we wish, to cling to the emphemeral or let it go; we are always outplayed by ourselves, and we know this, and somewhere there is still a Yes to our inmost nature— we do not want for the moment to characterize more than this "Yes" as "love"—a Yes with our will or without it, but at any rate a Yes forced from us. And if we commit suicide, we would still only be giving expression to our dissatisfaction with this finitude and it would once again be a (to be sure, foolish) way of admitting the direction of our flow.

This direction points us toward "unseen good things." Not only our eyes but our heart and our mind have no vision of them. All good things of which we have a concept suffer from an incurable contradiction: that we strive after them and are weary of them beforehand. We have to grasp after them, because we do not find in ourselves alone enough supplies to last the winter, and we still could not horde them because they run away from us: we lose them or they themselves lose their shine, their novelty, their attractiveness. They leave behind a hollow, pale emptiness, and it is not strengthened or refreshed that we look out for new good things, but exhausted and discouraged. We have once again the taste of frustration in our mouths, and we know quite well that it will be left over as well from the next adventure and the one after that. What should we do, you, our God? In what direction should we look? You tell us. You have prepared unseen good things for us. Inapprehensible for our desires that we take to be love. They are laid ready beyond a wide chasm, and the chasm is called dying. Radically dying to this kind of love that pretends to be our own flowing into the infinite. We should renounce such desire. That means to deny ourselves. It is an impure, selfishly tainted, mixed-up pressure that always wants both: you and us. You for us, us in you. We have ourselves in mind; we belong to the good things that in all our climbing always remain visible and reachable to us. And so we do not know if we should not simply suppress the word *love* completely, whenever the topic is our relationship to you. It is the deep-rooted desire that as creatures we trace back to our origin, burning and hollow. But with real love for you we cannot ourselves fill this hollow space. We cannot build the bridges that cross from us to you and your invisible good things. Even though you have made us for yourself and given us the promise of unseen good things, we are unable to be responsible to you in self-denial, in genuine repentance, unless your own Spirit purifies us, frees us from ourselves, and carries us over the abyss.

"Pour into our hearts the attitude of your love." Pour it in: become yourself one flowing for us, for our flowing does not carry us to you. Be rain in our dryness; be a river through our landscape so that it might have in you its center as well as the cause of its growing and bearing fruit. And if your water brings both blossoms and fruit in us, then we do not want to consider them as our own drives and results, because they come from you; and we want to consign them in advance to the invisible goods with you, over which you can dispose as you will. They are fruits from our land but brought forth by you, which you can use for yourself or for us; and we are indeed numerous, so that you can reserve what perhaps one person brings forth in superabundance for another who has nothing. For no tree enjoys its own fruits; its concern is only to make the seed, that it falls on good soil and a new fruit tree grows. But the sweet, meaty fruit that the tree brings forth with so much careful art is for whom? For the birds, for the worms. And finally for the owner of the tree. And still more ultimately for every hungry person who passes. Your trees, God, know this, and we do not know it. They bear a mystery of self-giving in themselves, that we still have to learn. They say not-I; but we say I and we still have to learn from you to say You. We are not the ones flowing: you are the stream, the blowing breath of love. You are yourself precisely inasmuch as you are the selfless one. The persons in you are not fixed points but soaring relationships, forms of self-giving, not fortresses one would have to capture, but opennesses of which only those who, surrendering, step out of their own fortress, gain a share. The attitude of love that we ask of you, is you yourself. You, Father, give your entire being as God to the Son; you are Father only inasmuch as you give yourself; you, Son, receive everything from the Father and before him you want to be nothing other than one receiving and giving back, the one representing, glorifying the

Father in loving obedience; you, Spirit, are the unity of these two mutually meeting self-givings, their We as a new I that royally, divinely rules them both—person become love!—which in both wishes for nothing else than to be crowned by absolute love: in the self-giving of letting go of every planning and disposing of one's own order to hand over the governance to love.

Is this Spirit which we beg of you perhaps already itself the quintessence of all unseen good things? But unfortunately for us spiritless sinners he is indeed quite invisible and in everything almost the opposite of what we prize and desire. He is indeed your Spirit, not ours; love according to your style, not according to ours. And if then in all important situations he demands our offering, then he always has need of precisely what we thought we would hold onto under the most sublime pretensions of using it for your greater glory, but also for our own. For us, individually or collectively, something should always look from within. Continually your Spirit has to change and reverse our direction with gentle force, has to tirelessly tie to his trellis the shoots that crawl about the ground, and to press those that strike out fantastically into emptiness to the hard, realistic wood. What we call earthly love and what is mostly self-seeking he has to penetrate with heavenly love; and what we call heavenly love and what is mostly a figment of our imagination, he has to test in the earthly sphere. He shows us the life of your Son, his cross. Here heaven and earth are united, in this roughhewn crossing. There is no more simple way. This cross we should daily take upon ourselves. Daily die to ourselves in all things in order to be a new human being in Christ. And these new human beings belong to the unseen good things; they are not at their own disposal. They notice from time to time something of the blowing and fragrance of the Spirit, the divine breath between Father and Son. But there is nothing to point to, neither the Spirit (who blows where he will), nor the human being in his wind. He works in an indeterminable place between heaven and earth.

"So that we may love you in all things and above all things." That precisely is our mysterious suspension between you and the world; it is something that we can not explain to ourselves, much less can we make it clear to others who look at us in amazement. In your Spirit we learn to love you in all things. People think that in that case we would not really love things, or at least not for the sake of their own goodness. They do not understand what your Spirit wants to make us realize: that you are the quintessence of all goodness, that all things are good and worthy of love from you and in you and for you. Yes, that it is impossible to love them, limited realities that they are, other than with a limited love, unless one sees them in you, the Unlimited,

and loves them as from you, together with you, in a no longer merely finite love. And then it is really you that we are loving in them, the better and the best in whatever is good; and because you will them and create them and love them in their createdness, there is no reason for us too not to love them, as they are and as you will to have them. But to love in all things, we must love you beyond all things; to be true to the earth, we must be true to you, Father in heaven. Otherwise our love becomes a tragic convulsion and ends in lies and self-rebellion. For this reason, may your Spirit teach us to give up all things for your sake; not to let them go packing, but to release them to you, with an impulse of love as it were, which releases them and lets them roll on your track. If it is an impulse of love, then they take our love along with them and we have provided ourselves a rendez-vous with you. Your Holy Spirit is so free that he always leads to liberation: spaces of divine freedom should reign among us creatures. Do not let us lower spiritual natures cling to one another; rather let our love be so illumined by renunciation that all who come in touch with it will thereby become more free, toward God, toward others, and toward themselves. It is a reverent making-free, for we know God's blood was used for this making-free. It is the kind of making-free, that results not from one's own fullness of power, but in free service to the divine freedom, in our making-space for the divine Spirit who is a Spirit of selflessness and of obedience. In all things and above all things we should love you: what a dynamic, history-filled space is opened for us there! Things can be quite close to us and in embracing them we can think, out of sheer proximity, almost to be embracing you before proximity; and then again they can be quite remote and alien, and then you, too, seem to disappear with them— and all at once we know: We are supposed to love you above all things; their remoteness opens new spaces for you; things set you free (for us); but then your free love for things immediately sends us back again to them. It is an endless fluctuation that can never come to rest: You are not the world, and you do not need it and yet you will not to be without it: it points to you alone, you point again back to it. The world points to you ambiguously: You are in it, but also beyond it; you are in it only when you are and can be above it; it points to you with its fullness and its emptiness, its proximity and its remoteness, its happiness and its bitter, insipid disappointment. You, in contrast, point unequivocally to it: Your finger signifies mission, the bringing of your love into the world. Grant, then, that we may love you before all, in things and above them; then we will be able, together with you, to love things unequivocally. Then the gift of your world will be for us like a huge overflow that comes to us unexpectedly as a reward for having sought to love you, the triune love, above all things.

"And so to attain those things, transcending all desire, which you have promised." Now the limitation that was in our desire has been transcended. We always wanted to measure your fulfillments by the standard of our desires. More than what our hollow space contains, so we thought, we cannot obtain from you. But when your Spirit began to blow in us, we experienced so much greater space that our own standard became meaningless to us. We noticed the first install-ment and pledge of a wholly other freedom, a promise that already began to be fulfilled by the Spirit and so gave to us a new kind of certainty. And we would not have been able to interpret this certainty to ourselves without the word and deed of Jesus Christ, who spoke to us of the kingdom of heaven and its explosive power, of dying in the earth and rising in the fruit of the ears of grain, of preparing dwelling places with the Father and coming to take us and send us his and the Father's Spirit to explain all things to us. The promise is already fulfilled in him: he is the eternal link between God and all his crea-tures. And the other promise is fulfilled as well: he has sent us his promising Spirit from the Father. And thus is fulfilled also the third promise which is the blowing Spirit itself in person: Because he blows the fulfillment toward us. He does it infallibly, if we are ready to allow ourselves to be surpassed in our desires. The religion and desire of all peoples means ultimately this: to get beyond one's own desires. And yet we do not want to say that this desire, this thirst for the absolute, is nothing, for it has been implanted in us by you. Only you in your triune love can bring its resolution to us: we ourselves must give ourselves up in order to be confirmed in your love by you. We were from the outset a gift which you have made to us. We give everything back to you. Dispose of it only according to your will. Give us only your love and grace, for that is what transcends all our desire and so it is enough.

Bibliographic Guide to the Work of Hans Urs von Balthasar

I

A full bibliography of von Balthasar's writings for the period from 1925 to 1975 is provided by: *Hans Urs von Balthasar, Bibliographie 1925–1975*, compiled (up to 1965) by B. Widmer, revised and enlarged by C. Capol (Einsiedeln: Johannes 1975).

II

Most of the secondary literature is supplied in Werner Löser, *Im Geiste des Origenes. Hans Urs von Balthasar als Interpret der Theologie der Kirchenväter* (Frankfurt theologische Studien 23; Frankfurt: Knecht 1976) 265–68; also in Giovanni Marchesi, *La Cristologia di Hans Urs von Balthasar* (Analecta Gregoriana 207; Rome: Universitá Gregoriana 1977) 408–10; and finally in Achiel Peelman, *Hans Urs von Balthasar et la Théologie de l'histoire* (Europäische Hochschulschriften, series XXIII, vol. 107; Bern/Frankfurt: Lang 1978) 194–200.

III

There are also some dissertations on von Balthasar's work. Those composed in German are:

1970 Willi Link, "Gestalt und Gestaltlosigkeit der Kirche. Umrisse einer personal-geistlichen Kirchenlehre bei Hans Urs von Balthasar"; Diss. Univ. Pont. Gregoriana.

1973 Pedro Escobar, "Zeit und Sein Jesu Christi bei Hans Urs von Balthasar. Umriss einer Christologie"; Diss. Institut Cath. de Paris.

1974 Michael Albus, "Die Unterscheidung des Christlichen nach Hans Urs von Balthasar"; Diss. Theol. Fakultät der Universität Freiburg/Br.

1975 Wolfgang Tinnefeldt, "Ekstasis der Liebe und Entfaltung des Glaubens. Eine Untersuchung zur Frage nach der Mitte und Einheit der christlichen Wahrheit bei Hans Urs von Balthasar"; Diss. Theol. Fakultät der Universität Mainz.

1975 Hanspeter Heinz, *Der Gott des Je-mehr. Der christologische Ansatz Hans Urs von Balthasars* (Frankfurt/Bern: Lang).

1976 Medard Kehl, "Christliche Gestalt und kirchliche Institution," in *Kirche als Institution* (Frankfurter theol. Studien 22; Frankfurt: Knecht; 2nd ed. 1978) 239–311.

1976 Werner Löser, *Im Geiste des Origenes* (see above, sec. II).

1979 Manfred Lochbrunner, "Analogia caritatis. Darstellung und Deutung der Theologie Hans Urs von Balthasar"; Diss. Theol. Fakultät der Universität Freiburg/Br.

IV

The spectrum of the works which Hans Urs von Balthasar has written, translated, and brought out as a publisher is broad. The following summary provides some representative titles from the various groups of his works. Unless otherwise noted, they were all published by the Johannes-Verlag in Einsiedeln.

A) Works in Philosophy and in the History of Philosophy

1937 *Apokalypse der deutschen Seele,* vol. I: *Der deutsche Idealismus* (Salzburg: Pustet; from the 2nd ed.: *Prometheus* [Heidelberg: Kerle]).

1939 *Apokalypse der deutschen Seele,* vol. II: *Im Zeichen Nietzsches;* vol. III: *Die Vergöttlichung des Todes* (Salzburg: Pustet).

1947 *Wahrheit,* vol. I: *Wahrheit der Welt* (Einsiedeln: Benziger).

B) Historico-Theological Studies

1941 *Kosmische Liturgie. Höhe und Krise des griechischen Weltbildes bei Maximus Confessor* (Freiburg: Herder; 2nd ed.: *Kosmische Liturgie. Das Weltbild Maximus' des Bekenners,* 1961).

1942 *Présence et pensée. Essai sur la Philosphie religieuse de Grégoire de Nysse* (Paris: Beauchesne).

1954 *Thomas von Aquin. Besondere Gnadengaben und die zwei Wege menschlichen Lebens. Kommentar zu Summa Theologica II–II, 171–82* (Deutsche Thomas-Ausgabe 23; Heidelberg: Kerle/Graz: Pustet).

C) Major Theological Works

1961 *Herrlichkeit,* vol. I: *Schau der Gestalt;* 2nd ed. 1967.

1962 *Herrlichkeit,* vol. II: *Fächer der Stile;* 2nd ed. 1969 in 2 volumes: vol. I: *Klerikale Stile;* vol. II: *Laikale Stile.*

1965 *Herrlichkeit,* vol. III/1: *Im Raum der Metaphysik.*

1967 *Herrlichkeit,* vol. III/2 pt. I: *Alter Bund.*

1969 *Herrlichkeit,* vol. III/2 pt. II: *Neuer Bund.*

1973 *Theodramatik,* vol. I: *Prolegomena.*

1976 *Theodramatik,* vol. II/1: *Der Mensch in Gott.*

1978 *Theodramatik,* vol. II/2: *Die Personen in Christus.*

1960 *Verbum Caro* (= *Skizzen zur Theologie I*). E.T. *Word and Revelation: Essays in Theology 1,* trans. A. V. Littledale with the cooperation of Alexander Dru (New York: Herder and Herder, 1964), and *Word and Redemption: Essays in Theology 2,* trans. A. V. Littledale in cooperation with Alexander Dru (New York: Herder and Herder, 1965).

1960 *Sponsa Verbi* (= *Skizzen zur Theologie II*). E.T. *Church and World,* trans. A. V. Littledale with Alexander Dru (New York: Herder and Herder, 1967).

1967 *Spiritus Creator* (= *Skizzen zur Theologie III*).
1974 *Pneuma und Institution* (= *Skizzen zur Theologie IV*).
1955 *Das betrachtende Gebet* (= *Adoratio I*), 3rd ed. 1965. E.T. *Prayer*, trans. A. V. Littledale (London: Sheed and Ward, 1961).
1963 *Das Ganze im Fragment. Aspekte der Geschichtstheologie* (Einsiedeln: Benziger). E.T. by William Glen-Doepel—British edition: *Man in History* (London: Sheed and Ward, 1968); American edition: *A Theological Anthropology* (New York: Sheed and Ward, 1968).
1969 "Mysterium Paschale," in J. Feiner/M. Löhrer, eds., *Mysterium Salutis*, vol. III/2 (Einsiedeln: Benziger) 133–326; separately published under the title: *Theologie der drei Tage* (Einsiedeln: Benziger).
1977 *Christlicher Stand.*

D) Lesser Writings on the Discernment of Spirits

1944 *Das Weizenkorn. Aphorismen* (Luzern: Räber; 3rd ed.: Einsiedeln: Johannes 1957 = Christ heute III/4).
1952 *Schleifung der Bastionen. Von der Kirche in dieser Zeit* (= Christ heute II/9); 4th ed. 1961.
1963 *Glaubhaft ist nur Liebe* (= Christ heute V/1); 3rd ed. 1966. E.T. *Love Alone*, trans. and ed. Alexander Dru (New York: Herder and Herder, 1969).
1966 *Cordula oder der Ernstfall* (= Kriterien 2); 4th ed. 1975. E.T. *The Moment of Christian Witness*, trans. Richard Beckley (Glen Rock, N.J.: Newman Press, 1969).
1969 *Einfaltungen. Auf Wegen christlicher Einigung* (Munich: Kösel).
1971 *Klarstellungen. Zur Prüfung der Geister* (= Herderbücherei 393; Freiburg: Herder; 4th ed.: Einsiedeln: Johannes 1978 = Kriterien 45). E.T. *Elucidations*, trans. John Riches (London: SPCK, 1975).
1971 *In Gottes Einsatz leben* (= Kriterien 24); 2nd ed. 1972. E.T. *Engagement with God*, trans. John Halliburton (London: SPCK, 1975).
1971 "Warum ich noch ein Christ bin," in H. V. v. Balthasar/J. Ratzinger, *Zwei Plädoyers* (= Münchener Akademie-Schriften 57; Munich: Kösel) 11–52. E.T. *Two Say Why: Why I Am Still a Christian by Hans Urs von Balthasar and Why I Am Still in the Church by Joseph Ratzinger*, trans. John Griffiths (London: Search Press; Chicago: Franciscan Herald press, 1971).
1974 *Der antirömische Affekt. Wie lässt sich das Papsttum in der Gesamtkirche integrieren?* (= Herderbücherei 492; Freiburg: Herder).
1975 *Katholisch* (= Kriterien 36).
1977 *Der dreifache Kranz. Das Heil der Welt im Mariengebet* (= Beten heute 9); 3rd ed. 1978.
1979 *Neue Klarstellungen* (= Kriterien 49).
1980 *Kennt uns Jesus—kennen wir ihn?* (Freiburg: Herder).

Index of Sources
and Abbreviations

The more detailed bibliographic data on the following works of Hans Urs von Balthasar are found under IV (C) on the preceding pages. Some works are found several times in this Index of Sources. Their titles are abbreviated as follows.

lected and trans. H. U. v. Balthasar (= Menschen der Kirche 1) (Einsiedeln: Benziger; 2nd ed., 1955) Intro.: 11–24; here 11–14.

101 "Mittler zwischen Ost und West. Zur 1300-Jahrfeier Maximus' des Bekenners 580–662," in *Sein und Sendung* 8 (1962) 358–61

102 "Exerzitien und Theologie," in *Orientierung* 12 (1948) 229–32

103 "Der 'kleine Weg.' Therese von Lisieux," in *Vaterland* no. 103 (30 December 1972)

104 Adrienne von Speyer, *Kreuz und Hölle* (= Die Nachlasswerke 3, ed. and intro. H. U. v. Balthasar; private

publication 1966) Intro.: 7–14; here 9–11

105 Madeleine Delbrêl, *Gebet in einem weltlichen Leben* (= Beten heute 4; trans. C. Capol and H. U. v. Balthasar; Foreword by H. U. v. Balthasar, 1974) Foreword 7–13; here 7–11

CONSUMMATION
106 W 84
107 Ge 64–69
108 PI 431–33
109 PI 434–41
110 PI 441–44
111 PI 444–47, 449–50
112 SC 472–79